WARS AND SOLDIERS IN THE EARLY REIGN OF LOUIS XIV

Volume 6 – Armies of the Italian States 1660–1690
Part 2

Text and Illustrations by Bruno Mugnai

'This is the Century of the Soldier', Fulvio Testi, Poet, 1641

Helion & Company

Helion & Company Limited
Unit 8 Amherst Business Centre
Budbrooke Road
Warwick
CV34 5WE
England
Tel. 01926 499 619
Email: info@helion.co.uk
Website: www.helion.co.uk
Twitter: @helionbooks
Visit our blog http://blog.helion.co.uk/

Published by Helion & Company 2023
Designed and typeset by Serena Jones
Cover designed by Paul Hewitt, Battlefield Design (www.battlefield-design.co.uk)

Text © Bruno Mugnai 2023
Images © as individually credited
Colour artwork by Bruno Mugnai © Helion & Company 2023
Maps drawn by Bruno Mugnai © Helion & Company 2023

Cover: German Mounted Life Guard, Grand Duchy of Tuscany, 1680 after Pandolfo Reschi, painted by Bruno Mugnai

Every reasonable effort has been made to trace copyright holders and to obtain their permission for the use of copyright material. The author and publisher apologise for any errors or omissions in this work, and would be grateful if notified of any corrections that should be incorporated in future reprints or editions of this book.

ISBN 978-1-804513-94-1

British Library Cataloguing-in-Publication Data.
A catalogue record for this book is available from the British Library.

All rights reserved. No part of this publication may be reproduced, stored in a retrieval system, or transmitted, in any form, or by any means, electronic, mechanical, photocopying, recording or otherwise, without the express written consent of Helion & Company Limited.

For details of other military history titles published by Helion & Company
Limited, contact the above address, or visit our website: http://www.helion.co.uk

We always welcome receiving book proposals from prospective authors.

Contents

Introduction		iv
1.	Medium and Minor Powers	
	The Papal States	9
	The Republic of Genoa	46
	Grand Duchy of Tuscany	71
	Duchy of Parma and Piacenza	100
	Duchy of Modena	109
	The Duchies of Mantua and Guastalla	118
	The Republic of Lucca	123
	Duchy of Massa and Principalityof Carrrara	137
	The Order of Malta	138
	The Republic of Messina	149
2.	Little and Great Italian Wars	
	Campaigns Against the Waldensians, 1655–1663	154
	The Savoy-Piedmont War Against Genoa, 1672–1673	171
	The Venetians in the Holy League War, 1684–1699	191
	The Second Waldensian War, 1686–1689	288

Appendix I: Imperial Fiefdoms, Independent Lordships and Republics in Italy (1659–1690)	292
Appendix II: Regiments and Tabular Data	295
Appendix III: Currencies in Italy in the Second Half of the Seventeenth Century	306
Image Commentaries	309
Colour Plate Commentaries	316
Bibliography	326

Introduction

According to some authors, a famous rhetorical statement concerning Italy and more specifically Italians seems, if carefully interpreted, to allude to exactly the opposite. This is the well-known definition of Italians as a people of poets, saints, warriors and sailors. Certainly there were worthy personalities among Italians in these matters, but according to some authors it is precisely in their anomalies that a different reality is perceived, namely a country with few warriors and sailors.[1] The result of these connotations, mutually amplified, has conditioned not only the entire history of Italy but even the daily existence of many of its inhabitants, and with it the knowledge of their past. After all, at the beginning of the sixteenth century this was already a sensitive topic.[2]

Today the concept of the small state in Europe applies to a few truly small territorial entities such as the Vatican City, the Principalities of Andorra, Liechtenstein, Monaco, the Republic of San Marino, and so on. Indeed, between the early modern age and the end of the Old Regime, it could refer to a plurality of geopolitical actors that interacted in various ways with the great national monarchies, guaranteeing their visibility and survival. Until a few years ago, historiography has rarely dealt with the ancient Italian states and even more rarely turned its attention to their 'military', even when certain factors interact with the study of society and its organisation. Among these, for example, the *bande* (militia) of the Grand Duchy of Tuscany, or those of the Papal State, prefigure a type of administration and take on characteristics typical of the compulsory conscription of the nineteenth and twentieth centuries. Concerning the overall numbers of this force it is obviously necessary to act with caution, but on several occasions the Italian states mobilised many thousands of men, and not only on paper. Just as obviously, these units could not compete with the regular troops in efficiency and discipline, however, the militia of the Genoese Republic successfully faced their enemies during the 1672 war against Savoy-Piedmont.

It is only in recent times that the debate has been taken up again thanks to excellent authors, who have investigated the role played by military

---

1　See various authors, *Studi Topografici e Strategici su l'Italia* (Milano, 1860), pp.620-623.

2　At the beginning of the Italian Wars, Nicolò Machiavelli warned his contemporaries in Chapter XII of *Il Principe* that 'the ruin of Italy is caused by the fact that for many years its security has been placed in mercenary arms'.

institutions in the formation of state apparatuses, bringing new knowledge and modifying many of the opinions that had been ingrained until then.³ Nevertheless, these contributions have relegated in the background the interest for the military participation of the ancient Italian states, so that apart from Savoy-Piedmont and Venice, a large part of the Italian military history consists almost exclusively of obsolete or ideologically conditioned works. At present, therefore, knowledge of Italian military institutions remains very fragmentary, pending the emergence of new knowledge from the rich repertoire preserved in the state archives of the Peninsula.

Recently, some historians have paid careful attention to the network of relations existing between the Italian states in the second half of the seventeenth century. Their research frequently reveals formal certificates of courtesy or pleasure on the occasions of marriage, papacy, monacation (entering a religious order), fairs and melodrama. There are also many circumstances of celebration, negotiation or exchange of hospitality in the passage to other states or religious places, in which the courts of princes are received by the holders of neighbouring states. These relations mainly concerned the princes dominating medium-sized territorial extensions of the Po Valley, namely the Gonzaga of Mantua, the Este of Modena and the Farnese of Parma. In this context the dukes of Savoy, the Medici in Tuscany and the less influential Cybo-Malaspina princes and then, from 1664, dukes of Massa, remain more reserved. Nevertheless, the sovereigns of Savoy-Piedmont, Tuscany and Massa were also necessarily involved in the epistolary rituals connecting the various Italian princes. In this interweaving of relations at a written level that sustained themselves with varying intensity and in certain cases could even be interrupted for long periods of time, as they were conditioned by geographical distance, the hierarchical gap emerges, the reciprocal antagonism, the need for protection and alliance, and again the weight of their marriage ties.⁴

---

3   Significant recent contributions include Alice Raviola Blythe, 'The Imperial System in Early Modern Northern Italy: A Web of Dukedoms, Fiefs and Enclaves along the Po', in P. H. Wilson and R. J. W. Ewans (eds), *The Holy Roman Empire, 1495–1806: A European Perspective* (Leiden-Boston, MS: Brill, 2012), pp.217–238; and 'Small States in Early Modern Italy: Definitions, Examples, and Interactions', in D. Bornstein, L. Gaffuri, B. Jeffrey Maxson (eds), *Languages of Power in Italy (1300–1600)* (Turnhout: Brepols, 2017), pp.3–16. To these works may be added Claudio Donati, 'Strutture militari degli Stati italiani nella prima età moderna: una rassegna degli studi recenti', in: *Società italiana di Studi Militari. Quaderno 2000*, P. Del Negro (ed.) *La storiografia militare in Italia e in Francia negli ultimi vent'anni. Due esperienze a confronto* (Venice, 27–28 aprile 2001), Napoli, E. S. I., 2003, pp.45–62; Virgilio Ilari, *Storia del servizio militare in Italia (1506–1870)*, vol. I, *Dall'ordinanza fiorentina di Machiavelli alla costituzione dell'esercito italiano*, Collana del Centro Militare di Studi Strategici (Rome: Rivista Militare, 1990). Regarding the panorama of recent studies on the military in Italy, see Nicola Labanca (ed.), *Storie di guerre ed eserciti. Gli studi di storia militare italiana negli ultimi venticinque anni* (Milan: Unicopli, 2011).

4   Alessandro Cont, 'Dialoghi della Sovranità. Gli incontri tra i principi italiani nel Seicento', in *Nuova Rivista Storica*, XCIX, January–April 2015, f.1, p.78.

From this viewpoint every Italian state was an 'artwork', as men had forged it for their own ends. However, one of the aspects that historians have rarely investigated is the relationship between the foreign policy of certain states and the reflection of this in military matters. The contradictions generated by the failed strategic challenges of the sixteenth century prefigured a limiting of the policy choices available. In the seventeenth century, with the exception of Savoy-Piedmont and Venice, most Italian states possessed a very small permanent professional force, supported by a militia that was more or less permanently joined in stable formations. Consequently every Italian state, even the smallest, pursued a geopolitics that was mainly geared towards a cheap defence of its borders and the attainment of a prominent international status. In this sense, the efforts of the Savoyards to free themselves from French tutelage must be considered, with the aim of providing themselves with an armed force capable of withstanding an enemy invasion and supporting them with modern fortifications. This was, moreover, the same objective pursued by apparently less threatened but much more exposed states such as the Republic of Genoa, the Grand Duchy of Tuscany, Modena, Parma, and even Lucca, the latter concentrating on the defence of the heart of the state by means of a massive urban fortification. It could not have been otherwise, considering that the invention and evolution of the *trace italienne* was the most obvious strategic outcome to respond to the changed scenario. In this period, Italian fortifications reached an unprecedented level of specialisation, combining the experiences developed in Italy with those matured in the Netherlands. Although no military engineer in Italy reached the fame of Vauban or Coehoorn, the number of engineers from the Peninsula is impressive.

At times, the defence of the state led some princes to forge alliances with distant foreign powers, as in the case of Modena when, through the marriage of Maria Beatrice d'Este to James II Stuart, Duke Alfonso IV tried to extend his network of relations as far as England: a choice that, after 1689, did not benefit him at all. Against this backdrop of insecure alliances it seems singular that, despite the fact that a league of Italian states had been formed twice in the seventeenth century against the Ottoman Empire, these relations did not give rise to a unitary confederation capable of producing results for the following centuries. This is even more peculiar considering that Italy was much more homogeneous in terms of language and especially religion compared to other European states.[5]

This age, therefore, also included a turning point for the Italian states, and although some pursued the most profitable strategy, the others on the whole did not remain as impassive as some historiography would like to portray. A careful study of the diplomatic sources yields an account of the awareness of the governments and courts on the most decisive issues. The long-term

---

5   As already mentioned, the next step, namely the creation of a lasting league of Italian states, was never realised, and in this epilogue today's geopoliticians can identify a recurring image of Italy, namely a substantially divided country in which particular interests ultimately prevailed over the collective ones.

causes and consequences did not escape their analysis. Evidence of this can be seen in the vast debate in certain courts such as that of the Pope, Tuscany or even princes who were actors of apparently contradictory choices, such as the Gonzaga in Mantua.

A product of long-term Italian geopolitics became the space of primary interest. This is represented by the area formed by the seas around the Peninsula, with a projection to Malta and the Aegean Sea, becoming Italy's actual border. Subservient to the Spanish sphere of influence, the Italian states played a fundamental role in the Mediterranean on the front opposing the other great empire of the time, the Ottoman Porte. The mutual membership of the Christian and Muslim worlds led to a further exasperation of the conflict, in which episodes of unprecedented cruelty were recorded on both sides. In the seventeenth century, belligerence between the two empires became endemic and continued into the next century without significant interruptions. Both factions faced each other in a ruthless privateers' war, punctuated by destructive actions in opposing territories, deportations of civilians, and reciprocal reprisals. In this context, the image of a peninsula uninvolved in the great international conflicts of the second half of the seventeenth century does not coincide with this state of chronic belligerence. The peninsular coastline was a military theatre that was unequalled throughout Europe in terms of duration and breadth of the front.[6] This scenario included the Spanish kingdoms of southern Italy as well as the mid-power states, and even the minor ones. No equivalent to the hundreds of armed coastal towers erected along the entire Italian coastal perimeter was built on the planet, including the Atlantic Wall; no other European territory in the modern age remained under the threat of raids from the sea for so long.[7] Although in the second half of the seventeenth century, none of the attacks reached the catastrophic violence of Otranto in 1480, or Agropoli in Salerno in 1630, the sighting of an Ottoman or North African sail was always cause for alarm and danger. It is a difficult task to establish the degree of military commitment provoked by privateer raids, and with it the extent of losses in terms of human lives and material, but it was certainly never a negligible item. Moreover, the adhesion in force of the Italian states to the war against the Porte shows how this threat was considered to be one of the most serious.

However, a process of consolidation of standing armies did not take place in Italy, opening – with the usual exception of Savoy-Piedmont – a season of strong military demobilisation that involved even a maritime power such as Venice. The crisis became evident, so much so that a talented historian could refer to this as a 'twilight' of a military vocation.[8] As already mentioned in

---

6   Claudio Donati, 'Le istituzioni di difesa nell'area italiana tra XVII e XVIII secolo: aspetti politici, economici e sociali', in R. Villari (ed.), *Controllo degli stretti e insediamenti militari nel Mediterraneo* (Rome: Laterza, 2002), pp.205–206.

7   Flavio Russo, *Guerra di Corsa. Ragguaglio storico sulle principali incursioni turco-barbaresche in Italia e sulla sorte dei deportati tra il XVI e il XIX secolo* (Roma: USSME, 1997), vol. I, p.7.

8   Gregory Hanlon, *The Twilight of a Military Tradition. Italian Aristocrats and European Conflicts, 1560–1800* (London: UCL Press, 1998).

the first part of this work, the unfavourable economic situation contributed to this twilight, which was more pronounced in the eighteenth century, however many signs of decline were already visible after 1659. Until recently, the historical trajectory of Italy during the Old Regime has been used as an element of comparison with Germany. In fact, in the second half of the seventeenth century, Germany and Italy offered very similar scenarios. Both countries were politically divided into many states, often with a history of recent bitter conflicts, and forced to move between the interests of Austria and Spain and those of Sweden and Louis XIV's France. This classical assumption then highlighted how, following a similar path, only two states were able to emancipate themselves from foreign influence: Brandenburg-Prussia in Germany and Savoy-Piedmont in Italy. And it was certainly not by chance that twentieth-century historians coined the term 'Brandenburg of Italy' to the Savoy state. However, in contrast to Italy, standing armies became an established reality in many other states including those with a smaller size and population than Italy, and above all, in Germany the profession of arms continued to involve a considerable part of the society of the Old Regime.

Certainly, many factors can be called upon to explain the negative trajectory of Italian military history. However, it is certain that the action of the Italian ruling class was not the same as in Germany. In Italy, the military vocation was destroyed by the very social glue that had enabled it to overcome the difficulties. It is something that has happened many times in the history of peoples, and the unreasonable and stubborn attachment to traditional values is the same that had enabled them to overcome difficulties in the past. In an interdependent society dominated by the aristocratic social bloc, the nobility was able to prevent anyone from introducing anything new. It was therefore a matter of the contrast between the short-term interests of the ruling class and the long-term interests of society as a whole.

1
Medium and Minor Powers

The Papal States

The negotiations for the Peace of Westphalia had shown the change of climate in international politics. Rome had found itself isolated from the European powers and both in Münster and Osnabrück the voice of the Papal envoy remained ignored. The renewed centrality of the Papacy achieved thanks to the Counter-Reformation, which had made Rome – with a fortunate expression – the 'grand theatre of the world', was entering a crisis.[1] The popes elected after 1648 took up the legacy of their predecessors in a European context that was becoming progressively more hostile over time, marked by the claims of monarchies and republics to reduce the privileges and prerogatives of the clergy in their states.[2]

By the middle of the century the Papal States took on a territorial and governmental pattern that remained stable until the crisis of the *Ancien Régime*. With an overall population of approximately 1,100,000 inhabitants, the Papal States were severely backward. Communication routes were poor, especially in the provinces south of the Apennines, and this naturally affected internal trade, which was also hindered by the presence of bandits organised into bands capable of challenging the regular troops. Although there were no large urban centres comparable to the cities of Northern Italy, Rome alone was the dominant city par excellence, symbol of the dual power held by the popes, and the only one with more than 100,000 inhabitants.[3] Therefore

---

1 G. Signorotto and M. A. Visceglia (eds), *La corte di Roma tra Cinque e Seicento teatro della politica europea* (Rome: Bulzoni, 1988), pp.13–14.

2 Elected popes from 1644 to 1692: Innocent X (Giovanni Battista Pamphili, 1644–1655); Alexander VII (Fabio Chigi, 1655–1667); Clement IX (Giulio Rospigliosi, 1667–1669); Clement X (Emilio Bonaventura Altieri, 1670–1676); Innocent XI (Benedetto Odescalchi, 1676–1689); Alexander VIII (Pietro Vito Ottoboni, 1689–1691) Innocent XII (Antonio Pignatelli di Spinazzola, 1692–1700).

3 A census from the early 1700s records a total population for Rome of 141,984 persons; of these, 62 were bishops, 2,824 priests, 3,811 friars and other religious persons, and 1,968 nuns. The list also includes 4,010 prostitutes. ASV, *Stato delle Anime della città di Roma dell'anno 1704*, c. n.n. f. 2.

'the eternal city' was the main reference point for careers and honours that could guarantee economic and political ascendancy. The remaining regional picture was fragmented into many medium-sized and small centres, which could not aggregate the economic activities of an entire region around them.

After Rome, the largest cities were Bologna, Ferrara and Perugia. These were the only centres to exceed 15,000 inhabitants,[4] and consequently, with the exception of Ferrara, enjoyed their own judicial and institutional autonomy.[5] Bologna was the only manufacturing centre of the state and the second most important city after Rome. Its ruling classes maintained relations with other Italian principalities, and the city's autonomy grew further during the seventeenth century.

Romagna had no cities capable of acting as a centralising pole. There was a reality made up of medium-small towns with Ravenna, Imola, Faenza, Forlì and Cesena among the most populous. All these centres had a patrician form of government that exercised a strong control over the countryside. The Romagna aristocracy, although small in number, was fully integrated into the service circuit between Rome and the province, and provided bishops, magistrates, governors and military. The Marche (or La Marca) had an urban, political and social profile similar to that of Romagna, and here too no great centre had imposed itself, which is why the picture was fragmented into towns with rather small districts. The territory was divided into two legations. In the first of these by extension, the most important centres were Ancona, Ascoli, Cingoli, Fabriano, Jesi, Macerata, Matelica, Osimo and Recanati. The major cities of the Urbino legation were Pesaro – which had become the regional 'capital' of the Marche – Senigallia, Camerino and Fermo. The ruling classes of the Marche had maintained their economic pre-eminence and retained an ideological bond with their past of self-government, yet during the century there was a profound demographic and economic crisis of the patricians and the entire provincial economy. The most obvious example of these difficulties can be found in Ancona, which suffered a sharp economic decline and demographic impoverishment of the entire social fabric of the city, with negative repercussions for the city's major infrastructures such as the port, fortress and roads. The economic downturn favoured the presence of people from the Marche in the army.[6]

---

4   The figures concerning the inhabitants of the communities are taken from a survey compiled in 1656 for the use of the congregation of the *Buon Governo*; the lists were drawn up in descending order of inhabitants. ASV, *Commissariato Armi*, 293, f. 77.

5   Luca Giangolini, *Le Armi del Papa. L'esercito pontificio tra burocrazia curiale e nobiltà. 1645–1740* (Rome: Università La Sapienza, 2018), p.80. Ferrara had lost its autonomy in 1598 and its territory had been reformed by Clement VIII in the early seventeenth century. Against this backdrop the city's nobles quickly linked themselves to the new Papal power, and probably with the loss of political autonomy, the memory of the previous organisation had also been lost.

6   Virgilio Ilari, *Storia del servizio militare in Italia (1506–1870)*, vol. I, *Dall' ordinanza fiorentina di Machiavelli alla costituzione dell'esercito italiano*, Collana del Centro Militare di Studi Strategici (Rome: Rivista Militare, 1990), p.289.

Like Romagna and the Marche, Umbria had many medium-sized towns, the largest of which were Spoleto, Narni, Terni, Città di Castello and Rieti. All these towns had a *contado* (countryside) similar in extension to that of the municipal age. In the course of the century the Umbrian centres had maintained a certain autonomy, and together with Perugia the province provided many personnel for the state magistracies and especially for the army.

Latium had a modest urban development, aggravated by the malaria that infested large parts of the region, including the Agro Pontino, where the sparse population was confined to a few villages. The main cities were Viterbo, Velletri and Alatri, all very small, and above all poor, with a purely agricultural and pastoral economy. Aristocratic families gravitated around Rome, as did the city economies. The only centre with a certain political importance was Orvieto, while in the southern area Velletri had a certain importance, with a patriciate that grew in size periodically thanks to new families coming from outside. In general the Latium area remained economically underdeveloped compared to other regions, and remained strongly conditioned by its relationship with Rome.[7]

The end of the territorial expansion of the state in the sixteenth century led to the need to reorganise the military apparatus, reducing it in peacetime to the minimum force necessary to protect the northern border. At the end of the sixteenth century in this area there were no modern fortifications, but within a few years, new impressive defence works were built. Now, the Papal frontier was articulated around a series of modern strongholds supported by a series of minor, weaker, centres of resistance. On the Adriatic coast new fortification plans were abandoned, entrusting the protection of the coastline to the fortified port-cities and to a set of coastal towers . These were far fewer in number than on the other Italian coasts due to the absence of Barbary pirates in the Adriatic, and sometimes these were supported by little forts and guarded by the usual pair or, rarely, three *torrieri* (watchtowers).

As the land border received more attention, Ferrara, on the branch of the Po known as the Po di Volano, quartered the major garrison on the northern border. Throughout the seventeenth century the city was subject to many improvements. The walls were reinforced with 15 bastions, three of which fortified the citadel, today known as Castello Estense.[8] This was situated on the northeastern edge of the city close to the river, and had a pentagonal and star-shaped plan, the remaining two bastions facing inwards, dominating the city, according to the classic scheme adopted by Francesco Paciotto between

---

[7] Giampiero Brunelli, 'Identità dei militari pontifici in età moderna. Questioni di metodo e uso delle fonti', in C. Donati and B. R. Kroener (eds), *Militari e società civile dell'età moderna Atti della XLVII settimana di Studio*, Trento, 13–17 September 2004 (Bologna: Il Mulino, 2007), p.313. 'People who approach the history of the papal army between the sixteenth and seventeenth centuries are struck by the disproportion between the conspicuous investments committed to the armed forces and the modest results achieved.'

[8] In sources after 1692, the Castello Estense is referred to simply as the *Cittadella*; the Castello Estense is not equivalent to the fortress of Ferrara, but they were two different places. See Lutz, 'L'esercito pontificio nel 1667', p.60.

1. Forte Urbano, fresco of the *Sala Urbana* in Bologna, mid seventeenth century. See image commentaries for more information.

1564 and 1568 for the citadel of Turin.⁹ On the opposite bank of the river the city was protected by a fortified structure in a barely visible semicircle, with three bastions.

Along the Po River there were some minor fortifications. Descending in an arc from north to south – from Ferrara to Bologna – passing west, the border with Modena was guarded by Bondeno on the Panaro River, and the village of Stellata, then by Cento, Secco, Crevalcore, Piumazzo, Bazzano and Castel San Giovanni (today San Giovanni in Persiceto). This was, quite rightly, the area most at risk and everyone in Rome remembered how the security of the borders had been threatened by the crisis of Mantua in 1629, when the Spanish-Imperial troops had descended along the Flanders Way to the Po Valley, bringing death, destruction and above all the plague.

Like all capitals, and because it was considered to be such, Bologna should have had a citadel as a strong defensive point. Instead, the Papal government had preferred to build something more and different, having the imposing Forte Urbano erected to the west of the city. Located about 25 kilometres from Bologna and only five miles from Modena, close to the village of Castelfranco near the Panaro River, Fort Urban had a powerfully bastioned curtain, designed in 1628 by Giambattista Mola da Como. The construction of the fort was entrusted to the architect Giulio Buratti, and the layout of the star-shaped fortress was 900 metres, with a ditch and an entrance with three lift bridges and equipped with a battery of 29 cannons.¹⁰

---

9 Ciro Paoletti, 'La frontiera padana dello Stato Pontificio nel secolo XVII', in C. Sodini (ed.), *Frontiere e fortificazioni di frontiera* (Florence-Lucca: Edifir, 2001), p.131.

10 Lutz, 'L'esercito pontificio nel 1667. Camera apostolica, bilancio militare dello Stato della Chiesa e nepotismo nel primo evo moderno', in *Miscellanea in onore di Monsignor Martino Giusti*

The particular position of Fort Urbano in relation to the city it was meant to protect stemmed both from a search for security and from a return of Papal policy to the expansionist aims of the previous century. The only point on which the Pope and the cardinals converged was in considering the northwestern frontier uncovered; and Fort Urban – named after the Pope – was the compromise solution between the defensive policy of the Pontiff and the offensive policy of the cardinals.[11]

Because of its location, Fort Urbano had the great advantage of serving as a base for concentrating the army in the countryside, as well as being an operational centre for defence from the west, a logistical terminal and main advanced warehouse for troops operating in the Po Valley, and finally additional cover for Bologna and secondarily Ferrara. The former was protected directly and frontally against attacks from the west, and indirectly against any other threat, because Bologna could not be besieged unless the fortress was neutralised, which in turn could not be besieged unless the city was neutralised. Fort Urbano thus represented an unprecedented optimisation of resources and a remarkable strategic innovation for this age. Its importance was immediately grasped by the neighbouring sovereigns and the fort was considered extremely dangerous by the Este in particular, who responded by erecting a citadel to protect Modena. The Venetians instead focused their attention on the main course of the Po, where they built the fort of Pontelagoscuro exactly opposite Ferrara. Rome considered Fort Urbano sufficient to cover the legations. For this reason it did not worry too much about the other centres in Emilia and left them with the fortifications already existing, making only some interventions on the wall structures, partially adapted to the growing use of firearms of various calibres.

The major fortress on the Adriatic coast was Ancona, which, however, was considered vulnerable from the land side. On the western shore the fortified port of Civitavecchia guarded the Tyrrhenian coast and housed the Pope's small war fleet. Rome was only fortified north-west of the Tiber River, thus exploiting the natural defence of the river and the Janiculum Hill. On the opposite side, where the ancient Imperial walls stand, the perimeter was overextended and for this reason the popes considered it too costly to modernise them with ramparts. An elevated corridor called Passetto di Borgo connected the Vatican palaces with the fortress of Castel Sant'Angelo, which had withstood the siege of the Lansquenets in 1527 and barred access to the main bridge of the Tiber. In 1626 the castle was provided with a modern rampart wall. The Passetto di Borgo was covered in 1627–30, again on the initiative of Urban VIII. The key to the defence of the *Urbe*, however, remained the Janiculum Hill. It was on the occasion of the First Castro War (1641–1644) that the Pope ordered the construction of a new defensive curtain. The work was entrusted to the architects Domenico Castelli and Giovanni Angelo Bonazzini. The new walls around the Janiculum Hill were later joined to the Vatican citadel, and the junction was carried out between Porta Cavalleggeri and Porta di Ripa Grande,

---

Prefetto dell'Archivio Segreto Vaticano, II (Città del Vaticano, Archivio Vaticano, 1978), p.61.
11   Paoletti, 'La frontiera padana dello Stato Pontificio', p.133.

Above, and facing page: 2. and 3. Plan of Ferrara and its pentagonal citadel, in two prints dating to the first half of the seventeenth century (author's archive). See image commentaries for more information.

which was set back to shorten the defensive circuit. The new wall included 12 new bastions and a new vehicular access: Porta San Pancrazio. These works were completed in 1644 under Innocent X.[12]

The largest arsenals and weapon factories were also located in and around Rome. The main arsenals were in Castel Sant'Angelo and Palazzi Apostolici. The Vatican armoury was located on the first floor of the east wing of the Palazzo del Belvedere, where today some rooms of the Vatican Apostolic Library are located.

On the southern border there were no modern fortifications capable of stopping the passage of an army from the Kingdom of Naples, an eventuality that in any case was considered entirely unlikely. Umbria also had no fortifications capable of stopping a possible invasion from the Tuscan Apennines, with the exception of the Pauline fortress in Perugia. Although mighty, the walls of the latter as well as the equally remarkable walls of Spoleto and Ascoli no longer held any strategic importance and therefore did not undergo any modernisation. The same was true for Benevento and Pontecorvo, as well as Avignon, which unlike the other two places was exposed to the invasion of a

---

12 Giangolini, *Le Armi del Papa*, p.67. The direction of all these fortifications in Rome and the modernisation of Fort Urbano were supervised by a prelate, Cardinal Vincenzo Maculano.

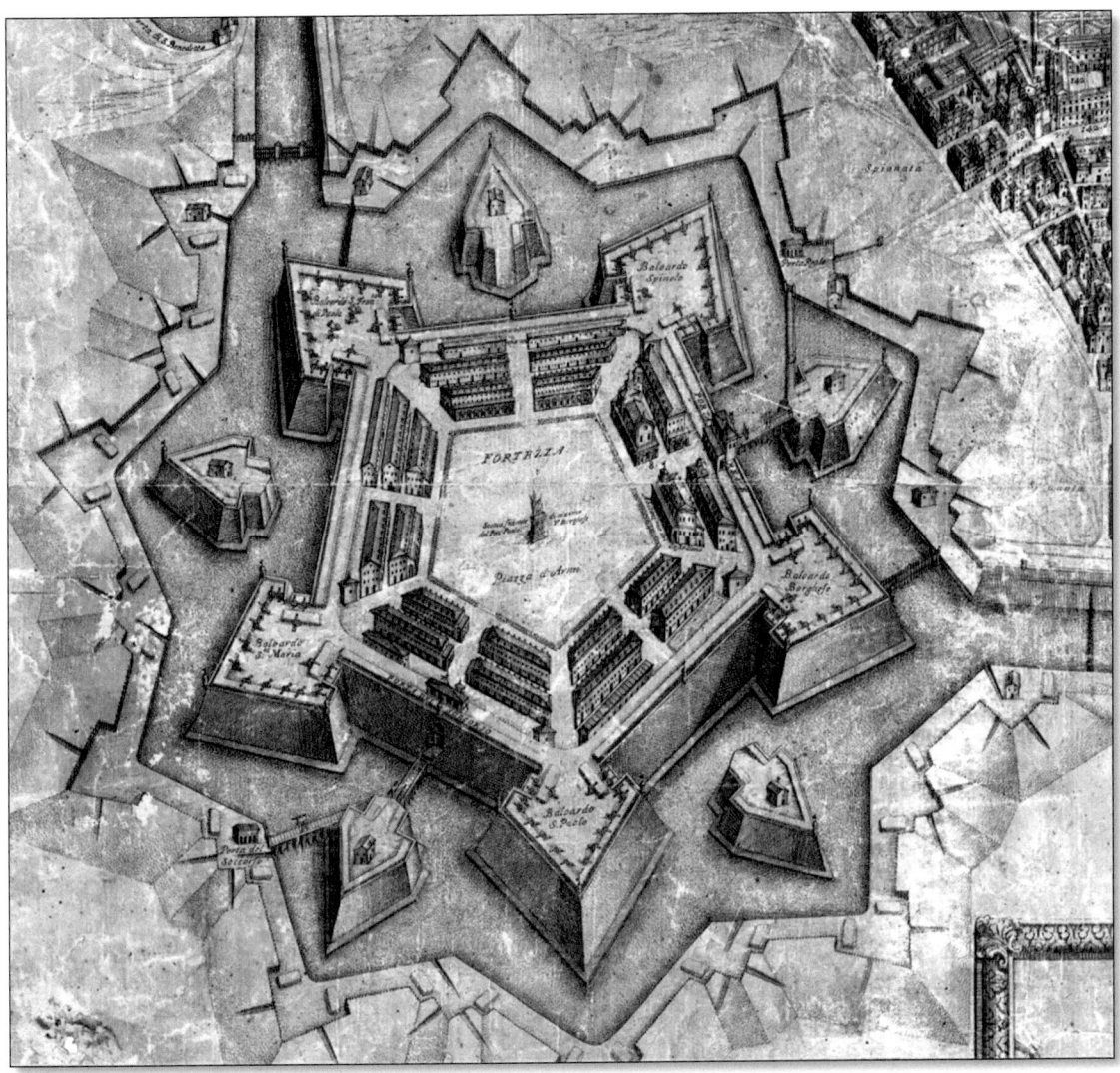

much less reassuring neighbour than the king of Spain, namely Louis XIV, who in fact occupied Avignon twice in 1662–64 and 1687–88.

Finally there were 31 fortified towers on the Roman coast, of which 12 were in the west and 18 in the east, including the tower of Fiumicino.

Despite the modern fortifications the state did not managed to remedy its chronic weakness. This condition was the consequence of two factors. The first was the preference for an aggressive policy, therefore being more concerned with preparing bases for attack than creating truly effective defensive systems. The second was the choice of Rome as the point of greatest concentration of resources. The legations were not to be neglected, but there was the problem of the high costs required to maintain strong military forces there. In order to get around this obstacle a dangerous solution was preferred: the setting back of depots and supplying the front only if and when it became necessary. In the event of war, men and materials from Rome went up the Via Cassia to Viterbo, the intermediate base for the concentration of resources generally destined for the north. If these were not necessary on the border with Tuscany they were sent along the Tiber valley to Orvieto and Perugia, making them cross the Apennines roughly at the height of Bagni di Romagna. From there they could either head towards Cesena and the sea or towards Forlì and the Po Valley. In the latter case, protected by the fortifications of Forlì, Faenza, Castel San Pietro and Imola, they would follow the Via Emilia to Bologna and then be distributed along the border.

The danger of the operation lay in the length of the route and the narrowness of the corridor to Umbria. If it were cut, the entirety of the Papal military forces in the Po Valley would be deprived of supplies. The alternative route was to move the supply along the Via Flaminia, routing it via Terni and Foligno to the Marche coast. There the materials could be forwarded to Rimini, from where they continued along the via Emilia towards Bologna and Forte Urbano. If, on the other hand, they were directed to Ferrara, the matter changed and they had to be conveyed by sea as far as the Po delta, taking the Po di Volano and going up it. This, however, could only be executed by having control of the Adriatic, or failing that, a good network of coastal fortifications; and the Papal States had neither.

'The Arms of the Holy Father'

By the 1650s the negative verdict on the Pope's army was a common opinion. The outcome of the Castro War had been very unsatisfactory despite the huge resources consumed, and this had at least persuaded the Holy See to reconsider its military policy. However, reform projects did not always proceed consistently, and the ambitions of a pontiff could be very different from those of his predecessors. In fact in 1663, almost 20 years after the end of the conflict over Castro, the Venetian ambassador Pietro Basadonna pointed out to Alexander VII Chigi (1665–1667), who intended to arm himself to oppose Louis XIV:

> His Beatitude (the Pope) told me that the hearts of the Romans were not afraid of the ravings of the Parisian youths, to which, I replied, that it is sometimes better to form an alliance with sensible old men than with reckless youths, who want to give vent to a whim of their own, venture even to the brink of precipices, and that to oppose those who have crickets in their heads, armies at their sides, iron in their hands, and millions under their feet, was no good for the Pontiff, who have but two fingers raised. I represented several times, that the king (Louis XIV) said that the pope was too ruined by the debt of fourteen million owed by the Camera, and now passed the fifty, and that in short His Holiness could not arm himself, and without arms he could not fight, and therefore was destined for certain defeat even without fighting the enemy.[13]

These words must have sounded mortifying to the Pope's ears, since the effort for defending the state with a modern and effective army had been

---

13 Nicolò Barozzi and Guillaume Bechet *Relazioni degli Stati europei lette al Senato dagli Ambasciatori Veneti nel Secolo Decimosettimo* (Venice, 1897), Serie II, Vol. III, *Relazioni di Roma*, pp.13–14.

significant and still recent. Indeed, the disproportion between resources employed and results achieved seems to have been a long-standing constant of the Pope's military policy.[14]

However, the Papal army was already a complex organisation with an administrative tradition that had been constantly updated. Theoretically, at the head of the army was the pontiff assisted by the *Congregazione della Sacra Consulta* (Congregation of the Holy Council). This body became permanent at the end of the sixteenth century and consisted of four cardinals, the Secretary of State as prefect, and a competent number of prelates, usually eight. It performed tasks of the utmost importance, such as the interpretation of laws, the resolution of jurisdictional, feudal, and administrative disputes, and the adjudication of conflicts between communities and governors. Consequently the congregation was called upon to intervene in all disputes between communities and soldiers, as well as in matters concerning the militia.[15] As guarantor of public order, the *Sacra Consulta* also managed the military force in charge of public order in the capital.

The delegated command of the armed forces was entrusted to the *Generale di Santa Chiesa* (General of the Holy Church). The office was normally attributed by the pope to his closest relative, brother or nephew; declared such by the pontiff with a special *breve* (brief). For the common opinion, the *motu proprio* had to guarantee a stronger institutional solidity, since the General had to be obeyed by all the troops of the state. The *Sacra Consulta* and the pontiff's *Maggiordomo*, as director of the pope's lifeguards, were to assist and support the general's actions. The appointment ceremony included the awarding of the general staff, and the oath of allegiance, which took place privately in the pope's residence. Contemporaries did not fail to point out the inexperience of these relatives, yet the position of Captain General of the Holy Church remained entrusted to the popes' relatives for a long time. As usual, Gergorio Leti commented with scornful irony on the awarding of the rank: 'and since the attribution of that office is concerned with blood, and not valour, it sometimes happens that it is given to people, who do not understand the Art of War, better than the horse they ride.'[16]

After the *Generale di Santa Chiesa*, the highest military office was the *capitano generale* (captain general). Originally this rank was conferred on princes and captains who had defended the Apostolic See, such as the dukes of Urbino, the kings of Naples and Aragon, and other members of important Italian families. The institutional contours of this figure gradually moved

---

14 Giampiero Brunelli, 'Al vertice dell'istituzione militare pontificia: il Generale di santa Chiesa (sec, XVI-XVII)', in A. Jamme and O. Poncet (eds), *Offices et papauté (XIVe-XVIIe siècle)* (Rome: Publications de l'École française de Rome, 2013), p.484.

15 The affairs of the militia were also managed by the Congregation of *Buon Governo*. As a rule, the *Sacra Consulta* was called upon in cases of violations of obligations, misconduct and abuse of power by individual militia members, while the Congregation of *Buon Governo* intervened in cases of excessive expenses demanded of the communities.

16 Gregorio Leti, *Itinerario della Corte di Roma o Vero Teatro Historico, cronologico e politico della Sede Apostolica, Dataria e Cancelleria Romana* (Valenza, 1675), vol. I, p.289.

4. Benedetto Odescalchi, pope as Innocent XI (r. 1676–1689) differed from his predecessors in his greater courage and decisiveness in the defence of Papal prerogatives. An austere pope of rigid principles, Innocent undertook important reform in the state's affairs, especially in foreign relations. Even more notable was his struggle against Gallicanism, which caused new tensions with Louis XIV.

away from a position of commanding an army enlisted by the Papacy, as the very name of the office implied.[17] In the following years a slow but profound change in the Roman political order matured. After a new phase of fierce nepotism under Clement IX (1667–1669) and Clement X (1670–1676), with the appointment of the former's brother, Camillo Rospigliosi,[18] and the latter's nephew, Gaspare Paluzzi degli Albertoni-Altieri, as *generale di Santa Chiesa,* Innocent XI (1676–1689) refused to appoint a titular officer. Shortly afterwards the last to be invested with the rank of Captain General, during the two years of Alexander VIII's pontificate (1689–1691), was Antonio Ottoboni.

With these major ranks the Secretary of State has to be considered too. Formally the Cardinal Secretary of State had no direct jurisdiction over the army, although on many occasions he communicated and intervened in military matters. The reason for this influence is due to the quantitative growth of the military bureaucracy and communication with other offices. However, the influence was also a consequence of the growth in importance of the figure of the Secretary of State in the changing balance of the *curia* in the second half of the seventeenth century. His main competence was to direct the pontiff's very important Particular Secretariat. He was responsible for the control and coordination of nuncios and legates, and was also in charge of correspondence with foreign sovereigns and princes.[19]

After the two major ranks, the *luogotenente dell'una e dell'altra guardia* and the *Eccellentissimo Castellano di Castel Sant'Angelo* followed in order of importance. The latter held command of the garrison, but the ordinary administration and military direction fell to his deputy, who was usually the captain of the first company quartered in Rome, and was therefore an officer by profession, while the titular *castellano* was chosen from among the prelates. The office itself was not traditionally granted to a relative, but under

---

17   Brunelli, 'Al vertice dell'istituzione militare pontificia', p.497.

18   In the same period Don Vincenzo Rospigliosi was appointed as *generalissimo* of the Allied fleet in 1668 and 1669, in the campaigns against the Ottoman at Crete. He was Pope Clement IX's nephew and belonged to a Tuscan family which had counted several knights in the order of St Stephen and St John, as was he himself before the election of his uncle. His experience in naval warfare, however, was not sufficient to avoid the unsatisfactory conclusion of the last naval campaigns in the Mediterranean.

19   Antonio Menniti Ippolito, 'Il Segretario di Stato e il Segretario dei Memoriali: la difficile ricerca di stabilità all'interno della curia papale prima e dopo l'abolizione del nepotismo (secc. XVII–XVIII)', in *Archivum Historiae Pontificiae*, 46 (2008), pp.79–85.

Alexander VII it was held by Carlo Chigi, Knight of Malta and member of the collateral branch of the Pope's family. There were also a further four, minor, offices of *castellano*, whose incumbents held the post in Ancona, Ascoli Piceno, Perugia and Benevento.

A fifth senior rank was the *Maestro di Campo Generale delle Soldatesche*, which, however, was assigned temporarily, although in the 1670s it was permanently assigned to a pope's nephew.

As examined by many historians,[20] the nature of the Roman *curia*[21] and the electability of the Papacy tended to disfavour career ministers in favour of relatives, and this was the more recurrent object of the complaints of people who commented on the structure and functioning of the Papal government. The presence of the relative as alter ego of the pope limited any possibility of replacing the curial 'nephew'. The nephew is a difficult figure to classify. In fact, he was not part of the court, but was above it, as an alter ego of the pontiff he was not part of the ordinary curial hierarchy. A younger trusted man than his elderly uncle, the nephew controlled the faction closest to the pontiff, supervised clientele and could manage the court with greater flexibility of action than the pontiff could. This stemmed from the exceptional and original character of the Papal figure, who in essence was an elected monarch. Throughout the seventeenth century there was no lack of political debates and encounters concerning the figure of the nephew. However, the debates never took on a substantial character as they did not produce a realistic alternative to the prevailing model of government, namely the creation of a cardinal relative with the characteristics of a worthy or favourite to act as a link between the court of Rome and the pontiff. In 1642 Urban VIII requested an opinion from the cardinals on the advisability of placing their relatives in positions of political and economic prominence.[22]

Among the measures proposed against nepotistic practices there was the plan to abolish all military charges assigned to the pontiff's blood relatives, starting with the rank of *Generale di Santa Chiesa*, and appointing a professional officer only in case of need.[23] In this regard, the treatment reserved to the pope's nephews in the last decades of the seventeenth century represented the start of a new phase. The changing context outside the *curia* made the debate on nepotism progressively more favourable to those who

---

20   Georg Lutz, 'L'esercito pontificio nel 1667', pp.39–95; Menniti Ippolito, 'Il Segretario di Stato e il Segretario dei Memoriali'; Paolo Prodi, *Il sovrano pontefice. Un corpo e due anime: la monarchia papale nella prima età moderna* (Bologna: Il Mulino, 1982).

21   The 'Roman Curia' comprises the administrative institutions of the Holy See and the central body through which the affairs of the Catholic Church are conducted. It is substantially the principal body of government of the Papal States.

22   Giangolini, *Le Armi del Papa*, p.39. The influence of the pope's relatives in the state's affairs was an old matter. The scenario began to change when Pope Paul IV (1555–1559) instituted the office of *sovrintendente dello Stato Ecclesiastico* (Superintendent of the Ecclesiastical State), initiating the phase of so-called 'moderate nepotism' or, with an expression that better describes the phenomenon, 'institutional nepotism'.

23   *Ibid.*

wished to put an end to this practice. However, about this delicate matter Cardinal Sforza Pallavicini had been very clear in his opinion addressed to Pope Alexander VII (1655–1667) just after his election as pope:

> Your Holiness cannot last without considerable help, and this he has proved he cannot obtain from foreign ministers, who lack but authority, love and confidence, ardour … The ministers mostly look to make friends and not enemies in the future, the cardinals do not want to spoil the hopes of the pontificate, so that the reigning pope has very few who are fully faithful to him, and those very few he does not see can not be trusted with prudence …[24]

Contemporaries did not fail to emphasise the inexperience of these relatives, yet the office of *capitano generale di Santa Chiesa* evolved in a way that cannot be reduced only to those judgements. The matter is somewhat different for the other posts of senior commander, always entrusted to relatives of the pope, which required military expertise, because they dealt with the actual command of an army on campaign. The nephew Camillo Pamphili was Captain General from 1645 to 1655, he was also Captain General of the galleys for only one year in 1644, commander of the Pope's lifeguard, and governor of Borgo and the fortress of Castel Sant'Angelo. Innocent X then decided to downgrade his nephew, thus the post of commander of the fleet passed to the more capable Nicolò Ludovisi, nephew of Gregory XV (1621–1623), while the post of commander of Sant'Angelo went to Andrea Giustiniani, another nephew of the Pope. Camillo Pamphili was a mediocre politician who occupied the traditional offices of his cardinal nephew. Innocent X's system of government then took the form of the so-called *cognatismo* (influence of the brothers-in-law), by virtue of the political prominence of his sister-in-law Olimpia Maidalchini, who had the politically insubstantial nephew Francesco Maidalchini appointed to the major offices.

A true debate on nepotism started with the aforementioned Alexander VII, who at first did not call his relatives to Rome. In 1656, during a session of the consistory, he asked the cardinals to express their opinion on the possibility of his relatives being transferred to Rome, so it was only a year after his election that the Pope granted positions to his own relatives. In another session, the Sacred College was unanimous in considering the practice legitimate, yet the fact that the Pope had sought such legitimacy shows how the institution of nepotism was no longer a foregone political fact.[25] These events and the decisions that followed had consequences for the Papal military. Indeed, during the pontificates of Innocent X (1644–1655) and Alexander VII there were some institutional developments for the offices that administered the permanent troops in the shadow of the Pontiff's prestigious relatives. After Alexander VII, with Clement IX (1667–1669) the role and influence of his nephew Giacomo Rospigliosi was inferior

---

24 Giangolini, *Le Armi del Papa*, p.58.
25 Antonio Menniti Ippolito, *Il tramonto della Curia nepotista. Papi, nipoti e burocrazia curiale tra XVI e XVII secolo* (Rome: Viella, 2008), pp.80–81.

to that of the Secretary of State, as well as that of Pope Clement himself, but the octogenarian Clement X Altieri (1670–1676) decided on a line of preservation, and not having a nephew he adopted one: Gaspare Paluzzi, who had married the Pope's only niece. Throughout his pontificate his nephew was *capitano generale di Santa Chiesa*; an interesting fact is that he held the position throughout the pontificate of Innocent XI (1676–1689). The end of the ancient equilibrium came with the election of Innocent XI, who made the first serious attempt to dismantle institutional nepotism. At the conclave of 1676 a new faction intolerant of nepotism coagulated, leading to the election of Benedetto Odescalchi as Innocent XI.[26] Efforts to approve a bill banning the practice of nepotism, however, did not have the outcome the Pontiff had hoped for, due to resistance in the *curia*, in particular from Cardinals Albizzi and Ottoboni, opponents of the Pontiff and influential supporters of the Holy Inquisition.

Pietro Vito Ottoboni, newly elected as Alexander VIII (1689–1691), quickly undid the institutional initiatives of Innocent XI and his collaborators. All the suppressed offices were reinstated, 'showing the magnificence and unwavering strength of the Church in the defence of its privileges'.[27] Consequently Alexander VIII granted military posts to his nephews: Antonio was appointed *capitano generale di Santa Chiesa* and created Duke of Fiano in 1690. His brother Marco received the office of lieutenant of the *due guardie*, general of the galleys and *castellano* of Castel Sant'Angelo.[28] In any case, to avoid emphasising the presence of the nephews, the four highest offices were always indicated without naming the titular officer.

Regarding military expenditure, this came under the responsibility of the *Reverenda Camera Apostolica*, the general administrative body of the Papal States, which was simultaneously in charge of the organisation and funds to manage all military expenditure. Originally these responsibilities were exercised by the General Treasurer. This office was entrusted to a prelate who acted as subordinate to the orders of the *capitano generale di Santa Chiesa*.[29] The chief officer of the administration was the *tesoriere generale*. Until 1634 this office extended his authority to all economic matters concerning fortresses, the war fleet and the Roman arsenal of Castel Sant'Angelo. Urban VIII removed

---

26 Brunelli, 'Al vertice dell'istituzione militare pontificia', p.14. 'Among the measures proposed against nepotistic practices, the project to abolish all military posts assigned to the pontiff's blood relatives stands out, starting with that of General of Holy Church, giving command to experts only in case of need. Subsequent comments by members of the College of Cardinals proved to be against the hypothesis, emphasising the inconsistency of excluding even a relative skilled in the military art and the risk of losing control of the troops without the activity of close relatives of the pope.'

27 Giangolini, *Le Armi del Papa*, p.61.

28 *Ibid.*: 'The reality, however, was quite different: besides the changes in European politics, nepotism as it had been conceived during the Baroque age was no longer financially sustainable. In two years, Ottoboni's nephews, who were on the verge of financial ruin, obtained around 700,000 *scudi* after the election of their uncle, almost a third of the State's annual income.'

29 Ruggero Pastura, *La reverenda Camera Apostolica e i suoi Archivi (secoli XV–XVIII)* (Rome: Archivio di Stato di Roma, 1984), pp.145–146.

5. Pope Alexander VII, the Tuscan Fabio Chigi (r. 1655–1667), came into conflict with Louis XIV in the 1660s. After him, his successor tried to avoid the involvement of the Church in the European conflicts inaugurating a foreign policy of low profile.

all military prerogatives from the *tesoriere generale* and granted these to a new cleric of the Chamber: Luigi Alessandro Omodei (1608–1685).[30] He received the title of *provisore e conservatore generale delle fortezze, armi e monizioni dello Stato Ecclesiastico* (*Provveditore* and General Conservator of the Fortresses, Arms and Ammunition of the Ecclesiastical State). The direct superior of this new prelate was still the *capitano generale di Santa Chiesa*, but he had to act in concert with the *Reverenda Camera Apostolica*. From this date the *tesoriere generale* only retained administrative authority over supplies to the troops on campaign. The new office acquired a certain importance and prestige thanks to the administrative expertise of Omodei, who held the post until 1654. In 1652 two *commissariati* were also established, respectively for the army and the war fleet, also dependent on the *Reverenda Camera Apostolica*. From the first of these, the *commissario delle armi*, depended the secretary of war, the *Uditorato Criminale*, the *collaterale generale delle Milizie* and the eight governors of arms: Romagna, Urbino, Velletri, Terni, Rome, Rieti, Ancona and Ferrara. Pope Alexander VII also made the office of Commissioner of Arms permanent in 1667.[31] The office was held by Niccolò Acciaioli from 1655 until 1667, and later by Buonaccorso Buonaccorsi from 1667 to 1668, and then by Girolamo Gastaldi, who would operate for just a couple of years until 1669.[32]

As for the *commissario del mare*, a position sometimes taken over directly by the *tesoriere generale*, he administered the navy, consisting of the galleys, the garrison of Civitavecchia, the prison of Castel Sant'Angelo, where those condemned to the oar of the galleys were kept, the ports of Anzio and Nettuno on the Tyrrhenian Sea, Senigallia and Pesaro on the Adriatic, and the 31 coastal towers on the Roman coast.

All military accounting was entrusted to the *collaterale*, a cleric of the *Reverenda Camera Apostolica*, who dealt with the control of all the expenditure of the garrisons, except for the legations, which had their own single *commissario camerale* (chamber commissioner) in Ferrara. Avignon, although also a legation, had its own chamber commissioner because of its distance from Rome. The most important garrisons had a paymaster.

The government administered its military expenditure through different means. The simple and most immediate method was the establishment of a tax for every military need. Communities were called upon to pay for the troops

---

30 Giangolini, *Le Armi del Papa*, pp.31–32.
31 Ilari, 'L'esercito pontificio', pp.581–582.
32 Giangolini, *Le Armi del Papa*, p.44.

of the garrisons they quartered, not only in the event of war. Recruitments that were made to increase the strength of the garrisons were partly paid for by the host and neighbouring provinces. For example, Alexander VII instituted two taxes in 1658, the first to reimburse Ferrara for the costs of housing the troops and the second, again for the benefit of Ferrara, for the equipment of the new recruits.[33] A second method of financing was the use of public debt. On the occasion of the War of Castro, bills of exchange were issued, half of which were *vacabili*,[34] while the permanent half was listed as *Monte Perpetuo Difesa*.[35] Finally, there was always the option of resorting to the Treasury of St Peter, which had an average value of about five million *scudi*.[36]

Military justice was managed by the aforementioned *Uditorato Criminale*. This office consisted of a military auditor, a civilian auditor, a chancellor and a fiscal auditor. The latter was in charge of preparing appeals to the tribunal of the *Sacra Consulta* to protect the rights of the military, especially if they were militiamen who appealed against community authority that did not recognise their privileges. The civil auditor reviewed the contracts and quarters, forwarded the commissariat's reports to the pope and counted the withholdings on the salaries of troops quartered in Rome. The *Sacra Consulta* did not only have jurisdiction over disputes between communities and soldiers. From 1670 the control of access and customs was directed by this office, which carried out this task with a special department with the functions of gendarmerie, acting against contraband and banditry.[37]

Alongside these permanent posts and offices the popes placed temporary magistracies, constituted according to need. The best known was the *Sacra Congregazione delle Armi*, or *Congregazione Militare*, as it is more often denominated in the sources. The mere fact that it was convened when needed testifies to its importance. In the seventeenth century it was convened three times: 1607, 1644 and 1663. In 1644 the congregation consisted of seven cardinals who had to limit authority and control the captain general. In 1663 Alexander VII convened the congregation in view of the possible war against Louis XIV; on that occasion the office comprised the *capitano generale di Santa Chiesa*, two generals and the general commissioner. The congregation also had its own secretariat.

---

33 Ilari, 'L'esercito pontificio', p.590.

34 Virgilio Ilari, 'L'esercito pontificio nel XVIII secolo fino alle Riforme del 1792–93', in *Studi Storico Militari 1985*, USSME (Rome 1986), p.591.

35 The interest rate of the *Monti* was four percent until 1684. Innocent XI reduced it to three percent. This brought considerable savings that created considerable budget surpluses in the following years. Domenico Strangio, 'La finanza pubblica a Roma e nello Stato Pontificio tra età moderna e contemporanea', in M. Cini (ed.), *Antico Regime e finanza pubblica: gli Stati italiani preunitari* (Pisa: ETS, 2015), p.112.

36 This reserve fund was established by Sixtus V in 1586 as the *Tesoro di Castel Sant'Angelo* and amounted to four million *scudi*, three million of which were in gold.

37 Ilari, 'L'esercito pontificio', p.587. *Vacabili* means that the title was extinguished upon the death of the subscriber.

Professional Troops

Throughout the century the pope's standing army ranged on average from a minimum of 3,000 to a maximum of 7,000 professional soldiers. The conflict for the Duchy of Castro (1641–44 and 1646–49) was the most imposing war effort undertaken by the Papal States during its history. In those years the army fielded approximately 20,000 men and the expenditure exceeded eight million *scudi*. After this massive armament the regular troops still in service after the end of the conflict were about 4,000 men.[38] This strength was divided among the major garrisons: Rome, where two fifths of the force generally resided; Fort Urbano; Ferrara; Civitavecchia; Ancona, each with a main garrison and a secondary garrison. Other localities had minor garrisons which were, however, functional to control the territory without having a strategic value.

An expenditure note dating to 1667 provides a picture of the Papal army some 20 years after the war of Castro. The source shows in good detail the number, quartering and salaries of the regular troops. This valuable document was written at the transition between the pontificates of Alexander VII and Clement IX.[39] The main contingent was located in Rome and Latium, and consisted of 1,600 infantry soldiers divided into the four large companies of the *Guardie di Nostro Signore*, and 175 cavalry divided in three companies. The maintenance expenditure of this contingent was 100,000 *scudi* per year, or about one third of the total military expenditure. These included salaries for soldiers and officers, bread and the rent of beds and accommodation in private houses. For the cavalry there were added the expenses for stable rent and fodder, on which they received the reimbursement. The garrison of Castel Sant'Angelo had two companies: one under the direct command of the *vice-castellano*, and the other under a captain. In 1667, they numbered 132 and 170 men respectively, with an artillery section attached.[40]

The only other regular cavalry in Rome was a company of 77 cuirassiers commanded by a captain. This small contingent on horseback cost almost half the required expenditure of the garrison of Castel Sant'Angelo, in view of the higher charges for the salaries of the members and officers, and of course the horses and their maintenance.[41] There were in Rome other mounted troops with special functions such as musicians, who performed during the ceremonies of the Papal court.

In 1667, 450 Swiss mercenaries organised in two companies were also quartered in Rome. They had been enlisted after the disbandment of the

---

38 Giangolini, *Le Armi del Papa*, p.23.
39 ASV, *Segreteria di Stato, Miscellanea*, Arm. III, vol. 122, ff. 168–176: *Nota della spesa annua che fa la Rev.ma Camera per la soldatesca tanto di leva che di presidii, come anco per le guardie di N.S. e per tutti gl'offitiali a guerra, con li nomi di chi possiede le cariche e spesa che si fa nella soldatesca di Dalmatia contro il Turco, descritta da principio sommariamente e più avanti con ogni maggior distinzione secondo lo stato presente de' 27 giugno 1667.*
40 Giangolini, *Le Armi del Papa*, pp.49–50.
41 Lutz, *L'esercito pontificio nel 1667*, p.71. The annual cost of the garrison of Castal Sant'Angelo was 20,566 *scudi*, of which 9,951 were for the maintenance of the *corazze* company.

MEDIUM AND MINOR POWERS

6. Private and officers of the Corsican Guard in 1660, from the book *La Corse Militaire* (1904) by Marquis Paul d'Ornano. The author has given this reconstruction of the appearance of the Corsicans in the service of the Pope, however, no source confirms this clothing.

Corsican troops in 1664. The Corsicans had been recruited in 1603 for the surveillance of law and order in Rome, but unlike the *esecutori* (policemen), they were professional soldiers employed like the modern gendarmerie, commanded by officers, non-commissioned officers and troop graduates, regularly dressed, armed, paid and maintained by the *Reverenda Camera Apostolica* like the other standing troops, and provided with their own flag. The episode that caused their dismissal took place in Rome on 20 August 1662, near the French embassy. According to contemporary chronicles the Duke of Crequì, French ambassador to the Pope, had irritated the Romans with his haughty behaviour. 'The people of his house, men who always push their master's faults to the extreme, committed the same disorders in Rome as the undisciplined youth of Paris, who then made it an honour to attack, every night, the Corsican picket guarding the city's gates.' It happened that, during one of these provocations, a soldier was wounded. The Corsicans, 'who were looking for a pretext to carry out a blind and unreasonable revenge, immediately gave the alarm to all the companies, which marched in arms towards the palace of the Ambassador with their officers, flags and drums.' Soldiers quartered in the barracks at the Trinità de' Pellegrini, near Palazzo Spada, also rushed to besiege the nearby Palazzo Farnese, seat of the French ambassador, demanding the delivery of those responsible for the wounding. A firefight ensued, initiated by the incidental return of the ambassador's wife to Palazzo Farnese under French military escort. The Corsicans killed a page and wounded several servants.⁴² This episode prompted a terrible diplomatic incident between Rome and Paris. The ambassador hired armed men and demanded reparation. At first the Pope tried to find a solution, disbanding the company of Captain Alfonso Franchi, identified as the main guilty party; but then, realising that the ambassador continued his acts of intimidation, the Pope also began to arm, planning to enlist 20,000 infantrymen and 3,600 cavalrymen.⁴³ The tension between France and the Holy See lasted two years, exacerbated even more when the Sun King ordered the occupation of Avignon. Eventually the matter was resolved by diplomatic means in 1664 with the Treaty of Pisa. Louis XIV evacuated Avignon, but the pope had to make an official apology and dismiss all Corsican troops.

At the end of the temporary service of the 450 Swiss infantrymen, in 1670 another corps of troops was therefore recruited to replace the Corsicans, always under the authority of the *Sacra Consulta*.⁴⁴ This took the denomination *Battaglione in luogo de' Corsi* (Battalion in place of the Corsicans), with a strength of 442 men divided into two companies, with permanent pickets at surveillance and customs services at the 16 gates of the capital, plus a periodic one for the Senigallia fair.⁴⁵

After Rome, the largest garrison was quartered in Ferrara. In 1667 this consisted of about 900 men for an annual expenditure of 41,628 *scudi*. The garrison included a mounted company commanded by *cavalier* Rasponi with 43 men, and four infantry companies. One company was commanded by an officer denominated *colonnello delle porte*, who in 1667 was Carlo Solieri.⁴⁶ Three companies garrisoned the citadel, whose command was entrusted to the *castellano*, in that year Francesco Massimi. A portion of the troops was also detached to the border fortifications along the Po, as far as the Adriatic coast. The Legate of Ferrara had his own Swiss guard of 40 men commanded, however, by a sergeant.

The third largest garrison in terms of cost and manpower was Avignon, 900 men in 1667, but this number may have resulted from the recent tensions with Louis XIV.⁴⁷ Unfortunately it is not possible to provide any more certain data for the 1660s and 1670s, due to the lack of information on the military

---

42   Luigi Paolo Lucciana, *Deux Documents Inedits sur l'Affaire des Corses à Rome (20 Aout 1662), Manuscripts de la Bibliothèque de Bastia* (Bastia, 1888), pp.408–409.

43   Ciro Paoletti, *Le Armi e le Chiavi – Storia militare degli Stati Pontifici nell'età moderna e contemporanea* (Rome: Commissione Italiana di Storia Militare, 2020), p.155.

44   Andrea Da Mosto, 'Milizie dello Stato Romano dal 1600 al 1797', in *Memorie Storico Militari*, n. 22 (Città di Castello, 1914), pp.242–245.

45   *Ibid.*, p.246.

46   Giangolini, *Le Armi del Papa*, p.72. 'It is unclear what powers this figure had over the militia *sergente maggiore* Michelangelo Braccin; mentioned on the sources after 1692, it is possible that he was a *governatore d'armi* with authority limited to the city fortifications.'

47   Lutz, 'L'esercito pontificio nel 1667', p.60. The garrison in Avignon cost 41,142 *scudi* annually. The hypothesis is supported by the fact that under Innocent X the expenditure for Avignon was 30,000 *scudi*, but it must be considered that Pope Pamphili ordered a sharp reduction in military

7. Avignon in 1635, after Matthäus Merian (author's archive). The Papal enclave in France had a medieval curtain, which did not prevent Louis XIV's occupations in 1662–64 and 1687–88.

affairs of this legation, but it is certain that the strength gradually decreased, down to 130 infantrymen and eight artillerymen in 1690.

In the Legation of Bologna, Fort Urbano was defended by about 500 men for 1,898 sc*udi* per month. They were organised into three companies, one commanded by the *castellano*, the others by two captains, in 1667 Bartolomeo Vittori and Baldassini and Giulio Boncambi. There was also a company of artillerymen of 20 men.[48] The Legate of Bologna was also entitled to its own Swiss guard, though the latter was not paid by the Apostolic Chamber but by the *Reggimento di Bologna*, an autonomous administrative centre, because of the administrative autonomy enjoyed by the city. In Bologna they were the only 'regular' troops, the service being entrusted to the city militia.

On the Tyrrhenian coast, Civitavecchia quartered about 350 regular soldiers, of whom about 100 formed the garrison of Fort Michelangelo and the detachments assigned to the gates, while a company of infantrymen was

---

expenditure for Avignon, so it is possible that the sums paid during the pontificate of Innocent XI between 1676 and 1689 were not the norm.

48 Giangolini, *Le Armi del Papa*, p.73. The total cost of the fort's garrison was 29,288 *scudi* per year.

quartered inside the city. However, this was the most variable garrison; in fact, Civitavecchia was reinforced every year between April and October, when there was a risk of raids by North African pirates. Other small contingents of no more than 50 men were stationed in various fortresses and castles in all the major centres of the state. Ancona was a partial exception, since its fortress could house up to 800 soldiers, but by the end of the century it had only 44 soldiers and three artillerymen. These garrisons acted as checkpoints for the military governor of the province, as an armoury, as a parade ground for the local militia and as an assembling point for regular troops in case of need. Lastly, Benevento and Pontecorvo, the Papal enclaves in the Kingdom of Naples, do not appear in the note. The garrison of Benevento was not under the Apostolic Chamber, and it was administered by the local *castellano*, who held the position of legate.

Overall, in 1667 the Papal army numbered about 5,065 men, a figure that did not include the 50 Swiss Guards of the Legate of Bologna. In detail, the regular troops consisted of 4,730 infantrymen, 270 cavalrymen and 65 artillerymen. There were 113 officers, including castellans, but this number could be higher.[49] Furthermore, the general figure does not take into account additional personnel who served in coastal watchtowers.

In 1670 Clement X reduced the army to about 4,000 men, the primary objective being to reduce military expenditure to 100,000 *scudi* annually. The numbers were therefore reduced, especially in the outlying garrisons. Fort Urbano quartered 330 infantrymen and 36 artillerymen; in Umbria and the Marches there were just 66 infantrymen distributed between Perugia with 25, Ascoli 13, Rimini 17 and other minor garrisons.[50]

In 1676, immediately after his election, Pope Innocent XI again reduced the strength of the regular troops and also suppressed most of the military posts. This reform, although only transitory, would immediately benefit the state's revenues. The accountants estimated a saving of around 100,000 *scudi*. However, this figure did not take into account some particularities, so it can be assumed that the actual earnings were higher than the figures given in the accounts. Even without taking this detail into account, the figures were considerable. The discharging of the troops in the Marches and Romagna brought 3,000 *scudi*, the cuts to the Papal navy brought another 10,000 *scudi*, that of the *corazze* yielded 9,000 *scudi*, eliminating the expenses for the stable, bread, wine and candles. The note concluded by calculating the total saving at 100,835 *scudi*.[51]

---

49 Lutz, 'L'esercito pontificio nel 1667', p.69.
50 Ilari, 'L'esercito pontificio', p.588.
51 Giangolini, *Le Armi del Papa*, pp.58–59. With a single act, Innocent XI suppressed the posts of *capitano generale di Santa Chiesa*, Legate of Avignon, *luogotenente* of the galleys, *capitano dell'una e dell'altra guardia*, governor of Benevento, *maestro di campo generale*, as well as the castellans of Ancona, Perugia and Ascoli.

MEDIUM AND MINOR POWERS

8. and 9. Swiss Guards after Vincenzo Maria Coronelli's *Ordinum Equestrum ac Militarium Brevis Narratio* (1715). The figure at top right shows an NCO with stick employed while carrying out public order duties.

WARS AND SOLDIERS IN THE EARLY REIGN OF LOUIS XIV - VOLUME 6 - PART 2

MEDIUM AND MINOR POWERS

Left: 10. According to contemporary accounts, in the seventeenth century Rome resembled a theatre, with its spectacular scenographies but also its dark backstages. Detail from the painting of Filippo Gagliardi depicting *La giostra dei caroselli*, staged in the Palazzo Barberini for Christine of Sweden on 28 February 1656. Two Swiss guards are trying to hold back a crowd of clerics.

Overleaf: 11 (top). and 12. The entrance of the *gonfaloniere di giustizia in Bologna*, by Giuseppe Maria Mitelli (before 1700), depicting the Swiss Guards with officers, NCOs, drums and fifes of the Legate wearing the traditional Swiss uniform. Some guards are armed with muskets. Note the circular objects hanging from the polearms, perhaps some type of bread. (Author's archive)

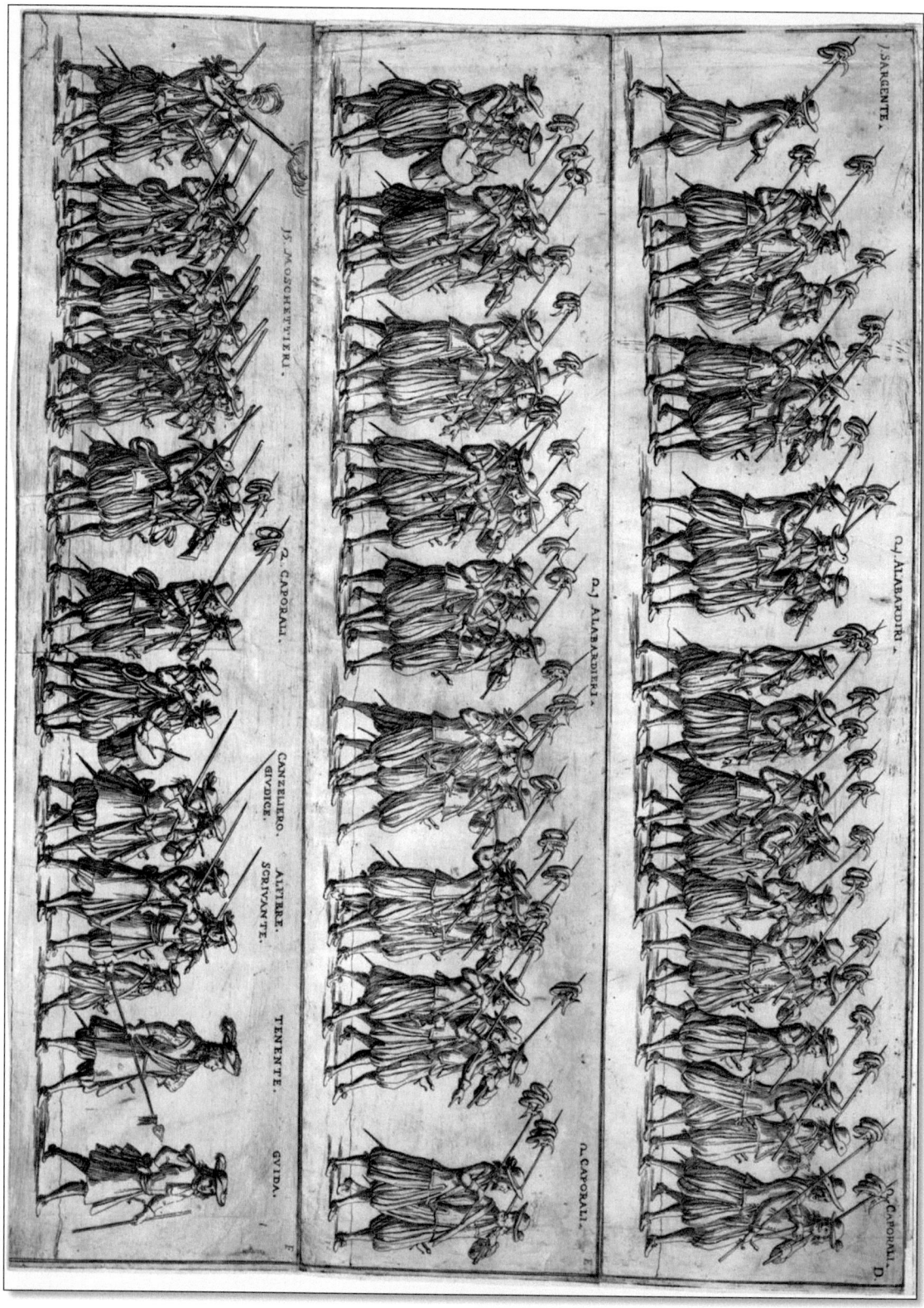

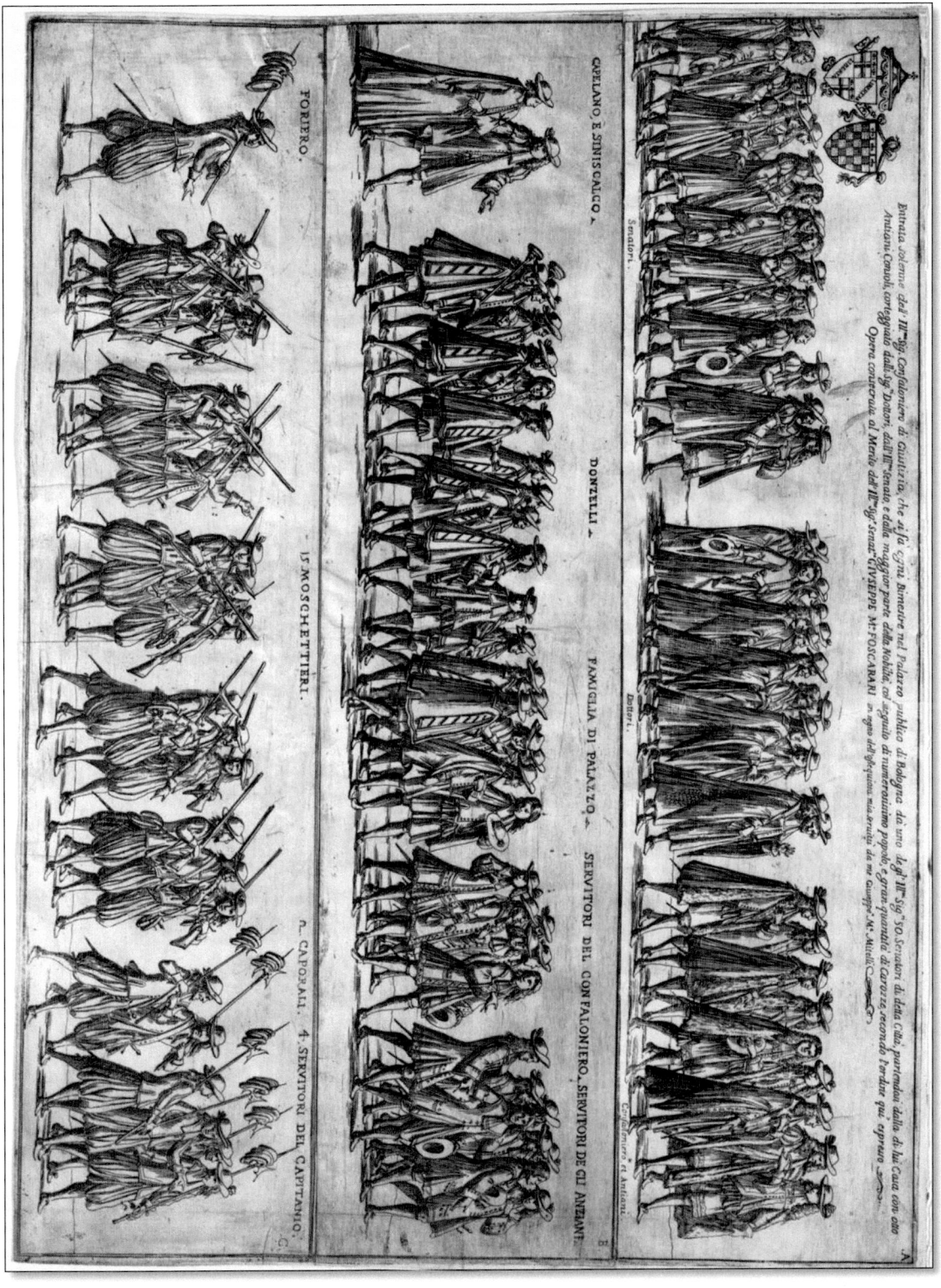

Above: 13. The city-port of Civitavecchia, base of the Papal fleet. A visit and sojourn in Civitavecchia could be just as detrimental as combat in terms of losses to combat strength, due to the insalubrious air for which the harbour and its surroundings were notorious, as remarked in the 1670 by the St John Order's chronicler Bartolomeo Dal Pozzo.

Left: 14. Swiss Guards wearing masks in a painting of Jean Miel, 1662–63. The contemporary iconography shows the Papal Swiss Guards wearing the traditional uniform in yellow, red and blue

MEDIUM AND MINOR POWERS

15. Celebration for the birth of Prince Carlos of Habsburg (later King Carlos II) in front of the palace of the Spanish Embassy in Rome, by Willem Reuter, 1662 (Gemaldegalerie der Akademie der Bildenden Küster, Vienna). According to the chronicles, the Spanish ambassador and cardinals were escorted by the *Guardia Corsa*, possibly depicted in the background wearing dark azure-grey coat and black broad-brimmed hat.

The decrease in strength was in all probability too drastic, so much so that by the end of the century the numbers increased again. In 1690 an incomplete list of troops puts the total 'regulated' strength of the army at 5,946 men, distributed mainly between Rome and Ferrara.[52] The latter city quartered the largest number of men, sent to reinforce the garrison due to the War of the League of Augsburg which was about to involve Northern Italy. The list includes 90 *corazze* in Rome and 134 dragoons in Ferrara, who together with the company of the cardinal legate of the city, were the only regular troops on horseback. Castel Sant'Angelo was manned by 240 foot soldiers in the main garrison and another 21 in the secondary, together with 32 *bombardieri*. The figures concerning Civitavecchia are also remarkable, since the harbour still deployed two garrisons, one of 300 and the other of 62 infantrymen in addition to 67 artillerymen. On the Tyrrhenian coast there were also five foot soldiers at Fiumicino and 24 at the port of Anzio, all under the *Commissariato di Mare*. In addition to them, 15 infantrymen served in Pesaro, and the same number in Senigallia; the port of Nettuno housed a

---

52 BAV, *Registri*, reg. 188 (1690–95). The annual expenditure was 412,498.04 *scudi*.

'garrison' of four infantrymen and one artilleryman, while Terracina had just two infantrymen.

Generally, the Pope recruited foreign mercenaries for his army by turning to private contractors, and rarely enlisted complete units from other states. However, this rule was not respected in 1663 during the crisis with France. Among the foreign troops there were also two regiments recruited by the Papal Nuncio at Vienna, Carlo Carafa. Both the units had been raised for Papal service by the Emperor and comprised one cuirassier regiment of 800 men and one infantry regiment of 1,200 men.[53] The contingent also included one squadron of cuirassiers divided in two companies, and a further free company of infantry. According to the *capitolazioni* agreed in Vienna, two Roman aristocrats were appointed as commanders. Colonel Giuliano Braida took the command of the cuirassier regiment on 15 February 1663, while on 21 February *sergente maggiore* Cesare Degli Oddi received the command of the infantry regiment. The cuirassier squadron served under Lieutenant Colonel Daniel Makley, also known as Pomer, while the infantry free company passed to the command of Count Ottavio Nigrelli. In April the Austrian contingent disembarked in Ancona; they were 1,134 infantrymen of the regiment Degli Oddi, divided between 10 companies, and 887 horsemen of the Braida cuirassiers, also with 10 companies. These figures included staff, *primaplana* and company officers like the Imperial regiments.[54] The cuirassier squadron numbered 154 men, and the free company had 156.

Apart from this contingent, the *Reggimento de' Corsi*, and the battalion that replaced it, throughout the seventeenth century the basic unit of the Papal army remained the company. The number of soldiers forming each company varied considerably according to contingencies, especially with regard to infantry. As elsewhere, the theoretical strength did not take into account the great volatility in numbers due to sickness, desertion and dismissal. The first two were the main causes of depleting the military potential of any army. The cavalry was organised into companies of 40 and 50 cavalrymen, the infantry 130 to 250 men: these were the numbers established by the notices, though in reality the infantry companies deployed very variable forces and the same was true for the cavalry. In 1655 the companies sent to Ferrara to escort Christina of Sweden on her way to Rome showed a maximum of 300 to a minimum of 112 men for the infantry, while the cavalry fielded a maximum of 82 to a minimum of 39 horses. Of the 16 infantry companies, five had

---

53 Da Mosto, 'Milizie dello Stato Romano', pp.308–310.
54 *Ibid.*, *Sul piede Alemanno*. For the enlistment conventions, the flags were to be provided by the Nuncio, and in Ancona all the companies received the ensigns. The infantry were given insignia of turquoise and yellow taffeta, *alla fiorentina*, while the cavalry had standards of turquoise damask embroidered in silver, with bows, fringes and *reticelle* of silver and turquoise silk. The only exception was a company of infantry that received a flag of turquoise, red, green yellow and white taffeta, with multi-coloured silk trimmings, and a company of cuirassiers, possibly the colonel, was given one of white damask.

more than 150 men and six more than 200; in the cavalry, out of a total of 10 companies, five had more than 60 men and three more than 40.[55]

In 1663, in order to ensure that the minimum number of soldiers was at least close to the established number, it was decided that officers' salaries would be paid after reaching at least 100 men for the infantry and 50 for the cavalry.[56] The companies, both infantry and cavalry, were commanded by the captain; sometimes, but very rarely, they were entrusted to a sergeant, when officers took advantage of leave of absence from duty for up to several weeks. The officer ranks also included a lieutenant and a captain's adjutant. The junior officers were the ensign for the infantry and the cornet for the cavalry. The non-commissioned officers were the sergeants and the quartermaster, while drummers and pipers ranked as corporals. Sometimes the unit had its own artillery section attached, with a *capo bombardiere*. The administrative and disciplinary personnel assigned to the major garrisons consisted of the auditor, paymaster, *collaterale*, the doctor, the surgeon, the barber, the armourer and the ammunitioner. The cavalry also had a smith and a saddler. Salaries were higher for the cavalry, but the soldiers quartered in Rome received even higher salaries in all ranks of both infantry and cavalry.[57]

The Papal Soldiers in Action (1647–1688)

After the War of Castro, for the rest of the century Papal troops never engaged military campaigns in Italy, but they participated in support for Venice against the Ottomans. Their first involvement occurred during the Cretan War. In the spring of 1647 the Pope raised an infantry regiment of seven companies. On departure from Rome it numbered 928 men commanded by *sergente maggiore* Marquis Federico Mirolli, but was reduced to 752 on arrival in Ancona due to desertions during the transfer. Arriving in Dalmatia in June, it was considered by *Provveditore Generale* Leonardo Foscolo to be badly trained, led by inexperienced officers, and included too many untrained recruits. Quartered at best in Zadar, in July the regiment was transferred to Sebenico, and after the muster the strength had further decreased to 650 men. Although poorly trained and weakened, the Papal regiment participated in the victorious defence of Sebenico (Šibenik); in this engagement Marquis Mirolli was wounded in the leg.[58] On 4 February 1648 Mirolli returned to

---

55　BAV, *Registri* (1655), ff. 10–11: *Infanteria e Cavalleria comand.ta a Ferrara*. The overall strength was 2,960 infantry, and 631 cavalry.

56　Giangolini, *Le Armi del Papa*, p.212.

57　According to Virgilio Ilari, 'L'esercito pontificio', p.652, there was compensation granted to officers when they resided in the city and thus had to pay rent for accommodation, which was then returned by the Apostolic Chamber. Officers in garrisons far from Rome, on the other hand, received lower pay because they used the accommodation in the fortress. However, the income of Roman officers was higher than that paid to the normal army officers. Moreover, the Roman garrison comprised the Guards companies so the higher income was also attributable to the prestige derived from belonging to the units that had the task of defending the pope.

58　Andrea Da Mosto, 'Milizie dello Stato Romano, 1600–1797', in *Memorie Storiche Militari* (Rome, Vol. X, 1914), p.483.

Rome with four companies. The remaining three, with a total strength of 500–600 men, remained in Dalmatia under *sergente maggiore* Tomaso Serughi. In April these troops caused some unrest, and thus the Papal infantry was sent to Split, where it participated in fortification works. In Dalmatia, the period 1649–50 saw few events and the Papal contingent also remained inactive. One of the three companies was suppressed, using rank and file to reinforce the other two. On 24 January the companies numbered 417 men, who on 6 March passed into the command of Colonel Giacinto Sgamba.[59]

In Dalmatia the companies took part in the failed attempt against Canina, where they lost 220 of the 300 men engaged as dead, wounded and prisoners. Despite the fact that the Venetians had repulsed the Ottoman attack on Perasto and concluded the cycle of operations with the conquest of much of the surrounding territory, the Pope decided to recall the regiment, which had been reduced to a meagre company, strongly criticised by the Venetians for its lack of discipline and effectiveness in battle.[60]

Thereafter, aid to Venice was intermittent. In 1653 the Pope sent an infantry *battaglione* to serve in Dalmatia under *sergente maggiore* Facchinetti, followed one year later by another battalion to serve on the galleys in the Aegean Sea alongside the Venetian fleet. In 1655 Alexander VII granted a levy of 2,000 men for the Venetian army, then in 1657 he issued licenses for recruiting in his state 4,000 volunteers, while the major Roman aristocratic families contributed economically to equip the contingents and the ships for transporting them. Finally, in 1665, the Pope sent to Dalmatia a regiment of 1,000 infantrymen.[61] The regiment was gathered in Orte, then marched to Ancona to embark and finally landed in Dalmatia under Count Marzio de' Baschi. Arriving in Zadar in early May 1657, it was moved to Sebenico where it remained in garrison. Again, especially due to the inexperience of the young colonel, indiscipline caused endless problems and forced the Venetians to transfer the regiment to Zadar again. Disturbances did not cease, desertions increased and there was an improvement only after the arrival of the new commander, *sergente maggiore* Agostino Molinari, who took command in March 1659. If desertions decreased, dismissal also increased, and by September 1657 the regiment numbered just 400 men. Until March 1658 the Papal troops remained at Zadar without sustaining any encounter, but it was necessary to enlist soldiers from other states to maintain a strength of at least 400 men.[62] In April all the companies were transferred to Candia, and finally disbanded in 1659 or 1660.

In 1665 a new battalion of 500 infantrymen was raised to join the Venetian army. This time the commander, Colonel Muzio Mattei, proved to be a skilled officer, but the quality of the troops had not improved. Desertion and dismissal reduced the strength, forcing Mattei to ask for new recruits. In 1667, 497 infantrymen were recruited to replace those serving in Dalmatia;

---

59 Paoletti, *Le Armi e le Chiavi*, p.146.
60 *Ibid.*
61 Mugnai, *The Cretan War*, p.113.
62 Paoletti, *Le Armi e le Chiavi*, p.149.

they arrived from Ancona in October divided into three companies under *sergente maggiore* Orazio Orlandini. A little less than a third of the recruits were enlisted along the road from Rome to Ancona and they were escorted by about 20 cuirassiers to prevent desertion. In early 1668 the battalion arrived at Candia alongside the five Papal galleys, in time to participate in the last defence of the city. On 5 March, in the terrible struggle around the Panigrà ravelin, Mattei was hit by the fragments of an explosion and died after 15 days of agony. Papal admiral Vincenzo Rospigliosi reformed the battalion and increased the strength to 952 men mustered on 1 September, and organised them in companies of 80 men following the Venetian pattern. In March 1669 the admiral appointed *sergente maggiore* Léonard de Cleuter, from Avignon, as new commander of the battalion,[63] and he found the strength decreased to 462 men in all. The Papal troops fought with admirable courage, led by the new commander who exposed himself and his men to greater danger.[64] After the surrender of Candia on 6 September 1669 the survivors returned home in March 1670, after spending three months in quarantine. They were 350 men in all.[65]

In 1684, with Venice's adhesion to the Holy League, Pope Innocent XI sent his contingent to the Levante just as the dispute over the expulsion of Cardinal Barbarigo was ongoing between Rome and the *Serenissima*.

The first Papal troops sent to the Levant were two infantry companies that served as landing troops for the small galley fleet. The contingent's strength was 486 men under the *sergente maggiore* Count Giuseppe Orselli from Forlì. In the summer of 1684 they joined the Venetians in the assaults on Santa Maura (Lefkas) and Prevesa. While on the island, Orselli fell ill and died within a few days. After being temporarily under the orders of Captain Montecchi, the contingent passed to the Cretan veteran Léonard de Cleuter. Reports of the campaign did not emphasise the Pope's troops except for an encounter alongside a Maltese infantry company in Gomenizze (Igoumenitsa in Greece); the episode was marginal, but it revealed the state of the troops' discipline and operative difficulties in inhospitable war zones such as Greece. The Roman troops landed with the Maltese near the town to provide water for the fleet's rowers. The Maltese commander went ahead to confirm water supplies in that place, where the Ottoman cavalry had repulsed other allied troops a few weeks earlier. As the operation neared completion the Papal soldiers scattered to the countryside to pick melons. Suddenly, enemy horsemen assaulted them. The Papal troops fled, and only Maltese intervention restored enough order for the Papal soldiers to return aboard the galleys. Nevertheless, the enemy assault resulted in several casualties and

---

63 In recognition of his valour, Cleuter was appointed captain *dell'una e dell'altra guardia*, continuing to serve the popes until a very late age. See Louis Lainé, *Archives généalogiques et historiques de la Noblesse de France* (Paris, 1829), vol. II, p.4.

64 Paoletti, *Le Armi e le Chiavi*, p.151. According to contemporary chronicles, Cleuter was threatened with being shot if he did not suspend his dangerous behaviour. He was wounded on 11 August during the defence of the Sabbionera bastion.

65 *Ibid.*, p.151.

among the fallen was a veteran Provencal officer from Avignon, the *ajutante* Audifredi.⁶⁶ The Papal infantry, numbering 300 men, joined the allies at the sieges of Corone and Calamata, where they temporarily formed the garrison. In May 1686 the Papal contingent was quartered on the island of Lefkada, where it was replaced by another *battaglione da sbarco* with 500 men. Papal infantry serving on the galleys usually belonged to the *Compagnie delle Guardie di Nostro Signore*, which in occasional rotation with other infantry from Civitavecchia and Ferrara participated in the campaigns.⁶⁷ The Papal troops participated in the siege of Old and New Navarino, Modone and Napoli di Romania, and this time the reports do not mention any particularly negative episode. On the contrary, the Pope's infantry was particularly appreciated at Modone in the digging of the trenches to approach the walls.

In 1687, the fear of an epidemic persuaded the whole Italian contingent to head for Dalmatia. The Pope's five galleys transported the battalion that participated in the successful campaign under Girolamo Corner, which culminated in the conquest of Castelnuovo (Herceg Novi). In 1690, after a two-year pause, the Papal troops resumed their participation in the war against the Porte. The new pope, Alexander VIII Ottoboni, a Venetian, increased the contingent to 1,400 men in two battalions under Counts Lodovico Montevecchio and Guido Bonaventura, with Colonel Léonard de Cleuter as commander-in-chief.⁶⁸ As barely half of the soldiers could be accommodated on the galleys, four vessels and four *tartanes* were also hired. After the surrender of Malvasia on 12 August 1690 the Papal troops, now under Marquis Monaldi, again joined the Venetians in 1692, sending a single battalion and five galleys until 1696.⁶⁹

The Pope's Lifeguard
The corps in charge of escorting the Pope and guarding his residences depended directly on the *Maggiordomo*. However, the command was entrusted to a relative with the aforementioned rank of *luogotenente dell'una dell'altra Guardia*.⁷⁰ He commanded three companies of lifeguards, two of horse and one of foot. The infantry company was the Swiss Guard, which in 1667 numbered 171 men, including the picket of 24 guards assigned to Urbino. The uniforms had to be renewed every eight months and cost 1,666 *scudi*, namely 12 percent of what was paid annually for the maintenance of the corps. The captain of the Swiss Guard received the highest pay compared to an army officer with the same rank, since he was colonel of all Swiss State Guards; the lieutenant and ensign were chosen from the men proposed by the canton of Lucerne.⁷¹ This corps enjoyed extensive administrative and

---

66 Bartolomeo Dal Pozzo, *Historia della Sacra Religione di San Giovanni Gerosomilitano, detta di Malta* (Venice, 1715), p.537.
67 Paoletti, *Le Armi e le Chiavi*, p.156.
68 ASVe, *Senato, dispacci, Provveditori di Terra e di Mar*, b. 1123, d. 38 (20 June 1690).
69 Paoletti, *Le Armi e le Chiavi*, p.158.
70 In the sources, the commander is sometimes referred to as *capitano*.
71 Da Mosto, *Milizie dello Stato Romano*, p.220.

legal autonomy with its own officers, including an auditor board for the examination of disciplinary cases.

The cavalrymen formed a special corps with exclusive ceremonial tasks, which benefited from high remuneration and consisted of cadets from the most important patrician families of the capital.[72] In 1667 the mounted companies numbered 94 men. In detail, each consisted of a captain, cornet, three trumpeters, 38 horsemen and three *lance spezzate* (broken lances) who joined as volunteers.[73] At the end of the century the Papal guards numbered nine *lance spezzate*, 84 horsemen, and 173 Swiss guards. In 1660 the Swiss Guard of the Legate of Bologna numbered 50 men, including a captain, two adjutants, one sergeant, four corporals, one drummer, one fife, one chaplain, and one cadet boy. They were paid by the city's Senate, which also issued the red uniforms with green *giustacuore* and grey broad-brimmed hat with plumes. The Swiss company of Ferrara had the same strength. In Urbino since 1631 a detachment of 24 men from the Swiss Company of Rome followed the Legate. This detachment continued to serve as the Legate's lifeguard, always depending on Rome. In 1663 a captain commander was appointed but subordinate to the commander in Rome.[74] In 1660 Ferrara also had 20 cavalrymen, while Avignon had 44 *cavalleggeri* (light cavalrymen), and 21 Swiss Guards.

Militia

The Papal militia had been established in 1563 and on paper could count on considerable numbers. According to the sources it reached 78,170 infantrymen and 5,160 horses in 1640: to what extent these figures were actually available is, however, disputable. At the beginning of the seventeenth century there were six military provinces, called colonnades, comprising the provinces of Romagna, Marca del Tronto, Marca del Chienti, Patrimonio, Campagna and Marittima. Later the provinces of Sabina and Montagna, Ferrara and Urbino were also added. In the second half of the century the provinces increased to 10 with the creation of the *colonnelato* of Civitavecchia.

Throughout the century the chain of command was fully established, and the troops were subordinated to a *maestro di campo* and a *sergente maggiore*. Under Urban VIII these senior officers were subject to a *luogotenente generale*, who controlled the militia of the most important provinces of the state, namely Marche, Umbria, Romagna and Ferrara. This officer also extended his authority over all troops in the province, including the permanent troops in the garrisons. The cavalry militia maintained its own command structure until the reform that probably took place in 1689 during the pontificate of Alexander VIII.[75] Originally the staff comprised the *generale della cavalleria*, the *luogotente generale della cavalleria*, who commanded the units of the

---

72 *Ibid*. Once again, the cost of the mounted units compared to those on foot stands out. The two mounted companies cost 16,170 *scudi* annually, while the Swiss Guard required 12,250 *scudi*.
73 Lutz, *L'esercito pontificio nel 1667*, p.51.
74 Da Mosto, *Milizie dello Stato Romano*, pp.221–222.
75 Giangolini, *Le Armi del Papa*, pp.85–86.

legations, and a *commissario generale*, who also commanded the cavalry of the Marche. The infantry was organised into *Terzi*, each divided into *bande* or *battaglioni*, the former comparable to battalions and the latter to companies, which were in fact commanded by a captain. The *Terzi* usually took their names from the provinces from which they originated.

In the second half of the century there was an institutional change, which helped to simplify the command system of the entire militia. This was exercised by a *sergente generale* in the legations, while in the other province of the state the command of the infantry *Terzi* was held by the *governatore delle armi*. On other occasions it was the *maestro di campo* who commanded the militiamen, assisted in both cases by the *sergente maggiore*. The *governatore* was superior in rank to the *sergente generale*, but it is not entirely clear what their respective functions were, and what the specific area of responsibility of both ranks was, nor even which of them was the deputy in the absence of the titular officer. The governors were often replaced by the *sergenti maggiori* of the provinces, since they did not reside in the capital of the region and often remained in Rome. An indication of a certain institutional uncertainty in this period is the affair of the sergeant majors, who were in charge of the ordinary service of the militia at least after 1682, when the office was restored after a brief period in which it was suppressed.

Ten military provinces had their own governors, two of which were named per city, while the militia of Bologna did not have a governor of arms, nor a sergeant major, but took orders from the *Reggimento*, the city's civil government body. Generally, each legation fielded at least one company of foot.

In 1692, at the beginning of the pontificate of Innocent XII, two 'veteran' colonels of the militia were still in service under the governor of the province, while there were no further appointments. Neither *maestri di campo* nor *luogotenenti generali* were in activity. All the militia, with the partial exception of Ferrara, were under the command of the *govrnatore delle armi* with a subordinate *sergente maggiore* with authority over the militia alone.[76] Similarly, other communities could control their militia in substantial autonomy through municipal bodies. These were Camerino, Ancona, Cesena, Ravenna, Forlì, Faenza and Monte San Giovanni.[77] The militia of Loreto depended on the Holy House. Avignon and Benevento had respectively a *maestro di campo* and a *sergente maggiore* depending from the Legate. These militias were usually composed of companies of 150–200 men.

The regulation of the service required of the militiamen was defined in the *privilegi* and *grazie* that were granted to people who actually participated in the training sessions and fulfilled the tasks. Periodically, printed editions of the chapters, orders and laws were issued throughout the provinces. By 1650, the institutional structure underwent some changes that led to the abolition of some military posts and a redistribution of competencies for the

---

76 Da Mosto, *Milizie dello Stato Romano*, p.409.
77 *Ibid.*, pp.85–86. The origin of these militias with special jurisdiction dates back to the sixteenth century, when banditry was endemic. The Papal legates in search of men to send against bandits resorted to confraternities called *Pacifici*. This legacy was still strong in the seventeenth century.

remaining ranks. The reforms also diminished the strength of the militia. Numbers, although decreasing compared to the first half of the century, remained high. In 1656, 55,956 foot and 5,547 horse were registered, for a total of 60,423 militiamen.

The strength briefly decreased to 5,237 infantrymen and 1,767 cavalrymen, when in 1659 Alexander VII imposed a one-off tax on each *miliziotto* – as they were called – to preserve the privileges associated with the registration of the roles. The same pope, on the occasion of the rearmament decided upon in 1663 to respond to French threats, had not resorted to mobilising the militia, except to a limited extent to enrol volunteers to join the regular troops. The tax introduced by Alexander VII was perceived by those concerned as so burdensome that Pope Clement IX was persuaded to withdraw it. In 1668, on paper, the militia could now field 68,471 foot and 7,752 horse, for 76,223 men overall. Under Innocent XI (1676–1689) the militia numbered to 64,924 men in all, of whom 57,150 were foot and 7,774 horse.[78] However, these data come from the *ruoli dei descritti*, namely the lists of subjects between 18 and 45 years residing in the state and registered as militiamen, and not from reviews and inspections, which were very rarely carried out.

In the second half of the seventeenth century, in spite of the reorganisations and updated versions of the militia *privilege* and *capitoli*, the communities' refusal to meet the tasks remained endemic. That membership of the Papal militia was above all a way to obtain tax relief and other privileges is indirectly confirmed by the classification introduced in 1642, and established on the presumed or actual level of military efficiency of the militiamen. On that occasion all the *descritti* were divided into three groups. The first of these, the *miliziotti scelti* (elite militiamen) comprised the bachelors, not fatherless, younger and more robust, and all people who according to their commanders 'would be fit, and comfortable to march, even as they allow'.[79] The chosen militia, according to the original plans of 1642, was supposed to field 20,000 foot and 3,000 horse. Then there were the *volontari*, who had no special requirements, but whom the government could send to other provinces of the state in case of need. Lastly there were the *ordinari*, those who did not fall into any of the previous categories, and therefore mostly represented a last resort in case of extreme danger. These were described as 'those, who through extreme poverty, or otherwise, are not fit to leave their homes'.[80] It appears from the sources that this militia was also selected according to the quality of the equipment the individual militiaman was able to procure.

Four times a year the company was assembled for the *istruzioni* (training). Every Sunday – except in winter and summer – the captains supervised the training of one quarter of the company in rotation. Weapons were distributed

---

78 Da Mosto, *Milizie dello Stato Romano*, pp.405–408.
79 Brunelli, 'Poteri e Privilegi. L'istituzione degli ordinamenti delle milizie nello Stato Pontificio tra Cinque e Seicento', in *Cheiron*, XII (1995), n. 23, pp.106–107.
80 *Ibid*.

by the state, but the foot militiamen had to procure the necessaries to use their muskets, while those serving as horseman had to provide their own mount. In 1656 a norm was established that anyone with more than 1,000 *scudi* of annual income would be enlisted in the cavalry.[81] On termination of service a special prize was issued that guaranteed the preservation of privileges for life, and the transmission of the same to related children for the duration of 10 years after the man's death. Obviously, loyalty and dedication were demanded in return. Prolonged absence on training days carried a penalty, at least on paper.

Junior militia officers did not perform any actual active service, except when their companies were mobilised, and only then did they receive pay. Usually it was the non-commissioned officers who trained the troops, the captains merely supervised their execution. The officers were also in charge of recruitment, or rather selection. The captains did, however, obtain an economic advantage from their service: they could receive money from the community when militiamen were mobilised to ensure public order, and collected 60 percent of the amount of the penalties imposed on the militiamen who did not fulfil their service. A part of these sums went to the *collaterale generale*, *cancelliere*, and *depositario*, the latter being officials who were appointed by the *commissario d'armi* to issue penalties. The remainder went into the company's funds.

These legitimate emoluments were raised by the illicit practices of the officers. Captains often used militiamen as servants, or employed them for private jobs. Moreover, it was prestige and influence in the community that made the rank of officer coveted. It was not necessary to be a nobleman to serve as an officer of the militia, but all commoners who could prove a sufficient income received the appointment. Furthermore, although the ranks in the militia had no equivalent in the regular army, in some cases the militia officers entered the standing troops as ensigns, the lowest officer rank in the regular army.[82] Sources and contemporary commenters, however, confirm that the Roman government placed little trust in the militia. Employment alongside regular troops was never considered a real possibility.[83]

In addition to the provincial militia there were also urban militias. The militia of the city of Rome provided, again on paper, an additional 10,000 men. Pope Clement VIII (1592–1605), granted the old Roman militia the prerogatives of regular troops, and subjected it to the authority of the Captain General of the Holy Church. In 1642 Urban VIII reorganised the urban militia, increasing the number to 12,000 foot and 1,000 horse, which was then again reorganised by Camillo Pamphili in 1646 with new *privilegi* and *ordini*.

---

81 Da Mosto, 'Milizie dello Stato Romano', pp.409–11.

82 Ilari, 'L'esercito pontificio', pp.634–5.

83 According to many authors, the militia became an institution dominated by the patronage of the curia. This system made the militia useless for providing effective support to the regular troops in times of war. In the second half of the seventeenth century, one can see how the Papacy and the court of Rome in general were aware of this and in fact the percentage of militia mobilised for the crisis of 1663 was minimal. See also Giangolini, *Le Armi del Papa*, pp.88–89.

However, this force rapidly declined over the course of the century, and by the beginning of the eighteenth century the only Roman militia that could be used was the *Compagnia de' Fanti dell'Inclito Popolo Romano*, which was only assembled in times of a vacant Papal seat to maintain public order in the city.

The scenario in Bologna was very different. The 'second capital' of the state had 22 companies of foot and three companies of horse, but this militia was a fully established corps, which dealt with the garrison duties in the city. The mounted companies, at least, even had their own uniforms. The three *Compagnie de Cavalli* of Bologna were the *decana*, namely that commanded by Captain Orsi, dressed in azure-blue coats, that of Captain Count Bovi dei Quaranta, patrician and senator of Bologna, in yellow coats, and that under Marquis Cospi, dressed in red.[84] Overall, the urban militia of Bologna could field about 7,000 men by mid century.[85]

The militia also had a corps of artillerymen trained in the bombardier schools. There were nine such schools: in Rome, the oldest and dating back to 1594; then Ancona, Pesaro, Rimini, Ferrara, Fano, Senigallia, Perugia and Civitavecchia. The *bombardieri* served on a voluntary basis and had to provide their own armament and the tools necessary for the handling of artillery pieces. Members were explicitly mentioned as 'craftsmen' of the four arts who could read and write. Later, simple shopkeepers were also allowed to join the corps. The greatest privilege these artillerymen enjoyed was the tax exemption they were granted as members of this guild. Promotion from assistant artilleryman to actual artilleryman took place through an exam, selecting the candidate by judgement of the senior officers. The actual number of militia artillerymen in the second half of the seventeenth century is unclear, however according to some authors 1,500 men were registered as *bombardieri* in 1667.[86]

The Republic of Genoa

Following Spain's downward parabola of the second half of the seventeenth century, Genoa left the stage of international politics just before Europe was preparing to become the battleground of Louis XIV's armies. Many contemporary commenters considered Genoa as just another gateway to Italy, finding itself squeezed between the aims of France and the traditional expansionist ambitions of its Savoy allies, with Madrid a distant and powerless spectator. In some respects the assault of Charles Emmanuel II in 1672, and above all, the French bombardment in 1684, punished the Republic's renunciatory policy by pushing it further under Madrid's shadow. Genoa's commercial interests dictated its policy. While theoretically neutral, the Republic was firmly bound with Madrid because the ruling class found it beneficial to act as the bank for the Spanish Empire. Genoese investments in

---

84   ASRo, *Congregazioni particolari deputate 1600–1760, congregazioni sulle armi*, t. 37, f. 5 (1686). Thanks to Ciro Paoletti for this notice.
85   Da Mosto, 'Milizie dello Stato Romano', pp.409–410.
86   Lutz, 'L'esercito pontificio nel 1667', pp.170–171.

the New World, in Spain and in the commercial and agricultural economy of Southern Italy were substantial. Despite their gradual naval decline, the Genoese were still redoubtable *asientistas* and continued to lease galleys to Spain. Genoa managed to maintain its independence, at least on a formal level, and this despite its military dependence on Spain, but remaining exposed to the threat from Savoy's dukes, who were skilled in moving diplomatically between Paris and Madrid.

On the whole, the Genoese domains were homogeneous if compared to those of other Italian states. By mid century the territorial extension included the provinces of the modern region of Liguria, except for the Spanish enclave of Finale, 20 among independent lordships and Imperial fiefdoms, and the territory of Oneglia belonging to the Duke of Savoy. In addition, Genoa ruled over the territories of Gavi, Ovada and Novi with their dependencies beyond the Apennines, collectively known as *Oltregiogo*. This territory was part of the traditional division along with the Riviera of *Levante* and *Ponente* to the east and west of Genoa respectively, which was the centre of gravity of the Italian domains. The Republic extended its rule on the overseas domains of Corsica – the third Genoese Riviera – the island of Capraia and the island of Tabarca, opposite the Tunisian coast, but used only for coral harvesting. However, all this territory was sparsely populated, and in total the Republic's subjects numbered around 500,000, of whom fewer than 80,000 populated Corsica.

Genoa was the heart and the main fortress of the state. In 1666 the Italian military writer Galeazzo Gualdo Priorato describes with admiration the imposing fortifications that protected the city to the land side. He also listed the aristocrat families who held power in the government, numbering them to 190, adding that half of them dressed in Spanish style, while the other half followed French fashion.[87] After Genoa, Savona was the second major city of the state, while among the other centre of the coast, Spezia, on the extreme eastern Riviera of Levante was the only town with more than 6,000 inhabitants.

16. Portrait of Doge Agostino di Saluzzo (1631–1700), 122nd doge of the Republic of Genoa between 1673 and 1675 (author's archive). See image commentaries for more information.

---

87 Galeazzo Gualdo Priorato, *Relatione della Città di Genova e suo Dominio* (Cologne, 1668), p.105. Among the Genoese aristocracy, the author mentions the family Garibaldi.

17. The Italian domains of the Republic of Genoa, 1660, including Imperial and other independent fiefs.

MEDIUM AND MINOR POWERS

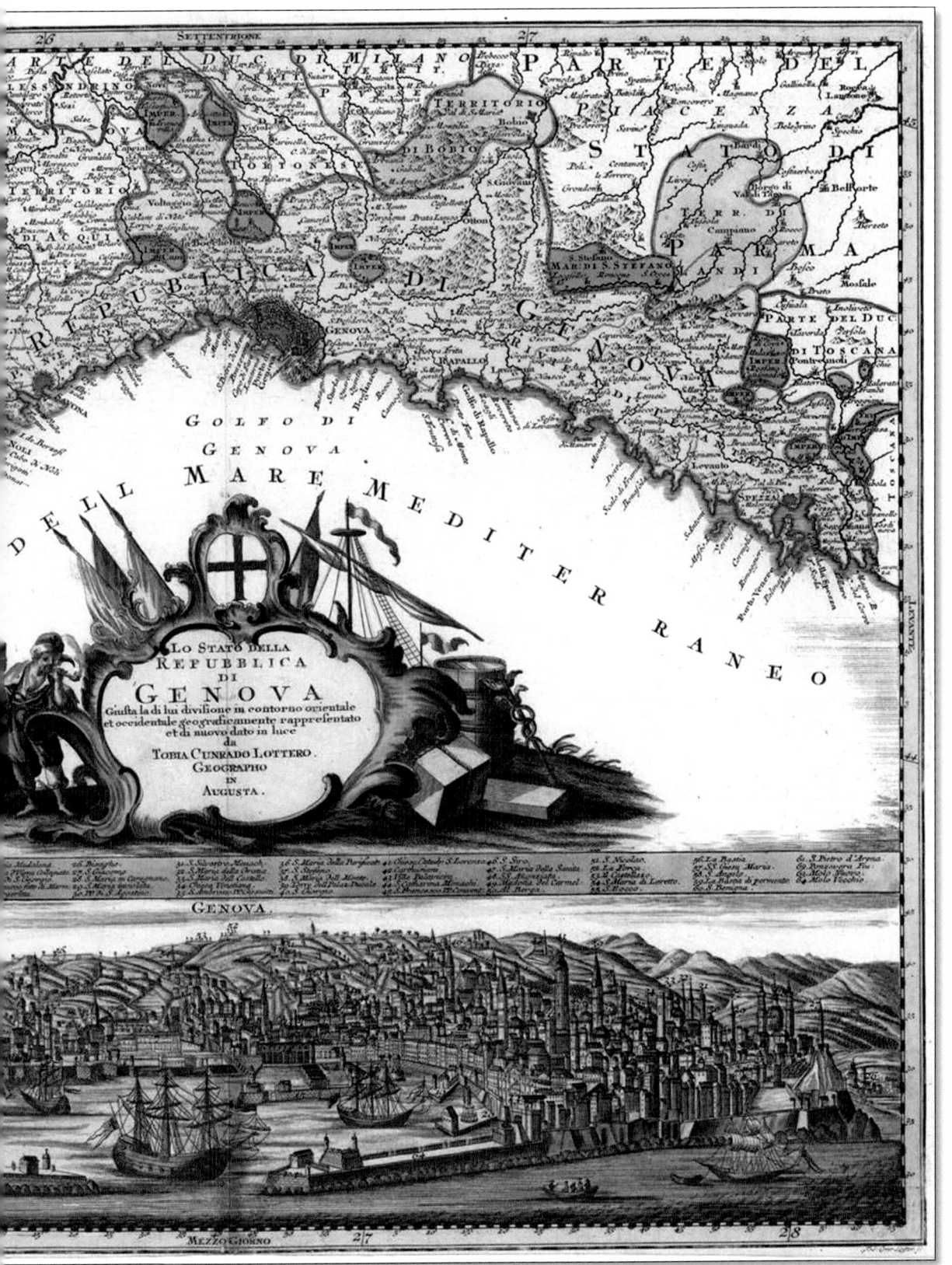

In Corsica the coastal towns, some of which were largely populated by Ligurians, especially Calvi, Bastia, Ajaccio and Bonifacio, enjoyed special privileges compared to those inland, such as tax exemptions or special immunities, thus constituting a world apart. In the inland towns, a class of notables referred to as the *principali* (principal ones) was thus free to develop.

The Other 'Most Serene Republic'

Genoa was a city-state governed by the aristocracy, which based its wealth on the trade of its harbour, and it may be compared with modern-day Singapore. For a seventeenth-century Genoese, the word 'state' meant only the city of Genoa and its surroundings,[88] while the remaining territory was the domain subordinated to the *Dominante*. There was no difference between Liguria and Corsica, both ruled by Genoa with the aim of safeguarding its independence and avoiding any competition at its port and, if this condition was accomplished, the domains were allowed a large amount of self-government.[89]

As in Venice, the Genoese aristocracy feared the concentration of authority, consequently all the offices were under even more direct control of the civil power than in the lagoon city. At the top of the Republic's legal system there was a particular category of norms, which comprised the constitutional laws of 1528, and the *Leges novae* (New Laws) also known as *Leggi di Casale*, issued in 1576. These latter continued to regulate the Genoese army throughout the next century, conditioning in a conservative attitude the military policy of the state.

The Genoese government comprised the *Collegio dei Governatori* (Senate), and the *Collegio dei Procuratori*, or *Camera* (Parliament). Both colleges operated as a single body, and all official acts were issued jointly, confirming that only these two powers exercised the most relevant political function, namely the government. To emphasise the indivisibility of the power, the colleges held the title *Serenissimi Collegi* (the Most Serene Colleges), sometimes also referred to as the *Serenissimo Trono* (the Most Serene Throne). The *Doge* was elected every two years, and though he did not formally have authority, with his opinion he could influence the decisions of the colleges, which he presided over as the highest dignity of the state. The colleges joined together the executive and legislative functions with the Senate at the head, formed by the *Doge* and eight *governatori* (governors) also in office for two years, and the *Camera*, to which eight procurators in office for two years and the former *Doges* as perpetual procurators belonged.

---

88 This territory was roughly equivalent to modern-day Genoa. The surrounding areas were traditionally called the *Tre Podestarie* (Three Districts), although they were actually four: Bisagno, Polcevera, Voltri and Sestri.

89 A decree issued in 1440 required all goods bound for Liguria and Corsica to be shipped through Genoa first; see Claudio Costantini, *La Repubblica di Genova nell'età moderna* (Turin: UTET, 1978), pp.364–365. Consequently, the harbour of Savona was blocked with stones. Paolo Giacomone Piana stated to the present author that the distrust of many parts of Liguria towards Genoa is still a major problem today(!).

MEDIUM AND MINOR POWERS

18. Genoa in a print dating to 1670, See image commentaries for more information.

The Senate took care of government matters, while the *Camera* supervised finance. Both bodies were, however, bound by the deliberations of the two *consigli* – Major and Minor – which were responsible for supervisory and foreign policy tasks, not least the power to declare war and to conclude peace treaties and alliance treaties, all of which were the sole responsibility of the Minor Council.[90]

For military matters, the most serene colleges extended their authority over the administration of troops, discipline regulations, garrison strength, fortifications, recruitment and licensing of troops, and the appointment of officers from captains up to the highest ranks. The *Camera*, as the body that supervised public finance, dealt with military matters as well, being the owner of the Public Armoury and the arsenals of the fortresses. This involved the purchase and manufacture of arms and ammunition, the casting of cannons, the supply of provisions, and the salaries of artillery personnel. All these matters were handled by two special procurators, designated *camerali deputati all'armeria* (chamber deputies for weaponry), while two other *procuratori alla scrittura* (administrative procurators) took care of the

---

90 Emiliano Beri, *Genova e il suo regno. Ordinamenti militari, poteri locali e controllo del territorio in Corsica fra insurrezioni e guerre civili (1729–1768)* (Genoa: Università degli Studi di Genova, 2009–2010), p.43.

economic side. It was only in 1688 that the Genoese government authorised the formation of a special military fund under the control of the *Camera* and administered by the *Banco di San Giorgio*: the Republic's bank.[91]

The Colleges were organised in such a way as to divide the work within them, forming mixed commissions of *procuratori* and *governatori*, called *Giunta*, which normally acted as advisory bodies, but could also exercise executive powers if expressly delegated. However, in the history of Genoa it was never necessary to set up a permanent council to deal with military affairs, and usually matters relating to the army that required in-depth examination were entrusted by the Colleges to the *Giunta della Marina* (Navy College), to the *Giunta dei Confini*, or directly to the *Camera*, without following a fixed procedure or regulation. As can be easily guessed, this resulted in an extreme dispersion of sources relating to military matters. In particularly serious emergencies, such as the war against Savoy-Piedmont of 1672 and the French bombardment of 1684, the government instituted an extraordinary *Giunte* with executive powers, composed of Governors, Procurators and members of the Minor Council to speed up decision-making. These were the *Giunte nuovamente erette*, *Giunte di esecuzione* and the *Giunte di difesa*.[92]

Since the government's main concern was to prevent the permanent occupation of positions of power by families or individuals, all the members of the magistracies and *Giunte* were subject to a high turnover. The negative effect of this was that people with military skills also entered the magistracies, although the government took this into account in times of emergency. There was also a suspension and ineligibility period between terms of office of at least one year to ensure rotation among the candidates.

In addition to this complex architecture of government, the *Serenissimi Collegi*, in agreement with the Minor Council, appointed magistrates who were responsible for directing the various aspects of the republican military machine. Therefore, there was no single body specifically in charge of military affairs, and these were entrusted to one or other of the various magistracies operating within the Colleges themselves with specific competences in recruitment, supply, officer appointments and other matters. Consequently, four different magistracies were in charge of military matters. The most

---

91 The *Banco di San Giorgio* exercised both the function of taxation and public debt management like modern central banks, as well as the collection of savings. In its activity it was one of the first deposit and loan banks in Europe, but also one of the first 'state banks', ancestors of the modern central banks. In 1625 the *Banco* was authorised to issue paper money, which had nominal value, payable on sight and transferable like modern cheques.

92 The *Giunte* should not be confused with the deputations, which were essentially executive bodies elected by the Colleges or the Minor Council, and which also included permanent or temporary deputations. Concerning this topic, Paolo Giacomone Piana and Riccardo Dellepiane, *Militarium* (Genoa: Brigati, 2003), p.27: 'The distinction is not always clear and in principle the *Giunta* was elected by the Colleges within themselves, while deputations included members of the two Councils, to which citizens not ascribed to the nobility could sometimes be added. In any case, the term *Deputazione* was often used to refer to *Giunta* with executive powers, while other deputations were normally called juntas.'

important of these, the *Magistrato di Guerra*, functioned like a modern general director of a ministry, whose responsibilities included the construction and maintenance of fortifications, regular troops and military justice. Artillery was entrusted to the *Magistrato alle Artiglierie*; the *Magistrato alle Galere* dealt with the fleet, while the *Magistrato di Veditoria* was in charge of all affairs relating to the administration of supplies. All these magistracies were collegial bodies, formed by a board of five members chosen by the *Camera*, and chaired by a procurator. There was also a hierarchy between the different magistracies, due to the importance of the functions exercised. This was expressed in the honorary attributes reserved for the war magistrate and the magistrate of Corsica, who were entitled to the title of *Illustre*, while those of the *Veedoria* and all the temporaries were entitled to the much more modest one of *Prestantissimo*.[93]

The *patente* letter was the document of dignity, and at the same time the decree appointing the officials to their rank. The heading is the usual one for all official government documents and included all the Republic's powers: *Duce, Governatori e Procuratori della Serenissima Repubblica di Genova*. The formula remained unchanged over the decades and the ceremony of appointment took place in the capital, with the candidates being summoned to the Ducal Palace for the oath of allegiance to the government. In 1661, following discussions regarding the 'royal dignity' of the Republic, the Palace mentioned in the patents from 'Ducal' became 'Royal'.

The Genoese constitutional organisation remained firmly hostile to the rise of any position of personal power, and this attitude constituted a problem of no easy solution for the appointment of a general commander. This was also the case in wartime, constantly obeying the principle of collegiality of offices first. In wartime, powers were given to special provisional bodies. In 1672 was established the *Deputazione sugli affari di Guerra* (War Deputation) composed of the *Doge*, four members of the *Collegi* and four of the *Minor Consiglio*. In 1684 the defence of Genoa was entrusted to the *Serenissima Giunta* composed of the *Doge*, four governors and four procurators. Also in wartime, the *Collegi* appointed various patricians as *commissari generali* with political and military powers in charge of the defence of territories under enemy threat.

Consequently, only in exceptional cases did the state confer extraordinary commands on a single personality.[94] However in 1672, during the war against Savoy-Piedmont, specific command authority was assigned to one or more

---

93 ASGe, *Archivio Segreto* n. 2691. In the archival sources, The *Magistrato di Guerra* is also denominated *Presidente della Magistratura di Guerra* and *Magistrato Eccellentissimo et illustrissimo di Guerra*.

94 In 1625, when the imminent attack by Carlo Emanuele I of Savoy was looming, Giovanni Gerolamo Doria, a Genoese patrician and former military officer in the service of Spain, was elected *Maestro di Campo Generale* as commander-in-chief, but with authority only over the local commissioners; the garrisons and the city of Genoa remained directly dependent from the *Collegi*. In the same year, the government entrusted the military command in the capital to Carlo Doria, Duke of Tursi, whose authority was however limited to the area within the walls. See Beri, *Genova e il suo regno*, pp.48–51.

commissari generali to the different border sectors. Each of them had as advisor a senior officer who combined the tasks of a chief of staff and commander of troops in the field. This was the role played by the *Sargente Generale di Battaglia* Pietro Paolo Restori, a Corsican who had served as an officer in the Venetian army, and by the *Commissario Generale delle Armi* or *Commissario di Guerra* (the sources use both terms) Gian Giacomo Grimaldi, who, having already been *Commissario Generale* of Corsica in the 1650s, was elected to this position at the end of the 1670s to flank Giovanni Battista Sopranis, his successor as *commissario generale*.[95] In 1684 Carlo Tasso, a Ligurian officer formerly in Spanish service, was appointed as commander-in-chief of the Genoese army during the French assault, receiving the title of *maestro di campo generale,* who related directly to the *Serenissima Giunta*.

In the Genoese chain of command, the *commissario generale* depended from the *Serenissimi Collegi*, while for other matters he referred to the military magistracies. The *commissario generale* represented the apex of the Genoese military machine, and under him there were the simple *commissari*. These officials were the ones who represented the government's power in the 'military' and dealt with many matters, such as the direction of garrisons, supplies, marine arsenals, and more. Although they were subordinate to the *governatore* or *commissario d'armi*, the commissioners had a certain degree of independence. Sometimes they temporarily replaced superiors for short periods.

The *Dominio di Terraferma*, whose territory was traditionally divided into *Riviera di Levante, Riviera di Ponente* and *Oltregiogo*, presented a large variety of situations, which was reflected in the different names of the districts that made it up: *consolati*; *castellanie*; *podesterie*; *commissariati*; *capitanati*; *governi,* and this was also reflected in organisation of the army. An actual territorial military division in the modern sense did not exist, with the partial exception of the militia, which after the abolition of the *colonnellati* was subject to the local authorities, whose official took the name of *commissario generale delle armi* in the major districts. By 1650 these were the Governor of Savona, the Commissioner of Sarzana and the Captains of Chiavari, Levanto and Spezia. They served under the direction to the *Serenissimi Collegi* and had full military authority over the territory under their jurisdiction, which could also include circumscriptions governed by lower-ranking officials. In turn, the one in charge of the territories that did not depend from the authority of a *commissario generale delle armi*, and who did not hold this rank themselves, depended on the Magistrate of War. From the 1680s a *commissario* was appointed in San Remo, who held the functions of *commissario generale delle armi* over the western territory between Noli and Ventimiglia.[96]

In several respects the Genoese *commissari* were a scaled-down version of the Venetian *provveditori*, but despite being a second-rate office, the

---

95   Giacomone Piana-Dellepiane, *Militarium*, p.32.
96   Giovanni Assereto, *La metamorfosi della Repubblica. Saggi di storia genovese tra il XVI e il XIX secolo* (Savona: Daner, 1999), pp.55–56.

19. The city of Savona, with the fortress of the Priamar on the right in a very schematic plan after the *Schauplatz des Krieges in Italien, Oder Accurate Beschreibung der Lombardey* by Thomas Fritschen, printed at Lipsia in 1702. The strong fortress of Priamar was called 'The Right Eye of the Republic' due its strategic location guarding against threats coming from the north-west.

government required assiduous commitment, just as the *provveditori* of the *Serenissima* did. A good *commissario* had to know how to administer stores to the garrisons, but this was probably not a difficult task for a Genoese aristocrat. Evaluating the prices of goods in the state's marketplaces was a congenial activity for many, as in the case of the commissioner of the fortress of *Priamar* of Savona in 1654, Giovanni Maria Spinola, who also acted as a consultant to the *Banco di San Giorgio*; or Giovanni Battista di Negro, commissioner in 1660, also known as an experienced textile entrepreneur.[97]

The most important names of the Genoese aristocracy such as Spinola, Doria, Pallavicini, Giustiniani, and Centurione are largely represented by the commissioners who served at all levels in the army of the Republic. It was common opinion, and a consolidated practice, that the state's offices and posts, including the military ones, were divided in Genoa into three classes of prestige: those reserved for the nobility; those entrusted to the bourgeoisie; and those attributed indifferently to one or the other class. The post of commissioner belonged to the first category. The delicacy of this position was such that only 'virtuous, prudent and loyal citizens of the public' were appointed as *commissari*.[98] Naturally, this meant restricting the number of eligible candidates and relying on a social class that perhaps possessed more business sense than state sense. In some cases, as often occurred in Savona, the post of commissioner was unwelcome and considered 'uncomfortable', and since it was reserved for a shortlist of candidates, it was difficult to find

---

97 Giovanni Rapetti, *L'Ochio Dritto della Repubblica* (Savona: Elio Ferraris, 1998), p.27.
98 Giacomone Piana-Dellepiane, *Militarium*, p.33.

anyone who would accept the appointment.⁹⁹ For this and other reasons, certain commissioners were very susceptible, and did not fail to protest whenever they felt there was little respect for them by addressing the government. On these issues, one commissioner harshly remarked that the *governatore delle armi* of Savona had ordered the city's guard corps to salute the commissioner 'without emphasis', believing it disproportionate to salute with firearms.¹⁰⁰

In addition to the difficulty of finding candidates for the post of commissioner, the decision to prolong the service was based on the need for more specialised professionals, and in fact, following the war against Savoy-Piedmont, the commissioner was often replaced by a professional soldier, a colonel or a *comandante d'armi*, especially in garrisons of greater strategic importance. Professional officers resided permanently in the major fortress to assist the *commissario* in military activities. It often happened that two commissioners carried out their activities at the same time in the same location, one in charge of the fortress and the other of the citadel. In these cases it was the commissioner of the latter who had the pre-eminence, in view of the presence of the arsenal and the greater strategic importance of the inner fortification. Halfway through the term of office it was the practice for the commissioners to exchange their posts. The presence of a double commissioner affected the Savona fortress until 1672, when the post of citadel commissioner was abolished and replaced by the *comandante d'armi* who therefore took command of the entire garrison.

Normally the commissioners held the office for two months, but this turnover was not always respected and it happened that the duration was as long as seven months. This was due to the difficulty in finding sufficient replacements. The problem became particularly serious in the 1660s, at least judging by the copious correspondence between the commissioners and the government in which warnings to the commissioners to go to their assigned posts abounded, along with requests for replacements due to termination of service. In this period the government realised that it was unable to secure a sufficient number of candidates, so in 1665 it changed the length of service to a full year, later reduced for special cases to six months in 1672.¹⁰¹

The commissioner was responsible for control of all the garrison service regulations, including those relating to the access of outsiders to the fortress, the exit of soldiers, NCOs and officers. He controlled the private correspondence of soldiers and their internal mobility, the guard duty, the management of the arsenal and food stocks, the verification of the conditions of the stores, and the gunpowder consumption. All correspondence

---

99 Rapetti, *L'Ochio Dritto della Repubblica*, p.28. There were frequent cases where commissioners asked to be replaced 'because, in substance, many people aspire to honour, but not to the weight of command.' For example, in 1663, Giovanni Agostino Lercaro, *commissario* of the Priamar fortress in Savona, asked to be replaced 'having to attend to his own affairs which are in serious prejudice to his interests.'

100 *Ibid.*, p.29.

101 Rapetti, *'L'Ochio Dritto della Repubblica*, p.32.

addressed to the government and military magistracies took place by means of coded letters. The authority conferred to the commissioners also included the faculty to punish and chastise officers and soldiers for irregularities and offences committed in service. During their term of office the commissioners assigned to the garrisons led an almost monastic existence that forced them to reside permanently in the assigned residence, and only from 1660 were they allowed to leave the garrison, and then only for short periods.

As far as the 'Kingdom of Corsica' was concerned, there was an autonomous organisation. Corsica depended on a particular magistracy based in Genoa, the *Magistrato di Corsica*, who operated directly under the highest organs of the Republic, the *Maggior Consiglio* and the *Minor Consiglio*. A Genoese governor resided on the island, assisted by a vicar and the *consiglio dei nobili dodici*, the latter being a collegial institution of medieval origin. In Corsica there were two *commissari generali*, both residing in Bastia, or sometimes one in Bastia and the other in Ajaccio, with three or four other commissioners subordinate to them. One resided in Ajaccio when there was no titular officer in post, and the others had their bases at Calvi, Bonifacio and on the island of Capraia. On several occasions the *commissario generale* of Bastia, the highest authority on the island, also had a *commissario generale alle armi* under his direct command, while in the 1660s the commissioners of Calvi and Ajaccio had their own *commissario alle armi* under their orders.

Corsica was therefore provided with an autonomous military organisation, a kind of independent colonial army, similar to the much more famous army of the Indian Empire during the British rule.[102]

Fortifications

The main instrument of Genoese defensive military policy, namely fortresses and their improvement, was a subject that received less attention than might be expected. In fact, it was only after 1625, with the danger of a Savoy-Piedmont siege, that the government recognised the need to remove the city population living close to the existing walls from the threat of the enemy artillery. The old city fortifications dated back to 1536 and had long been considered obsolete and unsuitable to withstand a siege supported by modern artillery. It was therefore decided to build a new and mighty city wall, using the natural amphitheatre that had its apex on Mount Peralto. From here began two ridges that descended towards the sea, skirting two main valleys, Polcevera to the west and Bisagno to the east. Taking advantage of the terrain conformation, the *Mura Nove* (New Walls) were built following the course of the ridges. The walls were not built close to the built-up area, leaving instead much of the natural environment wooded and difficult to pass through. Once completed in 1634, the city had a double circuit of curtains comprising 49 bastions, with redoubts at each corner, and eight gates into the city, the most important and monumental of which were Porta della Lanterna to the west and Porta Pila to the east. The bastions received further improvement in 1683 by an engineer sent by Carlos II of Spain, Domenico Sirena, who

---

102 Beri, *Genova e il suo regno*, p.77. The author attributes this statement to Paolo Giacomone Piana.

designed supplementary defences outside the curtain and projected new places for the artillery.

The same Domenico Sirena dealt with the other major fortress of the Republic: the strong *Priamar* of Savona. In 1683, at the end of a long debate on whether to maintain or dismantle this stronghold, the government decided to reinforce the bastions to face the modern siege artillery. Sirena proposed to double the bastioned curtains with highly complex advanced structures, tracing the two-line deployment adopted by the armies of the time. The fortress also had a well-located citadel with its own garrison. However, lack of resources forced the government to change its goal. Thus the aim was not to make a stronghold impregnable, but to delay surrender as long as possible to allow a relief army to arrive.[103] The fortress proved to be very useful, since Savoyard raids, both in 1625 and 1672, carefully avoided Savona's territory and the Priamar, testifying 'of what importance to our Republic is the fortress and citadel of Savona'.[104]

The other modern fortress guarding the sea was Santa Maria del Golfo, close to Spezia. Providing security for such an extensive and complex front was always rather problematic. Genoa was therefore forced to control and protect an extensive and articulated sea space that was not limited to the coasts of the two Ligurian rivieras but included a much larger area due to the possession of Corsica, which extended the maritime border much further south. This appeared as a large triangle with the vertices at Ventimiglia to the west, Capo Corvo to the east, and Bonifacio to the south. This space intersected with the routes of the Spanish ships sailing between the Balearic Islands and the *Estado de los Presidios*. For the Spaniards, Genoa and its sea were therefore the first safe harbour before or after (depending on where they came from) the stretch of sea off French territory. Genoa therefore devoted attention to the defence of the littorals, and of course in response to the requests for protection from the Ligurian and Corsican populations exposed to corsair raids, as well as its sea trade. This was no minor matter, and the scale of the losses was enough to persuade Genoa to intensify the protection of its commerce. From the mid 1640s to 1651 the government calculated that 20 million *lire* had been lost to French corsairs; of which two million at once when two very rich ships had been captured.[105]

Of other fortified towns which retained some strategic importance there was Sarzana, which guarded the border with the Duchy of Massa and Tuscan Lunigiana. On the coast, Vado, Chiavari and Levanto still quartered little garrisons for the surveillance of the harbours. On the northern border, the fortified village of Gavi controlled the route to the Po Valley. This was a stronghold comparable to the other major places of the Republic. After Gavi, Genoa could trust only to the obsolete fortifications of Ovada, to which the

---

103 Repetti, *L'Ochio Dritto della Repubblica*, p.26.
104 ASGe, *Archivio Segreto*, 2707-H. 1
105 Thomas Allison Kirk, *Genoa and the Sea: Policy and Power in an Early Modern Maritime Republic, 1559–1684* (Baltimore MD: Johns Hopkins University Press, 2005), pp.136–137.

20. The fort of Gavi, guarding the northern side of the Genoese domains. (Author's photo)

whole defence of the *Oltregiogo* was entrusted. The other major centre in this area, Novi, had just an old castle and a very outdated curtain.

Differently from these latter the fortresses of the Ligurian rivieras, whatever their size and wherever they were located, represented autonomous entities and depended directly on the Colleges. According to the provisions of the constitutional laws, the aforementioned Laws of Casale, the command of the major fortresses had to be entrusted to noble citizens aged over 30, who were 'particularly capable' and who had abstained from the mechanical arts for at least eight years. Only the command of minor forts could be entrusted to common people.

The minor forts, usually entrusted to a *castellano*, decreased considerably during the seventeenth century, when the territorial defence of the mainland was centred on the major fortresses, while the minor fortifications were demolished or abandoned. However, in certain emergency circumstances a *castellano* was appointed in the most exposed areas, although this position was usually taken over by the local civil official.

The Genoese Army

The orography of the territory, the organisation of the state, and Spanish protection were the factors that influenced the organisation, or rather the lack of development, of the Genoese army, which in fact retained an exclusively defensive role. Once the war against Savoy-Piedmont was over in 1625, the garrison of Genoa was established at a minimum of 2,000 regular soldiers, under a professional officer as city commander, with the rank of *Sargente Maggiore della Città*. The post was given, in turn, to one of the members of the *Magistratura di Guerra*, who alternated in the post every three months. In 1643 this arrangement, at first temporary, became definitive, and the commander of the garrison of Genoa took on the title of *Sargente Maggiore Generale*, or more simply, as it is often referred to in the sources, *Sargente Generale*, progressively taking on the task of executive body of the *Magistratura*.

In the following years some changes occurred. In 1644 the *magistrato di guerra* estimated that in 'normal times', namely when the Republic was not forced to defend its neutrality, 2,500 infantrymen were sufficient to guard Genoa, the mainland fortresses, and to supply the troops on board the galleys, which was entrusted to the regular infantry. For some time this figure represented the ideal strength of the army in peacetime, but in the 1650s the number of troops increased by a couple of hundred men.

The regular troops, all infantry, were designated according to the nationality of the soldiers who formed the companies: *oltramontani* (comprising Germans, Swiss and Grisons), *soldati di fortuna* (Italians recruited outside the Republican domains, but also Spanish and French mercenaries), *paeselle* (native recruits), and Corsicans. Each 'nation' had their own particular regulations and training, related to their traditions and employment. German mercenaries who had positively served the Republic were offered a position as a palace guard in the company of the *Guardia Alemanna*.

In peacetime the Italian soldiers of fortune were few in number and were mainly used for service on the galleys, while in wartime it was planned to increase their number by recruiting mercenaries in the State of Milan and the duchies of the Po Valley. The native *paeselli* were mainly employed for garrison duty in garrisons and fortresses, including Corsica, in both peacetime and wartime. The main task performed by the troops quartered in the various garrison of the rivieras and northern territory of the *Oltregiogo* was the maintenance of public order, as well as the surveillance of the fortifications and prisons of Genoa.[106]

In the 1660s the regular continental force climbed to 3,500 infantrymen. This was the regular force of the Republic and throughout the following decades it underwent only slight variations.[107] In Corsica there were a further 500 Italian, German and Swiss infantrymen, who formed the ordinary garrison of the island. Since 1651 the Corsican troops had been joined with the army of the mainland, and a rotation system was established for the garrison companies on the island coming from Genoa.[108]

In 1667 the peacetime establishment in the mainland decreased to 3,100 foot, divided into 18 independent companies: three German and one Swiss from Freiburg, called together *oltramontani*; six Ligurian or *paeselli*; two of *soldati di fortuna*, and six Corsican companies.[109] Five years later the war against Savoy-Piedmont brought a massive increase in the number of troops, and the effect of this rearmament was still noticeable in April 1673, three

---

106 Beri, *Genova e il suo regno*, p.57, and Ricci Jean-Baptiste, *Gênes e le maintien de l'ordre aux XVIIe et XVIIIe siècles (1568–1729): les effectifs* (Bastia: Université de Corse, Mémoire de DEA, 1998), p.44.

107 ASGe, *Guerra e Marina*, 1129, *Militarium* 1664–1666.

108 From this date the Genoese army assumed a stable structure, which remained unchanged for the next 80 years, until the outbreak of the insurrection in Corsica in 1729.

109 BCB, *Memorie Militari della Repubblica di Genova dal 1673 al 1747*, m. r. IV.5.6.

21. The *Guardia Alemanna* of Genoa in a painting of an unknown artist, 1670–1680 (thanks to Enea Mattia Solari for this picture). See image commentaries for more information.

months after the peace agreement. These were 1,720 *oltramontani* with 991 Germans, 315 Swiss and 413 Grisons; 4,061 *soldati di fortuna*, 720 *paeselli*; 3,052 Corsicans. All together they were 9,552 infantrymen, officers not included, and further companies were still in formation. One year later demobilisation had driven the infantry to its usual peacetime establishment of 3,500 infantrymen.[110] In the following years the army's strength varied according to the major or minor external threats. In 1681 the infantry decreased to 3,200 men, but in 1682–83 about 1,000 *oltramontani*, 500 Italian mercenaries and 500 Corsicans were recruited in a few months to face the growing French threat.[111]

The government was well aware that its army would not be able to withstand an open field encounter against an enemy as fierce as the French. But since it was expected that Louis XIV would attempt some naval action against the capital, military preparations were concentrated on the defence of Genoa and the nearby coastal fortresses, in order to maintain possession of key areas in the event of an assault, and then force the enemy into a regular siege. The recourse to German mercenaries was expressly requested by the College, having developed the conviction that they were the best and most reliable soldiers in case of an obstinate defence.[112] In May 1684 the French

---

110 *Ibid.*
111 Beri, *Genova e il regno*, p.59.
112 Giacomone Piana-Dellepiane, *Militarium*, pp.49–50.

navy prevented the Corsican levies being transferred to the mainland, but the governor of Milan sent 1,000 Spanish troops to the city. In a short time there were approximately 6,500 regular soldiers in and around Genoa.[113] Five years later, Corsicans and *oltramontani* alone composed four-fifths of the regular force. In detail, they were 1,104 Corsicans, 997 Germans, Swiss and Grisons, and 480 Italians.[114]

Originally the company was the administrative rather than the tactical unit, and in the 1660s usually had a strength of 300 men for the *oltramontani*, 120 men for the Corsicans, and 200 men for the other nations, with captain, ensign, sometimes also one lieutenant, one or two sergeants, corporals, musicians – drummer and fifer – and a couple of *enfant de troupe* boys as servants for the officers. In the 1670s the companies had a theoretical strength of 150 men each, with three officers and six non-commissioned officers, drummer and fifer; however, as always occurred, archive sources show that there were large differences between theory and practice. In 1674 an infantry company fielded on average 60–70 men.[115] In 1685, with almost 9,000 regulars, there were 53 companies equal to an average strength close to 150 men, but five years later with fewer than 4,000 regulars in service there were 40 companies, thus equal to fewer than 100 men each.[116]

For tactical exigency some companies could be joined in temporary *terzi* organised like the Spanish *tercios* under colonels *maestri di campo* appointed on occasion. While in 1625 the *terzi* were mixed, usually composed indifferently of Corsicans and soldiers of fortune, in the war of 1672 Corsicans served apart forming *terzi* from three to six companies under *maestri di campo* of the same nationality, while the Italian soldiers of fortune served in *terzi* commanded by Genoese patricians. In 1672 the *terzi* of Marco Doria, Francesco Maria Pallavicini, Pietro Luigi Saluzzo, Giovanni Prato, Giuseppe Serra were formed to facilitate the direction of the infantry on campaign. While the Ligurian and Corsican companies were composed of musketeers only, the German, Swiss and Italian companies usually included 20–30 pikemen. Grenadiers were first introduced in 1686 in the *oltramontane* and Italian companies.[117]

The government resorted to various methods to increase the standing force. In the 1660s the first and simplest of the methods was to increase the

---

113 Beri, *Genova e il regno*, p.59.

114 In the following decades this ratio did not change, considering that the Corsicans and *Alemanni* numbered 1,000 each, while the Italian soldiers of fortune numbered about 500. See Giovanni Rapetti, *L'Ochio Dritto della Repubblica*, p.40.

115 According to Paolo Giacomone Piana, the actual strength of companies on campaign is very difficult to determine, because the existing muster rolls dealt with administrative matters and thus registered everyone, including soldiers on detachment or those employed on non-combatant duties.

116 ASGe, *Magistrato di Veditoria, Rolli di milizie*, n. 229–233.

117 Quinto Cenni in *Genova e le sue milizie* (a manuscript conserved in the Vinkhuijzen Collection of the New York Public Library) reports the raising of a company of grenadiers early in 1679, but really it was only a proposal which was not carried out.

MEDIUM AND MINOR POWERS

22. The alleged 'red company' of the Genoese army in 1685, in a watercolour of Italo Cenni. As with many other reconstructions of this author, clothing and other details are based on guesswork. Cenni is also the author of the manuscript relating the Republic's military history from its origin until the end of the eighteenth century. This document includes an interesting but also inaccurate history of the war against Savoy-Piedmont of 1672.

number of soldiers in the companies by authorising the captains to enlist more than the established strength. This method was used when the increase was only a few hundred soldiers, otherwise new companies had to be formed. The method traditionally employed by the Republic was the *offerta di leve di truppe* (offer of levies) choosing the most economically advantageous proposals. The applicant, almost always a junior officer or a captain without employment, submitted within a certain date the company recruited at his own expense. The government granted the officer the command of the company and the right to propose officers, but always subject to the approval of the *Magistrato di Guerra*. The government issued equipment and weapons, and from the 1670s onwards, clothing.[118]

It was widely stated that the salaries paid by the Genoese government were the lowest in Italy, but the recruitment of a company could become a considerable and risky financial investment, especially as the sums were often borrowed.[119] Naturally, the captain-entrepreneur tried to recover as much money as possible by selling the subordinate posts and profiting from the sale of foodstuffs. He also relied on the length of service, but if the government decided to reduce the army, the result could be disastrous. This method became very unpopular, especially in times of economic crisis; consequently it caused a drastic deterioration in the quality of the troops, on whom the burden of the investment fell and who were consequently subjected to all

---

118 Giaomone Piana-Dellepiane, *Militarium*, p.68.

119 *Ibid.*, p.49.

23. Spanish-style sword, Italian manufacture, c. 1670 (private collection). This type of weapon was very popular in Italy among the infantry officers and soldiers. Overall length 109 cm.

kinds of economic harassment, which only the most desperate would accept, only to recover by resorting to crime. However, this method remained in force to raise companies of Italian mercenaries, whilst regarding the new companies recruited in Corsica it was only applied to recruit soldiers serving abroad: an eventuality that Genoa partially tried to limit, but at the same time allowed by realising that in this way it could avail itself of troops and officers trained according to the most modern drill.

Throughout the second half of the seventeenth century Corsica continued to be the Republic's main reservoir of recruits, and the *leve corse* (Corsican levies) became a typical feature of the Genoese army. When in case of necessity it was necessary to recruit a large number of soldiers in a short time, the government sent to the general governor of Bastia the captains' patents with the names blank, and left him free to choose the most suitable candidates by selecting the local notables, who in turn enlisted the soldiers by making use of their family ties and patronage. It should be emphasised that, although hastily recruited, the Corsican troops performed very well during the war against Savoy-Piedmont, especially on terrain suited to their characteristics, such as the rugged cliffs of western Liguria. As for the *oltramontani* troops, these were enlisted through five-year capitulations agreed with the company's commander or the Swiss and Grison authorities, while the *paeselle* were recruited by decision of the *Serenissimi Collegi*.

The defensive approach taken by the Genoese army was consistently supported by an infantry trained to fight in open order and behind shelters or, even better, inside fortresses. In this type of warfare, especially in the hilly terrain of Liguria, the Corsicans proved to be an excellent light infantry, able to hold their own with the contemporary Balkan irregulars of Venice. Like the *oltramarini*, the Corsicans avoided open engagement wherever possible. They would skirmish from a distance with their matchlocks, and made use of the natural cover provided by the terrain to perform what were clearly very effective ambushes. They showed a preference for defending river crossings and relied, where they could, on the difficulties of the terrain and the weather to deter the enemy. When obliged to fight in close formation, the Corsicans were able to engage in hand-to-hand combat with swords and even knives. According to contemporary accounts from the war of 1672 the Corsicans were 'a remarkable infantry, and the first in this kind of warfare'.[120]

---

120 Anonymous, *Carlo Emanuele II e la guerra del Piemonte contro Genova. L'anno 1672* (without place and date, USSME Archive), p.39.

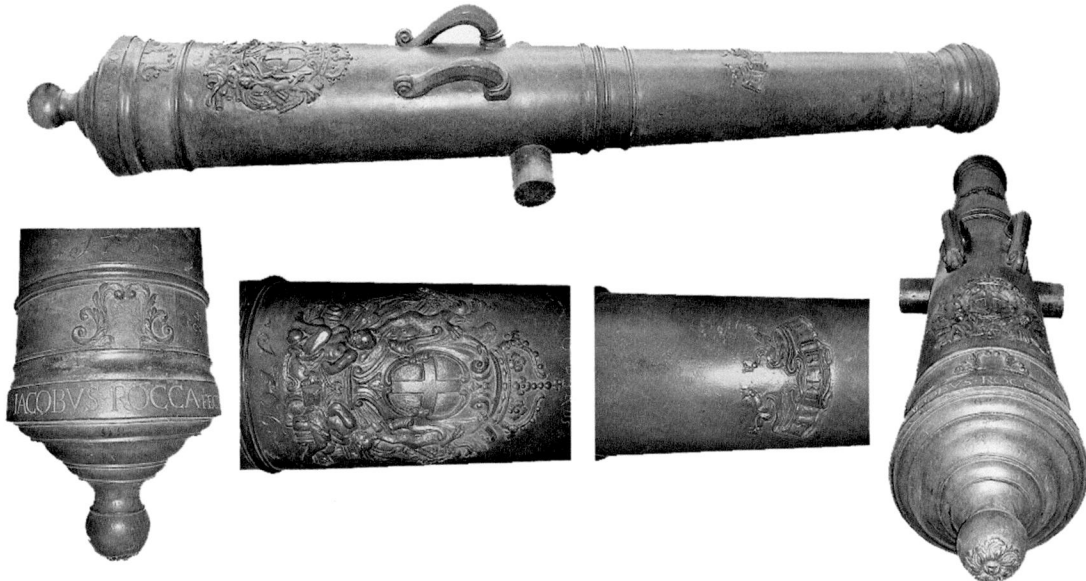

24. *Mezzo cannone*, cast for the Republic of Genoa by Giacomo I Rocca, late seventeenth or early eighteenth century, preserved in the Museo Nazionale di Artiglieria, Turin. (Author's photos)

As the Ligurian terrain was unsuitable for cavalry warfare, Genoa retained only a very small number of regular horsemen. After the *cavalleggeri* company of Sarzana was disbanded in 1657, the standing army in the Ligurian mainland comprised only a single cavalry company, operating in Oltregiogo, more precisely at Novi Ligure; it was denominated *Soldati a cavallo di Novi*, but was exclusively used for ceremonial purposes and escort for the local governor.[121] In 1672 some companies of horse arquebusiers were also raised, but they did not join the army on campaign and were soon disbanded. In Corsica there were further regular cavalry units, the *Dragoni di Bastia*, and the four *squadre* of horsemen of Bastia, San Fiorenzo, Portovecchio and Aleria.[122]

In the military organisation of the Genoese Republic the production and service of artillery occupied a special position, since people performing these functions were not considered soldiers but artisans, equated with the masters of a guild, with the associated privileges. This was also due to the fact that there was no field or siege artillery corps, and that the only task for which cannons and mortars were intended was the defence of towers, forts and fortresses. As a consequence there was neither an artillery train nor a field commander. The Genoese artillery personnel depended on the *magistrato dell'artiglieria* and were called *bombardieri*. The members were originally hired into service by individual contracts and permanently assigned to a specific garrison. In 1628 all the artillerymen in service were joined in the *Scuola*, or rather company of *bombardieri di Santa Barbara*, which continued to be a company of craftsmen, rather than an actual military corps, whose internal organisation was similar to that in the artisan guilds. A number of specialists were also attached to the

---

121 As for their actual military role, in the archival sources the *cavvalleggeri* are sometimes considered as mounted militiamen.

122 Beri, *Genova e il suo regno*, p.56.

company, such as a carpenter in charge of the manufacture of carriages and the technician who held the contract for the public cannon foundry, located in the Genoese quarter of the harbour's *Molo* (pier). The members of the company lived in their own homes, and when they were not on duty they could also practice another activity.[123] Their only obligations were to attend theoretical and practical lessons organised by the company and the shooting exercises, which were held monthly. Since artillerymen were not considered regular soldiers, they were not subject to military discipline, and if they left the service they could not be considered deserters.

However, with the decree of 23 March 1665 the government prescribed that personnel in service outside Genoa had to be replaced every three months, 'in order to prevent them from nesting in the same place with negative effect'.[124] To become a bombardier it was necessary to pass a theoretical and practical examination before a commission composed of the *magistrato dell'artiglieria* and presided over by a *procuratore* who issued the licence of appointment. Not all patented bombardiers belonged to the Santa Barbara company. In fact an autonomous artillery corps existed in Sarzana, while another was active in Corsica which depended on the local magistracy.

While the bombardier company was entrusted with the manufacture, maintenance and use of cannons, mortars came under the responsibility of another corps, separate from the previous one and denominated *compagnia dei granatieri bombisti*. This was a very special unit, almost a hybrid between regular troop and militia, considering that at the beginning of the eighteenth century officers and a certain number of men were counted among the regular troop while the rest continued to be listed in the militia ranks. The company originated in 1683, when a certain Francesco Maria Gazzo offered to train about 30 young men in the use of a light mortar he had designed. The Colleges accepted the offer and soon the company was established. In 1699 the new company was assigned to the coastal batteries of Genoa.[125]

Despite the defensive nature of the Genoese 'military', the Republic never raised a corps of military engineers, preferring to hire foreign specialists and civilian personnel. In 1672 Ansaldo De Mari, a patrician who was also an engineer, was temporarily appointed to improve the fortifications of the fortresses threatened by Savoyard attack. After the French bombardment of Genoa in 1684 the Republic started an extensive programme of improvement of fortifications, but only in 1690 was a military engineer with a lieutenant permanently registered within the officer corps serving in Genoa as *intrattenuti* (retained officers).

Stipendiati, Intrattenuti and *Giubilatii*

The term *stipendiati* (salaried) comprised several types of Genoese military personnel. Firstly, to this category belonged officers who were not on the staff

---

123 Giaomone Piana-Dellepiane, *Militarium*, p.67.
124 ASGe, *Guerra e Marina*, 359, *Magistrato artiglieria* (1663–1667), *Relazione all'Illustrissimo Collegio*, dated 7 May 1665.
125 Giaomone Piana-Dellepiane, *Militarium*, p.69.

of regiments, battalions and companies, generals, garrison officers' companies, garrison attendants, engineers, officers entrusted with the training of the militia, surgeons and even chaplains who served in the fortresses. Since the previous century it had been customary to keep a certain number of captains and other officers on duty without command of troops, in order to be able to use them in case of need. After the war of 1625 several of these *intrattenuti* were assigned to the command of fortresses as adjutants of the patrician commissioners, and from the 1660s onwards regular turns were established to assist the commanders of the major garrison. In Genoa, serving directly under the patrician *sergente generale*, a quartermaster was also assigned with the rank of captain and the task of supervising the barracks, gate guard, and night surveillance of the city.[126]

The spiritual assistance of the troops in peacetime was usually entrusted to local priests and religious. The health service was regulated on an identical basis: the few surgeons were assigned to the major fortresses, while sick soldiers were admitted to local hospitals at the expense of the *Magistratura di Guerra*, which recuperated the sum with a deduction from their pay. In wartime each company had a chaplain and a surgeon, but more often these had to provide for more than one unit at the same time.

The actual *stipendiati* were the officers in charge of training the militia, who were reserve ranked people engaged on half pay by the *Magistratura di Guerra*. Their origin dates back to the mid seventeenth century, when after the abolition of the *colonellati* one or two officers were assigned to each province to provide military training for the militia companies.

Another component of the Genoese army was the corps of the *giubilati*. They were elderly and invalid soldiers who were retired but continued to serve as guards, storekeepers and *ordinanza*. The number of *giubilate* was indefinite, as the rule was to grant this post to all the veterans with at least 30 years of service and 60 years of age, with an exception to the age requirement for people with disabilities justifying the inability to serve.

The Navy

The Republic never deemed it necessary to provide itself with a state naval force that was not purely symbolic. Throughout the sixteenth century the Genoese squadron – namely the private galleys of the *asentistas* in the service of Spain – represented the main naval force of the Republic. This consisted of some 30 galleys, and then considerably larger than the state's fleet.

Due to the change in the international scenario and the desire for a partial disengagement from Spain, from the beginning of the seventeenth century the *asentista* squadron was gradually reduced in size, while the state's squadron was increased to eight galleys.

The permanent fleet of galleys represented a very modest force fluctuating between two or three units, and six or seven in the mid seventeenth century, but possessed the quality of being completely state owned, namely financed entirely by the state. The Republic launched a programme to increase the

---

126 Beri, *Genova e il suo regno*, p.70.

25. The bombardment of Genoa by the French fleet in May 1684, in an *ex-voto* preserved in the church of Santa Maria di Castello (author's photograph). See image commentaries for more information.

permanent fleet, including the formation of an entirely state-owned squadron of sail ships. Genoese galleys employed slaves and convicted people, and in this regard there was an agreement with the Republic of Lucca for the sending of sentenced young males to the galleys' oars, who were specifically mentioned in the sources as *huomini da remo*.[127]

By 1638 the galley fleet was joined by the *squadrone di libertà* (squadron of liberty), composed of units of mixed public and private funding. This squadron originated from a private initiative for manning galleys with only free oarsmen, hence without slaves and convicts, recruited from the riviera communities through a system of maritime conscription. After the first favourable experiences the number of these units grew, reaching nine galleys by the 1650s. Their number varied from year to year depending on contingent factors. But as early as 1658, a few years after the most successful period, the experiment was dismissed and even the squadron of sail ships –

---

127 Salvatore Bongi, *Inventario del regio Archivio di Stato di Lucca* (Lucca,1876), Vol. II, p.406.

which reached a maximum of four units destined mostly for convoy escorting – represented nothing more than a parenthesis in the short space of half a century. In the last years of the seventeenth century the Genoese naval force was once again reduced to just six galleys in all; a figure that was destined to halve in the following century.[128]

The only Genoese help to Venice during the war against the Porte in 1684–99 came from the fleet. In 1686 one galley, *San Giorgio Genovese*, joined the allies, followed by a second unit the following year. In the same year a sailing ship with 70 guns and 300 crew and volunteers was armed on the initiative of the Genoese aristocracy, remaining with the Venetian squadron until the end of the campaign under captain Carattino.[129] In October the sail ship returned to Genoa together with the galleys, thus ending their participation for that year.[130] In 1689 Genoa offered two more galleys, to which three armed merchants were added in 1690.

Militia

Together with the regular troops, the Republic could mobilise the militia, the so-called *paeselli* or *cerne*. For this purpose the mainland domains were originally divided into 11 *colonellati* (districts): Sarzana, Spezia, Brugnato, Chiavari, Rapallo, Ovada, Novi, Savona, Albenga, Porto Maurizio, Ventimiglia. Each district formed 10 companies of foot, each with 150 men, which at least on paper would provide a considerable increase in men for the defence of the state. The captains were appointed by the government and selected from local 'experts in military matters'.[131] These officers were paid by the state, which is why they were known as *stipendiati*. They were entrusted with the tasks of training the militia, and with the distribution of armament and equipment, stored in arsenals belonging exclusively to them. In 1628 the *colonellati* were abolished and replaced by the territories with their governors and officials, the aforementioned *commissario generale delle armi*.

Once the war against Savoy-Piedmont in 1625 was over, the government decided to keep in service a contingent of militiamen called 'the chosen ones', to be deployed alongside the regular units in places of major strategic importance. This was a mild form of conscription of younger subjects, taking care to select candidates from the largest and wealthiest families, thus excluding orphans, heads of families and the poorest, although the government allowed them to enter the militia as volunteers.

All able-bodied peasants aged from 18 to 70 were expected to serve in the militia, but there was a further distinction between ordinary and selected militia. The *Milizia ordinaria* was obliged only to perform a limited service against pirates and outlaws, while the *Militia scelta* could be called

---

128 Luca Lo Basso, *Uomini da remo. Galee e galeotti del Mediterraneo in età moderna* (Milan: Selene, 2003), pp.206–311.

129 Nicola Beregani, *Historia delle Guerre d'Europa dalla comparsa dell'Armi Ottomane in Ungheria* (Venice, 1698), vol. I, p.450.

130 *Ibid.*, vol. II, p.23.

131 Rapetti, *L'Ochio Dritto della Repubblica*, p.32.

to arms in case of war. The latter's companies were formed by the voluntary or compulsory enlistment of men from 20 to 60 years, who were granted privileges such as tax exemptions, hunting, and the right to bear firearms. The companies were periodically assembled for military training under the direction of the *stipendiati* officers. The companies recruited in the territory around Genoa were to be the better trained, usually entrusted to a patrician ranking as captain and an experienced officer as lieutenant, who was expected to be effective in case of war. Contemporary commenters positively assessed the *scelti*, and indeed during the war against Savoy-Piedmont they fought better than German and Italian mercenaries.[132] In 1672 the companies of Laigueglia, Villanova, Alassio, Triora and Penna (today La Penne, in France) also aroused the government's admiration when they successfully engaged the regular enemy troops.[133]

In 1674 there were in Liguria 125 select militia companies: 50 in western Liguria, 57 in eastern Liguria and 18 in *Oltregiogo* between Novi and Ovada, with 39 *stipendiati*. In the area surrounding Genoa there were 29 companies organised in the four *Colonellati* of Bisagno, Quarto, Polcevera and Sestri.[134] In 1677 the select militia numbered on paper 25,000 men.

According to regulations the companies of the select militia had an establishment of 150 men, but many soldiers were unfit for active service so a company on campaign had a strength of around 60. The company was always the basic tactical formation, but in 1672 provisional military units called *battaglioni* were formed, led by local *stipendiati* and grouping companies drawn from the same territory. Though the *milizia scelta* had no regular military training, its members proved to be skilled marksmen and this provided valuable service when employed properly in its own territory. In 1684 the militiamen of Polcevera and Bisagno played an important role in repulsing the French landing.

There were several other types of militia in the Republic. Towns and villages had their own bourgeois militia, usually composed of the wealthy people. Their military skill was questionable, but they were useful for police duties. Genoa had no militia organisation, after the urban militia had been disbanded earlier in the seventeenth century for political reasons. The privileges allowed to the *milizia scelta* were granted to the small company of *granatieri bombisti*, and to the *capi-strada*, the officials raised in 1684 to run the civil defence organisation.

---

132 Gualdo Priorato, *Relatione della Città di Genova e suo Dominio*, pp.84–85.

133 Riccardo Musso, 'Compagnie scelte e ordinarie nello Stato di Terraferma' in *Liguria* LIII–1/2 (1986), pp.11–15. In subsequent years the prestige of this militia did not diminish. In 1691, the *scelti* of the upper Arroscia Valley formed the *compagnie paeselle* in permanent service. These were composed almost entirely of *scelti*, amounting to 582 men, employed with other soldiers in the fortresses of the mainland.

134 In 1639 a decree required formation of a fifth *Colonellato* called 'Between the old and new Walls' (*Tra le vecchie e le nuove mura*), enclosing the sparsely populated area between the old and the new curtains built after the 1625 war; but this order was carried out only at the end of the century. Thanks to Paolo Giacomone Piana for this information.

Grand Duchy of Tuscany

The historiography of the *Risorgimento* has generally attributed to Tuscany a policy of stubborn neutrality and consequently a military strength reduced to the needs of defence alone.[135] It was deep-rooted opinion that in Tuscany, the second half of the seventeenth century coincided with the progressive weakening of the military apparatus and consequently with the diminishing political influence of the Grand Dukes. It had served little purpose to show off during the War of Castro by overestimating the actual military force of the *descritti* (militiamen), the same who still retained the honours and name of the venerable *Bande della Milizia* instituted by Cosimo I de' Medici in 1556.[136]

Though less strategically exposed compared to other Italian states, Tuscany was not unaffected by the great powers' attempts at dominance. Therefore, similarly to the rest of Italy, the outcome of the duel in progress between France and Spain also reverberated in the Grand Duchy. Ferdinando II (1610–1670) was well aware that an excessive weakening of Spain or France would have been to his disadvantage, and in the second half of the century one of the constant concerns of the Grand Dukes was to avoid the French being overpowering in Italy, which would inevitably have jeopardised the independence of the Grand Duchy.[137] Therefore, caught between the demands of Madrid and Paris, Ferdinando II and his son Cosimo III (1642–1723) always tried to not displease either contender.

In the seventeenth century the borders of Tuscany corresponded only in part to the modern region, and although the Grand Duchy included part of Romagna with Castrocaro, Terra del Sole and Dovadola, the territorial extension was smaller overall than today. A considerable part of the coastline was under foreign sovereignty due to the presence of the Spanish *Estado de*

26. Portrait of Grand Duke Ferdinando II de' Medici (1610–1670), by Justus Sustermans (National Gallery, London). Like every Medici, Ferdinando was a protector of the arts, and despite the weakness of his state he managed to maintain Tuscany in a prestigious place in the Italian scenario of the second half of the seventeenth century.

---

135 Nicola Labanca, 'Le Panoplie del Granduca', in *Ricerche Storiche*, XXV n. 2 (May–August, 1995), p.298. 'The history of the relationship between armed forces and society in the seventeenth and eighteenth century Tuscany has long been neglected, and over time, the assertion prevailed that the Grand Duchy had no armies, but only policemen.'

136 Between 1659 and 1690 the Grand Dukes were Ferdinando II (r. 1621–1670) and Cosimo III (r. 1670–1723).

137 Jean Claude Waquet, *Le Grand Duché de Toscane sous le derniers Medici* (Rome: Ecole Française de Rome, 1990), pp.121–122.

los Presidios. The northern domains of Pietrasanta and Pontremoli, the latter acquired from Spain in 1658, were enclaves surrounded by other states, such as the Republic of Lucca and the Duchy of Massa and Carrara, or possessions of the Po valley sovereigns, namely the Duke of Parma in the Lunigiana and the Duke of Modena in the upper Garfagnana. Finally three-quarters of the island of Elba, and the Principality of Piombino were under Spanish-Neapolitan sovereignty. In the Archipelago, Tuscany held only Portoferraio on the island of Elba, Gorgona and the Giglio islands. Here lived a population of a few peasants, miners, fishermen, monks and soldiers, the latter often forced to serve in these remote garrisons as a punishment. The main Tuscan harbour was Livorno, a seaport celebrated 'as the most secure and convenient of Italy',[138] which became a neutral port in 1676,[139] a condition that in 1718 turned into an international limitation of grand ducal sovereignty by virtue of the Treaty of London.[140]

With a population of around 800,000 inhabitants, at the end of the century the Grand Duchy of Tuscany held the unhappy record of being the Italian state with the lowest birth rate.[141] Tuscany as a whole appeared to foreign travellers as diverse, with many inequalities. The attraction exerted by the artistic treasures preserved in Florence and the charm of the Renaissance architecture of many towns in the Grand Duchy were already a reason of interest to cultured Europe. Aristocrats and princes of reigning houses, but also wealthy bourgeois, came to Tuscany, which inaugurated the splendours of the grand tours across the Peninsula; but alongside such beauty and splendour, very few ventured into the poorest districts, where misery and endemic diseases did not favour social and

---

138 Galeazzo Gualdo Priorato, *Relatione della Città di Fiorenza, e del Gran Ducato di Toscana sotto il Regnante Gran Duca Ferdinando II, con tutte le Cose più degne e curiose da sapersi* (Cologne, 1668), pp.80–81.

139 As is well known, from the end of the sixteenth century England carried out a veritable commercial and maritime invasion of both the Christian and the Muslim Mediterranean. According to Carlo Maria Cipolla, *Il burocrate e il marinaio. La "Sanità" toscana e le tribolazioni degli inglesi a Livorno nel XVII secolo* (Bologna: Il Mulino, 1992), p.11: '[B]y increasingly replacing local merchant navies, the English trade also drew increasing profits from the business of transporting goods for hire and passengers from one port to another within the Mediterranean itself. Confirmation of the London intention to enter the area permanently lies in the Admiralty's decision, which in the spring of 1665, sent 8 galleons, four frigates and five smaller units in the Mediterranean to protect the English trade. Thus Livorno, which in the plans of the first Grand Dukes was to be the fulcrum of Tuscany's future maritime power, was practically transformed into an English base, and would remain so for the next two centuries.'

140 The treaty was definitively accepted by the last grand duke Medici only in 1736. The international imposition was then reaffirmed by the subsequent treaties of Vienna in 1738, Aix-la-Chapelle in 1748 and Paris in 1763 and only broken in 1793 by a convention imposed by England to use it as a base for the Mediterranean fleet. See Virgilio Ilari, Piero Crociani and Ciro Paoletti, *Bella Italia Militar: Eserciti e Marine nell'Italia pre-napoleonica 1748–1792* (Rome: USSME, 2000), p.342.

141 Leonardo Rombai, *Geografia Storica dell'Europa Occidentale, la Toscana tra '600 e '700* (Florence: Centro Editoriale Toscano, 1997), p.95.

economic growth. From the point of view of political-administrative organisation, Tuscany had the defect of having been constituted into a state by means of successive unifications of already defined territorial entities, which retained their legal autonomy with respect to the capital. An example of this scenario, is that there were the fiefdoms and local entities that escaped the control of the central government. An even more clamorous example was the de facto coexistence of the organisational structure of the Florentine and Sienese states, with their own laws, magistracies and still divided by borders, laws and even customs and trade restrictions between one entity and the other. This extreme disorganisation also existed in the local administration. A huge number of magistracies of medieval derivation were flanked, and often subordinated, to offices and local magistracies or *podesterie* of later creation. The result was a legislation that varied from area to area, which prevented a univocal action of government, theoretically possible through the vicariates of grand ducal nomination, but rendered ineffective in practice by the election of magistrates inspired by particularistic interests, when they themselves were not landowners, or acted linked to clientele of various kinds.

27. Cosimo III de' Medici (1642 1723), portrayed as a young prince by Justus Sustermans (Museum of Palazzo Corsini, Rome). See image commentaries for more information.

Also from an economic–fiscal point of view, there was a great lack of homogeneity. Taxes and duties of all kinds prevented the free transit of goods through the state, even to the detriment of the needs of the population. As far as communication routes were concerned, the overland road system had many shortcomings, especially for direct connection between the provinces. The road layout was practically the same as six centuries earlier, as was the state of maintenance of the roads, which started from the towns according to a radial pattern of medieval origin. The population was concentrated in the large agricultural areas of Valdarno, Valdinievole, and Casentino, where the living conditions of the residents appeared better and did not present the health problems that existed in other areas. However, settlements became increasingly scarce in the mountains, plains and coastal hills south of Siena, partly due to the presence of landowners who had little interest in new investment. This phenomenon produced over time an increasing depopulation of the territory, to the point of leaving entire villages of southern Tuscany completely deserted, and marshes and swamps returned.

Throughout the century, the activity of the population remained largely concentrated in agriculture and breeding, which absorbed more than half of the working population. Only in the cities was there a more articulated

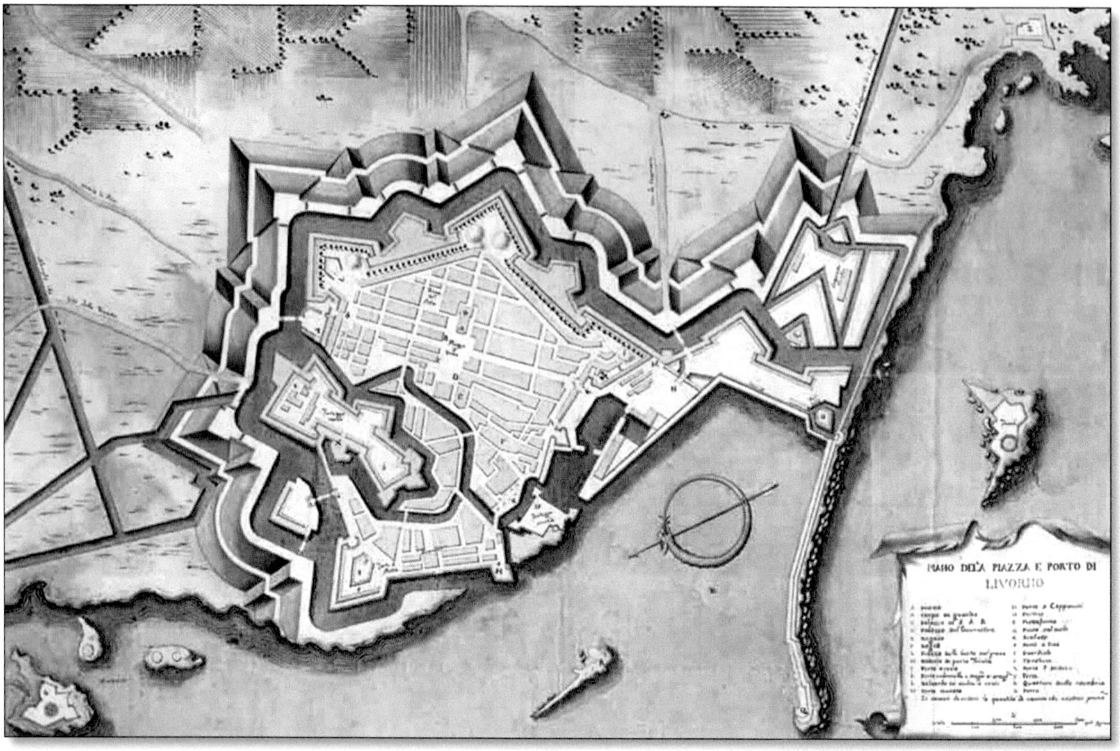
PIANO DEL'A PIAZZA E PORTO DI
LIVORNO

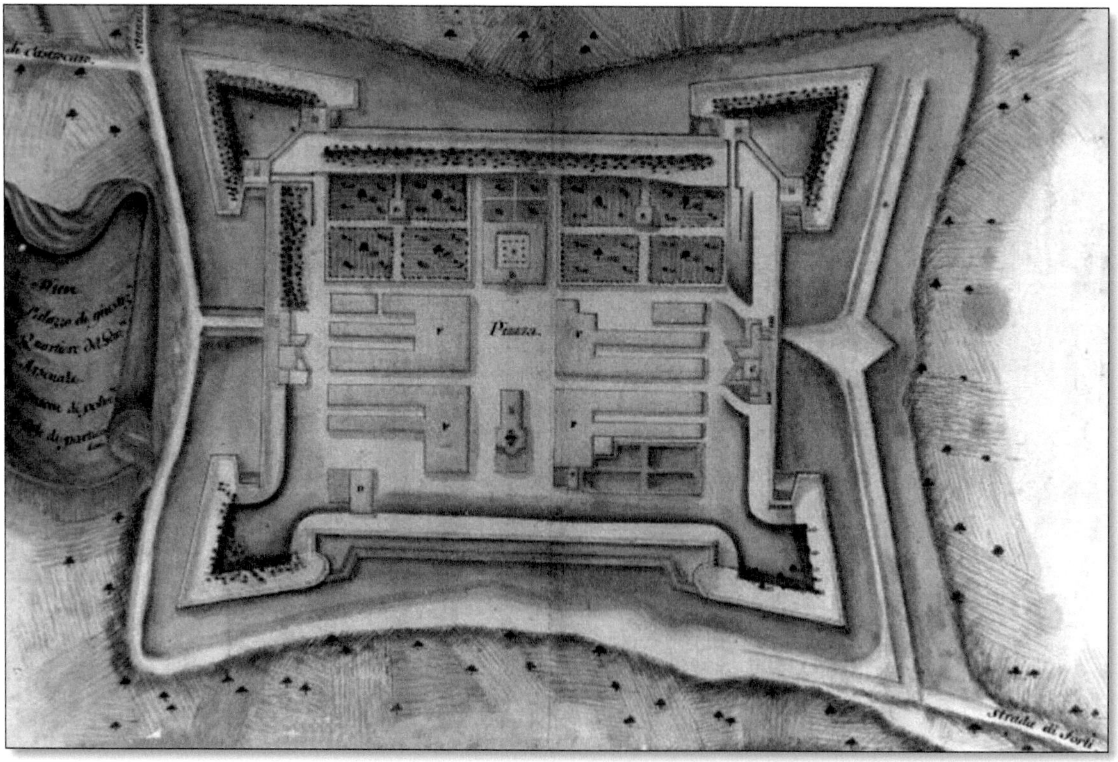
Piazza

MEDIUM AND MINOR POWERS

Facing page, top: 28. The fortifications of Livorno, in a late seventeenth-century print (author's archive). Since the 1660s Livorno had quartered the largest garrison of the Tuscan standing army.

Facing page, bottom: 29. Plan of the fortress of Terra del Sole. The fortress was built in 1564 by Grand Duke Cosimo I to guard the access to the Tuscan Romagna, a territory forming a triangle of approximately 5,800 square kilometres, most of which is now part of the modern province of Forlì. Terra del Sole is an admirable example of the new urban planning model introduced in the sixteenth century, after the theorisations and experiences of the Italian military engineers of the Renaissance. Today, Terra del Sole still retains a well-preserved curtain and is home to prestigious local historical institutions

Below: 30. The Florentine fortress of St John, or da Basso, built in 1531, was one of the first fortifications of Europe designed by Giuliano da Sangallo according to the *trace italienne* style. In the late seventeenth century, the fortress had lost its main strategic role, but still included a large arsenal and workshops for manufacture of firearms.

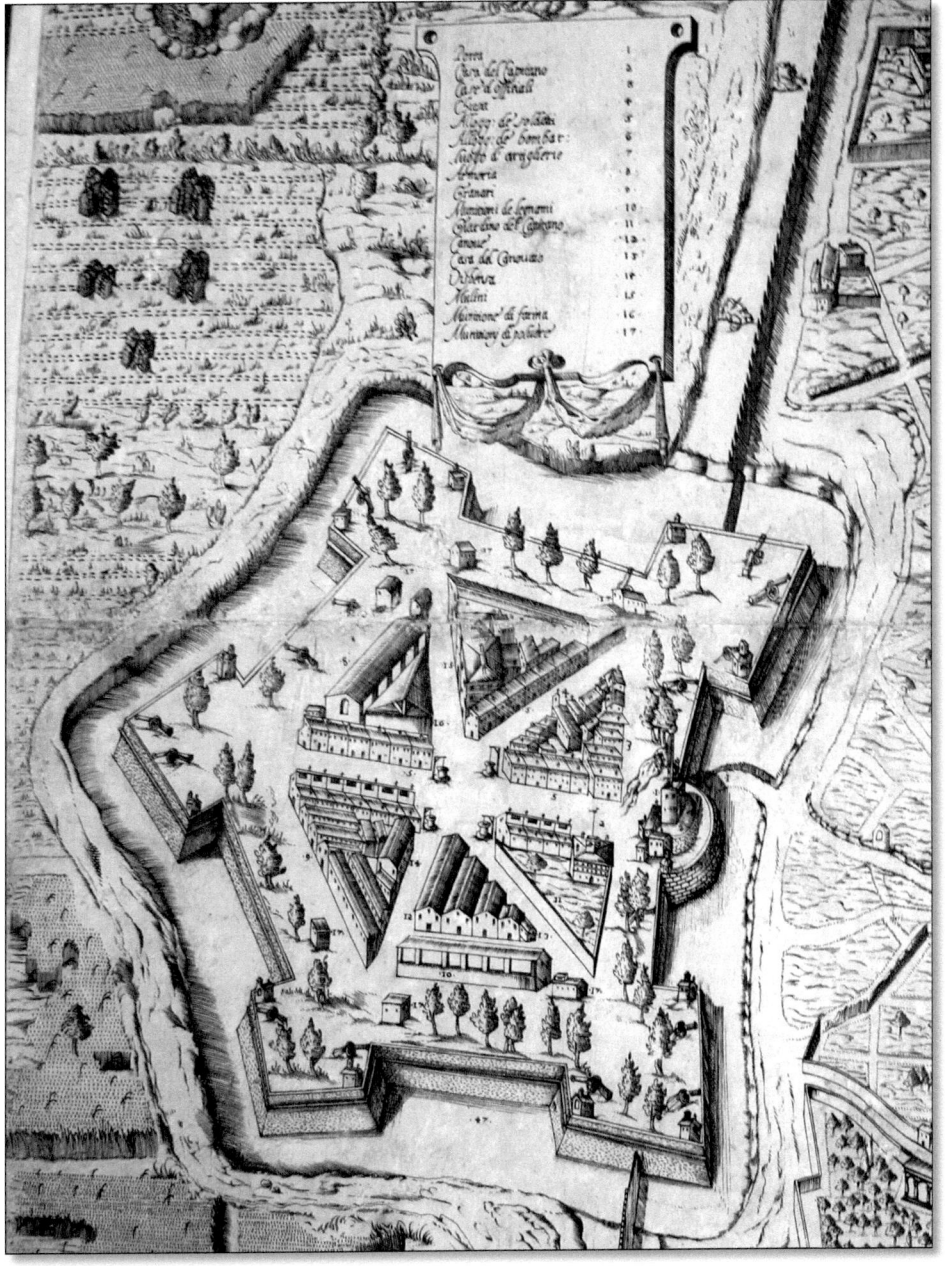

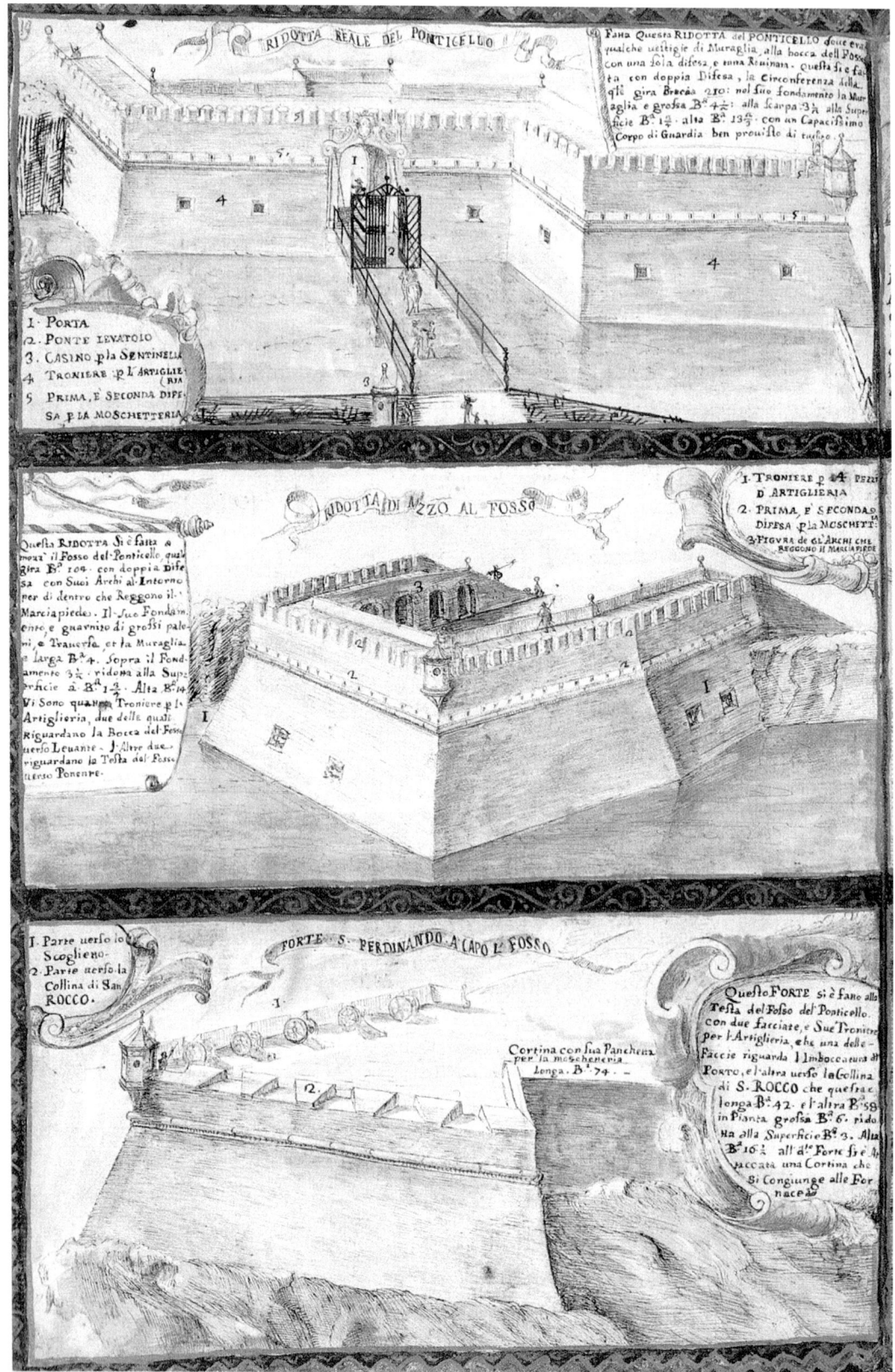

economy, and a greater diversity of activities.[142] In the 1660s Florence had a population of about 70,000 persons while Livorno housed about 18,000,[143] followed by Pisa, Siena, Pistoia, Arezzo and Grosseto, the latter with less than 6,000 persons. The economic and social imbalance between Florence and the rest of the territory was very strong. The few centres of manufacture were all concentrated in the capital, in Livorno and to a small extent in Arezzo, Pistoia, Pisa and Siena.[144] As far as the economic conditions of the aristocracy were concerned, the bulk of their income came from the exploitation of public offices, over which the nobility had always exercised an undisputed monopoly; and of course from land ownership.

Facing page: 31. Details of the artillery batteries of Portoferraio, after a 1697 drawing of an anonymous artist. (Maroniana Library, Florence)

Ercole Tirreno and His Geostrategy[145]

Certainly, Medicean Tuscany does not belong to the group of states that made arms the privileged means of their political initiative. Nor, however, is the traditional image of a country that remained cowardly and subservient to European powers to be accepted. The attempt of the Medici Grand Dukes to pursue a dynamic and autonomous foreign policy already dated back to the reign of Cosimo I. His successors had tried on numerous occasions to find territorial outlets that would allow them to increase their position on the European chessboard, as well as to increase their own prestige. This goal led his nephew Ferdinando I (1549–1609) to study very ambitious programmes of African conquests, including the possibility of colonising Sierra Leone. After him Cosimo II (1590–1621) seriously considered the conquest of Lebanon, supporting the Druze emir Fakr-ed-Din II, while the failed expedition of 1607 against Famagusta was part of a plan cradled by the Medici for a long time. The conquest of Cyprus, a possible advanced base for future ventures in the Near East, was not just the fruit of a passing mania, since it is demonstrated by the fact that again in 1629 the possibility of conquering and holding the island was carefully considered.[146]

---

142 Considering only the cases of Pistoia and Florence, located in areas where most of the Grand Duchy's population was concentrated, about a third of the labour force was employed in craft activities, while almost 40 percent were engaged in other activities such as construction, trade, domestic services and other paid occupations. See Furio Diaz, *il Granducato di Toscana. I Medici* (Turin: Utet, 1976), pp.344–346.

143 Gualdo Priorato, *Relatione della Città di Fiorenza, e del Gran Ducato di Toscana*, p.80 and p.109.

144 *Ibid*. In the cities the proportion of the ecclesiastical population was also high, almost 14 percent in the last decade of the century.

145 Until the sixteenth century, Hercules, the expression of strength and wisdom, had also been taken by the Medici as a symbol of warrior valour; painting and poetry joined this image with that of the dynasty's greatest soldiers and to the Grand Duchy itself. See Carla Sodini, *L'Ercole Tirreno. Guerra e dinastia medicea nella prima metà del '600* (Florence: Olschki, 2001).

146 As for Fakr-ed-Din, see G. Mariti, *Istoria di Faccardino Grand-Emir dei Drusi* (Livorno 1787); P. Carali, *Fakr Ad-Din. Il principe del Libano e la Corte di Toscana (1605–1635)* (Rome, 1936). As for Sierra Leone, the abandonment of the company was motivated by economic and strategic reasons. On this topic see P. E. H. Hair and J. D. Davies, 'Sierra Leone and the Grand Duke of Tuscany', in *History in Africa* vol. XX (Cambridge University Press, 1993) pp.61–69. For a

The Grand Dukes spared no expense in achieving their goals. Between 1625 and 1650, war expenses averaged around 50 percent of the Grand Duchy's total income, with a minimum of 30 percent in 1628, and a maximum of almost 67.5 percent in 1644.[147] The economic crisis in the Mediterranean, as well as the outbreak of the Thirty Years' War with its appendices, meant on the one hand a decrease in Tuscany's financial resources and on the other a greater military involvement of the Grand Duke – even if most often indirect – in the conflicts that bloodied Europe. The overall figure was probably even higher, as many other indirect expenses were not taken into account. These included the obligations that Tuscany had contracted with the investiture of the State of Siena in 1559. The agreement signed by Charles V and Cosimo I included the burden of a 'relief' of 4,000 infantrymen, and 400 cavalrymen provided by the Medici every time the State of Milan or the Kingdom of Naples was attacked. Although the Grand Dukes did everything they could to avoid this contribution, between 1625 and 1636 they had to send the required troops three times, with the consequent burden on the grand ducal finances.[148]

In 1626, on the occasion of the conflict between the Duke of Savoy and Madrid, the Grand Duke was asked to send a contingent to the Milanese area; but in Florence it was felt that since it was the Spaniards who had attacked, the conditions agreed in the investiture of Siena could not be applied and therefore there was no obligation to send troops. However, it was wise not to go against Spain. The only thing that Felipe IV obtained from Ferdinando II was a loan of 100,000 *scudi*, on condition that they be paid in cash.[149] This was a justified precaution, since the debts that the Medici boasted towards *Los Austrias* was huge. Between 1625 and 1642 about 1,800,000 *scudi* were lent to Spain, and Madrid's inability to honour its debts would have been one of the causes of the serious financial and economic difficulties that afflicted Tuscany in the mid seventeenth century.[150]

In the 1640s the creation of an axis between Mazarin and Urban VIII, in an anti-Habsburg function and to favour the Papal occupation of Castro, forced Ferdinando II to opt for a more pro-Spanish policy. Again, the Grand Duke tried to keep his distance from Madrid so as not to irritate Paris too much,

---

summary of the projects of Ferdinando I, see G. Uzielli, *Cenni storici sulle imprese scientifiche, marittime e coloniali di Ferdinando I, granduca di Toscana* (Firenze 1901).

147 ASFi, *Miscellanea Medicea*, f. 264, ins. 29, *Ristretto delle entrate ed uscite del granducato, 1625–1650*. It should be noted that these expenses, however high, are equivalent to, if not lower than, those of many contemporary European states. See Geoffrey Parker, *La Rivoluzione Militare* (Italian Edition, Bologna: Il Mulino, 1989), pp.103–105.

148 ASFi, *Mediceo del* Principato, f. 3250, f. 3251.

149 Waquet, *Le Grand Duché de Toscane*, p.120. The question of relief was always a *vexata quaestio* between Madrid and Florence, with the former demanding the sending of troops even in the event of danger of war in the Italian territories of the Spanish King, and the latter claiming, understandably, that the sending of soldiers was only due if the Spanish domains were attacked.

150 ASFi, *Mediceo del Principato*, f. 3250, ins. 2, *Ristretto del fatto circa i Soccorsi dello Stato di Milano dal 1614 al 1641, fatto dall'Auditor Vettori*.

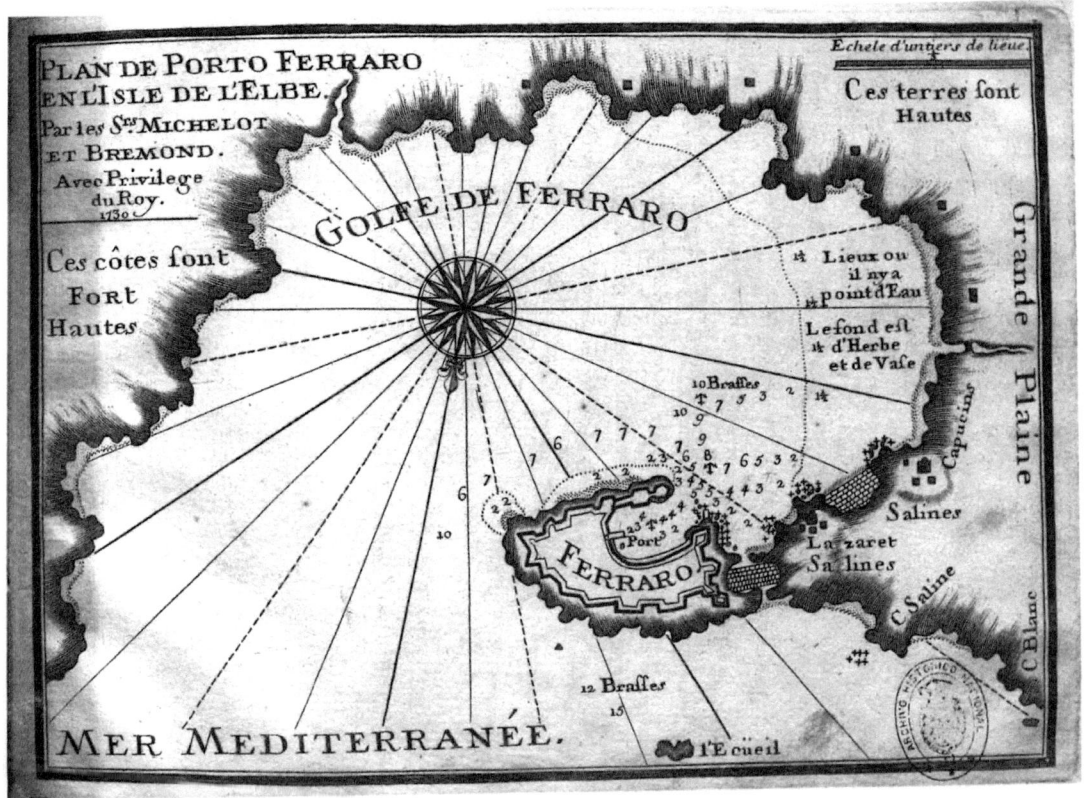

32. Portoferraio, on the island of Elba, in a Spanish print dating to the early 1700s (Archivo Histórico Nacional, Madrid). See image commentaries for more information.

even when Tuscany was forced to contribute money and galleys to Felipe IV's wars against France.[151] After Westphalia, when it became clear that Spain's fortunes were declining, Ferdinando II devoted greater attention to France, and this was confirmed in 1655 with the appointment as Secretary of War of Ferdinando de' Bardi-Magalotti, a former resident in Paris. However, the inclusion in the Grand Duke's circle of Bardi-Magalotti and other pro-French councillors is not indicative of a shift by the Medici in favour of France, but rather of the need to have people capable of understanding and dealing with situations at risk for Tuscany that might arise beyond the Alps. The rapprochement with France received new impetus in 1661, when Ferdinando II married his son and heir Cosimo to Marguerite-Louise d'Orléans, cousin of Louis XIV.

---

151 ASFi, *Mediceo del Principato*, f. 4652, Andrea Cioli to Ferdinando Bardi. This was a very delicate moment, especially after the appointment of the Grand Duke's brother Giovan Carlo de' Medici as general-admiral of the Spanish fleet, in the hope of counterbalancing the potential danger posed by the French–Papal fleet in the Mediterranean. In an attempt to appease the French government, Tuscan State Secretary Cioli instructed Bardi to inform the Cardinal that the Tuscan galleys had received orders to 'behave with every discreet term, on occasion of faction with anyone encountered at sea dependent from this Crown'.

However it was difficult, if not impossible, for the Grand Duke to sever his ties with Spain, due to the trade and personal relationships many of his subjects had with the Iberian Crown, contacts that would continue throughout the reign of Ferdinando II and beyond. In addition to the merchants in Cadiz[152] there were numerous Tuscans who served in the Spanish army, while others were members of military orders such as Santiago, Calatrava Alcántara and Montesa.[153]

However, it was not only the changed international balance and the Grand Duchy's uncertain foreign policy that led to the change in the Medici strategy: the turning point in the Grand Duchy's military policy was the war of Castro and its appendices (1641–44 and 1646–49). This event also precisely marks the turning point in the history of the Grand Duchy. It was this conflict that forced the Medici to pursue a land strategy instead of the naval one in vogue since the middle of the previous century, changing the Duchy's strategic objectives in the following years. After 1650 the problem for Tuscany, as for most of the Italian states, was the substantial inability to find sufficient resources to deal with sudden crises, military or otherwise. This meant that every slight event caused considerable burdens on the treasury.

A few years before the Medici dynasty died out, one of the ministers of the last Grand Duke, Marquis Luigi Viviani della Robbia, managed to summarise the military policy of the Grand Duchy in the years of the Medici regime into a few lines:

> Duke Alessandro, with the favour of Emperor Charles V, re-ordered his militia and the great Cosimo I increased them with laws and discipline, as in the course of the principality, and to this day, the narrowness of the country and the limitation of its revenue has never allowed the house of Medici to have a sufficient number of militia, apart from those that serve as garrison in the fortress or in other parts of the State.[154]

Tuscany had faced several threats during the seventeenth century, also going through phases of intense warfare, especially when the Grand Duchy had played an active role in the political framework of Italy or in the Mediterranean against Ottoman and North African corsairs. However, Viviani was right on

---

152 Rita Mazzei, 'Continuità e crisi nella Toscana di Ferdinando II (1621–1720)', in *Archivio Storico Italiano* (Florence: Olschski, 1998), vol. VIII, pp.67–68.

153 The presence of a strong pressure group linked to Spain for reasons of clientele could not fail to have an impact, still to be studied, on Tuscan foreign policy; not only with regard to the Spanish Monarchy and its Italian dependencies, but also the other states bordering the Grand Duchy. Moreover, the favour of the Spanish kings was necessary for the Tuscan merchant community to gain access to the markets of southern Germany, since the easiest routes to northern Europe passed through the State of Milan. See Angelantonio Spagnoletti, *Principi italiani e Spagna nell'età barocca* (Milan: Bruno Mondadori,1996), pp.202–206.

154 Luigi Viviani della Robbia, *Compendio Civile, Economico e Militare della Toscana* (1734), in S. Di Noto, *Gli ordinamenti del Granducato di Toscana in un testo settecentesco di Luigi Viviani* (Milan: Giuffré, 1984), p.247.

MEDIUM AND MINOR POWERS

33. The fortress of St George or di Belvedere, depicted on the left corner in the painting of Iustus Van Utens, on the hills of the left side of Florence (early seventeenth century).

the main point: after 1650 the Medici had no longer been able to dispose of adequate financial resources to maintain permanent armed forces in such numbers as to adopt a strategy other than defence. These considerations were obvious, and for this reason unquestionable. Looking at the records of the *Depositeria Generale*, between 1625 and 1650 an average of about 50 percent of the revenues were used for direct military expenditure.[155] Consequently, defence expenditure was leading to the virtual bankruptcy of the Grand Duchy.[156] The financial emergency soon caused side effects on the army, since the troops were not paid regularly. Taxes were also instituted to cope with

---

155 ASFi, *Miscellanea Medicea*, f. 264, ins. 29, *Ristretto delle Entrate Ordinarie e Straordinarie di S.A. Ser.ma, si come di tutte le Uscite Calculate dall'anno 1625 a tutto l'anno 1650*, Appendix, Tabulars 1–6. Certainly, the highest peaks in this regard were reached when Tuscany was in a state of war, with a ratio of 67 percent in 1644 between revenue and expenditure and defence costs, and this when the Grand Duchy's treasury had been replenished by the extraordinary tax known as *la gravezza universale*, with the result that in 1650 the budget deficit amounted to 129,117 *scudi*. This was not a large figure, but more than substantial when compared to the 926,000 *scudi* of revenue that year, and especially considering the serious financial crisis that occurred in this period. In fact, in 25 years, military expenditure had been rather low. Ferdinando II's liquidity problems were caused above all by unfavourable international circumstances, which led to the non-repayment of debts owed by Tuscany to the Spanish Monarchy; this becomes clear when we know that after 1660 when Tuscany experienced a period of economic recovery. See also Waquet, *Le Grand Duché de Toscane sous les derniers Médicis*, pp.315–318.

156 After the War of Castro, Tuscany could no longer bear the cost of a fleet, despite the prestige that came with it, also because there was an urgent need for cash. In 1647, the sale of three galleys to the prince of Monaco for 100,366 *scudi* not only gave respite to the Tuscan finance, but relieved

military crises, but it should also be considered that wartime mobilisations led to a fall in tax revenues from the subject communities, as the militia involved a large number of the labour force, the maintenance of which thus became another burden for the state economy. Recognising that further fiscal measures would prove to be unsuccessful, the only possible solution to solve the financial crisis caused by 20 years of emergencies was to consolidate public debt by reducing interest rates on government bonds by half and then three-quarters.[157] The failure to pay salaries is indicative of the serious financial crisis of this age.[158] The miserable appearance offered by the Grand Ducal troops in those years must have contributed to the negative image consolidated in subsequent years about the Tuscan 'military' of the last Medicis.

Though this was partly due to objective causes, such as the geographic conformation of the domains and their extension, another negative feature resulted from the tasks of static garrisons and maintenance of internal security. Given these assumptions, it is not surprising to note the virtual absence of regular cavalry and field artillery, given that the main function of the Tuscan 'military' consisted in dissuading potential enemies from invading the territory, relying on the deterrent constituted by the numerical strength of the militia to be mobilised in the event of aggression.

As for the fortresses, the only modern ones were Livorno, with a bastioned curtain on the land side and two citadels guarding the sea, and Portoferraio on the island of Elba.[159] A third stronghold, small but strategically relevant, was the fort of Terra del Sole, which controlled the border beyond the Apennine mountains. Florence had no modern defence except for the citadels of San Giovanni Battista or *da Basso*, and San Giorgio, or *di Belvedere*, which guarded the capital on both sides of the Arno River. Similar was the situation of Siena, whose defence depended on a single modern citadel.

The Grand Dukes had long known that Tuscany was virtually indefensible if attacked by a strong and determined enemy. The access routes to the Grand Duchy were too many to hope to control them, therefore it was unthinkable to rely on a defence based on an extensive system of fortifications, which

---

the administration of the thought of having to feed and maintain 395 slaves, 318 convicts and 157 *buonevoglie*. ASFi, *Notarile Moderno*, Protocollo 15644.

157 Eric Cochrane, *Florence in the Forgotten Centuries. 1527–1800* (Chicago IL: University of Chicago, 2013), pp.196–200.

158 ASFi, *Mediceo del Principato*, f. 2362. In 1655 the garrison of Livorno did not receive money for three months, and at Castiglione della Pescaia, a remote costal fortress in the Maremma, the garrison had not received salaries for eight months consecutively. The officers complained that 'without the slightest relief, as is the custom in all other fortresses'. The matter had reached the point where the local baker, in charge of supplying the soldiers, had decided to close the bakery 'and no one could be found to replace him … the hardships suffered by the garrison are also the effect of the poverty of this place, and the poor soldiers want to be dismissed for not having to live.'

159 The government did not remain inactive in the field of fortifications and studied a series of improvements which, however, remained at the draft stage. In the 1650s the modernisation plan was prepared by Annibale Cecchi (*c.* 1610–after 1662), who proposed traditional bastioned solutions for Portoferraio and Livorno.

would have had the sole result of diverting resources from other areas. How best to organise this defence became the subject of a debate that lasted almost into the next century. In 1625, during Savoy's assault on Genoa, and in 1636, following the Franco-Savoy occupation of Novara, Grand Duke Ferdinando II commissioned experts to analyse the situation should the war move to the borders of his states. Assuming that the Grand Duchy was easy to invade because there were no modern fortresses on its borders, the authoritative Giulio Borbolani di Montauto, admiral of the galleys of the Order of St Stephen, proposed to fortify the 'most opportune' sites exposed to a siege. According to his plan, Pisa had to become the centre of this defence. Meanwhile it would be necessary to complete the fortifications already begun. In addition, Pisa, though large, could count on the inhabitants of the countryside for its protection, and if 4,000 regular infantrymen were added to them, the city would be safe, as it was known that the militiamen would fight on a par with the regular troops if sheltered by the walls.[160] Montauto had good reason to extol the use of troops in defence rather than in battle, on the assumption that an enemy army would be weakened by an exhausting siege in an unfavourable location. His point was precisely this: the 'air of Pisa' which he described as 'very bad'. Moreover, due to the marshy ground, it would have been impossible for the besieging enemy to dig trenches. It was therefore sufficient to wait for the opposing army to break up spontaneously, due to the suffering and obstacles it would have to face. On the surface, Montauto's argument made sense. However it started from postulates that had not always proved accurate. Firstly, he did not consider the defence of the Apennines. As for the other routes on the northern frontiers, transit for an army, although difficult, was not impossible. In fact Pistoia was in danger of being conquered by Papal troops during the War of Castro, but the greatest weakness of Montauto's argument lay in considering a single line of defence sufficient. The limitations of the argument were evident from his own text. Although he recommended quartering 2,000 infantrymen in Livorno, in order to send them to where they were most needed, at the same time these troops were to be used to train and command the militiamen, although it was not advisable to remove the latter from their occupations, because of the economic damage this would cause to the state. Moreover Montauto, very optimistically, assumed that an assault from the sea could hardly take place due to the strong Spanish presence on the coast, while Florence could withstand a regular siege as occurred in 1529–30.

Montauto's plan was opposed by Bernardo Vecchietti. With his solid military experience gained in Flanders and on the Maltese galleys,[161] he gave an eloquent explanation of his opinions. Directly, Vecchietti had pointed out the vulnerability of the Tuscan defence system, especially in the event of the Spaniards failing to help. It was ridiculous, according to him, to concentrate

---

160 ASFi, *Manoscritti*, f. 740, Discorso di Giulio Montauto, c. 255.
161 ASFi, *Mediceo del Principato*, f. 2356, Reg. n. 6, p.12. Vecchietti would later become Captain General of the Maltese fleet; see in Ubaldino Mori Ubaldini, *La Marina del Sovrano Militare Ordine di San Giovanni di Gerusalemme di Rodi e di Malta* (Rome: Regionale Editrice, 1971), p.368.

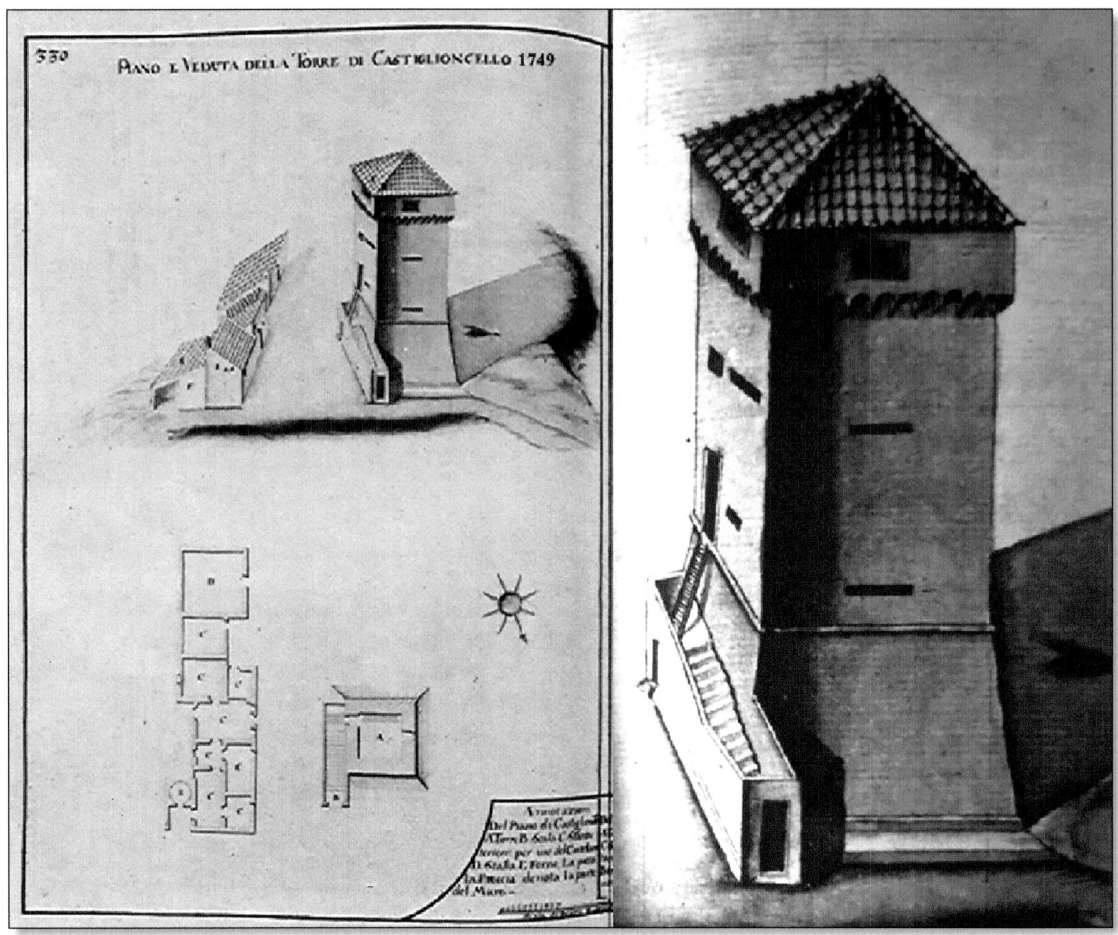

34. The watch tower of Castiglioncello, on the Tyrrhenian coast south of Livorno, in a mid-eighteenth century drawing (author's archive). See image commentaries for more information.

all the forces inside Pisa, '12,000 infantrymen with cavalry in proportion', while it was better to leave 2,000 soldiers in the city and place another 5,000 inside a fortified camp in the Empoli plain. This force could be distributed equally on both sides of the Arno, on which a pontoon bridge had to be built to allow the transit of troops from one bank to the other. The presence of this force close to Florence could protect the capital from any attempt to siege it. In addition, to close the road to an invasion from Genoa – alluding to the possibility of an assault from Piedmont by a Franco-Savoyard army – it was necessary to occupy and fortify Sarzana and Sarzanello, which were in Genoese territory, and all the places of Lunigiana starting from Lusuolo.[162]

However, Vecchietti's considerations, although solid from a military point of view, were deficient in other respects because they only considered one of the routes that an enemy army could have used to invade the Grand Duchy. Moreover, there were also other factors to consider, not least the complications that an eventual occupation of Sarzana and Sarzanello could have caused with the Genoese government. All these problems were well highlighted by

---

162 Lusuolo was donated to the Medici in 1574 by Ercole Malaspina.

Riccardo de Burgo (Richard de Burgh), an Irish officer in Tuscan service [163] who, again on the Grand Duke's orders, visited several places on the north-west frontier and then addressed his considerations to the sovereign.[164] He excluded the validity of fortifying the Lunigiana, both because of the expense this would have entailed and the fact that most of the posts were not on the route that an enemy coming from Liguria would have crossed. Moreover, in the event that Genoa fell, the same would have happened to Sarzana and then it would not have been necessary for the enemies to 'take every hillock in Lunigiana'. However, since it was a precise duty of the Prince to provide for the safety of his people, it was advisable to quarter troops in order to defend the territory from the invaders. The best measure to take in this area was to control the passage of the Serchio River, placing regular troops along it and fortifying the villages near the border, having the possibility of inflicting losses to the enemy if they tried to ford the river, and always with the idea of being able to retreat into Pisa.[165] Towards Massa there were the passes of the Salto della Cervia, the Rocca di Motrone, and Viareggio. Here the problem was that to effectively defend these access routes a very extensive field defence was required: an operation that, according to de Burgo, would not only be very costly, but would also have required a substantial number of soldiers. Moreover, this would certainly have irritated Lucca, who 'seeing themselves so pressed' would have taken 'every party to our detriment to free themselves from this yoke'. Consequently he agreed to reinforce the defences of Pisa, and as for the other areas exposed to an invasion, such as the Val di Nievole and Pistoia, the villages of Montecarlo and Altopascio were to be fortified, since they guarded the frontier and the marsh of Fucecchio; he warned, however, that the improvements should not be exaggerated 'by doing what the state can and not what it would like'. Similarly, all places that were suitable to defence could be fortified with little expense, being already strong due to their position. To complete the defence, it was necessary to reinforce Pistoia Empoli and Prato, and in this case the expense could have been limited by having the soldiers dig ditches and embankments, 'with a little more help than pay'.[166] In his report de Burgo had outlined all the limitations of the Tuscan defence system and in practice had shown how, even if these were modest improvements, considerable resources were needed, namely something the Grand Duchy did not possess. In the following years and until the end of the century, each time the problem of border defence returned to the agenda, the magnitude of the financial burden prevented the implementation of every large-scale fortification plan. This affair that developed in an almost comedy context, namely in the exhausting wait for an invasion, which did not happen.

---

163 From the family of the Counts of Clanricalde, and probably a veteran of the Spanish army in Flanders. See Brendan Jennings, *The Wild Geese in Spanish Flanders* (Dublin: Stationery Office for the Irish Manuscripts, 1964).

164 ASFi, *Mediceo del Principato*, f. 3155, *Discorso del Maestro di Campo Don Riccardo de Burgo sopra la maniera di difendere le frontiere di Toscana* (1625).

165 *Ibid.*

166 *Ibid.*

The Grand Duke's Household

The lifeguards or, more appropriately, the 'palace corps' were represented by the mounted company of the *corazze alemanne* and the foot company of the *lanzi*, also called *trabanti*. Both companies were also denominated *guardia ferma* (standing guard), and were originally composed of foreign soldiers: Germans for the *corazze*, and Swiss for the *lanzi*. The Medici had maintained good relations with the Swiss cantons, and already under Cosimo I it had become customary to pay a provision to a Swiss colonel, who, while remaining at home in peacetime, recruited troops for Tuscany if necessary. His successors had further strengthened this agreement by allowing the commanding officer to appoint one of his colleagues as lieutenant of the palace guard. The importance of this agreement was sanctioned by the fact that from 1592 it was decided that the foot guard was to be half Swiss and half German, the latter being in charge of the Grand Duke's mounted escort. In the seventeenth century new capitulations were agreed upon with the Catholic cantons for the enrolment of volunteers to serve as lifeguards in Tuscany, but despite the fact that the foot guards were Swiss-style, by 1660 the Swiss had almost disappeared from the ranks. Even their commander was not necessarily a Swiss, since in 1661 the captain was the Tuscan Francesco Piccolomini, brother of the famous Ottavio, *Feldmarschall* of the Imperial army. In 1660 the foot company numbered 112 men, mostly German, except two Burgundians, two men from Friuli, one Fleming and one man from Lorraine. Between 1666 and 1668 Gualdo Priorato reports that the 100 Germans, dressed like Swiss, formed the foot guard, while 100 *corazze* with 30 *lance spezzate* (cadets) composed the mounted company.[167] In 1685 the foot guards had decreased to 108 men, the vast majority of whom were still German, with the exception of 10 Swiss, two Italians, one Fleming and one Frenchman. The *corazze alemanne* had 112 men,[168] a figure slightly higher than the one found 20 years later, when there were 108 *corazze*, including one *capitano*, one *luogotenente*, one *cornetta*, three *brigadieri* and eight *sotto brigadieri*.[169] These fluctuations of strength were partly due to the progressive ageing of the members and consequent dismissal from the company.[170] In 1660, among the foot guards there were 47 married men, with 76 children,[171] but in spite of everything great care was always taken to ensure the quality of the soldiers who attended to the Grand Duke's person. Five years earlier a general reform had been carried out among the mounted company,

---

167 Gualdo Priorato, *Relatione della Città di Fiorenza, e del Gran Ducato di Toscana*, p.85.

168 ASFi, *RV*, f. 45, n. 1 *Ruolo della Compagnia della Guardia Ferma di S.A.S. di Corazze Alemanne*.

169 Gregorio Leti, *Ceremoniale historico, e politico. Opera utilissima a tutti gli Ambasciatori, e Ministri, e particolarmente à quei che vogliono pervenire à tali Carichi, e Ministeri* (Amsterdam 1685), vol. V, p.230.

170 Out of a total of 112 horsemen, eight appeared to be too badly off to serve, being afflicted with infirmities such as the *mal francese* (syphilis) or *mal caduco* (falling sickness), and there was a proposal to dismiss a total of 26 men, 'who are judged to be the worst in the company'. ASFi, *Commissariato di Guerra*, f. 726, ins. *Riforma dell'anno 1659 – Ruolo della Compagnia della Guardia ferma*.

171 *Ibid*.

enlisting 14 horsemen to replace 26 who had died or been dismissed, as well as considering the possibility of dismissing others to reach the regular number of 100 guards.[172] Probably, towards the end of Ferdinando II's reign the foot guard was not in the best condition, therefore in 1664 the regulations concerning the enlistment and conduct of its members were renewed.[173] The order specified that the foot soldiers of the *Serenissimo* Grand Duke were required to have 'good appearance, the greatest possible neatness in dress, and skill and courage in service'. They were also ordered not to blaspheme, to show respect for women, to keep their weapons ready and in order, and to observe 'modesty and decorum in their homes'. Above all, they had to be 'of good birth and educated in the Catholic religion', which they had to immediately communicate to the priest when they were enrolled in the rolls, and after taking an oath they had to promise to live in conformity with their faith, on pain of being dismissed without pay.[174]

In addition to command posts or posts of honour, the Grand Duke also had another means of attracting the nobility into his service, namely to include them in the ranks of the *Lanze Spezzate*: the third of the Medici guards. The corps had a political value, as it comprised a certain number of Italian noblemen of good lineage and financial means, able at least in theory to recruit troops in case of need.[175] But it would be wrong to consider this unit merely a collection of sinecures. Although there was a distinction between *Lanze Spezzate d'Honore* and *di Servizio*, many honorary members were also officers of the militia, such as Bernardo Rondinelli, Cammillo Martelli, Bettino Ricasoli and Sozzo Bardi, none of whom received more than the salary provided for a captain of militia.[176] In fact, the perception exists that

35. Imperial Feldmarschall Ottavio Francesco Eugenio Carlo Ferdinando Pio Pieri Piccolomini d'Aragona (1599–1656), portrayed by Anselm van Hulle (Deutsches Historisches Museum). The Thirty Years' War opened up a wide range of possibilities for Tuscan subjects, starting with Ottavio Piccolomini and Tommaso del Maestro, who with other officers commanded the cavalry regiment raised in 1620 by the Grand Duke for the Imperial campaign in Bohemia against the Protestants.

---

172 ASFi, *Mediceo del Principato*, f. 2499, *Informativa sulla guardia a cavallo*.

173 In 1689 there were 14 foot guards old or sick. One of them was 92 years old: he had entered the company 46 years before, but not served for 20 years. The youngest was just 54, 'but had not been active for six months, afflicted as he was by the falling sickness'. Another, 57 years old and with 33 years spent in the company, did all the guard work but his legs were so big and sore that the other soldiers did not want to sleep on his mattress. Finally three others, whose average age was around 70, had weak legs and could not see too well at night. See in ASFi, *Mediceo del Principato*, f. 340, *Ruoli delle Guardie di S.A.S.*

174 *Ibid.*, RV, f. 41, n. 6, *Lettere di diversi Principi*.

175 Gregory Hanlon, *The Twilight of a Military Tradition. Italian Aristocrats and European Conflicts, 1560–1800* (London: UCL Press, 1998), p.63.

176 ASFi, *Miscellanea Medicea*, f. 370, ins. 40, s. 50, *Ruolo de Provvisionati della Banca*, cc. 5–7.

during the reign of Ferdinando II the title of *Lanza Spezzata* (Broken Lance) was often bestowed together with a prestigious post: in 1624 Ruberto Obizzi, in addition to being *Lanza Spezzata*, was also *Cavallerizzo Maggiore* of the Grand Duke.[177] This practice would continue even afterwards: Giovanni Battista Sergiuliani from Sansepolcro, who entered the Grand Duke's service permanently in 1659, was appointed as a *Lancia Spezzata* in 1668 and sent to command the Aretine militia; the Sienese Dionisio Squarci entered the militia in 1660, and two years later received the title of *Lancia Spezzata* together with the command of Portoferraio. It must be added that both of the abovementioned officers received, along with these titles and positions, the rank of *sergente maggiore*, which evidently guaranteed them higher pay; something that did not happen to Fabiano Ricciardi from Arezzo, who in 1668 became a member of the *Lanze Spezzate* and commander of Siena's garrison, but nothing more.[178]

Professional Troops

After the diminution of military strength after the War of Castro, the Grand Duke's standing troops numbered around 3,000 men. In the early 1680s most of the infantry and artillery were located at Livorno, which had 18 companies with about 1,200 infantrymen, and 176 artillery pieces including cannons, mortars and *petrieri*. Portoferraio quartered 12 companies with 560 men and 107 artillery pieces. The two fortresses of Florence had six companies, amounting to 380 infantrymen and artillerymen in the fortress of San Giovanni and another 240 in the one of San Giorgio, with 101 cannons in all. Grosseto had a garrison of two companies with about 130 infantrymen. Pisa quartered a single company of 100 infantrymen, Siena another of 60, and a half-company with only 30 was in Arezzo. The remainder of the infantry defended a further 15 towns and forts located on the border as well as inland, with garrisons of 20 men or even fewer.[179] Finally, further detachments of three or four infantrymen were also assigned to the coastal towers and fortresses, who joined the titular officer, denominated *castellano* or *torriere*, who dealt with the local arsenal and the signals of alarm.[180]

Each company had its own officer staff with captain, lieutenant and ensign, with the customary sergeant, a couple of corporals, drummer, and a variable number of private musketeers and pikemen, usually of a ratio 3 to 1. The larger companies also had one or two volunteer *anspessade*, who served like exempts. However, it must be taken into account that the *piazze* (places, namely soldiers) could in the major garrisons also comprise women and children. In 1661, in the

---

177 *Ibid.*, *Mediceo del Principato*, f. 2356, reg.1, *Registro di tutti gli stipendiati*,
178 *Ibid.*, f. 2356, reg. 2, *Ruolo di tutti gli ufficiali in piedi*, cc. 25–27 and c. 114.
179 These were Pistoia, Barga, Terra del Sole, Pontremoli, Volterra, San Sepolcro, Pitigliano and Sorano, Giglio Island, Cortona, Castiglione della Pescaia, San Martino, Monte Carlo, Salto della Cervia, Radicofani, San Miniato.
180 ASFi, *Mediceo del Principato*, f. 3224, ins, 22, and *Miscellanea Medicea*, *Ruoli di tutti i capitani* f. 651. In the 1680s regular troops manned 25 coastal towers between the mainland and the islands of Elba, Giglio and Gorgona.

fortress of San Giovanni in Florence, out of 334 men of the garrison there were 86 married men, four soldier's widows, and 90 'male and female children over 10 years of age'. In total, including the 10 foundry workers, between 'soldiers and *particulari*' there were 524 people who received salaries and subsidies from the state.[181] The actual number of soldiers, which was often lower than established, combined with the isolation of the garrisons due to the distances separating the main centres – magnified by the lack of roads – and the variety of tasks the soldiers had to fulfil, acted as factors in the army's internal disintegration. After deducting the nominal figures from the companies – cadets, *piazzemorte*, those on half-pay, *passavolanti* – the men genuinely available were reduced to a small handful, often condemned to exhausting service turns, which for the unluckiest lasted whole days, especially on the coastal towers. This scenario gradually made the Tuscan army an increasingly discredited institution. Towards the end of the century the companies were completed by resorting to the forced enrolment of those convicted of small crimes, the so-called *discoli*, who were enrolled in the companies with the illusory hope that military service would return them better to civilian life, but who ultimately contributed to the further worsening of the quality of the troops. There were no differences between the companies, although salary differed from one place to another. As far as nationality is concerned, the available data suggests that the majority of soldiers came from Tuscany, with the foreign presence especially comprising Corsicans and Germans. The latter were probably still numerous in the early 1660s, and formed at least half of the garrisons of Livorno and Portoferraio.[182]

The artillerymen, in Tuscany also called *bombardieri*, were the second standing component of the grand ducal army. Artillery had always been an important element of the Tuscan army, receiving constant attention and funding. In some respects the Tuscan artillery had been in the vanguard, since around 1625 a standard definition of the types of pieces and their calibre had already almost been established. A list of the artillery dating to 1643 shows how, with the exception of the largest pieces, all guns were used in fortresses as well as on campaign, while in 1649 a distinction was already being made

36. Tuscan infantryman (right), in a drawing after the Manfroni Manuscript dating to 1668. The musketeer wears an undyed coat of grey cloth and pale-coloured broad headgear.

---

181 *Ibid.*, Scrittoio delle Regie Possessioni, f. 3927, *Rolo del Castel S. Giovanni et altra gente che in essa habita*.

182 *Ibid.*, Commissariato di Guerra, f. 726, ins. *Riforma dell'anno 1659*.

37. Officer of the *Corazze* or *Guardie Alemanne*, 1685–90, portrayed by Anton Domenico Gabbiani (private collection). Troopers and NCOs of the company were Germans or foreigners of various provenance, but the commander was a Tuscan subject appointed by the Grand Duke.

between the guns for the strongholds and the light ones for the field army.[183] The size of the Tuscan artillery establishment increased steadily during the seventeenth century, from about 700 in the 1660s to 946 at the end of the century.[184] How many of these weapons were actually serviceable, however, is open to question.

No longer needed to support troops in the field, in the 1660s the number of artillerymen required was established by the cannons in the fortresses, and thus this type of service assigned them to an exclusively static role. However, it should be noted that the number of artillerymen was insufficient to handle the fortresses' cannons. For instance, at Portoferraio 107 guns were assigned to 25 artillerymen, while the *Fortezza di Belvedere* in Florence had just 19 artillerymen for 101 guns.[185] This suggests that firing was to be executed by groups of cannons and that all guns of a battery were prepared in advance so that shots could be fired by a single gunner. A modest increase in personnel occurred in the following decades. In the 1690s there were 238 *bombardieri* with 16 NCOs and four lieutenants distributed between Livorno, Florence, Portoferraio and Grosseto, and one captain, who resided in the Fortezza Vecchia of Livorno.[186]

Alongside the force actually composed of military personnel, numerous artisans and labourers were employed in the maintenance of the fortifications and other works related to the garrisons. The presence of a not insignificant number of non-combatants reveals – as was happening in other parts of Italy – that the armed forces of the Grand Duchy had taken on characteristics similar to a welfare institution, in which the less fortunate component of society, lacking education, opportunities and the necessary means to emancipate itself, found employment.

The direction of this force was divided between three central offices: the *Segreteria di Guerra*,[187] the *Banca Militare*, which managed the funds for the

---

183 ASFi, *Scrittoio delle Fortificazioni di Firenze*, f. 1928, ins. 38, dated 6 November 1649.
184 *Ibid.*, *Mediceo del Principato*, f. 2602, cc. 22–23.
185 *Ibid.*, *Scrittoio delle Fortificazioni di Firenze*, f. 1722, ins. 16.
186 *Ibid.*, f. 1766, ins. 11.
187 It was Cosimo I who appointed a group of people loyal to him, to whom he had entrusted certain sectors of the administration, 'the Secretaries', forming a restricted council of the Prince, who turned to them to help him in domestic and foreign policy affairs. The practice of power by the secretaries inevitably led to an increase of their duties, and under Cosimo II the secretaries were at the head of actual dicasteries, although by then it was the *Consulta* instituted by Ferdinando I that did most of the political work, leaving the secretariats to deal with the administrative matters. A further restriction of

army,[188] and the *Scrittojo delle Fortificazioni*, in charge of the administration of fortification expenses. The last two offices operated in conjunction with the *Collaterale Generale della Milizia* and the *Provveditore delle Fortezze e Fabbriche di Sua Altezza Serenissima*. There was a command centre, comparable to a general staff, composed of the governor or *provveditore* of Livorno and the commanders of the Fortezza da Basso in Florence and the fortress of Siena. These three officers had the rank of *Sergente Generale* and formed the *Tribunale delle Bande* (militia). They were immediately followed by the eight *Maestri di Campo*, a rank attributed to the governors of Lunigiana, Pitigliano, Portoferraio and Grosseto, the *castellani* of Pisa, Volterra, the fortress of Belvedere in Florence and the commander of Prato. The other garrisons had their own *provveditore* who acted as military governor. There was also a control and inspection office, called the *Commissariato di Guerra*, based in Florence.

Much more than other Italian states, Tuscany maintained a close relationship with the Empire and other German states during the seventeenth century, through which a considerable number of aristocrats received a modern military training. They also served under the Sienese Ottavio Piccolomini and other famous generals, and the consequence was that in the second half of the century the Tuscan military apparatus was influenced by the 'German school', and no longer by that of Spain. This was also due to the fact that Ferdinando II's brother, Mattias, had spent many years in the Imperial army, thus learning the new techniques of warfare introduced by Gustavus Adolphus: a lesson that he introduced after his return in Tuscany. By the 1650s the Tuscan military establishment was dominated by veterans of the German wars. This was the case of Tommaso del Maestro, who had entered the Imperial army in 1620, appointed as cavalry commander of the militia in the 1660s. He was replaced in 1668 by the aged but still capable Jacopo Adami, from Pistoia, who closed his military career in Tuscany after his service in Bavaria until 1638, while Niccolò Bufalini, who had served with the Spaniards, and later with Condé and Turenne, was one of the *sergenti-generali di battaglia* of the militia. Veterans of the Thirty Years' War were still present to a considerable extent 20 years later. In the 1680s grand ducal officers included such personalities as Amerigo Attavanti, Fabio Corti and Tommaso Serristori, who had entered the military service in the Imperial army, and Nicolò Dal Borro, the son of the skilled Alessandro, who had served in Spain and later in Venice as *generale dello sbarco* until his death in 1656. Several of them had also participated in the War of Castro, which was considered a great merit. Besides the many junior officers who remained abroad, those who returned to Tuscany afterwards could aspire to obtain some form of employment within the Medicean military

---

their power was dealt by Ferdinando II's 'familiar' government, based on the subdivision of political-administrative powers to his brothers: Mattias for the 'military', Giovan Carlo for finance, and Leopold for foreign policy. See Niccolò Capponi, *L'organizzazione militare del Granducato di Toscana sotto Ferdinando II de' Medici* (Padova, Università degli Studi, 1998), p.35.

188 The *collaterali* of the *Banca Militare* also exercised their control over the cavalry of the militia, which for a variety of reasons received regular pay, as well as the choice of captains of the infantry in the *Bande* militia; see ASFi, *Magistraure Medicee* f. 475, i. 3.

38. Jacopo Adami, from Pistoia (1606–1674), cavalry general of the Tuscan militia in 1668. Like many other Tuscan officers he did his apprenticeship in Germany, where he served as captain of cavalry, aged 18, in the Bavarian army. Every young Tuscan, as well as other Italian noble cadets who wished to pursue a career in arms, had no other option than expatriation, hoping to survive long enough and gain sufficient knowledge to earn a post in the military establishment once he returned home.

system, usually as an *avvantaggiato* (beneficiary) or as an officer in the standing troops or in the militia. This was the case of Girolamo del Testa Piccolomini, from Siena, who served in Germany, Milan and Hungary, and after his return to Tuscany in 1668, he become two years later *castellano* of Grosseto.[189]

The *Bande della Milizia*

Some commentators of the early eighteenth century described how Grand Duke Cosimo III used the *Bande*, totalling almost 60,000 men, to demonstrate to foreign courts that he possessed the most powerful military strength in Italy.[190] Even if this statement is only partly true, it nevertheless shows us how high was the importance attributed to the militia in Tuscany. And in fact when compared to those of other Italian states, the constitution and the very structure of the Tuscan militia present peculiarities that influence the characteristic history of this institution, which already at its foundation appeared closely connected to the Grand Duchy's domestic and foreign policy.

A first distinctive element already lies in the overall strength of the *Bande*. In fact, comparing the data (albeit theoretical) of the Tuscan militia with the similar units of other states, it is not so much the high overall numerical value that is surprising, but rather that it is the same in comparison to the size of the regular stable forces. It must therefore be emphasised that in the seventeenth century, Tuscany had been one of the Italian states with the largest number of inhabitants involved in the militia system.[191] The percentage ratio between militia members and inhabitants was, alongside the Papal States, undoubtedly higher in Tuscany than in the rest of the Peninsula. In Italy the militiamen accounted on average for two to three percent of the whole population, while in Tuscany they accounted for over five percent. In any case, all sources point out that in the Grand Duchy there was an enormous disproportion between regular troops and militia.[192]

Originally the major cities such as Florence, Livorno, Siena and Pistoia had been exempted from the presentation of lists, reserving the task of preparing the contingents to the population of the countryside and smaller

---

189 ASFi, *Mediceo del Principato*, f. 2356, r. 2, *Ruolo di tutti gli ufficiali in piedi*, cc. 2, 4, 6, 15.

190 Franco Angiolini, 'Le Bande Medicee fra Ordine e Disordine', in *Corpi Armati e Ordine Pubblico in Italia (XVI–XIX sec.)* (Catanzaro: Rubettino, 2003), p.10.

191 Luciano Pezzolo, 'Le Arme Proprie in Italia nel Cinque e nel Seicento: Problemi di Ricerca', in: T. Fanfani (ed.), *Saggi di storia economica. Studi in onore di Amelio Tagliaferri* (Pisa: Pacini, 1998), p.56.

192 Angiolini, 'Le Bande Medicee', p.18.

towns. In the second half of the century the exclusion from the militia was reconfirmed for both the citizens of Florence and Pistoia; this also concerned the Sienese living inside the city. Livorno was also included, but excluding its citizens from the enlistment in the standing troops. These decisions, once deciphered, show the Grand Duke's constant attention to the question of political balance and not distracting his subjects from their occupations. The demographic aspect also had its weight. Citizens living in Massa Marittima, a town plagued by considerable depopulation, enjoyed perpetual exemption from the rolls of the militia. On the other hand the apparent favour reserved to Florence concealed a very different motive, since when the corps was constituted it was decided to leave out the Florentines because of their well-known political unreliability, while the Pistoiese were excluded because of the frequent disturbances that occurred in the city.[193] It was later decided that the exclusion of the citizens of Florence and Pistoia would cease when they lived in other towns or villages of the Grand Duchy. The absence of Florentines from the militia lists was a feature that survived into the eighteenth century. The ban on enlisting militiamen in Pistoia finished by 1650, when it was decided to create a *banda* in the city alongside another for the Pistoia's *Montagna* (mountain).

In the mid seventeenth century the method of recruitment of the militia was the same as established in chapter six of the regulations issued under Ferdinando II in 1646. The system served, at least in the intentions of the government, to give a proportion to the number of soldiers in a certain area of the territory in relation to its demographic resources, and at the same time to calibrate the enrolment of subjects with the needs of society at the time. For this purpose the Grand Duchy was divided into three parts, called *Terzi*; each corresponded to a certain number of *bande* and each had to be supplied by the population of the territory from which it came. It was then the communities, through the competent local authorities, who registered the lists of young men suitable for enlistment, denominated *descritti*. They were selected among the Tuscan subjects between 18 and 25 years of age, and after 30 years of service, or at the age of 50, the militiamen were finally dismissed. As elsewhere, the service was compensated with tax exemptions, permission to bear arms, hunting licenses, the right not to be prosecuted for community debts, and of course a salary commensurate with the actual service.

The lists, denominated *Ruoli dei Descritti delle Bande*, were sent to Florence and preserved by the *Magistratura delle Bande*. In addition to the name of the militiamen, these rolls also contained other useful information, especially when the mobilisation of a contingent was intended to avoid depriving the community of forces that would have compromised its economic and social equilibrium. Along with the name, age and paternity of the person described, the rolls also registered the occupation, the name of the wife if married, the number of children and siblings, the existence of other family members in the militia, and any persons away from the community. These

---

[193] Jolanda Ferretti, 'L'organizzazione militare in Toscana durante il governo di Alessandro e Cosimo I de'Medici', in *Rivista storica degli archivi toscani*, I (1929), pp.261–262.

39. A Swiss Guard or *Lanzo*, depicted by Ottavio Vannini from a detail of the fresco in the fourth room of the Casino Mediceo in Florence, c. 1650.

rolls were updated by the *Cancelliere delle Bande* of each district and ascertained during the reviews, namely in the inspections to which the militiamen were subjected each month, company by company. Each *banda* also had its own *depositario d'armi* in charge of maintaining the arsenal and the weapons. It was during the musters that the *descritti* thought to be unfit were removed from service due to age limits or physical problems, together with those who carried out activities that were no longer compatible with the functioning of the militia, or if absences caused their resignation. It was, as can be guessed, a system whose updating and effectiveness presupposed an equally effective and punctual control of the populations involved, as well as a continuous updating of information. The undoubted complexity of this work is more than sufficient reason to explain the gap that inevitably existed between the number of registered militiamen and their actual strength.

Some commentators asserted that the Grand Duke had a well-trained and numerous militia. In 1660 Gualdo Priorato, exaggerating, quantified the *bande* at 80,000 foot and 6,600 horse.[194] In 1659, according to the data registered in the chancelleries, there were 50,000 people registered as members of the *Bande*. However, once subtractions had been applied to the lists, such as the names of dead militiamen, those who had moved elsewhere, often even outside the Grand Duchy, and of those who were no longer capable to bear weapons because of illness, mutilation, crippling or, more simply, because they were too old, there remained only 35,210 men.[195] By 1680, the *Terzi* of Romagna, Lunigiana and Maremma numbered 36 *bande* of infantry, with a further 22 companies of cavalry divided into six companies of *corazze* and 16 companies of *Carabini* or *Cavalli*, which served as dragoons. Not included in the *Terzi* were Portoferraio, on the island of Elba, and Giglio, who both formed their own foot militia, but their companies served only in the respective territory. Usually, each unit was named after the district from which it came, but some units were identified by special titles, especially in the cavalry, such as the *Compagnia di Cavalli della Scoperta* at Livorno, and the *Carabini di Grosseto*.[196]

---

194 Gualdo Priorato, *Relatione della Città di Fiorenza, e del Gran Ducato di Toscana*, pp.84–85.
195 *Ibid.*, f. 2362, c. 201, *Ruolo delle Bande con i loro Capitani* (1659).
196 ASFi, *Mediceo del Principato*, f. 2356, reg. n. 2, *Ruolo di tutti gli ufficiali in piedi*, c. 48.

One of the recurring problems in the management of this considerable mass of men was that for some units there was no clear dividing line between militia and professional soldiers. Even if certain corps were composed of militiaman, it happened that the *descritti* were considered as standing troops, since by serving for the whole year they received a salary on a par with professionals. The typical case was that of the cavalry, nominally part of the militia, but the *corazze*, under the control of the Military Bank since the previous century, depended on the *Banca Militare*, while the *carabini*, considered as an 'unpaid cavalry', depended on the *Commissari delle Bande*. The difference between the two specialities was administrative as well as tactical-organisational, since the heavy cavalry always required more expensive equipment and horses than the other mounted troops, and therefore aid from the Grand Duke was needed in favour of the *corazze*.[197]

Each *banda* of infantry comprised four companies, which had their captain, ensign, sergeant, drummer, two adjutants and one corporal for every 30 militiamen. The cavalry companies had a similar organisation, but with one corporal for every 10 horsemen. While the cavalry coming from the district of the interior performed limited tasks, the companies of the coast formed the pickets in charge of the surveillance of the shores, communicating with the sea towers from Forte dei Marmi in the north to Cala di Forno in the extreme south. For the surveillance of the smaller coastal towers, namely the posts without regular *castellano* and soldiers, the militiamen of the *bande* formed units of *fazzionieri* with five or 10 men assigned in turn to the sentry duties. This was the least popular task, at least judging by the numerous documents containing requests for replacement and exemption due to the unhealthy air of the coastline, especially south of Livorno up to the border with the Papal States. The foot militia also provided the infantry embarked on the galleys that guarded the naval routes in the Tyrrhenian Sea. This service was carried out on a rotating basis, and involved all the *Bande*, even those from inland.[198]

Although the Grand Duke's propaganda overestimated the strength and efficiency of the militia, these were not a military corps of secondary importance. The militiamen had fought on a par with the regular army during the War of Castro, and like the professional troops they received clothing, precisely a coat, as early as the 1640s, but of undyed *bigio* (grey) cloth, and not of red as initially proposed: a decision that saved the state a lot of money.[199] Mostly the officers were veterans of the wars in Germany, or former NCOs, or noble cadets who had joined the *bande* as their main job. Throughout the age of Ferdinando II the grand ducal armed forces would be open up to the highest

---

197 Ferretti, *L'organizzazione militare in Toscana*, p.148.
198 In this regard a letter dated 1741, written by a former non-commissioned officer of the militia, who had served in a company of the *banda* of *Lunigiana* aboard the galleys in the late 1690s, asked for his sons to be given an 'honourable post' in the new militia that was being formed under the new government. ASFi, *Segreteria di Guerra*, f. 1126, *Suppliche*.
199 *Ibid.*, *Mediceo del Principato*, f. 5399, letter of Miniato Miniati to Mattias de' Medici (28 October 1642), c. 624.

ranks to talented people from all over Tuscany and the rest of Europe, never becoming the exclusive privilege of the capital's aristocracy. In 1644, out of 31 commanders of the *bande* only four were clearly identifiable as Florentines, while the others came mostly from the province, along with a few foreigners.[200] Forty years later, under Cosimo III, the percentage of officers from Florence was less than 25 percent, namely 21 out of 96, but more than half in the higher ranks of the military hierarchy. On the other hand there were 45 provincial officers, of whom 12 held higher command positions, although one of the two generals was the Aretine Marco Alessandro Dal Borro, son of the famous general commander of the Tuscan army during the War of Castro.[201]

The Grand Dukes' strategic choice of having a low-cost army allowed them to set aside funds to recruit mercenaries in case of emergency, but the economic situation had drained many of these resources, directing the government to reinforce the militia at the expense of the regular force. The convenience of this was obvious, given the enormous sums that a military force composed of professionals could cost. On the other hand the wars between France and Spain, as well as the resurgence of the Ottoman threat, forced the government to increase its military efforts in spite of the consequent increase in military expenditure. If the tax exemptions granted to militiamen were then added to the loss of income due to the loss of work days, the negative balance became larger, but still bearable for the Grand Duke's states.

'*Santo Stefano per Mare e per Terra*'[202]

After the involvement of the Grand Duchy in the war against the Porte in 1645, Ferdinando II sent the galley fleet to Crete, to join the Venetians in the unsuccessful attempt to retake Chaniá in September that year. The Tuscan galleys, formally belonging to the Order of St Stephen (Santo Stefano), participated in the sea campaigns in the Aegean Sea in 1659 and 1660. Then in 1666 the Grand Duke sent 400 infantrymen to Dalmatia under Marquis Filippo Pistolozzi. The Tuscan battalion departed two years later to Crete, where it was involved in the defence of Candia and where the commander was killed in action alongside two-thirds of the fighting force.

In 1684 the Order of St Stephen naturally adhered to the Knights' duties. Since the previous century the Knights had engaged in a war against the Ottomans and their North African vassals. As Grand Master of the 'Holy Religion of Saint Stephen', the Grand Duke had also opened his own channel of relations in the Levant with aims of establishing a protectorate in the predominantly Christian regions of the Middle East, along with a few other imaginative projects.[203]

---

200 *Ibid.*, f. 2331, c. 308.

201 *Ibid.*, *Miscellanea Medicea* f. 597, ins. 1, c. 1; *Mediceo del Principato*, f. 2356, reg. n. 2, *Ruolo di tutti gli ufficiali in piedi*, tab. 14–15.

202 'Saint Stephen by Sea and Land', after Cesare Ciano, *La Guerra Mediterranea e l'Ordine dei Cavalieri di Santo Stefano dal 1563 al 1716* (Pisa: ETS, 1985).

203 In the 1660s the Grand Duke, planned a raid to Jerusalem to dismantle the Holy Sepulchre and transport it to Florence. See Luca Calzetta, *Ferdinando I de' Medici e il Santo Sepolcro di*

MEDIUM AND MINOR POWERS

40. Tuscan infantry and knights of the Order of St Stephen (Santo Stefano) encamped before Modone in the Peloponnese, in 1686; after the Manfroni Manuscript. The knights wear full red, while the infantry have grey coats with red facings. Note the pikes arranged in the centre. Unlike the Venetian and Maltese infantry, The Tuscans retained pikes for the duration of their participation in the Greek campaigns.

The Order of St Stephen's successful privateering war against the Ottoman Empire earned it a stellar reputation regarding its fighting ability. Consequently the Republic of Venice regarded the skills of Tuscan officers, engineers, and many other technicians who accompanied the contingent in campaign with the highest esteem.

In the first months of 1684 a landing battalion was raised with remarkable speed and immediately headed to Livorno the following May. The battalion numbered six companies of approximately 696 men under the command of *Sergente Maggiore* Pietro Serrati from Pontremoli, a veteran of the Dutch War as a former officer of the French *Royal Italien* infantry regiment.[204] Each company consisted of 30 pikemen, 62 musketeers and eight grenadiers, with six corporals, one sergeant, one quartermaster, two drums, one *Ajutante* (warrant officer), one ensign, one lieutenant and one captain. With them, 50 knights of the order took place on the four galleys and sailed to Greece. The battalion and knights landed at Corfu on 13 June and joined the other allied forces. The Tuscan soldiers received their baptism of fire at the sieges of Santa Maura (Lefkas) and Prevesa. At the end of the campaign, as an officer laconically noted in his dispatch to Florence, the contingent returned to

---

Gerusalemme (Florence: Ars et Fides, 2018), pp.5–6.

204 ASFi, *Mediceo del Principato*: f. 2388, ins. 4, *Copia degli articoli da osservarsi in proposito alla leva di sei compagnie nello Stato di S.A.S., carteggi e miscellanea*; Alessandro di Chiarissimo de'Medici.

41. Ship's boy, sailor and knight of St Stephen, somewhere in the Mediterranean in 1677; after the Manfroni Manuscript. In Baroque Europe, men continued to fight the advance of Islam on a daily basis. Many considered themselves crusaders. Young noblemen from all over the continent, seeking adventure, joined the orders of Malta or St Stephen for campaigns against the Porte.

Livorno with 'large numbers of sick people'. Overall they suffered 252 losses including the commander Serrati, who died of illness in Prevesa.[205]

In a letter sent from Santa Maura, the same officer revealed the harsh conditions faced by Tuscan and other contingents: 'sad conditions of the soldiers who are sick and hospitalised in the galleys with little or no comfort … and my unsteady health makes the service more difficult. The crews are reduced to bad conditions and also the Roman galleys are suffering … every day we bury ten or 12 men.'[206] Even the Knights of St Stephen claimed 12 dead and just as many sick.

With the exception of 1687, when fleet and landing troops served in Dalmatia and Albania,[207] the Tuscans cooperated with the auxiliary contingent in all the Greek campaigns until 1688. Yet, their presence did not always coincide with the end of the campaign. The Tuscan admiral always returned

---

205 In a letter sent from Preveza dated September 30, 1684, the infantry captain Romolo Navarette informed the Grand Duke's war secretary that the 'regiment' was reduced to 222 healthy men and 'everyday someone falls sick, and after the departure of the galleys, eight soldiers have died and a few with severe disease will return'. ASFi, *Mediceo del Principato, Spedizione di Soldatesche in Levante dal 1684 fino al 1688*; f. 2219.

206 *Ibid.*, letters dated 11 September 1684.

207 According to Beregani, *Istoria delle Guerre d'Europa*, vol. II, p.325, the 300-man battalion fought with 'great zeal' and as per the experiment at Corone in 1686, the Tuscan mortars under the *bombista* Belmer targeted the city with accurate shots.

the fleet to Livorno before September to avoid Mediterranean's rough autumn seas. As the siege of Corone continued in mid August 1685, Admiral Camillo Guidi warned Morosini that the Tuscan battalion would have to re-embark within a few days. The following year two additional companies increased the battalion to 880 men, under the command of the Veronese *Maestro di Campo* Francesco Sansebastiani. Casualties incurred in previous campaigns pushed the Grand Duke to seek soldiers outside of Tuscany. He asked the Republic of Genoa for permission to recruit Corsicans, reputedly more resistant to deprivation than his subjects.[208]

Despite the formal cordiality between Florence and Venice, relations between Morosini and Guidi already deteriorated after the sudden departure in 1685. Morosini's comments during a fit of rage directed at the Tuscans eventually reached the ears of Guidi, which made matters even more difficult. Despite the far from peaceful climate, Tuscan soldiers provided satisfactory service, particularly at the Siege of Modone. Nevertheless, storms between the allied commanders returned, especially after the Tuscan admiral complained about his soldiers' rations.[209]

In 1687 the Tuscans joined the auxiliaries in Dalmatia, where they participated in the siege of Castelnuovo under the *sergente generale* Nicolò Dal Borro. On this occasion the Grand Duke's soldiers distinguished themselves for their excellent behaviour, admirably led by the 'audacissimo Dal Borro'.[210] The fourth campaign coincided with the unfortunate outcome of Negroponte. On more than one occasion, reports emphasised the Tuscan battalion's desperate attempt to overwhelm enemy resistance. In late July 1688 an Ottoman sortie swept the allied advances and nearly surrounded two Tuscan companies, but the Maltese infantry and the *Venturieri* saved them from destruction. A few days later the battalion distinguished itself in an assault on the palisades of the Ottoman defences. The Tuscans and the allies captured and held the position until the following day, when a violent enemy sortie repulsed them to their initial position. Additionally, losses due to epidemics of plague in the allied camp accompanied battle casualties. Furthermore, the

42. Possibly a portrait of Camillo Guidi (1635–1717), who led the Tuscan contingent in Greece. Unknown artist, 1685–88.

---

208 ASFi, *Miscellanea Medicea*, f. 598, cc. 12–14, *Reclutamento di truppe in Levante*.

209 Again, the sources do not agree on the reasons of the conflicts within the allied command. Tuscan historians do not refer to any particulars, while the Venetians argue that the Venetian *Provveditore all'Armata* considered Guidi's demands disrespectful, and '[Morosini] ridiculed the Florentines who did not get accustomed to the biscuit'. See also Locatelli, *Racconto historico*, vol. II, p.156.

210 Beregani, *Historia delle Guerre d'Europa*, vol. II, p.367.

auxiliary contingent's departure forced the Tuscans – reduced to a mere 300 men – to leave the siege. A note attached to the campaign report signed by Captain Cancellieri contains a list of losses suffered on 20 September 1688, numbering 93 dead and 91 wounded 'but not the sick soldiers, who it was not possible to list at the moment'.[211] Illness may have reduced the battalion to less than half of its original strength. The campaign of 1688 ended the Tuscan participation in the war against the Porte, but Nicolò Dal Borro asked permission to continue serving with the Venetians and remained in Greece until 1690.

Duchy of Parma and Piacenza

Due to its strategic position, the Duchy of Parma and Piacenza, like its main and natural antagonist Modena, was fatally exposed to invasion or at least was subject to involvement in military operations. This is what happened when the conflict between France and Spain shifted to the Po Valley in 1653. Parma, which sided with Madrid, bore the brunt of the military presence of the two main belligerents and until the Peace of the Pyrenees contributed to the defence of Spanish Lombardy with mercenary troops and money. Other military involvements had occurred in the meantime during the War of Castro, in which Parma and Piacenza played the main role against Pope Barberini. During the Cretan War the Duchy was among the first to send soldiers to Venice. In late 1645 he levied 2,000 men 'gathered in fine order', along with 300 dragoons, and offered to lead them personally against the Ottomans.[212] In 1652, Prince Orazio Farnese entered under the Republic's service with his 3,000 infantry recruits. However, these years were marked by a significant decrease in military forces that would never be reversed, since, after the military misadventure against the Papacy in the War of Castro, Duke Ranuccio II Farnese (r. 1646–1694) followed the path of peace in 1659.[213]

Compared to other Italian states of the time, the Duchy enjoyed homogenous territorial continuity, but included five independent states within its borders. In 1682, Duke Ranuccio II acquired the state of Landi, with approximately 10,000 inhabitants, bringing the overall ducal population to about 280,000 persons. Except for Parma and Piacenza, the Duchy did not had modern fortresses, and the border was guarded by castle or forts with outdated fortifications.

---

211 Gino Guarnieri, *I Cavalieri di Santo Stefano nella storia della Marina Italiana, 1562–1859* (Pisa: Listri Nischi, 1960), p.443.

212 Mugnai, *The Cretan War*, pp.112–113.

213 Gregory Hanlon, 'Parma during the era of Duke Odoardo, "the Great" (1630–1650)', in G. Bertini (ed.), *Storia di Parma* vol. IV (Parma: Monte Universitaria, 2014), p.31. Total ducal revenues declined from 800,000 *scudi* in 1619, to 600,000 in the 1640s, to only 400,000 in 1675, in the depths of the depression of the seventeenth century.

MEDIUM AND MINOR POWERS

The Farnese Army

The ducal family received its state for military merit in 1545.[214] The Farnese supplied many famous captains to Spain, and throughout the century the Duchy firmly sided with the Spanish monarchy. The core of the army had arisen together with the Duchy, but the first stable regulation was the one issued in 1581 which established the militia on a territorial basis. Like other Italian states at the end of the Renaissance, the Duchy also experimented with the constitution of a local militia gathered with a significant number of subjects, which in the case of Parma was a third of the whole male population. This was a theoretically unexceptionable measure, but it had the defect, common more or less throughout Italy, of being detrimental to the economy, because it subtracted many thousands of people from the work in the countryside. To deal with this problem, especially with the worsening economic crisis of the first half of the seventeenth century, the dukes granted permission to replace service in the militia with a *tassa militare* (military tax). In time this practice turned the militia into a revenue source for the ducal finances, losing its original character as a military force.[215]

The payment of the military tax served to hire mercenaries in case of need, but at the same time allowed subjects enrolled in the militia to keep their weapons and to serve, especially for public order, at celebrations, fairs and markets. Therefore even in the Duchy of Parma and Piacenza, the presence of a small *truppa regolata* or *di fortuna*, subject to considerable fluctuations of strength depending on the greater or lesser emergency, became the main feature of the Duchy's armed forces.

The Duke was naturally the head of all the armed forces of the state, and for this task he had a war secretariat with two separate sections: one in Parma and the other in Piacenza. In both cities was a *governatore delle armi*, on whom both the regular troops and the militia depended. In each city there were other officers whose duties were very limited, considering the small number of troops, but these appointments were mostly of a commendatory nature. In fact it was common for some positions to be held by the same

43. Ranuccio II Farnese, Duke of Parma and Piacenza (1630–94), portrayed by Jacob Denys (Parma National Gallery). The Duke's long reign covered the decades between 1660 and 1690, throughout which he remained strictly neutral.

---

214 *Ibid.*, p.2. The dynasty held Parma as a fief of the Papacy, who could deprive the prince of his state in case of rebellion. That the Pope was the ultimate lord of Parma was never in doubt; Piacenza was arguably a Spanish fief subject to Milan. One *memoriale* from 1627 recognised Farnese vassal status for Piacenza to the king of Spain.

215 Mario Zannoni and Massimo Fiorentino, *L'esercito Farnesiano dal 1694 al 1731* (Parma: Palatina Editrice, 1981), p.12.

person, as the *governatore delle armi* was often also the *comandante generale della fanteria* (infantry general commander), or *colonnello generale della cavalleria* (general colonel of cavalry), or *generale del cannone* (artillery general).[216] Moreover, confirming the honorary significance of these offices, the appointments lasted for life. The *cassa militare* provided for the expenses of the regular troops and militia and consisted of the *ufficio di veedoria*, from which depended the commissioners in charge of inspection tasks.[217]

Standing Forces and Household Troops

The only professional troops were the infantry companies forming the garrison of Parma and Piacenza, also denominated at Parma in Latin as *milites de Castro parmensi*. These companies were quartered in the citadels of the two main cities, in charge of guarding the fort and especially the arsenals preserved inside them. In Parma in the 1690s there were 140 infantrymen, while a lesser number manned the citadel of Piacenza. Both companies also included a surgeon and a physician. It is noticeable that the commander, who was awarded the title of *castellano*, had a personal Swiss guard of six footmen. The uniform of both companies is known: blue with yellow facing in Parma, and white with red facing in Piacenza, hence the name, *Bianchi*, given by the citizens to the soldiers.

Alongside these garrisons, between 1660 and 1690, some companies of *soldati di fortuna* were also raised, and their number varied between six and 10 companies with about 600–1,000 men in all. Each company numbered between 100 and 120 men; one-third of them were pikemen.[218] These companies were mainly formed by native recruits, since Duke Ranuccio II did not trust foreign soldiers and officers.[219] The main duty of these companies consisted of guarding the gates of the two cities, both day and night, divided into three groups. This rotation allowed each soldier to have two days off out of three. At dawn, the soldiers assigned to guard the four gates of Parma gathered at the Pilotta,[220] and then went to their assigned posts. In the city, a detachment formed the corps in the Piazza Grande, guarding the government palace. Other detachments formed the surveillance pickets at the two main bridges. In Parma, each gate was also defended by two light guns. In Piacenza the service followed a similar scheme, including the infantry guarding the Gotico.[221] Detachments also manned the posts on the border. In the 1690s there were two officers and 19 foot soldiers in the castle of Montechiarugolo,

---

216 *Ibid*. Practically, the *generale del cannone* only commanded the two companies of militia artillerymen, also called *bombardieri*.

217 ASPr, *Governo farnesiano, Computisteria*, n. 620.

218 Zannoni-Fiorentino, *L'esercito Farnesiano*, p.19.

219 *Ibid*., p.22.

220 The *Palazzo della Pilotta* is a group of palaces located between Piazzale della Pace and the Lungoparma in the historical centre of the city. Its name derives from the game of *pelota* played by Spanish soldiers stationed in Parma.

221 The government palace of Piacenza is denominated *Gotico* due to the presence of pointed arches in Gothic style.

another eight soldiers manned the *Rocca* of Rossena, and another 14 with one lieutenant were quartered in the castle of Compiano. The larger garrison was that of Bardi, which numbered 70 infantrymen and three officers.[222]

Another permanent unit formed by professional soldiers was quartered in the *Rocchetta* of Parma. This was the prison of the city and the guard service had been entrusted to Swiss soldiers who did not understand the Italian language, in order to avoid any familiarity between convicts and guards. Detention inside the Rocchetta was considered so harsh that the epigraph quoted by Dante in *L'Inferno* greeted the convicts at the entrance: 'Leave all hopes behind, ye who enter'. In 1691 the garrison numbered 42 men, with one *governatore*, one lieutenant, one sergeant, three corporals and 36 soldiers.[223]

The military tax collected in exchange for service in the militia also served to pay for the units assigned as lifeguards of the duke and princes. The duke disposed his own lifeguard, which comprised one company of foot, the *Arcieri della Prima Guardia* and one mounted company, the *Guardia del Corpo a cavallo di Sua altezza Serenissima*.[224] The foot company had been raised in 1581 after the German *Hartschieren*, and in the sources it was also denominated in Latin as *pretoria coorte*.[225] The strength of the company, 31 men, did not change throughout the years, including one captain, one lieutenant and three corporals. The *Arcieri* were the first unit of the Duchy and retained the attributes of the elite corps, having the precedence over all the other troops. The company was usually formed from retired NCOs, or people who did not attend 'mechanic' professions. They served as palace guardsmen in the ducal residence and escorted the duke or his family in Parma and had their quarter in the Pilotta. The service followed a scheme consisting of three turns of eight hours, each assigned to three *squadre* of eight men and one corporal.

The mounted company was also known by the population as *Guardia dei Collettoni*, after their *Kollet* leather coat usually worn by the German cuirassiers. In 1667, they were registered as *corazzieri alemanni della Guardia*, and their German origin is confirmed in the Latin denomination *Turma equitum germanorum*. The company numbered 68 men, comprising one captain, one lieutenant, one cornet, one chaplain, one sergeant, two trumpets, one kettledrummer, three corporals, three *sotto caporali*, and 54 horsemen.[226] The mounted company was the second duke's lifeguard in order of importance, and like the *Arcieri* the unit had its quarter in the Pilotta. They escorted the duke when he left Parma, and formed the foot guard when

---

222 Zannoni-Fiorentino, *L'esercito Farnesiano*, p.90.
223 *Ibid.*, p.89.
224 In the 1690s the strength was 25 foot guards and 50 *cavalleggeri*; see Heinrich Ludwig Gude, *Staat von Parma und Piacenza, Mirandula und Concordia, Massa und Carrara, Monaco, Doria, St. Piedro, Sesto St. Angelo und dei Fieschi* (1708), p.13.
225 ASPr, *Memorabilia civitas Parmae, 1688–1708*, ms. 55.
226 *Ibid.*

44. Parma in a print dated 1712. (Author's archive)

he was in Piacenza or another place of the Duchy. The mounted company formed *squadre* of 16 men that daily alternated in the active service.[227]

While the *Arcieri* dressed in Spanish style, the mounted guards retained the German cuirassiers' uniform, with pistol holsters and saddle cover of carmine cloth with yellow-gold edge, and an embroidered azure lily with gold edging on the corner of the saddle cover. Trumpeters wore a carmine coat with multiple yellow piping, and broad-brimmed headgear with blue plumes. Out of service, private guards wore full carmine with golden-yellow piping and facing, while the officers dressed in azure with golden lining, and broad-brimmed headdress with red or blue plumes. The cover of the kettledrums was azure (or carmine) cloth with gold edging and embroidering. The company had a square standard of blue silk with golden fringes, carrying the Farnese coat of arms, fixed on a long tournament-style lance.[228]

A further palace guard was raised for Princess (later Duchess) Dorothea Sophia of Neuburg, wife of the Duke's heir, Prince Francesco, after her marriage in 1690. The company, which took the denomination *Alabardieri*

---

227 Zannoni-Fiorentino, *L'esercito Farnesiano*, p.74. For reasons of economy, in 1698 the company was dismounted and when it had to escort the duke it took the horses of the militia on loan.

228 *Ibid.*

45. Piacenza in the early eighteenth century (author's archive). Parma and Piacenza were the only places in the Duchy provided with modern fortifications.

della Duchessa, numbered 39 men including one captain, one lieutenant, three corporals, three *vice-caporali*, and one drummer. The commander was a native of the Duchy, while the guards came from Switzerland, Germany and other northern European countries. The task assigned to the *Alabardieri* was the same as the other foot lifeguards, but they were quartered in private houses of Parma far from the ducal palace. Since the company should have consisted of Swiss, they were dressed like the coeval lifeguard recruited in Switzerland, and for this a tailor was appointed for manufacturing clothing *alla svizzera* or *alla tedesca*, of red cloth.[229] The company carried halberds and swords; the lieutenant's halberd had a blade with a golden profile.[230]

The Militia

The infantry of the militia was divided into *terzi* composed of a variable number of companies. At the end of the seventeenth century there were six *terzi* in Parma and four in Piacenza, to which were added the companies formed in the countryside. The latter formed the *milizia forese* or *milizia*

---

[229] Biblioteca Nazionale di Piacenza, G. Gondini, *Compendio Storico di Piacenza*, ms. Pallastrelli n. 162.

[230] Zannoni-Fiorentino, *L'esercito Farnesiano*, p.76.

suburbana, because it was composed of militiamen not resident in the two main towns. Denominated in Latin as *rustici milites*, this militia comprised all the able males aged between 18 and 50. The service lasted 25 years, and ended at 60. Each *terzo* took the name of the district where the militiamen were recruited. In the late seventeenth century these were Parma (the countryside surrounding the city), Colorno, Tizzano, Busseto, Piacenza (the countryside), the Val di Nure, the Val Trebbia, Belforte, the Val Tidone, to which in 1682 was added the pre-existing militia of the Stato di Landi. Each *terzo* was under a *colonello* who had his own staff with a *capitano-aiutante*, and they held the command of seven to 14 companies depending on strength. Each company had the usual three officers, *capitano*, *luogotenente*, *alfiere*, and a variable number of corporals and soldiers normally established at a maximum of 300 men.[231] On paper the overall strength was more than 30,000 militiamen of foot, but how many of them were actually available is questionable. Apart from the exemption of taxes and other privileges, service in the militia was less attractive. Only the officers wore clothing comparable to a military uniform, marked by a yellow sash worn over the shoulder or around the waist.

Residents of Parma and Piacenza, formed in turn the *milizia urbana*, composed of four companies in both towns, forming two battalions of 1,200 men each. In case of need, the urban militia were called upon to replace the soldiers guarding the entrances to the cities. In fact, the companies took the name from the cities' gates.

The militia also included mounted units. The most prestigious were the companies of the *Cornetta Bianca* (White Cornet) so called because of the colour of their standard. The companies were personally commanded by the duke, since in the event of war the nobility joined the companies, forming a corps of gendarmes. However, as the companies were no longer involved in war after 1649, these only served to attest to the nobility of their members.

The actual mounted force of the militia were the *corazzieri* and *carabinieri*. The former, called in Latin with the high-sounding appellation *cahtafractorum militum cohorte*, were recruited in Parma and Piacenza and formed two companies, both hierarchically positioned immediately after the lifeguards. The members were all *gentiluomini* and *cavalieri*. Many among them who were able to sustain the expense provided a replacement for active service. Cuirassiers did not pay military tax and had to provide for their own uniform, armament and horse. Membership of the cuirassier companies could be passed on from father to son. The strength of the companies ranged between 50 and 60 horsemen. As their service was similar to that of the lifeguards, the cuirassiers provided the additional escort to the duke or members of its family when needed. According to documents and iconography of the time, the two companies still wore a three-quarter corselet.

The other specialty of the mounted militia, and even the most numerous among them, were the *carabinieri*, or *carabini*, in Latin also denominated

---

231 ASPr, *Governo farnesiano*, Milizie, b.4.

equestris militia sclopetarum. In Parma and Piacenza there were two companies of 40 men each. The countryside formed a further 10 companies, one for each *terzo*, whose strength ranged between 40 and 100 horsemen. Like the cuirassiers, the carabineers had to provide their own horse, equipment and armament, or present a replacement. The horsemen were selected from among the *persone civili*, and held honours and rank like the *forese* militia officers. The *carabinieri* were the only mounted units of the militia that performed actual tasks, forming the escort to the duke's officials and patrolling the countryside and borders. At the end of the century a uniform was also established, which consisted of a dark blue jacket with red displays and a white cloak; the saddle cover and pistol holster were of red cloth edged with blue.[232]

The whole cavalry, including the mounted lifeguards, was under the command of the *colonnello generale della cavalleria*. The command of the militia was entrusted to the *collaterale generale* who had the function of administrator rather than field commander. The *collaterale*'s main office was in Parma and extended its authority over that territory, while in Piacenza there was another *collaterale* with the same prerogatives as the previous one. Both had to maintain and keep the rolls of the militia up-to-date and check that all payments were carried out regularly. They also had the task of seeing that no abuses took place against the militia in service by their officers, and having the companies carry out military exercises. In theory, once a month the companies had to meet for the training session, but more often these were limited to the *mostre*, namely inspections and counting.

The militia also supplied personnel for the artillery. Denominated as *bombardieri*, or in Latin *cohorte explosorum tormenti bellici*, they had been instituted in 1615, when two companies were raised in Parma and Piacenza. Between 1660 and 1690 their strength fluctuated between 400 and 500 men, with a staff in each city comprising one captain, two *gentilhuomini del cannone* (constables), five sergeants, four *consiglieri* (secretaries), one *depositario* (custodian), two fouriers, two ammunitioners, two *coadiutori* (adjutant NCOs), one *avviso alle salve* (shot warning deputy), four *cavapalle* (cannonball extractors), and one *notaio* (notary). These companies were a semi-professional force which served at the batteries of the two cities, formed by militiamen selected among artisans and even artists.[233] They received a salary according to their service and enjoyed the usual rights granted to the militia, such as permission to hunt and the right to bear swords and firearms in civilian life. In addition to training, under the direction of the *generale del cannone* the *bombardieri*'s duties included the maintenance of weapons, service at the batteries, and salvoes of honour and fireworks during the state festivities. The companies could be employed for the maintenance of the fortifications as qualified manpower. In Parma there were 93 cannons dating from 1505 to the end of the century, of calibres from 2 lb to 69 lb, plus 28 mortars and 1,866 rampart muskets. Piacenza had 62 guns of calibres from

---

232 ASPr, *Memorabilia civitas Parmae, 1688–1708*, ms. 55.
233 Zannoni-Fiorentino, *L'esercito Farnesiano*, p.111.

1 lb to 45 lb, seven mortars and other weapons.[234] In the late seventeenth century they wore a uniform consisting of an iron-grey coat with red facings and brass buttons.[235]

Among the professions that made up the militia there were also the *navaroli del Po* (Po River sailors) who, even if formally exempted by their service in the militia, formed the crew for the Duke's *bucintoro* (galleon) anchored in the fluvial port of Piacenza. The ship was richly decorated in gold leaf and covered with crimson velvet with golden embroideries. The oarsmen and the sailors were dressed in red *casacca* (jacket), breeches, and stockings; the *casacca* and breeches were laced with silver.[236]

Overall, in the 1690s the ducal militia numbered 10,000 infantrymen and 500 horses reputed as 'good troops'.[237] This force, however, did not preserve the Duchy from foreign occupations and the consequent disbursement of money for the winter quarters of the armies involved in the Italian campaigns of the League of Augsburg.

Parma and Piacenza Go to War

As hostilities against the Porte resumed in 1684, Duke Ranuccio II once again responded before any other Italian prince, sending an infantry regiment of eight companies to enter Venetian service. The unit arrived in Venice in the August 1684. Yet, a clause stated that this unit could not be employed on the fleet but only on the mainland, and for this reason the regiment was sent to Zadar in Dalmatia, and later the companies were distributed between Split, Traù, and Scutari. The Duke recalled his brother Alessandro, already a general in the Spanish army, appointing him to lead the troops in Dalmatia. The elderly prince dealt with the preparation of the companies and their travel to the *Levante*, but after a few months he returned to Parma, delegating command to his Lieutenant Giovanni Anguissola. In 1686 some companies appear in the Venetian battle order during the siege of the Ottoman fortress of Opus (today Opuzen, in Croatia). This action marked the Farnese participation at the war, since in 1687 the regiment was disbanded. Subsequent aid to Venice came only in the form of subsidies. However, Duke Ranuccio II permitted his officers and soldiers to join the Venetian army if they desired.[238] With the regiment, there arrived in Dalmazia the engineer Odoardo Odoardi, native of Ascoli Piceno but in the service of Parma. He was a skilled technician who prepared a detailed overview of the Ottoman fortification in Southern Dalmatia, and since 1685 he had served as *ajutante generale* of Prince Alessandro Farnese. In 1686 he participated in the conquest of Opus and Sinj, where in September he was killed in action.[239]

---

234 ASPr, *Governo farnesiano, Fabbriche ducali e fortificazioni*, b.9.
235 Zannoni-Fiorentino, *L'esercito Farnesiano* p.112.
236 *Ibid.*, p.111.
237 Gude, *Staat von Parma und Piacenza, Mirandula und Concordia, Massa und Carrara, Monaco, Doria, St. Piedro, Sesto St. Angelo und dei Fieschi*, p.12.
238 Beregani, *Istoria delle Guerre d'Europa*, vol. I p.469.
239 Thanks to Pier Filippo Melchiorre for this notice.

Duchy of Modena

After the interlude of the Castro War Modena found itself once again involved in a conflict against the neighbouring Duchy of Parma, in the Italian phase of the war between France and Spain. On that occasion Duke Francesco I d'Este (1610–1658) had formed an army larger than his state could sustain, enlisting mercenaries in Italy and Germany, which nevertheless earned him the conquest of Correggio, confirmed by the Peace of the Pyrenees in 1659.[240] In the following years the alliance with Paris was further strengthened. His sons had entered the French army and two regiments had been formed under their command. This was an unbearable burden for Modena's exhausted finances, which nevertheless became useful for the aid offered to Venice in the Cretan War. Modena became the base for the army set up together with the French for the unsuccessful expedition of 1660, which moreover cost the life of the promising Prince Almerico.[241]

In 1660, the extension of the Duchy included the territory of the modern provinces of Modena and Reggio Emilia, plus the northern Garfagnana with Castelnuovo, where lived a population of about 250,000 inhabitants. Lacking natural and above all secure borders, the Duchy also had few modern fortifications. The most strategically relevant fortress was Brescello, which together with that of the small satellite-state of Mirandola ensured a very uncertain control of the territory. Modena, Reggio and Correggio were also provided with modern fortifications, but in 1662 the Duchy went through a period of political uncertainty with the sudden death of Duke Alfonso IV. He left his son Francesco II under the tutelage of his mother Laura Martinozzi (1639–1687), niece of Cardinal Mazarin, and she ruled as regent until 1674. During the reign of Francesco II the alliance between Modena and France began to weaken. The deterioration of relations culminated in 1678 with the succession of Guastalla. After the death without heirs of Duke Ferrante III Gonzaga the strategic position of the small duchy, located on the right bank of the Po between Mantua and Modena, immediately aroused the interest of the two neighbouring states. In favour of the Este family was the close relationship with Ferrante's widow, Margherita, aunt of Francesco II's father. He was certain that in support of his claims France would intervene, especially after the Emperor and Spain supported the position of Mantua, whose troops had already occupied Guastalla. Louis XIV, on the contrary, was already secretly negotiating the cession of Casale with the Duke of Mantua, and this agreement, sealed in July 1681, highlighted the inconsistency of the alliance between France and Modena.

In 1685 the Duchy returned to assume a short international relevance with the marriage between James II Stuart and Mary of Modena, sister of Francesco II.

---

240 Between 1660 and 1690 the dukes were Alfonso IV (r. 1658–1662), the regent Duchess Laura Martinozzi (1662–1674), Francesco II (1674–1694).

241 In 1660 Modena contributed with 1,200 infantrymen and 300 oarsmen. Previously, 1,000 'volunteers' marched from Modena to Venice in 1653. See Mugnai, *The Cretan War*, p.263.

Below: 47. Portrait of Duke Francesco II d'Este (1660-1694), by an unknown artist (private collection). After a childhood spent under the tutelage of his uncles and physicians who constantly monitored his delicate health, at the age of 14, under the influence of his cousin Cesare Ignazio, Francesco ousted his mother and assumed the government of the Duchy. During his reign, Modena maintained a policy of rigid neutrality, yet Francesco II often neglected government affairs, devoting himself above all to his passion for music. An almost unique case in the Italian scenario, in 1675 the heir Prince Rinaldo entered a military career in a Lutheran German state, as colonel proprietor of an infantry regiment in Hanover.

Above: 46. Duke of Modena Alfonso IV d'Este (1634–1662), portrayed by Justus Sustermans (Isabella Stewart Gardner Museum, Boston MS). In 1655 Alfonso IV married Laura Martinozzi, Cardinal Mazarin's niece, thus strengthening the alliance with France. In 1659 the Franco-Spanish War came to an end and the Duke was rewarded with the town of Correggio for supporting France.

The Modenese 'Military'

Like every other ruler of the *Ancien Régime*, in the event of war Modena resorted to enlisting soldiers by turning to the international market of mercenaries; the scenario was somewhat reminiscent of the Renaissance. The network of relations extended to a wide range of territories. In July 1642 the Duke concluded a 'convention' with the Albanian ensign Casa-Gionima for the recruitment of a company of 100 infantrymen of his nation, while with Lieutenant Ippolito Pegolotti he concluded an agreement for the formation of a cavalry company to be recruited outside the Duchy. Before the end of the year an entire regiment of 1,000 Italian infantrymen entered Modena's service under the orders of Colonel Guido Rangoni.[242]

Like any other Italian state ruled by a prince, the sovereign was the head of his army. In Modena the Duke held command through a war secretariat and a *commissariato* with control and inspection functions, while financial matters were entrusted to the ducal treasury, which managed a fund for military expenditure and troop salaries. This was a very modest undertaking, considering the very small number of professional troops still in service after 1659.

The formation of companies of 'soldiers of fortune' regained some impetus in the 1660s, when Duke Alfonso IV instituted a tax on the militia which provided for the abolition of guard duties in the cities and other places of the state, and entrusted them to regular soldiers. In 1666, during the crisis with Mantua which led both states to the verge of a conflict, the number of mercenary troops increased but declined again at the end of the year. In the 1670s the service at the gates of the towns returned to being one of the duties of the city militiamen, known as the *caporioni*. However, in 1685 a company of 140 professional soldiers under the orders of Captain Antonio Maria Susari still composed the main garrison of Brescello.[243]

Also in Modena, the artillery personnel were called *bombardieri*. Only some of them were in permanent service and received a regular salary, while the remainder were volunteers, denominated *ausiliari*. They were craftsmen, carpenters, blacksmiths, masons, who formed a special militia summoned in case of need with a salary based on their service, and additional privileges. The organisation of the corps of *bombardieri* and *ausiliari* was re-established in 1660, and gave permission to the volunteers to carry the long or short harquebus in the city as well as in the countryside, where they could hunt certain prey. The corps was under the control of the *commissario del cannone*, who was also in charge of training the reservists, and established practice sessions for regular artillerymen. In 1657 the total number of professional *bombardieri* was 259, excluding officers, divided into companies of varying numbers based in Modena, Reggio, Brescello and Carpi, plus some pickets

---

242 Alberto Menziani, 'L'esercito estense ed austro-estense (1598–1859)', in A. Spaggiari and G. Trenti (eds), *Lo Stato di Modena. Una capitale, una dinastia, una civiltà nella storia d'Europa* (Modena, 1998), Saggi 66 – Ministero per i Beni e le Attività Culturali – Direzione generale per gli archivi, p.710.

243 *Ibid.*, p.711.

MODENA.
Das Cittadell
Der Marckt
Das Schloss
Secchia Fl.

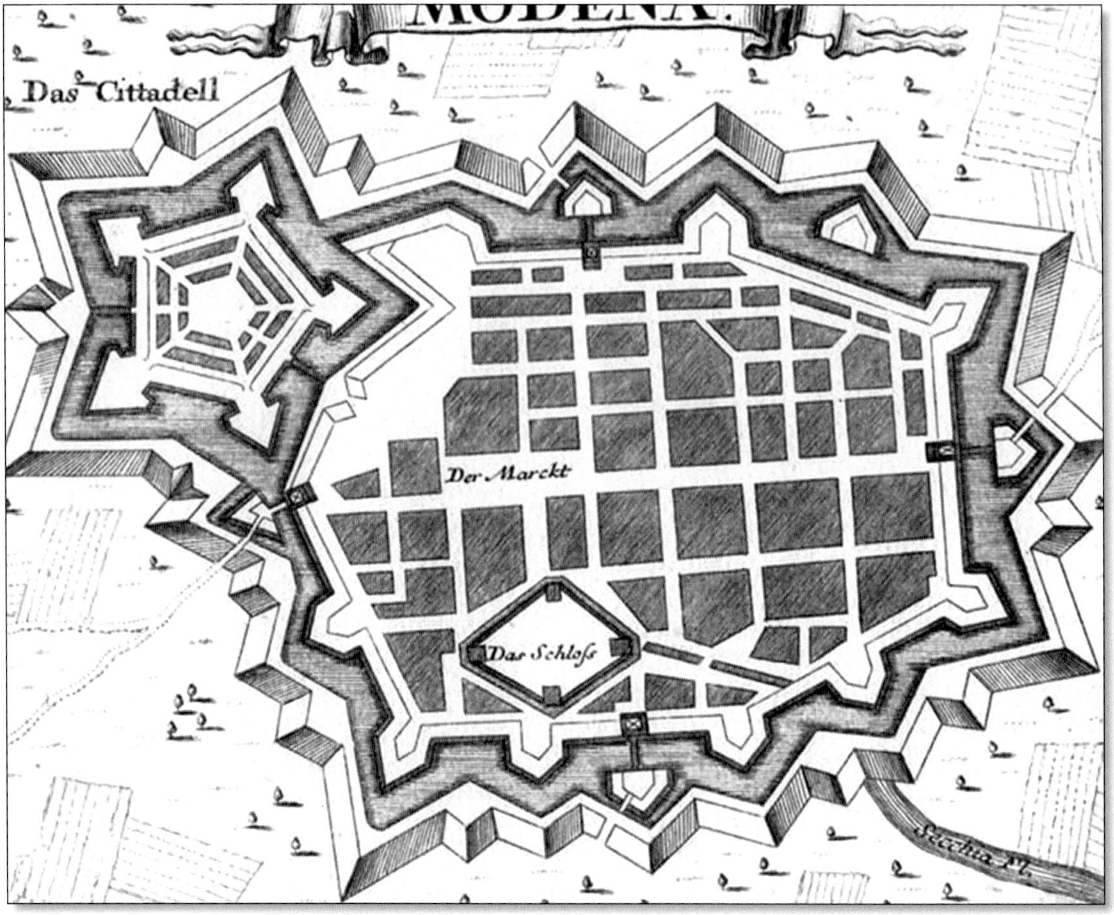

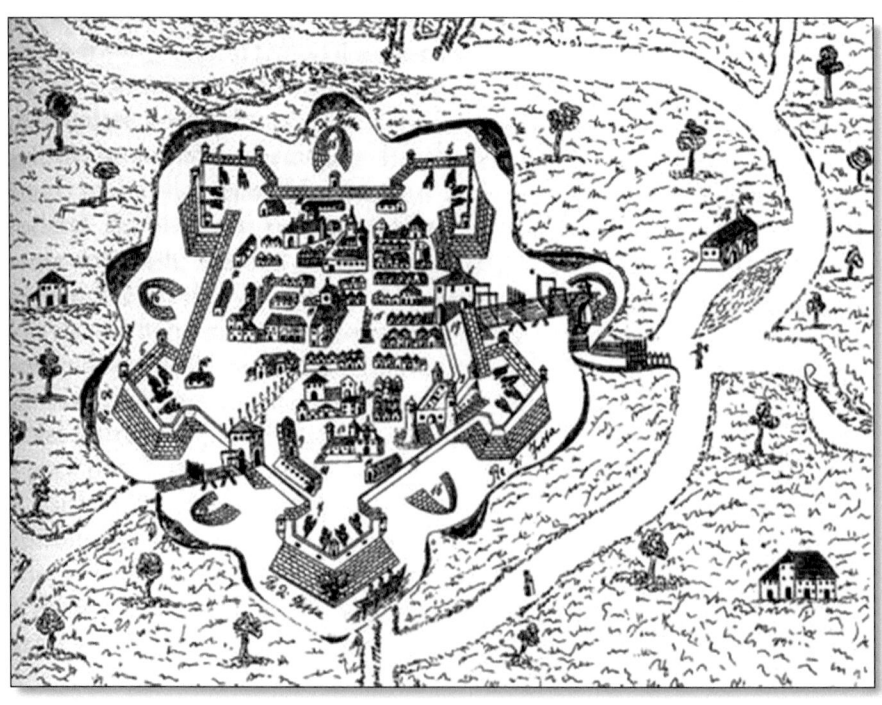

MEDIUM AND MINOR POWERS

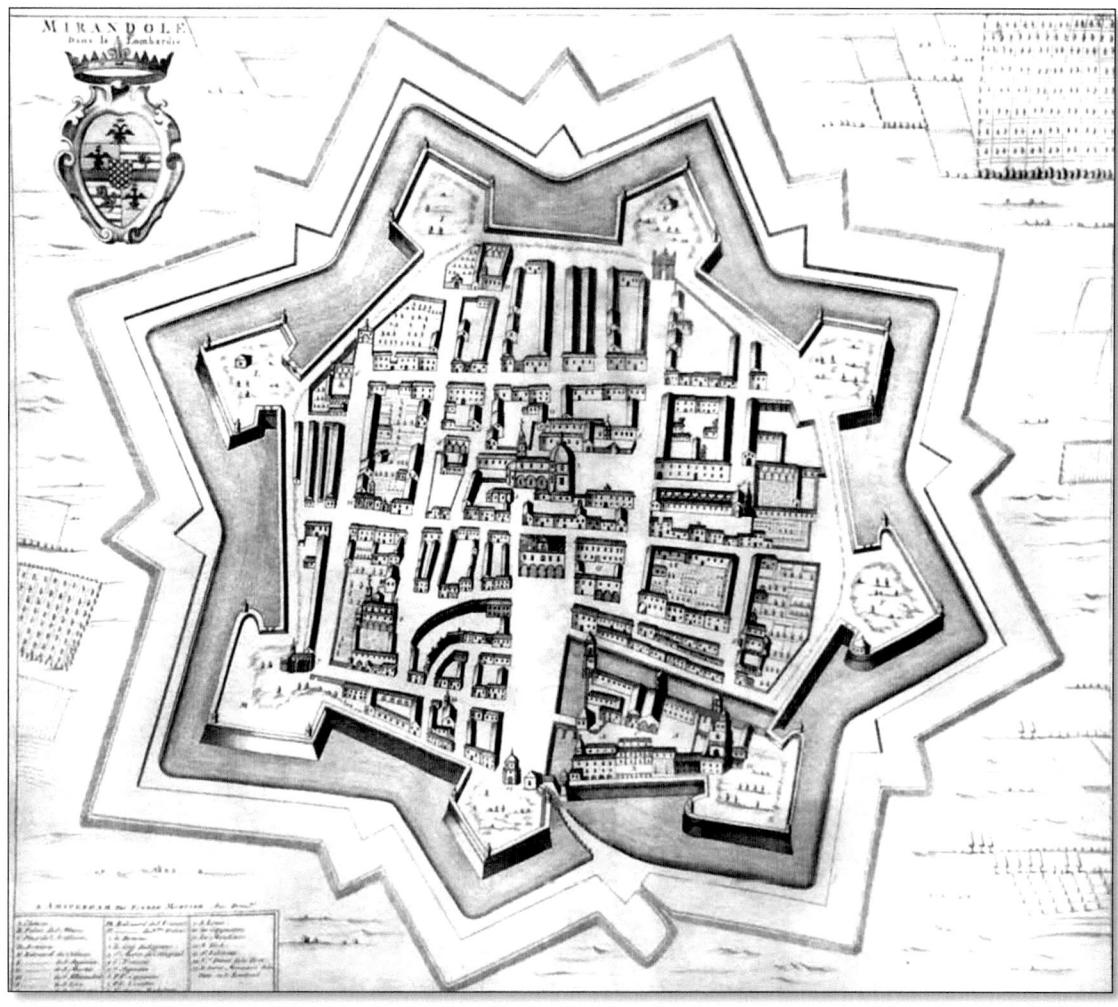

Facing page, top: 48. The fortifications of Modena in a German print dating to the early 1700 (author's archive). Modena had a modern curtain and an external citadel that reproduced the classical scheme of the *trace Italienne*.

Facing page, bottom: 49. The fortress of Brescello in the seventeenth century (author's archive). The fortress had been constantly improved and maintained by the dukes, but in 1704, after the French siege of the previous year, walls and bastions were destroyed. The demolition was entrusted to the Duke of Parma, who with much zeal provided 3,000 peasants who completed the work in six months.

Above: 50. The fortifications of Mirandola in a print dating to 1681. (Author's archive)

51. Modena militiaman, possibly a company of caporioni urban militia, wearing blue coats with yellow facings, in a watercolour dating to 1675. Note the NCO carrying a double-handed cutting weapon.

assigned to the batteries of Rubiera, Monte Alfonso, Sestola and Verrucole.[244] A year later the number of permanent artillerymen had risen to 531, distributed in the same locations. The corps continued to be included in the stable force until 1690, when it was abolished, only to be reconstituted in 1696 as an illusory deterrent to face the foreign armies violating the state's borders during the War of the League of Augsburg.

By the end of the seventeenth century 161 cannons were still usable, including five mortars and eight *petrieri*. The artillery had recently been renovated and was judged to be in excellent condition.[245] The inventory shows that the artillery still included cannons dating back to the sixteenth century. Of 47 bronze cannons, 21 had been manufactured between 1540 and 1590.[246]

---

244 'Capitoli dei Bombardieri del Ducato di Modena', transcribed by Carlo Montù in *Storia dell'Artiglieria* (Rome, 1933), vol. I, pp.768–771.

245 ASMo, *Militare Estense*, b. 142.

246 Most of these cannons were the work of the famous artillery foundryman Annibale Borgognoni, except one, cast by the Swiss Giovanni Lamprecht, who was his pupil. However, the employment

MEDIUM AND MINOR POWERS

Brescello was the most important fortress in the state, equipped with a pentagonal curtain wall with a bastion in each corner, and defended by 25 large-calibre cannons. Towards the end of the century the fortress was found to be in very poor condition; in fact, a report informed the Duke that Brescello was completely unprepared for a defence. As for the garrison, commissioner Claudio Ricci reported that the soldiers had no straw for their beds and those on sentry duty were better off than those sleeping, adding that the uniforms were also in poor condition. As for the artillery, of the 18 *falconi, falconetti, aspidi* and *sagri* positioned on the five bastions, only two were in good condition, while the others had broken carriages or were lying on the ground. The inventory of the fortress included a total of 40 cannons and other light

of cannons dating back to the previous century is not an indication of poor military efficiency, considering that one of the cannons abandoned by the French at Namur in 1695 had the monogram of Henry IV and thus dated back to the period 1594–1610.

artillery, as well as 40 rampart muskets.[247] Brescello was also the base of the brigantine and felucca of the Duchy's small river fleet, supporting the customs house where duties on trade were collected. Other fortified places were located in the Apennines, such as the *Sasso* (rock) of Rubiera, and Sestola, Verrucole, Monte Alfonso, near Castelnuovo in Garfagnana.

The ducal household comprised a lifeguard formed by 50 *cavalleggeri* and a company of Swiss with palace guard duties. They numbered 50 men at the end of the century.[248]

The Militia

The Modenese militia, both foot and horse, was recruited on a territorial basis and organised according to the regulation established in 1596 with the *Capitoli e Ordini sopra le Milizie e Ordinanze dello Stato*, issued by Duke Alfonso II. All the *descritti* – civilians registered in militia roles – were required to report periodically with the other militiamen for training and reviews of their strength. The foot militia also met once a year for a general muster in the presence of the colonel and at other times for special reviews. In return for service in the militia the Duke offered tax exemptions and a hunting licence. The service of the cavalry was regulated by the *Capitoli e Privilegi della Milizia a Cavallo del Serenissimo Duca*, issued in 1611. The regulation established that all subjects who were able to provide their own horse, equipment and armament could join the corps. For each mounted militiaman the Duke reserved the usual privileges and required the same training and inspection obligations as for the infantry. Each company was entrusted to a captain who received his licence from the Duke, but more often was under the lieutenant, assisted by a sergeant and some corporals. The militia was divided into the districts of Piana di Modena, Garfagnana, Reggio, Correggio, and San Felice.

Outside the disciplinary sphere, for having 'failed in the service of the Duke', the militiaman retained the ordinary status of subject but was benefited with special jurisdictional treatment. If a claimant or defendant in civil cases, in fact, he could not be submitted to the ordinary judge, but only to the court chosen by the ducal authority 'in every civil and mixed case', and only in the absence of the latter could he submit to the ordinary judge but with the permission of the captain or superior.[249] However, according to commentators of the time, the militia was negatively known for its lack of discipline and efficiency. During the Castro War the Duke's commissioners complained of the militia for 'poor discipline' and 'too open disobedience', and complaints also concerned the officers.[250] In June 1659 Duke Alfonso IV, not even a year after the beginning of

---

247 *Ibid.*, *Elenco degli Attrecci Militari della Ducal Munitione di Brescello*; the list includes muskets, pikes, partisans, *brandistocchi*, armour, bombs, cannonballs and 2,896 terracotta grenades.

248 Heinrich Ludwig Gude, *Der Staat von Florenz, Modena und Reggio* (1708), p.18.

249 Pierpaolo Bonacini, 'Per il gran bene della pubblica tranquillità e sicurezza … Giustizia e disciplina militare negli Stati estensi di Antico Regime (secoli XVI-XVII)', in *Historia et Ius*, n. 16 (2019), p.15.

250 *Grida Sopra la Liberatione de' Soldati delle Melizie della guardia di Modena, Reggio, Carpi, Correggio, Bersello, e altri luoghi*, in ASMo, *Militare Estense*, b. 215 (28 and 29 June 1659). Thanks to Alberto Menziani for this notice.

his rule, explicitly denounced the shortcomings of the system that, as a result, made the units unreliable: the 'poor discipline of the people of the country ... too open disobedience of the soldiers of these bands', and also widespread frauds among the officers who:

> either for friendship or for other reasons, release the wealthy and well provided of money from service, making the poor and wretched serve only during the necessary exchanges of fifteen days, who either flee while they are in service or, freed from service, abandon the country so as not to be forced again to do, in addition to their own parts, those of others.[251]

In an attempt to improve the service, the Duke exempted the militia from providing some tasks in exchange for the payment of a tax, so as to pay and raise a guard formed 'with volunteer and professional soldiers.'[252] After requests from numerous communities in the Duchy, militiamen were exempted from serving in the garrisons, in particular Modena, Reggio, Correggio, Carpi and Brescello.

Along with the ordinary militia the Duchy had an urban militia organised in 1625 into companies called *Centurie de'Caporioni*, formed exclusively by city residents, but with the exclusion of certain categories, such as servants and other people already part of corps such as the auxiliary artillerymen. Alongside Modena, in the 1680s urban companies were also raised in Reggio, Sassuolo, Correggio and Carpi.

Although the Duchy had a modest armed force, from 1674, with the end of the regency, the Modenese military experienced a period of enhancement at least as far as the militia was concerned. This mainly occurred on the initiative of Duke Franceso II's cousin, Prince Cesare Ignazio d'Este (1653–1713). Like his uncles Alfonso and Almerico he had been educated in France, and on his return to Modena in 1673 he was one of the protagonists of the removal of the Dowager Duchess from the regency the following year. Regarding Cesare Ignazio, historians outline an exuberant personality, developed to excess during his years at the court of the Sun King. Duke Francesco II appointed him as *Comandante Generale in Capo* of the Duchy's army, and he inaugurated a dynamic military policy that, however, was hampered by the meagre financial budget. Despite this the Prince did his utmost to establish the Duchy's militia as the best quality, issuing uniforms and equipment like the regular soldiers and taking as a model the French army. According to contemporary authors the militiamen numbered about 12,000 men in the last decade of the seventeenth century.[253]

52. A sketch depicting a Swiss Guard of the Duchy of Modena, black headgear with azure-white plumes, red coat with silver lacings and buttons, white stockings, azure baldric edged with silver, azure-white halberd pole. (New York Public Library, The Vinkhuijzen Collection of Military Uniforms)

---

251 *Ibid.*
252 *Ibid.*
253 Gude, *Der Staat von Florenz, Modena und Reggio*, p.18.

53. The fiery and pompous Cesare Ignazio d'Este of Scandiano (1653–1713), portrayed by Henri Gascard in 1675. (Gallerie Estensi, Modena). See image commentaries for more information.

The Duchies of Mantua and Guastalla

As the most exposed, and certainly the most threatened among the states of the Po Valley, the Duchy of Mantua was also conditioned by a disadvantageous territorial location. This included the territory between the Ticino and Po rivers enclosed within the borders of Modena, Parma, Venice and the Papal State, and the residual domain in Monferrato represented by the fortress city of Casale, which was separated from the capital by the territory of Savoy-Piedmont and the Spanish *Estado de Milan*. The overall population was reported to be approximately 200,000 persons, a figure that increased slightly in 1678 with the annexation of Guastalla after the extinction of the local Gonzaga rulers.[254] Despite this acquisition there were further satellites, principalities and counties ruled by other branches of the Gonzaga family in Sabbioneta, Bozzolo, Novellara and Bagnolo, and, after 1675 also in Castiglione and Solferino.

---

254 In 1692 the Duchy of Guastalla was restored, appointing Vincenzo Gonzaga as independent ruler.

The house of Gonzaga-Nevers, which had ruled since 1627 and survived the dramatic siege of Mantua in 1630, must have considered the geopolitical scenario of its domains as an actual viaticum for its survival.[255] Consequently Mantuan foreign policy was constantly in balance between France and Spain, and in the medium term the inability to assume an autonomous role was one of the causes of the Duchy's end in 1708. This does not mean the rulers of Mantua had renounced their desire to achieve emancipation from the tutelage of the two foreign powers, but unfortunate events played their part. Facing this unfavourable scenario, the dukes tried to insist in Vienna on their vicariate rights, particularly after 1657, when Emperor Ferdinand III appointed the duke of Mantua, Carlo II Gonzaga Nevers, as his imperial vicar and commissioner in Italy. After this success, in 1662 Duke Carlo II licensed the foreign garrison protecting Mantua without intending to create a force of his own to defend the state, pursuing a policy of neutrality and relying only on the state militia. After his death in 1665, the regent, Duchess Isabella Clara of Austria-Innsbruck (1629–1685) established close links with Spain, obtaining a subsidy from Madrid to raise a garrison of professional soldiers to man the strategic stronghold of Casale. In 1666 the Duchess also engaged in a border dispute with Modena along the Po River, but the arbitration of the Spanish governor of Milan resolved the tension.[256]

Coming of age in 1669, Duke Ferdinando Carlo played a more devious game. For a while the Duchy remained formally in the Spanish camp, to the point that Ferdinando Carlo's cousin, Prince Vincenzo Gonzaga, was appointed viceroy of Sicily in 1677. In the same year, the state finances were in very dramatic condition, but the Duke still went to spend Carnival in Venice 'in his usual debauchery'.[257] The Dowager Duchess had regained some authority and directed everything from her convent in the absence of his son. However, Ferdinando Carlo was firmly in the French camp, having concluded a secret treaty with Louis XIV in 1678, followed by the sale of Casale to France in 1681 after Spain was no longer able to pay the subsidy to maintain the local garrison.[258] For this cession, Ferdinando Carlo received 100,000 *scudi* from Louis XIV and the title of General of the French army in Italy. Although the pacts only provided for the cession of the town, the French commander Nicolas de Catinat occupied the whole territory of Casale. This act had very strong repercussions in all the European courts hostile to France, and irreparably undermined the reputation of the Duke, who became more famous for his parties and being an assiduous participant in the Venetian carnival than as a ruler of a state. In 1688 Ferdinando Carlo confirmed again his alignment with France, fortifying Guastalla with a

---

255 Between 1660 and 1690 the Duchy was held by Carlo II (1637–1665), Duchess Isabella Clara of Habsburg as regent (1665–1669), and Ferdinando Carlo (1665–1708).

256 Giuseppe Coniglio, *I Gonzaga* (Milan: Dall'Oglio, 1967), p.454.

257 Émile Laloy, *L'expédition de Sicile et la politique française en Italie (1674–1678)* (Paris, 1929), vol. III, p.545.

258 *Ibid*. The subsidy paid by Spain amounted to 20,000 *scudi* per year, a sum, it was said, that the Duke took away from his benefit.

54. Carlo II of Gonzaga-Nevers (1637–1665) in an engraving of Frans van der Steen (author's archive). The Duke is portrayed with the collar of the order of the Christ's Blood or *del Redentore*, which was a Mantuan chivalry order.

French subsidy in order to cede the place to Louis XIV at the first opportunity.[259]

Very little information exists on the military history of the Duchy of Mantua. Most sources had been dispersed over the years, and this was not always due to misfortune.[260] Archival sources therefore allow only a very approximate picture to be formed, and some information can only be reconstructed indirectly. Before 1680 the largest garrison was Casale, where in the late 1650s there were 2,460 men divided in four cavalry and 36 infantry companies.[261] In 1680 the same garrison quartered half this strength, which still represented the larger professional force of the Duchy, even financed by Spain. Although Duke Ferdinando Carlo had shown little concern for the affairs of the state, between 1682 and 1684 several reforms were introduced, including salaries for officers and troops *di fortuna* (mercenaries), the reorganisation of the artillery with the appointment of a commissioner and a disciplinary regulation. The latter act prescribed rather severe punishments ranging from the simple 'stretch of rope' to a prison term and capital punishment for the most serious crimes, such as armed aggression or desertion.[262]

With regard to the *soldati di fortuna* in Mantuan pay, some information can be found in the sources relating to the Duchy of Guastalla during the years between 1678 and 1692. On 13 January 1679 Duke Ferdinando Carlo in person came to Guastalla with 40 soldiers of fortune to establish infantry pickets at the town's gates.[263] The professional soldiers sent from Mantua continued to form the garrison of Guastalla, and in 1685 the force was established at 120 infantrymen, increased to 190 the next year, and finally to four companies, about 420–460 soldiers, in 1687 when work began on

---

259 Hanlon, *The Twilight of a Military Tradition*, p.200. In 1690, in the opening phase of the War of the League of Augsburg, the Spaniards dismantled the fortress, but in 1693 Ferdinando Carlo refortified Guastalla, this time as a Spanish ally.

260 After the annexation of Mantua the Austrians gave what remained of the Monferrato archives to Savoy-Piedmont, while all the papers concerning the army were transferred to the insane asylum of Mantua and distributed to the internees, who cut them up then burned the shreds to eliminate the most tangible memory of the Duchy's independence. Thanks to Ciro Paoletti for this information.

261 ASMn, *Archivio Gonzaga*, X n. 27, *Conto del pane distribuito alla soldatesca del presidio alla cittadella e castello di Casale*. In detail, there were 130 horse and 2,330 foot.

262 *Ibid.*, XI, s.n. dated 24 April 1684.

263 Biblioteca Municipale di Guastalla, *Cronaca Resta*, f. I, 7.

the fortifications.²⁶⁴ The documents regarding these troops contain mainly complaints about discipline. A report of the commander of Guastalla gives an account of the punishment inflicted on a soldier from Parma, who had chased another soldier with his sword with the intention of killing him.²⁶⁵ Several other complaints outlined the poor discipline of this soldiery. Overall, in the 1680s the Mantuan standing force could have been around 800–1,000 infantrymen. The gradual loss of Ferdinando Carlo's interest in Guastalla, and the destruction of the fortifications in 1690, left the city without a garrison, causing the decrease of the ducal standing troops by half. In addition to these meagre forces the Duke had a foot lifeguard consisting of 50 *Arcieri di Palazzo*.²⁶⁶

The decrease in professional forces reflected the strengthening of the militia, or at least the attempt to organise a territorial force capable of dealing with the defence of the state and maintenance of public order. In 1682 new *Ordini e Privilegi* were issued for the militia, each of them concerning the different components, namely, infantry and *carabini* mounted horsemen. Each district had its own *governatore delle armi* who dealt with the training and direction of the militiamen. Each company had three officers and NCOs and corporals, but the numbers of militiamen remained undetermined, wishing that the number could grow 'desiring we [the Duke] had time to increase the companies'.²⁶⁷

A notable feature of the militia of the Duchy of Mantua was that the *decritti* did not receive wages, and in return they benefited from tax exemptions and other rights such as indemnity from debt trials against private individuals. Apart from the infantry's equipment and weapons, which were distributed by the state, from 1691 each foot militiaman also had to provide his own uniform, consisting of a *habito* of grey cloth with red facings. In addition to the uniform the mounted militia also had to provide their own equipment, and of course the horse. The *carabini* were required to have a cloth *casacca* of an unspecified colour, a pair of boots, a bandolier, a *tasco* (ammunition pouch), cloak, saddle cover, and two pistol holsters. Officers wore a double-layered *colletto di Dante* (leather coat) in German style.²⁶⁸

55. Ferdinando Carlo of Gonzaga-Nevers (1665–1708), last Duke of Mantua and Montferrat, portrayed by Frans Geffel (Museum of Palazzo d'Arco, Mantua). Along with the military attributes worn by the Duke in the portrait, the yellow silk shoulder scarf is embellished with golden fringes and edgings.

---

264 Giorgio Sulpizi, 'L'organizzazione militare del ducato di Guastalla', in *Archivio Storico degli Antichi Stati Guastallesi* (Guastalla: Associazione Guastallese di Storia Patria, 2000), p.139.

265 *Cronaca Resta*, f. I, 8.

266 ASMn, *Archivio Gonzaga*, X n. 19.

267 Sulpizi, 'L'organizzazione militare del ducato di Guastalla', p.142.

268 *Cronaca Resta*, f. I, 10.

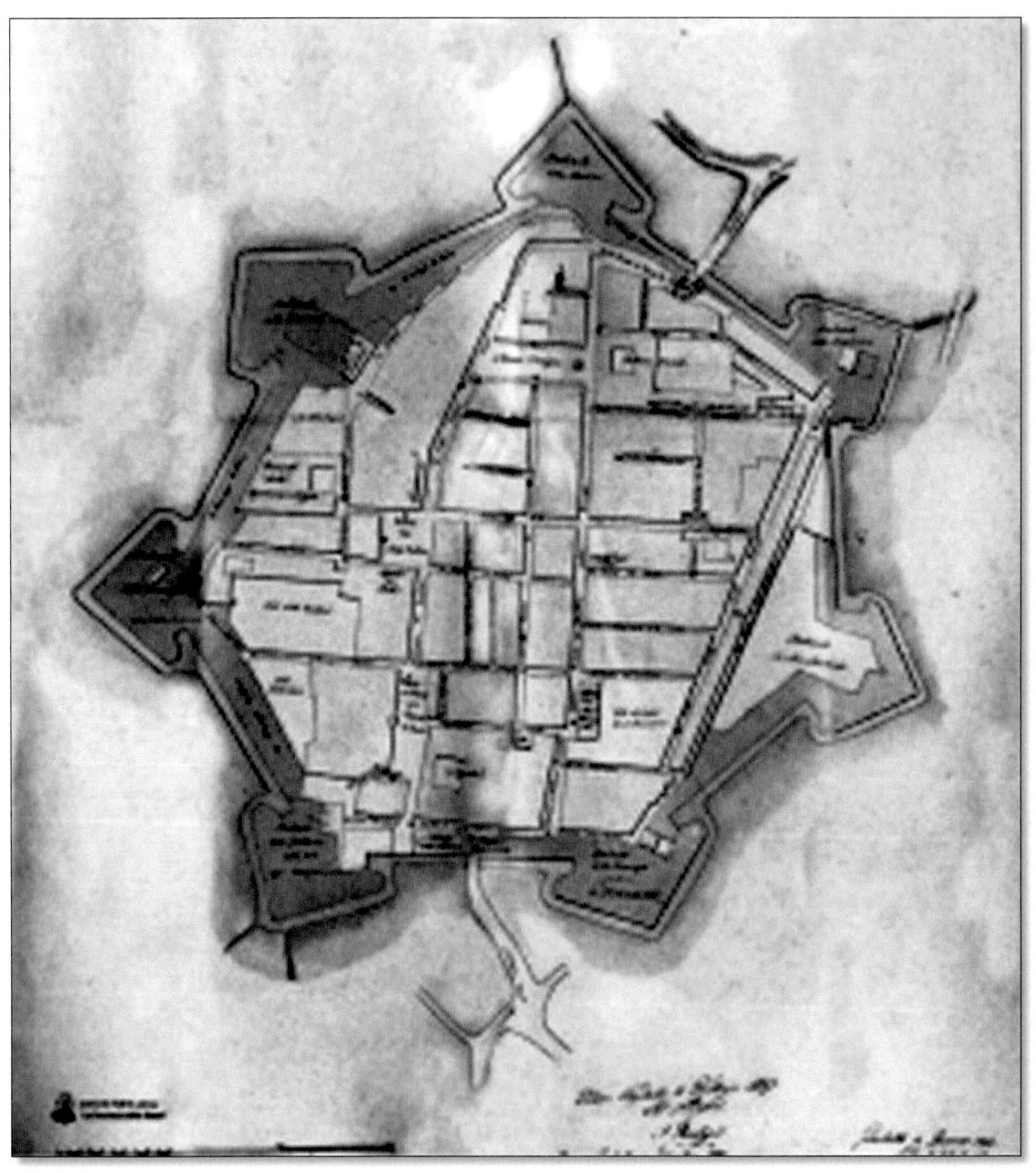

56. The fortifications of Guastalla in the 1690s, after a contemporary print. (Author's archive)

After 1690 the militia replaced the regular infantry in the guard service at the gates of Mantua. According to coeval reports, towards the end of the century Duke Ferdinando Carlo had 15,000 militiamen of infantry and cavalry. The arsenals were abundantly supplied with muskets and ammunition, and the Duke could dispose of a reserve of 12,000 horses ready to be distributed to increase the mounted troops.[269] This force also included the militia of Guastalla, which in 1690 rose to 1,600 men divided into two horse companies quartered in Guastalla and Luzzara, and nine companies of foot.[270]

The Republic of Lucca

General Raimondo Montecuccoli stated that a minor state could entrust its security to few entities except a couple of modern and strong fortresses. The Republic of Lucca had certainly adhered to this direction by choosing to defend the city regarded as 'the head of state'. Well aware of the size and low military strength of the state, the government had made immense efforts, in finances and men, to provide the city with mighty walls and bastions, and to maintain a military apparatus for defence. However, there were other considerations underlying this approach. First there was the well-founded conception that linked the fate of the state not so much to military power, but to the capacity of diplomacy, which could place Lucca in a game of international balances from which to obtain guarantees for its independence. The balancing between evaluation of military costs and the resources required by diplomacy had provided the Republic with a system of protection that had guaranteed the independence of the state during the tumultuous first half of the seventeenth century. Lucca had remained neutral during the War of Castro, and the government undoubtedly considered it advantageous that two of its most threatening neighbours, Modena and Tuscany, were heavily involved in a war with an uncertain outcome, and above all destined to consume huge resources that would distract them from other military adventures, at least in the short term.

The Republic's borders encompassed a territory of 1.175,66 square kilometres, with a population of approximately 117,000 inhabitants. The administrative division of the country had remained identical over the centuries and was still structured into *vicarie*, which in turn were divided into *comuni*. The territory was virtually uninterrupted except for the sector north of the Serchio River, whose communication routes ran through the Tuscan enclave of Pietrasanta. Within the Republic there were also two ecclesiastical fiefdoms. The first, comprising the territories located in the middle valley of the Serchio, belonged to the bishopric of Lucca until 1726, when the bishop ceded it to the Republic while retaining the title of count. The second, which remained semi-independent until 1799, belonged to the *Canonici* (Canonicals) of Lucca Cathedral and encompassed the communities located

---

269 Heinrich Ludwig Gude, *Staat von Mantua und Monferrat* (1708), p.38.
270 Sulpizi, 'L'organizzazione militare del ducato di Guastalla', p.150.

on the hills towards the sea. On these places the government of Lucca levied taxes and obliged military service, but respected the exemption, as for all members of the clergy, from taxes on purchases and wills. In turn Lucca ruled the little enclave of Montignoso, between Tuscany and Massa-Carrara.

Lying halfway between Genoa and Florence, the Republic did not have any places of particular strategic importance. The small port of Viareggio fulfilled Lucca's trade needs, and at the same time ensured the connection to its most important allies, Genoa and the Habsburgs.[271] The relations with neighbours, and above all with the Empire, whose borders theoretically included the state of Lucca, were still regulated by the *Diploma* granted by Emperor Maximilian back in 1509. With the exception of some modifications introduced over the years, Lucca had always appealed to this venerable document of international and political law and every 20 years had obtained from Vienna the reconfirmation of the privileges.[272]

The territory of the Republic was exposed on three sides, especially on the northeastern border, the Garfagnana, which was on the border between Modena and Lucca. This area represented the extreme periphery of the state and it was there that the last war fought by Lucca was conducted in 1613 against Modena. Despite this, Lucca, 'the head of state', had never been besieged, nor did its defenders ever see enemy armies approaching the city. The rulers were well aware of the security deriving from diplomacy, and hence derived their increasingly pronounced tendency to curb expenditure on military needs, the actual usefulness of which many doubted.

Political power was the exclusive prerogative of the nobility, which had become a closed group since the thirteenth century. From then on and until the end of the Aristocratic Republic in 1798 the *Nobili Mercanti* (Noble Tradesmen) represented an actual caste, a social class so impermeable to integration of new members that no other family ever managed to reach the rank of nobility. Out of a population of about 30,000 there were inside Lucca about 100 noble families. These provided the ruling class of the state, about 300 adult males in

---

271 More than a regular port, Viareggio used the Burlamacca canal, a tributary of the Lake of Massaciuccoli, to access the Ligurian Sea. The merchant ships, forced to stay offshore, were joined by small boats that took the goods to warehouses erected along the canal or on the shores of the lake, at the foot of Monte Quiesa. Loaded onto wagons, the goods finally reached the capital. According to Rita Fazzi, *La società lucchese del Seicento* (Lucca: Pacini Fazzi, 1977), p.95: 'Viareggio represented the obstinate will to survive of the oligarchic class, which saw the port as a potential escape route from the Florentine encirclement, and the irrepressible economic decline of a commercial society that could do without the crowded port of Livorno to satisfy its needs.'

272 Ugo Bernardini, *L'ultimo anno della Repubblica Aristocratica di Lucca* (Perugia, 1929), p.3: 'In Lucca, coins were minted, taxes were levied and the ruling class, belonging to families registered with the nobility, had begun to send ambassadors to other nations like any other independent state, but the link that still existed between Lucca and the House of Austria was kept alive through the homage paid to the Habsburgs at each new election to the Imperial throne.'

MEDIUM AND MINOR POWERS

57. (above) and 58. Swiss Guards of the Republic Lucca depicted in two sketches by Georg Christoph Martini (1685–1745), a German artist who visisted Lucca in the early eighteenth century (author's archive). Martini depicted these figures from life during a festive ceremony that occurred in the city. Both drawings are the first known representation of the Republic's Swiss Guards, and apart from a few details they could wear a uniform not very different from that of the late seventeenth century. Gualdo Priorato, in his *Relatione* of 1668, also gives some account of the uniforms, consisting of an azure doublet with red-white piping, breeches in Swiss style (possibly red and azure), azure stockings, and silver buttons.

59. Lucca in the late seventeenth century, copper engraving from *Curioses Staats-Kriegstheatrum in Bayern, Franken, Hispanien, Italien*, printed in Hamburg in 1702 (author's archive). See image commentaries for more information.

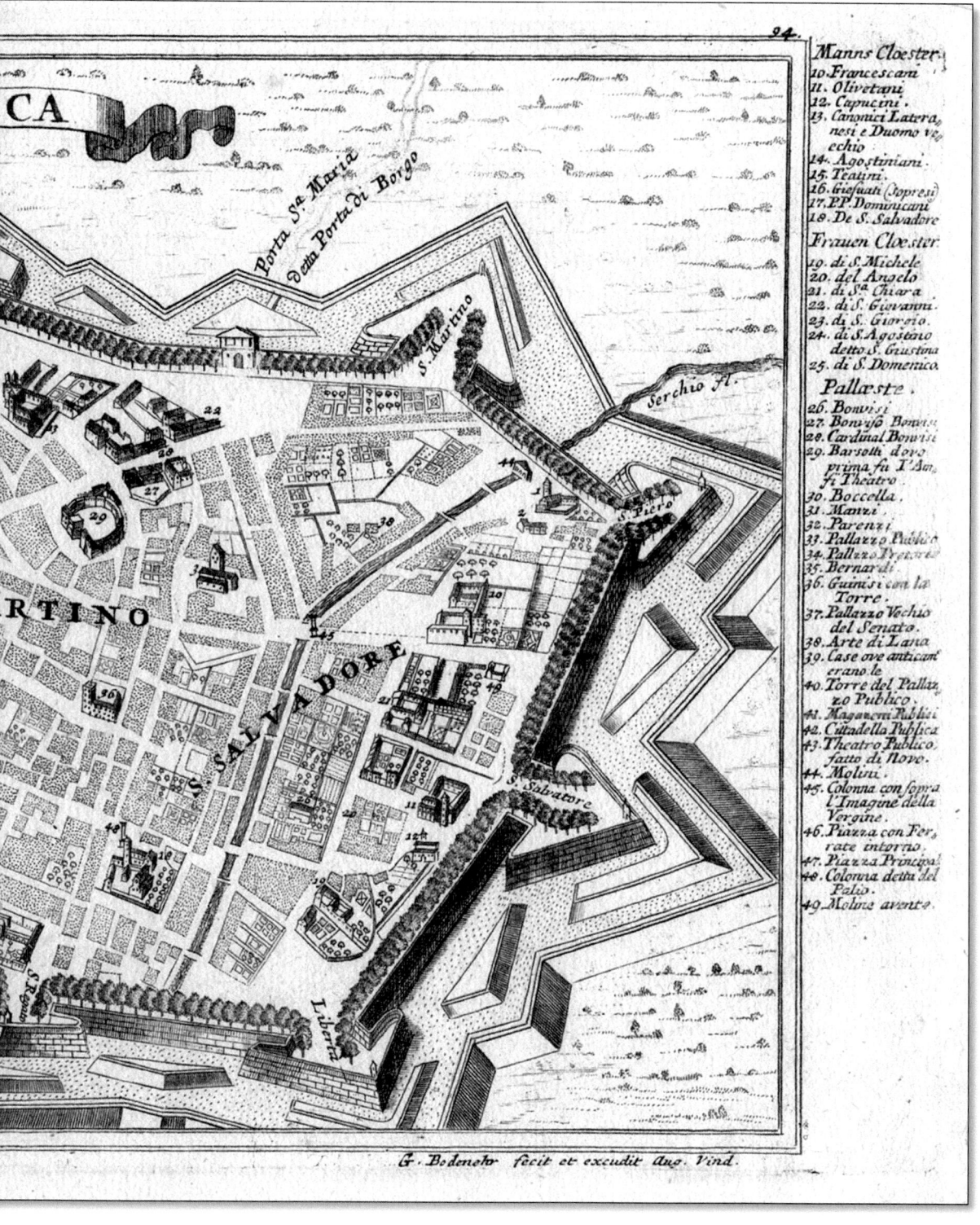

total.²⁷³ The network of mercantile interests and the legal mechanisms of trade, however, involved both patricians and common citizens.²⁷⁴

While the governmental organisation of the monarchies resembled each other, each Italian Republic had its own way of allocating power and functions. The main government's body consisted of two councils: the *Consiglio Generale* or *de' Juniori* (General Council, or Junior Council) a kind of parliament, and the *Consiglio degli Anziani* or *de Seniori* (Council of Elders or Council of Seniors), which elected the senators, namely the members of the *Consiglio Generale* (General Council). This was the legislative body par excellence and usually comprised 120 senators who held office for a single year. They joined the Council of Elders to discuss laws presented by the *Gonfaloniere* (equivalent to the *Doge*). During their mandate the elders were obliged to reside into the *Palazzo Pubblico*. A maximum of three Elders, including the *Gonfaloniere*, could be absent from the office, but only for short periods, coinciding with Republic festivities. The *Gonfaloniere* was assisted by the *cancelliere maggiore* and the *comandatore* chosen from among the elders, the latter replaced every three days. Also attached to the General Council were two particular offices: the *Invitati* (Invitees) and the *Conservatori della Legge* (Law Keepers), whose function was exclusively consultative. Similar to the General Council, the Council of Elders was in turn connected to the office of the *Colloquia* and the *consiglio dei 36*. The former was called on only to advise on specific matters of government, and the latter convened to elect members who were replaced every two months.²⁷⁵ The Council of

---

273 ASLu, *Carte Mansi*, 19, *Ristretto delle Anime della Città e dello Stato*. In the eighteenth century 11 families had become extinct, leaving the noble families at 88 and the number of adult male aristocrats at just 236. The clergy too was almost entirely composed of aristocrats, who directed their maidens, deprived of the opportunity of marriage for lack of an adequate dowry, and cadets, excluded from the logic of primogeniture and *fideicommissum*, to monastic life. While remembering that even the most powerful families never reached the levels of the aristocracy of Italy and Europe, the government provided honourable and useful offices for the most needy among its members, regardless of whether they had the necessary skills to exercise them. The fees were notoriously modest, but the less honourable deputies were nevertheless able to profit from the proceeds, tax revenues and other public incomes. See Antonio Mazzarosa, *Storia di Lucca dalla Sua origine al MDCCCXIV* (Lucca, 1833).

274 Fazzi, *La società lucchese del Seicento*, p.98: 'The population consisted of mild commoners and a small bourgeoisie. The quietness of the populace can be attributed to at least three elements: the focus on satisfying the material needs of the inhabitants, *a conditio sine qua non* for the preservation of the quietness of the state; the total absence of schools, a determining element of the widespread ignorance and disinterest in public affairs; the continuous vigilance implemented through the Magistrate of Secretaries (a kind of police minister) and the practice of *discolato* (compulsory military service as punishment). In addition, a large portion of the population lived as servants, in the houses of the nobility or had economic relations with them, while an equally large proportion held public office.'

275 *Ibid.*, p.102. The Council of Elders, composed of nine councillors, formed by three nobles from each *terziere* (district) of the city: San Salvatore; San Paolino; San Martino, and the *Gonfaloniere*, which held the executive function.

Elders appointed delegations, ambassadors, envoys and secretaries with licences and instructions for access to foreign courts. Their activities were supervised by the *cancelliere maggiore*. General affairs were taken care of by eight magistracies or *Offizi* (offices), whose tasks included the care of trade relations with other states and more generally public order, justice, religion, borders, health and defence. As representatives of the central power, the government appointed commissioners who had both political and juridical functions in the vicariates. They directly depended on the Elders and the Major Chancellor, but also corresponded directly with other offices.

Matters concerning the military apparatus were also regulated by specific magistracies. One of these was the *Offizio sopra la Buona Guardia*. The birth of this institution dates back to 1432, and in the mid seventeenth century it continued to administer the Republic's standing force. The organisational framework of Lucca's military structure was completed by the *Offizio sopra le Munizioni di Cortile*, which was responsible for the purchase of weapons, their maintenance and storage in the arsenals. Both these offices had their own commissioners to control the number of infantrymen and artillerymen with monthly musters.

The authorities showed their preoccupation with living in a situation of constant threat from their neighbours, and were always suspicious of the designs being prepared across the border. Lucca, it was said, 'lived like the turtle-dove next to the buzzard'.[276] The tension caused unexpected incidents. In 1642, fireworks on the occasion of a visit by a Tuscan prince to the communities near the border were mistaken for cannon shots, causing panic in the countryside. The town bells rang out for the militia and everything was prepared to defend Lucca from a siege that did not happen. Though Lucca managed to avoid any military involvement, the government allowed the friendly Republic of Venice to recruit volunteers. In 1645 Lucca released licenses to recruit 1,000 men, and in the last two years of the Cretan War sent 50,000 lb of gunpowder to Candia.[277] In 1672 Lucca offered substantial help to Genoa during the war against Savoy-Piedmont with recruits, weapons and ammunition.

Apart from Lucca there were no fortified places worthy of note. Gualdo Priorato, in his *Relatione*, enthusiastically praised the city's fortifications, calling Lucca 'one of the safest place in Italy'. He emphasised the presence of 11 strong bastions and underlined the thickness of the walls, which he considered remarkable.[278] He describes the quarter for troops and officers located at the gates of San Pietro, Santa Maria, San Paolino and San Donato. Foreigners were allowed to enter through San Pietro without firearms and only with swords if with the permission of the city authorities. He noticed that the garrison was composed of soldiers paid by the government.

---

276 Carlo Minutoli and Gerolamo Tommasi, *Sommario della Storia di Lucca* (Lucca, 1878), p.561.
277 ASLu, *Deputazione sopra le Milizie*, f. 244, c. 93, *Leva di truppe per Venezia*.
278 Galeazzo Gualdo Priorato, *Relatione della Signoria di Luca e suo Dominio* (Cologne, 1668), p.2.

Standing Forces

In 1664 the stable garrison of Lucca numbered 396 professional soldiers, including 71 officers and NCOs. Of this modest force, 109 men formed the corps guarding the city gates and the other 287 were stationed on the ramparts. The corps of the *bombardieri* numbered 291 men. Further professional soldiers formed the garrisons – more properly posts of observation – in Castiglione di Garfagnana, Viareggio, Camajore and Montignoso. While the infantry depended on the *Offizio sopra la Buona Guardia*, the artillery depended on the *Offizio sopra le Munizioni di Cortile*. Despite their small number, these troops represented the main expenditure of the State, amounting to 24,000 *scudi* annually.[279]

This strength varied little in the following decades. To ensure that this money was well spent, the government had established a severe selection process for recruits. To enter the permanent troop, candidates had to prove that they were healthy and able to handle musket, powder flask, ammunition, and sword. Available documents enable research that shows almost all candidates were natives of the Republic.[280]

By the 1660s the infantry comprised only musketeers, since pikemen were considered of poor utility in defensive warfare, however, the arsenals stored polearms such as spontoons, *corsesche* and forks. The surveillance service on the walls of Lucca was entrusted to the *ronda*, which consisted of 15 men: a standard bearer, a sergeant, four *lance spezzate* and nine private soldiers.[281] Every night a patrol inspected all the guards, checking that everything was regular.

As time went by, however, military service had become an employment for life, and therefore there were soldiers with more than 30 years of service often spent as a sentry on the same city gate or bastion. Moreover, to compensate for the very low salary, soldiers with families were allowed to earn additional income from other jobs. This resulted in a service that was judged to be very poor, as witnessed by the numerous complaints of the *Offizio*'s commissioners. On several occasions the government had addressed the problem by analysing the causes. According to some senators the excessively low pay only attracted the elderly, children 'and the strangling people who cannot move … and it is a pity to see under what eyes the city sleeps.'[282] In the following years the government tried to remedy the situation by increasing the number of soldiers and retiring the aged and unable soldiers, but periodically the problem came up again, a sign that the remedies had been ineffective. In 1671 the commander of the city garrison informed the authorities about the critical situation. As for the proposal for a new increase in the number of troops, he replied that the problem lay elsewhere and that it was the condition of these men, 'who of soldiers have only the name', and the low salary was the real cause of poor

---

279 ASLu, *Camarlingo Generale*, n. 66.
280 *Ibid*.
281 *Ibid*. To obtain the rank of *lancia spezzata* it was necessary to have served in war with the rank of corporal or to be a citizen of Lucca 'capable of the honours'.
282 *Ibid.*, *Uffizio Sopra la Buona Guardia*, *Relationi*, ff. 22–23, October 1671.

MEDIUM AND MINOR POWERS

60. The painting by Gerolamo Scaglia is a valuable source concerning dress and equipment of Lucca's garrison in the 1660s. Here is portrayed the captain of the artillery company. He wears black broad-brimmed headgear with red and white plumes, a leather coat over dark grey underclothes, red sash with silver fringes, carmine red breeches and grey stockings under white ones. This clothing complies with the first half of the 1660s, however the wide shirt collar is definitely out of fashion.

61. Artillery firing from a rampart of Lucca in 1664, detail after the painting of Gerolamo Scaglia, preserved in the church of Santi Paolino e Donato. A particularly serious event served as a pretext for the government of Lucca to reorganise the artillery. It took place on the occasion of the feast of San Paolino, the patron of Lucca. On 12 July, as every year, the feast was celebrated with a *gazzarra* which consisted of firing blanks with the artillery of the bastion of Porta San Donato. The event also attracted the population of the surrounding area, who gathered near the gate, while on the walls other people flocked, also wearing masked clothing. In 1664 it happened that instead of firing blanks, one of the cannons fired actual projectiles at the civilians outside the walls. Fortunately the firing caused no injuries and apart from the pierced clothes of some of the presents, there was only a great fright. The escaped danger was interpreted as a miracle of the saint, but at the same time persuaded the government to investigate the incredible negligence. Two artillerymen, identified as those who had loaded the cannon, were expelled from the corps, while all the others were subjected to a new selection to assess their knowledge. A month later, as a sign of gratitude for the escaped danger, a new *gazzarra* was set up at the same place and this time, to avoid any danger, the commander ordered that only the light pieces, called *i nani* (dwarfs), be loaded with blanks. According to the instructions received, all the guns were washed and inspected, and finally loaded with only two pounds of powder to avoid any risk. But at the moment of firing a spark fell on the barrel containing the powder, which immediately exploded, enveloping the entire bastion in a thick black cloud. When the smoke began to clear, once again it turned out that there had been no casualties and everything had been resolved with a few scratches and burns. Only one artilleryman, hit by the flames, was wounded in the head, risking loss of an eye, but considering the seriousness of the incident he could still count himself lucky, because in everyone's opinion the explosion could have incinerated him. Once again, for the people of Lucca, 'San Paolino' had protected the city.

MEDIUM AND MINOR POWERS

62. Another detail from Gerolamo Scaglia's painting shows a group of artillerymen of Lucca in 1664. The elderly officer on the left with the white hair is probably Filippo Stiavacci, then 75 years old, and a well-known figure of the artillery company, having served with the rank of adjutant since 1641.

63. Although conducting a policy of neutrality, the Lucchese aristocracy boasted strong relations with the major European powers, especially with Vienna and Madrid, and also with the Order of Malta. This painting portrays the knight *Fra'* Giuseppe Mansi in the early 1680s. Note the white cross of the Order of St John fastened at the waist. (Private collection)

service. 'These soldiers', the officer continued, 'perform guard duty very badly, tired from the manual exertions of the day, and pretend to take service without a sword and when they want.'[283]

It was a similar picture regarding the other professional standing force, the artillery. Although the gunners were specialists, and admission to the corps required a selection process that included tests in arithmetic and ballistics, by mid century they were described as 'a bilge of all vices'. From time to time, the government had introduced measures that on paper seemed to be able to remedy the shortcomings, but once implemented proved inadequate to repair them. The regulation issued by the government in 1555 established that the permanent force should consist of 100 *patentati* (examined) bombardiers, who were assigned a variable number of assistants and artisans. However, due to low pay and particularly harsh conditions of service, 20 years later the number had fallen to only 40 men.[284] In the next century the government offered higher salaries and tried to improve service conditions, which increased the number of *bombardieri* to 250 men. However, this was due not so much to government reforms, but mainly to worsening economic conditions. Therefore, in Lucca even the employment of artillerymen became a solution that today is called a 'social policy support measure'. Inevitably, control over the requirements to enter the corps became less rigorous and the examination of aspirant *bombardiere* turned into a formality. In addition to this, the need to save money caused a sharp drop in training sessions, and as a result there were gunners who had never had a drill worthy of the name for months or even years.

The report sent to the General Council in 1655 described a dramatic scenario, claiming that there were now 'more *bombardieri* in name than in fact'. Two years later the situation was the same, at least judging by the tone of the report, which stated that 'among the artillerymen there are people of very low status and that most of the time they are either on trial or in custody'. The situation was so bad that when it was necessary to assemble 18 or 20 gunners and assistants, barely six or seven could be put together because the others were in jail or could not be found. The most frequent complaints against the artillerymen concerned the stealing of powder to sell it illegally.

---

283 *Ibid*.

284 *Ibid*., The service on the ramparts was carried out in all seasons and even in rainy weather, so canopies were built to shelter the cannon batteries. However, in winter there were no adequate shelters and this made the tasks assigned to the artillerymen particularly undesirable.

In 1651 the Commissioner of the *Offizio* declared that adulterated powder had been found and consequently the cannon charges were unserviceable. In some cases the powder had been replaced with sand, while in other batteries it had been allowed to deteriorate, namely unsuitable powder had been retained in order to illegally speculate with newer powder. Officers and the Commissioner asked the government to intervene in order to remedy a pitiful situation that appeared irreversible. Using an incident that occurred on 12 July 1664 as a pretext, the government took drastic measures to restore discipline within the corps. One of the decisions taken was to subject all personnel to a new selection process, thus reducing the force to 225 salaried artillerymen under a *capitano* and an *aiutante* as officers. The repressive measures were followed by other initiatives to promote the efficiency of the service. Accepting a proposal from the officers, the General Council ordered regular training so that the service of artillerymen would not depend on luck, but knowledge.[285] At the same session, in order to achieve an improvement in discipline, the government granted the commander the power to arrest and imprison corps members, including non-commissioned officers.

The government also had a palace guard, composed until 1653 of young nobles, even exiles, as long as they were not from Tuscany, and from then on recruited only from Swiss Catholics in the canton of Lucerne.[286] In 1668 they were 90 men with one captain, one lieutenant, one ensign, one sergeant, one *cancelliere*, one chaplain and four corporals.[287]

Militia

The territory of Lucca was divided into three military areas: the city of Lucca; the *Sei Miglia* (Six Miles), namely the hilly belt around the city; and the *Vicariati*, the territories located on one side facing the sea, those to the north in the Garfagnana, and the others to the east and south along the course of the Serchio River. From an administrative point of view Lucca and the *Sei Miglia* were a single body, while the remaining part of the territory was divided into 14 vicariates.[288] The city militia and the militia of the Six Miles were divided into three *terzieri*, corresponding to the city districts, namely San Paolino, San Salvatore, and San Martino. This manpower was collectively called the *comandate*. In the event of an alarm, by means of signal fires lit on the city's highest tower, all militia members living inside and outside Lucca rushed to their *gonfaloni* (companies). According to Gualdo Priorato, 20,000 'well-disciplined militiamen' could be gathered in this way, forming 12 'regiments' complete with their field officers. To face a siege, there were inside Lucca arsenals capable of arming 30,000 men, and enough supplies to last one year.[289]

---

285 Carla Martinelli, *Il Miracolo di San Paolino. 12 luglio 1664* (Lucca: Pacini Fazzi, 1988), pp.80–83.
286 *Capitolatione, obligi e decreti per la compagnia svizzera del cantone di Lucerna destinata alla Guardia del palazzo dell'eccellentissimi signori Antiani* (Lucca, 1666), pp.1–20.
287 Gualdo Priorato, *Relatione della Signoria di Luca*, p.14.
288 The vicaries were Villa Basilica, Bagno, Borgo, Coreglia, Compito, Pescaglia, Castiglione, Gallicano, Minucciano, Montignoso, Capannori, Nozzano, Camaiore and Viareggio.
289 Gualdo Priorato, *Relatione della Signoria di Luca*, pp.15–16.

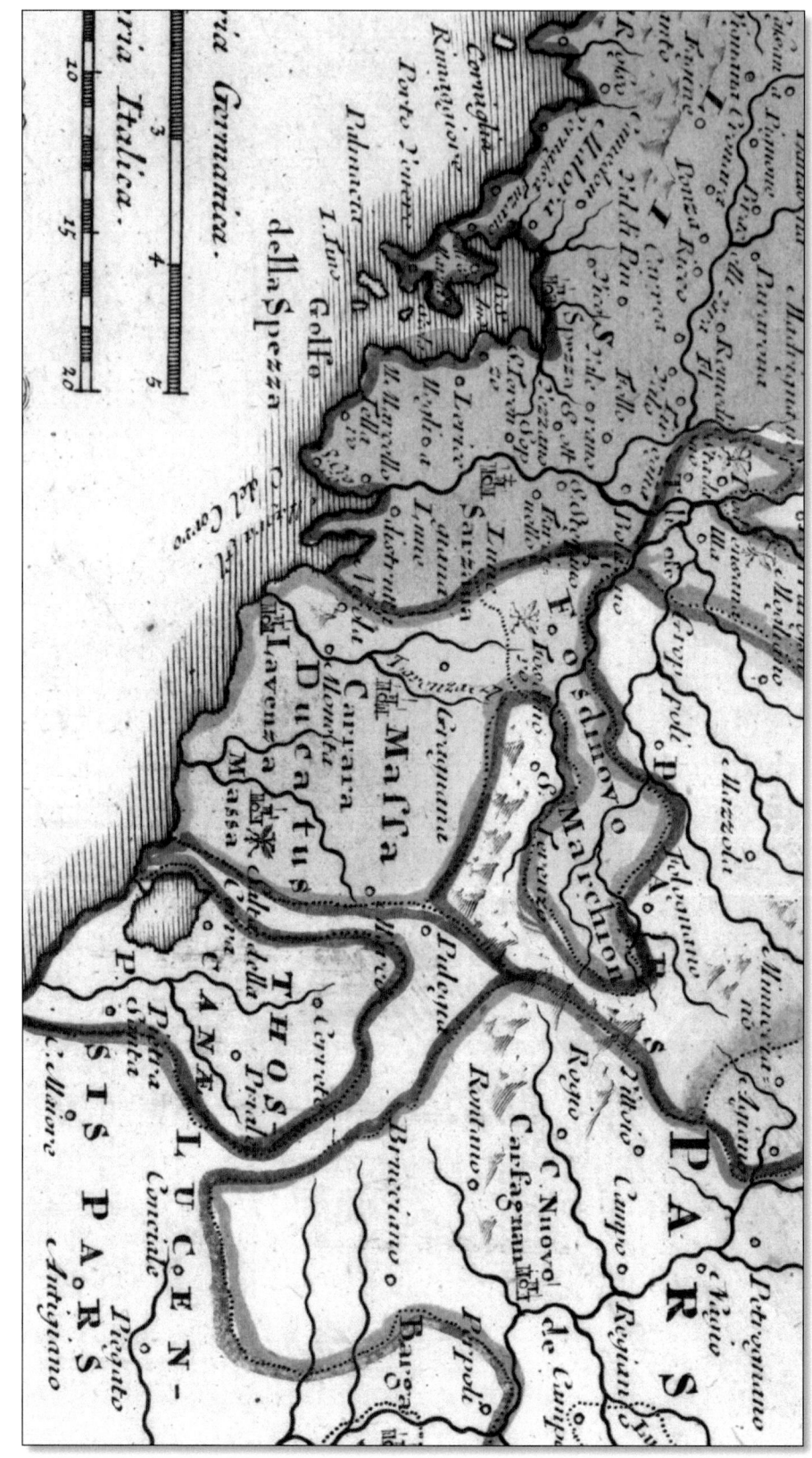

64. Map of the Marquisate of Fosdinovo, in Lunigiana (today modern Tuscany), detail from the map of Johann Baptist Homann's *Status Republicae Genuensis* (1715–30). The Marquisate was one of the many fiefs ruled by the Malaspina families. Relations between the members of the various branches were maintained on a level of formal cordiality, but despite the reduced ambitions of these lordships, local feuds and conflicts also occurred. In 1682 Marquis Federico Malaspina of Ponte Bosio disputed with Malaspina of Podenzana some properties in the nearby fief of Monti, and the use of the waters of the Tavarone stream, leading to bloody encounters between their subjects. Through the Tuscan governatore delle armi of the Lunigiana, whom the two families turned to for arbitration by Grand Duke Cosimo III, peace was restored. Shortly afterwards the warlike Marquis of Ponte Bosio came into conflict with the Malaspina of Suvero, once again over the exercise of feudal rights over Monti.

Duchy of Massa and Principality of Carrara

The little *signoria* of the Lunigiana was ruled since 1546 by the family Cybo-Malaspina.[290] The 'personal union' comprised the Principality of Massa and the Marquisate of Carrara. Further Malaspina branches and other sovereigns ruled as the Empire's immediate princes in 13 small lordships, which formed enclaves within the Duchy territory in a very intricate pattern. In 1664, as part of the House of Austria's renewed strategic interest in Italy, Emperor Leopold I raised Massa to the rank of duchy and Carrara to principality.

With a population of about 20,000 persons, the Duchy pursued no expansionist politics, enjoying the incomes from marble extraction and some trade with Genoa and Tuscany, and especially with Modena the export of salt. Set away from the main communication routes, it was considered even then as an almost 'mysterious' place frequented mostly by sculptors who went there on behalf of the pope or other lords to purchase marble for their commissioned works.

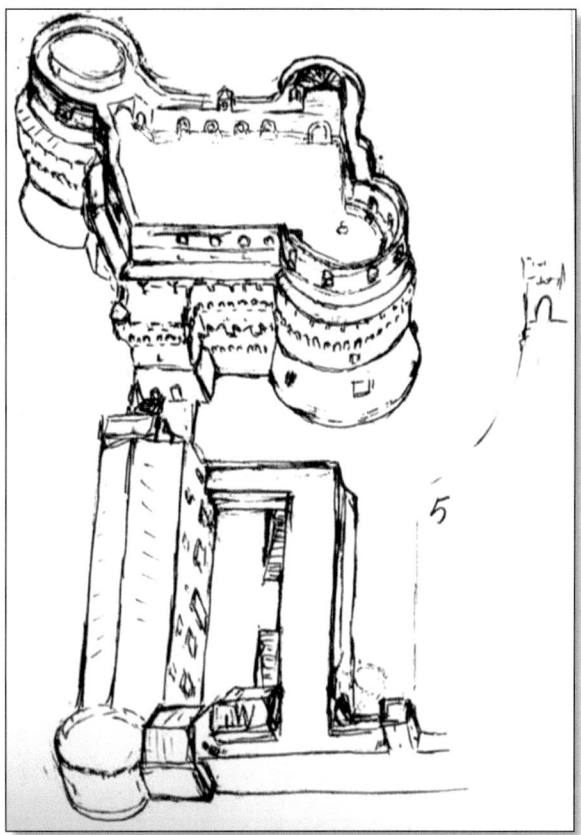

65. The fort of Avenza, in a sketch of the seventeenth century (author's archive). The fort was the only military building of the duchy, which also served as a customs point for the export of marble and station post for the change of horses.

The Duchy had not been in conflict for centuries and had not had a professional military force for a long time, with the exception of a small noble guard employed as a palace corps in the dukes' residences, and a mounted 'company' of 25 *cavalleggeri* for escort duties. According to contemporary estimations, by the end of the century the Duchy had a militia of 3,000 foot and 300 horse.[291] Fortifications dated back to the Middle Ages and gave the state a typical archaic appearance. The most modern fortification was the fort of Avenza, close to the shore. A report from the 1730s describes the state of the stronghold, that must have changed little since the end of the previous century. The fort was 'an ancient tower useful only to detect ships from afar or some troop passing through the surrounding countryside'. The battery numbered 33 cannons, some of which were of iron but with little ammunition, as well as various *spingarde* and muskets mostly unserviceable. The forts was judged to be 'falling down on all sides and capable of offering little defence'.[292]

---

290 Between 1660 and 1690, the rulers of Massa and Carrara were Carlo I (r. 1623–1662), and Alberico II (r. 1662–1690).

291 Gude, *Staat von Parma und Piacenza, Mirandula und Concordia, Massa und Carrara, Monaco, Doria, St. Piedro, Sesto St. Angelo und dei Fieschi*, p.36.

292 ASMo, *Militare Estense*, b. 98.

The Order of Malta

The domains of the Order of the Hospitaller Knights of Saint John were limited to the Maltese archipelago, comprising the islands of Medina and Gozo, and the uninhabited islet of Comino. In addition to these direct domains, the Order benefited from income from possessions in all the countries of the Catholic area. The order also had numerous terminals in Italy and other states consisting of fiefs or individual annuities from religious institutes. For military purposes, the permission to use the Adriatic port of Butrint guaranteed the Knights the supply of timber for the fleet.

The total population rose to approximately 70,000. The steady increase in Malta's population during the Order's rule (1530–1798), halted only by brief and temporary interruptions such as the plague of 1676, coupled with the influx of foreigners to the island's harbours from the four corners of the Mediterranean, helped to attenuate demographic decrease.[293] La Valletta, located on the east coast, was the largest maritime stronghold of the time and its fortifications enjoyed a great reputation, to the point of being considered a model that was difficult to surpass.[294] The city was built on the peninsula of Mount Sceberras stretching between the two inlets of Marsa Grande and Marsa Muscetto, which formed three distinct defensive structures, massively reinforced after the siege of 1556 and during the seventeenth century, inspired by the most up-to-date principles of the *trace italienne*. The central defensive core was located on the Santa Margherita hill, where a fort dominated the entire suburb, called Cospicua, surrounded by a continuous bastioned front known as Linee Margherita. Similarly, the Vittoriosa and Senglea quarters were also defended by a double wall. On the seaward side, access to the two inlets was protected by two forts: Sant' Elmo, completed in 1654, and Ricasoli, built in 1670 on the point of Renella. To the south, defence was entrusted to the forts Sant' Angelo and San Michele, which controlled access to the ports of Renella, Galere and Sanglea, while on the land side defence was entrusted to the fort of Burmola, where the main arsenal was located, and Cottonera. This fortification was located at the base of the Santa Margherita hill and consisted of a large semicircular bastioned curtain wall designed by the architect and engineer Antonio Maurizio Valperga, comprising eight bastions and two half-bastions surrounding the Margherita walls in a semicircle; outside the curtain walls were eight crescents in a large moat, and then the covered road and the ramparts. The works were begun in 1670, in the aftermath of the surrender of Candia, but were interrupted 10 years later for lack of funds. Once completed, Cottonera would form La

---

[293] Joseph Micallef, *The Plague of 1676: 11,300 Deaths* (Malta: self-published, 1985), pp.112–113. The plague of 1676 claimed the lives of around one-sixth of the island's population.

[294] Antonino Lentini, 'Lo sviluppo storico delle fortificazioni maltesi', in *Le misure del castello* (Ferrara: Istituto Italiano dei Castelli, 2006), p.7.

MEDIUM AND MINOR POWERS

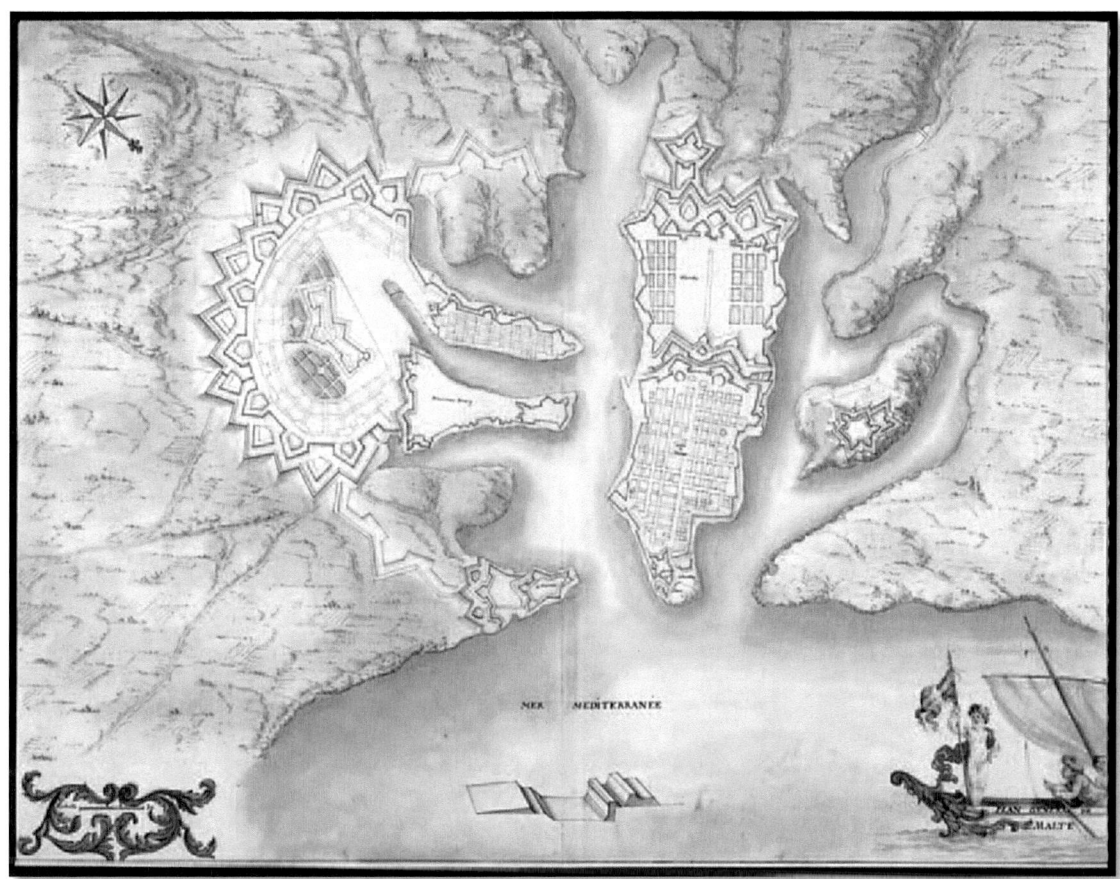

66. The fortifications of La Valletta with the improvement designed by Antonio Maurizio Valperga in the 1670s. (Author's archive)

Valletta's third and most impressive defensive ring.[295] Two other modern works continued on either side of the Cottonera, protecting the inlets of Sanglea and Renella from the landward side and joining Fort Ricasoli.[296] The inlets were also protected by a battery located on the islet opposite Valletta and on the point of Dragut.[297] The old city was surrounded by the Della Genga bastion, protecting the quarters behind the fort of St Elmo. On the rest of the peninsula laid the new quarter, named Floriana after

---

[295] Following the fall of Candia in 1670, the Order feared that the Ottomans were to invade Malta in a final effort to stamp it out. As a result, construction of the new curtains started in August. The new defence, which took the name *Cottonera* after the Grand Master Nicholas Cotoner, had to offer refuge to some 40,000 persons with their farm animals in the case of a siege. According to the contemporary commenters the *Cottonera* was the most ambitious work of fortification ever undertaken by the Order in Malta, and it was also the most expensive. It was only in the mid nineteenth century that the British finally completed the defence, albeit in a different manner than originally conceived, adapting it to the needs of modern warfare. Despite this, the *Cottonera* represents one of the greatest architectural wonders of Malta which unfortunately today remains hugely undervalued.

[296] Lentini, 'Lo sviluppo storico delle fortificazioni maltesi', p.8.

[297] In the following century, the forts of Manoel and Tigné were built on these sites.

67. Maltese knights, after Vincenzo Maria Coronelli's *Ordinum Equestrum ac Militarium Brevis Narratio* (1715). 'With the Habit of a Knight came to be dressed up as a new man.' Thus, according to *Fra' Jean Baptiste le Mariner de Cany*, the garment of a Hospitaller was a profoundly transformative experience. Hospitaller knights are often represented in heroic poses in contemporary paintings that recall the enduring image of the Christian knight.

the architect Pietro Paolo Floriani who had ingeniously fortified it between 1635 and 1636. The archipelago's defence also included 79 coastal towers and castles: 60 on Malta, 16 on Gozo and three on the islet of Comino.

The *Grand Maître* was an elective office for life, and he was chosen among the knights belonging to the eight 'languages' (nations) of the Order. These were Provence, Auvergne, France, Italy, Aragon, England, Germany and Castile. Each language had its own *procuratore* who had a seat on the council. By 1560 the language of England had been suppressed, but the number of procurators remained the same for representing knights who did not come from the other seven nations. Since the order was divided into eight nationalities, each of them was reserved one of the eight offices subordinate to the *Grand Maître*. The language of Provence occupied the first rank as the founding nation of the Order and its representative held the position of Grand Commander, the most important position after the Grand Master. The procurator of Auvergne, in turn, held the title of *Grand Mareschal*, which gave him command of the La Valletta garrison in the absence of the Grand Master. At sea his rank was equivalent to admiral, and he was also appointed as ensign of the marine infantry, to whom he entrusted the great flag of the Order. The language of France assigned its procurator the dignity of Grand Hospitaller, whose tasks were those arising from the care of the sick, tasks that originated from the duty of the Order at the time of its creation. This language comprised three *priorati*: France, Aquitaine and Champagne, and two bailiffs, one of whom took care of the administration as Grand Bailiff Treasurer. The language of Italy also had its own internal subdivision with seven grand priors or *commendatori*: Lombardy, Rome, Venice, Pisa, Capua, Barletta and Messina. The Italian nation also held six bailiffs, one of whom belonged to the Barberini family.[298]

The language of Aragon included the priories of Catalonia, Caspe and Navarre. The procurator of Aragon had the title of *Grand Conservateur*, in charge of overseeing the regularity of the knights' dress, purchases for the troops, their salaries, and equipment, including clothing.[299]

The procurator of the German language had the rank of Grand Bailiff, which extended his authority over all the fortifications of Malta and Gozo.

---

298 M. de Saint-Allais, *L'Ordre de Malte, ses Grand Maîtres et ses Chevaliers* (Paris, 1839), p.159.
299 *Ibid.*, pp.157–159.

The dignity of Grand Bailiff was assigned alternately to a German and a Bohemian knight. In addition to the priories of Germany and Bohemia, there were also those of Dacia, comprising Sweden, Denmark and Norway,[300] and that of Hungary; after 1606, this priory was always assigned to the Grand Bailiff in charge.

The language of Castile had the office of Grand Chancellor, entrusted alternately to the prior of this language and the prior of Portugal. Internally it was divided into three priories: Castile, Leon and Portugal.

The knights were divided into two categories, the *caravanisti*, and the knights residing in Malta. The first lived outside of Malta and participated in privateering actions aboard the Maltese galleys at least once per year. The second group manned the fleet all year long. The order was an international community formed by young Catholic aristocrats. Remarkably, fierce opponents such as the French and the Spanish fought alongside one another within the Order. In spite of the knights' varied languages, there were no differences in rank.

The four military posts were *maréchal*, *turcopoliere*, Grand Bailiff and admiral, usually held by Auvergne, England, Germany and Italy. Between 1596 and 1646 the military offices were reformed in a collegial body, unifying the land offices into a Congregation of War, headed by the Grand Bailiff, and one for the galleys, under the admiral. As commander of the fleet the admiral held 'possession' of the individual galleys of the captains and managed the hotel (residence) of the Italian 'language', which was the most numerous until mid century.[301] Gradually the French replaced the Italians, and in the last decade they represented a third of the Order's knights. However, the office of admiral was long claimed by the Italians and indeed, during the century, 22 of the 54 admirals came from Italy.[302] The post of *turcopoliere*, namely the commander of the light cavalry assigned to coastal surveillance, had disappeared in 1540 with the abolition of the language of England.

The Order had its permanent headquarter, the *Convento*, in La Valletta in charge of the ordinary military affairs for fleet and soldiers. Expenditure was administered by the Common Treasure, which was divided into seven different accounts: galleys, arsenal, biscuit, artillery, grain, invalids, pensions, to which the vessels account was added at the end of the century. Expenditure was managed by the two congregations through specific offices, called coffers and prodromes, directed by the respective commanders. There was an autonomous chapter of expenditure for the Grand Master's galley and

---

300 The term 'Dacia' originally represented Transylvania, Moldavia and Wallachia, but in the fifteenth century it was expanded to include the Scandinavian countries.

301 It is significant that admissions to the Order of Malta show a constant increase of Italian knights, both in absolute terms and in relation to other nationalities. As for the areas of origin, the supremacy belonged to the subjects of the Grand Duchy of Tuscany, followed by the Savoy-Piedmontese, Milanese, Neapolitans and Sicilians, Pontificals, and finally Venetians. See also Claudio Donati (ed.), *Eserciti e carriere militari nell'Italia moderna* (Milan: Unicopli, 1998), p.21.

302 Saint-Allais, *L'Ordre de Malte*, pp.158–159.

68. Nicolás Cotoner (1608–1680), the Catalan Grand Master of the Order who gave the name to fortification surrounding the Santa Margerita hill at La Valletta (author's archive). A strategist and a diplomat, he greatly increased the prestige of the order. In 1674 he funded in Malta a school of anatomy and medicine as an annex of the Sacra Infermeria. In the same year Cotoner drew up – in Italian – the constitutions and statutes of the order.

for the periodic renewal of the hulls, managed by the grand conservators of the galleys.

A constant concern of the Order was how find enough men for its military needs. Its gradual transformation into a military organisation committed to war against Islam compelled it to live in a state of official or undeclared warfare for hundreds of years, with the consequent need to find soldiers, shipbuilders, crews, and oarsmen. The gradual infrastructural and economic boost that the Hospitallers began to give to their 'military' resulted in a considerable growth that, combined with their chivalric ethos and maritime vocation, increased the demand for labour.[303]

News or rumours of raids by Muslim corsairs created even more pressing worries for the archipelago's administration. Gozo, smaller and more vulnerable than Malta, had to be garrisoned and reinforced whenever the *Convento* – the Order's headquarters – received more or less reliable information that the sister island was at risk of attack by Ottoman or Barbary forces.

Despite this demographic increase, however, the Order could never really stop relying on the voluntary or forced influx of healthy adult labourers through its seafaring activity. Their self-imposed religious and military mission compelled the knights to act as predators in a Mediterranean Sea at war and participate in concerted campaigns against the infidel. At one point, in 1620, the Order had to come to terms with rumours emanating from Rome that its galley squadron was also recruiting heretics (Protestants) as soldiers, a rather embarrassing accusation to direct at a Catholic State in Counter-Reformation Europe whose destiny was so reliant on Papal endorsement.[304]

The Order's systematic aid to Venice in the long Cretan War is emblematic in the periodic strain that that conflict exerted on the Hospitallers' manpower resources. The Order had to recruit sailors, oarsmen and soldiers for its fleet of galleys for the seasonal campaigns in the *Levante*, thus increasing the vulnerability of its island seat due to the displacement of the fleet and soldiers for months on end. Since 1645, waiting in the eastern Sicilian port of Augusta to

---

[303] Ivan Grech, 'Dealing with Manpower Shortages in the Mediterranean: the Order of St. John's Labour Force problems during the Long Seventeenth Century', in C. Vassallo and S. Mercieca (eds), *The Port of Malta* (Malta, 2018), p.77: 'In 1552, Sicilians were brought to work on the island's fortifications and, in the immediate years following the siege of 1565, an increase in migration to Sicily and internal population displacements towards urban centres left patches of rural areas depopulated.' The problem could be even more acute in Gozo, the smaller island of the archipelago, where the adult male population was often insufficient for the military infrastructural work dictated by the state of constant war. In 1601 workers had to be sent over from Malta to Gozo to work on the fortress walls overlooking the small harbour of Mġarr, and the governor of the island was given the authority to recruit foreigners to make up the necessary numbers on the construction sites. See Alison Hoppen, *The Fortification of Malta by the Order of St. John, 1530–1798* (Edinburgh: Scottish Academic Press, 1979), p.137.

[304] *Ibid.*, p.82: 'In the second half of the seventeenth century, Protestants from Hungary did end up on Catholic galleys, but as convict crews (*forzati*, convicts condemned to hard labour) and, in any case, Spain could easily afford to ignore any potential remonstrance directed at its behaviour from Rome.'

69. Another portrait of Giuseppe Mansi from Lucca, here wearing the full dress of a Maltese knight (private collection). The red-white livery pattern of Malta was also used by the Tuscan order of St Stephen, differing only in the nuance of the red: carmine for Malta, and vermillion for Tuscany.

be joined by the Papal galleys before sailing east could keep the Hospitaller squadron idle for a month, in the meantime more sailors would be sent over from Malta to bolster the crews.[305] Once in the Cretan War the infantry battalion on occasions numbered between 300 and 400 soldiers, including more than 60 knights, would be left behind at the expense of the Order's treasury for up to eight months; if necessary, galleys plying the Mediterranean under the Order's flag were briefed to relocate their efforts to aid the Venetian fleet.[306] The ensuing casualties, temporary or permanent, were inevitable. In June 1669, the last year of the war, it was reported that up to the early days of that month 17 knights and 142 Maltese soldiers had lost their lives fighting inside besieged Candia, while many others had ended up injured or infirm, stimulating the Order's sense of paternal solidarity into providing one *scudo* a month and four bread loaves a day to the widows of the deceased for the rest of their lives.[307]

Since the beginning of the Cretan War in 1645, the plausibility of another serious Ottoman attempt at an invasion was a nightmare for the Hospitallers. Following insistent rumours of naval preparations specifically directed against Malta, the danger resurfaced with dramatic urgency as the fall of Crete appeared to be approaching fast. In Malta the Order's satisfaction must have been great when, in 1650, the Ottomans did not resume the siege of Candia after the two massive assaults of 1648–49. Although the danger appeared less imminent, Malta did not cease to support the Venetian war effort, and during the 24 years of war the Order sent the fleet with marine infantry and knights on board in 13 campaigns: six galleys until 1647 and then seven from 1656.[308] Grand Master Nicholas Cotoner, whose magistracy covered the last six years of the war and was therefore in a position to assess its overall impact and predict possible consequences, made sure his complaints and concerns regarding the conflict's repercussions on Malta were heard from Sicily to Savoy. He made it clear in his official writings that Candia had cost the Order and Malta troops, supplies, munitions, and galleys, forcing the Hospital to stretch its human, technical, and financial resources to dangerous limits at a time when it was a justifiable fear that the Porte, if Candia were taken, would direct all its energies west,

---

305 AOM 1443, Nicholas Cotoner to General Del Bene in Augusta, dated 24 May 1667, ff. 42–43.
306 Grech, 'Dealing with Manpower Shortages', p.79.
307 AOM 1444, dated 25 June 1669, Nicholas Cotoner to Receiver Gherardi, f. 92.
308 Mugnai, *The Cretan War*, p.141. In comparison, the Pope sent his galleys on campaigns 10 times up to a maximum of five ships; the Grand Duke of Tuscany sent his five-galley squadron in 1645, then only two galleys in 1659 and three in 1660.

and attempt another full-scale invasion of Malta.[309] In the summer of 1667 the perception was that the Ottomans wanted to conclude the Candia affair in order to turn their attention to Malta.[310] The following year the Order was restocking its arsenal with munitions in preparation for an eventual siege, and in the early months of 1669 it looked increasingly evident that Candia's fall was imminent.[311] In a propagandist invocation in favour of his Order's devotion to the Catholic cause, and denouncing what in March 1669 already seemed an inevitable defeat, Grand Master Nicholas Cotoner stated that the timely remanning of his island post in case of an enemy attack would undoubtedly be one of the Order's most pressing tasks.[312]

The sinister presages evoked by Cotoner did not come true, but the problem of manpower came up again in 1684, when the Order joined the Holy League called by the Pope for a new war against the Porte. Apart from paid sailors, galleys needed a permanent complement of oarsmen. On the Order's galley, as on those of the Tuscan Order of St Stephen, oarsmen were mainly composed of slaves, while *buonavoglie* (men who served at sea to pay off their debts or as a salaried workforce), and *forzati* were few.[313] This partly solved the problem of finding oarsmen, but sailors and soldiers continued to be critical issues for the Order. The use of mercenaries was not very popular in Malta, both for economic reasons and because of the lack of trust for this type of troops. In this regard, there were bitter memories. The Order's contemporary chronicler Bartolomeo Dal Pozzo, in his rendering of the last days of the siege

---

309 Grech, 'Dealing with Manpower Shortages', pp.79-80: 'Cotoner emphasized the difficulties of replacing the troops lost or maimed in Candia. He voiced his irritation at the inquisitor's insistence on behalf of the papacy for the Order to keep sending troops to the Levant and expressed his frustration to the Sicilian viceroy that the knights' example and dedication in sustaining the Catholic mission was not being sufficiently emulated by the other European princes who, according to the Grand Master, were lukewarm in translating their confessional commitment to practical collaboration with Venice.'

310 *Ibid.*, p.80.

311 AOM 1444, Nicholas Cotoner to Ambassador Verospi, dated 10 March 1669, ff. 29-30: 'And it must also be considered that this is not a place to be depopulated by the people of arms: Those who were sent to Crete have left, of whom very few will return, and if more were to leave, we do not know who will be able to guard these walls if they are attacked by the enemy, as we are not without thought that the war will be over, which could happen very soon … and it is certain that in the island there is much less than half the number that would be needed, and for the order to send the galleys this year to the Levant armed with the usual number of soldiers is not insignificant, because many of those who were sent to Crete were removed from the armament of the galleys, and we will need no small amount of work to find the usual number to fill them. This [Malta] then is not a place where one can find people so easily, as someone may think; on the contrary, everyone was amazed that we could find those who were sent to Crete.'

312 In 1669 an anonymous report written from Constantinople urged Pope Innocent X to free the prisoners and even to call the bandits to arms to strengthen the ranks of the Order to relieve Candia. See Paolo Piccolomini, 'Corrispondenza tra la Corte di Roma e l'Inquisitore di Malta durante la Guerra di Candia (1645–69)', in *Archivio Storico Italiano*, n. 41 (1908), pp.120-124.

313 Lo Basso, *Uomini da remo*, pp.232–236.

70. *Fra'* Bartolomeo Varisano-Grimaldi di Castrogiovanni (1626–1682), a Sicilian knight who served Venice and the Maltese Order between 1669 and 1681, portrayed as *cavaliere di Gran Croce* (author's archive). See image commentaries for more information.

of Candia, records how the Order had to lend funds to the captain general for the payment of the troops in order to avoid defections to the Ottoman side.[314]

For Venice, Malta was certainly the most redoubtable ally. Their small but highly effective fleet, proverbial courage, and especially their landing infantry, earned the Hospitallers a reputation as an elite force able to prevail against any opponent. Their equally proverbial pride, however, represented their downside. They unhesitatingly resorted to any means necessary to assert their precedence in the division of the spoils, in all matters related to protocol formalities, and the recognition of their dignity. The war's history is dotted with countless episodes of rivalries between the Maltese knights and other auxiliaries, sometimes even the Venetians. Additionally, the rules of the Order forbade the fleet, thus the landing infantry, to remain in campaign beyond September. This restriction sometimes meant the cancellation of military plans.

The war against the Ottomans served as a pretext to mobilise all the members. However, the Order never interrupted its corsair activities even in peacetime, and justified them as a direct retaliation against the North African pirates. Additionally, the knights began to operate against the Ottomans by May 1683 near Castelrosso (today Kastellorizon) and Hierapetra on the southern coast of Crete in the following June. Mobilising these knights required monastic orders to accommodate the *caravanisti*, who travelled to Hungary to participate as volunteers against the Ottomans.[315]

Venice's accession to the Holy League mobilised the order on its traditional front: the eastern Mediterranean. In 1684 the Maltese began their campaigns with a number of solitary actions on the North African coast. The war against the Porte represented a significant opportunity to gain spoils of war proportionately distributed among the allies, and such proceeds could materialise through prisoner ransoms and especially the slave market. During the 1684–99 war, estimates suggest that the Knights of Malta alone deported

---

314 Bartolomeo Dal Pozzo, *Historia della S..Religione Militare di San Giovanni Gerosolimitano dettà di Malta* (Venice, 1715), pp.367–368. The author also laments how the Order's troops were depleted by disease owing to gangrene and what he calls 'bad air', which were causing more damage than the Ottomans themselves, so much so that at one stage the battalion from Malta was even exempted from doing guard duty.

315 The Council granted each knight who had recruited 100 men at their own expense and fought in the war for a year a promotion to galley commander; see Dal Pozzo: *Historia della Sacra Religione di San Giovanni*, p.496.

no less than 18,000 Muslim civilians as slaves.[316] Indeed, considering the captive population in the *bagni* of Livorno in the same period, the size of the market for men and women was significant and profitable.[317]

In preparation for their campaign alongside the Venetian fleet and other auxiliaries, the Order increased its galley battalion to 900 soldiers: 'chosen among all people capable of being employed in any actions on sea and land'.[318] Like the Knights, the infantry comprised a mix of nationalities. The Order enlisted soldiers among the Knights' servants and through many pre-existing supply channels for recruits. Duration of service varied according to the capitulations granted, and the prospect of getting rich from the Order's corsair activities encouraged continued service. However, in the first months of 1684, to complete the companies the Council voted to levy 300 recruits from the island.[319] A knight of Auvergne, Michel de Saint-Julien Saint Marc, commanded the regiment, leading the Maltese infantrymen in the conquest of Santa Maura and Preveza alongside the Venetians. The following year, however, the regiment was reformed to 800 men and divided into 16 musketeer companies with another autonomous grenadier company embarked on the Maltese flagship. Campaign reports often record protests related to the position of honour and prerogatives for greetings between the fleets. In the spring of 1685 the Knights refused to cede the right side to the Tuscan fleet; as a result, Admiral Guidi refused to participate in the council of war. Morosini tried to settle the matter and restore harmony between the allies, but eventually Papal diplomacy was required.[320]

After the first regiment's commander fell ill another knight of Auvergne, Hector la Fay, Count La Tour-Mauburg, replaced him. This new officer soon became popular and distinguished himself in all actions of the 1685 campaign – not only for courage, but also for his generosity towards the soldiers and his attention to the sick and wounded, 'sustaining them in large numbers at his expense'. The brave commander led the decisive assault during the siege of Corone but was mortally wounded in the leg. His passing filled the allied command with dismay. Chevalier de La Barre, the French lieutenant of la Tour-Mauburg, who proved to be no less brave than his predecessor, took the command. The Maltese contingent paid a particularly high price in the 1685 campaign, claiming 150 killed and wounded at the

---

316 See Ordine di Malta: *Sovrano Ordine dei Cavalieri di San Giovanni di Gerusalemme*, cap. XIV (Roma, 1954).

317 At the end of the seventeenth century the largest Muslim community in Italy lived under slavery in the *bagni* in Livorno. They were used as privately rented labour by the Grand Duke through the Knights of St Stephen; see Jean Pierre Filippini, *Il Porto di Livorno e la Toscana* (Naples: Edizioni Scientifiche Italiane, 1998), p.158.

318 Dal Pozzo: *Historia della Sacra Religione di San Giovanni*, p.498.

319 Dal Pozzo: *Historia della Sacra Religione di San Giovanni*, p.496.

320 The compromise allowed the Maltese to maintain the position of honour and the right to receive the first greeting, while the Tuscans 'honourably' formed the vanguard army; Dal Pozzo, *Historia della S..Religione Militare di San Giovanni*, p.516. Other conflicts occurred in the following years, this time also involving the Milanese officers.

71. The Maltese contingent at the siege of Modone, 1686, after the Manfroni Manuscript. The knights are recognisable by the white cross on the red tunic, while the infantrymen are uniformed in green with red facing. Note the infantry weaponry consisting only of muskets.

siege of Corone alone, and another 60 died upon their return to Malta. For the Knights' part, the conquest of the enemy fortress cost 13 casualties. Even higher losses incurred the following year during the Siege of Napoli di Romania (Nafplio). Afterwards, the regiment could only deploy 350 soldiers and 38 knights, a mere fraction of the 900 soldiers and 112 knights who left Malta four months before. Count Claude François de Méchatein, again from Auvergne, commanded the infantry during this campaign, with La Barre as his second in command. A levy of 400 Maltese islanders reconstituted the companies. These recruits were divided into 18 companies and embarked on the galleys and *tartanes* of the Order's fleet.[321] Numbering 10 captains, the French company commanders confirmed their prevalence in the officer corps, followed by five Italian, two Spanish, and one German.[322]

The Maltese landed in Patras and Lepanto during the campaign of 1687. The risk of epidemics compelled the allied command to allocate the auxiliary and Maltese troops to Dalmatia and Albania. Here, two battalions under the captains de' Marevile and Lusignano, further distinguished themselves alongside the knights at the Siege of Castelnuovo. The following year the Maltese infantrymen fought with their usual valour at Negroponte but lost 24 knights and a further 400 infantrymen among the dead, wounded, and sick. The regiment participated

---

321 The *tartane* was a lateen-rigged, single-masted ship used in the Mediterranean.

322 Dal Pozzo, *Historia della S..Religione Militare di San Giovanni*, p.680. The Italian knights were Carlo Caraffa, Mario Fondodari, Giovanni Battista Faella, Paolo Peruzzi, and Francesco Ventura-Saracini.

in all subsequent campaigns as landing infantry, sometimes even independent from the rest of the Allied fleet. The Maltese fought again at Malvasia in 1689 and 1690, then in Albania in 1691, Chaniá in 1692, and Chios in 1694. The negative outcome of the last campaigns ended the major actions of the Maltese infantry and the fleet.

The Republic of Messina

In the mid seventeenth century Messina was a wealthy city populated by 150,000 persons. It enjoyed significant autonomy, and considered itself a Republic under the protection of the King of Spain. Since the Middle Ages the city had been granted fiscal privileges, and the inhabitants were exempted from military service and recruitment. Spain maintained its authority through the captain general appointed by the king, who retained the medieval denomination of *stratigoto*. The city council was dominated by a few patrician families, who had strong ties with the bourgeoisie and common people thanks to the favourable economic trend. In 1663 the Spanish government had granted Messina the monopoly on the export of silk, but after strong protests from other Sicilian ports, Madrid withdrew the concession the next year. There were no immediate disturbances, but the nobility and upper bourgeoisie of the city became increasingly hostile to Spain. The Spanish *stratigoto* Luis de Hojo conceived the plan of turning the common people against the upper classes through a display of charity and devotion, and through planning an artificial shortage of food for which the senate of the city would be blamed.[323] As a result the artisans threw out the patricians in 1672, but did not dispute Spanish rule. Two parties emerged, the *Malvezzi* and the *Merli*, which inaugurated a bitter struggle.[324] The Prince de Ligne, Viceroy of Sicily, was alarmed by the disturbances, and had Hojo removed. When the disorders continued and there was talk of using force against the rebels, Ligne also resigned.

On 7 July 1674, new disorders involved the parties in a violent fight. The *Malvezzi* outnumbered the *Merli* by 20,000, routed them and seized most of the city.[325] News of the revolt reached Palermo from where the governor, Francisco Bazán de Bonavides, Marquis of Bajona, moved with some troops.

---

323 Carlo Botta, *Storia d'Italia continuata da quella del Guicciardini*, vols VII–VIII (Paris, 1853), Libro VII, p.228.

324 *Ibid.*, p.232: 'These two opposing parties did in Messina what the Guelphs and Ghibellines had done in Italy, the Blacks and Whites in Florence; the Malvezzi resembled the Guelphs, the Merli the Ghibellines; the former sided with the senate, the latter with the *stratico*; the latter esteemed themselves as adherents of the king, the other against him.'

325 *Ibid*. The crowd forced the Spanish soldiers to retreat into the palace of the stratigoto, the Marquis of Crespano, who had replaced Hojo in 1672. He locked himself into the palace to prevent the furious crowd from attacking him, and ordered the artillery of the forts to repel the assault with fire. Days later the common people, united with the patricians in a revolt against the Spanish rule, drove out the Spanish garrison and gained control of the city. Four of the five forts of Messina were seized while the insurgents besieged Crespano in his palace.

Once he reached Messina by sea and tried to negotiate with the rebels, promising a full amnesty, he was met by cannon fire from the rebels and was forced to retreat. Bajona then asked the governor of Naples to intervene and sent to Sicily 800 Spanish and Italian soldiers by sea.[326]

Soon, the newly appointed government of Messina sent deputies to the French ambassador in Rome and to Admiral Louis Victor de Rochechouart de Mortemart, Count de Vivonne, who was sailing off Catalonia.[327] On 17 August the rebels achieved a victory against the loyalist troops at Lombardello, but failed at Rometta on the same day. In the following weeks, the Hispanic troops coming from continental Italy and other garrisons of Sicily managed to besiege the city by land and blockade it by sea.

The inhabitants organised a resistance, but after two months the diminishing of resources was about to force Messina to surrender. However, relief materialised after an appeal to France. On 27 September 1674 Vivonne sent his second in command Jean-Baptiste de Valbelle to help the rebels, with a convoy of supplies escorted by a squadron of seven warships and three fireships. The Spanish galleys, also supported by the Genoese fleet, returned to their ports, avoiding the encounter. Thus the French squadron managed to bring into Messina enough provisions for about five weeks, along with 300 infantrymen. With this regular force Valbelle helped the Messinese expel the Spanish from the last fort, the *Faro* at the harbour entrance, but lacking sufficient provisions and troops to further act against the Spaniards, he left to ask for more effective assistance.

In the 1670s many of the fortresses of Sicily were found to be in a poor state, lightly-garrisoned, semi-completed or suffering serious defects of one sort or another.[328] Consequently, the idea of conquering the entire island made its way in the King's war cabinet, and Louis XIV and his ministers thought of the rebellion as a useful diversion of Spanish resources from other war theatres. On 2 January 1675 Valbelle's squadron returned, bringing 3,000 good troops under Lieutenant General Valavoire. With their arrival, the siege turned into an inconclusive campaign. The Spanish army was camped outside Messina, had retaken some villages, and seemed to be about to seize the city, but the fleet was unable to close access to the harbour, allowing the French to supply Messina by sea. The help received from Louis XIV encouraged the senate of Messina to elaborate ambitious plans. Primarily it was necessary to ensure necessary

---

326 Piero Gazzara, 'La rivolta antispagnola di Messina e la battaglia di Lombardello (1674)', in F. Imbasi (ed.), *Sicilia Millenaria. Dalla microstoria alla dimensione moderna* (Messina: Università degli Studi, 2019), vol. I, p.187. According to Laloy, *L'expédition de Sicile et la politique française en Italie*, vol. I, p.285, Bajona planned to ask the Viceroy of Naples for 4,000–5,000 militiamen from Calabria to the viceroy of Naples and 400 Neapolitans whom he had raised. He had resolved to raise in Sicily 3,000–4,000 infantrymen. Thus in a short time he would have 8,000 to 9,000 infantrymen (including 1,000 Spaniards, 300 of whom transferred from Naples), 500–600 horses and the company of his guard.

327 David S. T. Blackmore, *Warfare on the Mediterranean in the Age of Sail. A History, 1571–1866* (Jefferson NC: McFarland, 2011), p.95.

328 Luis Ribot, *La Monarquía de España y la guerra de Mesina, 1674–1678* (Madrid: Actas, 2002), pp.102–103.

MEDIUM AND MINOR POWERS

72. Execution of loyalists in Messina in a Spanish print dated 1674 (author's archive). See image commentaries for more information.

supplies for the city and avoid relying on the French fleet. It was therefore decided to occupy towns and villages around the city. The offensive brought modest results, and by the spring of 1675 Messina only controlled Taormina and Augusta, which alone had joined the rebellion.[329] Further French attempts to seize Palermo and other parts of Sicily by sea had failed. While the French troops continued to increase the garrison of Messina, Vivonne, who had joined Valavoire in March 1675, assumed the command of the city. Although the Spanish troops withdrew some distance away, Valavoire did not have enough forces to advance inland and provisions soon ran low again. The siege turned into a war of position, but the oar ships of Valbelle offered the opportunity for punitive actions against enemy infrastructure, destroying windmills and farms, becoming a viable tactic to weaken the besiegers.[330] After weeks of negotiation, on 28 April 1675, Messina swore an oath of obedience to Louis XIV, represented by Vivonne as viceroy. With this act, Messina passed under French protection and the viceroy, for his part, 'swore by the cross of Christ,

---

329 Laloy, *L'expédition de Sicile et la politique française en Italie*, vol. II, p.202: 'Taormina has been taken, San Placido and Scaletta will fall of their own accord …. We would then have the whole coast from Messina to Augusta, which would be all one could wish for, since this country provides crops, wine, meat and all other kinds of food in abundance. Moreover, all the villages in the mountains would be on our side, for they have no garrison and if they did not want to submit, we would force them to do so, and thus, step by step, we would have conquered the whole kingdom, leaving out only Syracuse, which is a very strong city.'

330 Ribot, *La Monarquía de España y la guerra de Mesina, 1674–1678*, pp.89–90.

73. The Battle of Augusta (Sicily), fought on 22 April 1676 between the Dutch–Spanish and the French fleets, in the painting of Ambroise-Louis Garneray (Palais de Luxembourg, Paris). See image commentaries for more information.

and his four holy Gospels, to observe the chapters, privileges, immunities and freedoms granted in the past by kings or emperors to the city of Messina, and its district and dependencies, as well as the uses, customs and good habits of the city, and other prerogatives that would be granted in the future, commanding all and any officials to guard, respect and observe them.'[331]

For the remainder of 1675 the French increased their strength in Sicily. In June the senate drew up a plan for the formation of a regular force, trained and equipped by the French. At the beginning of the revolt the only armed force in the city was the city militia, consisting of 500 men under the orders of Don Jacopo Averna, who on 6 August 1674 had succeeded in seizing one of the strongest fortresses held by the Spaniards in Messina, Forte Castellazzo. Although the majority of the population adhered to the new order, they had been accustomed to not attending military service for centuries. Among the privileges granted in return for the submission of the city to France was one that exempted citizens from fighting, except for the defence of the city and surrounding territory.[332] According to a contemporary chronicle, 'on all sides one could see works of war, here workshops for making gunpowder and balls, there forges for making and forging firearms and cutting weapons;

---

331 Botta, *Storia d'Italia*, p.250.
332 Laloy, *L'expédition de Sicile et la politique française en Italie*, vol. II, p.764: 'The inhabitants were exempted from fighting against the Spaniards, except for the defence of their land; the land was to retain all its jurisdictions over the villages dependent on it, as well as its rights as a 'district land' of Messina. The inhabitants of the countryside were in turn exempted from paying taxes, except for those earmarked for the needs of the cult or owed to the city of Messina.'

in this place cannons were being led, in that one soldiers were practising.'[333] However, the expectations were deluded and the creation of a regular force had to wait months before becoming a reality. Between 1675 and 1676 a single regiment of foot had been raised under Colonel Averna, but only in January 1677 did the government issue a *bando* (order) to raise four regiments of 500 men each,[334] which took the French organisational structure of 10 companies of 50 men. The regiments were entrusted to *maestri di campo* belonging to the most important families of Messina, such as Ventimiglia, Campolo, Gallero and the aforementioned Averna. The aristocracy promised to raise at its own expense 1,200 horsemen, but ultimately just half of this force was gathered.[335] It is not known whether the decision not to form more native units in Messina was due to the French viceroy, however even the militia, which on paper could muster more than 50,000 men, was not increased, gathering about 8,000 militiamen in total: a sign that Vivonne did not trust such a large number of armed civilians. Therefore the defence of the city was then entrusted to the French troops, which in early 1677 numbered about 11,000–12,000 inside the city, 2,000 on the sail fleet and a further 1,200 on the galleys. These forces, supported by 2,000 troops of Messina, faced an increasingly number of besieging Spanish troops, which had increased to 11,012 foot and 1,180 horse in the summer of 1677.[336]

The French garrison and the entire city depended on French supplies by sea, a cost that became exorbitant. Restrictions caused desertion.[337] In the meantime the international scenario was changing, and the growing French presence in the central Mediterranean became one of the pretexts used by Charles II of England to enter into war on the side of Spain. In early 1678 Louis XIV sent François d'Aubusson de La Feuillade from Toulon, ostensibly to replace Vivonne as viceroy in Sicily but in fact to evacuate the French troops. La Feuillade proclaimed viceroy with great pomp on 28 February 1678, then 15 days later embarked the French troops on the pretence of an expedition against Palermo. The viceroy then informed the senate of Messina that the French were leaving the city. A few hundred leading families were also allowed to embark before the fleet left. The Spanish viceroy returned to Messina without opposition, having promised a general amnesty, a promise that was not kept.

---

333 Botta, *Storia d'Italia*, pp.213–214, and p.254: 'The senate, whose cause was especially at issue, spared no means to inflame spirits, and order what was necessary for defence, divided the population into regular companies, and subjected them to the discipline of men, most of them nobles, fervent in their intent, endowed with extraordinary courage, and uncommon expertise in military matters.'

334 Laloy, Émile, *L'expédition de Sicile er la politique française en Italie*, vol. II, p.815.

335 *Ibid*.

336 Davide Maffi, *Los últimos tercios, el ejército de Carlos II* (Madrid: Desperta Ferro, 2020), p.258.

337 Laloy, *L'expédition de Sicile et la politique française en Italie*, vol. III, p.278: 'On 7 September the deserters exaggeratedly estimated that only 3,000 Frenchmen and 500 Messinese remained in the city, mainly used to guard the former, most of whom would otherwise have fled, 'so badly treated were they'. According to them, there had been a sedition in Messina, and the garrison had taken refuge in the fortresses.'

2

Little and Great Italian Wars

Campaigns Against the Waldensians, 1655–1663

Relations between Piedmont's Waldensian Protestant communities and the Savoy ruling house had always known ups and downs. However, from 1602, thanks to an agreement signed between the Duke and the Reformed religious leaders, freedom of belief was established at an acceptable level of tolerance, at least for that age. This act followed the Cavour agreement, signed in 1561, which had recognised and regulated the presence of a Protestant enclave in the Duke's states.[1] The legal framework of the existence of this religious minority in the Duchy permitted the exercise of the Reformed belief within predetermined territorial limits.[2] However, the Waldensians, driven by the increase in population to about 18,000–20,000, had settled in the plains not far from Turin, tending to expand into areas judged by the government to be outside the permitted limits. This became a source of dispute, since some of these 'limitations' had not been granted by the Dukes.[3]

A substantial change occurred after the death of Duke Vittorio Amedeo I, in 1637, when the struggle between *madamisti* and *principisti* led both sides to attempt to gain the support of the Catholic Church. As a result, the ducal government gradually reduced the rights of the Waldensian communities. The strategy of Turin aimed to contain as much as possible the Reformed communities within a restricted territory, since they represented an insidious

---

1 Stefano Tron, *Le Pasque Piemontesi e l'Internazionale Protestante* (Turin: Società di Studi Valdesi, 2005), p.7: 'Even in the presence of increasing discriminatory measures at the fiscal, social and symbolic levels, it should be noted that in regard to the Protestant population [of Piedmont] there were no formal prohibitions from holding and acquiring property even outside those limits.'

2 The contested limits comprised the villages of Luserna, Bibiana, Bricherasio, Campiglione, Fenile, and surrounding areas, which were predominantly Protestant.

3 On the Savoy side there was a tendency to make the territorial limits allowed for free preaching coincide with those of the home, with the clear intention of containing the Waldensians as far as possible; see Davide Jahier, *I Valdesi sotto Vittorio Amedeo I, la reggente Cristina e Carlo Emanuele II (1630–1665)* (Società di Storia Valdese, February 1932), p.7.

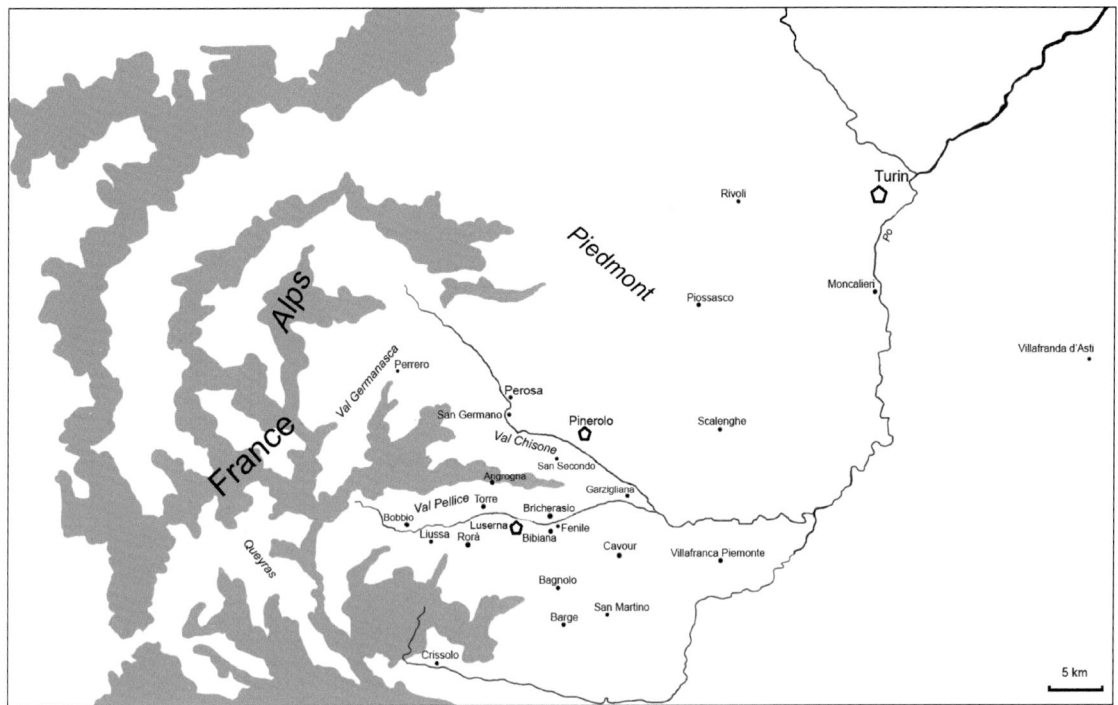

Map 1. Theatre of operations of the war against the Waldensians, 1655–63

bridgehead of the Protestants on the southern side of the Alps. Therefore the government strongly encouraged conversions to the Catholic faith through the preaching of missionary friars. The Waldensians were gradually confined within a 'ghetto' formed by the territories of the Val Pellice, Val Chisone and Valle Germanasca, and subjected to periodic controls on compliance with an agreement that prevented them from proselytising, and condemned to capital punishment all those who acted against the conversions to Catholicism within the communities. The following years saw the proliferation of new edicts, orders, ducal rescripts, and a plethora of acts aimed to impose new limitations, or aggravating and interpreting the previous agreements in the most restrictive possible way. Certainly one of the major functions of the issuing of all these legislative measures, was for the court the flow of money into the often empty coffers of the State, because these acts provided an opportunity to open, from a position of advantage, long and complex negotiations with the 'heretics'. The negotiations, which began in the form of 'humble appeals' and 'heartfelt supplications' addressed to the sovereign, ended almost regularly with a new *capitolazione*, namely a substantial cash disbursements in exchange for the partial acceptance of the Waldensian demands.[4] The edict issued on 15 May 1650 further threatened the rights of the communities, since this abrogated many of their privileges in favour of Catholic penetration in the valleys. Through payment for expansive guarantees the problems with the government had

---

4   After 1602 new edicts were issued in 1603, 1622, 1633, 1640 and 1644, each more or less aimed at a restriction of the Waldensians' prerogatives except for the payment of new taxes.

always been solved in favour of the Waldensians, even if only precariously, but after this act relations deteriorated. Mutual suspicion and the growing Catholic interference caused incidents and riots. According to some sources, in March 1653 the Waldensian synod of Boissel, under pressure from the most 'radical' leaders, would have voted in favour of expelling the Catholic priests and friars present in the valleys.[5] In the same month the population of Villar (today Villar Perosa) rose up and drove the Capuchin friars out of the convent, which was set on fire together with the church. As soon as news of these events reached Turin, the government sent soldiers to restore order and arrest the seditious. By the end of the month there were dead and wounded on both sides, but in April a truce was reached, granting a ducal pardon to all except those responsible for the events at Villar.[6]

After a period of relative quiet, tensions resumed. The hostility was fuelled by the constant pressure exerted by the *Concilium Novum de Propaganda Fide et Extirpandis Haereticis* (New Council of Propagation of the Faith and the Extermination of Heresy), an institution of the Roman Catholic Church established in 1650 which regularly convened in the palace of the Archbishop of Turin.[7] Accusations of opposition to conversions, which was followed by convictions and confiscation of properties, provoked further incidents in the valleys, which culminated in the village of Fenile with the murder of

---

5   Paoletti, *Dal Ducato all'Unità*, p.139. In the years that immediately followed, the campaigns against the Waldensians were the subject of numerous reconstructions, almost always partial and sometimes manipulated, both by Catholic and Protestant authors. With regard to the Catholic side Alessandro di Saluzzo, *Histoire Militaire du Piémont* (Turin, 1818), vol. IV, pp.334–352, supplies a full pro-Savoyard version, but includes an interesting account about the Geneva–Savoy crisis of 1666–67. As for contemporary sources, the chronicles written in exile by the Waldensians contain valuable details, although they represent a clearly biased version of events. The first, and most important, account is the *Récit véritable de ce qui est arrivé depuis peu au Vallées de Piémont* (Leyden, 1669) by Jean Léger. There are few Savoy-Piedmontese chronicles of the events, but it is possible to access court and ecclesiastical correspondence to add some details, and to understand the attitude of the Catholic Church. The latter does not hide its satisfaction with the outcome, employing terms such as 'elimination' and even 'extermination' regarding the fate of the heretics. As for the military operations against the Waldensians, Alexis Muston, a nineteenth-century French Protestant pastor based in Bordeaux, offers a detailed but incomplete chronicle of the event in his *The Israel of the Alps – a complete history of the Waldenses of Piedmont and their colonies* (London–Glasgow–Edinburgh, 1866). Among the recent contributions, Ciro Paoletti, in his *Dal Ducato all'Unità*, provides a version decidedly biased in favour of the Savoy and the Catholic side, blaming the Waldensians for their hostile acts against the government, which would have caused the bitter reprisal against them. Among the other studies recently published it is worth mentioning the aforementioned essay by Daniele Tron, *Le Pasque Piemontesi e l'Internazionale Protestante*.

6   The instigators of the riots at Villar Perosa were identified in the family of the pastor Mondet. See Paoletti, *Dal Ducato all'Unità*, p.139.

7   Muston, in *The Israel of the Alps*, vol. I, Part I, Chapter III, claimed that neither Duke Charles Emmanuel II of Savoy nor the Waldensians themselves had sought to wage war, and both parties were content with maintaining the peace.

74. Dutch print denouncing the atrocities against the Waldensians in the late 1650s (author's archive). It is difficult to establish how much and how brutal the persecutions of the Piedmontese Protestants were, but it is certain that religious hatred led to a fight without quarter.

a Catholic priest.[8] Then, on Christmas Day 1654, an eyewitness reported that in the village of La Torre in the Val Pellice, a parade with a donkey disguised as a priest was staged in mockery of the Catholic processions.[9] This news reached the ears of the Archbishop, who asked the Duke for a strong response. The Duke's reaction was peremptory. On 25 January 1655 an order was issued to all Waldensians who held activities outside the 'limitations' to return to their home within three days on pain of confiscation of the properties, unless they proved their conversion to Catholicism within 20 days.[10] Convinced that, as in the past, their return would be obtained in a short time through a new negotiation, and several demands for talks were immediately sent to the court, the expelled Waldensians obeyed orders. Then in the middle of winter, with their household goods, they returned to the upper Val Pellice leaving a few men on guard to prevent the highly probable

---

8   Paoletti, *Dal Ducato all'Unità*, p.139.
9   Ibid.
10 The order specified 'That every head of a family, with the individuals of that family, of the reformed religion, of what rank, degree, or condition soever, none excepted inhabiting and possessing estates in Luserna, San Giovanni, Bibiana, Campiglione, San Secondo, Lusernetta, La Torre, Fenile, and Bricherasio, should, within three days after the publication the order, withdraw and depart, out of the said places, and translated into the places and limits tolerated by his highness the Duke of Savoy during his pleasure; particularly Bobbio, Angrogne, Vilario, Rorata, and the county of Bonetti. And all this to be done on pain of death, and confiscation of house and goods, unless within the limited time they turned Roman Catholics.' Jahier, *I Valdesi (1630–1665)*, p.9.

looting of the abandoned houses, while awaiting an answer from Turin. But this time the course of events was not what the Waldensians expected, since a plan had been designed 'in order to defend the true faith and eradicate the heresy once and for all'.[11] The conditions demanded by the government were impossible to accept. While waiting for an answer to the request for negotiations, the Waldensians turned to the European Protestant Churches to receive support and advice. The Reformed Swiss cantons offered their mediation, while the Republic of Geneva offered weapons and money. Moreover, vague and imprecise news had come from Switzerland and France about the possibility of military action in the valleys. Indeed, in mid April the Marquis of Pianezza, Carlo Emanuele Filiberto Giacinto di Simiana, one of the most influential members of the Turin Court and an active member of the powerful *Concilium Novum* instituted in 1650, had decided to settle the matter by force of arms and put pressure on the regent, *Madama Reale* Christine of France.

On 17 April 1655 the Marquis of Pianezza appeared at the entrance to the Val Pellice with 700 soldiers. This force comprised the infantrymen of the regiment *Livorno* and a company of Irish mercenaries under the governor of Villanova d'Asti, Count Antonio Francesco Gentile.[12] The regular force also comprised two cavalry companies under the Marquis Galeazzo Villa. With them a number of peasant militia from Saluzzo and the villages of Barge, Bagnolo and Costigliole, referred to as 'volunteers' and enticed by the promise of plunder, had joined the regular troops days before. The arrival of Pianezza was not unexpected. The Marquis found the village of San Giovanni completely abandoned, but realised that the heights before La Torre were defended by armed villagers, commanded by Bartolomeo Jahier: a strong and clever local leader who had been elected to the rank of *capitano*. After a brief skirmish, which caused some casualties to the ducal troops, in the evening they seized La Torre thanks to the action of the cavalrymen, who outflanked the defenders and entered the village from the north. Jahier and his men managed to escape capture. On 18 May the Marquis established his headquarters in the village, from where he directed future operations. Soldiers and militiamen plundered all the houses, but the following day the ducal troops could only carry out demonstrative actions, as the limited number of men did not allow them to continue the offensive. The situation remained at a standstill until 20 April. Talks commenced, but without result. Bringing a definite advantage for the ducal troops came the news of the imminent arrival in Piedmont of the French army heading for the siege of Pavia.

With the permission of the regent, *Madama Reale* Christine of France, Pianezza was ordered to arrange the transit and quarters of the French by directing them to the Waldensian valleys. With these troops he could 'raise

---

11 Muston, *The Israel of the Alps*, vol. I, Part I, Chapter III.

12 They were Catholic Irish prisoners of war expelled by the English government in 1653, and enlisted in the army of Savoy-Piedmont the next year; see Denys Murphy, 'Cromwell in Ireland', in *The Irish Monthly*, Vol. III (1875), pp.398–408. According to Muston, *The Israel of the Alps*, vol. I, Part II, Chapter VII, this company behaved brutally towards the Waldensian population.

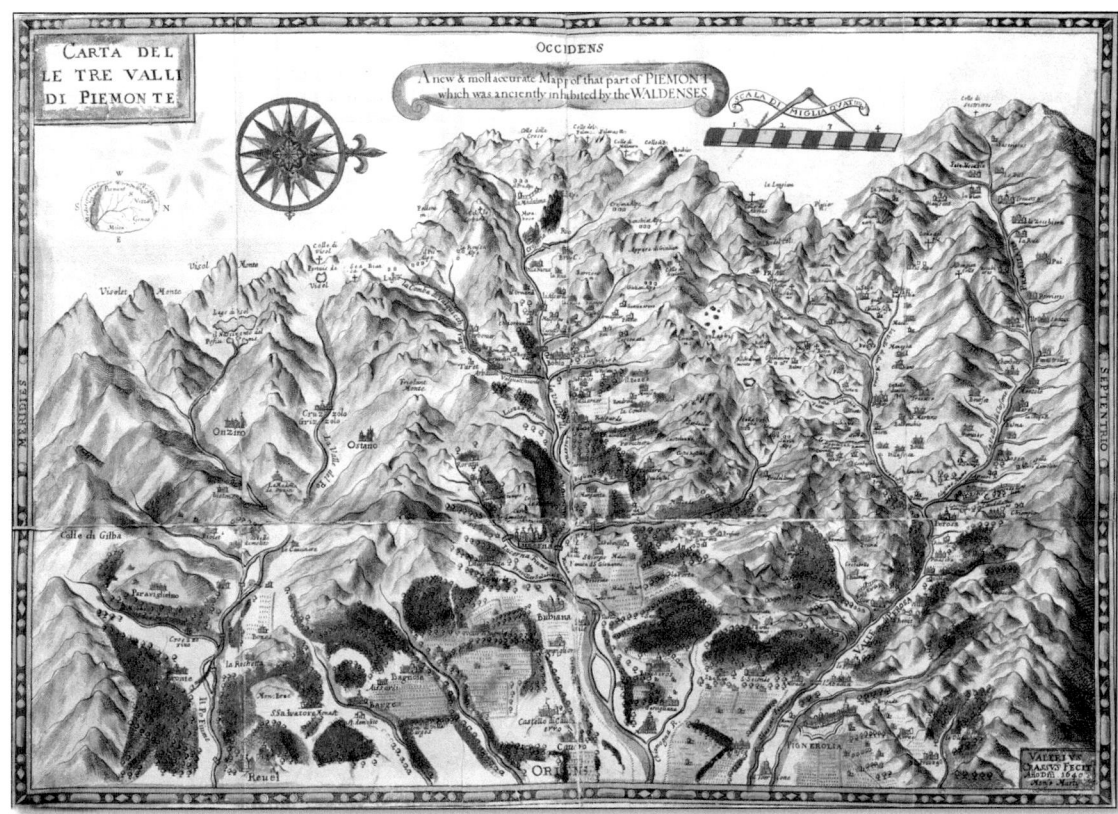

75. The Waldensian valleys in a French print of the seventeenth century. (Author's archive)

the tone' and 'give the last extermination to the rebellion and heresy that infects the most beautiful places in Piedmont'.[13] Meanwhile a battalion of the infantry regiment *San Damiano* headed to La Torre, while a Bavarian infantry regiment was hired to join the troops in the Val Pellice. Thanks to the agreement between Paris and Turin, since 19 April Pianezza could exploit the presence of six French infantry regiments. The arrival of these troops is summarised by the letters written by the Marquis. The first regiment was composed of Irishmen under Sir James Preston, which was quartered in the Val Pellice, followed by regiments *Chamblay, Grancey, Villa, Carignan*, which arrived between 21 and 23 April, and finally *Montpezat* on the 29th; they were approximately 4,000 men.[14] The first acts of violence against the inhabitants occurred on 22 April. For five days the villages of the Val Pellice

---

13 Tron, *Le Pasque Piemontesi*, p.12. Other sources gives different figures which are clearly exaggerated, such as the 18,000 French and Ducal soldiers stated by Jean Léger in 1655. As for the housing of soldiers at the expense of the inhabitants, it was a well-established measure, which could easily be transformed into a brutal instrument of repression. The infamous *dragonnades*, the painful experience which the French Protestants knew in 1685–86, were the evolution of this practice.

14 Nicola Borello, *I valdesi in armi* (Bergamo: Soldiershop, 2019), p.11. According to letters of the Marquis of Pianezza to the Court of Turin, the force under his command numbered 5,000 men; see Tron, *Le Pasque Piemontesi*, p.13. This figure is also confirmed in E. Balmas and G. Zardini Lana, 'La vera relazione di quanto è accaduto nelle persecuzioni e i massacri dell'anno 1655', in

were subjected to the looting, devastation, and killing of civilians: these were the tragic events that nineteenth-century historiography passed down under the name of 'Piedmontese Easter' or 'Bloody Easter', as it occurred during the Protestant Easter week.[15] The rumours of the looting alarmed the inhabitants of the villages further north, who fled their homes to find a safe place, but cold and starvation caused the death of many among them.

On 28 April a strict order was issued requiring all people still living beyond the limits to leave their homes within 24 hours, on pain of confiscation of all property: this was punishment for supporting the heretics of Luserna, thus depriving them of the rights established in the capitulations previously granted. On the same day the Marquis Galeazzo Villa wrote from Bobbio that 'not a soul is to be found in those surroundings', while on the 29th a second round-up in the Val d'Angrogna, following the attack in force at Pra del Torno on 24 April by the French regiments of *Preston Irlandaise* and *Grancey*, still produced a large amount of booty, especially livestock that had not yet been taken. Only the villages of Bobbio and Villar retained some inhabitants, namely those who had abjured and 'gone to holy mass'.[16] Overwhelmed by the fury of the attackers, the population offered no resistance, except at Rorà. Here, the peasants tried to organise a defence under the direction of the local leader Josué Janavel. While the devastation raged on, a large part of the population of the small community, around 25 families in all, continued to conduct normal activities, relying on the assurances of their Lord, Count Cristoforo di Luserna, who claimed to have obtained their exemption from military quartering. In spite of these assurances Janavel remained on the alert and maintained surveillance on the access routes to the village, accompanied in practice only by his family members and trusted companions. However, they were no more than a dozen in all. Janavel's concerns soon proved to be well-founded. On 24 April a first unsuccessful assault was launched by some 'volunteer militiamen' eager for booty, who were repulsed by the reaction of the small but determined group.[17] The next day, however, the assault was repeated. In this second battle, Janavel, having sent some of his men out to scout, was able to know in time the path followed by the enemies, so was able to choose the most suitable place to face them, establish a plan and arrange the men to defend the village. He now

---

Le 'Pasque Piemontesi' del 1655 nelle testimonianze dei protagonisti (Turin, 1987), pp.183–186. However, this figure suggests that Pianezza would have lost 200 regular soldiers in just one week.

15   Giorgio Vola, *Mais où sont les neiges d'antan: la colletta inglese del 1656 per i valdesi*, in BSSV, n.155 (1984), p.6. According to a document compiled in 1656 in order to distribute the solidarity aid of the European Protestant churches, the victims were 1,712. This figure must not be far from the truth, considering that Catholic sources propose even higher numbers.

16   *Ibid*. A ducal document dated 10 May fixes the number at 116 inhabitants in Bobbio and 289 in Villar, to which at least 106 new Catholics must be added from La Torre, who had taken refuge at Villar.

17   Tron, *Le Pasque Piemontesi*, p.21. The population of Rorà, very worried about what had happened, complained to Count Cristoforo, who replied that 'the assailants are nothing more than thieves, vagabonds or peasants, and certainly not soldiers of the army', and that he would in any case take the necessary measures to suspend these assaults.

had 18 men, of whom only 12 were armed with muskets; the other six were equipped with slingshots and cutting weapons. Janavel divided his men into three groups, so that the vanguards of the enemy, already tired from the steep climb, suddenly found themselves exposed to fire from different points. The impression of being surrounded by superior forces drove the militiamen to flee in the direction from which they had come and which had been purposely left clear by Janavel. The flight of the militiamen spread panic throughout the squadron, which retreated hastily. Rorà was attacked again on 26 April and 1 May, but without better results: Janavel's defence, always conducted with a handful of men, proved effective. Finally, on 3 May the Marquis of Pianezza sent against them no longer only the peasant militia but regular troops, and also used the French troops to seize Rorà. The first attempt failed, but the second succeeded on 4 May thanks to the arrival of further troops, including the French regiment *Chamblay*, the Irish company of Francesco Gentile, who 'made wonders', and the militiamen under the infamous brothers Mario and Bartolomeo Malingri, Counts of Bagnolo.[18] By the evening of 4 May the village had been seized, the houses destroyed and the livestock captured. Janavel and his meagre group of partisans, after fighting all day without ammunition and provisions, took refuge in the mountains. The escape was not a final abandonment, but a way to continue the fight. After crossing the snow-covered heights, Janavel and his men headed for the Queyras where other Waldensians had already taken refuge.

As soon as the occupation of that valley was completed, Pianezza turned his attention to the others. On 5 May, marching from Bobbio and through mountain sentries, the Ducal–French troops entered the Val Germanasca and obtained the submission of the local civilians, who already knew the fate of their co-religionists of the Val Pellice. On 6 May, taking advantage of knowledge of the mountain paths, a handful of 'Partisans' led by Bartolomeo Jahier assaulted the village of Perrero. They destroyed the Prevost's home, fired the Catholic church and looted the convent.[19] A new action occurred the day after, but one after another the other Waldensian villages submitted, allowing the Marquis Galeazzo Villa to occupy the whole valley on 8 May. As for the Val Chisone, on 2 May the French–Ducal force under the Marquis of San Damiano marched into the valley. The inhabitants of San Germano and other villages tried to face the enemy, raising an improvised defence, but left their homes after a few days. The inhabitants of Perosa and San Martino, pressed by the Ducal troops, passed the border at the Abres Pass or simply crossed the Chisone River to find refuge in France, but were forced to abjure

---

18   *Ibid.* According to the letter of Pianezza, about 40 civilians were killed and many others taken prisoner, as happened to Janavel's wife and three daughters. The Marquis claimed the loss of four men.

19   These actions resulted in the capture of a number of prisoners, including a 'gentleman' or a cavalry officer, and two monks whose lives were spared by Jahier, who released them safely. These actions, with some divergences in the details, are also reported by Pianezza in a letter dated 9 May, and with greater emphasis in an anonymous *Relazione de' Successi seguiti nella Valle di Luserna* in the year 1655, attributed to the Marquis himself.

in exchange for the right of asylum.[20] According to the Ducal commander, all the valley was now uninhabited, '[the civilians] having taken away even the window bars with them'.[21]

On 9 May the Marquis of Pianezza informed the court that the operation had been successfully concluded and therefore dismissed the French troops. Three days later the French resumed their march towards the Milanese, with a stop at Villafranca d'Asti. Two days before the departure of the allies the Marquis had left his headquarters in the Val Pellice and returned to Turin. In triumphalist tones, he reported that the 'partisans of the Val Pellice with their leaders had been driven out of the valleys': two pastors of Villar and Bobbio were his prisoners, and the others were on the run; as for the notables, some had been executed, numerous others had been captured and taken as hostages to Turin. On 18 May, 'the third day of the feast of Pentecost, about forty prisoners, including the two religious ministers, were forced to abjure during a sumptuous ceremony in Turin Cathedral in the presence of the highest civil and religious dignitaries of the state, as a tangible sign of the triumph over heresy, also witnessed by a pamphlet celebrating the event'.[22]

However, despite the killings, devastation and submissions, the action led by the Marquis of Pianezza had not annihilated the Waldensians' will to resist. The day after the departure of the French troops, thanks to the initiative of the 'valiant and indomitable captains' Bartolomeo Jahier and Josué Janavel da Luserna, two bands of partisans were raised and equipped with weapons received from Geneva. Moreover, the atrocities perpetrated against the civilians, including women and children, aroused the dismay of the Protestant nations. In England Oliver Cromwell took up the desperate appeal of the people who had escaped capture and interested Puritan England in the salvation of the Piedmontese Reformed community.[23] In the Dutch Republic, Sweden, Denmark and also in Germany and France, public fasts were held for the Waldensians, and subscriptions were opened.[24]

---

20 Hopes of salvation lay in seeking asylum in French territory, where there were several communities of co-religionists able to provide rescue: either in the Queyras through the Col de la Croix, or in the part of the Val Chisone subject to King Louis XIV, passing through Col Giulian or from the Pramollo valley through the Colle de la Vaccera; see Tron, *Le Pasque Piemontesi*, p.14.

21 *Ibid.*, letter of Carlo Lodovico d'Agliè, Marquis of San Damiano.

22 *Ibid.*, letter of the Marquis of Pianezza.

23 With feverish diplomatic work he immediately interested Geneva, the Swiss Protestant cantons, and also Cardinal Mazarin, to impose an end to 'the destruction of a people that was not a mere part of the Protestant world but represented the link between Protestantism and the apostolic age'. The poet John Milton wrote a sonnet about the events, entitled *On the Late Massacher in Piemont* (sic). See Muston, *The Israel of the Alps*, vol. I, Part II, Chapter VIII.

24 Tron, *Le Pasque Piemontesi*, p.29. On 27 April 1655, the leadership composed of pastors and notables headed by the Pastor of San Giovanni Jean Léger addressed a heartfelt appeal to the brethren across the Alps to denounce them and implore diplomatic, economic and military help. The future author of the *Histoire Génerale* wrote that, after having fortunately escaped with his family to safety in France, and having ascertained the futility of the appeals made to the

Plate A

The early 1660s
1. Papal States, *Guardia Corsa*, musketeer, 1662; 2. Grand Duchy of Tuscany, musketeer, 1661;
3. Duchy of Modena, musketeer 1660
(Illustration by Bruno Mugnai © Helion & Company 2023)
See Colour Plate Commentaries for further information

Plate B

1660–75

1. Republic of Lucca, artilleryman, 1664; 2. and 3. Republic of Genoa: field officer or galley commander, early 1670s; Italian infantry, musketeer 1672

(Illustration by Bruno Mugnai © Helion & Company 2023)

See Colour Plate Commentaries for further information

Plate C

1675–80

1. Duchy of Modena, infantry NCO, 1675; 2. Duchy of Modena, foot militia, pikeman, 1675;
3. Republic of Lucca: musketeer 1681–85

(Illustration by Bruno Mugnai © Helion & Company 2023)

See Colour Plate Commentaries for further information

Plate D

Venice's allies, Malta 1680s
1. Knight in livery dress, 1685–88; 2. Knight in campaign dress, 1686;
3. Marine infantry *battaglione*, musketeer, 1686
(Illustration by Bruno Mugnai © Helion & Company 2023)
See Colour Plate Commentaries for further information

Plate E

Light infantry and *soldati di fortuna*
1. Republic of Genoa, Corsican infantry, musketeer 1684; 2. Francesco Morosini's Lifeguard, *schiavone*, 1685–88; 3. Duchy of Mantua, *soldato di fortuna*, musketeer, 1687–88

(Illustration by Bruno Mugnai © Helion & Company 2023)
See Colour Plate Commentaries for further information

Plate F

Heavy cavalry
1. Papal States, German cavalry field officer, 1663;
2. Grand Duchy of Tuscany, *Corazza Alemanna*, 1675–80

(Illustration by Bruno Mugnai © Helion & Company 2023)

See Colour Plate Commentaries for further information

Plate G

Palace guards
1. Papal States, *Guardia Svizzera*, 1665; 2. Grand Duchy of Tuscany *Guardia Ferma de' Lanzi*, 1650–60;
3. Parma and Piacenza, *Guardia Alemanna*, or *Arciere Prima Guardia*, 1680–90
(Illustration by Bruno Mugnai © Helion & Company 2023)
See Colour Plate Commentaries for further information

Plate H

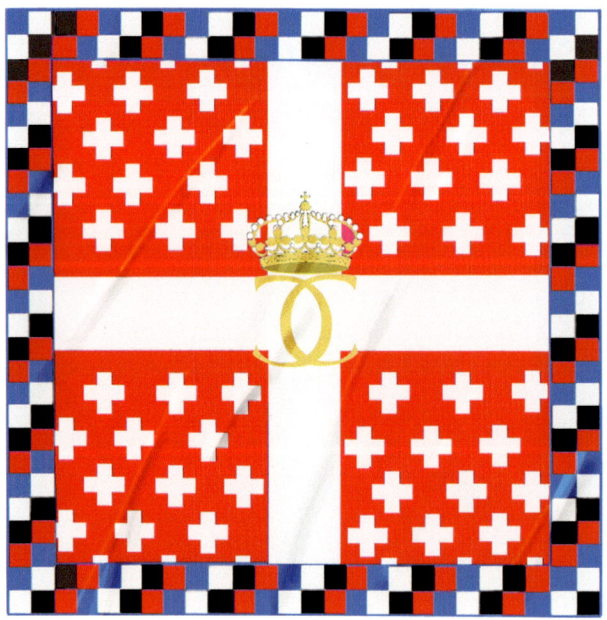

Savoy-Piedmont ensigns, 1672–73: *Guardie* Regiment
1. Colonel's ensign, 2. *Ordinanza* ensign. Reconstruction after Stefano Ales, *Insegne militari preunitarie italiane* (1671–1870). Approximate size 240×240 cm.

(Illustration by Bruno Mugnai © Helion & Company 2023)

Savoy-Piedmont ensigns, 1680–90
Ordinanze for infantry, 1680s–1690s
(Illustration by Bruno Mugnai © Helion & Company 2023)
See Colour Plate Commentaries for further information

Plate J

Venetian infantry ensigns, 1680–90

1. Traditional rectangular colour with yellow-golden lion; 2. Ensign, copy from a watercolour of the Bassan collection, Venice; 3. Colonel's company ensign, *Waldeck* infantry regiment; 4. Company ensign, infantry regiment *Hohenlohe*, 1694

(Illustration by Bruno Mugnai © Helion & Company 2023)

See Colour Plate Commentaries for further information

Plate K

Papal infantry and cavalry colours

1. Papal States: infantry ensign for the *Guardie di Nostro Signore*, 1667–69; 2. Standard of the *Corazze* company, papacy of Innocent XI Odescalchi (1676–1689); 3. Standard of the second militia mounted company of Bologna, 1689

(Illustration by Bruno Mugnai © Helion & Company 2023)

See Colour Plate Commentaries for further information

Plate L

Genoa and Tuscany infantry colours
1. Genoese infantry ensign; 2. Tuscan infantry ensign
(Illustration by Bruno Mugnai © Helion & Company 2023)
See Colour Plate Commentaries for further information

Plate M

Modena and Lucca infantry colours
1. Modena, infantry colour, second half of the seventeenth century; 2. Lucca, infantry colour
(Illustration by Bruno Mugnai © Helion & Company 2023)
See Colour Plate Commentaries for further information

Plate N

Malta and Messina infantry colours
1. Malta, infantry colour, end of the seventeenth century;
2. Republic of Messina infantry colour, 1675–77

(Illustration by Bruno Mugnai © Helion & Company 2023)

See Colour Plate Commentaries for further information

Plate O

Knight of the Order of St Stephen, 1685
See Colour Plate Commentaries for further information

Prince Cesare Ignazio d'Este of Scandiano (1653–1713), portrayed by Henri Gascard in 1675 (Gallerie Estensi, Modena)

See Colour Plate Commentaries for further information

LITTLE AND GREAT ITALIAN WARS

76. The fort of Luserna in a print dated 1700 (author's archive). This stronghold controlled access to the Val Pellice, where the larger Waldensian community of Piedmont resided.

A few days after returning across the border, Janavel returned to the Val Pellice, choosing the Liussa valley to the right of the river as his base of operations. He had more and better equipped men at his disposal and immediately went into action, attacking the villages of Bibiana and Lusernetta, but without succeeding in seizing them. In this action he was wounded in the leg by a musket ball that he would carry with him for the rest of his life. In the meantime the other and more numerous band under Jahier had continued to operate in the San Martino and Perosa valleys, being able to exploit the base represented by the Val Chisone under French rule. An increasingly irritated and embarrassed Pianezza claimed that Pinerolo had become a veritable rebels' hideout and the French governor La Bertonnière, in particular, provided a shelter to numbers of refugees, and turned a blind eye to the blatant support given to the 'heretics' by the Reformed communities in France. Gradually Jahier extended his control to the upper Val Pellice by moving his headquarters to Verné, near Angrogna, which was more defensible. Finally, Jahier and Janavel established contact and decided to join forces to conduct

---

Marquis of Pianezza to put an end to the massacres, as Moderator of the Waldensian Churches he tried to take the first steps towards organising resistance. He urged the community leadership who held civil and religious offices not to be discouraged and not to think of a diaspora in foreign countries, according to the pessimistic predictions of the survivors, and designed a plan to obtain the support of the other Protestant churches in Europe.

77. Alleged portrait of Josuè Janavel (1617–1690), the skilled Waldensian leader and military chief who organised the resistance against the Savoyards in 1655–63.

a coordinated campaign against the enemy. To the original nucleus of a few dozen partisans, the two Waldensian leaders were able to add other co-religionists eager for revenge, as well as a growing number of volunteers from France, Switzerland and elsewhere, including Protestant aristocrats, officers and professional soldiers who wanted to join the 'Waldensian army'.[25] In May, Janavel and Jahier had almost 1,000 men under their orders. With these forces they began to conduct an assiduous and effective guerrilla campaign that extended outside the perimeter of the valleys, menacing the communities that had joined the regular forces with their militia. The village of San Secondo was under threat several times, until half of the Irish infantrymen of Francesco Gentile's company was sent as a garrison. The presence of regular troops did not discourage Jahier, who had been elected *generale* of the army, indeed it stimulated him to design an even bolder plan. Before the end of May San Secondo was attacked twice, and in the second assault the Waldensians managed to set fire to the castle where the Irish soldiers were quartered. They all died, and then the action was concentrated against the settlement. People found in possession of objects and animals from the looting of the previous month were executed. Two monks belonging to a convent particularly disliked by the rebels, were also killed and their bodies sent on a cart to Turin, to the dismay of the population. Almost the entire settlement was destroyed and the surviving population fled to the capital, increasing the consternation of the court. Between May and June, the partisans blocked the castle of Mirabouc and assaulted Fenile, Garzigliana, Luserna, San Giovanni, Bricherasio, La Torre, and Crissolo in the Po Valley, from where Jahier came back with livestock, which later he sold in Pinerolo.

Pressed by the need to suppress the guerrillas and resolve the issue with arms before foreign diplomacy intervened in domestic affairs, the regent Duchess convinced her son to replace Pianezza. The designated substitute was Francesco di Mesmes, Lord of Marolles and Count of Chiavazza, *maestro di campo* of the Guards regiment, General Lieutenant of the infantry, and knight of the Supreme Order of the *Santissima Annunziata*. He arrived in the Val Pellice and soon realised that the regular forces were not sufficient to control the area. He called for further soldiers, who arrived in late June to reinforce La Torre, Bricherasio and Luserna, and in the latter he installed his headquarters. These were the centres from where he could control the

---

25 *Ibid.*

partisans installed at Angrogna, and intercept their actions with some chance of success. In fact, rather than organising a new campaign, it was a matter of keeping the 'rebels' at bay and defending the Catholics and converted people from their reprisals and supplying actions. Marolles led some counter-attacks, but with the aim of allowing the Catholic peasants to do their work undisturbed.

On 18 June Janavel was seriously injured in one of these encounters, remaining out of action for six weeks. Another serious event affected the Waldensians on the same day: Bartolomeo Jahier, having recklessly ventured out of the Val Pellice to raid cattle and probably deceived by a traitor, was ambushed by the Ducal cavalry and killed, along with 60 of his men.[26] However, the successes achieved by the House of Savoy were limited to this.

The scarcity of resources offered by the now almost uninhabited Val Pellice worsened the soldiers' conditions. There was no longer even the incentive of booty, because the few remaining inhabitants were Catholics, and nothing could be gained from them, 'since these poor peasants are all naked and have not a money in their pockets'; desertions became numerous and frequent, and Marolles himself complained about this to *Madama Reale* Christine and Duke Carlo Emanuele II.[27]

Although deprived of their two commanders, the Waldensians did not lose heart and elected in their place Giacomo Jahier, brother of Bartolomeo, and Francesco Laurenti dei Chiotti. In late June they moved to a more easily defensible position, climbing to La Vaccera at 1,460 metres altitude. In the meantime other volunteers had arrived from Switzerland, Languedoc and the Dauphiné to help them with soldiers and officers and who organised a small cavalry corps. On 12 July the horsemen took part in the fighting around the Col de la Vaccera, with disappointing results, but it came as a surprise to Marolles, who immediately informed the court. Another attempt to expel the Waldensians from their position occurred on the evening of 13 July. The ducal infantry, accompanied by 'volunteers' from the Piedmontese villages, advanced on their way to attack Angrogna, but the Waldensian sentinels spotted them and managed to warn their comrades in time. The next day the ducal troops attacked, being repulsed after a day of fighting. A few days later an expedition by the garrison of Torre Pellice was again repulsed, and the Waldensian counter-attack reached the edge of the village, from which they were forced to retreat due to the arrival of the ducal garrison of Luserna. This was the last major action since, thanks to the intervention of the Swiss cantons and the other European Protestant powers, the preliminaries for a peace agreement had been started.

Soon the echo of the events spread across Europe, increasing support for the Waldensians' cause. The exiled leaders skilfully exploited their

---

26 Tron, *Le Pasque Piemontesi*, p.26. On 23 May the Savoy had issued an edict that sentenced 37 'rebels' to death, and offering the sum of 600 *ducats* for the capture or death of Bartolomeo Jahier and his brother; he offered as many *ducats* for the main political leader Jean Léger, but only 300 for Josué Janavel.

27 *Ibid.*

network of relations not only to receive weapons and money, but also to place the blame on the House of Savoy all over Europe.[28] From 27 April the Waldensian leaders involved foreign diplomacy, and this mobilisation transformed the small and geographically remote religious minority into an 'affair' that dealt with the European chancelleries. The cantons of Bern and Zurich addressed their concerns about the episodes of violence in Piedmont to Savoy's court, while Cromwell sent to Turin the able Samuel Morland to form an exhaustive picture of the events.[29] Other letters urging intervention in favour of the Waldensians were sent to the States General of the United Provinces of the Netherlands, the kings of Sweden and Denmark, the Elector Prince of the Palatinate and even to the Prince of Transylvania. The severity of the accusations made against the ducal government also provoked strong reactions in France, where the Reformed community asked for a reprisal against the Duke of Savoy.[30] The Waldensian question was carefully examined by Mazarin, precisely when he was negotiating with Cromwell an alliance between France and England against Spain. Consequently, and unfortunately for the Duke, French support to him could become a problem for reaching an agreement, since on a diplomatic level the House of Savoy was severely embarrassed in the presence of the campaigns denouncing the

---

28 Among the many initiatives taken by the Waldensians during the persecutions of 1655, that of resorting to the widespread distribution of chronicles proved to be very effective, and denotes their ability to exploit relations within the international Protestant network. These chronicles were printed several times in the space of a few weeks in different countries, with numerous variants, and some fragmentary updates on the news coming from the Valleys, demonstrating that these were not sporadic but a well-concerted plan.

29 Morland's mission to Turin, about which he himself provides many details in *The History of the Evangelical Churches of the Valleys of Piemont*, published in 1658, and which in the British Isles would become a classic of Waldensian history, lasted almost two months and apparently achieved no greater results than the missions of the Swiss cantons. *Madama Reale* and the Duke also countered the Waldensian version, insisting on describing their subjects as 'rebels' and defining the punishment inflicted on them as 'legitimate'. As for the massacres, *Madama Reale* and the Duke stated that Morland must really have been misinformed, because in Turin noone had knowledge of crimes, although they did not deny the presence of victims, caused by climatic adversities after fleeing to the mountains, or as consequences of the encounters with the rebel partisans. However, Morland's mission served to dispel Savoy's illusions about the possibility of resolving the Waldensian question as a matter of domestic policy. See Jahier, *I Valdesi (1630–1665)*, pp.21–22.

30 Tron, *Le Pasque Piemontesi*, p.32. Concern about the turn of events in France is reflected in a letter sent to Turin by Savoy's agent in Paris, the Abbot Bailly. He notes with disappointment, regarding the Regent Christine, that 'the Waldensians have sent to Béarn, Bretagne and all the Reformed Churches in this kingdom reports about the facts involving the Duke's troops in their vallyes, giving such a horrible representation of it that one has never seen such an emotion as this false piety has excited in the spirits of the Huguenots … I met in Amboise a gentleman from Bretagne, who told me that many of his [Protestant] creeds were throwing fire and flames against Turin, and were waiting for nothing more than to get in arms and array themselves in battle.'

atrocities against the civilians.[31] What for the court in Turin was merely an internal affair was turning into an international problem that revealed the fragility of the state in the political scenario of those years.[32]

Actual negotiations were opened thanks to the Swiss cantons. On 28 May Gabriel von Weiss, councillor and diplomat of Berne began the first of his two missions on the same day as the second Waldensian assault on San Secondo. Weiss was received at the castle of Rivoli by the Duke, to whom he delivered a letter of intercession from the Swiss Protestant cantons in favour of the Waldensians. He also met the Marquis of Pianezza and later the Waldensian representatives in exile in France. However, as he had no real mandate to negotiate, he only succeeded in obtaining the promise of lenient treatment of the 'rebels' from the Duke, if they laid down their arms. After a second negotiation at Court on 3 June, he returned to Bern. The following month he made a new mission to Piedmont, during which he delivered to the Savoyard authorities a further invitation from the Cantons to exercise moderation. Letters of protest arrived also from the Prince of the Palatinate, the Duke of Württemberg, and the Landgrave of Hessen Kassel. However, concerted action on an international level would only occur with Cromwell's intervention.[33] After the Lord Protector, Mazarin also intervened and instructed the ambassador to Turin to commit himself to the Waldensian cause. Decisive support also arrived from prominent personalities in France, such as Henry de la Tour d'Auvergne, better

---

31 *Ibid.*, p.40. The Savoy representative in Paris met Mazarin on 11 June, the same day Morland presented Cromwell's missive to the Cardinal. However, neither on this nor any other occasion did he succeed in obtaining the promise of a commitment of any kind: 'and which is required in the name of holy principles, holy faith, and the advancement of the Catholic cause'. The Cardinal opposed the reasons of politics, the peace in the kingdom, the necessity of keeping the Huguenots, 'who are still powerful' and quiet the alliance with England, 'which is to be concluded to the greater glory of France against Spain, but which involves the Protector being silenced in his tumultuous demands in favour of the Piedmontese Protestants'.

32 *Ibid.*, p.33. The international pressure and the condition of encirclement in which the Savoy court found itself also caused a diplomatic incident with the Dutch Republic. The letter sent by the States General on 27 May was judged to be particularly forceful in tone, and above all the Dutch forgot to address the Duke using the title of *Altezza Reale* (Royal Highness) and consequently the Duke refused to reply.

33 A month after the military operations in the Val Pellice the English press, strictly controlled by the government which was well aware of the potential effects on public opinion, took a leading role in denouncing the atrocities committed by the French–Piedmontese soldiers. The first news appeared in *Mercurius Politicus* on 27 May. Cromwell's instruction to Morland included the possibility of an English war fleet 'demonstration' against Nice and Villafranca. As for the possibility of turning the strategic situation, using the small army raised by Jahier and Janavel to take the war into the ducal territory, London thought about it for a moment; but as Secretary of State Thurloe wrote on 27 July, 'nothing can be done without the Swiss, and the Swiss are backing down'. As for the other forces that could have militarily helped the Waldensians, there were the French Huguenots, who according to the Savoy ambassadors flaunted warlike intentions. However they remained politically immobile, limiting themselves to vigorous denunciations of the atrocities and gathering relief. See also Jahier, *I Valdesi 1630–1665*, pp.20–21.

78. Waldensian footmen involved in a fight in a painting of the late 1650s (courtesy of the Accademia di San Marciano, Turin). The Waldensians wear civil dress and only the figure depicted from behind, a commander, wears a red scarf over his shoulder. To his left, a drummer with embroidered sleeves and a red headdress incites his co-religionists to fight.

known as Turenne, who in 1655 was still a Protestant. Thanks to the growing international support, the Swiss cantons sent a new delegation to Turin led by Councillor Salomon Hirzel from Zurich, joined by the French ambassador de Servient. An agreement for a truce was finally reached on 18 August 1655 in Pinerolo with the issuing of the *Patenti di Grazia* (Patents of Pardon). This act was signed before English and Dutch delegates present in the city, since Savoyard diplomacy had manoeuvred to put them before a *fait accompli*. The agreement granted a 'pardon' to the Waldensians for their rebellion in arms, and restored at least part of their original civil and religious freedoms, but introduced some restrictions concerning the settlement outside the three valleys.[34] Janavel was excluded from the pardon and remained a fugitive. He was accused of continuing the armed resistance, and was sentenced to death in absentia in 1661.

After 1655 the court of Turin introduced a change of strategy. This was imposed by circumstances, but the underlying attitude did not change. The

---

34 Jahier, *I Valdesi (1630–1665)*, p.23. In particular, a ban was established on residing on the right bank of the river Pellice in Luserna, Lusernetta, Bibiana, Campiglione, Fenile, Garzigliana, Bricherasio and San Secondo of Pinerolo.

goal was that of containing the Waldensians within the limits in the most authentic sense of the term, namely, not only confining them within the territory established in 1650, but also restricting their civic autonomy as much as possible with a rigorous application of the 'concessions' contained in the patents and with a stronger military control. The instrument of this policy was the immediate erection of a fort on the hill above La Torre, with the emblematic name of *Santa Maria*. The location of the fort was unsuitable to defend the valley from an invasion from the mountain side, and in fact the purpose was only to keep the Waldensians under constant threat. The construction had begun even before the signing of the patents, and during the negotiations the Waldensians had insisted on its demolition, but without success.

With such assumptions, the peace agreements were destined to failure. In 1660 the Waldensian synod declared that the terms of the patents were not fully respected; the harsh demeanour of the governor Count of Bagnolo, 'who with truly over-soldierly methods ran the government of that place',[35] contributed to worsening the situation. Pastor Jean Léger reacted, and tensions between Turin and the Waldensian community resumed in 1662. In response to the actions of the Waldensian leaders, the Turin senate condemned Léger to death, ordering that his mansion be demolished and an 'infamous column' erected in its place as a warning to his followers. In February a senator was sent to execute the sentence with 115 soldiers from the Guards regiment and 40 mounted gendarmes.[36]

The fire continued to burn under the ashes for over a year, until 1663, when Jean Léger and Josué Janavel led a new insurrection which began in March with an assault on Luserna. About 500 Waldensians under Janavel moved to the plain, but he decided to abandon any further offensive action when his men encountered the resolute defence of the inhabitants of Bibiana, supported by the few regular soldiers led by the Count of Bagnolo. Janavel made his presence felt again on 11 May by storming the fort at Torre Pellice, and having failed to achieve any appreciable results, he headed east, threatening Bricherasio.[37] The Duke's reaction materialised in June, when three infantry columns of approximately 3,500 men marched against the valleys under the Marquises of Angrogna and Fleury and the Count of Bagnolo. Janavel concentred his forces in the Val Pellice, and advantaged by the carefully chosen positions on the heights he managed to push the enemy back for three weeks. The ducal troops intensified their efforts, and marched to Angrogna with regular infantrymen including the Duke's Guards and some squadrons of cavalry.[38] The Marquis of Villecardet de Fleury held command of this force,

---

35 Domenico Guerrini, *La Brigata dei Granatieri di Sardegna. Memorie storiche* (Turin, 1902), p.219.
36 *Ibid.*
37 Borello, *I valdesi in armi*, p.20.
38 Guerrini, in his *La Brigata dei Granatieri di Sardegna*, p.221, states that the Guards were on campaign with only 10 companies. His statement is intended to refute some chronicles of the events that double this figures. However, it is unlikely that there were more than 15, considering that in 1663 the regiment deployed this number.

which numbered approximately 1,200–1,500 men. On 5 July the ducal troops dispersed the Waldensians, who were reaping their grain. This action triggered a major encounter, which went down in history as the victory of Angrogna. On 6 July Fleury divided his force into three columns, in order to engage the enemy sited not far from the village of Angrogna, and assaulted them from behind with an outflanking manoeuvre. About 500 Waldensians were deployed on the spurs and immediately offered a strong resistance. Fleury's plan was thwarted by the impassable terrain, allowing the Waldensians to retreat into the mountains to prevent the Marquis attacking from the rear. In vain the ducal infantry assaulted the enemy. The situation on the field was now in favour of Janavel and his men, who counter-attacked and induced Fleury to order the retreat of all the troops, who arrived late in the evening at San Secondo and Bricherasio, pursued by the Waldensians.[39] The lack of fresh forces and the shortage of ammunition prevented Janavel from exploiting the victory and forced him and his men to take refuge on the mountains. Once again ducal repression was very harsh and resulted in further cruelty against the civilians. The encounters continued with minor skirmishes, but in December, not far from Angrogna, the Waldensians ambushed a ducal column and killed some officers.[40] Unfortunately international support for the Waldensians was almost nonexistent, and in France the attitude had changed now that Louis XIV ruled. In early winter the political unity of the Waldensians came to an end: the synod disavowed Janavel, who had to expatriate to Geneva, while Jean Léger moved to Leiden.[41] In January 1664, after a new mediation of the Swiss cantons, the Duke of Savoy issued new patents which restored a peace that would last until new persecutions in 1685.

---

39 *Ibid.*, p.223. The casualties are not known, and each side claimed figures too different to be reconciled. In any case, the defeat had strong repercussions, as the Marquis of Fleury was replaced in command by the Count of San Damiano.

40 Borello, *I valdesi in armi*, p.22.

41 The Waldensian diaspora into Geneva led to repercussions in relations between the Protestant republic and the Duchy of Savoy. By 1664, the protests of the clergy on both sides regarding their respective jurisdiction over the border communities had further stiffened relations between the two governments, In Turin it was also well known that Geneva was the main base for Waldensian resistance in exile. In October 1666, following a dispute over a trial against a Savoyard officer arrested in Geneva for crimes committed in Savoy, worsened the situation. Protests were followed by threats. The issue involved the Swiss cantons, who split in half: the Protestants for Geneva and the Catholics for the Duke. The Geneva government responded by mobilising the militia, which was followed by the arrival of the Marquis of Pianezza with 4,000 regulars to Lake Leman. This move did not intimidate the government of the Republic, which appointed the Count of Donat (the former Protestant commander of Orange) as commander-in-chief, and obtained help by way of men and weapons from Zurich and Berne. This situation continued throughout 1667. The parliament in Geneva came out in favour of a settlement, but at the same time declared that the Republic would never give satisfaction to the Duke of Savoy. In 1668, after two diplomatic missions and the negotiation of France, the crisis was resolved, thanks to an agreement that revised the borders. See Saluzzo, *Histoire Militaire du Piémont*, vol. IV, pp.348–352.

The Savoy-Piedmont War Against Genoa, 1672–1673

Italy is like an artichoke, which the House of Savoy has to eat one leaf at a time.
(Duke Carlo Emanuele I of Savoy; 1562–1630)

The Savoy enclave of Oneglia and the western borders between Piedmont, Nice and the territory of Genoa had been a source of many local conflicts between the Duchy and the Republic. Since the fifteenth century the dukes of Savoy had sought to annex the Roya valley to connect their domains with Oneglia, in order to develop the salt trade by circumventing Genoese customs duties. But the valley had remained in Genoese possession, thwarting the dukes' trade plans. A new opportunity to circumvent the Genoese customs came with the acquisition of Tende in 1572. This possession allowed for a connection between Nice and Piedmont, but the path was long and difficult and could be travelled only in spring and summer. Furthermore, the Savoyard domains wedged into Genoese territory with the castles of Maro and Prelà, located in the valleys of the Impero and Prino torrents, causing new mistrust and friction between the two neighbouring states. To make coexistence even more difficult there were the robberies by the local inhabitants, described by a contemporary historian as 'fierce as wild boars'.[42] The Oneglia road, on the other hand, was passable all year round, but the tract from Pornassio to Col di Nava was Genoese territory and the Republic had every interest in maintaining possession of it.

Frictions between Genoa and Turin continued, since the boundaries of this area, which had last been established in 1625, became the subject of disputes by local communities who claimed exploitation rights over woods and pastures. The ownership of these territories was often subject to partisan interpretations, but the rulers did not intervene to resolve the disputes. Complicating the scenario, in 1652 came the question of the inheritance of the Marquisate of Dolceacqua, close to the western border of the Republic of Genoa, and not far from Oneglia. The heir of Marquis Carlo Doria, Francesco had made an agreement with Regent Christine of France to cede the territory to the Duchy of Savoy. This included not only Dolceacqua, but also the villages of Perinaldo, Apricale and Isola (today Isolabona).

Over time, a heated rivalry arose between the population of the villages on the Republic's side and those beyond the border ruled by the Duke of Savoy. Disputes had degenerated into armed confrontation over claims for access to water sources, or timber from the surrounding forests, whose paths crossed the insecure borders. In November 1664 a clash between the inhabitants of Castelfranco and Pigna for the property of the woods on Mount Gordale resulted in the wounding of a subject of the Duke. The Savoyard authorities, in the opinion of contemporary chroniclers, did not miss the opportunity to magnify the incident, and once the news reached the court of Turin, the Regent ordered the mobilisation of the militia in the municipalities of the

---

42 Anonymous, *Carlo Emanuele II e la guerra del Piemonte contro Genova. L'anno 1672* (without place and date, USSME Archive), p.9.

WARS AND SOLDIERS IN THE EARLY REIGN OF LOUIS XIV - VOLUME 6 - PART 2

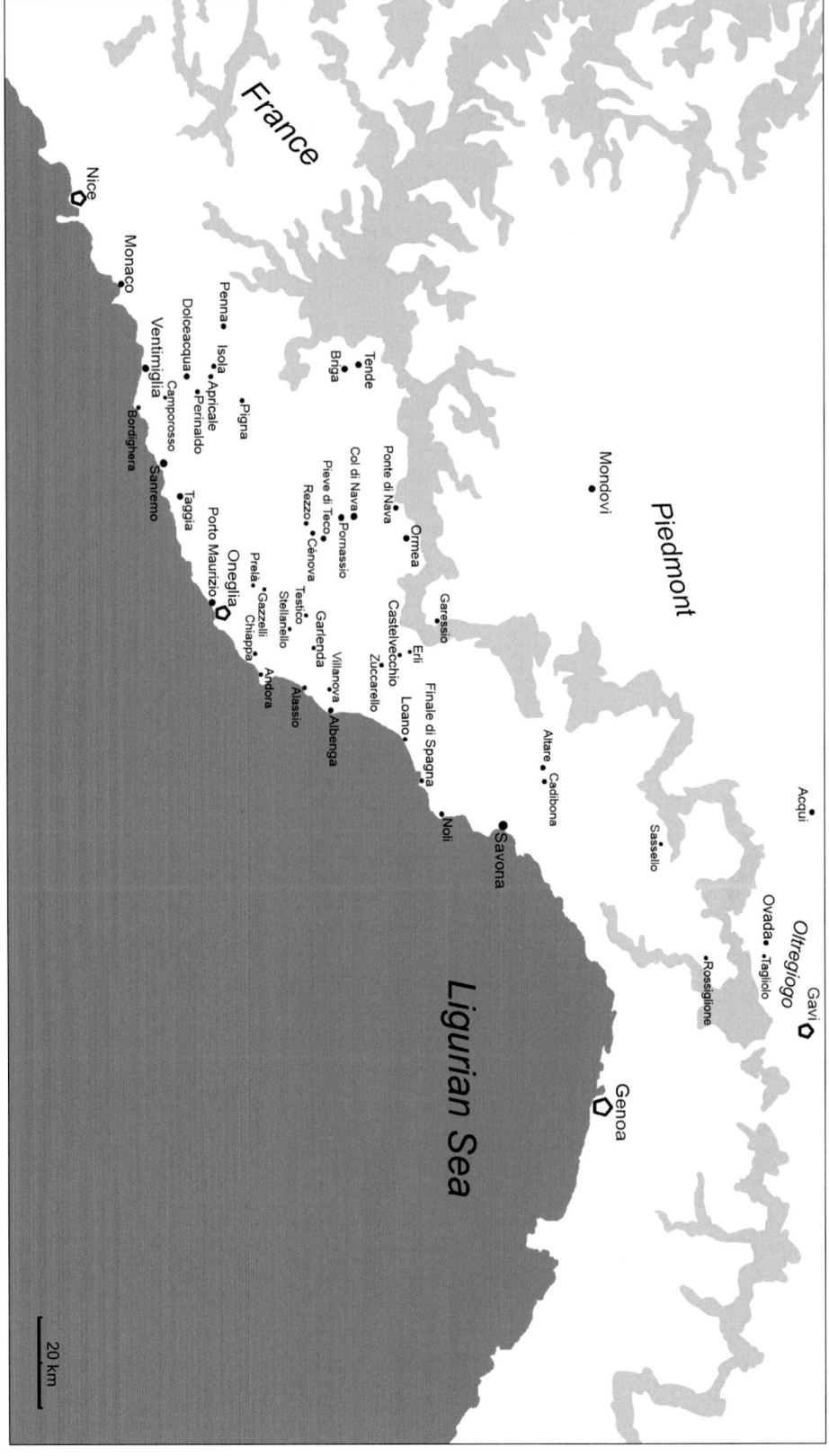

Map 2. Theatre of operations, 1672

region.⁴³ The movements of troops near the borders, albeit only of militia, alarmed the Genoese government, which immediately sent its soldiers to the border. For the moment the conflict died down due to the intervention of France and Spain, whose ambassadors in Turin and Genoa convinced the parties to interrupt the escalation of war.

In 1670 the border disputes this time involved the inhabitants of Briga, subjects of the Duke, and those of Triora, ruled by Genoa.⁴⁴ The winds of war returned to blow, but once again the intervention of French diplomacy restored peace between the two contenders after the intervention of the Abbot of Servient, son of the French ambassador in Turin.⁴⁵ The mediation had lasted a whole year, and in the end neither side was satisfied. Meanwhile further incidents, this time with cattle theft, involved the villages of Rezzo and Cénova, which accused each other of invading the territory. The Duke ordered an investigation, and to this end sent the governor of Oneglia to Cénova to gather information and deliberate over countermeasures. He then sent his emissaries to make contact with some bands of brigands in Genoese territory to support the population of Cénova against the oppression of the more populous Rezzo.⁴⁶

Carlo Emanuele II, resentful about the composition of the disagreements that he considered unfavourable, and also because he considered it dishonourable to come to terms with the government of a Republic, began to meditate on entrusting the question of borders to arms.⁴⁷ But if the Duke had not already made up his mind to go to war against Genoa, his finance minister, Giovanni Battista Trucchi, pointed out the proximity of the Rezzo territory to that of Pornassio and that a military action could solve the problem of supplying salt from Oneglia.⁴⁸

The Duke, however, was aware that a war against Genoa would provoke the reaction of Spain, which feared Savoy for the threat repeatedly brought on its Milanese possessions. Furthermore, on the French side there was also interest in preventing an increase of the ducal territories. It was therefore necessary to wait for the right opportunity; the moment in which both powers

---

43 Francesco Maria Viceti, *Compendioso Racconto De principali Successi della Guerra mossa l'anno 1672 Alla Repubblica di Genova Dal Duca di Savoia Collo stabilimento della Pace nell'Anno 1673 Descritta Dà Francesco M:a Viceti* (Archivio Storico del Comune di Genova, Manoscritti, Ricci, 136, after 1673), p.13.

44 Some militiamen from Briga had captured two men from Triora with firearms in the ducal territory and handed them over to the Savoyard authorities who, after a quick trial, had executed one of them. The death sentence on their fellow citizen provoked the reaction of the inhabitants of Triora, who crossed the border and kidnapped a peasant from Briga. The Genoese opened fire on the people who had rushed to help the peasant. Anonymous, *Carlo Emanuele II e la guerra del Piemonte contro Genova*, p.16.

45 Ibid.

46 Ciro Paoletti, *Dal Ducato all'Unità. Tre secoli e mezzo di storia militare piemontese* (Rome, USSME, 2011), p.148.

47 Anonymous, *Carlo Emanuele II e la guerra del Piemonte contro Genova*, p.17.

48 Ibid., p.21.

would have diverted attention from those places, perhaps because they were engaged in a new war. It was also necessary to find a more solid pretext than a border dispute between peasants and muleteers. A first opportunity came at the beginning of 1672: the council of the small Republic of Noli, associated with Genoa through a perpetual alliance since 1202, declared its dissatisfaction with the protecting Republic, and attracted by the Savoyard agents asked to join the ducal states. In Genoa, however, the negotiations were discovered and all the members of the Noli council were arrested; the councillors found guilty paid for this action with their lives.[49]

A further, unexpected opportunity materialised in the spring of the same year. In 1671 the Genoese patrician Raffaele Della Torre, exiled for debt and theft by the Republic, had made contact with the ducal authorities in Oneglia, assuring them that he, thanks to his accomplices in Savona, could deliver the city to the Duke of Savoy. He had also explained his plan to important people of the court, such as Marquis Carlo Giovanni Battista di Simiana, Marquis of Livorno di Piemonte, son of the influential Marquis of Pianezza, who had met him years earlier in Genoa. Thanks to the interest of the Marquis of Livorno, the unscrupulous Della Torre was summoned to Turin to introduce his plan directly to Carlo Emanuele II. The plan, after being amended several times, found agreement among the Duke and his advisors, including the Marquis of Livorno, the general auditor and *sovrintendente generale di guerra* Carlo Antonio Blancardi, the Marquis Ghiron di Villa, a veteran of the Cretan War, and of course the minister of finance, who pursued his plan concerning the Oneglia salt trade. The plan was opposed by the Marquis of Pianezza, who had long since retired to the convent but was summoned by the Duke for important decisions.

A council of war was convened in the presence of the Duke, who agreed on a plan of operations that included a rapid advance on Savona, where according to Della Torre a strong anti-Genoese party was ready to rise up. Meanwhile the latter, with mercenaries he had enlisted with the Duke's money in Monferrato and Parma, would advance on Genoa through the Bisagno valley, arriving by the night of 24 June, the day of St John the Baptist, the city's patron saint. He counted on taking advantage of the festivities in which the soldiers of the garrison usually participated. Della Torre's local partisans would then open the gate of San Simone, allowing the men enlisted by him to enter the city and set fire to the Acquasola arsenal, causing the panic of the population. Della Torre would then open the prisons, occupy the ducal palace and the harbour and seize the treasure of the Banco di San Giorgio. As soon as this feat was accomplished, the Duke's troops were to march from Savona in the direction of Genoa to defeat any remaining resistance and complete the occupation of the Republic's territory.[50]

The plan was audacious and complex, and above all it did not take into account any setbacks that could jeopardise its operation, nor did the Duke and his advisors investigate the truth about the partisans who Della Torre

---

49   *Ibid.*, p.18.
50   *Ibid.*, p.25.

boasted to have inside Genoa in order to complete his bold action. In partial defence of the Duke and his councillors, Della Torre had managed to assure the support of authoritative people such as Angelo Maria Vico, who had actually recruited mercenaries in Monferrato, as well as the support of a strong band in Chiavari, with the order to be ready to march on Genoa. On June 16 the ducal army with 4,000 infantry of the regiments *Guardie*, *Savoie*, *Piemonte*, *Monferrato* and *Nice*, three Swiss companies, and 850 cavalrymen was assembled at Altare, close to the Ligurian border.[51] As commander-in-chief Carlo Emanuele appointed Count Catalano Alfieri, a man who was already aged but reputed to be an expert officer trained in the war against Spain.[52] The Marquis of Livorno had been designated as lieutenant with the rank of *tenente generale della cavalleria*, who, much younger than Alfieri, was reputed an officer no less valiant than the commander-in-chief. Among the senior commanders there were other important and authoritative officers, such as the Marquis of San Damiano, the Marquis of Parella, the Count of Piossasco and the Count of Magliano, son of the commander-in-chief. Everything proceeded according to plan, and without the Genoese noticing the movement of troops on the border.

On 22 June, however, the events took another direction. Angelo Maria Vico, realising that the plan to seize Genoa was destined to fail, and fearing the consequences of his betrayal – which would have consigned him to the executioner – revealed to the governor of Mallare, Giovanni Battista Cattaneo, the plan prepared by the Duke of Savoy and Della Torre. The news caused the astonishment of the Genoese government, but immediately afterwards the Senate sent as many troops as possible to Savona with the fleet, at the disposal of the governor Girolamo Spinola. Once reinforcements were received, the governor had to send part of them to the border in order to block the way of the Savoyards. The government ordered the arming of four war vessels and all the galleys for the defence of the *Ponente*, then sent the commissioners Mario Doria and Giovanni Battista Gentile with 1,000 Corsican infantry and foot militia in the Bisagno and Polcevera valleys, and the commissioner Ansaldo de' Mari, to reinforce the fortress of Vado with other infantry. Della Torre managed to escape just in time and fled to neutral territory.[53] Overall, the Republic had on paper 3,500 regular troops dispersed over the whole

---

51 Paoletti, *Dal Ducato all'Unità*, p.148.
52 Catalano Alfieri was born in 1602, the eldest son of Count Urbano Alfieri. Since a very young age he was educated to a career of arms by his father, who was killed by a cannonball in battle while standing at his son's side. Catalano inherited the family lordship in the territory of Castagnole delle Lanze as lord of Magliano and Castagnole. In 1633 he obtained the license of colonel-proprietor of an infantry regiment, which later became *Piemonte di Sua Altezza Reale*. He was always at the service of the dukes of Savoy, showing great courage and skill, especially in the conquest of the Fortress of Ceva (1635), of which he was later governor for several years, as well as in the reconquest of Asti in 1643, Turin in 1652 and Trino in 1658.
53 Raffaele della Torre disappeared from the scene, only to return in 1675 when the Regency expelled him from Aosta, where he had received asylum. He wandered for some time in France, Alsace and the Netherlands. In 1681 Della Torre was in Venice, where he was assassinated by

territory and only 2,500 between Genoa, Savona and western Liguria, with which numbers it was impossible to repel an invasion, and therefore ordered the enlistment of other troops in Corsica, Liguria and friendly Italian states.

Meanwhile, on the Piedmontese border, the march was proceeding according to plan, but on the evening of 24 June the Savoyard advance was suddenly delayed by an illness of Alfieri; the command was temporarily taken over by the Marquis of Livorno. From the border, the Marquis moved at the head of the vanguard in the direction of Altare, but as soon as the troops crossed the border he learned from a friar that Della Torre's conspiracy had been discovered and that the Republic was sending troops and ships to defend Savona.

On the opposite side, on 23 June, Spinola had sent a Corsican and Italian infantry corps from Savona under Captains Alfonso Gentile and Girolamo Bagigalupo with the task of defending Altare and Cadibona before he even received the order from Genoa. On 24 June reinforcements sent by the government landed in Savona under the orders of Corsican *sergente maggiore* Pier Paolo Restori, a veteran of the Cretan War who was reputed a renowned and strong commander. The day after, the Marquis of Livorno gathered his officers for a council of war. Understandably he was very disappointed at the outcome of the Genoese affair and also suspected that Alfieri had feigned illness to intentionally leave him in charge of operations.[54] Before taking any decision, the Marquis sought Alfieri's advice and sent a messenger to Turin to inform the court of Della Torre's failure. Initially the Duke decided to renounce the enterprise, but on 26 June he sent the order to proceed and crossed the border with all the troops. The acquisition of Genoa was intended as the culmination of Savoyard mercantilism, and the Duke's plan was to take advantage of Louis XIV's preparations for the Dutch War of 1672.[55]

Having recovered from his illness, Alfieri retook command on 26 June, and marched with the troops on Garessio, where the Savoyards entered in the evening. The troops stopped for a day, then the offensive resumed and continued with the action of the militia of Oneglia, which at the end of a short fight seized Ponte di Nava, a strategic location for securing the march on Savona. On 28 June the Savoyard infantry under *sergente maggiore* Bonard assaulted Pieve di Teco, whose small Genoese garrison surrendered without resistance.[56] Alfieri, in the name of Duke Carlo Emanuele II, issued a *manifesto* in which he declared that his soldiers had to protect the inhabitants of Cénova from the harassment of the Republic's subjects, and exhorted the local authorities to negotiate an agreement with the Republic

---

unknown killers during carnival; see anonymous, *Carlo Emanuele II e la guerra del Piemonte contro Genova*, p.86.

54 Saluzzo, *Histoire Militaire du Piémont*, vol. IV, p.360.

55 *New Cambridge Modern History* (Cambridge: Cambridge University Press, 1964), vol. V: 'The Ascendancy of France, 1648–1688', p.470.

56 Anonymous, *Carlo Emanuele II e la guerra del Piemonte contro Genova*, pp.29–30. Alfieri stated that the Duke was ready to withdraw if Genoa agreed to entrust the settlement of the dispute to a college of doctors from Bologna.

to resolve the quarrel. Meanwhile reconnaissance carried out by the cavalry informed Alfieri that the paths towards Savona were manned by the enemy. The Savoyard commander, therefore, decided to carry out the offensive in the valley of the Empire and establish a contact with the garrison of Oneglia.

The Genoese government gave no credence to Alfieri's conciliatory proclamations and did not doubt what the Savoyards' real objectives were. It therefore ordered the rectors of the provinces to mobilise the militia to reinforce the regular troops, and the manning of the passes and access routes, and then entrusted the command of the troops to its most trusted officers: Domenico Doria, Ambrogio Imperiali, Jacopo Grimaldi, Gerolamo and Agostino Spinola, and the aforementioned Restori.

Gradually, other troops arrived from eastern Liguria. A column of fully equipped troops under Ambrogio Di Negro received orders to march on Pieve di Teco and deploy to protect Albenga. They were followed by captains Carlo Lorenzo Spinola, Gerolamo Zerbi and Giovanni Durazzo, at the head of Italian and Corsican troops. The garrison at Albenga was reinforced with another 200 regulars, and finally Porto Maurizio, in front of Oneglia, received a company as reinforcement, under the command of commissioner Ansaldo de' Mari. The government called upon the population of the capital to contribute donations of money and provision to recruit and support more troops, and both patricians and commoners responded enthusiastically. Within a few days a sum capable of paying for 6,000 mercenary infantrymen was assembled.[57] As for external aid, the Republic of Lucca offered troops and money, but the government politely declined, declaring however that they would ask for it if needed, and for the time being Genoa negotiated the purchase of arms and ammunition at a reduced price.[58] *Doge* Alessandro Grimaldi, a man of great ability and charisma, became the soul of the resistance against the Duke of Savoy.

At the end of a week of fruitless negotiations between Alfieri and the Genoese authorities, the situation in Pieve di Teco became increasingly critical. The population, subjected to harassment by the Savoyard soldiers, had fled into the woods and begun to react with weapons, to the point of forcing the occupying Savoyards to garrison the access roads from the village to Ponte di Nava and to have to fight their way out to supply themselves with water from the stream.

The Genoese found an unexpected ally in a bandit named Antonio Folco, known as 'the Turk' and already condemned to the death penalty, who in exchange for forgiveness and greedy to commence looting, received authorisation to carry out guerrilla operations against the Savoyards. Folco and his band, made up of about 70 people, kept the enemy troops on alert and on 11 July finally attacked the Ponte di Nava garrison. The bandits were about to prevail, but the Count of Magliana came to the rescue with all the companies of *Piemonte* and some of the *Monferrato* regiment. The Savoyards,

---

57   *Ibid.*, p.31.

58   Between July and August Lucca supplied Genoa with 1,000 flintlock muskets. ASLu, *Camarlingo Generale, Deputazioni*, f. 229, *delibere* (1672).

however, were repulsed by a violent rainstorm that disordered the troops, obliging the Count to order the return to Pieve di Teco.

In response to the Republican government, which had hired criminals to fight them, the Savoyards in turn hired the Piedmontese brigand Sebastiano Contrario, who was also sentenced to death, entrusting him with the task of harassing the Genoese troops.[59]

On 15 July, therefore, the Duke of Savoy ordered Alfieri to resume the offensive. The following day a column of infantry under the Count of Piossasco, comprising the three Swiss companies, the *Savoie* regiment and some volunteers headed to Rezzo. After dispersing the 200 armed villagers guarding the village, the Savoyards destroyed the fortifications and set fire to the castle. On the same day the bulk of the troops marched to Pornassio, which was occupied without encountering resistance.

In Genoa, meanwhile, a flying corps of 1,500 Italian mercenaries and 500 Corsicans was formed selecting the best and most trustworthy troops, and entrusting it to the 'valiant' Pier Paolo Restori.[60] The first action directed by him took place on 18 July, but the expectations were not rewarded. After gathering detailed information on the situation in Rezzo, Restori headed towards this location and sent a vanguard commanded by his second Vincentello Gentile, also a Corsican, to take up position and prepare to assault the enemy if they moved from Rezzo.[61] At the same time, Restori took up position a short distance away at a paper mill on the Arroscia stream, so as to rush in support of Gentile or cut off the Savoyards if they advanced towards the sea. As expected, the Savoyards came out from Rezzo and began to be targeted by enemies hidden in the bushes. The sound of musketry alerted Restori who sent some troops to engage the enemies. The Savoyards responded to enemy fire and maintained their order of march, despite the narrow paths and ravines that facilitated ambushes.

A reconnaissance had warned Alfieri of the Genoese presence in the paper mill. The Savoy commander sent two companies of gendarmes to outflank the enemy position, while with the infantry headed towards the paper mill to trap Restori and his men. The Genoese had meanwhile entrenched themselves firmly on all sides and were ready to engage the enemy who were advancing on open ground. Behind their entrenchments and protected by the bush, the Genoese opened fire on the enemy infantry, who began to suffer heavy losses. Alfieri launched more troops to the assault, then advanced himself with the Guards regiment and finally succeeded in defeating the stubborn resistance of the Corsicans, who retreated to the mountains, avoiding the arrival of the enemy cavalry which was slowed down by the dense forest terrain. Alfieri's

---

59 Anonymous, *Carlo Emanuele II e la guerra del Piemonte contro Genova* p.33. The two bandits continued the guerrilla operations, each taking care, however, not to cause the least damage to each other.

60 Viceti, *Compendioso Racconto*, p.33.

61 Vincentello Gentile became later *maestre de campo* of the Corsican infantry regiment in Spanish service. See Mugnai, *Wars and Soldiers in the Early Reign of Louis XIV*, Volume 4, pp.152–153.

victory cost many lives, including four officers, and among them the Marquis of Cavour.[62]

Discontent was spreading among the Savoyard troops and militiamen, the latter especially complaining about the strong discipline, the still unpaid salaries, and the poverty of the region which thwarted any hope of plunder. The situation was worsened by the growing irritation of the Marquis of Livorno towards Catalano Alfieri, which undermined the direction of operations. The news of the quarrel between the two commanders reached Turin, and induced the Duke to send his bastard uncle Don Gabriele of Savoy with some infantry companies of regiment *Saluzzo*, volunteers of the Piedmontese militia, provisions and ammunition; the Duke entrusted Don Gabriele with the command of the campaign and ordered him to proceed rapidly to the conquest of some important towns on the western *Riviera*. Alfieri and the Marquis of Livorno were to remain with the troops as his lieutenants. The decision turned out to be a bad one: the two commanders, surprised and irritated at being placed in subordination, soon reached an alliance, both siding against Don Gabriele and opposing his designs.

The new commander had a summary knowledge of the territory and its dangers, having travelled there a few weeks earlier, sent by the Duke to obtain information on the progress of operations. However, he had formed an opinion by studying the maps of the region, which were very inaccurate.[63] At the council of war on 20 July, Don Gabriele proposed dividing the troops into two columns and directing one to Oneglia and the other to occupy the village of Zuccarello, north of Albenga. The two columns were eventually to rejoin at Testico, more or less halfway between Zuccarello and Oneglia. During the march the two columns would take over all fortified places held by the enemy. The plan was very complex. The troops in Pieve di Teco were to make a wide turn via Garessio instead of proceeding by the more direct route, which was judged to be not comfortable, but exposed to enemy ambushes. The rush to get to the sea was a serious strategic mistake. As important as it was to occupy coastal locations, the destruction of enemy forces was still the main task of a military campaign. Circumstances, moreover, favoured the Savoyards: Restori's flying corps was isolated and far from its bases, and if Don Gabriele forced it to retreat, his troops could pursue it and exploit their numerical superiority, and with a bit of luck cause it to rout. The discarding of this option had decisive repercussions on the course of the war.[64]

On 21 July the march to the sea began. Don Gabriele, with the *Guardie Savoie* and *Nice* infantry regiments, the Swiss companies, 400 volunteers and part of the cavalry headed towards Oneglia, where he arrived the next day.[65]

---

62 Anonymous, *Carlo Emanuele II e la guerra del Piemonte contro Genova*, p.37.
63 Saluzzo, *Histoire Militaire du Piémont*, vol. IV, p.377.
64 Anonymous, *Carlo Emanuele II e la guerra del Piemonte contro Genova*, pp.40–41.
65 Regarding the composition of the contingent under Don Gabriele, a contradiction should be noted. The *Guardie* regiment, assigned to his column, was later involved in the fighting that involved the corps under Alfieri. However, it is probable that, as it was the largest unit, it was assigned to both commanders.

Having left some reinforcements with the local garrison, in the afternoon he resumed the march to Testico to meet the other column. Once in front of Diano, Don Gabriele demanded the surrender of the Genoese garrison, composed of 150 local militiamen under Raffaele Giustiniani. The Genoese captain refused to surrender, thus the town was assaulted and sacked, and the garrison taken prisoner. Then without suffering any losses, and despite the fire from the Genoese galleys that were cruising along the coast, Don Gabriele advanced, burning the countryside, and heading menacingly towards Andorra.

In the meantime Alfieri, after destroying the fortifications of Pieve di Teco, took governor Gaspare Maria Gentile and some prisoners to accompany the troops under his command, comprising the *Piemonte* and *Monferrato* infantry regiments, a battalion of militia and the remainder of the cavalry. He headed to Garessio, where he joined the companies of the *Saluzzo* regiment and 400 volunteers of the militia under the Marquis of Brianze. After a one-day stop in Garessio the column resumed its march on Zuccarello, hindered by the locals who tried to block its way with boulders and felled trees. On 23 July the Savoyards occupied Castelvecchio after breaking the obstinate resistance of the defenders. Among them, some Piedmontese deserters were recognised, who were immediately executed. In the evening the march came to a halt at Zuccarello, at which point Alfieri ordered another one-day halt to give the troops, exhausted from marching in the middle of summer on the rugged terrain of Liguria, a chance to recover. The column was joined by other militiamen led by the Marquis of Parella and Sebastiano Contrario's band. On 26 July Alfieri resumed the march to join Don Gabriele in Testico, where he believed the commander was already expecting him. To be on the safe side, Alfieri left a rearguard between Castelvecchio and Erli formed by the infantry of the *Saluzzo* regiment and the militiamen of Brienze.

In Genoa, several pieces of news of enemy movements followed one another. On 22 July the Commissioner General, Senator Gian Luca Durazzo, arrived in Albenga which he had chosen as the base of operations. Here he met Restori returning from the interior to organise the countermeasures to be taken. The information gathered confirmed that the Savoyards had split into two corps, so it was decided to send the flying corps to take up position on the heights between Alassio and Albenga. Two days later Restori learned that Don Gabriele's column was marching on the ridge of the hills between the villages of Chiappa and Cervo, while Alfieri had been spotted near Albenga. The Corsican commander placed some sentinels on the Mount of Madonna della Guardia, from which it was possible to observe the enemy's march. After a brief council of war with his officers, and after receiving some reinforcements of Corsican troops led by *sergente maggiore* Frediani, Restori decided to deal first with Don Gabriele's column, which appeared to be the most threatening.[66]

On 24 July Restori engaged the approaching enemy with his Corsican infantrymen nearby Chiappa. The Savoyards had prepared some

---

66 Viceti, *Compendioso Racconto*, p.40.

entrenchments, but the continuous pressure of the Corsican troops, who took advantage of the terrain to approach the enemy and hit them on the flanks, prevailed after two hours of fierce fighting. The Savoyards retreated in good order and by the evening they were near the village of San Bernardo. The next day they fell back on Stellanello. Restori ordered his men to halt, as Stellanello was an Imperial fief and Genoa's peremptory orders were to avoid any territorial infringement. However, the Savoyards suffered an unexpected setback when a cart carrying gunpowder exploded, killing some soldiers and an adjutant, the Marquis of Luserna.

On 26 July Alfieri learned of Don Gabriele's retreat, from whom he was separated by a few miles of easily passable terrain. He therefore decided to move his troops towards Albenga and along the way set fire to the houses of Bastia, and from there he thought to reach Villanova and finally Testico. Durazzo, informed of Alfieri's advance, alerted Restori, who immediately moved his troops to the heights south-west of Albenga, threatening Alfieri's troops marching on the left flank. Durazzo then mobilised the militia of Albenga, which together with the inhabitants of Villanova barred Alfieri's way. Restori's evasive tactics, which took advantage of the wooded terrain and did not allow the Savoyards to be fully aware of the Genoese forces, caused the joint march to be halted for a whole day. On 28 July Don Gabriele marched again in the direction of Testico, but Restori attacked him on one flank, after Frediani had arrested the column by attacking it frontally. This time the action was perfectly coordinated. The Genoese succeeded in routing in succession the *Nice* regiment, the Swiss, the militiamen and the cavalry, which was useless on that terrain.[67] The Savoyards loss many soldiers in the fight, and as many were taken prisoners, and only by taking refuge once again in Stellanello did they avoid an even greater disaster.

Another encounter occurred on 28 July between Garlenda and Castelvecchio. It involved all the Savoyard force, which held firm and forced the Genoese to retreat. Confident in the better quality of his troops, Alfieri sent all the troops at his disposal against Frediani's Corsicans, but taking advantage of the terrain he repulsed every assault in turn. The Marquis of Livorno also intervened, leading the *Monferrato* regiment to the assault and opening the way in the intricate terrain, but after one hour of fierce fighting he ordered a withdrawal without achieving appreciable results. Manoeuvring by internal lines, Restori was able to maintain his strong position until sunset. Despite the continued deployment of fresh forces, the Savoyards had failed to expel the enemy from the hills, and thus, late in the evening, they left the battlefield. With this defeat, the last chance to win the war also vanished.

During the night of 28–29 July Alfieri's column gathered its stragglers and returned to Villanova, with the cavalry in rearguard, followed at a fair distance by the Genoese patrols. The following morning, reconnaissance revealed to

---

67   The chronicles do not mention the *Guardie* regiment, which was also part of the column of Don Gabriele. Paoletti, in *Dal Ducato all'Unità*, p.150, claims that the Genoese assault isolated the guards, preventing them from marching with the column. The regiment succeeded in joining Alfieri the day after.

79. Genoese infantry and militia marching against the Savoyards before the battle of Garlenda, on 3 August 1672, in the reconstruction by Italo Cenni. The Savoyards had planned the invasion with great care, using mules and other pack animals to transport ammunition and supplies through the region's rugged paths, but the effectiveness of the Genoese guerrilla warfare and serious strategic mistakes by the Savoyard commanders resulted in a bitter defeat.

the Savoyard commanders that the enemy had surrounded them, closing off all ways of retreat, and cutting off communication with both Oneglia and Piedmont. Don Gabriele, furious at the failure to rejoin Alfieri's column, who he accused of cowardice, decided to make his way to the nearest friendly territory, namely Oneglia. After leaving 800 men at Stellanello, he headed with his remaining 900 in the direction of the sea. The plan was certainly dictated by the scarcity of available provisions, but with that move Don Gabriele abandoned Alfieri, leaving him in a decidedly dangerous situation. Arriving at the border with the territory of Oneglia, the Savoyards found the access blocked by the militia of Triora under Giuseppe Maria Centurione, while behind them were marching the Corsicans of Vincentello Gentile, who had just arrived as reinforcements. The sun was going down, and to prevent his force being surrounded Don Gabriele took advantage of the darkness to send the drums along a different route from the one he intended to take, so as to divert the enemies' surveillance as he headed north with the troops. The expedient worked, and by marching quickly Alfieri and his men reached Briga, in Piedmontese territory. To march faster, the Savoyards had abandoned 200 mules loaded with ammunition and provisions.[68] Don

---

68 Anonymous, *Carlo Emanuele II e la guerra del Piemonte contro Genova*, p.54.

Gabriele also managed to send 800 men to reinforce the garrison of Oneglia, who, with much luck entered the city the following day.[69]

Now that Don Gabriele was no longer a threat, the Genoese could deal with Alfieri, who was unaware of the retreat of the other column. He was camped with troops at Zuccarello and therefore posed a threat to the plan drawn up by the *illustrissimo* Durazzo: with the troops just arrived to reinforce him from Genoa, he intended to besiege Oneglia and conquer it as quickly as possible. Once he had completed the operation, he would be able to enter Piedmont and repay the enemy with requisitions and seizures at will. Leaving part of the troops on the border with Oneglia, and blocking the city from the sea side with galleys, Durazzo sent some companies to guard the roads to Piedmont, while with the other troops he approached the area between Pieve and Zuccarello, where he had been informed that Alfieri's column was camped. He then alerted Restori, and ordered him to head for the same area to close the enemy in a trap. On 31 July the Savoyard commander was still unaware of the evolving situation, but after fruitlessly trying to make contact with Don Gabriele's column, Alfieri realised he was isolated and decided to move from that position. Once the camp was raised, the Savoyards set fire to the surrounding villages while the cavalry screened the column's march. The next day Alfieri stopped and laid the camp on the road to Garessio not far from Garlenda, and decided to stay there two days waiting for Don Gabriele; he still had 3,600 men.[70] The stop was fatal. Restori managed to reach the enemy column and carefully set up an ambush. On 3 August the Savoyards resumed their march along the route to Garessio. Slowed by a violent thunderstorm and the foraging for cavalry and train, Alfieri ordered the Count of Scalenghe to advance with the cavalry and the *Saluzzo* regiment at the head of the column. As soon as the enemy vanguard had passed, on both sides of the road Restori and Frediani's Corsicans opened fire on the column, cutting it in two. Fighting flared up along the road, which ran between thickly wooded cliffs. The Genoese infantrymen quickly advanced, overwhelming the carriages, and only encountered resistance when they attacked the Marquis of Parella and his men in the surrounding hills. In the meantime the Genoese also attacked the Savoyard rearguard, but even without taking advantage of the surprise, Restori's men prevailed on Count de la Trinité's militiamen, who fled the battlefield and dispersed into the woods. In the centre, the *Piemonte* and *Monferrato* regiments formed two squares and held out for hours on unfavourable terrain. Despite the chaos, Alfieri kept his cool enough to rally the troops and fall back on Castelvecchio. He tried in vain to draw back the vanguard, which had unexpectedly continued in the direction of Garessio regardless of the noise of the fighting. The Genoese pursued their enemy so closely that they arrived in the village almost together with them, and the fighting continued in and around the village. Count Durazzo sent more troops to support Restori, but Alfieri managed to keep possession of

---

69 *Ibid.*, p.54. The reinforcement comprised the infantry regiment *Savoie*, one company of *Nice* and the three Swiss companies.

70 *Ibid.*, p.62.

the village and castle, preparing to resist. The Genoese took the next day to close off all access to Castelvecchio and to place the artillery that had arrived with reinforcements. Restori's forces numbered now about 3,000 men. On 5 August Alfieri rejected an offer to surrender. During the night he had sent a messenger to Garessio to take contact with the vanguard and make them turn back and assault the enemy from behind. The mission succeeded, and on the afternoon of 5 August the Count of Scalenghe with 1,000 infantrymen and horses headed to Castelvecchio. However, the Genoese sentinels spotted the enemies and informed Restori, who ordered Frediani to engage the approaching columns. The numerical superiority was to the advantage of the Genoese, who easily routed the enemy.[71]

In vain, Alfieri had attempted a sortie as soon as he became aware of Scalenghe's arrival, but was repulsed after a fierce fight. The situation inside Castelvecchio was becoming increasingly difficult for the Savoyards. Now short of ammunition, provisions, and above all water as the Genoese kept the wells under control, resistance was hopeless and Alfieri assembled a council of war and planned a general sortie on 6 August. The action took place between three and four o'clock in the morning. The attack was carried out with speed and audacity and allowed Alfieri, the Marquis of Livorno, some officers and 234 infantrymen to reach safety at Garessio, but at the cost of 600 dead and wounded.[72] The Marquis of Parella, repulsed inside the castle at the end of the sortie, burned the flags of the *Guardie* regiment and surrendered at discretion with 50 officers and 1,000 men.[73] The prisoners were despoiled by the victors and transferred to Albenga, where Durazzo had them refreshed before sending all the prisoners to Genoa.

On 9 August Durazzo gathered his troops to invade the territory of Oneglia, and after dividing them into several columns he crossed the border the day after. The Genoese met strong resistance at the village of Gazzelli, where the inhabitants had erected barricades. However, late in the evening the Genoese entered the village, and after plundering the houses set fire to them. Durazzo occupied the other localities around Oneglia and each time he encountered resistance he reserved to the inhabitants the same treatment as that inflicted on Gazzelli. For the siege of Oneglia, Durazzo assigned 3,000 regulars and 1,000 militiamen. On 14 August the Genoese troops were deployed on the hills around the town. To the west there were 800 Italian mercenaries raised with funding from the Genoese aristocracy; on the opposite side another 1,000 Corsicans under Frediani and Restori

---

71 Biblioteca Naciónal de España, Madrid, *Carta Escrita del Rev. N. al Ill.no continuando la novedades que resultan de las hostilidades, entre la Serenissima Republica di Genova, y el serenissimo Ducque de Saboya, y con mas distinta relacion del encuentro de Castel Vecchio* (1675); 31. Leg. 2, n. 18.

72 Anonymous, *Carlo Emanuele II e la guerra del Piemonte contro Genova*, pp.73–76. Several officers had died in the action, among them the Count de la Trinité, who managed to escape from Castelvecchio but was captured and killed by the villagers of Erli, despite having offered them a large sum to spare him.

73 *Ibid.*

LITTLE AND GREAT ITALIAN WARS

80. The ruins of Castelvecchio (author's photograph). The ancient castle was the last stand of the Savoyard troops under Catalano Alfieri on 3–6 August 1672.

closed the ring alongside a further 800 Corsican and Ligurian foot under Giovanni Prato. Finally, the militiamen under Giovanfrancesco Pallavicini-Sforza formed the reserve corps. The Savoyard garrison, some 1,300 regulars and town militiamen under Count Antonio di Castelgentile, tried to slow down enemy progress with four sorties, but under threat of bombardment from the heights and from the sea, on 15 August the Count accepted an offer to surrender. The following day Durazzo entered Oneglia, and left a garrison of 700 regulars there.

News of the debacle reached Turin. Responsibility for the failure was attributed to Catalano Alfieri and the Marquis of Livorno; the Count of Castelgentile, guilty of surrendering without permission, was sentenced to death in absentia.[74] The Marquis of Livorno received a pardon, but Alfieri was ordered to withdraw to his possessions with a ban on leaving.[75] Now it was necessary to provide for the defence of southern Piedmont. With a 'manifesto' already circulated throughout Piedmont on 18 July, Duke Carlo Emanuele called the population to arms, which according to *Risorgimento*

---

74 Paoletti, *Dal Ducato all'Unità*, p.154.
75 Alfieri was accused of treason, imprisoned in Turin, tried, tortured and sentenced to death. Before the execution took place, Alfieri was mysteriously found dead in his cell on 14 September 1673. In 1675, when Duke Carlo Emanuele II also died, Catalano Alfieri was recognised as innocent and his memory rehabilitated by the regent Duchess Giovanna Battista of Nemours, who returned the confiscated property to Catalano's son, Carlo Emanuele.

historians, responded enthusiastically to the call, to the point that there were not enough weapons for everyone.[76] Moreover, the Duke turned to his network of relations to obtain aid and troops in Bavaria, Mantua and Parma.

In the meantime the Genoese army had grown to 10,000 men, of whom over 6,000 were destined for the campaign in Piedmont. The first target was Briga, a choice expressly ordered by the Genoese Senate, on which a corps of 1,600 Corsicans marched under the orders of Restori, now proclaimed as 'the hero of the Republic'. On 28 August, at the end of a strong but useless resistance, the village was conquered and set on fire. The Corsicans took prisoner the local Savoyard representative, Count Antonio Lascaris. The following day Restori prepared the troops to march in the direction of Nava and invade Piedmont, but the news that French galleys had appeared off the Riviera di Ponente made him change his plans and return to Oneglia. While Restori was engaged in Briga his second in command Frediani, with 1,000 Corsicans, and the governor of San Remo, Francesco Maria Spinola-Cibo with an equal number of militia from San Remo and Taggia, marched on Perinaldo for a punitive expedition. The village stood on a location that was difficult to approach and had a strong medieval curtain. The population offered fierce resistance and the fighting resulted in 50 deaths on both sides. By the evening, the militiamen had been repulsed, but on 30 August Frediani's Corsicans managed to penetrate the village and sacked it, not even sparing the churches. News of the events at Perinaldo caused the immediate submission of all the communities in the area, agreeing to pay a large sum to the Genoese government.[77]

The echo of these events had meanwhile also reached Paris, and Louis XIV came to the Duke's aid, as it was in the King's interest that none of his vassals be defeated by a republic allied to Spain. Two squadrons of French galleys had sailed from Toulon under the orders of the Sieur de Vivonne and their presence in the Ligurian Sea prevented the Genoese from sailing west. French diplomacy, for its part, prevented the Republic from enlisting 3,000 Swiss.[78]

Taking advantage of the pause in operations, Charles Emmanuel reconstituted his forces with the recruits enlisted with the *Manifesto* of July and decided to start a new offensive with 6,000 infantrymen and 1,000 horse, gathered between Asti and Canelli. A further 2,000 regulars were assembled at Nice. To support these forces, the Duke had again mobilised the Piedmontese militia and this was joined by 200 Waldensians hired for their expertise in fighting in mountainous terrain. The plan called for a diversion against Ventimiglia to divert the Genoese from their main objectives, which were Ovada and Novi in the *Oltregiogo*.

In early September the Savoyards moved to the offensive. The first encounters took place at Col di Nava, where they managed to destroy the enemy's fortified camp. This time the plan was successful and attracted the Genoese into the threatened sector, but a second diversionary action led by the Marquis of San

---

76 Anonymous, *Carlo Emanuele II e la guerra del Piemonte contro Genova*, pp.87–88.

77 *Ibid.*, p.93.

78 *Ibid.*, p.121.

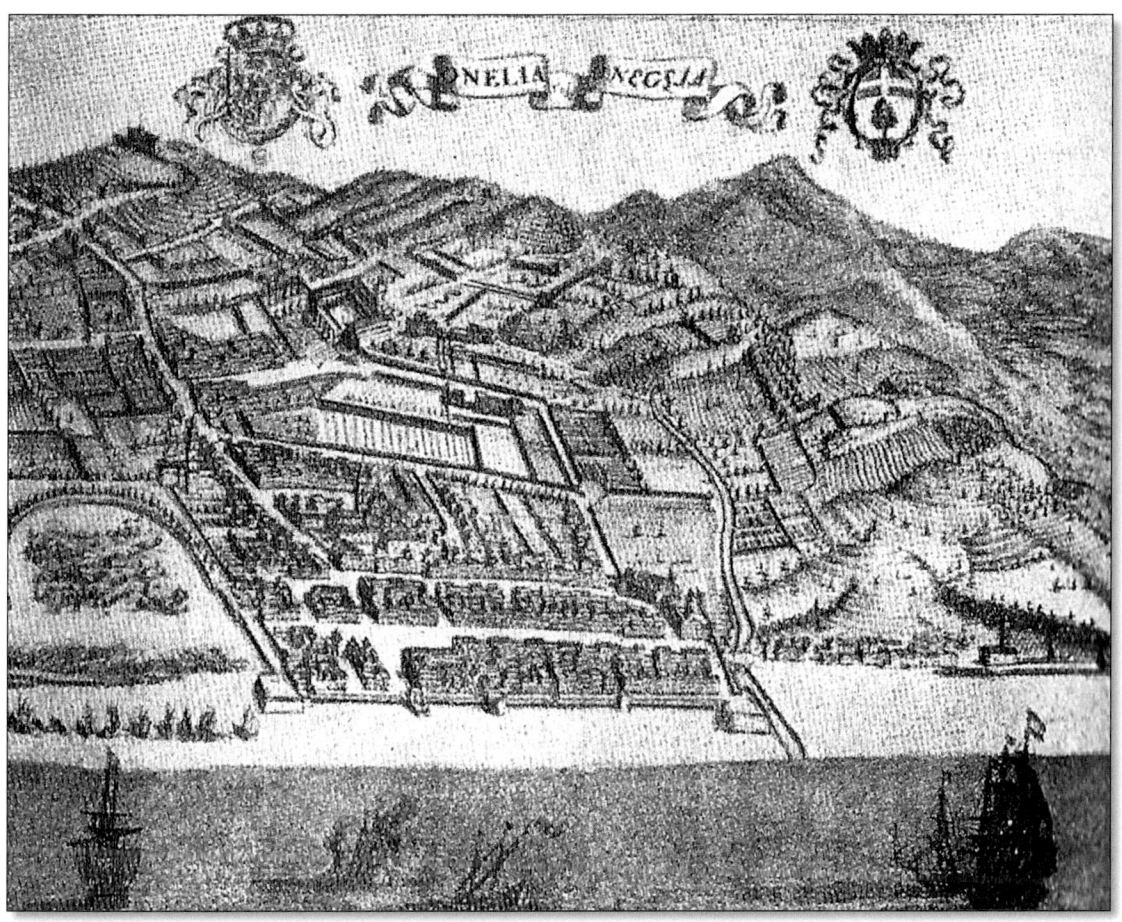

81. The town of Oneglia, now part of modern Imperia, in a seventeenth-century print (author's archive). Blocked by land and sea, the Savoyard enclave surrendered on 15 August 1672.

Damiano with 3,000 regulars and militiamen from Nice advanced through the Roya Valley to Ventimiglia. During the march the Savoyards retook Perinaldo on 4 September, chasing away the small Genoese garrison.

However, the Savoyards encountered an unexpected obstacle at Penna, where the castle and the fortified village controlled the road to Ventimiglia. Here, the route approaching Penna was just a path where troops could only advance in two-man lines. San Damiano had formed a vanguard with 2,000 regular infantrymen and artillerymen under the orders of the *Commendatore di Malta* Cesare Badat, of the *Crocebianca* infantry regiment. Penna was defended by 500 militiamen under Captain Girolamo Maria Gastaldi, who successfully repulsed the first enemy assault. San Damiano, worried by the delay in the advance, decided to leave the siege. He recalled Badat, and soon moved to Dolceacqua, and from there towards Camporosso, east of Ventimiglia, where Frediani with his Corsicans was heading in the meantime. Informed by the inhabitants of the enemy presence, on 6 September, in the evening, Frediani intercepted San Damiano's column and repulsed it at the end of a fight in the middle of the bush, where the Corsicans, as always, excelled.

The Savoyard threat had intensified work to improve the defences of Ventimiglia, directed by the governor and commissioner Ottavio Doria, who died of natural causes in early September and was replaced by Giovanni

Prato. The new commissioner intensified preparations for the defence and for responding to the enemy offensive. After the Battle of Camporosso, Frediani had fallen back on Bordighera and then moved to Penna, urged on by Prato who had received news that Badat was preparing a second siege. Reinforced by Ranuccio Ornano's Corsican regiment, on 10 September Frediani arrived just in time to relieve Penna, stubbornly defended by Gastaldi who had retreated into the castle with the few men still able to fight.[79]

In the meantime Don Gabriele of Savoy, and the Marquis of Livorno with the main army, began the march towards the Genoese border of the *Oltregiogo*, where they arrived at the end of September. The access points were guarded by the local militia, commanded by commissioner Ambrogio Imperiali, who had skilfully organised the defence. The Genoese held off the enemy vanguard under Count Maffei for days, and then with the arrival of reinforcements and other militia, forced the Savoyards to withdraw to Acqui. Don Gabriele, resolved not to repeat the terrible experience months before, ordered the Marquis of Livorno to carry out a diversion with a mixed corps of infantry and cavalry, while on 8 October with the bulk of the troops he took possession of the village of Sassello, capturing the small garrison and four guns. Genoese troops from Rossiglione tried to relieve Sassello, but were defeated. From here, Don Gabriele could now outflank the Genoese positions and march on Ovada.

On 9 October the Savoyards arrived before Ovada, and after placing the artillery Don Gabriele invited the garrison to surrender. The day before, the Genoese had managed to reinforce Ovada with 200 regulars, and although the commissioner, Imperiali, knew that the town was unlikely to resist a regular siege, he rejected the offer. Imperiali had drawn up a plan to evacuate Ovada and had therefore stationed the militia in the hills to the south to secure a route of retreat. Two mines had been prepared to be triggered at the appropriate time. This moment came the following day, when the Guards regiment stormed the wall. The explosion of the mines destroyed part of the houses and killed almost 400 Savoyard soldiers. Once the smoke cleared, Don Gabriele, horrified by the massacre, targeted the town with the artillery and ordered the cavalry to close every exit from Ovada. The Savoyard infantry entered Ovada through the breaches opened by the explosion, and 100 Genoese soldiers were trapped and captured. Meanwhile the explosion caused a fire and some powder barrels exploded, killing another 100 Savoyard soldiers. Convinced they had been lured into a trap, the Savoyards turned to the prisoners and mercilessly massacred many of them. Imperiali with half of the garrison had managed to get away from Ovada, but they failed to rejoin the militia and were captured by the Savoyard cavalry, who confiscated all their weapons but had to set them free because they had managed to take refuge in the Imperial fief of Tagliolo.

On 12 October the Savoyards resumed their offensive, conquering other villages in the *Oltregiogo* including Rossiglione, which guaranteed control

---

79 *Ibid.*, p.104. To force Gastaldi to surrender, Badat allegedly threatened to hang the Genoese captain's sons.

LITTLE AND GREAT ITALIAN WARS

82. The town of Ovada, main centre of the Genoese *Oltregiogo*, in an early eighteenth-century print (author's archive).

of the main route to Genoa. The conquest of Ovada was a dear price to pay, but it at least served to persuade Genoa to turn to a diplomatic resolution of the conflict. The war was consuming huge resources, and also from a strategic point of view the continuation of the struggle benefited the Savoyards, who were able to increase their forces with foreign mercenaries while Genoa found itself increasingly isolated. Nor could relief be expected from Spain, since Madrid was focused on the developments of the French invasion of the United Provinces of the Netherlands. On the western border too, the situation appeared uncertain. In an attempt to close the access to the sea to enemies coming from the north, commissioner Giovanni Prato and *sergente maggiore* Bacigalupo, with 1,200 men divided into 12 infantry companies, half Corsican and half Genoese, marched on Camporosso and then headed to Dolceacqua, where they arrived on 11 October. The Genoese had prepared a mine, when the news of the fall of Ovada interrupted the siege. On 12 October Prato and Bacigalupo began their retreat, pursued by the defenders of Dolceacqua on the march. Meanwhile Don Antonio of Savoy, governor of Nice, with 5,000 men including regulars and militiamen, advanced against Penna which was besieged for the third time. Against all odds Penna resisted until 29 October, when an armistice was reached at the behest of France.[80]

---

80 *Ibid.*, p.112. During the third siege the heroic Captain Gastaldi was mortally wounded. The senate rewarded him with a gold chain and a pension for his children.

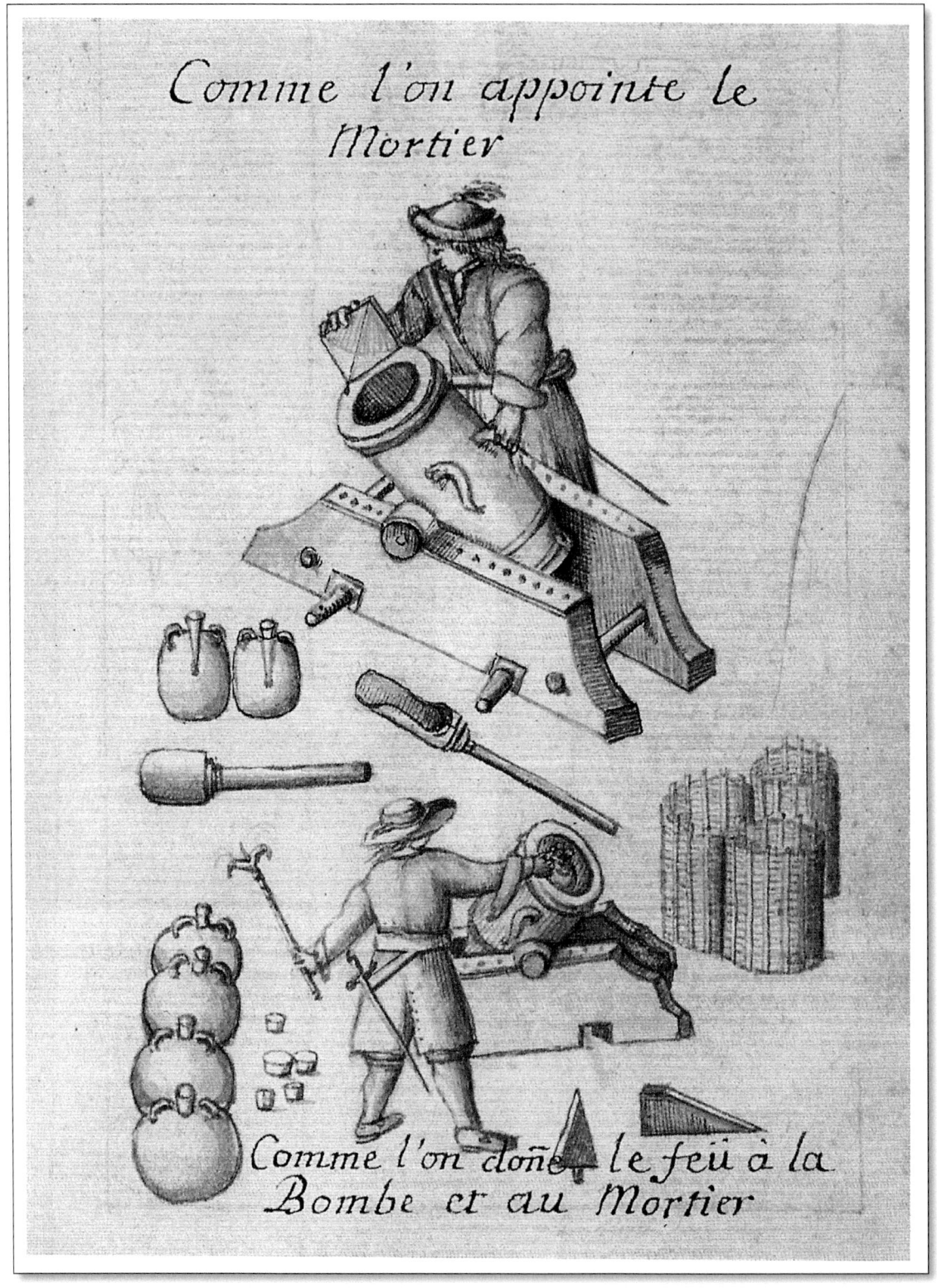

Negotiations lasted until 18 January 1673, concluding with a draw as the parties agreed to an exchange between Ovada and Oneglia, although the Genoese senate was reluctant to cede the conquered town. Louis XIV was the guarantor of peace and agreements. The King's tone was friendly, but the content appeared threatening.[81] Genoa had been saved from invasion, but the future looked ominous, especially now that Spain's help was no longer so certain.

The Venetians in the Holy League War, 1684–1699

On 10 May 1684 the *Serenissima* declared war on the Sultan, interrupting 15 years of a foreign policy centred on appeasement.[82] It was an important episode in the Republic's history, because for the last time the Senate agreed on an offensive war of large proportions. Historically Venice had always reacted to external aggression with a state of emergency, and since the sixteenth century every war had been fought to defend its domains, not to gain new territorial conquests. Now, despite the proactive approach, Venice's military preparation was no better than the past. Despite the truce with the Porte officially signed in 1671, the Republic had to remain on the alert, as the worries and annoyances caused by its untrustworthy neighbour remained a constant concern. Frequent incidents between the Christian Morlach subjects of Venice, and the Muslim Bosnians continued to trouble the Dalmatian border. In this region brawls and other punitive expeditions between the borders quickly degenerated into bitter local conflicts with potentially disastrous consequences. In January 1671, just before the signing of the peace, Ottoman border horsemen led by Mehmed *Paşa* of Bosnia launched an unsuccessful *coup de main* against Risano. According to the Venetian sources the Porte generally showed outrageous bad faith, and constantly threatened the Senate with the reopening of hostilities, an event that the Republic feared more than anything else.[83] Armed confrontation was the result of a permeable and ill-defined frontier. Battista Nani, who in 1669 was the designated commissioner in charge of negotiating the borders in Dalmatia and Albania with the *paşa* of Bosnia, realised that the Porte had no interest in establishing a definitive agreement on this issue.[84] Despite the intimidation of the Ottoman government, the discussion for the border

Facing page: 83. Savoy-Piedmont artillerymen, early 1680s, copy from a manuscript preserved in the Biblioteca Reale of Turin. Note the different projectiles and the fur cap worn by the men at the mortar, an alternative to the broad-brimmed cap: a symptomatic feature of the larger autonomy reserved to the artillerymen of every country in matters of military clothing, in the last quarter of the century.

---

81 Paoletti, *Dal Ducato all'Unità*, p.160.
82 Venetian senator Andrea Valier, writing on the conflicts between the Serenissima and the Ottoman, stated that 'All the wars, of which there were many, ended only to the detriment of kingdoms and considerable provinces. For this reason, the greatest application of the Republic was directed to maintaining peace, and to procuring it with all offices and by all other means.' See Andrea Valier, *Historia della Guerra di Candia* (Venice 1679), p.2.
83 Houssaie, *Histoire du gouvernement de Venise*, pp.123–127.
84 *Relatione* of *bailo* Giovanni Morosini, in Nicolò Barozzi and Guillaume Berchet, *Le relazioni degli Stati Europei lette al Senato dagli Ambasciatori Veneti nel secolo decimosettimo* (Venice, 1856–1878), p.206. According to the Venetian diplomats, it seems Grand Vizier Köprülü Ahmed did not seriously consider the possibility of a truce.

WARS AND SOLDIERS IN THE EARLY REIGN OF LOUIS XIV - VOLUME 6 - PART 2

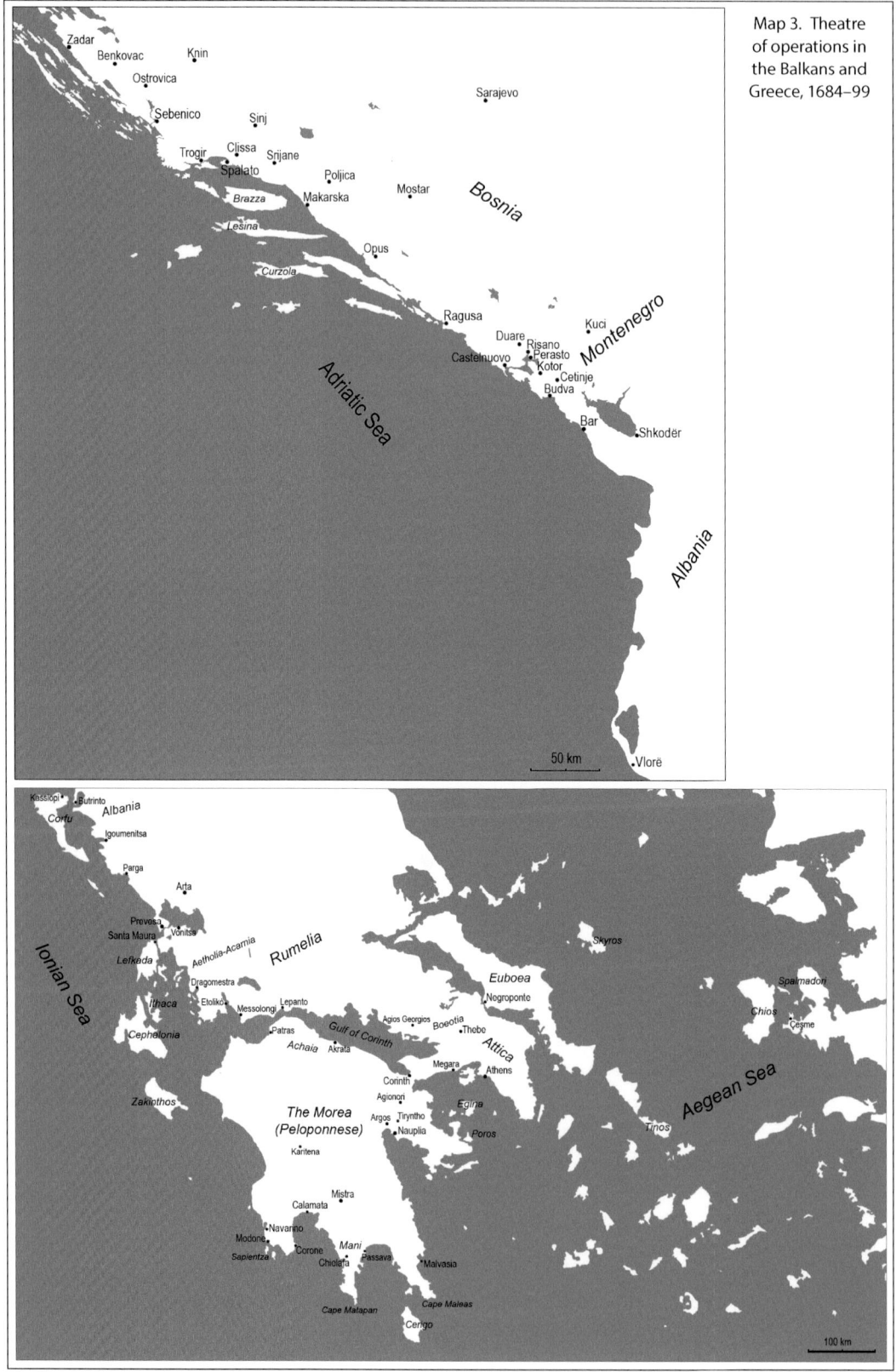

Map 3. Theatre of operations in the Balkans and Greece, 1684–99

continued, but with reciprocal distrust. In the years following 1671, Ottoman pressure decreased and relations became more 'polite', interrupted in 1674 by the notice of an imminent Ottoman landing on Corfu, which pushed the Senate to allocate relevant sums for the improvement of the defences.[85] However, when Ahmed Köprülü died in 1676 this temporary improvement was only a memory. New Grand Vizier Merzifonlu Kara Mustafa exploited every opportunity to humiliate the Venetian representatives. In 1677 he asked *bailo* Giovanni Morosini for compensation for the loss and plunder of a ship that had run aground in the Venetian Island of Grabusa (today Gramvousa, Cretan archipelago) three years earlier. As soon as Pietro Civran arrived in Istanbul in January 1680 to replace Morosini, the scenario got worse. In May a dozen Christian slaves took refuge on two Venetian warships, then two Venetian traders were accused of molesting some of the Sultan's subjects, forcing Venice to pay a considerable sum as compensation.[86]

In September 1682, while the Ottomans and their Hungarian allies were already campaigning against the Imperial troops in Upper Hungary, the Morlachs under their chief Mitrovič ambushed an Ottoman corps of 100 or 200 men in the Ottoman Bosnian territory.[87] News of the encounter, which ended with the massacre of the Ottomans, was reported by the *paşa* of Bosnia and reached Constantinople in January 1683, infuriating the Grand Vizier. However, obeying the Sultan in order to avoid a new war, he ordered the newly appointed *bailo* Giovanni Battista Donà to hand over 224 Venetian subjects to be executed. The Venetian ambassador and the Ottoman *divoan* finally agreed on an onerous monetary compensation. This was not a peaceful time, and the *bailo* was well aware of the gathering of troops throughout the Empire. It was rumoured that the Ottoman army's objective was Austria, but more than once the Porte had disguised its offensive plans in order to head for other targets. In doubt, Donà agreed to pay the enormous sum, which caused his recall to Venice and replacement by the secretary Giovanni Capello.[88]

As early as April 1683 the Count de la Tour, the Imperial ambassador to Venice, had represented to the Senate the imminent danger that threatened Christian Europe and tried in vain to invite the Republic to join the alliance with the Austrian Habsburgs. This embassy must have delighted the older senators, who remembered that in 1657, in similar circumstances during the siege of Candia, the Republic had sent a delegation to the Diet of Frankfurt,

---

85 Giovanni Morelli, 'Che musica intorno alla Guerra di Morea?', in M. Infelise and A. Stouraiti (eds), *Venezia e la guerra di Morea. Guerra, politica e cultura alla fine del '600* (Milan: Franco Angeli, 2005), p.286.

86 For having given in to blackmail, contrary to government instructions, Civran was removed from office but remained in Constantinople until 1681, as no replacement was available. See Pietro Garzoni, *Storia della Repubblica di Venezia. Dalla Sua Fondazione Sino l'Anno MDCCXLVII* (Venice, 1751), vol. I, p.365.

87 Camillo Contarini, *Istoria della Guerra di Leopoldo Primo Imperadore e de'Principi collegati contro il Turco* (Venice, 1710), vol. I, p.249.

88 Kenneth M. Setton, *Venice, Austria, and the Turks in the Seventeenth Century* (Philadelphia: The American Philosophical Society, 1991), pp.258–259.

in order to obtain the help of the Emperor, but without result. In June, when the Ottoman troops were converging on Vienna, Austrian Count Martinitz received the same courteous refusal.[89] Although the Senate was necessarily very interested in the Ottoman invasion, as well as in the treaty of alliance between the Emperor and the King of Poland, a majority was reluctant to embark on a dangerous adventure.

However, the news of the Ottoman defeat in Vienna had reached Venice on 15 September. Agents and diplomats of the Republic as well as of the other Italian states, who were equally concerned about this dramatic duel, had constantly reported to their sovereigns on all stages of the siege. In the weeks that followed, as the news continued to be excellent and the extent of the Ottoman defeat became clearer, the reports from the Venetian ambassador to the Imperial court were formal: the Viennese court was clearly showing its desire to continue the war. Before the end of September, Count Caprara spoke with the Venetian ambassador to Vienna, Domenico Contarini, with the aim of bringing the *Serenissima* into the League by mentioning they could possibly 'try to regain the lost', obviously referring to Crete and other ancient domains of the Levant.[90]

For some time in Europe, the most informed observers regarded the decline of the Ottoman Empire as irreversible, but for many governments, Venice included, a war against the Porte was still a worrying reality. Among the Christian princes who thought war was inevitable was Pope Innocenzo XI. For him, the defeat in Vienna was the auspicious occasion for a 'Holy League'. In order to exploit the unique opportunity to defeat the Ottoman Sultan and ensure that he was no longer a threat, the Pope's plan for a crusade gained widespread popular support throughout Italy, including Venice. Roman propaganda claimed the Ottoman Empire was 'half as powerful as it shows to be'.[91] Adopting an even more optimistic tone, Papal supporters claimed that

---

89 Roberto Cessi, *Storia della Repubblica di Venezia* (Florence: Giunti, 1981), p.645, and Dore Levi-Weiss, 'Le relazioni fra Venezia e la Turchia dal 1670 al 1684 e la formazione della Sacra Lega', in *Archivio Veneto* (1925–26), p.109. Ultimately, pursuing a policy of neutrality in the midst of this chain of events seemed increasingly untenable, as Levi-Weiss rightly states: 'If therefore Venice did not first begin negotiations of agreement, it was for fear of being left alone.' It should not be forgotten that almost a quarter of a century earlier, Emperor Leopold I had also hesitated for a long time to take up arms, for fear of being abandoned by the Venetians. The latter could have signed a separate peace with the Porte on advantageous terms, as occurred in 1573. In the end, the opposite was true.

90 To turn that part of public opinion less favourable to a new war against the Porte, travel reports began to circulate in which the backwardness of certain regions of Greece was admitted, but was said to be due to poor Ottoman administration, whereas the air was declared healthy, the population strong and the land fertile. According to these reports, Mistras, the ancient Sparta, was still rich in gold and goods, and in Athens the air was so good that an old man of 130 and another of 118 were still alive. See Infelise, 'L'ultima crociata', p.10.

91 Jean Coppin, *Le bouclier de l'Europe ou la Guerre Sainte, contenant des avis politiques & Chrétiens, qui peuvent servir de lumière aux Rois & aux Souverains de la Chrétienté, pour garantir leurs Estats des incursions des Turcs, & reprendre ceux qu'ils ont usurpé sur eux...* (Lyon, 1686), pp.48–51.

the Ottomans' numbers were still overestimated, their empire was almost devoid of modern fortifications, and the war fleet was almost nonexistent.[92]

However, in the autumn of 1683 Venice's entrance into the anti-Ottoman alliance with the Emperor, the Pope and Poland still appeared uncertain. The Papal emissaries reported the stalling of the *Serenissima*, complaining that 'The Venetian aristocracy seems to be fallen into idleness and indolence.'[93] On 5 December Count Leopold Wilhelm Königsegg, Vice-Chancellor of the Empire, officially reiterated to Venice that Spain, the Grand Duchy of Tuscany and the Maltese Knights would also be invited to join the alliance. On 18 December Count de la Tour spoke to the Senate, but his arguments were considered too vague, even evasive, especially regarding the conditions for joining the League. On 1 January 1684 the senators studied the reports requested from some veterans of the Cretan War. Andrea Corner estimated the military requirements in the event of joining the League at 30 sail ships, as many galleys and six galleasses. Francesco Morosini, the last Captain General of the previous conflict, estimated much more, recommending the armament of 40 galleys, with 8,000 crew for the fleet, and 16,000 soldiers as landing troops.[94]

After weeks of negotiations many senators were still hesitating, but some pointed out that, once peace had been restored between the Emperor and the Sultan, the latter would soon avenge the attacks of the Morlachs of Mitrovič that were multiplying along the border in Dalmatia. To persuade the Senate to join the League, even Father Marco d'Aviano came to Venice, and his

---

Part of the text had been completed in 1683 with the title *Projet general de la guerre contre le Turc*. The plan was largely utopian, however some elements became an essay of Papal propaganda for a crusade against the Porte.

92 According to 'Reverend Father' Coppin, the invasion forces of 50,000 soldiers had to be provided by every part of Europe, primarily by France and Spain, but also by other countries: England, Portugal, the Dutch Republic and the Maltese Knights, followed by the Pope 'with all Italy'. Since the general assault was to be by sea, the Emperor, Poland and Russia were to adopt a purely defensive strategy, without undertaking anything on their side, although the navy chartered by the same nations would be 200 ships strong.

93 Not all Venetians and not all the patriciate sided for the war. Indeed, there were people who questioned the utility of a war that absorbed endless resources without promising any concrete compensation, except in terms of international reputation. In this regard Mario Infelise, in 'L'ultima crociata', p.15 writes: 'City venues were stages where the war, its progress, and future moves were carefully discussed. There are even notices of "public academies" announced by posters displayed around Venice and other locations. These venues promised public confrontations on topics such as "whether it is convenient for Venice to win or lose the war", as was debated in the summer of 1687 in the palace of Quintiliano Rezzonico, a newly made aristocrat. The event caused quite a stir because it was held in front of a large number of people "of all nations, and of French, Austrian and other parties." The partisans of the Emperor and those of the King of France, who was considered an ally of the Sultan, debated openly whether the news of a victory was true and sometimes became a pretext for brawls and aggression.'

94 Pinzelli, *Venise et la Morée*, p.50.

propaganda inflamed the people, while other personalities proposed the most bizarre plans.[95]

The day of 15 January 1684 was decisive. Count de la Tour, by express order of Leopold I, harangued the Senate once again. This time the Imperial envoy knew how to use the right words, delighting the Venetian patricians with the promise of easy conquests, soothing their worries with the guarantee of a perpetual defensive alliance. There were heated debates in that session and over the next two days. Among the counsellors who were against the war, Michele Foscarini, senator and member of the *savi*'s council, declared that 'an empire possessing 430 kingdoms could not be defeated by the misfortune of a single day', and finally adding that 'the war is always a financial drain, and the Republic is still in a major distress'. Moreover, with no valuable generals available and no seasoned troops, declaring war in these conditions meant fighting a defensive, not an offensive battle. As for trusting the Pope for promised grants, 'He has lavished much gold on other princes, but to us he will only give words!'[96]

The advocates of the alliance emphasised that failure to adhere to the offer of the Holy League would condemn the Republic to isolation, exposing it to the contempt of all of Christian Europe. Among the speeches made by those in favour of joining the League, that of the *savio* Pietro Valier made a great impression when he declared 'Better a war that preserves us than a peace that destroys us!'[97]

The council of 19 January ended with 125 votes in favour of war, 71 against and two abstentions. Ambassador Contarini was given the authority to begin negotiations in Vienna; the Emperor and the King of Poland cordially congratulated the Republic. In the following days the ambassador in Rome, Giovanni Lando, confirmed the Papal willingness to grant substantial war subsidies to Venice. However, the economic scenario was worrying enough to make the government's action and subsequent strategy in the new war even more cautious than before. In the week following the vote of 19 January, numerous decrees were issued. The fleet commanders requested 30 galleys, six galleasses, 24 sailing ships, six fireships, with a land force of 9,000 foot and 300 horses, a request considerably lower than that made by Francesco Morosini one month earlier.[98]

---

95 The Marquis of Parella, who had fought at Vienna, demanded to be appointed *generale* of the Morlachs to invade Bosnia. See Levi-Weiss, 'Relazioni', p.110. Some reports hint at the existence of contacts between the Morlach leaders, already at war with the Ottomans, and the Austrians, who had every interest in seeing the situation in Dalmatia worsen in order to force the Venetian Republic to join the alliance.

96 Pietro Garzoni, *Istoria della Repubblica di Venezia in tempo della Sacra Lega contra Maometto IV e tre suoi Successori* (Venice, 1712), vol. I, pp.48–57; Contarini, *Istoria della Guerra*, vol. I, pp.254–259. Both authors give accounts of these speeches, with roughly similar content in substance but with different words.

97 Mario Infelise, 'L'ultima crociata', in Infelise and Stouraiti (eds), *Venezia e la guerra di Morea*, p.10.

98 Pinzelli, *Venise et la Morée*, p.52. The arsenal was ordered to launch four galleys, eight galleasses and five sail ships, to recruit crews and to charter ships from foreign nations. The Republic

LITTLE AND GREAT ITALIAN WARS

On 12 February the senators studied the clauses of the treaty between Poland and the Austrian Emperor, agreeing to use this text as the basis for the final drafting of the new articles. The Republic agreed to provide a strong fleet and prepare the campaign in Dalmatia at the same time. The consultations began on 1 March in Linz, under the auspices of Nuncio Francesco Buonvisi, in the presence of Domenico Contarini, the Emperor's representatives, and the Polish ambassador. There were lively discussions, particularly regarding Articles 9 and 12, concerning the forces to be provided by each coalition, and their respective fields of action. Indeed, the Venetian senator made no secret of the Republic's desire for reconquest of the ancient kingdoms. The Imperial court and the Poles, however, preferred to see the *Serenissima*'s fleet engaged in a blockade of the Dardanelles. The effect would have been particularly useful for the former, since it could cut off supplies from North Africa to the capital and beyond to the Ottoman armies in Central Europe, but certainly not very fruitful for Venice. Moreover, the blockade of the Dardanelles had been put into practice during the Cretan War, and since then the canal had been reinforced with fortifications and artillery on both sides, so that a repetition of the task would be difficult. Despite these conflicting interests it took only a few days to iron out the differences, and on 5 March the treaty of alliance was signed. The treaty defined the permanence of members in an association with offensive and then defensive purposes at the end of the conflict. Pope Innocent XI was proclaimed protector of the alliance; in his hands Cardinals Pio for the Emperor, Francesco Barberini for Poland and Pietro Ottoboni (the future Pope Alexander VIII) for Venice, swore the oath to the treaty on behalf of the three united nations. A peace treaty with the Porte, the only designated enemy of the Holy League, could not be contemplated without the universal consent of the allies. Venice, which was the only naval power in the League, was granted the right to obtain revenge, *ad vindicanda, et recuperanda ab hoste ea, quae perdidit*, as Article 12 read, without further specification, namely reserving to the Republic the right to change its objectives in the eastern Mediterranean.[99] All the articles, sent by Contarini to Venice, were studied and approved in the Senate in the session of 11 March and ratified on 25 April 1684, the day of the Republic's patron saint, a happy omen and sign of heavenly providence which could only favour the incoming enterprise.[100] The entry into the war was publicly announced to the sound of trumpets in Venice and throughout the *Terraferma*.[101]

Now it remained to declare war on the Sultan. For the first time in the history of the Venetian Republic, it was the *Signoria* that had the satisfaction of breaking off relations with the Porte. In the 'ducal letter' of 29 April the

---

acquired the *San Vittorio* and the *San Giovanni Battista Grande*, owned by the Duke of Savoy, which the Duchess had acquired in Holland in anticipation of her young son's union with the *Infanta* of Portugal.

99 *Ibid.*, 'To avenge and recover from the enemy what [the Republic] has lost.'
100 Garzoni, *Istoria della Repubblica di Venezia*, vol. I, p.61.
101 Beregani, *Historia delle Guerre d'Europa dalla comparsa dell'Armi Ottomane in Ungheria* (Venice, 1698), vol. I, pp.136–137.

Senate informed Giovanni Capello about the alliance, advising him to leave Constantinople to escape possible reprisals. The letter arrived in the Ottoman capital on 11 June. Capello took the declaration of war to the Grand Vizier's residence and fled on board a merchant ship, disguised as a sailor.

1684

The Senate devoted the following councils to the appointment of the commander and the *capi da mar*. The candidates were all veterans of the Cretan War. On 11 March 1684 Francesco Morosini, the last defender of Candia, was elected Captain General; his main rival Girolamo Corner held the office of vice-commander as *provveditore straordinario all'Armata*.[102] Alessandro Molin was appointed as *capitano straordinario delle navi*, a post that he already held in 1669. Other commanders came from prominent families such as Alvase Pasqualigo *provveditore generale* in Dalmatia with Domenico Mocenigo as *provveditore straordinario*, and Antonio Zeno *provveditore straordinario* at Kotor. In the fleet, Girolamo Garzoni was appointed *provveditore ordinario all'armata*, Benedetto Sanudo *capitano in Golfo*, Marino Bragadin *governatore dei forzati*. As commander of the landing troops, the Senate naturally turned to Count Carlo di Strassoldo. This experienced officer, who came from an old family of Udine, had already spent a long career in the Imperial army under Piccolomini and Montecuccoli. The Emperor agreed to let him enter the service of Venice. The post of Lieutenant General of Artillery went to Filippo Besseti di Verneda, certainly the most experienced technical officer of the Republic, who already served as principal engineer and superintendent for the fortifications.

For over a decade Francesco Morosini held various positions, but not with the fleet. In 1670 he was appointed *provveditore alle artiglierie*; then from 1681 he was in charge of the fortifications in the Italian mainland, at Legnago and Crema, and from 1683 in Friuli. In the Senate he did not belong to the interventionist party, but was in favour of a limited use of the fleet, mainly aimed at interrupting Ottoman supplies from Anatolia to the Balkans. Practically, a repetition of the strategy implemented during the Cretan War.

The preparations started at full capacity. In the *Arsenale* there were 29 galleys, six galleasses, and 12 other ships nearing completion. The Senate also increased the number of commissions to accelerate the recruitment of troops and appointed new senior officers.[103] Despite the efforts of the carpenters, when Alessandro Molin embarked on 6 May, his squadron was still incomplete. Considering that the declaration of war had not yet been delivered, the Senate had invited the Captain General to take advantage of surprise, as Senator Pietro

---

102 He was the brother of Caterino Corner, killed in action at Candia on 13 May 1669. His appointment followed the balance of power typical of Venice's policy.

103 ASVe, *Senato mar*, Reg. 150 (1684), f. 87. Appointment for senior officers' posts were issued to Count Francesco Salvadego, Filippo de Toy and Alessandro Vimes, the latter being a veteran of Crete. Other patents were issued to Leandro Molviz, Gerolamo Bachielli, already *governatore degli albanesi*, and two *sergenti maggiori in Terraferma*, Fabio Lanoia and Lauro d'Andria. ASVe., *Senato mar*, Reg. 150 (1684), f. 87.

Valier expressly indicated, by using the fleet.[104] Senator and *savio* Giorgio Corner proposed the conquest of Castelnuovo di Cattaro (today Herzeg-Novi in Montenegro), but the final decision of the campaign's strategic approach was left to the council of war. On 8 June Morosini set sail from Venice, the day in which the military adventure actually began, on board the *galea bastarda* (flagship) reserved to the Captain General, escorted by three galleys and two galleasses. On 17 June the Dalmatian squadron joined the fleet at Lésina, and soon a council of war was called at Curzola.

The main task of the sail ships squadron was to guard the routes of the Aegean Sea, in particular the waters between Cerigo, Tinos, and the Venetian fortresses off Crete, and to intercept enemy convoys if the opportunity came. The council of war guessed that, expecting a Venetian attack, the Ottomans considered Crete to be the most probable target. Evidently the news of the war preparations had not gone unnoticed in Constantinople, since the *kapudan paşa* had sent 40 galleys with supplies and troops to Crete.[105] Relying on their intuition, the Captain General and his commanders were confident that they could deal a major defeat to the *kapudan paşa* and put the enemy fleet out of action for that year. The Venetian expectations were disappointed, since no significant naval encounters occurred in the war's early years, especially because the Ottoman fleet avoided such encounters as much as possible.[106] Morosini and the *capi da mar* also examined the possibility of an assault on the objective proposed by the Senate, and instructed engineer Verneda to prepare a report on the fortifications of Castelnuovo, but in the end the objective was discarded. After listening to the opinions of the other commanders, Morosini choose the first objective: the fortress of Santa Maura, on the island of Lefkada, which served as a haven for the North African corsairs.

The Venetians resumed sailing, and after a stop in Ragusa (Dubrovnik) on 3 July, dropped anchor at Corfu: the journey had cost the lives of 112 sailors, oarsmen and soldiers.[107] Some days later, the allies joined the Venetian fleet at Corfù off Kassiòpi. They were seven galleys and three sail ships of Malta under don Giovanni Battista Brancaccio, who also led 100 knights and 1,000 infantrymen; the Tuscan admiral Camillo Guidi with four galleys and one sail ship, 20 knights of St Stephen and 600 infantrymen; followed by five galleys with 300 foot soldiers under Paolo Emilio Malaspina sent by the

---

104 Senator Pietro Valier considered the fleet as the best instrument to perform naval campaigns in the Mediterranean, comforted by the experience achieved during Cretan War. In this perspective, his opponents were more conservative and they preferred to reinforce the interactions of sail ships and galleys which had performed equally well in the last conflict. See Guido Candiani, 'Vele, remi e cannoni: l'Impiego congiunto di navi, galee e galeazze nella flotta veneziana, 1572–1718', in G. Candiani and L. Lo Basso (eds), *Mutazioni e Permanenze nella Storia Navale del Mediterraneo, secc. XVI–XIX* (Milan: Franco Angeli, 2010), pp.131–132.

105 Contarini, *Istoria della Guerra*, vol. I, pp.271–272.

106 The Ottoman fleet's only action was an attempted landing on Tinos in August of 1684, which was repulsed by the island garrison.

107 ASVe, *Senato, Dispacci, Provveditori di Terra e di Mar*, b. 1070, n. 5, dated 3 July 1684.

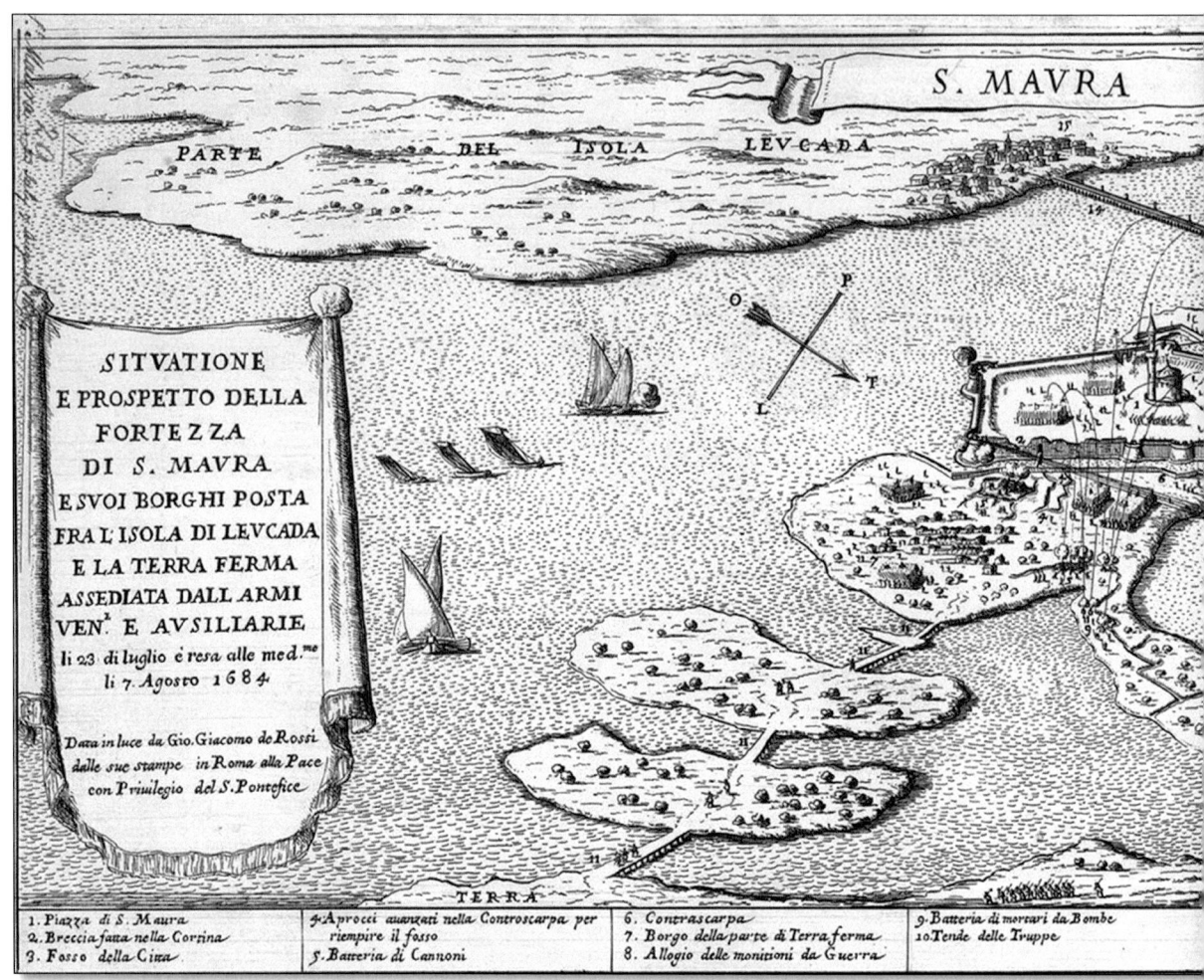

84. The siege of Santa Maura (Levkas) on the island of Lefkada, in a print from Rome celebrating the first Venetian and allied victory in the campaign of 1684.

(Author's archive)

Pope.[108] After the arrival of all units in Corfu, a new council of war met on 12 July. Shortly before the arrival of the Captain General, Girolamo Corner had tried to take the fortress of Santa Maura by surprise. The *provveditore straordinario* had received assurances from the inhabitants that the Ottoman garrison was weak, and they could support Corner and his squadron to seize the fortress. The information turned out to be wrong, because Corner found the garrison ready and resolute, as if someone had warned them of the arrival of the Venetians.[109] The surprise effect had therefore vanished, yet Morosini decided to concentrate all available forces on this objective.[110]

---

108 *Ibid.*

109 Contarini, *Istoria della Guerra*, vol. I, pp.339–340.

110 BNM, *Diario anonimo della guerra di Morea* (1684–1687), ms. It. VII 2592 (12484), f. 4v. The council of war examined the possibility of attacking Negroponte, in order to use the Euboea

LITTLE AND GREAT ITALIAN WARS

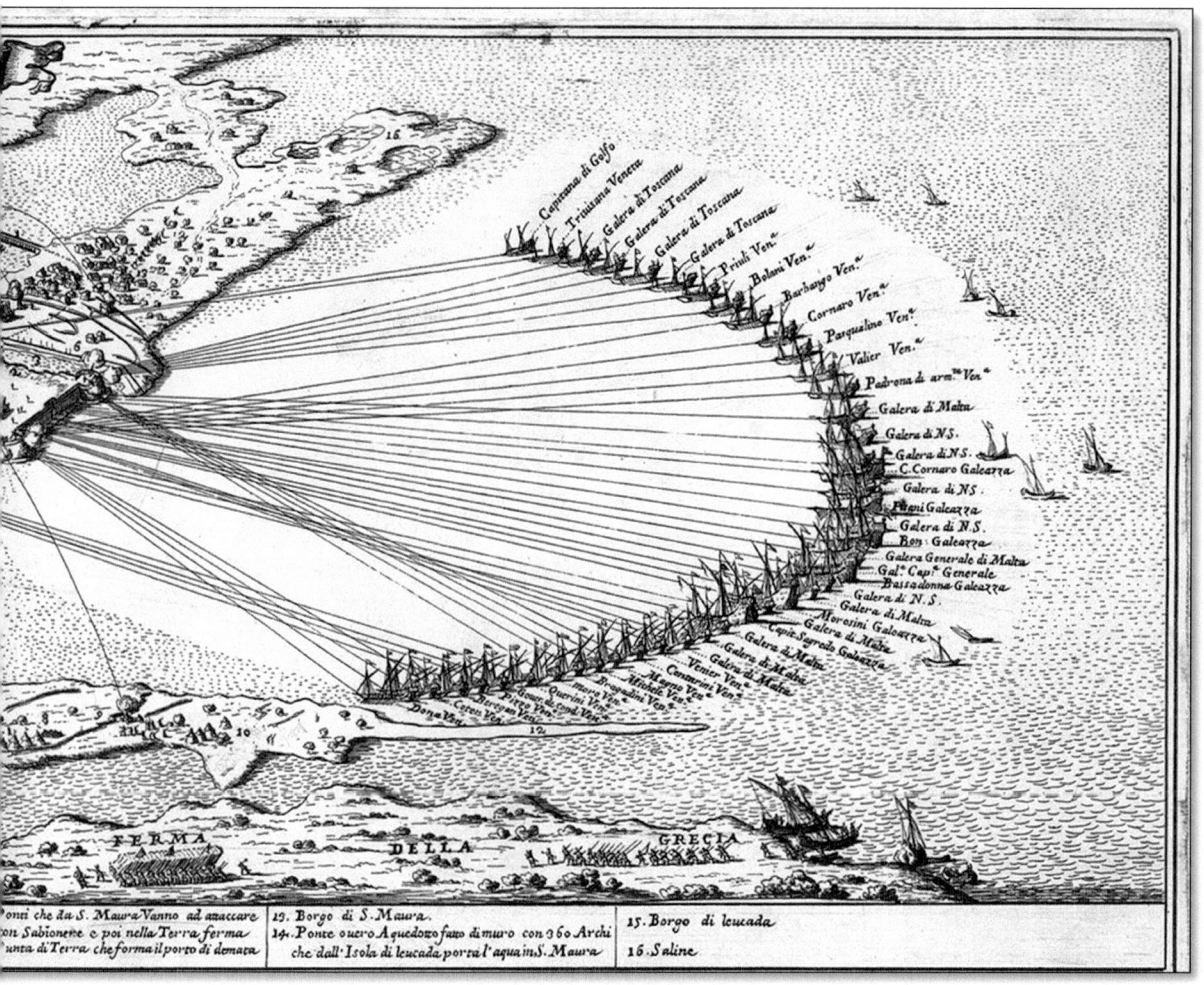

On the evening of 20 July the troops began their landing, about 1,200 metres from Santa Maura. On the same day two brigantines from Corfu, with 2,000 Greeks from the Ionian islands, and a galley commanded by the famous privateer Stai Maneta from Mani with 150 men, joined the Venetians. Santa Maura had a modest curtain reinforced by ramparts, but its position across the island and the continent favoured defence. To be effective, the siege had to be conducted simultaneously on the two opposite sides of the fortress, which was protected on the north-east side by an extensive lagoon and on the south-west by the sea. Strassoldo managed the deployment of the infantry. On the eastern side there were the troops under the orders

---

Island as a base for raids in the north of the Archipelago and the Dardanelles. Another proposed option was to seize Albania and the entire coastline between Scutari and the Dalmatian border.

of *sergente maggiore di battaglia* Jouy, with Jacques Milhau-Verneda,[111] an engineer, and his colleague Sebastiano Alberti as second in command. The infantry formed three 'battalions' under Colonels Maron, Mirabaldo, and Bianchi, supported by the Maltese, Papal and Albanian infantry. On the western side, the *sergenti maggiori* Salvadego and Bonsio, with the engineers Mauro and Benoni, commanded the battalions of Gabrieli, Catti and Tasson, supported by Tuscans and *schiavoni*. The siege started in a quite chaotic series of actions. On the morning of 21 July Stai Maneta, at the head of his men, seized without resistance a place called *Chirebbe*, belonging to the son of the *aga* of Santa Maura. Meanwhile Colonel Metaxa led the 2,000 Greeks who had arrived the previous day to plunder the countryside in the vicinity. The next day the Orthodox Bishop of Kefalonia arrived in person with 150 men of his retinue, pretending to come to the aid of the Venetians, but he returned almost immediately after trying in vain to collect part of the spoils as a contribution to his church.[112]

On the same day, Morosini ordered the Ottoman garrison to surrender, and after receiving a negative response he ordered the galleys to open fire on Santa Maura. The strong wind and rough sea impaired the effectiveness of the artillery, persuading the Captain General to land 15 heavy guns and four large 500 lb mortars. Although the rugged terrain did not allow for regular batteries, the artillery caused numerous fires in the town, since the majority of the houses were of wood. During the night, Maneta and his men tried to extend the fires by launching flaming darts inside Santa Maura. The artillery targeted the town for six days, causing the collapse of a rampart, but Strassoldo and Morosini waited for better results. Two days later, the fleet targeted the town from the south. The Ottomans replied with their artillery, which succeeded in killing a tenth of the besiegers, including the engineer Benoni. However, the defenders were running out of projectiles, and on 31 July the damaged rampart definitively collapsed. However, the siege suffered complications. Having learned that enemy reinforcements had just arrived at Prevesa, less than a day's march from Santa Maura, Morosini directed a diversionary naval bombardment against this place on the evening of 2 August. While the batteries continued to target Santa Maura, fearing of an enemy attack from behind, Morosini sent Maneta with 500 Greeks to patrol the area and make raids around Prevesa.

The breach in the walls of Santa Maura was now wide enough, so on the evening of 5 August Morosini ordered Strassoldo to prepare a general assault for the following morning. As planned, the infantry advanced but the besiegers reacted with determination and the assault was repulsed. Forty men were killed, and many more wounded. However, the assault brought an end to the garrison's resistance; perhaps running out of ammunition, they realised that the end was near. On the evening of 6 August the Ottomans hoisted the white flag, and after a brief negotiation the commander agreed to surrender. On 7 August, 700 soldiers and 3,000 civilians left Santa Maura. The

---

111 He was the nephew of Filippo Besseti di Verneda.
112 Pinzelli, *Venise et la Morée*, p.89.

85. The conquest of Prevesa, which occurred on 29 September 1684, was preceded by a brilliant amphibious operation by the Venetians and their allies, who routed an Ottoman corps entrenched not far from the city. (Engraving by Vincenzo Maria Coronelli from Alessandro Locatelli's *Racconto Historico della Veneta Guerra in Levante*, Venice 1691)

Christian soldiers entered the town and rushed in, taking all that remained to be seized. The spoils of war consisted of 126 cannons, 33 of which were of iron, and 42 Black slaves, mostly women and children.[113] Ninety Christian slaves were released. The siege of Santa Maura lasted 18 days and cost the lives of 127 soldiers, including two engineers; the auxiliaries and allies alone claimed 112 casualties. The Maltese paid for their participation with the loss of the knights Francesco Magallon and François Morienne.[114]

In the days following the capture of Santa Maura, the council of war did not consider assaulting Prevesa, despite the risk posed by this fortress so close to the island of Lefkada. Moreover, in his report of 17 September, Morosini estimated that he did not have enough troops for such an undertaking. But there was still another alternative: to raid the southwestern part of Acarnia, a region without protection apart from the old castles of Crysovitsa and Angelocastro. Captain Maneta was nevertheless sent to Prevesa to carry out an exploration and diversionary manoeuvre. On 2 September troops under

---

113 Contarini, *Historia della Guerra*, vol. I, p.345; Garzoni, *Istoria della Repubblica di Venezia*, vol. I, p.57; Locatelli, Alessandro, *Racconto historico della veneta guerra in Levante* (Cologne, 1691), p.63. A few prisoners were sent to the galleys; two Black slaves were entrusted to Léonard de Cleuter, the commander of the Papal infantry, to be presented to the Swedish queen Ulrike Eleonore, and the others were distributed among nobles and officers.

114 Pinzelli, *Venise et la Morée*, p.91.

Carlo di Strassoldo landed at Dragomestra (today Astàkos), west of the River Ahelòos. A local Ottoman corps of 1,500 infantrymen and 300 cavalrymen immediately tried to stop the Venetian advance, but it was defeated at the first engagement. Acarnia was now at the mercy of the Venetians and their allies. The troops ravaged and plundered the region, pushing as far as Etolikò and Messolòngi, which paid a heavy price. Morosini, taking advantage of his naval supremacy, raided the coastal regions by surprise wherever he wished, multiplying the false alarms among the enemies. The Tuscan galleys, reinforced by six Venetian oar ships, appeared before Prevesa. Three other Venetian galleys went near the entrance to the Gulf of Corinth with the Maltese squadron. On 10 September the troops were embarked at Petala, near the mouth of the river Ahelòos. Two days later, Camillo Guidi took leave and returned with the Tuscan galleys to Livorno.

In dictating his dispatch, Francesco Morosini for the first time considered the possibility of further conquests on a much larger scale. During the Cretan War he had the opportunity to discover locations such as Egina, Megara and the Saronic Gulf, and the strategic importance of the isthmus had not escaped him. Now, almost 30 years later, Morosini proposed to occupy this area and to raise a new *Examilion*, if the Senate gave him the means to exploit this goal.[115] While waiting to attack as far away as Corinth, the council of war decided to besiege Prevesa. This fortress, the main one in southern Epirus, controlled the entrance to the Gulf of Arta and dominated a very fertile area. However there were also other, more worrying, considerations if the *consulta* chose this option. Informants reported that an enemy corps of nearly 3,000 foot and horse was gathering there. By not intervening quickly, the Venetians risked finding themselves under siege in Santa Maura, which could not withstand another siege. The Captain General, loyal to his favoured tactic, was in favour of defeating the enemy by means of a surprise attack despite – or perhaps because of – his own numerical inferiority. At 66, the old sailor still felt ready to repeat the daring actions that had made him famous during the Cretan War.

86. Carlo Strassoldo (1647–1685) was a Venetian subject who had served in the Imperial army since the 1670s before entering the *Serenissima*'s service. See image commentaries for more information.

---

115 ASVe, *Senato, Dispacci, Provveditori di Terra e di Mar*, b. 1070, d. 12: 'When I could, in such a prosperous opening, have a corps of 10 or 12,000 soldiers and 300 horses, with the necessary provisions, it would not have been difficult to conquer the Castle of Lepanto, and then pass on to Corinth, and fortify the Isthmus that divides the Morea from Greece with the help of the inhabitants ...'

LITTLE AND GREAT ITALIAN WARS

To prepare the surprise, the Captain General feinted to attack Igoumenitsa by sending five galleys and the six galleasses. At Prevesa the Ottomans had entrenched themselves near the beach to prevent a possible landing; the Venetians had to carry out a 'commando'-style operation to allow the troops to land while avoiding casualties. This perilous mission was entrusted to Stai Maneta and the Corsican privateer Vitali, who had joined the Venetians some days before.[116] During the night of 20–21 September their ships sailed into the darkness without the slightest noise, within musket range, and entered the Gulf of Arta. They were followed by 11 other brigantines and feluccas with 1,400 men on board. Taking advantage of the dark night, Morosini disembarked all troops still available, including *Leventi* and *Scapoli di Galere*, on a beach far from the fortress, where the Ottomans did not expect them.[117] The Venetians marched against the enemy camp; the battle began at dawn on 21 September. Confident of their numbers, the Ottoman cavalry moved against the Venetians, but they were repulsed and abandoned their positions in disorder. Strassoldo then landed the regulars to the west of the fortress; the Maltese and Papal troops occupied a hill, called Mehmet Efendi, which dominated the town. The Venetians landed mortars and heavy guns that had already been used against Santa Maura. Having wanted to summon the garrison to surrender, the bearer of the message was greeted by musket fire. The bombardment began at once. However, Morosini quickly realised that the cannons were not effective in opening breaches, and called on the engineers to destroy the fortifications with mines. However, the garrison of Prevesa did not resist as long as that of Santa Maura: after just eight days, the defenders asked to surrender, demanding to take weapons and baggage, agreeing to leave only the slaves. Morosini only reluctantly accepted these largely favourable conditions granted to the Ottomans. On 29 September, 1,500 people evacuated Prevesa; they were escorted to Arta. In the town the Venetians found 44 cannons and 500 kantars (27.5 tons) of gunpowder. The Ottomans had to free 16 Christian slaves and Morosini sent 19 renegades and 16 Black people to the galleys' oars. The crews were immediately put to work to repair the damage caused by the siege and to clear the trenches. The lieutenant general of the artillery, Verneda, took charge of drawing up the plan of Prevesa. It was out of the question to undertake too much work, and only a palisade was raised.

Eight days after the conquest of Prevesa, Morosini sailed with some galleys to the castle of Vonitsa, located 15 km away, on the southern shore of the Gulf of Arta. According to the sources, either the lieutenant general of the artillery Verneda or his nephew accompanied him. The Venetians found the old Byzantine fortress abandoned: the occupants had fled and there was no artillery.[118]

---

116 He was the nephew of the skilled Giorgio Maria Vitali, who was very esteemed by Morosini during the last phase of the Cretan War.
117 Foscarini, Michele, *Historia della Republica Veneta* (Venice, 1696), pp.186–187.
118 Locatelli, *Racconto historico*, p.81.

The 1684 campaigns were coming to an end. There had been success also in the other theatres. In the Adriatic, after the initial skirmishes occurred in the spring, the Venetians took the offensive, and between June and August the *provveditore straordinario* Domenico Mocenigo seized some fortified villages in Bosnia, and in September extended the Morlachs' incursions in the Makarska valley. In Albania the Venetians launched raids against Duare and Risano, destroying crops and raiding cattle.

In his relation to the Senate, Morosini praised his soldiers and officers, and among them he especially remarked the behaviour of Count Carlo Strassoldo, whose experience had favoured the successful outcome of the Ionian campaign. Unfortunately the veteran commander fell ill at the end of October and retired to Corfu for better treatment, but died in early January 1685.[119] The news reached the Senate, which had to find a replacement to lead the naval troops. The senators could choose between two people who had already served the Republic during the Cretan War: Count Claude de Saint-Paul-Longueville, or Baron Hannibal von Degenfeld. The choice fell on the Count, who certainly reassured the senators because of his age and consummate experience.[120]

In 1684, Venice turned its attention to Montenegro in an attempt to open another front in the region, in order to divert the Porte from northern Greece. In its effort to win over Montenegrins to their side, Venice sent troops and aid to Montenegro, while a corps of irregulars demonstrated their intent with a night attack on Castelnuovo di Cattaro (Herceg Novi) on 22 August 1684. The *paşa* of Skhoder, Bushati Süleyman, after threatening and pacifying the Montenegrin clans of Kuči and Kelmendi, gathered more troops and marched towards Cetinje, where the Venetian irregulars accompanied by some Montenegrins decided to make a last stand. The confrontation resulted in the Battle of Vrtijeljka, where the Ottoman forces defeated the Venetian irregulars and their allies and entered Cetinje. After plundering the town, Bushati retreated.

1685

Meanwhile, the next campaign had to be prepared. In the autumn, Morosini was already planning to extend his conquests towards the Peloponnese. Perhaps through the intermediary of Stai Maneta, or perhaps through direct correspondence with the Mani's chiefs, the captain general was trying to stir up these populations against the Porte. The strategic scenario appeared favourable for concluding an alliance between Venice and the Maniotes, like the one that had united Venice and the Morlachs during the Cretan War. In mid October, during the council of war, Francesco Morosini proposed to go personally to the Mani peninsula with two galleys and the galleasses. He informed the Senate that the Mani Peninsula had risen up and the local

---

119 According to Beregani, *Historia delle Guerre d'Europa*, vol. I, p.138, Morosini trusted Strassoldo, whom he said was 'very fiery', but he knew that the general was disliked by the troops because of his excessive severity.

120 Locatelli, *Racconto historico*, p.113.

chiefs were besieging two Ottoman fortresses. This was the ideal time to offer help and to bring about a rapprochement based on a community of interests.[121] The *consulta* refused to let the Captain General leave, but the latter, with obstinacy, did not abandon the project.[122] The death of Strassoldo, and the absence of a commander capable of directing the landing troops made it possible to support the rebellion of Mani, and above all to restore the conquered fortresses. In February and March, Morosini inspected Santa Maura and Prevesa. In the former, where the walls had been largely restored, the Captain General left 1,280 men, half of this figure was left to guard Prevesa.[123]

To carry out this second campaign, the Republic needed new recruits. Infantry regiments were recruited in Germany with private colonels and the Duke of Brunswick-Lüneburg Kalemberg, while a regiment of dragoons was raised through the initiative of a colonel from Avignon. These new troops arrived in Corfu between May and June 1685. As usual, the Senate made its suggestions concerning the objective. While the reconquest of Crete was still the main dream, the possibility of extending the offensive into other regions appeared more and more concrete, considering that the Ottoman Empire appeared more vulnerable than before, now that it was attacked on three fronts. Therefore, the conquest of the Peloponnese – the ancient kingdom of Morea – seemed a possible achievement.

A great council of war held on the Captain General's galley with the Maltese commanders Giovanni Battista Brancaccio and Jean Hector Count de la Tour-Maubourg, who had also fought in the Cretan War, *governatore* Paolo Emilio Malaspina, three *provveditori*, the Count of Saint-Paul and Prince Maximilian Wilhelm of Brunswick, all under the chairmanship of the Captain General. Some historians do not mention the presence of Baron Degenfeld, who immediately began to violently challenge Saint-Paul about the direction of the landing troops.[124] Last but not least, the question of pre-eminence between the Knights of Malta and the Knights of St Stephen was

---

121 Foscarini, *Historia della Republica Veneta*, p.217. According to Foscarini, the chiefs of Mani were ready to provide 10,000 men and 2,000 pack animals as soon as Venetian troops appeared in Morea.

122 In his dispatch of 21 October, Morosini asked the Senate to send him 10,000 muskets to deliver to the insurgents of Mani. He also asked for other material, especially tents, and twenty 50 lb cannons of a better alloy than the one used until then. He also needed qualified personnel: four surgeons, 100 bombardier apprentices and 30 *capi*, including Gravella of Bergamo and Pallavicino of Treviso. For the incoming sieges he requested 12 qualified mortar servants (*bombisti*), and 20 miners 'exercised in the wars of France', in order to compensate for the weaknesses encountered during the siege of Prevesa. There were also promotions: *cavaliere* Alcenago of Verona became a *sergente maggiore di battaglia* and Pietro Cechina was appointed *governatore* of the Albanian troops. In ASVe, *Senato, Dispacci, Provveditori di Terra e di Mar*, b. 1070, d. 16.

123 *Ibid.*, d. 28 and 30. The entire restoration had cost 7,820 *Reali*. According to Morosini, the same works in the Venetian mainland would have cost 100,000.

124 Alberto Guglielmotti, *La squadra ausiliaria della marina romana a Candia ed alla Morea* (Rome, 1883), p.392–393.

resolved to the disadvantage of the latter, causing the withdrawal of Camillo Guidi from the council. At this meeting the generals discarded the idea of attacking Patras and the castles that closed the entrance to the Gulf of Corinth, since reports indicated the gathering of large contingents of enemy troops. Instead, the council of war decided to set sail for the island of Sapientza, quite close to the Mani Peninsula, to help the local insurgency against the Porte, and then turned to Modone (Methoni) as the main objective. The fleet, consisting of 76 large and small ships, arrived off Modone on 22 June 1685. On board there were 6,900 Venetians, Dalmatians and Germans, as well as 1,900 auxiliary troops and volunteers.[125] The Venetian Captain General asked the Count of Saint-Paul, one of the Verneda, and the engineer Giovanni Bassignani to prepare a relation on the fortifications, and all three stated that a regular siege was 'very difficult'.[126] A new council of war agreed to move towards another objective, and the choice fell on Corone (Koroni).[127] The fortified town quartered a garrison formed by 800–900 Ottoman irregulars with guns and mortars. The fortifications were not of a modern type and had a triangular shape, but these were built on high ground, with several ramparts and a tower castle on the side opposite to the sea, which was described as 'very strong'. The port was of negligible size, and could contain just four galleys. About 500 houses formed the settlement.[128]

The fleet approached the shore and the *oltramarini* were the first to seize a fortified tower guarding a village not far from the town. The garrison only performed a timid sortie, which was immediately repulsed. By the end of the day, despite the enemy fire, the tower and the village fell into the hands of the Venetians. These initial operations had cost them two dead and nine wounded. Two days later, four 50 lb guns were unloaded from the galleys under the orders of Leandro Molvis, *provveditore alle artiglierie*. To accelerate the operations, the oarsmen were promised a reward if they volunteered for the task. Over the

---

125 They were in detail: 3,000 Venetians, 1,000 *schiavoni* (Dalmatians), 500 dragoons, 2,400 infantrymen from Brunswick-Lünburg, 120 Maltese knights with 900 infantrymen, the Tuscans with 100 knights of St Stephen and the *battaglione da sbarco* with 400 men, the Papal battalion with 300 infantrymen, and 60–80 *venturieri* (volunteers). These figures are reported by various sources, including Contarini, *Istoria della Guerra*, vol. I, p.434; Leonard, Jean, *Histoire des conquestes des Vénitiens depuis 1684 jusques à present* (Bruxelles, 1688), and ASFi, *Mediceo del Principato*, f. 2138; *truppe in Levante*. Contarini does not provide details about the auxiliaries, but states an overall strength of 9,500 men.

126 Garzoni, *Istoria della Repubblica di Venezia*, vol. I, p.82. Reports claimed that the greatest difficulties lay in the use of artillery, not because of the distance of the city from the landing point, but because of the presence of dangerous suburbs.

127 The reasons why the council of war chose Corone are reported differently according to the sources. For Hammer-Purgstall, *Histoire de l'Empire Ottoman* (Paris, 1838), vol. XII, p.219, Morosini allegedly received a message from the Mani Peninsula that diverted him from besieging Modone. For the author of the *Diario anonimo*, BNM, ms. It. VII 2592 (12484), f. 43, Morosini did indeed meet a messenger sent by some 'Christian villages', who told him that 'Corone is in great fear, and misses everything'.

128 Foscarini, *Historia della Republica Veneta*, pp.219–220.

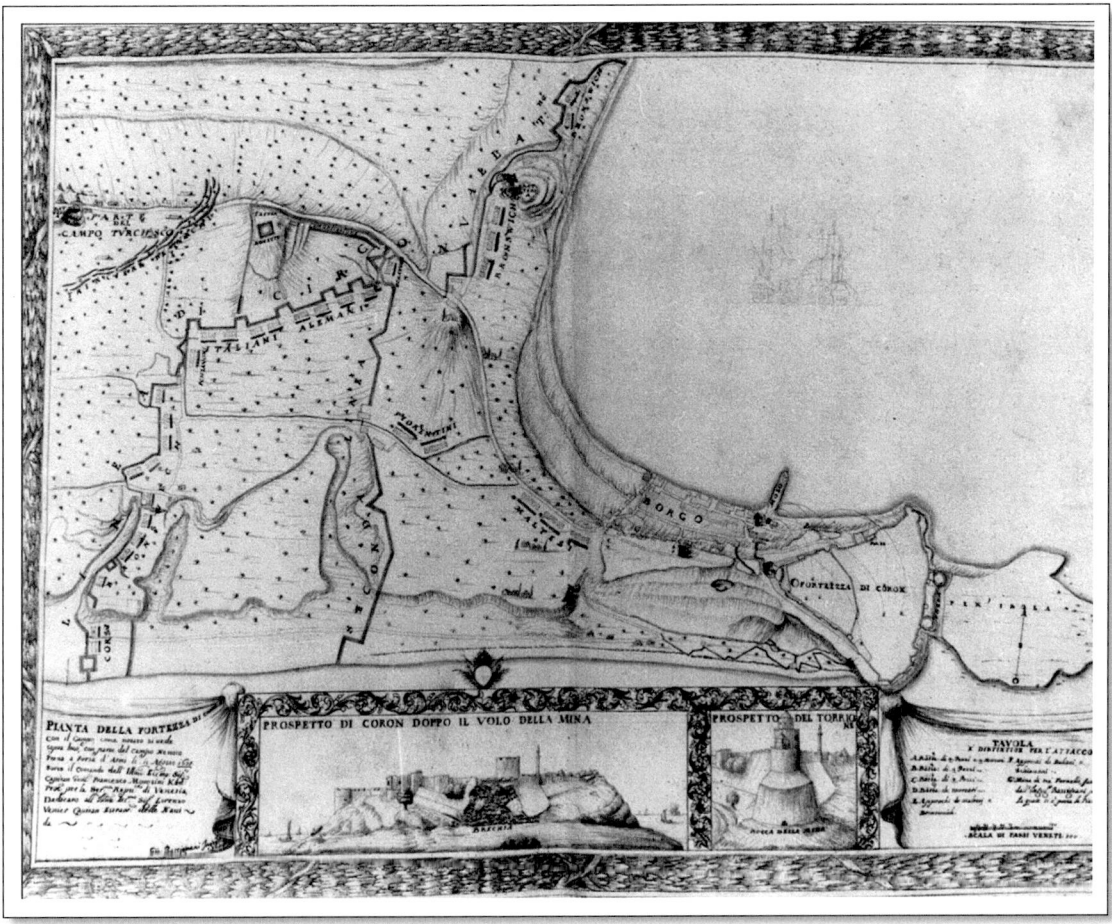

87. Plan of Corone and the deployment of the allied besieging army in July 1685 (author's archive). The siege engaged the Venetians and their allies for 48 days.

next few days, the besiegers dug the circumvallation, and Morosini inspected the earthworks on 1 July. To face any sortie from Corone, a four-gun battery directed fire against the large bastion at the western corner.[129] On 2 July four 500 lb mortars were also deployed, and all the artillery began to target the town. The Ottoman artillery returned fire. As the artillery duel had gradually died down on both sides, the besiegers assumed that the garrison was already on the verge of surrender. A Greek from Mani managed to escape during the following night, and informed the Venetians that the town was short of food, but the garrison was awaiting reinforcements, which was confirmed by two Greeks captured a few days later.

The next day, thanks to Greek informers, it was also learned that an Ottoman relief corps of 500 horsemen and as many infantrymen was only 14 km from Corone. However, as this corps was commanded by Sabbam Ağa, the same who, at the head of the relief force under Prevesa in September of the previous year, had turned back in the first engagement, the Venetians considered this threat negligible. On the same day a Greek tradesman from

---

129 Pinzelli, *Venise et la Morée*, p.102. Ironically, the tower had been built in 1463 by the Venetians against the assaults of the Ottomans.

Zakynthos brought valuable information. Thanks to the French consul in Patras, he had learned that the *paşa* of Lepanto had informed that of Corone that the Porte had ordered the defence of the fortresses at the entrance of the Gulf of Corinth, 'and not the ones of all the Morea'. This was therefore auspicious news, which allowed the allied commanders to know the intentions of the enemy.[130] The next day Morosini offered the surrender to the garrison, which replied negatively. Two other heavy guns were then unloaded, and positioned in the battery to be used against the town. However, the artillery was insufficient to force the defenders to surrender. As the ground around the fortress was soft, Morosini immediately considered digging a mine under the walls.[131]

The enemy relief force sporadically carried out reconnaissance and sometimes engaged in skirmishes with the Venetians. On 7 June, in one of these actions, the Ottomans managed to capture 16 soldiers, including some Maltese.

Further interrogations allowed the council of war to have a better knowledge of the situation. On 9 June the Venetian sentinels took a Greek renegade escaped from the Ottoman camp, and brought him before the Captain General. The fugitive reported that Ottoman reinforcements were arriving daily, but that they were short of ammunition, and were waiting for the arrival of the *paşa* of Lepanto with more troops. The Ottoman commander was planning to send a message to the defenders of Corone to urge them to make a sortie as soon as his troops had taken the Venetian trenches with an assault from behind.[132] Further information confirmed this scenario. The allies estimated the enemy troops, assembled under the command of Halil Paşa of Lepanto, at 3,400 foot and horse.

On 12 June, with the advance of the Ottomans threatening the allied trenches, the Count of Saint-Paul led three infantry regiments to face the enemy who, after a short skirmish, withdrew to their positions. In the following days, the Ottoman relief force advanced with trenches towards the besiegers' camp, while the allied battery continued to bombard the fortress, and the engineers advanced with their mines. On 20 June a mortar shot fired from a galleass fell on one of the tunnels and destroyed the vault, killing

---

130 *Ibid*. Information from locals was valuable, however Morosini was suspicious of them and always ordered a strict control. In this regard, on 14 June a Greek who had escaped from the Ottoman camp brought news that Halil Paşa of Lepanto had arrived with reinforcements. Morosini, who interrogated him, considered this news to be disinformation intended to spread panic in the allied army, and ordered the arrest of the renegade. Morosini immediately convened the council of war, but in the meantime another fugitive arrived in the Venetian camp. This man, who claimed to be a native of Cephalonia, claimed in turn that Halil Paşa, appointed vizier – actually *serasker* – of Morea by the Sultan, had just reached the Ottoman camp with 1,100 men and a single cannon.

131 Contarini, *Istoria della Guerra*, vol. I, pp.443–444. The work was led by three engineers: Jacques Milhau-Verneda, Giovanni Bassignani and Sergeant Major 'Marscè'; the latter was killed on the evening of 11 June by a musket ball that hit him in the head.

132 BNM, *Diario anonimo*, ms. It. VII 2592, f. 46 v.

two of the miners and wounding several others. Despite this, on 23 June the mine prepared by Milhau-Verneda was almost ready. About 1,200 men were divided into three corps to storm the breach after the explosion scheduled for the following day. When the 100 barrels of gunpowder exploded, the Christian troops were about to attack from several sides at once, but the breach in the wall was smaller than expected, and the assault was suspended. Meanwhile, Halil took advantage of the confusion and launched an assault against the besiegers' trenches. An advanced position was captured and all the defenders massacred. The Greeks, Albanians, and the dragoons of the Marquis de Courbon counterattacked, immediately supported by the Knights of Malta. The fight raged for three hours, when a barrel of gunpowder exploded as the Ottomans were retreating from the conquered position. The brave Maltese knight, Jean Hector de la Tour-Maubourg, was killed, while the commander of the Albanians, Pietro Cechina, had his left arm amputated. The besiegers claimed 120 killed, of which 80 Maltese, and many wounded. The battle had been followed with apprehension from the fleet, but when the red flag with the white cross of the order was hosted as a signal of the victory, immediately the Maltese sailors and oarsmen shouted *viva Malta!*.[133] In the encounter, the Ottomans lost 17 ensigns and 300–400 men; 130 of them were beheaded and their heads, stuck on poles, were exposed to the view of the besieged garrison.[134]

Despite the fact that the enemy threat had been neutralised and the catastrophe avoided, Morosini made negative remarks about his *generale dello sbarco*, the Count of Saint-Paul, who did not prevent the enemy assault. The Captain General complained openly to the Senate, judging Saint-Paul 'too old, too clumsy, certainly not combatant enough'.[135] Furthermore, the Ottomans were receiving reinforcements daily from Euboea and other places of the Morea. The Venetians and allies received knowledge of the enemy progress from Ottoman deserters, who included people of all nations. On 27 July a Greek from Zakynthos, a Frenchman and even a Russian slave of Halil *Paşa* arrived at the besiegers' camp with useful news. The Ottoman commander had now gathered 7,000 men, but his main concern was to establish contact with the garrison inside Corone.[136]

The siege continued unabated, and to intensify the bombardment of the defence Morosini required more heavy cannons from the galleys. On 30 July a deserter informed the Venetians about the incoming Ottoman assault. This time, the besiegers had strengthened their defence around the

---

133 *Ibid.*, f. 48.

134 *Ibid.*, 'to bring down the pride of these dogs'. This kind of ferocious practice was often carried out in the merciless wars between Christians and Muslims.

135 ASVe, *Senato, Dispacci, Provveditori di Terra e di Mar*, b. 1070, N. 45.

136 BNM, *Diario anonimo*, ms. It. VII 2592, f. 49 v. According to information gathered from the deserters, the *paşa* had offered prizes to volunteers who crossed the enemy lines to deliver his messages to the besieged town. The chronicler remarks that 'A black slave had managed to reach Halil's camp by leaving Corone at night, but had refused to take the reverse route despite being offered a large sum.'

circumvallation with embankments and palisades, and these improvements were effective, since after an intense exchange of musketry the Ottomans withdrew in disorder leaving 300 dead and wounded. The allies claimed 70 casualties. Although another threat had been neutralised, news from Cerigo alarmed the besiegers. Girolamo Marcello, *provveditore* of the island, informed the Captain General that the Ottoman fleet was sailing with 40 sail ships to the Morea. The *kapudan paşa* had escaped the surveillance of Alessandro Molin and Daniele Dolfin, who had been chasing him since June, and with whom he was conducting a cat-and-mouse duel. The news was worrying, as the Ottoman admiral could have landed reinforcements to overturn the balance of power and caused the siege to fail. Morosini immediately convened a council of war with all his commanders. It was clear that no more time was to be lost. The Captain General sent word to the whole army, to all the volunteers and to the crews of the fleet, to launch a general assault against the *serasker*. After giving his order, Morosini managed to gather a further 1,500 men from the fleet. He joined this force with all the available infantry, leaving just a thin line around Corone, and prepared the assault for 7 August. At midnight, in silence, the Venetian and allied troops, were divided into two corps and deployed in the trenches on the flanks of the enemy camp. At dawn both corps advanced, taking the Ottoman sentinels by surprise and opening a continuous fire. The surprise was complete and the Ottomans fled leaving all their artillery, ammunition, supplies and tents behind. An eyewitness reported that the enemy ran to safety 'just with shirts, others without underwear, some barefoot, some on horseback and some behind'.[137]

The battle of 7 August 1685 sealed the fate of Corone. Morosini was determined to exploit this outcome and that evening sent a messenger to demand the surrender of the town. Once again, but after more hesitation, the answer was negative. The council of war, meeting on the morning of 8 August, decided to make use of the mines. The gallery ran under the western bastion where it divided into three chambers. The most important chamber was further enlarged, and the miners placed 200 barrels of powder taken from the Ottoman camp in the previous days.[138] While the preparations were nearing completion, Morosini had a talk with the Count of Saint-Paul, Giorgio Benzon and Lorenzo Venier in order to prepare the troops for the assault on the breach that was to be created. On 11 August, at dawn, the mine exploded and ruined the main tower; however, the explosion also killed 30 Venetian soldiers who were in the advanced trench. The troops then attacked simultaneously on the side of this new breach, as well as on the side of the smaller breach made by the artillery. The battle, which raged for three hours,

---

[137] Juge de Pierrelatte Aymar, *Histoire du Marquis de Courbon, Maréchal des camps et armées de la Serenissime Republique de Venise* (Lyon, 1692), pp.106–107. The Ottoman commander himself fled without clothing.

[138] Anonymous, *Relazione del Glorioso acquisto della Fortezza di Coron, Capitale del Regno di Morea, fatto sotto il prudente Valoroso Commando dell'Eccellentiss. Signor Cavalier e Procurator Francesco Morosini Capitano Generale da Mar, il giorno 11 Agosto 1685* (Venice, 1685), p.17.

was bloody but the Venetians and their allies were eventually repulsed with very heavy losses: 400 soldiers, including 32 knights of Malta.[139] However, some of the troops had managed to enter the breach where they barricaded the position with sacks and fascines. Meanwhile the siege artillery redoubled its intensity, and as a new assault seemed imminent, the Ottomans finally decided to surrender. On 12 August, while negotiations were taking place, a cannon shot fired from the fortress killed a dozen Venetian soldiers. The episode was the pretext for the troops to enter the city, climbing over the breach and walls and spreading through the streets, looting without restraint and slaughtering soldiers and civilians.[140] The Venetians captured 105 cannons, 62 of which were of bronze. In 48 days of siege the besiegers' casualties totalled 653 dead and 762 wounded.[141] The Maltese paid the highest toll with 13 knights and 220 soldiers and sailors killed.[142]

In the following days, three infantry regiments of the Elector of Saxony arrived with the convoy of the *provveditore* Alvise Marcello. These reinforcements proved to be very useful after the losses suffered during the siege. After the departure of the auxiliaries, with 1,800 wounded and sick, and after the 1,000 men left as a garrison in Corone, Morosini had only 4,000 soldiers, and now the Saxons added 3,000 men.[143]

News of the surrender of Corone, 'the most superb and strongest fortress in the Morea' spread quickly and instilled courage in the Mani Peninsula, which rushed to the call of the local leaders who besieged Zernata, the largest Ottoman stronghold of the region. In early September, reconnaissance confirmed to Morosini that the siege was in progress. On 6 September Venetian galleys arrived in sight of the port of Zernata and the fortified village of Citres, defended by a small Ottoman garrison. According to the sources, Morosini decided to act cunningly. Having intercepted Halil's correspondence from Calamata, the Captain General sent a false message of the *serasker* informing the commanders of Citres and Zernata that he could not rescue the fortresses due to the presence of the Venetian fleet in the Mani's waters. The trick took effect, and on 11 September 600 people evacuated the forts without suffering any injury or damage. Morosini judged

---

139 Foscarini, *Historia della Republica Veneta*, p.227.

140 Garzoni, *Istoria della Repubblica di Venezia*, vol. I, p.95; Contarini, *Istoria della Guerra*, vol. I, p.449. Beregani, *Historia delle Guerre d'Europa*, vol. I, pp.324–325; anonymous, *Relazione del Glorioso acquisto della Fortezza di Coron*, p.18. According to the Venetian sources, about 3,000 people died, 325 men were taken alive and sent to the galleys, of whom 69 were consigned to the auxiliaries. The women, children and Blacks, who had not been killed, were also distributed: 1,207 were counted, the Republic retained 861.

141 The good performance of engineer Giovanni Bassignani had facilitated the conquest of Corone, and he was rewarded by Morosini. Giorgio Benzon was appointed extraordinary *provveditore*, Giustin da Riva ordinary *provveditore*, Count Alessandro Vimes 'governor' of the garrison.

142 Bartolomeo Dal Pozzo, *Historia della Sacra Religione Militare di San Giovanni Gerosolimitano detta di Malta* (Venice, 1715), p.591.

143 Friedrich Constantin von Beust, *Feldzüge der Kursächsischen Armee* (Hamburg, 1803), vol. II, p.89.

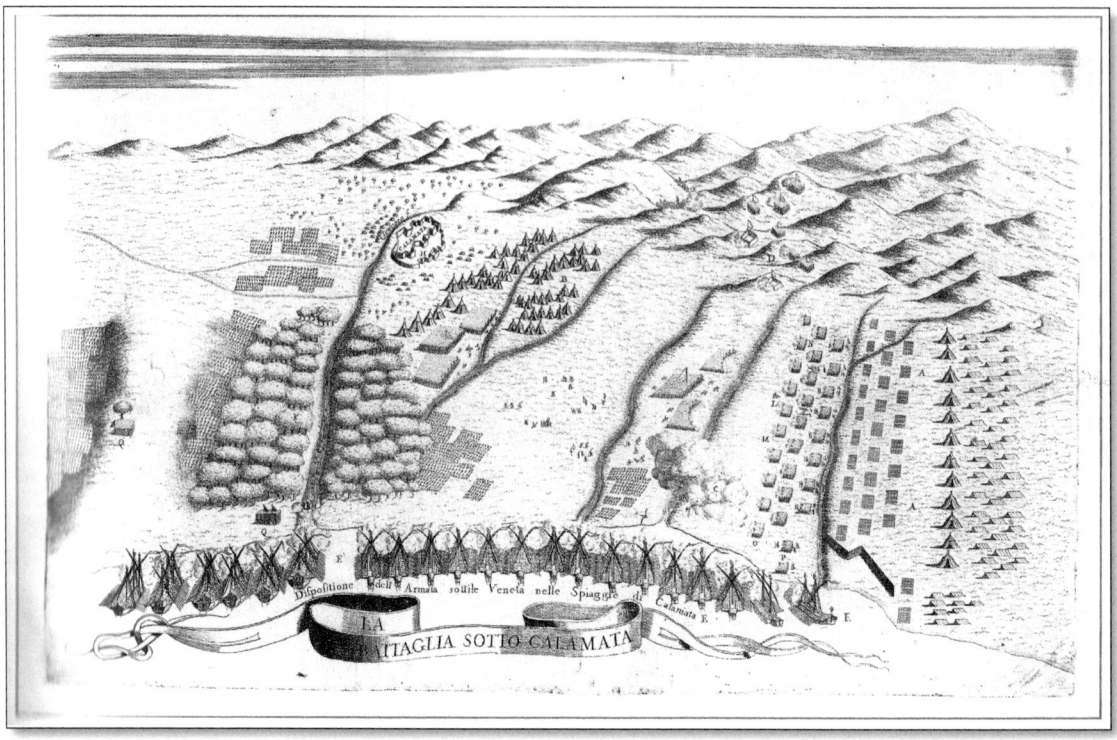

88. The battle of Calamata, fought on 14 September 1685 (author's archive). Morosini performed a very successful amphibious action that routed the Ottomans in their late attempt to relieve the besieged Corone.

that it was in his interest to show clemency on this occasion, since the garrisons had surrendered at the first intimation. This could induce other enemies to follow.

Despite the conquest of Zarnata, the presence of the Ottoman fleet posed a real danger. Spies informed the Captain General that Halil *Paşa* was gathering 10,000 men at Calamata to move against Corone. Morosini realised that the Ottoman fleet should be driven out as soon as possible, since this would encourage the rebellion of the Mani Peninsula and clear Corone from any possible threat. On 13 September, with all forces at his disposal, Morosini directed the fleet to the coast and landed at Agia Ston, east of the Calamata plain, at the foot of Mount Kalathio. The day after, the two armies encountered each other near Calamata, early in the morning.[144] The allied troops under General Hannibal Degenfeld, 8,000 strong, disposed in two lines preceded by 10 *oltramarine* free companies with 800 men deployed as skirmishers.[145] The left wing, on the beach side, commanded

---

144 This location must have brought back many memories to Morosini, who certainly had not forgotten how the Chevalier de Grémonville, under his command, had already defeated the Ottomans at Calamata 26 years earlier.

145 Pinzelli, *Venise et la Morée*, p.110. 'While the Count of Saint-Paul had already retired to Venice, Baron Degenfeld joined Morosini. Officially, Degenfeld had come to take leave and also return to Venice, but Morosini was not fooled and realised that the baron had come to compete for the post of general-in-chief of the landing troops. Degenfeld therefore had no problem staying and taking command of the embarked infantry.'

by the Saxon general Johan Rudolf von Scheenfelt, was supported by the cannons of the galleys under the orders of the *capitano della Guardia in Golfo* Sanudo. The Italian troops occupied the centre and the Brunswick infantry formed the right wing. On the far right, 1,500 Maniotes took position on the heights dominating the Nedonas valley. According to the well-informed Nicola Beregani, Degenfeld is said to have hesitated, and the attack was only decided by the council of war thanks to the intervention of Prince Maximilian Wilhelm of Brunswick. The Ottomans reacted by engaging the left wing and the *oltramarini* with 2,000 *sipahis*, while their infantry faced the infantry under Prince Maximilian. The battle was not particularly fierce, and soon the better deployment and discipline of the allied infantry prevailed over the poor coordination of the enemy. Within a short time the Ottomans began to retreat and eventually fled, leaving 200 of their own on the field. The Venetians claimed 110 casualties, mostly Saxons and *oltramarini*.[146] The Ottoman defeat also caused the Calamata garrison to flee, abandoning the fortress after destroying all the ammunition. The Venetian avant-garde occupied the place and Morosini ordered the firing of the houses and breached the walls. The castle of Chielafà, besieged by the Maniotes, also surrendered on the same day. The agreements for the evacuation were identical to those granted to the garrison of Zarnata: the defenders could leave the fortress with arms and baggage, with the obligation to release prisoners and slaves.[147] The following day, Passava also laid down its weapons without firing a shot, as soon as the dispirited defenders saw the *schiavoni* and Maniotes preparing for the assault. On 12 October Morosini went to Passava, where the Council of war decided to dismantle the defences. The ancient castle, located in an unfavourable place to be conveniently defended, could be conquered too easily by the enemy and was therefore demolished.[148] In October the 1685 campaign had ended even more favourably than the previous one. The Venetians had conquered a series of bridgeheads in the Peloponnese, the enemy relief forces had been defeated twice on the field, and the Mani Peninsula was freed from the 'Ottoman yoke'.

In dispatches written in the autumn, Francesco Morosini commented on the situation of the troops in the Levant and sent numerous requests to the Senate. He asked for a sufficient number of artillerymen for the conquered fortresses, as well as for engineers, since Verneda was 'impotent', his nephew had been wounded in the leg, and only Giovanni Bassignani was still in service.[149] In mid October Morosini learned that an epidemic had affected

---

146 Beregani, *Historia delle Guerre d'Europa*, vol. I, pp.368–369. The Saxon Obrist-Lieutenant Franz Salomon von Freuther was among the casualties.

147 Pinzelli, *Venise et la Morée*, p.112: 'On the morning of 24 September, the Ottomans evacuated Chielafa. Morosini estimated them at 1,000, of whom 350 carried arms. They had to be escorted by Venetian troops to the shore to the shore where Pisani's ships were waiting to transfer them to a safer place. The armed escort was to keep them out of the hands of the Maniotes and ensure their safety, than to ensure their departure.'

148 *Ibid.*

149 Beregani, *Historia delle Guerre d'Europa*, vol. I, p.383.

the garrison of Prevesa. He therefore decided not to send the troops there, but to accommodate them at Corfu to avoid contagion. Diseases had hit harder than the battles, since more than twice as many soldiers, sailors and oarsmen wounded in battle, died in hospitals than those sick and malnourished.[150]

As the weather permitted other enterprises, on 11 November Morosini sent Alcenago with 500 *schiavoni* to assault by surprise the village of Igoumenitsa, a natural port in continental Greece close to Corfu. The Venetians easily seized the old fortress, captured 12 bronze guns, and then dismantled the walls.[151]

Throughout December 1685, information was gathered about Ottoman movements in Corinth and Mistra, where Caffer Ismail *Paşa* had gathered 4,000 men, and for this Corone seemed directly threatened. As for the *serasker*, he was risking his head if he failed to retake the fortresses in the Morea that had fallen into Venetian hands. At the end of December there were some skirmishes around Corone, but the 1,300-strong garrison seemed to have enough biscuit and ammunition to hold out until March. However, the fortifications, badly damaged during the siege, were still not sufficiently repaired. Lieutenant General Verneda, who was increasingly ill, submitted a project to restore the fortress with some improvements.[152] Meanwhile in the Mani Peninsula, Lorenzo Venier, appointed *provveditore* of this sensitive region, had succeeded in setting up a local militia, 24 companies of 200 men each to guard the crossing points.[153]

On the Bosnian–Dalmatian border, the terrain favoured the development of a warfare that was initially a matter of small columns numbering a few thousand men, marching along the routes of the major rivers and seeking each other out in sparsely inhabited and inhospitable terrain. In October 1684, in Dalmatia, the Venetians had tried to seize Sinj in the Cetina valley, but failed. The following year they had returned twice in March and April 1685, but always without success. In both attempt the Venetians had received help from the community of Poljica, which had rebelled against the Ottoman sovereignty that lasted since 1513. To take revenge on Poljica, the Ottomans under the *paşa* of Bosnia attacked Duare in June 1685, but the mixed garrison of regular soldiers and militiamen repulsed the enemy assaults.

1686

On 26 March 1686 a neutral brigantine docked at Corfu, informing Morosini that an Ottoman corps was advancing into the Mani Peninsula, having

---

150 The statistic is based on Alexander Schwenke, *Geschichte der Hannoverischen Truppen in Griechenland*. The author states that 256 Brunswick-Lüneburg soldiers had died in battle and another 736 ended their lives in hospital.

151 ASVe, *Senato, Dispacci, Provveditori di Terra e di Mar,* b. 1070, d. 51–53.

152 Not having recovered from his fatigue, Verneda had obtained permission from Morosini to retire. The old engineer was replaced by the Count of San Felice, Antonio Muttoni, who had acquired great credit in Venice. Now, without an immediate superior, the Count had a free field. ASVe, *Senato, Dispacci, Provveditori di Terra e di Mar,* b. 1070, d. 68 – 26 March 1686.

153 ASVe, *Senato, Dispacci, Provveditori di Terra e di Mar,* b. 1070, d. 51–53.

opened the passage by driving out the Maniotes guarding the passes. True to his habit of acting in the shortest possible time even without more detailed information, on 27 March the Captain General embarked 4,000 German, *oltramarine* and Italian infantrymen on the fleet and headed for Chielafà. On 1 April Morosini became aware that 9,000–10,000 Ottomans were besieging the fortress defended by the *provveditore* Marino Gritti. The landing took place far from the fortress, but as soon as the *schiavoni* on the vanguard came in sight of the enemy camp, the Venetians realised that the Ottomans had left the siege, abandoning a considerable number of cannons. The retreat had been precipitous, since the besiegers had also abandoned many supplies and some camels.[154]

The council of war took place in the presence of all major allied officers. The susceptibility of Brunswick's officer had to be handled with great caution. The Duke, aware of the importance of his own contribution to the victories of the 1685 campaign, pushed his son Maximilian Wilhelm to impose his ascendancy in the council of war. As soon as he arrived, the Prince visited the admirals and the fleet as if he were commander-in-chief, and presented Morosini with a letter from his father Ernst August. The Duke requested that his brigadier, Herman Philipp von Ohr, be given the rank of *sergente maggiore di battaglia*. The Captain General apologised for not being able to grant the request, blaming the Senate, which was responsible for promotion and to whom he forwarded the request. To keep the peace, the Prince received three camels as a gift, but he remained a constant source of worry for the Captain General.[155]

At the same time, Count Otto Wilhelm von Königsmarck, chosen by the Senate as the new landing general, also took up his duties. The Count had come into contact with Venice during negotiations for the enrolment of a battalion of 500 Swedish infantrymen. He had arrived in Venice with an impressive retinue, as was then customary for such a prestigious figure, comprising engineers and other technicians who had served the King of Sweden.[156]

While waiting for the arrival of the auxiliaries, large manoeuvres were organised on 21 April, when the troops were arranged in order of battle; the muster registered an overall force of 13,060 infantrymen and 1,240 dragoons.[157] On 25 May the auxiliary squadrons were finally in sight. The eight Maltese galleys, with 120 knights and 800 men, were commanded by

---

154 *Ibid.*, d. 70, 1 April 1686.

155 ASVe, *Senato, Dispacci, Provveditori di Terra e di Mar*, b. 1070, d. 65, 26 February 1686.

156 A member of the Königsmarck family had served as volunteer during the Cretan War, and this was another detail took in consideration by senators who formed a concrete opinion of the warlike qualities of this this family. See Pinzelli, *Venise et la Morée*, p.116.

157 BNM, ms. It. VII 2592 (12484), fol. 56. The vanguard consisting of 17 platoons each with 60 *oltramarini* was placed under the command of Lauro d'Andria. Behind them there were 18 battalions of 400 men each, with three dragoon squadrons of 120 men on the right wing and four on the left. These corps were commanded by the Prince of Brunswick, Herman von Ohr, *sergente maggiore* Enea Rapetta and the Marquis de Courbon. The reaguard, or reserve, under

Count Johann Joseph von Herbestein, Grand Prior of Germany and Hungary. The Papal squadron, with five galleys and 450 men, was under the command of Count Camillo Ferretti, who had just been appointed *governatore*.[158] All the generals paid a visit to Morosini, who explained the views of the Consulta to the new arrivals, to which they agreed. The Venetian fleet was then composed of 26 galleys, six galleasses and a further 70 ships of various tonnage, excluding auxiliary units.[159] The departure was set for 28 May, and while the sail ships and galleasses under Carlo Pisani and Alessandro Priuli sailed to the Gulf of Navarino, the galleys led by the Captain General headed towards the Gulf of Corinth, in order to lure the Ottomans. To this end Morosini landed 1,000 *oltramarini* on the morning of 30 May, but the Ottomans, who had entrenched themselves, held their positions.

The galleys set sail for Patras that evening, only to change course abruptly at nightfall to rejoin the rest of the fleet.[160] The success of this diversionary operation depended on the speed with which the galleys could rejoin the sail ships. Unfortunately a headwind at Cape Kilini forced the galleys to seek refuge in Zakynthos until the following day. This caused no immediate consequence, and after the wind had changed the two squadrons were able to join up on 2 June. The landing began immediately, on the beach north of Old Navarino (today Pylos), probably in the cove of Voidokilia, without encountering enemy opposition. The town, standing on the southernmost point of the small, rugged peninsula of Koryphasion, had a natural position that was difficult to attack, but the walls had long been neglected. The occupants, just 400 civilians and soldiers, were well aware of the weaknesses of the fortifications. At the first intimation of surrender sent by Königsmarck, when the landing had just begun, the defenders decided to capitulate. On 3 June, around noon, the surrender agreement was agreed. It stipulated that the garrison could freely evacuate the place with their families, weapons and baggage, while waiting to be transported by ship to Alexandria: 'not trusting themselves to stay in the Morea so as not to leave their heads there ...'[161] The next day the Ottomans left the city, abandoning 43 bronze cannons.[162] With this easy victory, the campaign of 1686 began under the best auspices.

On the same day, the Tuscan squadron led by Camillo Guidi arrived with four galleys and four galleasses, carrying about 900 men including

---

sergente maggiore di battaglia Alessandro Alcenago, formed another line with nine infantry battalions flanked by two squadrons of 100 light horsemen on each side.

158 Camillo Ferretti (1646–1733), of the family of the Counts of Ancona, see in Valori, *Condottieri*, p.147.

159 According to another author, the figures are slightly different. According to him, the fleet that left Porto Glimino was composed of 30 galleys, six galleasses, 12 galleots, 40 ships and 34 other vessels. See Giovanni Battista Burgo, *Viaggio di cinque anni in Asia, Africa, e Europa* (Milan, 1688), vol. III, p.436.

160 Anastasia Stouraiti, *Memorie di un ritorno, la guerra di Morea (1684–1699) nei manoscritti della Querini Stampalia* (Venice: Fondazione Querini Stampalia, 2001), p.51.

161 Contarini, *Istoria della Guerra*, vol. I, p.562.

162 Garzoni, *Istoria della Repubblica di Venezia*, p.126.

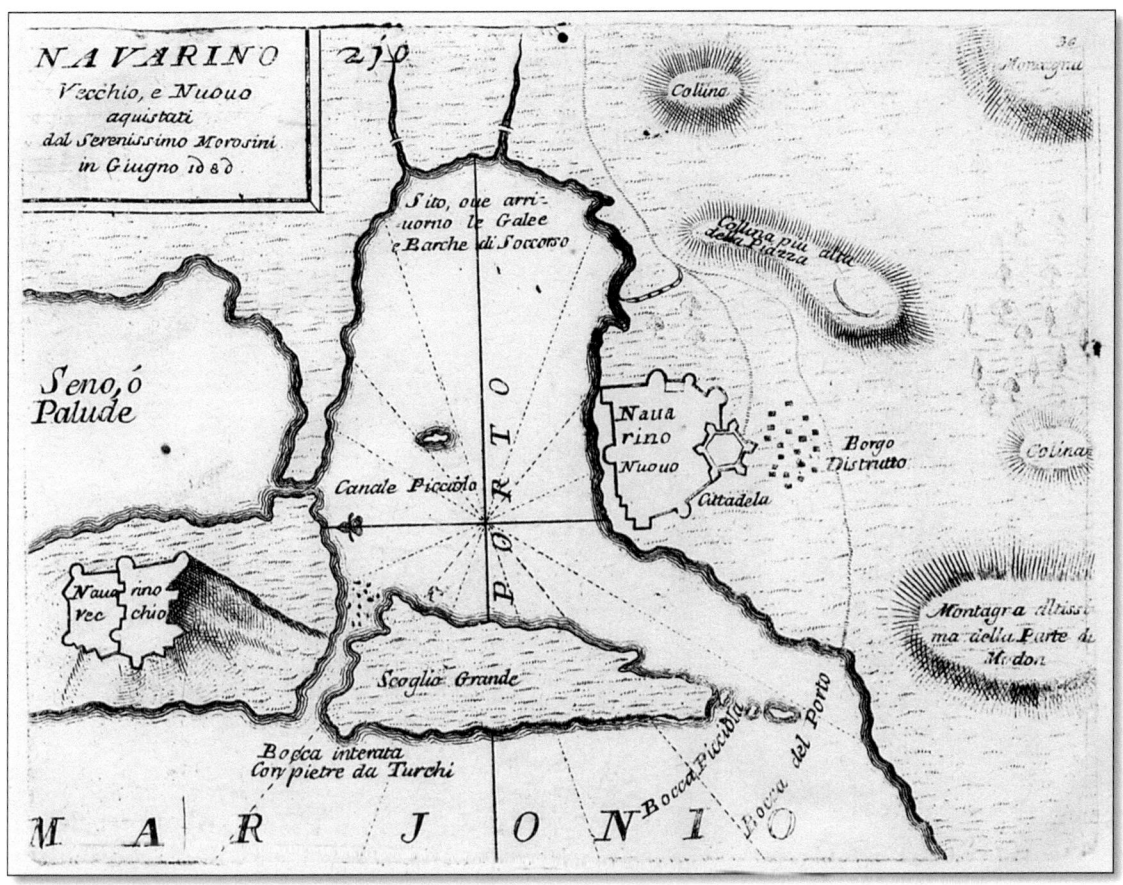

89. Old and New Navarino in an early-eighteenth century print by Vincenzo Maria Coronelli (author's archive). Both fortresses were seized by the Venetians in the opening phase of the campaign in June 1686.

marines, knights of St Stephen and volunteers. The next move was to lay siege to Navarino Nuova (Neokastron). On 5 June the troops moved along the Osmanaga marshes and then onto the plain that bordered the northern part of the bay, to camp east of the fortress. A problem immediately arose. The city had been built on rock and the surrounding terrain was rocky and barren, which prevented the construction of entrenchments. The dwellings near the fortress were built of stone, and finding straw for the faggots was also a problem. The camp *provveditore* Daniele Dolfin, assisted by Filippo Maria Paruta and Angelo Emo, had to deal with all these logistical problems. Water was brought to the camp from a distant stream with pack animals, but there was no shortage of food and wine, so that with some drunkenness 'the soldiers get by cheerfully'.[163] On 6 June the sentries sounded the alarm when 250 soldiers in 'Turkish dress' approached, but this was actually a group of Albanians bringing over 2,000 head of cattle taken from the area, enough to keep up the troops' morale.[164]

After a reconnaissance of the terrain to find the best alternative for an attack, the Count of Königsmarck ordered the bombardment of the city,

---

163 BNM, ms. It. VII 2592 (12484), fol. 54.
164 Pinzelli, *Venise et la Morée*, p.127.

WARS AND SOLDIERS IN THE EARLY REIGN OF LOUIS XIV - VOLUME 6 - PART 2

Questo è un accampamento dei Venetiani et erono 8. battaglioni distribuiti in più luoghi A° Quartiere del Sig.r Gen.le Chinismart. con suoi padiglioni. 8. Luglio

Alcune Baracche & stalle della guardia di d.o Sig. Gen.le attorno al suo quartieri. 13. Lug.o

LITTLE AND GREAT ITALIAN WARS

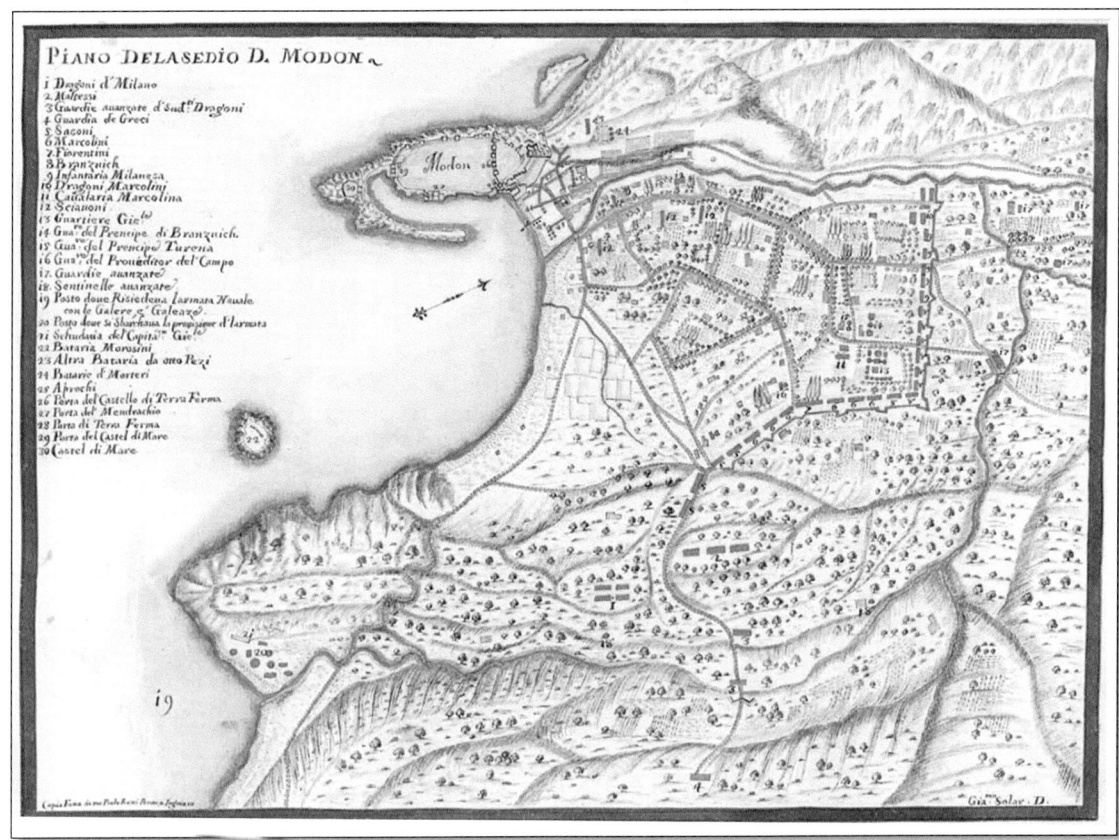

Facing page: 90. (top) and 91. Scenes from the Venetian encampment before Modone, July 1686, after the Manfroni Manuscript. In the Peloponnese, the hot summer created a punishing physical environment that was difficult to endure for the majority of soldiers, especially mercenary troops arrived from Germany or Switzerland. In this harsh environment diseases like smallpox, cholera and typhoid wiped out the less-accustomed troops, causing more deaths than any battle. As a result the soldiery greatly suffered, since they were supplied with poor and unreliable rations and faced a constant lack of clean water. Officers often neglected their men, while hygiene and medical support were mostly nonexistent. Privation, disease and famine were the usual companions for armies in the field, which were ill-equipped to resist them.

Above: 92. Plan of the siege of Modone in July 1686 showing the deployment of the besieging army. (Author's archive)

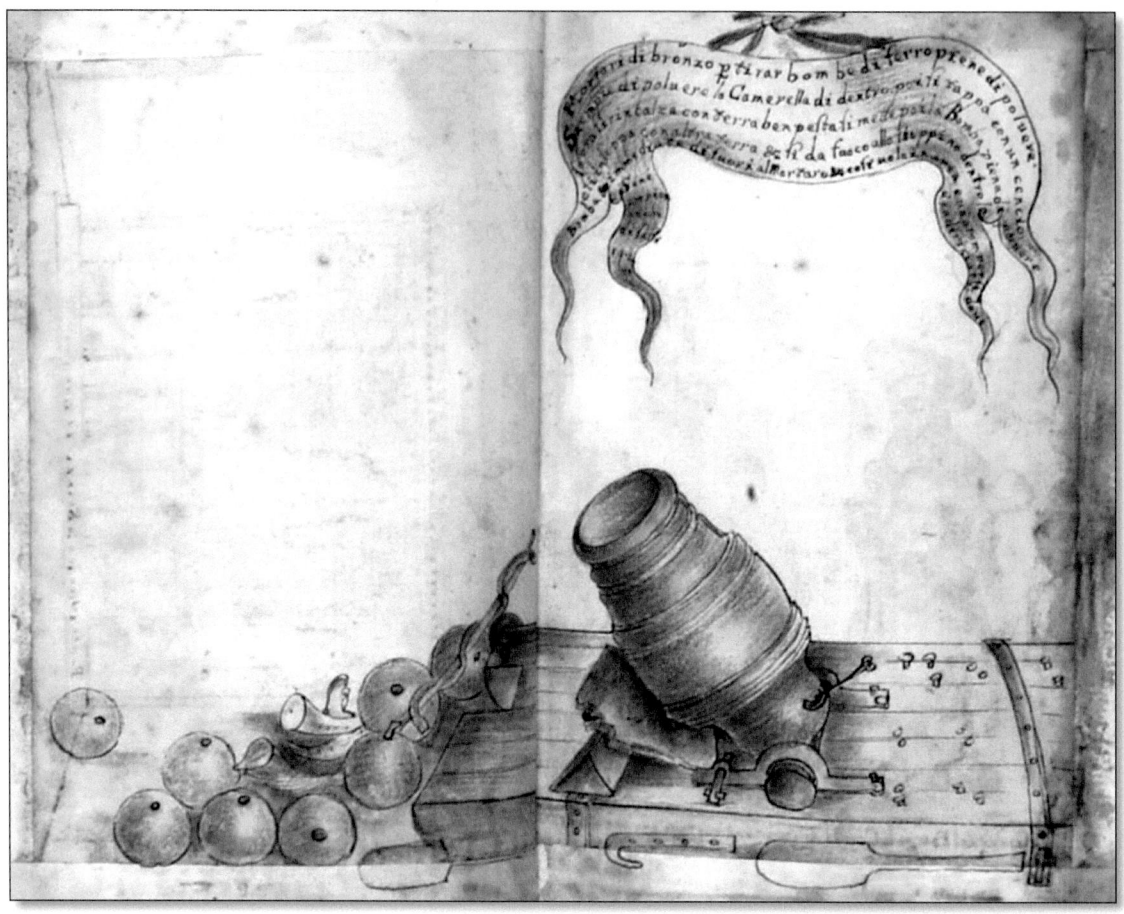

93. Another drawing from the Manfroni Manuscript, depicting one of the celebrated Tuscan mortars employed in the sieges of New Navarino and Modone in 1686.

estimating that a full-scale assault by troops on that terrain would cost too many men their lives. The plan drawn up with Morosini was first for the galleys to enter the harbour. However, this was a very dangerous mission because the defenders had placed two batteries with 16 cannons to defend the entrance, and even entering at night was a real challenge because of the full moon. Despite these difficulties, 11 galleys managed to get through during the night, and on this occasion the enemy gunners showed their inexperience. The first two galleys were led by *provveditore* Donà, with Königsmarck on board, and Pizzamanno.[165]

The Count Antonio Muttoni di San Felice was given the task of directing his company of *bombardieri* using his 18 heavy mortars located between the encampment and on the island of Sfaktiria. The first shots were catastrophic, with bombs exploding in the air or falling far from the target, and only one sixth of the shells actually reached the target.[166] Morosini expressed his concern, judging the action of the artillery and its commander negatively. Camillo Guidi then landed two more mortars and soon the accuracy of the

---

165 Burgo, *Viaggio*, vol. III, p.440.
166 BNM, ms. It. VII 2592 (12484), fol. 54.

trajectories improved, reassuring Morosini.¹⁶⁷ On 8 June Königsmarck sent an ultimatum to the garrison, whose leader, Seffer Ağa, replied to buy time, assuring them that he was ready to discuss the surrender, provided that the *serasker* Ismail *Paşa* was first defeated in the open field. The latter showed up on the morning of 14 June with 8,000 irregular infantrymen and 2,000 provincial *sipahis*.

Morosini entrusted Alcenago with the task of continuing the siege. The battle began around noon. Several patricians participated as volunteers, among them, the most beautiful names of the Venetian aristocracy stood out: Pietro Basadonna, Bortolo Erizzo, Filippo Paruta, Fabio Bonvicini and Pietro Marcello. The battle is described by most contemporary commentators as a succession of clashes that followed the attack by the dragoons of the Marquis of Courbon, who engaged the enemy without the support of the infantry. In vain Königsmarck would have ordered him to retire, but due to the existing rivalry, Courbon continued his action. The Ottomans managed to surround the dragoons, who soon found themselves in trouble. During the fighting the Marquis de Courbon, the Prince of Turenne, and the Baron of Colombier did their best to rally the squadrons, which retreated and fought their way to a safe position. The *schiavoni* arrived to aid them in time to repel the enemy, who retreated in good order. According to some reports, the arrival of the Maltese infantry and two field pieces restored the situation and the whole Venetian army, reorganised and reassured, was ready to fight again. At that point the Ottomans no longer offered any opposition and abandoned the battlefield, leaving 50 barrels of gunpowder, camels, provisions and more than 300 tents, including that of the *serasker*, which Courbon offered to Morosini after spending the night.¹⁶⁸

Without hope of relief, the Ottoman commander of New Navarino agreed to surrender after Morosini's second ultimatum. The *ağa* requested only that they exit the town freely within four days and be sent to Alexandria. Hostages were also exchanged. The allied fleet was able to enter the bay of Navarino on Sunday 16 June 1686, however, the surrender did not go as planned. The following night a tremendous explosion shook the fortress when an ammunition depot exploded, killing 150 people including the Ottoman commander.¹⁶⁹ It was probably an accident, although there were rumours that the *ağa* was behind this suicidal act. The next day 3,000 people, including almost 1,000 soldiers, evacuated New Navarino. They had to hand over 138 Black slaves and 200 horses, which were divided between the different contingents; 53 bronze cannons, six iron cannons and 16 *petriere* were found in the fortress.¹⁷⁰

---

167 ASFi, *Mediceo del Principato, Spedizione di Soldatesche in Levante dal 1684 fino al 1688*; f. 2219.
168 Pinzelli, *Venise et la Morée*, pp.128–129.
169 Burgo, *Viaggio*, vol. III, pp.446–447: 'In the meantime, there followed a serious disturbance in the fortress … As the fire was first ignited by bombs in some of the houses of the fortress, although it was largely extinguished, it was always secretly going on, so much so that when it reached a powder store, it killed Seffer Aga, Commandant of Navarino, with another 250 Turks and six Christians, leaving another 15 wounded outside the city.'
170 Pinzelli, *Venise et la Morée*, p.130.

Morosini immediately appointed Pietro Bassadona and Steffano Lippomano as *provveditori* of New Navarino, while Pietro Grioni was put in charge of Old Navarino. The bay of Navarin had been entirely occupied in less than 20 days and the rout of the *serasker* made it possible to optimistically envisage the conquest of Modone, 15 km to the south.

The campaign was delayed by the relief of Chielafà. In early June the Venetian fleet landed 1,500 Mainots along with another 8,000 regular soldiers near Cape Matapan, forcing the Ottomans to abandon the siege.[171] After this action the council of war decided to march the troops overland, while the fleet set sail on the morning of 22 June. The fleet and the troops arrived in sight of the fortress that evening. Modone, the only stronghold still in Ottoman hands in Messenia, was much better built and located than all the strongholds conquered until then. The ancient Greek fortress, extensively improved by the Venetians in the fifteenth century, consisted of a 500-metre peninsula, with the sea on all sides except the north, where a ditch with a width of 20 to 50 metres separated it from the mainland. When Königsmarck got close enough to it, he could not help but notice that reconnaissance efforts had greatly underestimated the place. Morosini too was overconfident, hoping that the Ottoman garrison would capitulate on his approach, or at worst on the first warning. It was therefore a bitter surprise to find that the enemy artillery offered intense fire as the Allied fleet approached. On 26 June, after deploying troops and artillery, Morosini sent an officer with the surrender demand to the Ottoman commander but he, citing the fate that befell Corone, rejected the offer with such disdain that Morosini was disgusted.[172]

After the failure of the negotiations, the mortars shelled the city and set many buildings on fire. According to a contemporary account, during the first day 500 bombs targeted the city, but 80 of them completely missed the fortress and 30 others exploded in the air before impact.[173] On their side the Pope's troops, supported by the Maltese and Tuscan infantry opened two trenches 500 paces from Modone during the night of 29/30 June. They worked so diligently that by morning the trenches were only 50 and 75 paces from the walls.[174] On the evening of 30 June Königsmarck again tried to force the Ottomans to surrender. The commander asked for a ceasefire for the night, declaring that he would consider the offer, but in fact used this truce as a pretext to move the ammunition to a safer place and to reposition the artillery. This information was reported through the escape of a Greek. When the *paşa* asked for a new suspension of the siege for 15 days, in order to

---

171 Camillo Contarini, *Istoria della Guerra*, p.386.

172 Garzoni, *Sommarii*, p.58. The Ottoman *paşa* answered that he and his soldier were ready to perish, 'with finally setting fire to the city, provided it was never to come into the hands of Christians.'

173 Léonard, *Histoire des conquestes*, p.104. According to Beregani, *Historia delle Guerre d'Europa*, vol. II, p.28, some projectiles hit the Maltese infantry causing several wounded.

174 *Ibid.*: 'Infantry of all nations, Papal, Maltese, Brunswick, Saxons and Florentine infantry competed in digging trenches for generous emulation.'

contact the *serasker* and ask for permission to surrender the place, a furious Morosini declared the truce broken, and the siege operations resumed. The operation of mining the baluards began under the direction of Verneda and Giovanni Bassignani, as in Corone the previous year.[175] The Tuscans landed four mortars from their galleys and targeted the city with greater success.[176]

On the evening of 6 July, Morosini asked for the third time that the commander of the garrison surrender. This time the proposal had more effect, especially as the Ottomans could only note with fear the progress of the mining work and the 4,000 bombs already dropped, which had almost completely destroyed the town. On 7 July the white flag was raised on the walls. The whole day was spent in bitter negotiations before an agreement was reached and finally accepted by both parties. On 8 July the defenders were given three days to evacuate Modone before being transported to North Africa like the garrison of New Navarino. The conquest of Modone had cost minimal losses, and the surrender this time took place without incident. 1,000 soldiers and 3,000 civilians left on 11 July. When the besiegers finally managed to enter Modone, they found a desolate city and a spectacle of destruction on an unimaginable scale.[177] It took days of work for the fleet crews and the soldiers to clean up the city and resume normal activities. In Modone, Morosini left a garrison of 500 infantrymen under the *venturiere* Filippo Paruta.[178]

It was then the middle of July, far too early to stop military operations, especially with the favourable conditions of the moment. On 17 July Morosini ordered the council of war to take place the next morning, but the meeting was brought forward to the same day. The generals and admirals had a lively discussion to decide which new conquest to turn towards. The objectives proposed were Patras and the castles at the mouth of the Gulf of Corinth, as well as Lepanto, Malvasia (Monemvasia), and Nauplia (Nafplio). It was the latter that was chosen by a majority of only one vote, but certainly the allied generals were confident that all the Peloponnese would fall if they succeeded. On the morning of 27 July 200 men and 20 horses were distributed to each galley; overall, about 10,000 men and 650 horses took their places on board in an extremely small space. The two largest galleys were assigned to escort the convoy, while the other three remained anchored at Navarino. The following morning, the fleet sailed along the Mani Peninsula and rounded Cape Matapan. At the end of the day the sail squadrons reached Cape Sant'Angelo (Cape Maleas) where the headwind, as often happens between the mainland and Cerigo, temporarily disunited the sail squadron. The galleys, under Morosini, continued sailing and arrived on the morning of the 29th in sight

---

175 Burgo, *Viaggio*, vol. III, p.449.
176 Beregani, *Historia delle Guerre d'Europa*, vol. II, p.28.
177 Garzoni, *Sommarii*, pp.61–62: 'the houses everywhere in ruins, the ramparts largely open and smashed, the stinking corpses thrown into the streets and scattered everywhere, caused horrendous spectacle in the sight of the present, in such a way that it became impassable to enter the city because of the great stench of such stinking corpses.'
178 Beregani, *Historia delle Guerre d'Europa*, vol. II, p.34.

94. The painting by Romeyn de Hooghe depicting the battle of Nauplia fought on 29 August 1686. The conquest of Nauplia was hampered by several obstacles, first of all disease and then an unexpected Ottoman resistance. In the last major action of the 1686 campaign, Morosini's and Königsmarck's errors of judgement risked defeat with a disastrous outcome for the continuation of the war.

of Malvasia, where they stopped for a few hours to stock up on fresh water.[179] As usual, Morosini did not waste time and immediately sent an ultimatum,[180] but the garrison firmly rejected it, as the fortress had the means to resist a siege for a long time, which future events would confirm.

Heading north, the galleys entered the Argolis Gulf and on 30 July reached the bay of Tolo, a few miles from Nauplia. After disembarking the troops, a few patrols of *oltramarini* were sent out to gather information. The arrival of the allies gave courage to several Christian slaves to flee and join the *oltramarini*. One of them, a Frenchman who had been enslaved for 34 years, provided a lot of valuable information to Morosini. He told how the garrison had hurriedly locked itself in the fortress upon hearing the news of the arrival of the allied fleet, refusing entry even to stragglers returning from the campaign. The garrison numbered about 1,000 men, the only ones able to

---

179 Pinzelli, *Venise et la Morée*, p.134.
180 BNM, ms. It. VII 2592 (12484), fol. 60: 'to see if the consternation in the city could be allowed to surrender the fortress'.

carry weapons, and could count on a good supply of food and ammunition.[181] The Frenchman also stated that there were 400 Christian slaves in the city. Another escaped slave, a Russian, told of an incident in which barrels of gunpowder had exploded, killing about 20 soldiers and putting the main cistern out of action. Inside the walls – a quadrilateral of 400 by 200 metres, dominated by the high ground of Acronauplia – were crammed about 7,000 people and their livestock.

As for the *kapudan paşa*, he had just raised anchor a few days earlier for Negroponte (Chalkis), leaving behind him two galleys in the port of Nauplia where there were also two galliots and an English vessel. With this new information, Morosini ordered Königsmarck to set out with the troops the following morning. The strategic point that was to be occupied as a priority was Mount Palamida, which dominates the city from a height of 216 metres just a musket shot away. Some enemy parties that had entrenched themselves on the high ground were dispersed and the Venetian troops were able to start digging in under fire from the garrison. The Ottomans also executed a sortie with 200 men to destroy the work of the attackers. The Venetian dragoons repulsed the threat; during the skirmish, the *Sergente Maggiore di Battaglia* Lauro d'Andria was wounded in the foot. The following day, however, a battery of four cannons opened fire from Mount Palamida on the town below.[182] On 2 August the *serasker* Ismail *Paşa* encamped at Argos, some 15 km away. He had with him about 4,000–6,000 men of good troops.[183] This presence made the surrounding countryside dangerous and the besieging army paid the price, for in just three days 120 soldiers were wounded or captured by the enemy as they approached the allied camp and put it in a state of awe. The next day, the Venetian fleet finally arrived and the troops on board could reinforce the besieging army, which now consisted of 11,500 soldiers, including 900 cavalry, including auxiliaries.[184] On 5 August the council of war agreed to chase the Ottomans from Argos, and to this end 1,500 infantrymen continued the blockade of the city, while the remaining troops under Königsmarck headed to the plain of Argos to face the enemy. The allies deployed in order of battle and the *serasker* accepted the challenge. Divided into three large squadrons, the Ottomans deployed their infantry in the centre, while the allied troops, this time greatly superior in numbers, advanced in a single line. The Prince of Brunswick held the command of the left wing, and Königsmarck directed the action from the opposite wing. He ordered his subordinates to hold their positions and only open fire within a short range. The main charge of the *sipahis* focused against the right of the Christian position, where two *oltramarine* regiments and Courbon's

---

181 Burgo, *Viaggio*, vol. III, p.454. According to this author, a spy would have estimated the garrison to be 3,000 strong, to which 300 men sent as reinforcements had joined.
182 Beregani, *Historia delle Guerre d'Europa*, vol. II, p.79; Léonard, *Histoire des conquestes*, pp.124–125.
183 Morosini estimated the Ottomans at 4,000 horsemen and 3,000 infantrymen, ASVe *Senato, Dispacci, Provveditori di Terra e di Mar*, b. 1070, d. 85.
184 Pinzelli, *Venise et la Morée*, p.134.

dragoons were located. The Ottomans had placed two field pieces which fired seven or eight times without success; the Venetians used instead rapid-fire falconets which surprised the enemy. In the battle the Prince of Turenne, Carl Johan von Königsmarck and Courbon distinguished themselves by their bravery; the horses of the latter two were killed.

While Königsmarck confronted the Ottomans in the plain of Argos, the Captain General directed a landing of 2,000 men under the command of Colonel Magnanini, to take the enemy by surprise from behind. After several unsuccessful attempts to break Königsmarck's battalions, the Ottomans finally abandoned the battlefield. But they did so in good order, with cavalry covering the troops on foot, allowing them to break camp and carry their baggage to safety, and retreat to the Isthmus of Corinth. The small garrison of Argos followed the *serasker*'s example: when the Venetian vanguards reached the castle, they found the place deserted and unarmed, and there were only two cannons and six petrieres. Despite the apparent violence of the battle, the allies suffered few casualties.[185] The balance of Ottoman losses is always more difficult to assess: perhaps 100 dead, perhaps up to 400.

Meanwhile, the siege had not stopped. Under the *provveditore* Daniele Dolfin, the incessant bombardment of the city had ignited fires which propagated in the interior of the walls, the houses being partially built of wood. In the evening, after the Battle of Argos, Morosini tried to persuade the Ottoman commander to surrender, but his ultimatum was firmly rejected. As a result, a new battery of eight 50 lb cannons was displayed on Mount Palamida and started firing on the morning of 10 August.[186] With a further two 20 lb guns and two additional mortars employed under the orders of Faustin da Riva, the bombardment of the city became more intense hour after hour, with up to 500 bombs fired per day according to Morosini.[187]

Exasperated by the terrible conditions, the civilian population mutinied and asked to surrender. This episode was reported by several Greeks who had escaped from the city. The Ottoman commander managed to restore order, promising the arrival of the *serasker* with new reinforcements within a few days. But the situation of the defenders was not reassuring enough to prevent the *ağa* who held the command of Thermis, an old castle located on the Gulf of Hydra, offering to surrender in exchange for a passage to Negroponte for himself and his 40 soldiers. A delegation of Greeks from the surrounding area came to the Captain General to inform him of this offer. A few days later, the Ottomans did not hesitate to surrender and abandon the castle, and the crews of the Venetian galleys went to Thermis and removed the five iron cannons and the ammunition that was there. Morosini assigned a local Greek notable to survey the castle.[188]

---

185 *Ibid.*, p.135. The Venetian sources claim only 24 killed and about 40 wounded.
186 The battery was manned by particularly skilled or very lucky artillerymen, since their very first shot centred an enemy standard at 600 metres. Beregani, *Historia delle Guerre d'Europa*, vol. II, p.81.
187 ASVe *Senato, Dispacci, Provveditori di Terra e di Mar*, b. 1070, d. 85.
188 Locatelli, *Racconto historico*, pp.279–280.

However, the resistance of the Ottoman garrison of Nauplia continued, despite the progress of the Maltese approaches against the eastern curtain, and despite the new battery of four 50 lb guns on Mount Palamida, which began to target the city on 16 August. On 17 and 18 August, rain delayed the besiegers. Moreover, the defenders received an unexpected and unstoppable help: a terrible epidemic was spreading in the Christian camp, although it was not clear what the disease was. One of the first to be affected was the provender of the Dolfin camp himself, who was struck by a *febbre quartana*[189] Among the sick were the governor of the *galeotti* Bragadin and the *capitano straordinario delle navi* Lorenzo Venier. By 20 August only 300 of the Maltese troops remained available, compared with the contingent's original strength of 1,000. Every day, 20–30 people were taken by violent fevers, and many died within a few days.[190] The regiments of Braunschweig-Lüneburg were not much better off, since 1,550 men were still able to serve, but another 1,200 were either wounded or ill.[191]

While the allied troops were plagued by the epidemic, the *serasker* appeared again on the plain of Argos on 19 August, this time with many more reinforcements, probably at least 10,000 men, 3,000 of whom arrived from Egypt. For greater security the eight mortars under the Count of San Felice were transferred to the first line of the circumvallation to face the enemy threat. The position of the Venetians and the auxiliaries became increasingly untenable. The siege was progressing when, on the evening of 23 August, *sergente maggiore di battaglia* Alcenago was killed by a musket ball to the head. This veteran of the Cretan War and a companion of Francesco Morosini was a myth among the Venetians, who regarded him as 'an officer universally beloved by all, of much credit, and one of much expectation, and perhaps the most devoted to the Republic'.[192] Alcenago was not the only illustrious victim. In the following days, the disease took the convicts' governor Bragadin and his brother Marino, the galley *governatore* Francesco Loredan, Count Barnabò Maria Visconti, commander of the Spanish-Milanese dragoon regiment, and on 26 (or 27) August it was the turn of Carl Johan von Königsmarck, the nephew of the *generale dello sbarco*, who had lived adventurously to fight for Venice, only to come to die aged 27 of a contagious disease in Greece. The epidemic had put so many officers out of action and left so many companies without officers that Morosini turned to the *venturieri* to enter the regular service.

On 26 August the besiegers' situation became even more precarious with the arrival of 2,500 Albanians to reinforce the *serasker*.[193] For their part, Morosini and Königsmarck tried to prepare the troops for the assault

---

189 The symptoms are those of malaria, as the *febbre quartana* is often associated.
190 Garzoni, *Sommarii*, p.68.
191 Alexander Schwencke, *Geschichte der Hannoverischen Truppen in Griechenland, 1685–1689* (Hahn, 1854), p.182.
192 Foscarini, *Historia della Repubblica Veneta*, p.275. His death led to the suspension of work in the night between 23 and 24 August.
193 Pinzelli, *Venise et la Morée*, p.138.

that seemed imminent. All the available privateers, sailors and volunteers, in all nearly 3,000 people, were enlisted in order to take the Ottomans by surprise if necessary. According to the Maltese source, on the evening of 28 August a Polish slave came to bring vital information, with all the details about the assault that was planned for the next day. But this warning was not taken seriously. Only a detachment of 30 *schiavoni* was left on Mount Palamida. Consequently, the Venetians and their allies were very confused by the intensity of the attack at dawn. The Ottoman infantry, 3,000 strong, had marched all night to bypass the Venetian entrenchments, which stretched 1,400 metres from west to east, and take them by surprise from the heights. Before sunrise the Ottomans assaulted the Venetian lines with their war cries, and Magnanini's *oltramarine* troops, posted on the right of the circumvallation, suffered the full violence of the enemy assault and were forced to retreat. This move involved the Maltese infantry, which routed, and in a few minutes the Ottomans could advance to the centre of the allied encampment.[194] According to the sources, the Prince of Turenne with his retinue fiercely defended themselves, barricaded within their quarter.[195] But the actual turning point of the battle came when Königsmarck decided to move a large part of the troops recruited by Morosini from the entrenchments and to launch a bold counter-attack on the enemy left wing. When this miscellaneous corps entered the field and engaged the Ottoman infantry on the flank, the latter finally withdrew in disorder, pursued by the *oltramarini* and Courbon's dragoons.

The battle had lasted three hours. For the first time it almost turned to the advantage of the Ottomans, whose victory would have changed the course of events. Thanks to the coolness of Königsmarck, whose horse was killed during the engagement, the day which had begun under such bad auspices, had turned into one of unequivocal victory which left the door open for further conquests. Once again it is impossible to specify the number of casualties, which, however, were significant for both contenders.[196] After sighting the routed army disappearing over the horizon, the last hopes of the Ottoman garrison vanished. Barely an hour after the end of the battle, the white flag

---

194 Aymar, *Histoire du Marquis de Courbon* (Lyon, 1692), pp.147–148: 'These Infidels having entered made a great slaughter of ours and defeated some regiments of which few soldiers escaped, and the whole terror bringing such a great disorder in the camp that it was thought that all was already lost. Some officers of the defeated regiments, who were frightened by the massacre of their men, fled wherever they could, and threw the fear into the minds of the others without being able to stop them, so that the Marshal of Conismarc [sic], not knowing what to do to remedy the evil, found himself in no little pain.'

195 *Ibid*.

196 The turn of events suggests that the allied losses were at least as great as those of the Ottomans, but some authoritative sources, such as Léonard, *Histoire des conquestes*, pp.136–137, and Burgo, *Viaggio*, vol. III, pp.464–465, claim 1,400 Ottomans killed against 300 of the allies wounded and killed. In Pietro Garzoni's *Sommari*, pp.68–69, the anonymous Maltese chroniclers gives very different figures: 200 Ottomans killed against 60 of the allies killed or wounded. This kind of data is always subject to caution, and its reliability can vary according to the use made of it.

was raised on the walls of the besieged city. Morosini agreed to negotiations, and gave the Ottomans eight days' respite before they evacuated the fortress to be transported to the island of Tenedos. On 3 September 4,000 people, including 1,200 soldiers, left Nauplia; 135 Black slaves who had survived were distributed among the Venetians and the auxiliaries. Finally, of the 61 captured horses, 27 were confiscated without permission by the auxiliaries, and most of these were assigned to the Spanish dragoon regiment of Milan.[197] Nauplia had suffered so much from the bombardment that it was necessary to wait a few days before celebrating the victory inside the city.[198]

After the conquest of Modone, a violent contrast arose between Königsmarck and the Marquis de Courbon, commander of the dragoon Regiment. Reciprocal jealousy and discourtesy escalated, fuelled by acts of banditry attributed to the Marquis' dragoons. The storm broke out during a review of troops. The Marquis verbally challenged Königsmarck in front of the troops, thus the clash became inevitable and other officers intervened to separate the two commanders. The incident was serious and could not go unpunished, thus Morosini had Courbon arrested and confined him to a galley.[199]

Moreover, such a conquest came at a high price. The epidemic continued to ravage the allies; among the Maltese contingent, 19 knights and 200 soldiers had died during the siege. The Order's general took leave at once, and the galleys sailed on the 7 September alongside those of the Pope, followed by the Grand Duke's squadron the next day. Fear and discouragement spread at all levels. The Marquis de Courbon died of fever; the Count of Königsmarck fell sick from 18 September onwards, and soon it was his wife's turn. Her condition worsened rapidly, and soon she was considered hopeless. Countess Katarina Charlotta fell so deeply asleep that she was not believed to be alive. The Count had already lost his nephew and was inconsolable, talking of leaving the Venetian service and returning to his homeland. The Countess's health improved, then she had a relapse: she was not out of trouble until mid December.[200] Most of the officers implored Morosini to grant them license to return to Venice. The evil was blamed on the 'quality of the local climate', and running away seemed the best solution. But the Captain General remained firm, and decided to take the winter quarter for the troops in Nauplia, and to give a better example he decided to stay there too. Seeing that the situation was worsening, at the end of September he ordered a meticulous inspection of all troops. The sick were to remain in the city, those who were healthy were

---

197 BNM, ms. It. VII 2592 (12484), fol. 68. According to Contarini, *Istoria della Guerra*, vol. I, p.586, the auxiliaries insisted that the 180 Jews who resided in the city should also be similarly distributed, but the Captain General succeeded in imposing his opinion that they should be allowed to stay in return for an annual contribution in cash.

198 Beregani, *Historia delle Guerre d'Europa*, vol. II, p.100.

199 Pinzelli, *Venise et la Morée*, p. 32. Shortly afterwards, he was freed thanks to the intervention of the Prince of Turenne on his behalf, although the reasons for this intercession are unclear.

200 *Ibid.*, p.125; the recovery was attributed to the zeal and skill of the surgeon of the Brunswick-Lüneburg regiments.

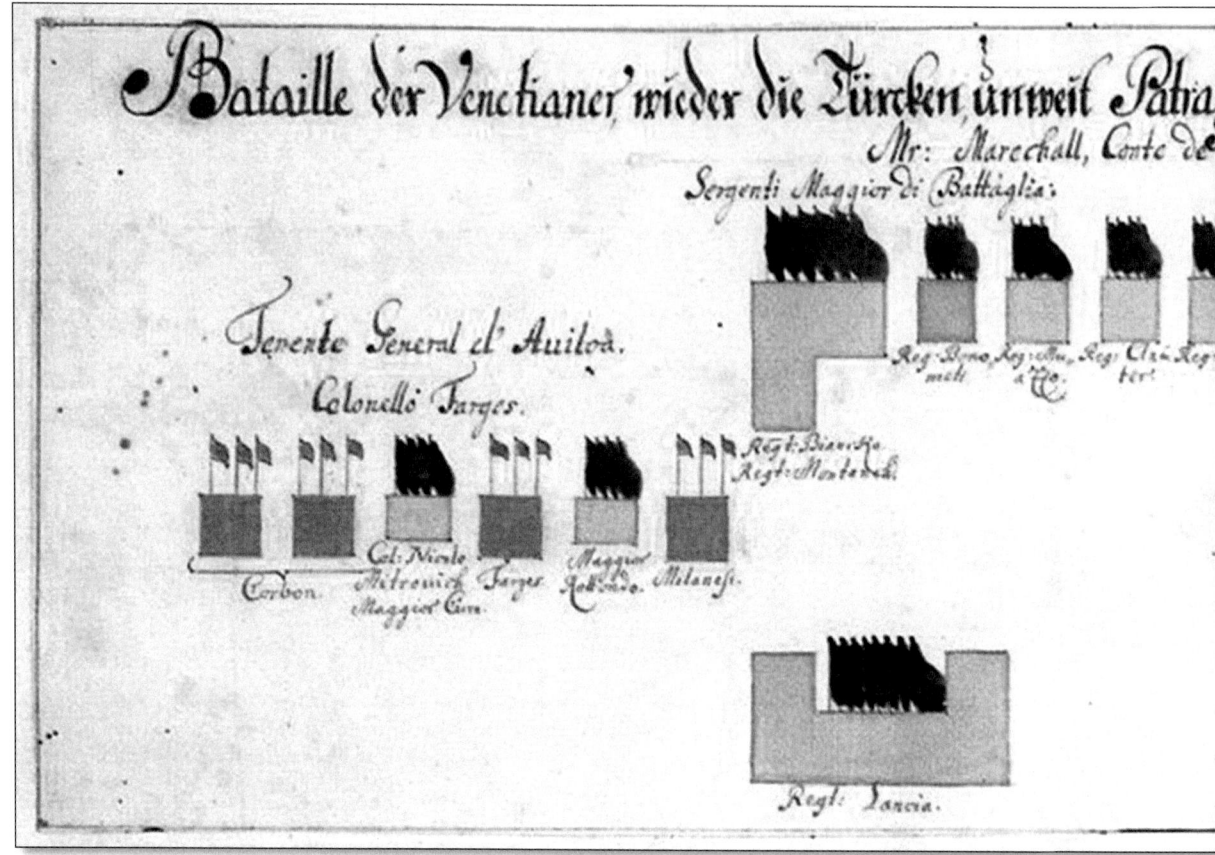

95. Deployment of the Venetian army at Patras on 27 July 1687 (Collection of the Hessische Archiv, Marburg). The amphibious campaign of 1687 was Morosini's masterwork, which brought the conquest of Corinth and the sealing of the last Ottoman places in the Morea.

transferred on the fleet. Königsmarck was of the opinion that this was useless. In October the sick Brunswick-Lüneburg troops and the Milanese were sent to Zakynthos. Despite all the measures taken, from the end of September to the end of October more than 1,000 soldiers died, 227 belonging to the Saxon contingents. Morosini himself did not know the number of victims among the soldiers in Zakynthos. The epidemic was killing so many people because the officers left their men virtually abandoned, not providing them with sufficient food or medicine. The spectacle was terrible, since the corpses of soldiers had been left unburied. This certainly did nothing to improve matters, as desertions multiplied.[201]

These concerns did not deter Morosini, who supervised the restoration of Modone's fortification, which was proceeding well thanks to the work of Giacomo Corner but which was far from being completed at Corone, where the Count of Vimes was supervising. In Nauplia Morosini and Königsmarck realised that the fortification of Mount Palamida were difficult to achieve. Engineer Verneda also gave his opinion on the work to be carried out, considering it impossible to fortify that position. He agreed on the raising of a new battery on the high ground of Acronauplia, to conveniently oppose the

---

201 ASVe, *Senato, Dispacci, Provveditori di Terra e di Mar*, b. 1070, d. 89–95.

LITTLE AND GREAT ITALIAN WARS

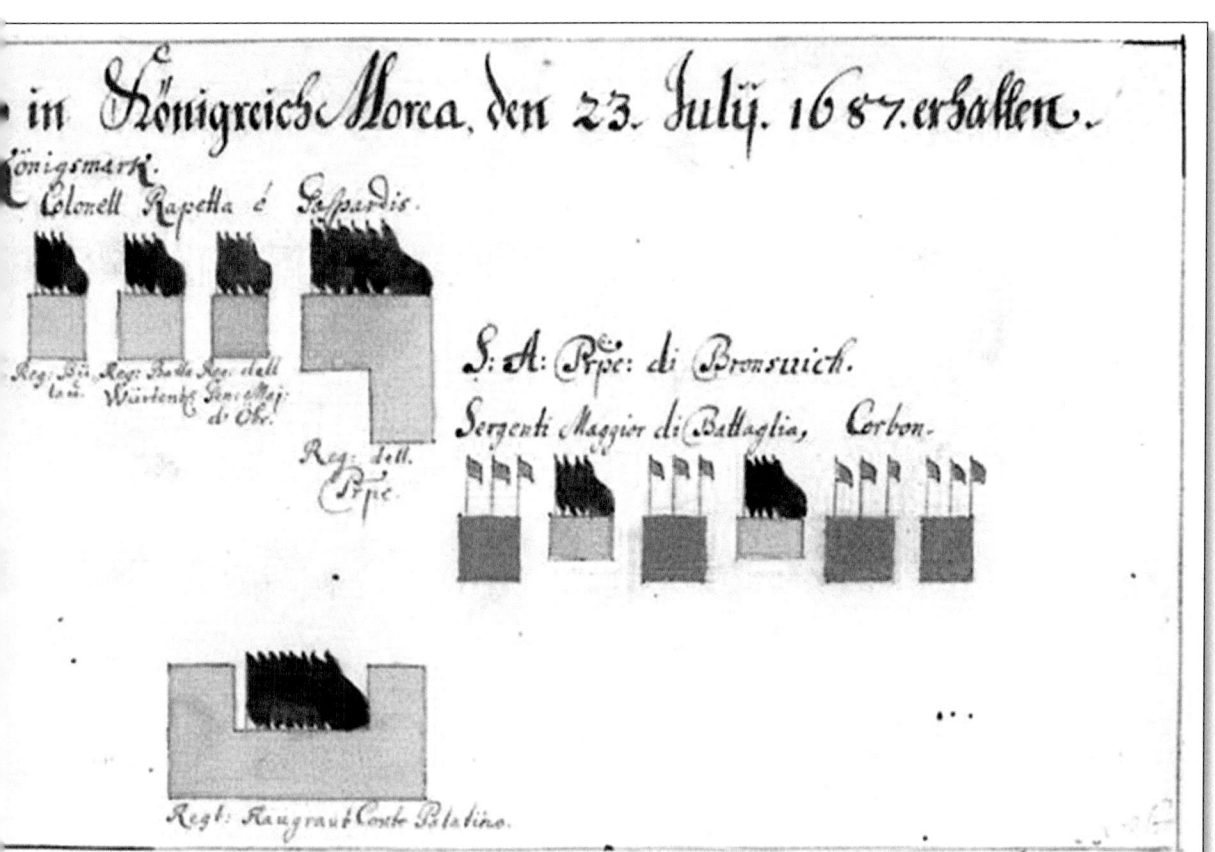

threats of Mount Palamida, and that a gallery be dug under the counterscarp of the ditch with new underground branches.[202] In September Morosini, probably afflicted by the situation in which the army found itself, asked for the first time to be released from his obligations. Certainly, aged 68 and after a life entirely devoted to the war, his rest would have been well deserved. Captain General for three years, his office had legally expired, but Morosini's good faith in this matter is far from obvious.[203] In October he learned how the Ottomans of Negroponte had demanded the presence of the *serasker*, but the latter had received orders from Constantinople not to leave the Morea if he wanted to save his head. The Ottoman commander thus divided his troops between Patras and Mistra. As for the garrison of Negroponte, it consisted of 3,000 men who represented a serious obstacle to an attempt against this place, while the fortifications were just being improved there.

Despite Morosini's attempts, the Count of Königsmarck, who had been ill until the beginning of October, had spoken repeatedly of leaving the army, so

---

202 *Ibid.*, p.91. However, 30 years later these works, still incomplete, could not prevent the fall of the city to the Ottomans.

203 *Ibid.*, p.142: 'Perhaps he was only trying to make himself indispensable to the Republic, which he certainly was.'

much so that at the end of the month the Captain General asked the Senate to find a replacement. However, at the end of December Morosini finally managed to change Königsmarck's mind. To prepare for the next campaign, the Captain General wrote directly to the *Savio alla Scrittura* requesting *chevaux de frise*, field pieces and bayonets.[204] With regard to health issues, the measures decided by the senate at the end of 1686 met with some success, but this was due to the natural decrease in cases of illness during the winter season.

In Dalmatia the Ottomans took the initiative in July 1686, trying to surprise the Venetian outpost of Dolac and Srijane, but each time they were repulsed with heavy losses. With the irregulars from Poljica, Morlachs, and the infantry sent by the Duke of Parma, the Venetians prepared a counter-offensive. After seizing Fort Opus (today Opuzen, in Croatia) in June, on 28 September with the assistance of General Saint-Paul, the Tuscan Nicolò Dal Borro and the engineer Camuccio, Girolamo Corner had succeeded in storming Sinj, which finally fell into Venetian possession on 30 September.

The 1686 campaign also saw the first naval battles occur in the waters off the island of Naxos and in the Mytilene Channel. However, both encounters resulted in only some exchanges of shots before the Ottoman fleet managed to escape, avoiding a full engagement.[205]

1687

Preparations for the new campaign took place in the uncertainty of the epidemic. In April, when there had been no reported cases of contagion for several months, the secretary of the Greek Archbishop of Nauplia and an oarsman on the Loredan galley died suspiciously. According to Pietro Garzoni and Camillo Contarini, the disease had been brought on a French *tartane* from the Archipelago. Although Garzoni later insisted that the disease had spread to the whole of the Morea, in reality the outbreak was very mild: only 50 of the crew died, and 53 recovered.[206]

In April the Venetian *inquisitori di stato* executed the musters of the available troops for the new campaign. On Angelo Michiel's newly arrived convoy, of the 1,026 troops originally embarked, only 732 arrived safely. When asked to explain the causes of this loss, the officers responsible blamed death, desertions and illness. Of the 22 companies mustered at Zakynthos, 445 men were missing when reviewed at New Navarino, not counting the 123 others

---

204 ASVe, *Senato, Dispacci, Provveditori di Terra e di Mar*, b. 1070, d. 98.

205 Guido Candiani, 'Vele, remi e cannoni: l'Impiego congiunto di navi, galee e galeazze nella flotta veneziana, 1572–1718', in G. Candiani and L. Lo Basso (eds), *Mutazioni e Permanenze nella Storia Navale del Mediterraneo, secc. XVI–XIX* (Milan: Franco Angeli, 2010) pp.140–142. Before this encounter the Venetians had lost their first units in October 1684, when a storm off the coast of Skopelos in the Aegean had driven two vessels, the *Costanza Guerriera* and *Venezia Trionfante*, onto the rocks. This wreck killed almost the entire crew, including the commander Pietro Grimani. Four years later a blizzard caused two more vessels to sink off the Isthmus of Corinth, which killed 400 crewmen including *Almirante* Zaguri.

206 James Morton Paton, 'A Florentine officer in the Morea in 1687', in *American Journal of Archaeology* n. 38 (1934), p.59.

LITTLE AND GREAT ITALIAN WARS

96. Mistra, which surrendered to the Venetians in 1687. See image commentaries for more information.

who were officially hospitalised there. The three regiments of Brunswick-Lüneburg were no longer composed of more than eight companies, and the Saxons were in no better condition. As for the 1,357 men of the Milanese contingents, in April 1687 only 535 remained, a consequence of the scant care shown by the officers who, according to Morosini 'neither paid, nor fed the troops'.[207] The commissioners estimated that only 4,670 men were still fit to bear arms, while the *serasker*'s army camped around Patras had an estimated strength of around 12,000 men.

In May, the fleet set sail. Morosini inspected the Morea's fortress in Venetian hands, then in June the Captain General awaited the arrival of the other officers and auxiliaries. No new cases of disease had been reported, however the auxiliaries did not take the risk of joining Morosini's troops in Greece but headed to Dalmatia, where *provveditore* Girolamo Corner could take advantage of this unexpected reinforcement for an offensive campaign in Bosnia and Albania.

The Saxon contingents had returned to their homeland, but the senate succeeded in recruiting new mercenaries in Württemberg, Hessen Kassel, Ansbach-Bayreuth, Brandenburg-Bayreuth Culmbach, Brunswick-Wolfenbüttel, Waldeck-Pyrmont and even Liège. With these troops, the new recruits destined for the campaign in the Morea also arrived in Lefkada at the beginning of July. Morosini had the pleasure of finding Prince Louis de Turenne and the sergeant general, Ohr; Königsmarck, wounded in the leg by a rush of his horse had left Zakynthos on 8 June to join the Captain General on his galley. In the councils of war called in the early summer of 1687, now formed only by Venetian and German commanders, it was decided to move against Achaia to proceed to the conquest of the Peloponnese. Despite the late start of the campaign, as early as mid March Morosini had ordered the *provveditori*

---

207 *Ibid.*, d. 111.

of Messenia and Mani to move against the enemy's rear. Reinforced by local irregulars, Civran and Polani advanced first to Karitena in the Arcadian mountains, and then besieged Mistra with 6,000 Greeks, most of them from Mani. Once the town outside the walls had been looted, the Greeks withdrew with the booty and returned to their homes.[208]

On 20 July, the troops were finally embarked and the fleet was able to weigh anchor in the evening at the entrance of the Gulf of Patras: it was composed of 26 galleys, six galleasses, 14 galliots and 87 sail ships of various sizes.[209] The Venetians numbered about 9,000–10,000 foot and horse. The next day the oared fleet approached the northern shore and discovered that the Ottomans had dug trenches. Morosini decided to feint to land on this side and then turn quickly to take the troops to the opposite shore. The operation was carried out with precision and by dawn on 22 July the galleys were in front of Patras. It was a few miles west of this location, in a rather swampy area, where the *oltramarini* landed first, followed shortly after by the other troops. The landing could proceed unhindered, as the Ottomans did not move until their cavalry attacked the Venetian right wing. The naval artillery supported the land troops and the combined fire of infantry and galleys repulsed the enemy assault without difficulty.[210]

The rest of the afternoon was used to unload horses and equipment. Morosini did not want to give the enemy time to get organised or to receive reinforcements from the units deployed on the opposite shore. At nightfall the *Capitano in Golfo* Sanudo rowed between the channel of Lepanto with the galleys of Polani, Venier, Nani, Foscari and Emo. His mission was to cut the lines of communication between Rumelia and Achaia. At the same time, Königsmarck marched with 4,000 men to assault the Ottoman camp at Patras by surprise at dawn, making a wide diversion of about 15 miles. The night march was arduous and tiring. At dawn the troops stopped to refresh themselves. The Venetian vanguards and the Ottoman sentinels came into contact and began to exchange fire. Königsmarck deployed the troops in battle order, with the infantry in the centre protected by the cavalry squadrons on the flanks. The Ottomans had been estimated to have about 10,000 men.[211] According to an eyewitness, the squadrons of dragoons commanded by the Marquis of Courbon went too far and had to take refuge in the bush under the pressure of enemy cavalry: the Marquis was wounded in the knee by a mace blow.[212] Meanwhile the infantry on the right wing, formed by the Brunswick-Lüneburg soldiers, fired from too far away without receiving the order, allowing the Ottomans to advance, cheering with war cries. However, they clashed with the *chevaux de frise* and the bayonets of the troops of Prince Maximilian. The German mercenaries were thus able

---

208 *Ibid.*, d. 116–117.
209 Paton, 'A Florentine officer in the Morea', p.62.
210 Foscarini, *Historia della Repubblica Veneta*, pp.325–326; Locatelli, *Racconto historico*, p.330; Beregani, *Guerre d'Europa*, vol. II, p.290.
211 Pinzelli, *Venise et la Morée*, p.147.
212 Beregani, *Guerre d'Europa*, vol. II, pp.291–295.

to take advantage of these defensive weapons, and fired more regularly, until they maintained a continuous fire. After three unsuccessful attempts, the Ottomans hastily abandoned the battlefield. They fought valiantly, but the muskets and the defences formed by the *chevaux de frise* and bayonets proved to be decisive.

The *serasker*, fearing to see his retreat interrupted by the enemy landed behind him, fled towards the Isthmus of Corinth without attempting resistance. His troops, left to fend for themselves, followed him. The garrisons of Patras, the castles of Rumelia and the Morea, and even Lepanto garrisons, in panic, abandoned their posts. All these strongholds fell simultaneously into the hands of the Venetians. The Ottomans left behind over 2,000 dead and wounded, 160 guns and many supplies. The Venetians also captured 14 ships, and the enemy commander's own standard.[213] Morosini went up the Gulf of Corinth with the galleys and quickly reached the isthmus in pursuit of the *serasker*. Upon seeing the Venetian fleet, the Ottomans set fire to the ammunition and food depots and halted their retreat only at Thebes, where the *serasker* set about regrouping his forces. It was the most important victory ever achieved. The landing and night action planned by Morosini and Königsmarck had prevailed despite the inconveniences that occurred, thanks to the discipline of the troops and timeliness of the fleet.[214]

Morosini quickly called for the council of war to plan the future operations. Corinth had to be the next objective in order to complete the conquest of the northern Peloponnese. The Venetians followed up this success with the reduction of the last Ottoman forts in the Peloponnese: Chlemoutsi surrendered to Angelo De Negris *oltramarine* troops on 27 July, while Königsmarck marched east towards Corinth. The Ottoman garrison abandoned the defences of Acrocorinth as the enemy approached after torching the town, which was captured by the Venetians on 7 August. Morosini now gave orders for the preparation of a campaign across the Isthmus of Corinth towards Athens, before going to Mystras, where he persuaded the Ottoman garrison to surrender, while the Maniots occupied Karitena, abandoned by the Ottoman garrison. Now the Peloponnese was under complete Venetian control, except for Malvasia (Monemvasia) in the south-east.

On August 10 the cavalry and infantry quartered in Corinth. The following day Morosini and his generals inspected the city and visited the isthmus in detail, accompanied by all the senior officers and engineers. Königsmarck

---

213 Ioannis Chasiotis, 'The Decline of Ottoman Power' in G. A. Christopoulos and I. Bastias (eds), *History of the Greek Nation, Volume XI: Hellenism under Foreign Rule (1669–1821), Turkocracy-Latinocracy* (Athens: Ekdotiki Athinon, 1975), pp.25–26 (English translation kindly provided by the publisher).

214 The Florentine Count Francesco Arrighetti, eyewitness and volunteer, declared in a triumphant tone: 'In just three days we landed before the enemy, beat the army, became masters of two cities and two castles, cannons and ammunition, and all the houses full of goods, and in a country so delicious and fruitful that it does not suffer the comparison with our Italy.' Paton, 'A Florentine officer in the Morea', p.64.

97. A seventeenth-century print depicting Corinth and the Acrocorinth, the latter standing on a rocky outcrop overlooking the city. See image commentaries for more information.

was enthusiastic about the idea of completing the great unfinished work of Emperor Nero, the digging of a canal linking the Saronic Gulf to the Gulf of Corinth. But when the engineers had measured the distance between the two opposite shores and found that there were 3,256 geometric steps (5,659 metres), it was found that the task seemed really colossal, which was confirmed by the observation of the remains of the ancient works.[215]

The council of war accepted Morosini's proposal to embark the troops and sail to Malvasia, assuming that the conquest of the whole Morea would have convinced the Ottoman garrison to surrender as soon as the fleet was sighted.[216] The *capitano straordinario delle navi*, Lorenzo Venier, was sent to the waters of Laconia with one squadron of the sailing fleet to demand the capitulation of Malvasia, arriving there on 27 August. But Venier was unable to bend the determination of the citizens to resist, who, according to the reports, comprised pirates and Greek merchants loyal to the Porte. Morosini reached Venier in early September, but he too had to acknowledge the city's willingness to resist. Despite a brief but intense four-day naval bombardment,

---

215 Pinzelli, *Venise et la Morée*, p.150. It would take 206 years for the King of the Hellenes Georgos I to finally be able to open the Corinth Canal in 1893.

216 ASVe, *Senato, Dispacci, Provveditori di Terra e di Mar*, b. 1070, d. 123.

the garrison refused all offers to surrender. The Ottoman artillery managed to set fire to a 70-gun Genoese ship that had been chartered by the Republic, the *Santa Maria* commanded by the *Cavaliere* Marc'Antonio Carattino.[217] The enterprise had to be abandoned; the *Serenissima* had more ambitious projects.

After the conquest of 'the gate of the Peloponnese', as Corinth was rightly considered, the Venetians and their allies were faced with the choice of which objective to turn their attention. The initial plan to remove the Morea from the Ottomans had almost been completed, and the inhabitants of Malvasia would probably soon capitulate as had happened elsewhere. The council of war discussed whether to take advantage of the weakness of the Ottomans and continue with other conquests or to fortify the Isthmus of Corinth and wait for events. Negroponte, 48 nautical miles from Corinth, was a real threat, because it was an important enemy stronghold and a hub of communication between northern Greece and Attica. Some commanders, such as Morosini, planned to carry the next offensive in this direction. Other generals proposed to move the fleet to the other side of the isthmus, bypassing the entire Peloponnese. In the meantime the army had to wait in Corinth, in a large encampment under the *provveditori* Benzon and Dolfin, before being embarked when the sail ships returned. Therefore it was planned to turn the fleet towards the vicinity of Negroponte, to attract the enemy, and if conditions allowed, to point it towards Athens.[218] On 15 September Königsmarck was received by the Captain General and two days later Morosini convened a new council of war to study new possibilities of conquest. He returned to support his original plan: the attack on Negroponte. Most officers felt the season was already too late, and the Ottomans well prepared, with a garrison estimated by spies at 5,000 men. The fortifications had just been strengthened with the construction of a new fort called Kara Baba, 'the black father'.[219]

Finally, on 18 September, the council of war decided to move against Athens. The only ambition of this expedition was to carry the danger further into territory still occupied by the enemy, thus distancing the latter from the isthmus, and above all to hold the population to ransom by demanding the immediate payment of a large war tax. Morosini did not consider for a moment that Athens could be held for a long time. The fortress of Athens, the

---

217 The anonymous author of the manuscript n. 1347 preserved in the Fondazione Querini Stampalia Cl. IV, Cod. XCIII, ff. 160–161, gives another name to the ship which was destroyed in front of Malvasia: *La Concetione*. Thanks to Eric Pinzelli for this notice.

218 ASVe, *Senato, Dispacci, Provveditori di Terra e di Mar*, b. 1070, d. 120 and 122. Morosini's opinion was that the fall of Negroponte should result in all of Boeotia, Attica and central Greece also falling into Venetian hands.

219 This fairly modest fort, built on the rock, was the work of the renegade Girolamo Galoppi from Guastalla, former dragoon NCO of the Courbon regiment, who would desert during the siege of Nauplia following a conflict with Daniele Dolfin. Burgo, *Viaggio*, vol. III, p.550: 'Galloppi deserted from the Venetian Army and fled to Negroponte, where, posing him as an engineer, he had the entire city mined, built a palisade, and constructed a large battery in the harbour, in revenge for four beatings he had received.'

Acropolis, being situated nearly 10 km from the shore, was difficult to defend for a mainly naval force.[220] The troops, consisting of 9,880 infantrymen and 871 cavalrymen, were embarked on 20 September, and the fleet set sail the same evening, crossing the Saronic Gulf during the night with a favourable wind. The following morning the fleet entered Piraeus, which was then called *Porto Lione* or *Porto Draco*,[221] without difficulty. The Ottoman garrison, some 1,500 *azab*s and armed civilians under Murad Paşa, took refuge on the Acropolis as soon as the Venetian fleet appeared, determined to hold out as long as possible, and hoping for relief. Morosini immediately gave the order to occupy the city, which had no walls, and the troops led by Königsmarck entered divided into two long columns. In the evening the Venetian troops laid their camp among the olive groves at the foot of the Acropolis, dominated by the imposing Parthenon which had, until the autumn of 1687, fairly well resisted the ravages of the year. However, of its former glory, Athens retained only the name and the temple of Athena. The Acropolis served as a fortress and place of residence for the Muslims and their families; while the Greeks and the few Latins living in Athens were excluded. The latter lived in the suburbs on the northern and southern slopes of the hill. The city was inhabited by 10,000 inhabitants, a not insignificant number compared to other coeval Greek cities.[222]

On 22 September the galley oarsmen were tasked with transporting the siege artillery, consisting of six cannons and four mortars, to the camp. Daniele Dolfin was once again appointed as camp *provveditore*. The batteries were placed to the west of the Acropolis, under the command of the Count of San Felice, and opened fire around midday on 24 September. According to various sources, Morosini and Königsmarck were unsatisfied by the fire of the artillery, indeed, an eyewitness stated that some projectiles missed the Acropolis altogether and scattered into the city below, causing the disappointment of the Greek population, who went to Königsmarck to ask for an explanation. On the evening of 26 September a furious Morosini was about to replace the *provveditore all'artiglieria* Leandro Molvis when a bomb hit the Parthenon, and penetrated the ammunition depot that had been stored inside the ancient temple.[223] This shot, described as 'a lucky shot' by

---

220 Pinzelli, *Venise et la Morée*, p.153.

221 So named because of a beautiful three-metre marble lion at the entrance of the harbour.

222 The English traveller Bernard Randolph visited Athens between 1671 and 1679, and left this description of the city: 'The Houses are better built here than in any part of the Morea, most having little Courts, with high walls, in which are arches with marble pillars; few houses above two story high. They also patcht up with the ruines of old Palaces, and in most walls are abundance of old inscriptions … The Greeks live much better here than in any other part of Turkey (Scio excepted) being a small common-wealth amongst themselves.' *The present state of the Morea* (London, 1689), p.23.

223 The literature on the explosion of the Parthenon is enormous. The destruction of the famous temple caused great embarrassment in Venice, and for a time the responsibility for the incident was attributed to various actors in the affair. In the study days dedicated to the 400th anniversary of Morosini's birth, Irene Favaretto, in 'Le antiche vestigia di celebri ed erudite memorie … Francesco

98. Plan of the Acropolis of Athens, during the Venetian siege of September 1687 (author's archive). See image commentaries for more information.

Morosini, caused a devastating explosion that destroyed the Parthenon and killed 300 soldiers and civilians.[224]

On the Acropolis, the fire raged for two whole days, but it was not enough to make the beleaguered defenders give in, since they were still waiting for help. This finally arrived at dawn on 28 September, but the relief force numbered just 2,000 horse and 1,000 foot, who soon withdrew when Königsmarck marched against them with some squadrons of dragoons and the *oltramarini*. The garrison had to rely on the generosity of the Venetian Captain General, who gave the Ottomans five days to evacuate the place, with the right to take only their personal belongings.[225] Morosini appointed Daniele Dolfin as *provveditore* of Athens and Colonel Pompei as governor of the Acropolis.

Before the news of the conquest reached Venice, the Great Council had already decided to pay homage to Morosini. The senators granted him the title of *Peloponnesiaco* (Peloponnesian) and had a marble bust erected in the saloon of the Council of Ten. The event was truly extraordinary as Venice, for the first time, elevated one citizen above all others by dedicating a statue to him while he was still alive. Morosini thus accumulated yet another honour, after he had already been elevated to the rank of hereditary knight following the conquest of Nauplia, an honour from which his grandson Pietro benefited. The Count of Königsmarck was not forgotten either, and in fact the Senate voted to increase his salary by 6,000 *ducats* per year.[226] Meanwhile, in late September the fleet sailed to Egina, which was conquered without encountering resistance. In Morosini's plan, the island represented a useful base for an offensive against Euboea and the northern Aegean.

Morosini e le spoliazioni del Partenone', in G. Ortalli, G. Gullino, E. Ivetic (eds), *L'inestinguibile sogno del dominio. Francesco Morosini* (Venice: Istituto Veneto di Scienze, Lettere e Arti, 2021), pp.198–207, summarises the event with some rough errors regarding the composition of the besieging army. The author focuses on the animated discussion arose between Königsmarck and the Count of San Felice, who was accused, once again, of lacking competence and of firing shots that were too short. The 'credit' for hitting the Parthenon would therefore be attributed to a lieutenant of the Brunswick-Lüneburg troops who intervened on Königsmarck's orders to rectify the Count's ballistic errors. According to the chronicle of Cristoforo Ivanovich, in James Morton Paton, *The Venetians in Athens. 1687–1688* (Harvard–Cambridge, 1940), pp.10–11, the Captain General had learned that the Turks were using the Parthenon as a munitions depot, and he expressly requested that the temple be targeted: 'Having warned His Excellency that the Temple of Minerva was occupied by the Turks together with their main women and children, and considering themselves safe there due to the thick walls and faces of the temple, he ordered Count Antonio Muttoni of San Felice to concentrate mortar fire on the historic building.'

224 Pinzelli, *Venise et la Morée*, p.155.

225 On 3 October 3,000 civilians and 500 soldiers left for the port where an English ship, two French *tartanes* and three Ragusan polacres were waiting to take them to Smyrna at their own expense. On the way to Piraeus some of them were harassed and robbed by soldiers who had escaped the control of the officers. See Antonio Muazzo, *Guerra coi Turchi*, Biblioteca Nazionale Marciana, Manoscritti Italiani VII n. 172 (8187), f. 56.

226 Locatelli, *Racconto historico*, vol. I, p.353

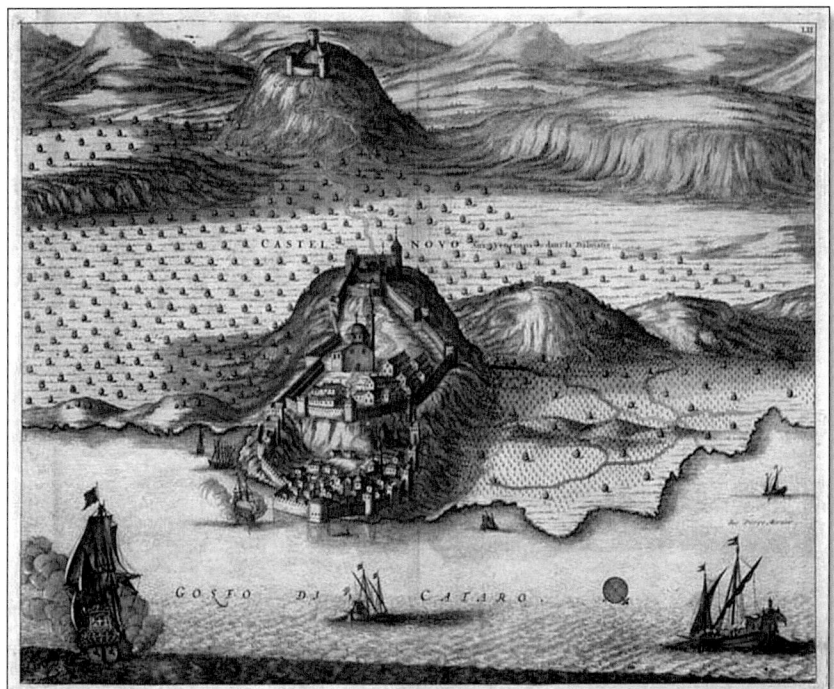

99. The Gulf of Kotor with the fortress of Castenuovo, in a late seventeenth century engraving by Pierre Mortier (author's archive). The conquest of this fortress was the only success achieved by the Venetians in the 1688 campaign.

If the campaigns in Greece had been a triumph, those in the Balkans were no less, since Girolamo Corner, the major Morosini adversary and 'other thunderbolt of war' according to the expression coined by the Cretan Nicolò Calliachi, had been appointed *provveditore* of Dalmatia at the end of 1685.[227] In the spring, clashes occurred in Podgoritza following a Montenegrin raid that destroyed the Ottoman mills in Duralik. In July the Morlachs of Makarsca had advanced on Mostar and set fire to six Bosnian villages, deporting the population, horses and flocks.[228] On 30 September 1687, after a 26-day siege, the Venetians and their allies seized the strong fortress of Castelnuovo (Herceg Novi), at the entrance to the Bay of Kotor, a victory that amply redeemed the failure at Santa Maura in 1684.

The Ottomans had been defeated everywhere, but at a high cost. According to the detailed report of the *provveditore*, Zorzi Emo, between July 1686 and July 1687 the casualties numbered 7,983 for the army, and 793 for the navy; a further 1,197 men had deserted, and 277 had been dismissed due to disciplinary measures.[229]

---

227 Anastasia Stouraiti, *Memorie di un ritorno, la guerra di Morea (1684–1699) nei manoscritti della Querini Stampalia* (Venice: Fondazione scientifica Querini Stampalia, 2001), p.177.

228 Beregani, *Historia delle Guerre d'Europa*, vol. II, p.260.

229 ASVe, *Senato, Dispacci, Provveditori di Terra e di Mar*, b. 1249, d. 54. In detail, the casualties of the army were 3,307 Italians and nationals, and 4,676 foreigners dead. The navy claimed 198 sailors, 189 *buonevoglie*, 272 convicted oarsmen and 134 prisoners of war dead. Among the deserters, the Italians were 715 and the foreigners 706. The navy registered 176 deserters in all, with 120 sailors, 33 *buonevoglie*, 12 convicts, and 11 prisoners of war.

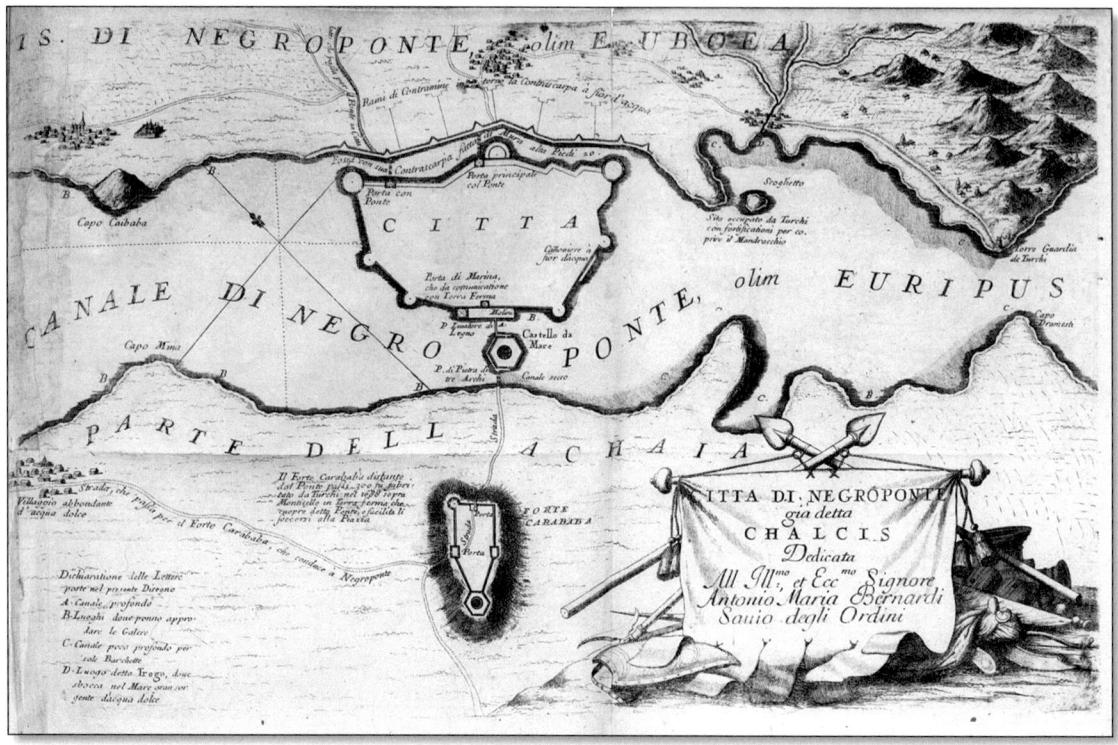

100. The strong natural defences of Negroponte appear in this print after Vincenzo Maria Coronelli (author's archive). See image commentaries for more information.

The Venetian field army spent the winter in Athens where the good weather lasted until the end of January 1688. This was suddenly ended by a strong decrease of temperature and the arrival of snow accompanied by violent winds. The troops did not remain totally idle, however. The four redoubts between Athens and Piraeus had to be guarded and a regular sentinel service was organised. Skirmishes were frequent, as were raids, such as the one carried out in mid December by the *sergente maggiore* of the *oltramarini*, Lauro Darduino, which resulted in the seizure of a herd estimated by Morosini at 4,000 head.[230]

Königsmarck had agreed to continue his service, but Morosini had granted the Princes of Brunswick and Württemberg, as well as the Prince of Turenne, permission to return to Venice with their people, all together being about 100 'very spirited' people.[231] In the council of war held on New Year's Eve, decisions were taken with far-reaching consequences. Firstly, the evacuation of Athens. Wintering in Attica had kept the troops away from the Morea, where cases of plague had been reported with increasing frequency. However, maintaining the city was a serious problem: fortifying it was too costly; a garrison could be besieged and caught in a mousetrap, and men were much needed for new campaigns. It was therefore necessary to retreat, without forgetting to organise the repatriation of the Greek population to the Morea, to protect them from

---

230 *Ibid.*, b. 1070, d. 132.

231 *Ibid.*

the revenge of the Ottomans on their return.²³² In his dispatches addressed to the Senate, Morosini insisted a great deal on the importance of the next campaign, the fifth consecutive that he had directed. On 17 December he wrote that 'this campaign must be the decisive one and the most important of all', without however knowing what the next target would be. It was on 2 February 1688 that Morosini informed the *Signoria* of his intention to attack both Negroponte and Crete, requesting the opinion of the senators and the means to carry out the ambitious operation.

1688

Meanwhile the departure of Athens' inhabitants left the city open to soldiers for looting, which although punishable by death, became increasingly widespread. Cases of plague had appeared in Athens itself, and the troops were hit hard.²³³ Daniele Dolfin tried to stop the progression of the epidemic by burning the contaminated areas. Morosini created a *magistratura alla sanità* composed of three patricians, and a *Lazzaretto* (hospital) was also organised, but these measures were not effective, since the epidemic continued to spread. It was necessary to leave as quickly as possible, because, as the superstition suggested, Athens seemed to take revenge against Morosini and his soldiers, by striking those who had reduced it to the status of a ghost city.²³⁴

The artillery was moved out of the city on 21 March. When all the civilians were evacuated, the regiments were finally able to march to Piraeus where the fleet awaited them. The embarkation took place on 8 April with the destination Poros, an islet near the eastern shore of the Peloponnese. The sick were isolated and hospitalised on boats pulled by galleys. But this measure was only a paltry palliative: every day 60 to 70 soldiers, rowers or sailors fell ill and about 30 died. In the following weeks there was a truce, but in his dispatch of 6 May Morosini informed the Senate that in the meantime 574 soldiers and 52 sailors had died.²³⁵

---

232 Paton, *The Venetians in* Athens, p.20; Pinzelli, *Venise et la Morée*, p.168. For the population of Athens, the abandonment of their homes and homeland to seek asylum elsewhere was another tragedy. The evacuation had begun quietly in February, but there were few boats available. In middle of March, realising that the troops would leave Athens, the inhabitants panicked at the thought of being left behind and 'were rushing to board their belongings on vessels destined for them'. The richest were transported to Nauplia, the others were divided between the islands of the Saronic Gulf, or in different cities of the Morea, waiting for the houses abandoned by the Muslims to be assigned. The most fortunate families landed in Zakynthos, while the lower class of Athenian society, composed mainly of Albanians, headed towards Corinth and the isthmus. Morosini intended to make good use of them: they could lodge in the caves of the region and live at the expense of the enemy.

233 Kenneth M. Setton, *Venice, Austria, and the Turks in the Seventeenth Century* (Philadelphia: The American Philosophical Society, 1991), p.342. The disease was studied by the chief physicians of the fleet, Lorenzo Braga and Emanuele Sepilli.

234 Pinzelli, *Venise et la Morée*, p.168.

235 ASVe, *Senato, Dispacci, Provveditori di Terra e di Mar*, b. 1070, d. 142.

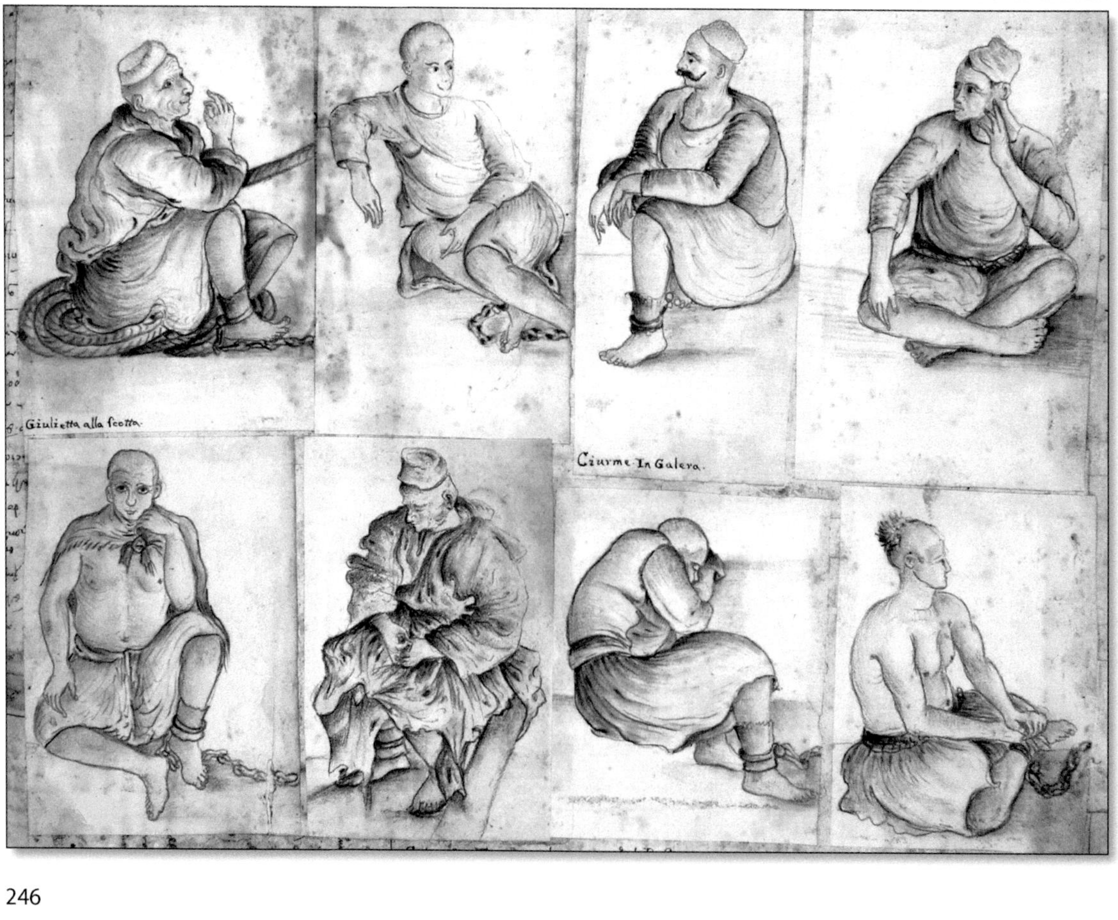

WARS AND SOLDIERS IN THE EARLY REIGN OF LOUIS XIV - VOLUME 6 - PART 2

Giulietta alla scotta.

Ciurme In Galera.

LITTLE AND GREAT ITALIAN WARS

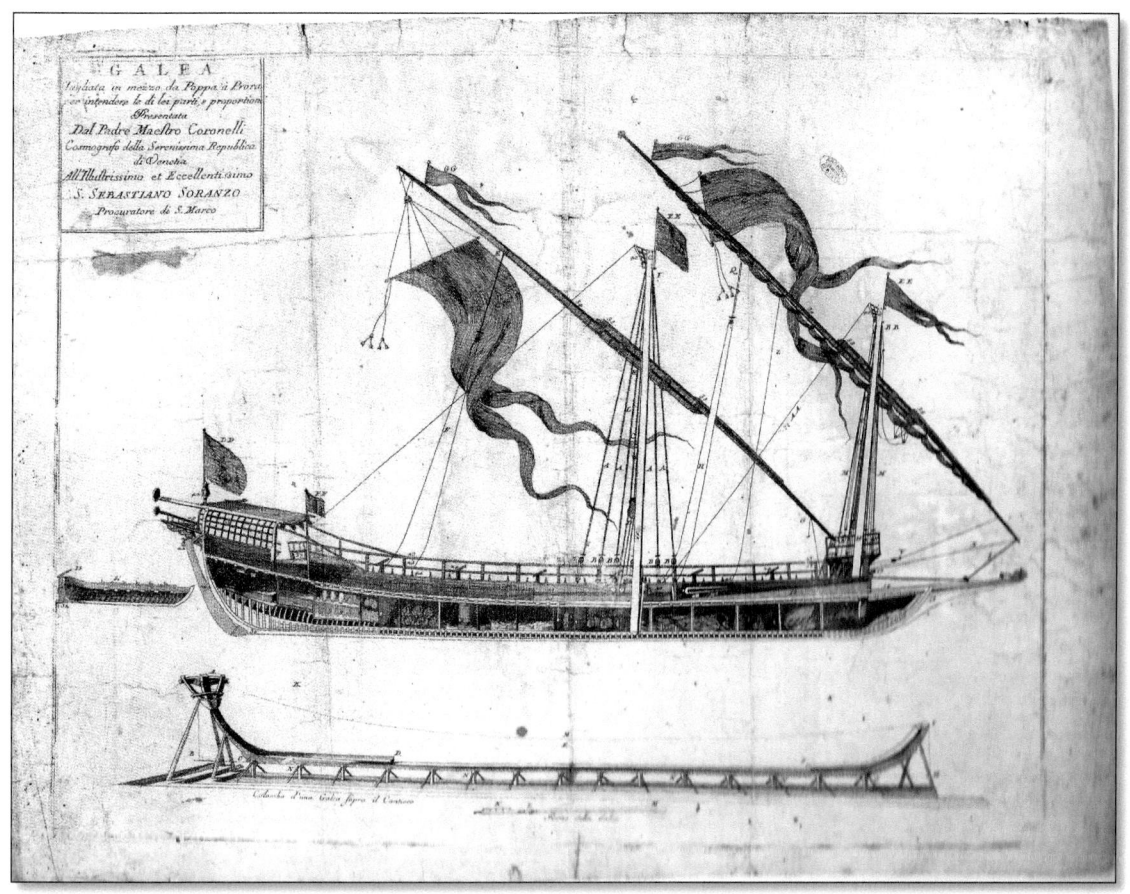

Facing page, top: 101. Two sleeping knights of the Order of St Stephen on board a Tuscan galley, after the Manfroni Manuscript, before 1688. Living conditions on the oar ships were very harsh and even ranked personnel had to be accommodated in the poor facilities of a galley, since the ships only had cabins for the officers. Contemporary accounts often mention the presence of vermin, which tormented crew and passengers. The French Dominican Father Labat, speaking of his galley voyage from Civitavecchia to Messina in June 1709, recounts that he escaped the assault of bugs because he slept in a hammock on which he had taken care to put a lot of glue, so that the insects would stick to it and not reach him. But, Labat admitted, he had not been able to save himself from those that walked on the ceiling and fell on him. In 1741 the Venetian playwright Carlo Gozzi, for a time an officer in the army, wrote: 'in two painful nights I was able to learn the difference between staying overnight at home and staying in a galley'.

Facing page, bottom: 102. The 'engine' of the galley fleet, the oarsmen, after the Manfroni Manuscript, before 1688. Venice tried to limit the use of slaves as oarsmen wherever possible, however it did resort to every source of supply abroad. Among the thousands of men who served on the benches of the Venetian oar fleet, there were probably also Royalist English and Scottish prisoners of war, sold by Oliver Cromwell to the Serenissima. In September 1648 1,000 Scots captured at the end of the battle of Red Bank, along with other 'traitors and papists', were embarked for an overseas destination, however their fate remains uncertain. Recently some connections have been discovered between these prisoners and the negotiations that took place between London and Venice to hire 'soldiery and labour force' for the Levant. Although the negotiations concerned the formation of one infantry regiment, no 'English' unit was raised in Venice in those years, but it is not unlikely that the final fate for these men was the oar of a galley. Along with the lamentations of the many languages of the Mediterranean, there would also have been those in the Scots Gaelic of these unfortunate prisoners. Thanks to Paul Beckmann for this information.

Above: 103. A Venetian galley in a drawing of Vincenzo Maria Coronelli (author's archive). Developments in technology and naval strategy ascribed sailing ships a central role at the expense of the galleys. Since Morosini maintained direct control of the fleet in the first phase of the war, he procrastinated about finding a way to close the gap between oar ships and sail ships. The change of naval strategy that occurred after 1694, which moved tactical superiority to the sail ships, caused a political earthquake in Venice.

It was at Poros that Morosini learned the news of his election as *Doge*, the logical completion of his long series of services for the *Serenissima*. On 23 March 1688, after four years spent as major dignity of the Republic, Marc'Antonio Giustiniani died at the age of 69. The election took place on 3 April, and gave rise to great celebrations at the Morosini Palace: ballets, cantatas, and masquerades followed one another for three days. Francesco Morosini was the new *Doge*, but also remained Captain General, an event which had previously occurred only on two occasions.[236]

The appointment, important as it was, could not remedy the dramatic reality. Aware of the miserable state of the army's financial resources, on 23 April Morosini decided to send Lorenzo Venier with a squadron of eight sail ships and a galliot with mortars in the direction of Salonica to ransom the city. But the population of the Macedonian capital held steady, encouraged by former Morea *serasker* Ismail *Paşa* who commanded the garrison. After a short artillery duel, Venier had to retreat and returned empty-handed to Poros on 16 May. Morosini now had to await the reinforcements promised by the Senate. They arrived slowly, at the rhythm of the convoys. On 6 May, 1,220 new recruits from the Duchy of Brunswick-Wolfenbüttel landed at Poros. The regiments from Ansbach and Culmbach were detached from Dalmatia. However, the quality of these troops was mediocre and most of them had never been in a fight. The Count of Königsmarck did his best to train and discipline them in record time. As for the veteran troops, the regiments of Brunswick-Lüneburg had already been involved in serious disorders on 17 April, while they were still in garrison at the Lido of Venice, enough for the Senate to be concerned and to open an investigation.[237]

Further problems concerned the Captain General. In early 1687 the Senate had agreed to raise an infantry regiment of 2,000 Swiss soldiers, recruited from the Lucerne and Schwyz cantons. This unit endured a very short but troubled history. Since the cantonal authorities lethargically dispatched recruits to Venice until late summer, only a few hundred soldiers were ready to embark for the Levant in September 1687. Moreover, the flow of recruits halted during the following winter as mountain passes closed. In early June 1688, 1,000 Swiss arrived in Venice and were quartered at the Lido. The Venetian *Inquisitori* discovered, however, that many recruits did not qualify to serve as soldiers. Furthermore, as a result of their journey, many arrived critically sick and required hospitalisation. The commissars discovered recruits 'still novices' and even two women. Before the end of the month, 800 Swiss were shipped to Corinth. Unfortunately, after entering the Gulf, Algerian pirates attacked the fleet and captured some transports, including those carrying the Swiss recruits. After this episode, their destiny was lost in the North African slave markets. Under the Walloon Colonel

---

236 Mario Nani Mocenigo, *Storia della marina veneziana* (Rome, 1935), p.267.
237 ASVe, *Senato da mar*, r.154 (1688), f. 114.

Count de Lannoy, the Swiss regiment finally landed in Greece but with just two thirds of the expected strength.[238]

On 26 June Morosini assessed the forces available: with the arrival of the 1,147 Swiss on the Mocenigo convoy, the personnel amounted on paper to 14,615 men, including infantry and cavalry. However, on closer inspection the 1,700 sick people, servants, porters, drummers and other *passavolanti* had to be excluded from this figure, and therefore only about 10,000 men, of whom 929 were dragoons, were actually available.[239] This force was increased in the spring by the auxiliaries: Camillo Guidi joined the allies with four galleys, two transport vessels, 10 infantry companies (800 men) under *sergente maggiore generale* Girolamo Cancellieri and 45 knights of the Order of St Stephen.[240] Meanwhile the Maltese contingent under the command of General Claude de Méchatein counted about 1,000 men between soldiers and knights.[241]

The choice to operate against both Negroponte and Crete was prevented by the lack of available forces, and this persuaded the Venetians and their allies to choose only one target, which was Negroponte. Morosini explained in detail the reasons for this choice. Attacking Crete or any other remote island would have required him to leave at least 3,000 men to defend the Isthmus of Corinth. Attacking the capital of Euboea instead, all enemy forces would have rushed at once to defend the island, leaving the Peloponnese safe. In the event of a cavalry raid, the 8,000 Greek militiamen armed by the Venetian authorities could suffice to repel the threat. As for the possibility of an Ottoman landing, Venetian naval superiority was certainly capable of preventing such an improbable action. The decision to besiege Negroponte was strategically correct, but in this decision Morosini made a serious error of evaluation, which became apparent as soon as a reconnaissance of the city was carried out.

The city of Negroponte is located on the western half of the island of Euboea and was connected to Boeotia by a fortified five-arched bridge over the Euripus, the narrow arm of sea barely 30 metres long that separated the island from continental Greece. The western end of the bridge and access road to ancient Chalkida was overlooked by the hill of Kanethos, where the Ottomans, under the direction of the renegade Galloppi, had just built the fort of Kara Baba. This work was by no means imposing, considering its rather small size: 260 metres by 90 metres. The allies probably thought they could seize Kara Baba by surprise and prevent Ottoman reinforcements from relieving the garrison. Certainly, the allied commanders made another

---

[238] Giacomo Diedo, *Storia della Repubblica di Venezia. Dalla Sua Fondazione Sino l'Anno MDCCXLVII* (Venice, 1751), p.461.

[239] Muazzo, in *Guerra coi Turchi*, f. 67, refers a strength of 16,600 men, including 8,000 Germans, 4,000 Italians, 1,500 *schiavoni*, 800 dragoons, 2 000 Suisses et 300 Milanese. The number of Swiss is only a paper figure, since they never arrived with the expected number. Locatelli, in *Racconto historico*, vol. II, p.102, gives an overall strength of 13,070 foot and horse.

[240] Gino Gurrieri, *I cavalieri di Santo Stefano* (Pisa, Nistri-Lischi, 1960), p.270.

[241] Ubaldino Mori Ubaldini, *La Marina del sovrano militare Ordine di San Giovanni di Gerusalemme, di Rodi e di Malta* (Rome: Regionale Editrice, 1971), p.456.

serious mistake when they decided to besiege the city without taking Kara Baba, which was essential to the success of the siege. The city formed a wide trapezium encircled by a solid medieval wall with towers dating back to Venetian rule in the fifteenth century. Outside the walls there was an unfortified quarter where the Greek inhabitants lived. The population was estimated at between 14,000 and 15,000.[242] On the land side there were two gates, defended by a wide moat and an eight-metre-high counter-carpet. Palisades, trenches, redoubts with batteries and other external works had been added the previous year and extended up to the Kanethos hill, which the Ottomans called *Maslakat Tepesì*. The entire peninsula on which Negroponte lay was thus defended by external works at least 250 paces, sometimes even 350 paces, from the city walls. The rocky terrain was another advantage for defence, since it made it impossible to open mines under the fortifications. The garrison was estimated at 4,000–5,000 *azab*s and other *serhaddkulu*, commanded by Mustafa *Paşa*, who resided in the city, and Ibrahim *Paşa*, who held the command in the citadel. The latter was a man of experience, who had previously served as an officer in the Janissary corps.[243] The *serasker*, the newly appointed Halil Ibrahim *Paşa*, was gathering troops in Boeotia. Initially undecided whether to launch an incursion into Attica or wait for events, the Ottoman commander camped with the troops at Thebes from where he could control the enemy's next moves.

Headwinds and strong currents delayed the allied landing operations, and only on 13 July could the galleys approach the shore, about 10 km south of the city. The camp was set up in a place located, according to Morosini, between woods and marshes, in fact on the northern coast east of the city. Königsmarck had to wait another 12 days before the fleet with the troops arrived at their destination. The sail squadron under Lorenzo Venier anchored in the waters north of the city.

An increasingly impatient Königsmarck placed five batteries with a total of 24 guns and five mortars on the ground east to the city, and finally opened fire on 30 July. A ditch was also dug to protect the artillery from enemy sorties. The Ottomans, for their part, quickly took countermeasures and women and children were evacuated to Thessaly; messengers brought information that the *serasker* was camped with his troops at Thebes, 32 km away. The defenders' artillery succeeded in destroying two 30 lb guns of the besiegers, while at the same time the latter suffered the accidental explosion of four other guns. It all started badly for the allied army, especially as, with unprecedented intensity, a new epidemic returned to strike, sparing no one. As early as 4 August Königsmarck was struck down by a high fever that did not leave him for 11 days; *provveditore* Daniele Dolfin, sergeant general Carl Ludwig Raugraf von Pfalz and the veteran Grand-Combe were also confined to bed.[244] Sergeant Major Gaspardis died of an illness that Morosini described

---

242 George Wheler, *A Journey into Greece* (London, 1682), p.457.

243 Pinzelli, *Venise et la Morée*, p.174.

244 *Ibid.*, p.175. Samuel Lacrois de Crozat (1637?–1699), *seigneur* de Grand-Combe, had served three years as a lieutenant colonel of the Lorraine regiment d'Harcourt during the siege of

in his dispatch of 7 August as 'a kind of *febbre terzana*, which, as it becomes continuous, degenerates into malignancy'.[245] By then, more than 3,000 men were already sick. The Swiss regiment paid the highest price, and 400 soldiers died in the first month, including the colonel, while the contagion spread to the rest of the companies in a short time.[246] The approaches were constantly hindered by the sorties of the Ottomans, who regularly received reinforcements from Thebes. On 17 August 2,000 Ottoman infantry and 400 horsemen launched a violent attack, which succeeded in driving the allies out of their positions before they were recaptured by Baron Karl von Sparr of the Bayreuth troops, supported by the Maltese who lost five knights in the clash. Count Henri de Lorraine, Prince of Harcourt, another prestigious volunteer who had just arrived, received two musket wounds.

Realising that the time was favourable for the defenders, Morosini decided to throw all the forces at his disposal into the battle. The hill of Maslakat Tepesì was chosen as the first objective, and the assault was planned for August 20. Victory was obtained after a violent fight, at the end of which 39 guns, of which 26 bronze, and four mortars of 500 lb fell into the hands of the allies. However, the victory had been acquired at high cost: 130 dead and 300 wounded, and among the dead the *provveditore* Girolamo Garzoni (brother of the public historian of the *Serenissima*), as well as the Capuchin friar Antonio d'Asiago, chaplain of Morosini – who incited the troops with a large crucifix – shot in the head while trying to aid Garzoni.[247] The conquest of the hills allowed the allies to seize the external works and to place an artillery battery with 32 guns and 20 mortars, four of which were served by the Tuscan artillerymen. A new convoy had just landed more reinforcements, including the third Brunswick-Lüneburg regiment, and the last Swiss recruits discharged from the Lido hospital. But the losses, mainly due to the epidemic, were so high that the besieging troops were without officers. All the engineers were sick, dead, or seriously wounded. Among these, Captain Giacomo Verneda and his brother Giovanni, nephews of the lieutenant general of the artillery, were killed a few days later, but also the engineers Pierre Romagnal, Rinaldo de la Rue, Samuel Rudolf Miller, all killed by musket fire while they directed the work in the trenches. Since Giovanni Battista Bassignani, the Count of San Felice, and Grand-Combe had all been

---

Candia, where he became familiar with siege techniques and fortifications. At the end of the war, the Venetian Senate rewarded him with a gold medal. After serving in the French army, and under the *Infante* Dom Pedro of Portugal, he became Vauban's aide-de-camp. In the spring of 1688 he contacted the Venetian ambassador in Paris to volunteer in the Levant once again. His proposal, supported by Lieutenant General Verneda, was accepted and Grand-Combe was appointed *sergente maggiore di battaglia*.

245 This was not plague, like the epidemic in Athens, but malarial fever.
246 ASVe, *Senato da mar*, r. 155 (1688), f. 223.
247 According to Schwencke, *Geschichte der Hannoverischen Truppen in Griechenland*, a letter of a Brunswick-Lüneburg officer reports 271 dead and 890 wounded.

injured from the start of the operations, soon there was no officer capable of directing the approaches with the necessary competence.[248]

The situation worsened daily for the allies as the Ottomans resisted, regularly compensating for losses by letting reinforcements enter Negroponte thanks to the unguarded land access. On 27 August 1,500 men joined the garrison, while a small corps sent by the *serasker* was encamped near Kara Baba's fort, in case the enemy attempted to conquer it.

In the besieging camp many volunteers decided to return to their countries, as did the Count of Harcourt at the end of August. These departures further encouraged the Ottomans who saw new sails take to the sea every day. The continuous sorties slowed the progress of the besiegers, who also had to face the danger of mines in their path. Around noon on 6 September, in the pouring rain, the Ottomans returned to the counter-offensive, relying on humidity to take advantage of their superiority in close combat. They were repulsed anyway, but the allies were playing their final cards. Three days later the Captain General decided to attempt an assault against the keep on the sea side, that is, the bastion at the northern end of the city walls. The attack started well, but ended in debacle with an explosion that caused panic among the troops who fled in disorder.

Meanwhile, Königsmarck was fighting his last battle against the disease, which overcame his resistance. On 12 September he spoke a few more words during a lull in the fever, but he was now bothered by a bad cough. Three days later, the Count died at 49 years old.[249]

Since the siege continued, Morosini persisted in attempting the impossible. Engineer Giovanni Bassignani had recently returned to service and was preparing a mine when he was again wounded. This time the bullet wound to the head nearly killed him and put him out of action for several months.[250] There remained at least one senior officer of great value, the Marquis de Courbon, but he too fell on the field on 9 October, hit by a cannonball. A last attempt was made to reinforce the troops with volunteers from the fleet's sailors, armed with spontoons, but this failed.

Since the beginning, the siege involved the both sail and oar ships. The sailing fleet assisted the besiegers by carrying reinforcements and ammunition to feed that frightening furnace; the light fleet (the oared vessels) simultaneously engaged in coordinated operations with the field forces

---

248 Garzoni, *Istoria della Repubblica di Venezia*, vol. I, pp.278–281, and Locatelli, *Racconto historico*, vol. II, p.128. The direction of the approaches therefore passed to the young captain of the miners Antonio Giansich, who, if he lacked experience, on the other hand overflowed with goodwill and learned a lot during this siege, thus starting his long career as an engineer.

249 Pinzelli, *Venise et la Morée*, p.179: 'With the heatwave, it was necessary to take rapid measures for the preservation of the body until he was transferred to The Hague, where according to his will he had asked to be buried with his ancestors. On the same day, his body was embalmed. The following evening his viscera were buried in a nearby Greek church in the presence of German and Italian officers, who later came to offer their condolences to the Countess. She had to wait until the end of the campaign to leave the island of Euboea with the rest of the fleet.'

250 Locatelli, *Racconto historico*, vol. II, p.134.

during the last unsuccessful assaults in September. The galleys performed a mock landing action to deceive the defenders, but without results.[251] On that occasion, artillery aboard the ships and galleys provided limited support to the siege of Negroponte, since the key defences were located far from the sea.

The siege of Negroponte resulted in a bitter failure. At the beginning of September only 4,000 men were available; the artillery was largely out of service; the ammunition exhausted. The Maltese had lost 24 knights and no less than 400 soldiers, and the Tuscan contingent was now reduced to half the force deployed in June. Morosini convened the council of war on 15 October with the remaining officers. The Germans vehemently demanded immediate departure, and in the end the *Doge* had to yield. Two days later, he gave the order to prepare for departure. The Greeks who had collaborated with the besiegers had to follow the retreating fleet. The siege was lifted in disorder, everyone eager to leave those inauspicious shores. On the evening of 20 October, 3,450 survivors were transferred aboard the galleys, but the sky did not spare the vanquished, and the cold and the rain accompanied them to Thermis where Morosini quartered the remains of the regiments to spend the winter in Morea. The aristocrat volunteers, meanwhile, returned to Venice as was customary. All battle reports agree that, in spite of the great valorous acts of the Venetians and their allies, the siege's failure was inevitable because of serious strategic mistakes. First of all, the allies neglected to complete the encirclement of the city, which could be supplied and reinforced by land. Casualties had been very high. Whole regiments numbered one third of their original strength; out of the 11,442 Germans deployed during the campaign, 4,748 soldiers and 1,190 officers had survived.[252]

The only success achieved by the Venetians in 1688 occurred in the Balkan theatre. In March and May 1688 Paşa Bushati Süleyman attacked the Montenegrin highlanders of Kuči, only to suffer a devastating defeat twice, with 1,500 casualties, and lost Medun to them. In the summer, Montenegro officially recognised the Venetian protectorate,[253] and the Republic established a garrison in Cetinje and fortified the monastery. Even more significant was the conquest of Knin, in Bosnia. The fortress surrendered to Girolamo Corner after a 12-day siege on 11 September.[254]

Dismay and bitterness met Morosini upon his return to Venice. However, it was necessary to consolidate the Venetian presence, and for this it was necessary to take away the conquest of Malvasia, the only outpost left to the enemies in the Peloponnese. Already in the spring of 1688, when the Negroponte adventure was about to begin, Morosini had ordered the *provveditore generale* of Morea, Giacomo Corner, to prepare the land

---

251 Diedo, *Storia della Repubblica di Venezia*, p.411.

252 Pinzelli, *Venise et la Morée*, p.396.

253 In 1689, Metropolitan Visarion thus invited nobleman from Kotor Ivan 'Zane' Grbičić to Cetinje, who was then elected the first Montenegrin *Guvernadur*. See Gligor Stanojević, *Montenegrina – digitalna biblioteka crnogorske kulture i nasljedja*.

254 The conquest marked the end of the successful Venetian campaign in Inner Dalmatia, and determined the final border between Dalmatia and Bosnia and Herzegovina still existing today.

blockade of Malvaisia. The *provveditore* of Mani, Antonio Lascari, was appointed to supervise the operations on the ground. On 22 September the *Doge* also ordered the erection of an embankment reinforced by gabions to control the bridge leading to the town. Morosini's plan was to employ 150 soldiers from Nauplia with 2,000–3,000 peasants from the surrounding area in the work, in order to complete the work in 15 days before the rains arrived. To supervise the work a senior Venetian official was needed and Giacomo Corner sent his second, Antonio Molin, while the *provveditore straordinario* Zorzi Benzon dealt with the situation at Corinth. The operation at Malvasia was very badly organised. In October the engineer appointed to take care of the technical details fell into an ambush with his escort and was saved by a miraculous rescue. In the meantime Molin had not moved, and all responsibility for the operation fell on Lascari who, arriving late and with only 500 Greeks, was attacked by the garrison and forced to flee. This setback cost the lives or freedom of almost 200 people.[255] As a result, the Ottomans remained undisturbed in Malvasia until the following year.

Facing page: 104. Girolamo Corner, *provveditore straordinario* in Dalmatia, here portrayed like a Renaissance Condottiero in an engraving dating to 1686 (author's archive). Corner obtained significant success against the Ottomans in Bosnia and Albania from 1686 until 1688. His career is exemplary in the Venetian military: in 1684 he was appointed *provveditore all'armata*, and in 1689 after his service in Dalmatia he replaced Morosini as *capitano generale da mar*.

1689

Venetian preparations continued during the winter, and new recruits were enlisted to fill the losses of the last terrible campaign. Troops were also now necessary since the Papal and Tuscan contingent had not recovered from the previous campaign, and their respective governments had informed the *Serenissima* that they would not participate in new operations.

The year 1689 brought another fundamental event. On 24 September 1688 Louis XIV had invaded the Palatinate, opening the conflict against the League of Augsburg. This event had forced the German princes to recall all their troops from the Danube to the Rhine to face the French, obliging the Emperor to change his plans for war against the Porte. The Senate feared that the balance of forces resulting from the new scenario could turn into an advantage for the Ottomans, at least against Venice.

In February Morosini recovered from a brief illness, and on 4 April, after discussing the plan of fortification in the isthmus of Corinth, he convened the council of war. It was decided to send the *provveditore* Giacomo Corner with 2,000 men, six galleys, five vessels and other ships under *capitano strordinario delle navi* Lorenzo Valier to blockade Malvasia. Corner estimated that the construction of the two forts ordered by Morosini would take more than 80 days with 600 workers and 34 masons. Thirteen days later, the first Venetian convoy anchored in Nauplia. The nine ships brought the newly formed *Stiron* regiment and several companies of Italian and *oltramontane* infantry, for a total of 1,926 men. The Tuscan *sergente generale di battaglia*, Marquis Nicolò Dal Borro, previously at Castelnovo, was in the convoy as a volunteer. On 31 March Morosini learned that the Senate had found a replacement for Königsmarck in Charles Félix de Galiens, Duke of Gadagne. He was a veteran of the French army with an impressive military curriculum, started at the age of 14 in the *Régiment des Galères*. In 1689 he was 66 years old, but

---

255 Pinzelli, *Venise et la Morée*, p.188.

the Senate had chosen him for his experience in amphibious operations.[256] Gadagne embarked on 12 May in Venice and on 9 June he was in Malvasia. On 10 June he participatated in a council of war where the possibility of a new attack on Negroponte was unanimously rejected. The following option, a siege of Malvoisie, was confirmed. Two forts were built, to the right and left of the stone bridge leading to the islet. Nicolò Vendramin was appointed *provveditore* of the encampment, as in the previous year. With the Maltese finally having reached the theatre of operations with their galleys, Morosini again convened a new council of war that called into question the decision of 10 June. Opinions continued to diverge completely at a new meeting on the morning of 29 June. The generals continued to present their opinions for or against Negroponte and Malvasia. In the end the wisest option was adopted, and the current siege continued. The army was then 10,000 infantry and 600 cavalry. Gadagne sent all the cavalry to Corinth and detached 3,500 infantrymen to guard the isthmus. The Venetians feared that *serasker* Ibrahim and the bands of Liberachi, 'the *bey* of Mani', who now sided with the Ottomans, could hit the army from behind.

The bombardment of Malvasia began on 12 July, but the new mortars soon proved defective, with most bombs exploding as soon as they were fired into the air.[257] Weeks later, a commando-type operation was launched at dawn. Three incendiary boats were to be launched against the Ottoman ships under cover. This attack was supported by four warships while 150 men were to provide a diversion on the bridge side. But the headwind prevented the manoeuvre from being carried out, which resulted in five dead and 30 wounded on the Venetian side. The most notable loss was that of Lorenzo Venier. The captain had approached the shore to observe the attack, and a ball fired from the fortress hit him in the head and killed him instantly.[258]

In late August Morosini was recalled to Venice. His replacement, Girolamo Corner, *provveditore generale* in Dalmatia, had been in the city since 5 August, and he in turn had been replaced by Girolamo Dolfin. On 13 September Morosini set sail for the lagoon, taking with him the Count of San Felice, who was preparing a new kind of mortar bomb for the next campaign. Corner, did not stay long in the waters of Malvasia, having to visit the conquered towns. He left there Carlo Pisani, who had replaced Lorenzo Venier, with four galleys and 10 ships. Some Greeks who had escaped from the place confirmed that the garrison could resist for a long time, lacking neither water nor ammunition, even collecting the cannonballs fired by the

---

256 Gadagne took part in the Battle of the Dunes, the capture of Dunkirk and Ypres in 1658. As a lieutenant general he was in the army of Lorraine and then commanded the expedition against Gigeri in 1664. Gadagne continued to serve during the Dutch War, before retiring to his estates, disappointed because he had not been made *maréchal* along with d'Estrades, Vivonne and La Feuillade. According to some commenters, Louis XIV said 'If Monsieur de Gadagne had been patient, he would have been among them, but he withdrew, he became impatient.' Thanks to Éric Pinzelli for this notice.

257 Beregani, *Historia delle Guerre d'Europa*, vol. II, p.338.

258 *Ibid*. The same shot also decapitated Marquis Caravioli, nephew of the General of Malta.

Venetians and sending them back. The situation at Malvasia remained at a standstill for the rest of the year.

In 1689, after the field army progressed into the Peloponnese, the sailing fleet was deployed to a different operational theatre from the galleys and galleasses, and once again demonstrated the naval division that occurred in the Cretan War's final years, when Francesco Morosini had directed this choice. While the light fleet focused on amphibious operations – one of the keys to success in previous campaigns – the sailing fleet tried, with little success, to engage the weak but elusive Ottoman fleet in the Aegean. Supported by fortified ports on Chios and Rhodes, the Ottomans checked the Venetian fleet. Furthermore, Venetian commanders lacked logistical support and sometimes even the patience to implement long blockades like those carried out 30 years earlier in the Dardanelles. Nevertheless, the Ottoman fleet's prudence did not help their army. Two major naval encounters occurred off the island of Naxos and in the Mytilene Channel, the same waters as the encounter of 1686, but once again the Ottoman fleet, comprising both sail ships and oared ships, managed to escape and avoid destruction. On that occasion, for the first time the Venetians only deployed sailing ships, just as the Ottomans had done three years before. Because the Ottoman ships carried strong armament on the fore and aft, the Venetian sailing vessels focused on defence, but the line tactics enabled them to prevail over the galleys. Though Morosini and Königsmarck repeatedly defeated Ottoman troops in the Peloponnese, the Porte was able to save its navy for a more opportune time. A long-expected victory attributed to the new sailing fleet never arrived, and this created bitter frustration among the Venetian commanders.

1690

In March 1690 Girolamo Corner returned to Malvasia and ordered the *Almirante* Alessandro Valier to collect a war contribution in the archipelago. Valier came out with the fleet visiting the Aegean islands, which on the way back was attacked by *kapudan paşa* Hüseyn Mezzomorto with two Algerian and 10 Ottoman ships en route to Malvasia. This caused the loss of two Venetian vessels, including Valier among the casualties. The fight lasted several hours, and at the end of it the Ottomans captured about 30 Venetian sailors.[259] With the favour of darkness, 18 of them managed to escape by sailing to Milos.

In early May the Duke of Gadagne arrived in front of Malvasia and decided to go resolutely on the offensive. On the evening of his arrival he gave the order to *sergenti maggiori* Tomeo Pompei and Bonometti to take position with their infantry at the foot of the wall, under the cliff where the fortress lay. The two Venetian commanders moved to the assault and managed to occupy the position, but the next morning the Ottomans overwhelmed the enemy who, outnumbered and unprotected, had to withdraw, losing about 30 soldiers

---

[259] Pinzelli, *Venise et la Morée*, p.193. Captain Agostino Petrina from Zadar, commander of the sail ship *San Iseppo*, his son, and one of his nephews were among the prisoners. Petrina died in Constantinople in 1693.

105. The fortified city port of Malvasia, in a late seventeenth century drawing by Vincenzo Maria Coronelli (author's archive). See image commentaries for more information.

including the brave Bonometti. A council of war was convened, and Gadagne's proposal for a new assault was opposed by the other senior officers. Finally, the council decided to wait for the auxiliaries and further reinforcements before attempting another assault, and in the meantime strengthen the blockade of Malvasia. The auxiliaries arrived in mid June, followed by reinforcements. The Maltese squadron, commanded by the bailiff Claude de Moreton Chabrillan, and the Papal squadron, led for the first time by Anton Domenico Bussi, numbered 2,500 men. The convoy of Bortolo Contarini had on board Dal Borro and Sparr, as well as engineer Giovanni Bassignani. With these forces, two Genoese galleys also joined the fleet. On 28 June Girolamo Corner held a council of war. All the senior officers took part: the Duke of Gadagne, the *Marquis* Dal Borro, Barons Sparr and De Rose, Count Rapetta, the *Chevalier* de Manville, Lieutenant General of the Maltese battalion, Counts Lodovico di Montevecchio, and Guido Bonnaventura, commanders of the two Papal battalions, the *sergenti maggiori di battaglia* San Felice, Montanari, Pompei, and Lanoia, as well as the engineers Jean Bernard, Giovanni Battista Bassignani, and Giacomo di Solari. Embittered by the failure of May, the Duke of Gadagne summarised the proposal to abandon the offensive. Now, it was better to continue to hold the present positions, even if it meant reinforcing them, because a full-scale attack on the town would seem too risky.[260] The besiegers had now entrenched at the western and eastern ends of the islet, and Gadagne asked the engineers to make a report and a detailed plan to see if it was useful to keep troops on both sides. On 3 July the report stated that the positions to the east of the town were untenable and subject to attack from three different directions. The engineers' point of view was accepted and the soldiers were withdrawn from positions deemed too dangerous. The besiegers took a more rearward position, but Corner had received information a+9bout the lack of provisions of the besieged, which made him optimistic about the success of the blockade.

On 25 July a convoy led by the *provveditore straordinario all'armata* Giacomo Contarini brought more reinforcements. As the days passed, the allies were not content to wait for the surrender, and Gadagne decided to advance some artillery pieces which, well protected, began to target the bastion at the southern end of the curtain, opening a breach. The shelling was successful, and the Ottomans demanded a truce. They were probably also short of ammunition, and asked for 30 days to evacuate the place, remove the artillery from the city, and retain all their personal goods. Corner accepted all the requests except that regarding the artillery, and finally, the day after, the garrison of Malvasia agreed to surrender.[261] On 12 August 1690, 1,200 people, including 300 soldiers, made their exit. They had succeeded in forcing Morosini and Corner in wait for 17 months of uninterrupted siege, but the conquest of the Morea was now complete. During the siege, the sail ships supported the troops and shelled the city until the final surrender on 12 August.

As the campaign had already progressed, the Captain General turned his attention to the fortress of Vlorë in Albania, where the main base of the Ottoman pirates in the southern Adriatic was located. He informed the council of war of his decision and all the senior commanders agreed to move the war into Corner's favoured theatre. The Maltese contingents, despite the limit of their term, joined the Venetians in the action. The light fleet set sail on the evening of 8 September, stopping briefly in safe harbours. On 13 September the troops landed under the protection of the galleys, but instead of attacking Vlörë the troops laid siege to Canina, a fortress on the heights in the interior. After three days the garrison capitulated, and Corner forced the defenders to leave the place without conditions. On 17 September 3,000 people, including 526 soldiers, evacuated the fortress. Terror then gripped the garrison of Vlörë, to whom the Venetian Captain General sent a message that he would give no quarter if they tried to resist. On the evening

---

260 ASVe, *Senato, dispacci, Provveditori di Terra e di Mar*, b. 1123, d. 39 (2 July 1690).

261 Antonio Pinelli, *Distinta Relatione dell'acquisto di Napoli di Malvasia fatto dall'armi della Serenissima Republica di Venetia sotto il prudente, valoroso comando dell'illustrissimo et eccellentissimo Signor Cav. e Proc. Girolamo Corner, capitan general da mar, li 12 Agosto 1690* (Venice, 1690), pp.2–3. Inside Malvasia, the besiegers captured 78 bronze and iron guns and two mortars. Corner also obtained the delivery of the artilleryman who had killed Lorenzo Venier in 1689. He was an Italian renegade who refused to abjure his new faith, and was condemned to execution by being tied hand and foot to four galleys and torn apart.

of 18 September all the Ottomans fled from the town. Corner had succeeded in seizing two strongholds in just six days.[262] Further north, at the end of an autumnal campaign, *the provveditore in Dalmazia* Girolamo Dolfin had managed to conquer Vrgorac on 26 November, which opened the route towards the Imotski and Mostar regions.

The 1690 campaign had ended without the enemy having tried to relieve the besieged places. Too busy facing the Imperials on the Danube, the Ottomans were now resigned to sacrificing their possessions in Greece and on the Dalmatian border. Fate was also favourable to the Venetians at sea, and despite the defeat suffered at the beginning of the year, in September the sail fleet finally obtained a success. The captain of sailing ships Daniele Dolfin, with a squadron of 12 vessels and two fireships, managed to intercept an enemy convoy en route to Mytilene, escorted by 32 ships and 26 galleys. After the battle the Venetians claimed few casualties, although Dolfin himself was seriously injured in the leg. The Ottomans lost at least three ships and six galleys, which sank during the night due to damage suffered in combat. The battle was a significant success, but the main strategic objective, namely the annihilation of the enemy naval forces, was not achieved.

The situation was now favourable for Venice, but unexpectedly Girolamo Corner died on 1 October 1690, at the end of a short illness; he was 58 years old. To replace Corner, the Senate called upon Domenico Mocenigo. He was another veteran of the Cretan War, who had been appointed *provveditore generale* of Dalmatia in 1683, but who had been quickly dismissed for incompetence at the very beginning of the hostilities. Raised to the rank of captain general at the age of 66, this patrician accomplished no miracles, as he was a much less intrepid man than his two illustrious predecessors. Mocenigo had only one tactic during the few months he was Captain General: to defend above all the newly conquered 'kingdom' of the Morea. Talks between the Porte and the Holy League were continuing, so it was necessary to hold on, in order to negotiate from a position of strength. As a member of one of Venice's leading families, Mocenigo was appointed to Captain General as a clear sign of the government's desire to stall, pending an armistice with the Sultan. The necessity of limiting war expenditure conditioned this phase of the conflict. Consequently the council of war, which met on 2 October, agreed with the *provveditore della Morea* Antonio Zeno, who judged sufficient the field force under Gadagne: 6,179 infantry and 500 dragoons in all, for controlling both Dalmatia and the Morea.

1691

Domenico Mocenigo reached Corfu towards the end of December 1690, and as soon as he arrived he learned the situation from the generals. According to them, Canina and Vlöre could be directly threatened by enemy winter attacks; both the officers and engineers generally considered that it was difficult to hold both strongholds. The Captain General wanted to see this for himself, by going

---

262 BQS, cl. IV, ms. n. 186 (442), *Ristretto de successi seguiti nelle conquiste di Malvagia, Valona e Canina presi dall'armi venete unite a quella della Sacra Religione Gierosolimitana*, ff. 95–103.

there with the whole council, but the bad weather conditions dissuaded him. Mocenigo did not want to take any risks and therefore decided to abandon Canina, having first dismantled it so that it could no longer be used by the enemy. This mission was entrusted to the *governatore dei forzati*, Carlo Pisani, who was already there with four galleys. On the evening of 16 January 1691, explosives were used to collapse Canina's walls.

While this was happening, Mocenigo received alarming news from Pisani, who reported that more than 3,000 janissaries with artillery were marching against Vlöre. The Captain General then convened an emergency council of war which decided to abandon this place as well. To provide better cover for Pisani, who as at Canina was charged with destroying the walls, Baron Sparr was hastily sent to Albania with 1,000 infantrymen. In the meantime much news arrived, making the situation on the ground less and less clear. In a new letter, Pisani recommended to the Captain General that they hold Vlöre, but everything was ready to detonate the charges, so Pisani asked for a new confirmation before carrying out the task. Mocenigo declared that he could not decide and therefore left the decision to Sergeant General Spar who, once before Vlöre, would be able to assess what to do.

But events took the Venetians by surprise. On 7 February a new message from Pisani announced that the Ottomans had already been besieging Vlöre for three days. Moreover, the Venetian spies had underestimated the enemy forces. Halil *Paşa*, the former *serasker* at the time of the siege of Negroponte, together with the Albanian Kaplan *Paşa* and Süleyman *Paşa*, had assembled a force of 8,000 irregulars and 16,000 diggers, and now they were only 150 paces from the counterscarp. The besiegers had also placed a battery of three cannons and another of mortars that were wreaking havoc inside the city. Sparr, held up by a headwind, only reached Vlöre on 5 February. He managed to enter the city, and with the reinforcements the garrison was 1,200 strong. The Venetians launched successful sorties to hinder the enemy approaches, but from prisoners Sparr learned that the Ottomans were determined to besiege Vlöre with all their means.[263] On the morning of 18 February the Venetians suffered a considerable loss caused by friendly fire: a cannon shot fired from the citadel beheaded the valiant Sergeant General Sparr, who was watching the enemy's progress. Pisani replaced him at the command of the defence, and the fighting continued fiercely. On 27 February Pisani tried to seize the enemy artillery but the sortie failed. Meanwhile, Mocenigo was becoming increasingly worried, since he feared that the siege of Vlöre was an expedient to divert the Venetians from the Morea. Now estimating the forces defending the Peloponnese as insufficient and fearing an assault in force in the Isthmus of Corinth, on 13 March the Captain General ordered the evacuation of Vlöre. He had thus inaugurated his office with a setback disguised as a wise retreat. Carlo Pisani, dejected at having to give up the fight, was the last to leave the fortress, blowing up a few sections of the walls in front of the besiegers.[264] In his dispatches of May,

---

263 ASVe, *Senato, Dispacci, Provveditori di Terra e di Mar*, b. 1125, d. 16 (1 March 1691).
264 *Ibid.*, d. 19 (14 March 1691).

Domenico Mocenigo spoke about a possible attack in force by the Ottomans against the Morea, of which the Grand Vizier himself would have to take command. However, with the death of Sultan Süleyman II on 10 June, and the political complications that followed, Grand Vizier Mustafa Köprülü had many other domestic concerns. Eleven days later Mocenigo mentioned the change in the disposition of the Ottomans, who were evidently preparing no offensive.[265] However, after leaving Vlöre the Ottomans had recovered control of northern Epirus.[266]

Between May and June the council of war discussed the next possible objectives. These were Chaniá, Chios, Tenedos or a new assault on Negroponte, but each target was excluded in turn for a host of reasons. Finally, the captain general proposed to go and confront the enemy navy, but operations were no better on the sea. In combination with the exhaustion of the amphibious strategy in 1689, this frustration probably led to the fleet's first joint operation in 1691, joining oar and sail ships. The combined offensive, which resulted in an exhausting and unsuccessful raid into the waters of Bozcaada, did not yield the expected results. The Ottoman fleet continued to evade confrontation, remaining safe in the Dardanelles protected by castles on both shores. Furthermore, problems of a technical nature affected the Venetians. Combining the fleets brought to light the oared ships' struggle to maintain formation and speed with the sailing vessels. Moreover, the galleasses showed their inferiority in open water, especially in rough seas. The new sailing ships could exploit the wind more efficiently than previous designs and continued their slow but steady technological evolution. Meanwhile, galleys and galleasses struggled to manoeuvre in the difficult conditions common to the northern Aegean.[267] After several weeks of waiting for a hypothetical confrontation, the allied fleet returned to the Archipelago, finally reaching the Morean ports from where the Order's squadron sailed to Malta. Mocenigo finally decided to act in early September, when the Ottoman cavalry approached Corinth. On 4 September some Turkish squadrons carried out a reconnaissance at the isthmus, but as the Venetian cavalry approached, the enemy units retreated and returned without a fight to Thebes. The next day, Mocenigo arrived with galleys on the Saronic Gulf side and landed 1,200 *oltramarini*, but the enemy was already far away.

---

265 *Ibid.*, b. 843–844, d. 28 (23 July 1691).

266 For the next two years the local inhabitants, particularly in Chimeria (Himara), were subject to reprisals, which led many to flee to Corfu and others to convert to Islam to save themselves. See Ioannis Chasiotis, Ἡ κάμψη τῆς Ὀθωμανικῆς δυνάμεως (The Decline of Ottoman Power)'. In Georgios A. Christopoulos and Ioannis K. Bastias (eds), Ἱστορία τοῦ Ἑλληνικοῦ Ἔθνους, Τόμος ΙΑ΄: Ὁ Ἑλληνισμὸς ὑπὸ ξένη κυριαρχία – περίοδος 1669-1821, Τουρκοκρατία - Λατινοκρατία (*History of the Greek Nation, Volume XI: Hellenism under Foreign Rule – Period 1669–1821, Turkocracy–Latinocracy*) (in Greek) (Athens: Ekdotiki Athinon, 1975), pp.32–33.

267 Candiani, 'Vele, remi e cannoni', p.152. The author specifies that in summer the *Meltemi*, northerly winds, occur for most of the season. These conditions forced the fleets to narrow their range of action and climb towards the main Ottoman bases if they wanted to take the initiative. This situation was a disadvantage especially for the galleys, which were heavier and less manageable. Candiani, 'Vele, remi e cannoni', p.152.

In June, peace negotiations had resumed on the initiative of the British and Dutch ambassadors to the Sublime Porte. In fact, the Prince of Orange was doing everything he could to end the conflict in the Balkans, which would allow his Austrian allies to transfer all their forces to the fight against France. For his part the French ambassador, de Croissy, had every interest in not distracting the Ottomans from their warlike plans, but in the summer of 1691 the Porte began to listen to truce proposals. On 28 August 1691 the new British ambassador, Sir William Hussey, again confirmed to the allies that the Ottomans were ready to open negotiations. The Venetian diplomats advanced their proposals: Negroponte was no longer demanded, but the Republic still wanted its dominion over the Morea to be confirmed. In addition to this, the Republic had wide-ranging territorial claims on the Dalmatian hinterland, but also on the regions north of the Gulf of Corinth, from Parga to Attica.[268] Negotiations came to a halt and the war resumed its course.

Before the end of the year the Venetians suffered a defeat, slight militarily, but important strategically. On 6 December the fortress of Grabusa (Gramvousa) north-west of Crete surrendered to the Ottomans after the betrayal of the local commander.[269] To prevent further incidents, the *provveditore straordinario all'Armata* Bortolo Contarini was immediately sent to Crete to reinforce the garrisons of Suda and Spinalonga. The *provveditore* of the latter fortress, Vincenzo Pasta, was approached by the French consul Fabre, who also offered him a large sum of money to deliver the place, but the patrician refused.[270]

Except for the siege of Vlöre, the campaign of 1691 was remarkable only for the almost total absence of events, however in July and August the Montenegrin allies achieved some success repulsing the attempts led by Bushati Süleyman during his expeditions against Piperi and Bjelopavlići.

1692

Crete or Negroponte were precisely the objectives towards which the Captain General was planning the new campaign, having learned that the Greeks of Chios, favoured by the Sultan, would take up arms to assist the Ottomans in

---

268 BNM, ms. It VII 1882 (9073), *Ambascierie della Repubblica Veneta all'Imp:r di Germania 1687-1692*, f. 128.

269 Pinzelli, *Venise et la Morée*, p.205. Along with Suda and Spinalonga, Grabusa was one of the last Venetian possessions in Crete. The garrison commander, Luca Della Rocca, was a Neapolitan former outlaw who had entered the service of the *Serenissima* in 1685 in Dalmatia. In 1687 he entered the regular army as an infantry ensign. During the siege of Malvasia he obtained permission from the *provveditore* of the Morea Giacomo Corner to raise a company formed with convicted soldiers. In Greece he had married a woman 'of bad life' who led him down a wrong path. Della Rocca, who had only been in Crete for a few months, got in touch with Ottoman agents, and when most of the soldiers were outside, together with a compatriot accomplice named Peroni, he took the Venetian officers hostage: the governor Valentino Negretti, Major Belisario Graziano, the chancellor, and the *provveditore* Francesco Donà, and consigned them to the *paşa* of Chaniá.

270 According to Pinzelli, *Venise et la Morée*, p.207, Pasta embodies the actual 'model' of patrician, the one who dedicates his life to Venice to the ultimate sacrifice of his life.

the event of an enemy assault, while Negroponte had been discarded as a new siege was again deemed too dangerous. In 1692 the Venetian fleet resumed an ambitious, cooperative campaign to land in Chaniá on Crete that involved the sail and oar fleets. The Senate believed that this campaign could reclaim the kingdom lost in 1669, and simultaneously force the Ottoman fleet into a decisive battle.[271] This campaign also involved the Papal and Maltese fleets, which each raised a sailing vessel to transport their landing troops.

On 12 July 12,000 infantrymen including many *venturieri* volunteers, and 800 cavalrymen, under the new *generale dello sbarco*, Count Sigismund Joachim von Trauttmansdorf, landed undisturbed on the beach of Plataniàs, to the west of the city. Chaniá, which had been largely spared during the Cretan War, was the most populous and industrious city on the island. The defences were in good condition and the Ottomans, apparently warned by the French, were able to offer good resistance. According to local spies there were in Chaniá 3,000 soldiers, including 800 janissaries and *kapikulu* professional artillerymen.[272]

The Venetians and their allies established their batteries to the south of the town and concentrated their fire on the San Dimitrio bastion. At the end of July an external redoubt was seized and reinforced by the engineer Camuccio. After the placement of further artillery, the besiegers managed to damage the western flank of the bastion. However, the allies were soon faced with an insurmountable problem, namely the digging of the approach trenches. Since foreign mercenaries were exempt from digging work, the engineers resorted to recruiting locals, but 'the villagers around Chaniá feared the reaction of the Turks' and then the siege progressed slowly.[273] Differences between Mocenigo and Trauttmansdorf caused further concerns. Furthermore, troop desertion[274] and the crews' indiscipline emphasised the Venetian weakness and poor organisation. The unexpected Ottoman resistance, increasingly supported by relief forces from Candia and Réthymnon, losses in combat including several brave officers, and desertions, convinced Mocenigo to convene a council of war on 17 August. Trauttmansdorf proposed to take Chaniá by assault, but on 29 August a new council of war decided to leave the siege after a mere 39 days.[275] The Cretan expedition was the last major Venetian amphibious operation of the war.

---

271 The other objectives proposed and voted by the Senate were Chios, Mytilene, and a new assault against Negroponte. Apart from the last one, the others were clearly identified as the key strategic points of Ottoman sea traffic.

272 ASVe, *Senato, Dispacci, Provveditori di Terra e di Mar*, b. 1124, d. 60 (29 April 1692).

273 Diedo, *Storia della Repubblica di Venezia*, p.449.

274 *Ibid.*, pp.449–450. The Venetian historian specified that desertion was particularly high among French mercenaries, 'who took salaries from the Ottomans'.

275 *Ibid*. The commanders of the Maltese and Papal fleets also attended the council of war. The votes were split in half, and ultimately the Captain General opted for suspending operations and returning to the Morea.

Though Mocenigo blamed the Austrian general for the failure, the Captain General was severely criticised, but he was aware of elements to take into account. In July, Mocenigo had removed Antonio Zeno from the post of *provveditore* of the Morea on the grounds of corruption; Zeno was suspended from duty and brought to trial in Venice, and replaced by the *Provveditore all'Armata* Marino Michiel. To assist him, two new extraordinary *provveditori*, Alessandro Bon and Pietro Duodo, had arrived in July.[276] Moreover, Mocenigo learned that in early August the Maniote leader Liberachi (Limberakis Gerakaris), who now sided with the Porte, and the *serasker* were concentrating their forces at Negroponte, and that the Ottomans were opening a new route to the isthmus. On 6 August a vanguard of 100 *sipahis* came to test the defences around Corinth, before retreating to Megara, where Liberachi along with the Ottoman *paşas* were camped with 10,000 men. Four days later the Maniote warlord advanced with his troops and the Ottoman cavalry to camp in sight of Corinth. As they marched against the Venetian positions, the Greek militiamen armed by the *provveditori* fled, leaving the regulars to their fate. In the battle, Giovanni Strel's dragoon regiment lost 115 men, almost the entire unit. The rest of the troops had to retreat to Acrocorinth.[277]

106. Portrait of *capitano generale da mar* Antonio Zeno, by Isabella Pacini, after Vincenzo Maria Coronelli's *Ritratti di personaggi celebri* (Venice, 1703).

When the Ottomans had appeared before Corinth, Michiel immediately tried to warn the Captain General by sending three letters by as many different ships, but the southern Aegean was so infested by corsairs that none of them reached their destination. In another encrypted letter, Michiel took a dramatic tone, describing in detail all the depredations committed by the enemy. This time the message reached its destination, since Domenico Mocenigo abandoned the siege of Chaniá.[278] Unfortunately for him, the Ottomans crossed the isthmus again on the evening of 25 August. Thus, the Captain General unwittingly thwarted an enterprise that was well on its way to success because the crucial information arrived too late.

Two months later Marino Michiel reported on the devastation caused by the enemy in the Morea. In the area around Corinth 67 houses had

---

276 Pinzelli, *Venise et la Morée*, p.207. Michiel himself fell seriously ill and had to delegate his authority to *sergente maggiore* Fabio Lanoia and his nephew Angelo, who had been the first *provveditore* of Corinth in 1687 before serving in Suda.
277 Contarini, *Istoria della Guerra*, vol. II, pp.345–346.
278 Pinzelli, *Venise et la Morée*, p.208.

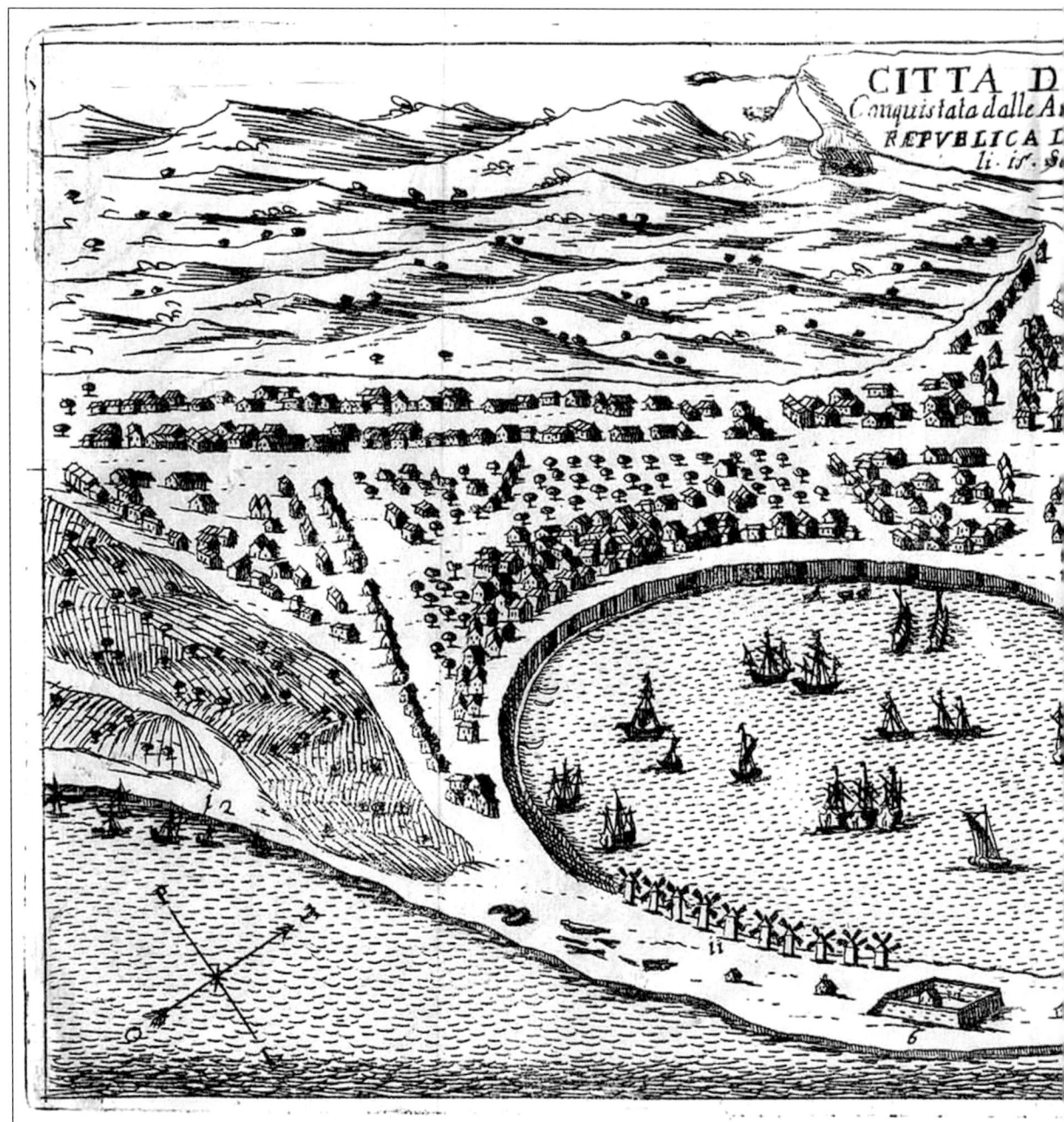

107. The island of Chios seized by the Venetians and their allies in 1694, in an engraving after Girolamo Albrizzi (author's archive). The conquest took place easily and the soldiery, which for years had not had the opportunity, indulged in their favourite activity of looting. The troops made up for lost time, although they had not been authorised to pillage, and Antonio Zeno admitted that nothing escaped their rapacity, 'neither the shops of the Turks, nor those of the Greeks, nor the houses'. If the Venetians had come to free the inhabitants from the Ottoman yoke, they certainly did so in the worst way. Almost everyone took part: the Baron of Rosen, the adjutant of the *generale dello sbarco* Steinau, had taken so much advantage of this that the captain-general wanted to have him arrested, but the culprit managed to escape on board one of the auxiliary galleys. A year later, overly concerned about an Ottoman offensive in the Morea, the Venetians abandoned the island.

LITTLE AND GREAT ITALIAN WARS

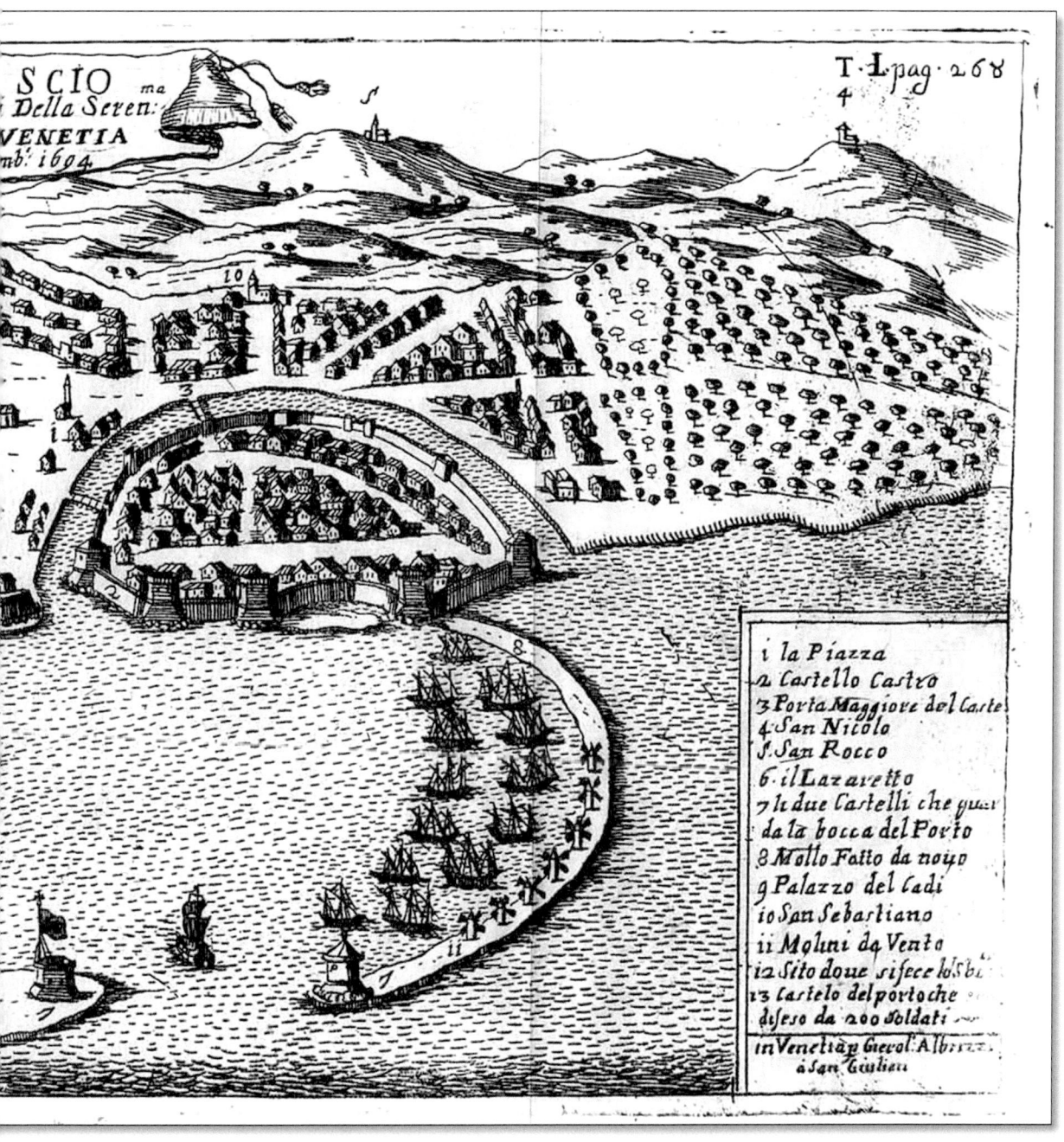

been destroyed, 1,256 in the whole region, as well as 19 churches.[279] As for Mocenigo, this new failure sounded the death knell of his career. Recalled to Venice, he was found innocent of charges of negligence and misconduct of the campaign but was largely discredited, and the Republic sent him to Vicenza to fill a subordinate position. Now the *Serenissima* had to designate a new captain general.

After the death of Girolamo Corner, Venice had achieved no more successes, and doubts grew into senators' minds. However, the Republic still had a skilled soldier in the person of the *Doge* himself. Despite being aged 74, he was an exceptional man who had so often prevailed against the Ottomans that it was difficult to keep an exact account. Francesco Morosini was a talisman, a guarantee of success; it was therefore natural that the Republic would choose him as captain general for the fourth time. On Christmas Day 1692 a body of 200 patricians gathered in the *Sala dello Scrutinio*. The decision was unanimous: the *Doge*'s name was chosen with 95 votes against Girolamo Dolfin's 27, while the rest of the votes were divided between 22 other candidates. A second vote in the *Maggior Consiglio* was necessary to confirm the decision, but it was only a matter of principle, as the response validated the will of the majority. Of the 847 patricians present, 797 supported Morosini's appointment, only 34 opposed it and 12 did not vote.[280] Morosini addressed his speech to the Senate, but according to contemporary reports, he was a tired and worried man.[281]

Problems also occurred in the Balkans with the Montenegrin allies. In 1692 the Metropolitan Visarion Borilović Bajica died under mysterious circumstances, and popular conspiracy theory has it that he was poisoned by the Venetians. In September Bushati Süleyman launched another large campaign against Montenegro. The Venetian forces had no intent of facing the Ottomans like they did seven years earlier and in turn retreated to the sanctuary of Cetinje monastery. The Ottoman army reached Cetinje almost without a fight, with only a handful of Montenegrins offering resistance. After negotiations the Venetian army was allowed to retreat from Cetinje. Before their departure they mined the monastery, destroying it permanently. This move was unpopular among the local population and resulted in Montenegro turning its back on Venice.[282]

---

279 ASVe, *Senato, Dispacci, Provveditori di Terra e di Mar*, b. 845, *dispacci di Marin Michiele dal 1691 al 1693*, dd. 7–13.

280 Pinzelli, *Venise et la Morée*, p.209.

281 According to Ivone Cacciavillani, *Francesco Morosini nella Vita di Antonio Arrighi* (Venice: Fiore, 1996), pp.215–216, Morosini expressed his gratitude to the senators by declaring: 'For the fourth time you have called me to the supreme command. My deep gratitude is mixed with embarrassment at the difficulty of the undertaking, with the deepest respect for the will of the City, and even more so for my profound devotion to the Fatherland. As long as I have life, it will be in the service of the Fatherland. I leave, supported more by my affection for the Republic than by the confidence I have in my abilities. I can assure you of only one thing only, that I am ready and that everything possible will be done for the greatness of the Republic, as God is my witness.'

282 Stanojević, *Montenegrina – digitalna biblioteka crnogorske kulture i nasljedja*.

1693

The opening weeks of the new year went by with negotiations between Morosini and the Senate. The *Doge* asked that a war fund of 200,000 *scudi* be financed and that Antonio Muttoni, Count of San Felice, be promoted to sergeant general of the artillery alongside other three officers.

On 1 June Morosini embarked for the Levant on board his galley. The Count of Trauttmansdorf, as *generale dello sbarco*, Lieutenant General Salzburg, Sergeant General Enea Rapetta and the newly promoted artillery sergeant-generals were also part of the expedition. Antonio Zeno had preceded them by 15 days: after being formally exonerated by his peers in mid April, he too was returning to the Morea. Morosini arrived in Corfu on 16 June, then resumed his journey and headed for Nauplia. Mocenigo, who was awaiting his arrival so he himself could return to Venice, gave him a detailed report on Negroponte. The capital of Euboea had just received reinforcements and the fortifications had been restored, and thus even for that year, the conquest of the Euboea was deferred. According to a contemporary chronicler, the Senate submitted to the *Doge* the request to take a direct action against the Ottoman capital to stop the war. The idea of forcing the Porte to peace by striking directly at the heart of the Empire was not new, as it had been considered several times during the Cretan War. Imperial and Polish delegates had suggested it in 1684 during the Treaty of Linz, but once again the enterprise was deemed too hazardous.[283]

On 24 July, after much discussion, the council of war decided to defend the Isthmus of Corinth. In his dispatches to the Senate Morosini acknowledged the strategic impasse, describing an army and fleet in a pitiful condition. Of the 11,000 infantrymen and 2,000 cavalrymen under his command, many were sick and the mounts 'unskilled'.[284] Consequently the *Doge* seemed determined not to make any attempt, which caused many Venetian patricians to whisper that this admission of weakness would damage the interests of the Republic and that the Ottomans would consider the need to make a peace less urgently.[285]

For his part Morosini set off with the oar and sail fleet in search of the enemy, after the presence of North African vessels was reported at Smyrna. The Venetian fleet sailed the Aegean Sea for the rest of the summer and early autumn, but the enemy fleet did not materialise. The *Doge* meditated on sailing to the Dardanelles, but by then the auxiliaries wanted to return to their bases and nothing could hold them back. The galleys therefore withdrew to the Morea, since Antonio Zeno had been sending warnings about the Ottoman preparations in progress at Thebes since the beginning of August. Trauttmansdorf received orders to prepare the troops encamped

---

283 Pietro Garzoni, in Biblioteca Querini Stampalia, classe IV, cod. n. 168 (424), *Diario del Senato tenuto da P. G. dal 1693 sino al 1732*, ff. 15–16. The crossing of the Dardanelles had cost the life of the brave Lazzaro Mocenigo in 1658, and since then no one had dared venture into the straits, which were defended by an extensive network of fortifications and coastal batteries.

284 ASVe, *Senato, Dispacci, Provveditori di Terra e di Mar*, b. 845, d. 35 (24 July 1693).

285 Garzoni, *Diario del Senato*, f. 18.

in Corinth for the defence of the isthmus. In mid October Liberachi left Boeotia for a reconnaissance and took the road to Corinth with 3,000 men. Morosini arrived in the Saronic Gulf with the fleet, but Liberachi withdrew and returned to Thebes before the *Doge* could land the troops in his rear to trap him.

Meanwhile, Morosini's health was deteriorating rapidly. Bladder stones were already causing the *Doge* constant pain. In October and November, despite the excruciating pain, Morosini was mainly concerned with the defence of the isthmus, requesting that the skilled engineer and gun caster Sigismondo Alberghetti be sent to erect fortifications there. The *Doge* then retired to Nauplia to rest. On 2 January, on his deathbed, he dictated his last dispatch to the Senate. Four days later he passed away. News of the *Doge*'s death reached Venice on 13 February; Marino Michiel temporarily held the command.

1694

As soon as the *Doge*'s death became known, the senators considered that a replacement for the office of captain general should be chosen as a matter of priority, and that the election of the *Doge* could wait. On 14 February Antonio Zeno was elected in the Senate and this choice was immediately ratified by the *Maggior Consiglio*. The election of the *Doge* was held on 23 February, when Silvestro Valier was appointed to succeed Morosini. With Zeno promoted to captain general, Marino Michiel was confirmed as provost general of the Morea. In April, Zeno and Michiel had an army corps of 11,259 infantrymen and 1,705 cavalrymen.[286] They met on the *galea bastarda* off Nauplia. Antonio Zeno entrusted Michiel with the task of defending the isthmus, leaving under his command about 4,000 men, namely 2,746 infantrymen, and all the cavalry available.[287] By the end of May the army and fleet were already assembled near Nauplia, ready to go on the offensive. It remained to be decided what the objective would be this time. There were four councils of war that month, and finally the senior commanders agreed to seize Chios. The island was considered an important cornerstone of the Ottoman sea routes, both for Ottoman trade and for the war fleet, which had an excellent base for navigation along the Anatolian coast. Everything was ready, or almost: the general of the landing was still Trauttmansdorf, at least until his successor arrived on the scene, for the Republic had reserved the right to replace him with a more qualified officer. The replacement was on his way, and as a result, Trauttmansdorf went on a real strike to show his dissatisfaction, causing preparations to be delayed.

Already during the previous year, the Senate had begun the selection of candidates for the rank of *generale dello sbarco*, considering Trauttmansdorf's service as unsatisfactory. In April 1694 the choice had fallen on Baron Adam Heinrich von Steinau (1650?–1712), a Saxon officer who had served in the Imperial and Bavarian armies. He was considered a specialist in sieges and warfare against the Ottomans, having served in Hungary as an artillery

---

286 ASVe, *Senato, Dispacci, Provveditori di Terra e di Mar*, b. 1129, dispatch dated 13 March 1694.
287 *Ibid.*, b. 846, d. 11 (30 July 1694).

general. Steinau's appointment suffered a setback due to the Baron's financial demands, but after further negotiations the new *generale dello sbarco* took office the following June.²⁸⁸ In late July, as soon as he arrived in Nauplia, Steinau insisted on reviewing the troops to get an idea of the situation. He was satisfied with the Italian regiments, but concerning the *oltramontani* he declared that they were of 'very poor quality' and that it was a waste of money to recruit such units, whereas the *schiavoni* were, in his opinion, much better.²⁸⁹ Steinau also took the time to visit the camp at Corinth, and gave his consent to the erection of four forts below the fortress, before asking to board one of the galleys bound for Chios. Zeno offered to take him aboard his own ship and Steinau graciously accepted.

For weeks the ships and galleys were scattered and battered by violent headwinds. The whole fleet was then able to gather at Andros and Tinos, to anchor in front of the port of Chios on the morning of 7 September. The whole day was used to prepare for the landing, which took place at dawn the next day. Supported by naval artillery, the battalions of *oltramarini*, led by *sergente maggiore* Ioannis *Zuanne* Ghica, were the first to land. The troops advanced encountering no resistance and formed up in battle order according to the instructions of Steinau, who arranged them in two lines.

Chios had an ancient citadel built by the Genoese on the edge of the sea to defend the town and the harbour. The walls were strengthened by five round towers on the sea side, and a modest ditch on the land side. The interior was almost entirely filled with narrow houses, inhabited only by Muslims or occupied by the Latin population, which still included a few Genoese merchant families. External redoubts and entrenchments guarded the entrance of the harbour and the countryside. Silihtar Hasan *Paşa*, son-in-law of the late Sultan Mehmed IV, held the command in Chios. Information gathered by Zeno indicated that the garrison numbered 1,400 men, but that more than 2,000 would be needed for its enclosure.

On 9 September the Italian infantry, supported by platoons of grenadiers, took possession of a fortified height on the edge of the suburb. Then 400 grenadiers and six battalions led by *sergente maggiore di battaglia* Luigi Citadella seized the suburb after a violent fight. The Ottomans were forced to fall back into the fortress, while Steinau ordered the digging of the circumvallation line. On 10 September the Baron studied the ground and gave the necessary orders for the deployment of the artillery. Thanks to the work of the oarsmen, led by the *provveditore al campo* Alvise Mocenigo, the artillery was operational the next day. During this siege an officer of the German regiment Degenfeld stood out for his brilliant skill in raising plans

---

288 Pinzelli, *Venise et la Morée*, pp.216–217: 'Steinau, through his representative baron von Rosen, had made an express request that the Senate considered "unusual" since he demanded that his wife should receive 4,000 *ducati* a year for life in the event of his death, a real life insurance policy that the Countess of Königsmarck had not enjoyed.'

289 ASVe, *Senato, Dispacci, Provveditori di Terra e di Mar*, b. 1129, d. 12 (8 August 1694).

108. A print of Giuseppe Maria Mitelli, dating to 1694. The war against the Ottoman Empire was marked by strong propaganda. See image commentaries for more information.

and directing attacks.[290] After four days of bombardment a breach was opened and the counterscarp destroyed. Seeing that the assault was then feasible, Steinau sent an ultimatum to the Ottoman commander. Hasan *Paşa* accepted the offer and agreed to evacuate Chios within three days, with permission to take weapons and baggage, and to then be transported to Cesme. Zeno estimated the spoils of war at 100 artillery pieces, not counting the various boats that were in the port, including three galleys from Negroponte and Rhodes, and immediately freed more than 600 Christian slaves.[291]

Antonio Zeno appointed Giustin da Riva *provveditore* of Chios. The Captain General sent an emphatic dispatch on 29 September, praising the officers who had distinguished themselves in the action: the Count of San Felice, the

---

290 Pinzelli, *Venise et la Morée*, pp.218–219. He was the Frenchman Pierre de La Salle, a name that was to be closely linked to the whole story of Venetian rule in the Morea.

291 BNM, ms. It VII 656 (7791), *Venezia e il Turco (Miscellanea)*, 'Relazione Copia di lettera scritta al Sig Capitan Santo Marchetti à Venetia, doppo l'acquisto di Scio con la relation di quanto è seguito nella presente campagna 1694, ff. 76–80. The Ottomans, around 6,000, soldiers and civilians, evacuated Chios in time. In addition to Hassan *Paşa*, there were among them remarkable personalities, such as a former mufti, and the old Ali 'Mazzamamma', *kapudan paşa* at the time of the Cretan War, Beşir *Paşa*, owner of a large part of the island, and the *beys* of Negroponte and Rhodes, who had been surprised by the siege when they had arrived in port.

Sieur de Saint Hilaire *Gentilhuomo Francese* who had just joined the Venetian army, and above all General Steinau, for whom Zeno was full of praise.

The evacuation of Chios proceeded without incident; then on 18 September the Ottoman fleet was reported near the Chios channel, between the island and the Spalmadori islands (Oinousses). It consisted of 20 sailing ships and 33 galleys. The next day Zeno met it with 19 ships, 32 galleys and four galleasses, but on his approach the Ottoman squads separated and headed for the ports of Anatolia. The *kapudan paşa* headed with the galleys to Mytilene, while the sailing ships pursued by Zeno for four days and four nights managed to take refuge in the port of Smyrna. When the Captain General arrived on the spot, the consuls of France, Holland and England forced him to retire without trying anything.

While the bulk of the troops were held back in the Archipelago, the Ottomans and their ally Limberakis Gerakaris did not remain idle. First, in August, the 'perfidious Liberachi' came to camp at Megara, and on 22 August he advanced with 1,000 men to the isthmus to observe and test the Venetian defences. His men tried to penetrate further forward, under cover of the darkness; having been spotted, they withdrew after a few skirmishes and returned to their camp, then went to Thebes, in case the Captain General came with reinforcements and cut them off from their bases. Marino Michiel then sent some bands of Albanians to harass the enemy in the region of Megara. Two hundred of them returned in mid September, claiming to have attacked some Ottoman convoys near the village of Koundoura, between Thebes and Megara, killing nearly 150 people. To prove their story, they brought back 20 prisoners and 30 beasts of burden loaded with provisions.[292] Having learned that Liberachi had abandoned his camp at Megara, Michiel sent these same irregulars to destroy the enemy posts.

For the *provveditore* of the Morea the die was cast, and the Ottomans were not going to return any time soon, especially since the rain was starting to fall, signalling the arrival of the cold season.[293] Nevertheless, for the Venetians to establish themselves in the newly conquered kingdom required a great deal of effort, since the Isthmus of Corinth remained on a permanent war footing. Irregular Ottoman bands from the Megara region frequently crossed the Isthmus and attacked the enemy outposts. Venetian forces usually repelled these raids successfully, even though the damage was serious. Among the raids of the period, mention should be made of that which occurred in autumn 1694, during which the Agios Georgios district was the epicentre of fighting between the two sides.

In Constantinople, the loss of Chios had caused great consternation. To create a diversion, *serasker* Ibrahim *Paşa* received the order to attack the Morea, and in order to facilitate the gathering of the troops he was granted full powers over all timariots of mainland Greece, and the command of the 1,000 *kapikulu sipahis* quartered in Negroponte. In early October, fires sited

---

292 Garzoni, *Diario del Senato*, f. 25, 4–9 September 1694.
293 ASVe, *Senato, Dispacci, Provveditori di Terra e di Mar*, b. 846, d. 14–16, from 23 August to 19 September.

on the hills warned that the Ottomans were already approaching the isthmus. As the Count of Trauttmansdorf was still in Nauplia waiting to find a place on a ship heading for Venice, Michiel sent him to Corinth to organise the available troops. In a council of war, Trauttmansdorf and his lieutenants agreed to advance with the cavalry and engage the Ottoman vanguard, which was expected to be tired by its march, as soon as it passed the Gerania mountains. Consequently the squadrons left the Corinthian camp on the night between 4 and 5 October and headed east, commanded by the Count of Trauttmansdorf himself. However, when he realised the significance of the enemy forces, the Count preferred to turn back and return to the entrenchments under the Acrocorinth.

On the 6 October the Ottoman force, accompanied by the irregulars of Liberachi, set out from Megara and crossed the Isthmus. The size of the attacking force was reckoned by the Venetian authorities to number 13,000.[294] A large quantity of ammunition and supplies was transported by 1,500 horses and 150 camels. This large force advanced into the interior of Corinth. After passing Agionori it encountered the Venetian force, approximately 5,000 regulars and militiamen supported by some Albanian irregulars which had taken up a position in battle order on the plain of Agios Georgios near the village of Petri, held by *sergente maggiore generale* Fabio Lanoia. This inexperienced officer engaged the approaching enemy, contravening the order to maintain the defensive. The Ottomans repulsed the bold assault and the result of the clash was a defeat for the Venetians, who lost 311 men killed or missing.[295]

Michiel was judged harshly by his peers. During the session of 30 November the *Maggior Consiglio* decided to transfer him to Vicenza as a simple captain, a sentence that was undoubtedly excessive in view of the actual situation on the terrain, since with the forces at his disposal, the *provveditore* certainly could not have done better.

Continuing raids in the Corinth region were a source of anxiety to the Venetians, who sought ways to remedy the situation. Among the plans which were drawn up, those of Steinau, which he submitted to commander-in-chief Antonio Zora at the time, stand out. Steinau was a passionate advocate of lines of defence. According to his detailed plan it was necessary to fortify all the passes of the Isthmus.[296] The purpose of these fortifications, despite not being strong, was to slow down the enemy's advance, leaving the Morea under constant threat.

---

294 ASVe, *Senato, Dispacci, Provveditori di Terra e di Mar*, b. 846, d. 17 (9 October 1694). According to an eyewitness the colonel of the Croat cavalry, Antonio Medin, fled back to the seashore, 'where he looked for a boat to leave, just to say in what confusion the soldiers found themselves'.

295 *Ibid.*, b. 1129, d. 20. In addition to the loss of human life, 200 other soldiers deserted and went over to the enemy.

296 Angeliki G. Panopoulos and Kostas G. Tsiknakis, 'Historical Research on the District of Agyos Georgios in the Second Period of the Venetian Rule', in S. Kourakou-Dragona (ed.), *Nemea Beloved Land of Zeus and Dionysos* (Athens: Foinikas Publications, 2011), p.199.

In mid October Antonio Zeno began to realise how dangerous retaining the island of Chios could be. He had heard about the defeat in the Morea, and every day received more information about the Porte's determination to reconquer Chios. No doubt it was necessary to choose between the Peloponnese and his new conquest. With growing anxiety, in the dispatches of the late autumn of 1694, the Captain General complained bitterly of a lack of money, biscuits, and at the same time painted a pitiful portrait of the situation in which he found himself, and the difficulties he encountered.[297] Once again, the strategic impasse would affect the next campaign, and with it the fate of Zeno.

1695

While land operations languished, only the fleets conducted armed confrontations, and in 1695 the Aegean Sea turned into the epicentre of war.[298] The first two battles were fought off Chios, and unexpectedly the Ottomans prevailed. From both a strategic and tactical level, both episodes clearly outlined that cooperation between sailing ships, galleys, and galleasses was too difficult. With the advent of new tactics, oared ships could not find a suitable place for their characteristics and ultimately hampered the sailing ships' actions. In the absence of wind, galleys could haul sailing ships into battle position, but it was preferable to leave the water in such conditions. In a battle north of the Spalmadori islands on 9 February 1695,[299] oared ships formed the vanguard of the fleet, and sailing vessels fought separate battles. In this decisive episode, the Venetian Commander of Sailing Ships, Girolamo Priuli, headed north with his 21-vessel squadron. Galleys hauled these ships to gain a windward advantage over the 16 Ottoman *sultana* sailing ships. The Ottomans designated four other vessels to face the five Venetian galleasses, while the Venetian galleys encountered 24 Ottoman galleys. Priuli, who had assumed his rank a few days earlier, prematurely ordered the rope to be cut, and only five ships managed to be in position. The others remained cut off for much of the fighting. This error proved fatal to Priuli when he was killed on the flagship *Stella Maris*, which exploded together with two other vessels targeted by six enemy ships. The providential arrival of another Venetian sail ship saved the two remaining units, which managed to exploit a favourable change of wind. While the sailing ships suffered a crushing defeat, the galleys fought an equally confusing, though less bloody, battle. Demoralised, some Venetian galleys escaped from the fighting. Even the galleasses obtained poor results. The galleys had to rescue them to deal with the four Ottoman sailing ships that engaged them in combat. Nevertheless, the galleasses decisively repelled the Ottoman galleys' onslaught in the battle's final phase. The Ottoman and Venetian galleys took protection in the ports of Smyrna and Chios, while the *Serenissima*'s ships remained in the Spalmadori. The Ottoman sail ships dropped anchor near the Anatolian coast, where for 10

---

297 Pinzelli, *Venise et la Morée*, p.225.

298 Candiani, 'Vele, remi e cannoni', p.152.

299 For this reason, the battle is recorded in Venetian sources as *Spalmadori di Scio*.

days Mezzomorto took care of the necessary repairs. On the Venetian side, Bartolomeo Contarini replaced Priuli as captain of the sail ships.

The second naval encounter happened 10 days later in the same channel, but south of the Spalmadori. The rough sea prevented the oared ships from participating in the battle, thus only the sail ships fought. The two fleets, deployed in line, made several attempts to cut each other's route, but neither side prevailed nor gained a windward advantage. Since the Venetians were too far away from their bases, however, they departed towards their port for repairs.

News of the double failure came to Chios, where an increasingly distressed Antonio Zeno convened a council of war on 20 February, which met on board his galley in the port of Chios. According to sources hostile to him, Zeno called for a vote to abandon the island. Pietro Querini and Carlo Pisani would have agreed, but General Steinau – who claimed that Chios was stronger than Belgrade – the captain of the galleasses Sebastiano Mocenigo and *provveditore* Giustin da Riva would have been fiercely opposed. The fortress could be defended, they said, and at worst it would be necessary to capitulate only after a long resistance. However, Antonio Zeno ordered immediate evacuation, and he was the first to walk away from this conquest which had momentarily covered him with glory. Deprived of leadership, the Venetian army never made so poor a retreat. Everyone tried to save their lives by finding a place on board, and in the chaos the transport ships *Abbondanza* and *Ricchezza* ran aground. The 280 crew and passengers fell into the hands of the Ottomans. On the island, the company of artisans, hundreds of soldiers, horses, more than 80 cannons of various calibres, food and ammunition for six months were abandoned.[300] Furthermore, the mines that should have destroyed the fortifications of Chios had not been fired. The inhabitants of the island, especially the Latins, could expect bloody reprisals, and very few were able to escape. After hastily abandoning Chios, it returned to Ottoman possession. On his arrival in Nauplia on 29 April Antonio Zeno was arrested and the Senate removed him from office, and together with the Captain General many officers were put on trial.[301]

On 12 April the government appointed the *provveditore generale di Morea* Alessandro Molin as the new captain general.[302] He had risen through the ranks by always serving in the fleet and was unfamiliar with land warfare. This limitation affected his actions to the extent that on many occasions he did not attend the councils of war to discuss field operations, delegating

---

300 Muazzo, *Guerra coi Turchi*, f. 295.

301 After this failure, 10 *sopracomiti* and one ship's captain were removed from command. Both *Provveditori all'Armata* Pietro Querini, Carlo Pisani, and 11 other governors of galleys or ships ended up in prison. Antonio Zeno died in prison a year later, before his trial. The same fate befell Pietro Querini. Mario Nani Mocenigo, *Storia della Marina Veneziana* (Venice, 1935), p.289.

302 Girolamo Dolfin, who was performing an excellent service in Dalmatia, had also been considered, but he was dismissed for mainly political reasons. As for the Morea, Agostino Sagredo, former *provveditore ordinario all'Armata*, was designated to the office. During this session the Senate also elected two new *provveditori all'Armata* who were to correct past mistakes: they were Francesco Grimani and Paolo Nani, former commissioners of the fleet.

Steinau for this task. Molin arrived in Nauplia on 12 May. Two days later the *provveditore straordinario* of the Morea Giustin da Riva sent a messenger to inform him that *serasker* Halil Ibrahim and Liberachi had just crossed the isthmus. This time the Ottomans and their ally set up camp in sight of Corinth. No doubt they were awaiting the arrival of reinforcements to be transported by the *kapudan paşa* Hüseyin Mezzomorto. Every day Da Riva sent a new message to Molin reporting on the events. On the 26 May he estimated that the enemy forces consisted of about 12,000 soldiers including 3,000 horsemen, and this time the enemy had an actual artillery train, consisting of 19 cannons drawn by pairs of oxen, and six others by horses. To transport food and ammunition, this army was accompanied by 7,000 mules and horses, and by more than 200 camels.[303]

The council of war held in Nauplia on 16 May, attended by Molin with Baron Steinau and all the fleet commanders, decided to send the cavalry to Poros while the infantry was embarked on galleys to be landed on the isthmus. On 27 May the fleet set sail for the Saronic Gulf while the convoy of the *provveditore all'Armata* Sagredo was sailing to Nauplia with new troops. Marino Michiel was left in command of Nauplia with a garrison of 800 men and a reinforcement of 1,000 new recruits, all under the command of *sergente maggiore di battaglia* Pietro Frachia. According to the *provveditore* of Tinos, the Ottoman fleet was not yet ready to set sail from the Dardanelles, allowing time to plan a manoeuvre that would stop the invasion. But the Ottomans also had their informers and Molin learned that two dragoons and a French sergeant had deserted and gone into the enemy camp. Consequently, the ongoing plan was now known to the *serasker*. The latter was camped near the Hexamilion, while Liberachi had encamped near the fortress with 1,300 of his men. From the evening of the 20 May the Ottomans prepared against a possible counter-attack, setting up several outposts to control the approaches to the isthmus. To control the coast and warn the *serasker* in case of enemy landings, cavalry squadrons patrolled the shore of the Saronic Gulf.

Alessandro Molin depended more than ever on his intelligence service. He sent spies to Constantinople and Smyrna; other informers wrote to him from Athens, Aegina and Megara, but the information was contradictory. On the morning of 3 June a privateer brig arrived in Tinos and informed him that the enemy fleet was still in Constantinople due to a lack of timber for the masts. Other information gathered during the capture of an Ottoman ship in the waters of Naxos indicated that on 11 May, 23 sail ships, 17 galleys and 18 merchantmen were about to leave the Dardanelles. At Phocaea, seven Barbary ships were waiting for three others from Algeria and Tunisia. A spy in the pay of the Porte had been discovered and arrested in Patras.[304]

Meanwhile, on 28 May, the Ottomans had suddenly raised their camp before Corinth and were heading to Nauplia through the mountain paths. Molin was openly concerned about this news, knowing that the fortifications of the Morean capital were still incomplete and especially because the Greek

---

303 ASVe, *Senato, Dispacci, Provveditori di Terra e di Mar*, b. 1130, d. 9.
304 Pinzelli, *Venise et la Morée*, p.232.

inhabitants of the region, or those who had come from Athens in 1688, seemed to him to be 'of doubtful faith'.[305] This was an important detail, especially since Ibrahim *Paşa* was spreading a declaration by the Grand Vizier calling on the Greeks to take up arms against the Republic and threatening them with all manner of evil if they did not. Every countermeasure to respond to the threat was considered. The *provveditore* of Laconia Bartolomeo Moro proposed to assemble a corps of Maniote mercenaries, and succeeded in quickly rounding up 4,000 of them. Colonel Antonio Muazzo was sent to take command, but shortly afterwards he abandoned the mission, believing that nothing could be gained from such a band of plunderers.[306]

The *consulta* decided to proceed towards the isthmus as planned. Bartolomeo Contarini headed towards Aegina with the sailing ships, while Molin at the head of the galleys advanced towards Poros. But a message from Marino Michiel changed all plans: the enemy, except Liberachi who was plundering Acadia, was in sight of Nauplia, encamped around Argos since 1 June. The *serasker* attempted to seize the castle of Larissa, defended by Giuseppe Frachia, son of the *sergente maggiore di battaglia*. The latter had managed to repel all attempts by the enemy. The *serasker* also tried to buy the loyalty of the inhabitants, but without success. The Venetian fleet therefore reversed its course, but was delayed by a headwind and only managed to land the troops in Nauplia on 5 June. The *serasker*'s army was well entrenched in the foothills of Larissa, the left wing covered by the cultivated fields of Argos and the hill of Aspis, the right wing by the marshes where the village of Nea Kios now lies, the settlement created by the exiled inhabitants of Chios in 1695.

All the information gathered from deserters or captured foragers confirmed that Ibrahim *Paşa* intended to wait for the reinforcements coming with the Ottoman fleet. Alessandro Molin realised that time was on the enemy's side, especially since the castle of Argos was also in danger of falling into enemy hands. General Steinau and *provveditore* Sagredo led the army on the field. There were 10,000 infantry and 1,200 cavalry deployed behind the remains of the ancient city of Palaiokastro (Tiryntho) three kilometres north of Nauplia, on the eastern edge of the Argos plain, in which the *sipahis* could move with ease. Even in ruins, the mighty walls still offered an appreciable shelter, since Steinau carefully assessed the best terrain in which to engage the enemy advantageously. In his report of 6 June, Alessandro Molin betrayed his concern. If the outcome of the clash had been negative, the Ottoman cavalry – far superior to the Venetian cavalry – would have easily pursued the fugitives and cut them to pieces before they reached Nauplia, but the risk

---

305 ASVe, *Senato, Dispacci, Provveditori di Terra e di Mar*, b. 847, d. 1. According to Molin, an Orthodox priest from Kalavrita named Papa Dimantin, 'a dastardly man', had gone to Constantinople six months earlier to assure the Grand Vizier that upon the arrival of the Ottoman troops, all the Greeks would rise up against the Venetians to welcome and support them. This priest apparently had a whole network in the Morea, but since then the Grand Vizier had him put in irons for lack of tangible results.

306 *Ibid.*, b. 847, d. 16 (24 September 1695). Following this reply, Moro had Muazzo arrested and imprisoned in Nauplia.

of losing Argos or seeing the arrival of the Ottoman reinforces was increasing by the hour. The troops were growing impatient and desertions were increasing. On 7 June a council of war was held in the presence of Steinau, Agostino Sagredo, *sergenti-generali* Fabio Lanoia and Valerio Castelli and other senior commanders. The result of the discussion was communicated to Molin. The generals advised the Captain General to hold the position and wait and observe the enemy's moves, even if this meant not taking advantage of a favourable situation, relying on the fact that the enemy, lacking supplies, would be forced to retreat.[307] Two days later, at the end of another council of war, the general opinion changed, believing that it was necessary to go on the assault. Alessandro Molin proposed a surprise attack by landing troops on the beaches between Lerna and Miloi, to catch the enemy by surprise. The plan was carefully prepared: to this end, two corps of *oltramarini* were to go there on 10 June before dawn. The famous engineer Sigismondo Alberghetti, who arrived in Greece together with Molin, was entrusted with the task of supervising the manoeuvres of the fleet's artillery, as the Captain General intended to use the cannons of the galleys and galleasses to target the enemy.

All preparations were in vain: that very morning of 10 June, Ibrahim *Paşa*, who had recalled Liberachi, decided to move on the assault and forced the Venetians to accept battle. Having probably exaggerated notices about the Venetians' weakness from the interrogation of deserters, the *serasker* detached two corps of 500 *sipahis* in the direction of Palaiokastro. The Baron of Steinau immediately informed Molin, demanding an explicit order before engaging in combat; the Captain General decided to go all out, and ordered the assault. All the sources relating the battle outline that Steinau had meticulously deployed the troops in order to perform a series of manoeuvres to divert the enemy. He deployed his forces in two lines. In the first he placed eight regiments of Italian and *oltramontane* infantry, four in the centre and four on the sides, alternating with six squadrons of cavalry. The second line also comprised eight regiments of infantry and two squadrons of the *Onigo* dragoon regiment. The centre of the line was empty, apart from the *oltramarine* battalions on either side. Infantrymen of the *Rossi* and *Veneto Real* regiments closed the sides of this large quadrilateral with four squadrons of *Fenicio* and *Gualtieri* dragoons. Each infantry regiment carried Frisian horses to place in front of the line. Steinau held the command, assisted by Marino Michiel who served as a volunteer, and by Agostino Sagredo. The right wing was under *sergente generale* Lanoia and *sergente maggiore di battaglia* Magnanini; the left wing being entrusted to *sergente generale* Castelli and *sergente maggiore di battaglia* Teodoro Volo; the *oltramarine* battalions in the centre were under *Zuanne* Ghica.[308] The Venetians numbered about 11,000 foot and horse. In the early afternoon the Venetian army advanced in the direction of the village of Dalamanàra, and the Ottoman

---

307 *Ibid.*, b 847, d. 3.

308 BNM, ms. It. VII n. 94 (10051), plate 94: *Dissegno d'informatione de l'ordine di battaglia dato alli Turchi, dell'Eccellentissimo Baron di Steno Generale della Serenissima Republicha di Venetia sotto il comando dell'Eccellentissimo Signor Alessandro Molin Capitan Generale da Mar... Adì 10 di Giugno 1695.*

parties tried to draw the enemy towards the artillery with a few skirmishes at a safe distance. Ibrahim *Paşa* then opened hostilities. The Ottoman infantry on the left wing attacked the enemy's right, supported by cavalry charges, but the Venetians repulsed the assaults. Steinau feinted to assault the Ottoman centre, and then turned the whole deployment to the right, intending to establish himself on the hill of Aspis and the suburb of Argos in order to engage the *serasker*'s army from an advantageous position. The latter guessed the aim of the manoeuvre and sent all his reserves against the Venetian wings, but especially against the left, where the Ottomans charged with 2,000 elite horsemen supported by 1,000 infantrymen. The assault was successful. The Frisian horses were broken and the enemy pressure disordered the *Rossi* infantry regiment and *Gualtieri* dragoons. Steinau immediately went from one wing to the other in front of the line at a gallop, sword in hand, without worrying about the danger. He rallied the fugitives and sent the Corsican infantry regiment of Nicolò Grimaldi, the *oltramarini* and the infantry regiment *Salzburg* into the fight. The close combat lasted more than an hour. *Oltramarine* commander Ghica was wounded in the foot, Colonel Giansix received a sabre blow on the shoulder, and Pietro Sagredo, son of the *provveditore* Agostino, lost an arm to a cannonball. The Ottoman assaults extended all along the front but were arrested by musket fire at short range, and in the late afternoon the Ottomans retreated to their entrenchments. Steinau continued to advance cautiously, and before nightfall the Venetians had entered the suburb of Argos without encountering opposition. At nightfall there were a few exchanges of fire from both sides, and then everything stopped; the Venetian troops bivouacked where they were and rested. Throughout the battle the small garrison of Argos had done its best to disturb the Ottomans by targeting them from behind.

When the sun came up, the Venetians were delighted to see that the enemy had disappeared. Taking advantage of the darkness, Ibrahim *Paşa* and Liberachi had retreated, abandoning nine culverins, two mortars and two falconets. The Venetians also found a large quantity of ammunition, 12 wagons and some tents, however, no food was found, a sign of the famine that had affected the Ottoman camp for days. Upon entering the camp the Venetians also discovered the horribly mutilated bodies of the deserters. Before leaving, the Ottomans had presumably taken revenge on them for having discovered incorrect information about the Venetian strength.[309] Agostino Sagredo and Alessandro Molin gave an accurate account of the losses suffered by the Republic's troops: 108 dead and 164 wounded. An estimate of Ottoman casualties is always more difficult to establish, although Venetian sources propose 700–100 dead.[310] The Battle of Argos had been a Venetian great victory; the army of the Republic had once again triumphed over the 'hereditary enemy'. No one could have known that this was the last field encounter of the war.

---

309 ASVe, *Senato, Dispacci, Provveditori di Terra e di Mar*, b. 847, en annexe de la depeche no 3: *Nota di quello che si trovò nel Campo Turchesco nella Campagna d'Argos*, and b. 1130, d 10.

310 BMC, ms. Morosini-Grimani n. 557, f. 54, *Nota de' Feriti è morti nel giorno di 10 Giugno 1695*.

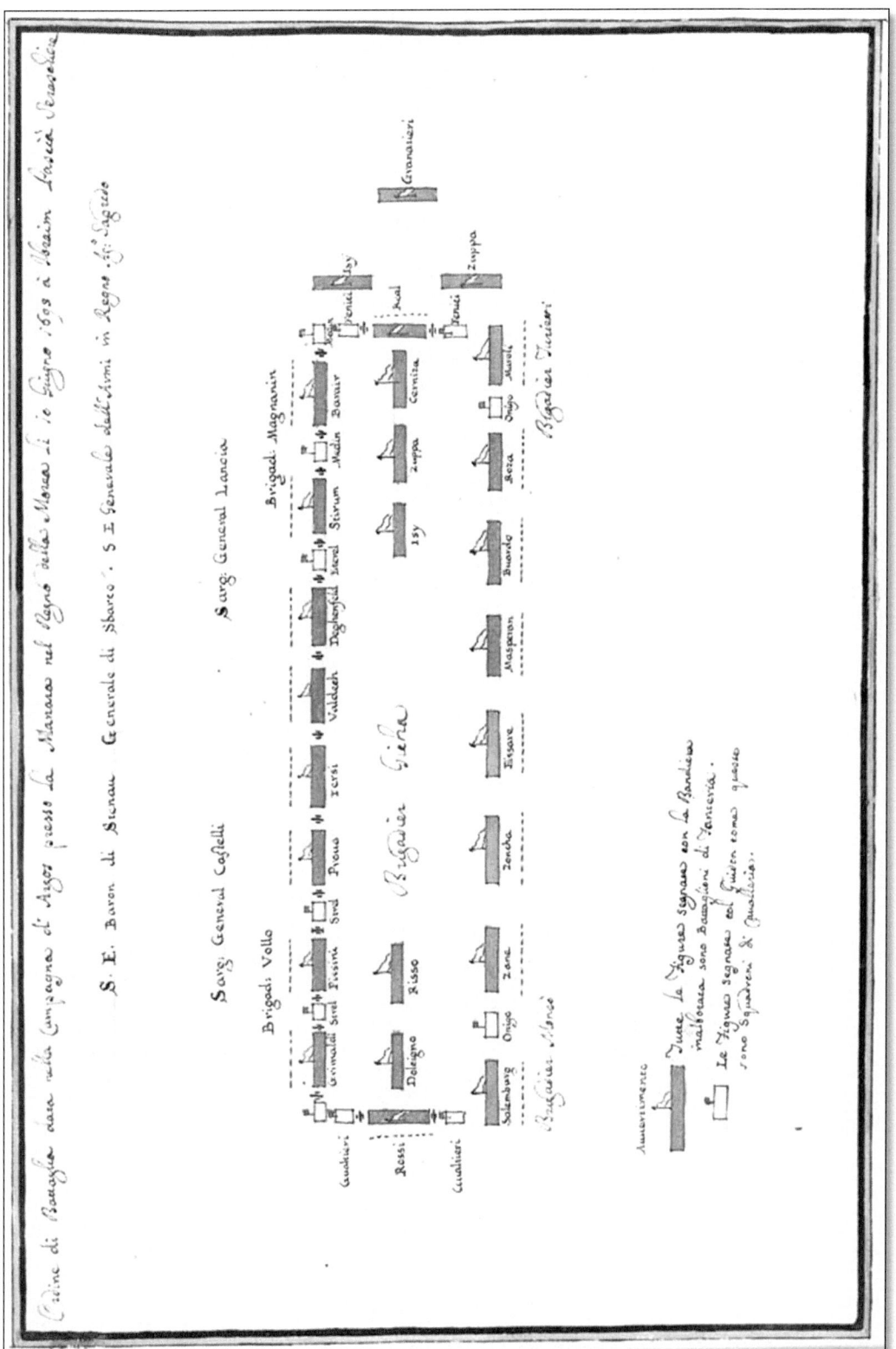

109. The Venetian order of battle at Argos, on 10 June 1695. With this victory the *Serenissima* had shown that it was still militarily competitive and could sit, with equal dignity, in the assembly of the major European powers. It mattered little if the enemy forces encountered were far inferior to those that had opposed the Emperor: what mattered was that the honour of the state, greatly diminished after Candia, had been restored.

Ten days after the victory at Argos, Agostino Sagredo proposed concluding the campaign with a raid on Thebes. The provost explained that by landing at Megara, on the coast of Boeotia, the troops were only two days' march from Thebes. The weakened Ottoman forces could not offer much resistance, and once the city was burned the *serasker* could no longer use it as a base for his raids. The Captain General was not of the same opinion, and conditioned by his training as a sailor he considered it more important to ensure Venetian supremacy on the sea. For that moment, the *provveditore straordinario* Giustin da Riva was sent to Corinth to direct the fortification works on the isthmus that had been decided years before, but had always been postponed for economic reasons. Once completed, the Republic hoped that these would become an obstacle for a future invasion of the Morea.

For a two-week period the Venetian carpenters did their best to restore the fleet to its proper condition: 7,300 infantrymen were taken on board, 250 per galleass, 110 per galley and 150 per sail ship. On 25 June the fleet left the port of Nauplia in search of the enemy. Molin left 3,300 soldiers in the Morea to defend the isthmus, not including the garrisons of Corinth and Nauplia, which numbered almost 1,000 men each.[311] Molin had set sail for Andros, but was hampered by a headwind for 15 days. When the fleet reached its destination the Captain General learned that the Ottoman fleet commanded by Hüseyin Mezzomorto was still anchored in the Dardanelles with 27 sail ships, 13 of which belonged to the North African regencies. Another seven *sultanas* were sent to Rhodes and Cyprus to collect money and troops in Egypt. Once assembled, the *kapudan pasa*'s forces would grow to 33 sailing ships and 22 galleys, while Molin had only 19 *navi pubbliche*, another four hired sail ships and four fireships; his light fleet consisted of six galleasses and 24 galleys.[312] At Andros, the Venetians learned that a few weeks earlier, 10 French ships had embarked 4,000 to 5,000 soldiers in Alexandria, were about to land these reinforcements in the Morea, when a storm prevented them from the journey. After the retreat of the *serasker*, this convoy stopped at Negroponte, before heading for Thessalonica, where the Egyptian reinforcements disembarked and finally joined the army on the Danube. On 9 August the auxiliary squadrons comprising seven Maltese and five Papal galleys joined the Venetian fleet anchored at Andros. Molin, who was aware of the enemy's movements, knew that Mezzomorto had left Mytilene for Phocaea, and from there had sailed to Chios. Apparently, the former barbarian pirate had decided to abandon his galley and board the sail ship. This was a revolution, confirming that the Ottoman navy was turning resolutely towards sail ships, something that the more conservative Venetian nobility were not yet ready to accept.

Before the end of the year, two naval battles were fought in the Aegean. The first occurred on 15 September, again in the waters south of Chios. The sea conditions prevented the oared ships from participating in the battle, but the sail squadron also suffered. The sailing vessels fought at a disadvantage

---

311 ASVe, *Senato, Dispacci, Provveditori di Terra e di Mar*, b.1130, d. 12.

312 *Ibid.*

110. The battle of Mytilene, fought on 20 September 1698, was the last naval engagement of the war against the Porte. See image commentaries for more information.

since they simultaneously protected the galleys and galleasses, which were in danger of being overwhelmed by the Ottomans. The encounter involved 27 Venetian ships against 32 Ottoman; for six hours they exchanged fire with poor results. The same pattern was repeated three days later at Mytilene; this time however, the oared ships, increasingly unable to provide support due to the rough sea, managed to take cover. This left the water open to the sailing ships under Bartolomeo Contarini. The Venetian fleet was about to prevail, when an accidental explosion destroyed the 42-gun vessel *Giovanni Battista Piccolo*. All the crew members and passengers perished: 96 sailors, 135 officers and soldiers, plus 20 members of Steinau's family, since this ship usually served as the Baron's headquarters, even though he was not on board at the time. The explosion put the Venetian fleet in disarray and caused the hired vessels to flee.[313]

The dangers that oared ships presented, and their infrequent support in the encounters of 1695, fuelled tension between the new Captain General Alessandro Molin – who in fact commanded only the light fleet – and the

---

313 Pinzelli, *Venise et la Morée*, p.242. The Venetians also lost 83 men and had 177 wounded on the rest of the fleet. Among the dead were several patricians: Angelo Bembo, Girolamo Michiel and Zuanne Zen.

commander of the sail ships Bartolomeo Contarini. Even worse, in order for Molin to effectively exercise his role as commander-in-chief, the Senate denied him permission to direct the action from a sailing vessel. Thus, the Senate's order allowed Contarini to act in full freedom and without having to worry about the oared ships. The 1695 campaign ended with these encounters. The fleet returned to Nauplia after suffering a serious blow, and the troops were distributed to winter quarters. The sea campaign's unfortunate outcome was attributed to the oared ships, and many captains were suspended or jailed, which inflicted a decisive blow to the galleys' prestige. Nonetheless, the government avoided the implied consequences of this change. Instead, it adhered to tradition and the Captain General continued to raise his insignia on the *galea bastarda*. This fuelled further internal conflict.

1696

In January 1696, Baron Steinau was back in Venice with all the senior field commanders. Apparently disappointed by the reception he received, Steinau resigned his post and withdrew to his estates in Germany.[314] The Senate, which had not remained insensitive to the loss of his family in the disaster of 18 September, had offered him 3,000 *ducats* and a gold vase as a gift, but this was little comfort. Thus, in December, the Republic took into service Count Antonio Zacco from Padua, already a senior officer in the army of the Elector of Bavaria. Zacco was appointed as a lieutenant general.[315]

With regard to the next campaign, in the late spring of 1696 the Senate addressed the main objectives to be pursued by the Captain General: the defence of the Morea, and of the other states; the reputation of the fleet; and possible damage to the enemy.[316] To accomplish these tasks, Alessandro Molin had about 14,000 men at his disposal, of which about 4,800 were camped in Corinth. But the Venetians did not fear much on this side, as the new *serasker* Miseroglu Ali could only count on 2,500 men, especially as his ally Liberachi had just deserted him and gone over to the Venetian side with his brother Georgos and many other friends.[317]

---

314 After serving with little success in the Saxon army against the Swedes, in 1706 Steinau entered the service of Venice for a second time. He was the main actor of the reorganisation of the Venetian army in 1708.

315 Contarini, *Istoria della Guerra*, vol. II, p.536.

316 ASVe, *Senato, Dispacci, Provveditori di Terra e di Mar*, b. 847, d. 40.

317 *Ibid.*, b. 1132, b. 42. Liberachi had been in secret contact with the *Serenissima* authorities since 1691 through Pietro Davich, a long-time Venetian friend, and he weighed up for a long time what he could gain by betraying the Ottomans. Seeing his star fade and no longer feeling safe with the new *serasker*, in May 1696 Liberachi laid down his conditions: that the Senate should knight him, offer him an estate with a pension, and that he should be allowed to come into the service of the Republic with 15 people from his entourage, who would also receive an endowment of land. Of course, it was also necessary to facilitate and cover his escape. All this was given to him, and having gone to Lepanto with nearly 300 of his men, two Venetian galleys came to embark him and bring to safety. In mid July Molin proudly announced to the Senate that the *bey* of Mani was on his galley.

Eager to end the fleet's accumulated series of failures, Alessandro Molin devised a plan to attack the enemy fleet in the Aegean near the island of Andros, more sheltered waters near the Venetian bases in the Peloponnese. A landing in Boeotia was planned, to accompany this naval attack in July; the landing aimed to destroy the Ottoman camp at Thebes which supported the devastating raids against Attica and Morea in 1695. Yet, news that the Ottoman fleet had been sighted within a day's sailing suspended the landing. This time only the sailing ships deployed for battle, since the galleys no longer represented the main element of the two fleets. For several weeks the Ottomans and Venetians manoeuvred off the coast of Andros and unsuccessfully tried to attack each other with the advantage of wind. Finally, Molin with six galleasses and 31 galleys, including the Papal and Maltese galleys and vessels, joined the fleet on 22 August. After another fruitless day of fighting against the *Meltemi* winds, the Captain General assumed control of the entire fleet. This prompted bitter resentment from Contarini, who had gained a windward position towards the enemy fleet the night before. The next day, however, the wind weakened and changed direction, and this allowed the Ottoman fleet to move into an advantageous position. Molin ordered the oared ships to haul the sailing vessels further north to ensure the upper hand, and further irritated Contarini by using this opportunity to change the sailing ships' formation. Although violently targeted by Ottoman ships, the galleys performed their task very well and hauled the sail ships around the head of the opposing fleet. Yet, the Ottomans reduced the distance between their ships and engaged their larger numbers against the Venetians. Perhaps due to the dispute between Molin and Contarini, the Republic's fleet failed to do the same. However, despite numerical inferiority the Venetians valiantly responded to the enemy attack, and after a few hours the Ottomans began to falter. Upon observing that the rigid tactic of the line and the lack of wind prevented other Venetian ships from engaging in battle, Molin brought the oared ships into action. The Captain General had already dispatched six galleys to the tail of the enemy formation, but unexpectedly the powerful culverins were unable to inflict serious damage to the Ottoman ships, which were effectively protected by stern guns. Indeed, the galleass had also lost its calibre advantage, the primary reason it had remained in service. Initially the galleys' action seemed to shift the battle's outcome to the Venetian side: the oared ships assaulted the disordered line of Ottoman ships and repeatedly hit the hulls with their guns. Nevertheless, these enemy vessels were more powerful than those in the Cretan War, and the galleys failed to damage these stronger hulls. After recovering the cohesion of the line, favourable winds allowed the Ottoman vessels to tack and withdraw without suffering serious damage. This battle sounded the death knell for the galleasses, and the Senate asked for the withdrawal of at least two of them. Even though the galleys had performed valiantly and came close to victory, ultimately they proved unable to prevail over the enemy.

The arrival of the cold season forced Molin to return the fleet to Nauplia, and then went to the isthmus to see the progress of the works. Agostin Sagredo also reported to him about Liberachi's failed attempt against the villages of Etolia-Acarnia. The Greek warlord tended to want to act independently, and on this occasion Molin had a serious discussion with him about his duties towards the Republic. The Senate, reluctant to trust a man as dangerous and volatile as Liberachi, ordered Molin to keep the Maniote leader close to him in order to better control his activity.[318]

1697

During the winter of 1696–1697, the Venetians were mainly concerned with improving the defences of the Acrocorinth. According to the Captain General, for the first time in years the inhabitants of the surroundings began to plant and sow again, a sign that confidence had returned.[319]

During the 1697 naval campaign the Ottoman and Venetian fleets met three times in the waters off Tenedos and Andros. However, the unsolved problems concerning the relationship between sailing ships and the light fleet came to a head again. Before the end of June the Venetians decided to perform a deep attack by dispatching the fleet in front of the Dardanelles. The fleet consisted of 25 ships, six galleasses, and 20 galleys. The Republic intended to repeat a blockade like the one in the 1650s. The Ottoman fleet, however, had anticipated them. On 5 July both fleets were sited off the coast of Bozcaada and manoeuvred into battle positions. Once again, the Ottomans and the Venetians were prepared to fight with only their sailing ships. After a few skirmishes, the onset of darkness led Bartolomeo Contarini to suspend the action: compounded by difficult synchrony between the two fleets, the bitter rivalry between Molin and the commander of sailing ships proved toxic for continued action. To make matters worse, a strong current hindered the clumsy galleys' approach to the Ottoman line. By midnight Molin asked Contarini to intercede between the galleasses, dangerously close to ending up in the midst of the Ottoman ships. The manoeuvre succeeded, but the Venetian ships lost the windward advantage. Despite efforts to maintain battle formation, on 6 July the conditions forced Contarini to move to the assault to rescue the oared ships. This encounter, known as the Battle of Lemnos, lasted 10 hours and was a confused melee. The galleys tirelessly sought to cut the route of the enemy ships, but divided the Republic's fleet in half. At the end of the battle the Ottomans captured a galley. One week later, both the Venetian squadrons met off the island of Skyros in the western Aegean. The Battle of Lemnos was the last battle of the war that witnessed oar and sail together. Molin deemed the galleasses responsible for the failure, and finally, instead of ignoring the problems that the galleys caused, they were excluded from the battle fleet. Moreover, Molin was dismissed shortly afterwards, and the *Armata Grossa* fought the last battles of the war without the presence of oared ships. The latter were sent to another theatre of war.

In the Morea, the only remarkable action was the offensive led by the newly appointed *serasker* Yuruk Paşa at the beginning of September 1697, when Agostino Sagredo, suffering from illness, was temporarily replaced by Paolo Nani. The Ottomans advanced with 6,000 men to the isthmus, but

---

318 Garzoni, *Diario del Senato*, f. 58, 16 February 1697.

319 ASVe, *Senato, Dispacci, Provveditori di Terra e di Mar*, b. 1131, d. 59.

Alessandro Molin immediately sent reinforcements. On 9 September the *Molin* and *Tenach* regiments were landed at Cenchrées by the two galleys and came to take cover behind the line. The day after, 500 Timariot *sipahis* advanced to the shore. They were caught in the crossfire of the field guns of Fort Riva and a Corfu galley anchored in the Gulf of Corinth. A first assault was attempted by 100 horsemen from Megara, who were sent out as scouts and dispersed by the heavy fire of the defenders. The second attack, a little later, was made by a corps of 3,000 *sipahis* who went into battle 'with little motivation' and were again easily repulsed. On 11 September news reached the camp that the *serasker* was withdrawing, and the next day both Venetian regiments retreated.[320] The only officer killed in these skirmishes was Lieutenant Colonel Giovanni Labar of Strel's dragoon regiment. A few days later Liberachi was betrayed by one of his relatives, who informed Vincenzo Lio, Paolo Nani's secretary, about the secret and very friendly correspondence between the former 'bey of the Mani Peninsula' and the *serasker*. It was clear that Liberachi was ready to desert again to the enemy, and thus Nani had him arrested on 6 October. The unscrupulous warlord and his brother were transferred to Italy: Liberachi to Brescia and Georgos to Palmanova, where both died in prison.

1698

In 1698 the last actions of the war took place. On the Venetian side, Captain General Alessandro Molin had reached the end of his term of office and the senators elected Giacomo Corner as his successor. In the Morea, Francesco Grimani had just replaced Agostino Sagredo as *provveditore generale* of the Morea. Peace was known to be close at hand. However, hostilities had not yet ceased. At the beginning of June, Grimani mentioned the preparations of the *serasker* who was gathering troops. The latter had just received the assistance of Captain Garbei, a deserter from the Medin Croat regiment, and the renegade Spiro, who threatened the Republic with destruction and revenge.

Giacomo Corner had left all the cavalry in Morea, 1,757 strong, which took up position in Corinth as usual, with 1,066 infantrymen under Lieutenant General Antonio Zacco, while *sergente maggiore di battaglia* Gregorio Dir led the companies of miners and artisans engaged in the works of fortification of the Corinthian isthmus. The Ottomans did not remain inactive. On 20 July the *serasker* and the renegade Spiro left their encampments in Boeotia and reached the isthmus two days later, with troops estimated at only 1,600 men. This raid was primarily intended to reconnoitre the Venetian defences, as in the previous year, and if possible take prisoners, but the alert had been given in time. The inhabitants of the surrounding villages had been able to take refuge behind the Corinthian line.

Meanwhile, on 13 June, the Venetian fleet set sail for the northern Aegean, intending to confront the enemy ships as soon as they left the Dardanelles.

---

320 Garzoni, *Istoria della Repubblica di Venezia*, vol. I, pp.619–620; Contarini, *Istoria della Guerra*, vol. II, pp.604–605; ASVe, *Senato, Dispacci, Provveditori di Terra e di Mar*, b. 848, d. 60 (12 September 1697).

Commander of the sailing fleet Daniele Dolfin led his 27 sail ships for this final campaign. Having reached Lemnos on 26 June, he disembarked a few men on the island and sacked the defenceless villages to force Mezzomorto to accept the challenge. But it was in vain; Dolfin then went to Imbros where he waited for the next few weeks. On 27 August, the Venetian squadron sailed to Thasos, and after days of patrolling, the two fleets finally met on 1 September off Andros. The battle was a Venetian tactical success, but Dolfin's ship, the *Rizzo d'Oro*, which had been rammed by the *San Lorenzo Giustinian* because of a wrong manoeuvre, was almost lost.[321] The last clash, fought on 20 September near Mytilene, ended with another modest tactical success for the Venetians.

The following winter there was complete calm in Greece, no events to report, no enemy troop movements for the first time in 15 years. As a sign that peace was coming, an Ottoman merchant came to Corinth to sell his goods. The local authorities, a little taken aback, had him quarantined for safety.[322]

Venice's representative signed the Treaty of Carlowitz on 26 January 1699, by which the Peloponnese was incorporated formally into the Venetian state, but until 1701 further negotiations continued to establish the border in Dalmatia and Albania. Efforts were made by the new occupiers to organise the conquered territories more effectively, and to exploit their productivity. However, the international environment was becoming unfavourable to Venice's geostrategy.

The Second Waldensian War, 1686–1689

In 1664 the Waldensians had returned to their homes in Piedmont, but secretly formed a clandestine resistance force financed with money from the 'Protestant International' that had mobilised in their support. Concerns now came from France, which had inaugurated a wave of persecution against the Protestants. In 1685 Louis XIV revoked the Edict of Nantes and initiated a persecution against French Protestants, including the Waldensians of Pinerolo, who were forcibly converted to Catholicism. Pressured by Louis XIV and the Pope, on 31 January 1686 Duke Vittorio Amedeo decreed the prohibition of the Reformed religion in all of Savoy-Piedmont. Waldensians under pastor Henri Arnaud (1641–1721) resisted the ban, and on 22 April a new war broke out.

In the spring of 1686, under the watchful eye of the French ambassador in Turin, who came to the field to personally witness the military operations, the French and Savoyard armies competed with each other to show their efficiency. Louis XIV, for the occasion, assigned the command of the troops to Marshal de Catinat. Vittorio Amedeo responded by fielding the best of his army, leaving only a single infantry regiment and the village militia to

---

321 Nani Mocenigo, *Storia della Marina Veneziana*, pp.302–205.
322 Pinzelli, *Venise et la Morée*, p.262.

garrison Turin and the rest of the country. The Savoy troops led the way with light field artillery, which they took to even the most inaccessible areas, and by making extensive use of the grenadiers recently introduced into the infantry regiments. On 17 April 1686 they found themselves deployed at Bricherasio, where the Duke had established his headquarters. He had with him as 'adjutant' Carlo Emilio San Martino Marquis of Parella. In the advance through the Val Pellice, which began on 23 April, the column even included the *Gardie del Corpo*, dismounted, assigned with the *Monferrato* infantry regiment to the right column under the orders of Don Gabriele di Savoia.

The Waldensians had about 3,000 rebel soldiers at their disposal, which sought to protect around 12,000 non-combatant civilians. However, the Waldensians fell into the error of relying too much on the successes of the previous war, and closed themselves into a sort of mental Maginot line that prevented them from developing a strategy to respond to the changes that had occurred in the European armies, including those of France and Savoy.[323] The Waldensians were unable to oppose an effective resistance and were quickly defeated. The surviving leaders of the 1655–1664 resistance were either too old, or were in exile abroad. The guerrilla tactics devised 30 years earlier were not entirely ineffective, but the Waldensians lacked an adequate overall defence plan and coordination in the face of a much more powerful enemy than those they had fought in the past. They were no longer the mercenary and peasant soldiers who had faced the Waldensians in 1664, but troops mainly composed of regiments of ordinance, grenadiers, dragoons and artillerymen, given modern training and capable of developing a continuous volume of fire. Consequently, the Second Waldensian War took place in a different context than before.

The ducal troops numbered around 4,500 men, supported by thousands of local militiamen and 4,000 French regulars under general Nicolas Catinat. In May, Vittorio Amedeo marched with his forces towards the Val Pellice, while the French troops flanked the Waldensians from the French fortress of Pinerolo. All organised resistance was crushed within three days. About 2,000 Waldensians were killed in the encounters or massacred afterwards, and almost all the population in the Val Pellice was taken prisoner and abducted to Turin. Some 3,000 survivors, mostly children, were forcibly converted to Catholicism through baptism and placed in Catholic homes. The remainder of about 8,500 prisoners were imprisoned in the Piedmontese fortresses. Only 3,841 people had survived by the time they were released

111. Portrait of Henri Arnaud (1643–1721). See image commentaries for more information.

---

323 Borello, *I valdesi in armi*, p.45.

in March 1687. Between 1685 and 1687, about one third of the Waldensian population fled to the Grisons, Switzerland or Germany. A small number of rebels continued fighting until June, and raids continued until November. The valleys, which were only inhabited by about 2,500 pre-1686 converts to Catholicism, were resettled by Catholic subjects from elsewhere as part of a government colonisation programme to confiscate and resell the Waldensian properties. In July 1686 the Duke promised to release the prisoners, and to return the forcibly Catholicised children back to their Waldensian families abroad. On 3 January 1687, the released prisoners were granted permission to leave the country, and 2,565 reached Geneva.[324] Many Waldensian refugees resided in Brandenburg, Württemberg, Hessen Kassel and the Palatinate from 1687 to 1689.[325] Two Waldensian attempts to penetrate into Piedmont occurred in 1687 and 1688, but failed.

When the War of the League of Augsburg (the 'Nine Years' War') broke out in September 1688, Vittorio Amedeo gradually took the side of the League, although he would not formally accede to the coalition until June 1690. Due to his intentions to ally himself with the Protestant-dominated Dutch Republic and England, which was undergoing the Dutch Protestant-led 'Glorious Revolution', he was put under pressure to cease his persecutions of his Protestant subjects. However, there was no need to reach a final agreement between the Waldensians and the Duke. During the summer of 1689 a fresh development added to the mounting tension between Vittorio Amedeo and Louis XIV. In August, Arnaud raised in Geneva a corps of about 1,000 exiled Waldensians and French Huguenots, with the aim of returning home and regaining possession of their valley. On the night of 26–27 August this force left Geneva on an epic march that would become known as the *Glorieuse Rentrée*. Arnaud and his men traversed Savoy, crossed the Mont-Cénis, and having avoided annihilation by Savoy troops at Giaglione di Susa, and despite the loss of many of their number during the journey, defeated at Salbertrand a French infantry contingent blocking their path. Then, by forced marches they regained their native valleys on 6 September. Here they ravaged the farms of the new colonists and ambushed French and Savoyard patrols, spreading alarm far and wide. The surprise attack, even though it involved no more than 1,000 of men, was profoundly disquieting to Louis XIV. Furthermore, a force of armed and defiant Protestants close to the border of Dauphiné might well stir the large Huguenot population there into revolt; all through the summer of 1689 the French Protestants were in ferment, awaiting an allied invasion and nurturing hopes of deliverance. The return of the Waldensians might well provide the spark to ignite this volatile mass, and in fact the next autumn a few bands from the valley crossed the mountains into Dauphiné in an ill-fated attempt to foment insurrection. It was therefore essential for Louis XIV to crush the Waldensians at once, before they could endanger the security of his southeastern frontier and

---

324 Lovisa Barbro, *Italienische Waldenser und das protestantische Deutschland 1655 bis 1689* (Göttingen: Vandenhoeck & Ruprecht, 1994), pp.30–31.

325 *Ibid.*

its communication with Pinerolo, now of prime importance to the French King in view of Vittorio Amedeo's wavering loyalty. Louis XIV accordingly demanded that the latter cooperate with him in destroying Arnaud's band. At first the Duke seemed ready to comply, and a Savoyard contingent under the Marquis of Parella with some French troops engaged the Waldensians from their advanced positions in the Val Pellice and the Val Luserna. The enemy offensive hemmed Arnaud and his followers into the inaccessible mountain stronghold at La Balziglia, in the valley of Massello, where in the spring of 1690, they repulsed a siege. Now, reduced to less than half of their original force, they were finally reintegrated into their former possessions thanks to the change of alliance of the Duke of Savoy, who meanwhile had adhered to the League of Augsburg.[326]

---

326 Having reconciled the Waldensians with the Duke, the valiant 'pastor-colonel' Henri Arnaud was a Savoy-Piedmont secret agent at the League of Augsburg; but with Vittorio Amedeo's rapprochement with Louis XIV, he organised the exodus of French refugees to Baden, Hesse and Württemberg and in 1699 became pastor of the Schönenberg community in Württemberg.

Appendix I

Imperial Fiefdoms, Independent Lordships and Republics in Italy (1659–1690)

In Lombardy and Piedmont

1. Marquisate of Fortunago, Gravanago, Montepicco, Sant'Eusebio, Stefanago, Staghiglione, ruled by Malaspina local branch
2. Marquisate of Godiasco, Pianocozzo, Trebbiano ruled in condominium by Malaspina' branch of Oramala, Valverde and Sant'Albano, Malaspina-Piumesana, and Counts Adda and Ghislieri
3. Marquisate of Varzi, ruled by Sforza di Santafiora
4. Marquisate of Sagliano, ruled by Malaspina local branch
5. Marquisate of Valverde e Sant'Albano, ruled by Malaspina local branch
6. Marquisate of Santa Margherita di Staffora, ruled by Malaspina local branch
7. Marquisate of Pregola, ruled by Malaspina local branch
8. Marquisate of Pregola-Campi, ruled by Malaspina local branch
9. Marquisate of Orezzoli-Volpedo, ruled by Malaspina local branch
10. Marquisate of Fabbrica-Curone, ruled by Malaspina local branch
11. Marquisate of Bosmenso-Monteforte, ruled by Malaspina local branch
12. Marquisate of Piumesana, ruled by Malaspina local branch
13. Marquisate of Montemarzino, ruled by Malaspina local branch
14. Marquisate of Cisterna (principality by 1670), ruled by Acerbo, and after 1665 by Dal Pozzo
15. Principality of Masserano, ruled by Ferreri as the pope's vassals
16. Lordship of Montesegale and Castignoli, ruled by Gerolamo-Gambarana
17. County of Desana, ruled by Tizzoni di Vercelli (annexed to Savoy-Piedmont in 1693)
18. Marquisate of Gazzuolo-Dosolo-Pomponasco, ruled by Ippoliti di Gazzuolo
19. Marquisate of Gazoldo, ruled by Ippoliti of Gazoldo
20. Marquisate of Vescovato, ruled by Gonzaga local branch
21. Lordship of Castellaro, ruled by the Prince-Bishop of Trento
22. Lordships of Limonta, Campione and Civenna, ruled by the Abbot of

APPENDIX I

Sant'Ambrogio (Milan)
23. Lordship of Valsolda, ruled by the Archbishop of Milan
24. County of Maccagno, ruled by Borromeo-Arese
25. Barony of Retegno and Bettola, ruled by Trivulzio
26. Principality of Sabbioneta and Bozzolo, ruled by Gonzaga local branch
27. Principality of Castiglione and Solferino, ruled by Gonzaga local branch (created in 1675)
28. County of Novellara and Bagnolo, ruled by Gonzaga local branch
29. Duchy of Guastalla, ruled by Gonzaga local Branch
30. Princedom of Soragna, ruled by Meli-Lupi
31. State of Landi, ruled by Doria-Landi (annexed in 1682 by Parma and Piacenza)
32. Marquisate of Zibello, ruled by Pallavicino local branch
33. Marquisate of San Secondo, ruled by Rossi di San Secondo
34. County of Mezzano del Vescovo, ruled by the Bishop of Parma
35. Duchy of Mirandola and Concordia, ruled by Pico
36. Marquisate of Rolo, ruled by Sessi
37. Princedom of San Martino in Rio, ruled by Este local Branch

In Liguria
38. Marquisate of Torriglia, ruled by Dora-Landi
39. Marquisate of Campo Freddo, ruled by Spinola
40. Marquisate of Savignone and Crocefieschi, ruled by Fieschi di Lavagna
41. Marquisate of Bobbio, ruled by Dal Verme
42. Marquisate of Montemarzino and Montegioco, ruled by Spinola de los Balbades
43. Marquisate of Borgo Adorno and Cantalupo, ruled by Botta Adorno
44. Marquisate of Orezzoli, ruled by Malaspina
45. Marquisate of Cabella, Fontanarossa and Cremonte, ruled by Spinola-Pallavicini
46. Marquisate of Ottone, Garbagna, Vargo and Garrega, ruled by Doria
47. Marquisate of Gorreto and Campi, ruled by Centurione-Scotto
48. Marquisate of Grondona, ruled by Malaspina
49. Marquisate of Mongiardino e Vergagni, ruled in condominium by Fieschi and Spinola di Luccoli
50. Marquisate of Roccaforte, Montessoro, Rocchetta and Castel di Pietra, ruled by Spinola
51. Marquisate of Pregola and Zerba, ruled by Malaspina local branches and Centurione Scotto
52. Marquisate of Dolceacqua, ruled by Doria local branch
53. Marquisate of Balestrino, ruled by Del Carretto di Balestrino
54. Principality of Monaco, ruled by Grimaldi
55. Lordship of Rezzoaglio, ruled by Della Cella
56. Lordship of Bagnaria, ruled by Doria
57. Lordship of Stellanello, ruled by Divizia
58. County of Loano, ruled by Doria
59. County of Tagliolo, ruled by Gentile
60. Republic of Noli

In Lunigiana and Lucca
61. Marquisate of Fosdinovo, ruled by Malaspina local branch
62. Marquisate of Mulazzo, ruled alternatively by Malaspina del Castello and Malaspina del Palazzo
63. Marquisate of Castegnetoli, ruled by Orsini
64. Marquisate of Aulla and Podenzana, ruled by Centurione
65. Marquisate of Olivola, ruled by Malaspina local branch
66. Marquisate of Podenzana, ruled by Malaspina local branch
67. Marquisate of Licciana-Nardi, ruled by Malaspina local branches
68. Marquisate of Villafranca, ruled by Malaspina local branches
69. Marquisate of Castevoli, ruled by Malaspina local branch, inherited in 1678 by Malaspina di Villafranca
70. Marquisate of Suvero, ruled by Malaspina local branches
71. Marquisate of Ponte Bosio, ruled by Malaspina local branch
72. County-Pieve of Piazza al Serchio, ruled by the Bishop of Lucca
73. Jura of Massarosa, ruled by the canons of Lucca's cathedral

In Tuscany
74. Principality of Piombino, ruled by Buoncompagni-Lodovisi
75. Marquisate of Santa Maria del Monte, ruled by Bourbon-Del Monte
76. Marquisate of Petrella and Sorbello, ruled by Bourbon-Del Monte
77. County of Montauto, ruled by Barbolani di Montauto
78. County of Chitignano, ruled by Ubertini (under the protectorate of the Grand Duchy of Tuscany)
79. County of Elci, ruled by Pannocchieschi
80. County of Carpegna and Pincipality of Scavolino, ruled by Della Rovere local branch
81. County of Vernio, ruled by Bard

In the Papal States
82. Republic of Cospaia
83. Republic of San Marino

In the Kingdom of Naples
84. Republic of Senarica
85. Duchy of Benevento and Pontecorvo, ruled by the pope

Appendix II

Regiments and Tabular Data

Savoy-Piedmont Regiments (1659-1690)

Id.	Year	Colonel or Denomination	Engagements	History	Uniforms
SI-1	1619	**Cheynez**, 1630 **Boydanid**, 1645 Carlo Emanuele Giacinto di Simiana Marquis of Pianezza; 1649 Carlo Giovanni Battista di Simiana Marquis di Livorno di Piemonte, 1674 Coudray (**Monferrato** in 1664)	Campaigns against the Waldensian (1655–53) Chiappa, Rezzo, Garlenda, Castelvecchio, Ovada (1672)	Disbanded in 1798; reformed as *Reggimento Monferrato* in 1814	(1671) Private: black headgear, red cravat, grey coat and breeches, red stockings, brass buttons[1] (1680) Private: black headgear, white cravat, light grey coat with blue cuffs and lining, red breeches and stockings, brass buttons[2] (1687) Private: black headgear with yellow edge, white cravat, light grey coat with blue cuffs and lining, red breeches and stockings, brass buttons[3] Drummer: black headgear with yellow edge, white cravat, red coat with blue cuffs and lining, red breeches and stockings, brass buttons.
SI-2	1621?	(1654) Françoise de Mesmes-Marolles Count of Chiavazza, 1665 Carlo Emilio San Martino Marquis of Parella (*Regiment aux Gardes* or **Guardia di Sua Altezza Reale**)	Campaigns against the Waldensian (1655–63) Pieve di Teco, Chiappa, Rezzo, Garlenda Castelvecchio, Ovada (1672)	Became *Gardes à pied* in 1659 and *Guardie del Re di Sardegna* in 1715	(1670) Private: black headgear, white cravat, medium blue coat faced and lined of red, red breeches and stockings; white metal buttons[4] (1680) Private: black headgear, white cravat, medium blue coat faced and lined with red, red breeches and stockings; white metal buttons[5] (1690) Private: black headgear with white edge, white cravat, medium blue coat faced and lined with red, red breeches and stockings; white metal buttons[6]

1 ASTo, *Materie Militari, Ordini militari dell'Altezza Reale di Carlo Emanuele II dall'anno 1648 sin all'anno 1674*, m. 3, 8-1671.
2 BRT, *Manoscritto Militare*, Ms. 134.
3 ASTo, *Camerale, Piemonte, Contratti* (1688), *Monferrato*.
4 ASTo, *Materie Militari, Ordini militari dell'Altezza Reale di Carlo Emanuele I*, *dall'anno 1648 sin all'anno 1674*, m. 3, 6-1670.
5 BRT, *Manoscritto Militare*, Ms. 134.
6 ASTo, *Camerale, Piemonte, Contratti* (1690), *Estat d'un habit de soldat selon lequel nous avons habillé en l'année 1690, seicents vint soldats du Regiment de Gardes de S.A.R.*

Id.	Year	Colonel or Denomination	Engagements	History	Uniforms
SI-3	1624	Fleury (French), 1631 Françoise de Mesmes-Marolles Count of Chiavazza (French), 1654 Pierre Millet de Challes (French), 1659 Francesco Sigismondo Marquis d'Este, 1670 Francesco Provana Count of Leyni di Piossasco (**Savoia di Sua Altezza Reale** in 1664)	Rezzo, Testico, Oneglia (1672)	Disbanded in 1798; reformed as *Reggimento Savoia* in 1814	(1671) Private: black headgear, red cravat, grey coat, blue breeches and stockings, brass buttons[7] (1680) Private: black headgear, white cravat, light grey coat with blue cuffs, blue breeches and stockings, white metal buttons[8] (1687) Private: black headgear with yellow edge, white cravat, light grey coat with blue cuffs and lining, blue breeches and stockings, brass buttons[9]
SI-4	1636	Carlo Catalano-Alfieri, 1664 Carlo Emanuele Alfieri Count of Magliano, 1672? Marquis of Saluzzo di Valgragna, 1685? Baldassarre Pobel de Saint'Amand de la Pierre (**Piemontese di Sua Altezza Reale** in 1641, **Piemonte di Sua Altezza Reale** in 1664)	Chiappa, Garlenda, Castelvecchio, Ovada (1672) Oudenarde (1674)	Ceded to France from 1673 to 1678	(1671) Private: black headgear, red cravat, grey coat and breeches, red stockings, white metal buttons[10] (1680) Private: black headgear, white cravat, light grey coat with red cuffs, red breeches and stockings, white metal buttons[11] (1687) Private: black headgear with white edge, white cravat light grey coat with red cuffs and lining, red breeches and stockings, white metal buttons[12]
SI-5	1636	François d'Havard de Senantes (French), 1651 count of Challant (Savoy), 1660? Senantes, 1685 Francesco Provana Count of Leyni di Piossasco (**Aosta di Sua Altezza Reale** in 1664)		Ceded to France in 1689	(1671) Private: black headgear, red cravat, grey coat and breeches, red stockings, white metal buttons[13] (1680) Private: black headgear, white cravat, light grey coat with crimson red cuffs, crimson red breeches and stockings, white metal buttons[14] (1687) Private: black headgear with yellow edge, white cravat light grey coat with red crimson cuffs and lining, crimson red breeches and stockings, white metal buttons[15]
SI-6	1637	Reynero		Disbanded in 1667	

7 ASTo, *Materie Militari, Ordini militari dell'Altezza Reale di Carlo Emanuele II dall'anno 1648 sin all'anno 1674*, m. 3, 8-1671.
8 BRT, *Manoscritto Militare*, Ms. 134.
9 ASTo, *Camerale, Piemonte, Contratti* (1687), *Savoie*.
10 ASTo, *Materie Militari, Ordini militari dell'Altezza Reale di Carlo Emanuele II dall'anno 1648 sin all'anno 1674*, m. 3, 8-1671.
11 BRT, *Manoscritto Militare*, Ms. 134.
12 ASTo, *Camerale, Piemonte, Contratti* (1687), *Piémont*.
13 ASTo, *Materie Militari, Ordini militari dell'Altezza Reale di Carlo Emanuele II dall'anno 1648 sin all'anno 1674*, m. 3, 8-1671.
14 BRT, *Manoscritto Militare*, Ms. 134.
15 ASTo, *Camerale, Piemonte, Contratti* (1687), *Aoste*.

APPENDIX II

Id.	Year	Colonel or Denomination	Engagements	History	Uniforms
SI-7	1643	1649 Carlo Lodovico d'Agliè, Marquis of **San Damiano**, 1659 François Joseph de Mesmes-Marolles Count of Chiavazza, 1662 François de Willecardel Marquis de Fleury of Triviero-Martigliengo, 1665 Carlo Emilio San Martino, Marquis of Parella (**Nizza di Sua Altezza Reale** in 1664) **Nice**	Campaigns against the Waldensian (1655–63) Testico, Col di Nava. Penna (1672)	Ceded to France in 1689	(1671) Private: black headgear, red cravat, grey coat and breeches, red stockings, white metal buttons[16] (1680) Private: black headgear, white cravat, light grey coat with red cuffs, red breeches and stockings, white metal buttons[17] (1687) Private: black headgear with white edge, white cravat light grey coat with crimson red cuffs and lining, crimson red breeches and stockings, white metal buttons[18]
SI-8	1649	La Loubière, 1661 Coudray		Disbanded in 1664	
SI-9	1654	Badant (German)		Licensed in 1659	
SI-10	1653	Bellino		Disbanded in 1660	
SI-11	1655	Giovanni Bartolomeo Malingri di Bagnolo	Campaigns against the Waldensian (1655–63)	Disbanded in 1659?	
SI-12	1658	Ghimitieres	Dalmatia and Crete (1659–60)	Disbanded in 1660	
SI-13	1659	Kalbermatten (Valais)		Licensed in 1660	
SI-14	1660	Ayazza, 1665 La Cerverie	Crete (1660-69)	Disbanded in 1670	
SI-15	1660	Malabayla, 1660 Mezerac, 1662 **Arborio**	Crete (1660-69)	Disbanded in 1670	
SI-16	1660	Dogliani (1660) **Masino**	Crete (1660-61)	Disbanded in 1661	
SI-17	1667	Cesare Badat, 1674 Saint-Giles de Caderousse, 1690 Arduino Tana (Crocebianca, in 1680 **Crocebianca di Sua Altezza Reale**)	Col di Nava, Camporosso, Penna (1672)	Became *Piemonte* in 1710	(1671) Private: black headgear, red cravat, grey coat and breeches, red stockings, white metal buttons[19] (1680) Private: black headgear, white cravat, light grey coat with red cuffs, red breeches and stockings, white metal buttons[20] (1687) Private: black headgear with white edge, white cravat light grey coat with crimson red cuffs and lining, crimson red breeches and stockings, white metal buttons[21]
SI-18	1667	Carlo Filiberto **d'Este**, Marquis of Dronero		Disbanded in 1668	
SI-19	1668	Vittorio Amedeo di Savoia **Principe di Piemonte**		Disbanded in 1672	
SI-20	1672	La Marina		Ceded to France in 1672	

16 ASTo, *Materie Militari, Ordini militari dell'Altezza Reale di Carlo Emanuele II dall'anno 1648 sin all'anno 1674*, m. 3, 8-1671.
17 BRT, *Manoscritto Militare*, Ms. 134.
18 ASTo, *Camerale, Piemonte, Contratti* (1687), *Nice*.
19 ASTo, *Materie Militari, Ordini militari dell'Altezza Reale di Carlo Emanuele II dall'anno 1648 sin all'anno 1674*, m. 3, 8-1671.
20 BRT, *Manoscritto Militare*, Ms. 134.
21 ASTo, *Camerale, Piemonte, Contratti* (1688), *Crocebianca*.

Id.	Year	Colonel or Denomination	Engagements	History	Uniforms
SI-21	1672	Eugéne de Géneve Marquis de Lullin, 1675 Marquis of **Bagnasco**, 1678 Count of Masino, 1683 Amedeo del Pozzo Marquis of Voghera and Prince of Cisterna (**Saluzzo** in 1680)		Disbanded in 1798	(1680) Private: black headgear, white cravat, light grey coat, cuffs and lining, light grey breeches and stockings, white metal buttons[22] (1687) Private: black headgear with white edge, white cravat, light grey coat, cuffs and lining, light grey breeches and stockings, white metal buttons[23]
SI-22	1672	San Severino	Ovada (1672)	Disbanded in 1674	
SI-23	1672	San Michele	Ovada (1672)	Disbanded in 1674	
SI-24	1672	Chablais	Ovada (1672)	Disbanded in 1674	
SI-25	1672	Val d'Isère		Disbanded in 1674	
SI-26	1683	Francesco Provana Count of Leyni di Piossasco, 1685? Carlo Francesco Aldobrandino-Biandate Count d'Ales (**La Marina**)		Ceded to France in 1689	(1683) Private: black headgear, white cravat, light grey coat with green cuffs, green breeches and stockings, white metal buttons[24]
SI-27	1687	Gaspare Roussillon Count of Bernezzo or Chablais		Disbanded in 1703	
SI-28	1690	Cavalier Cerruto (**Mondovi**)		Disbanded in 1694	
SI-29	1690	Giuseppe Filiberto Costa Count de la Trinité (**Fucilieri di Sua Altezza Reale**)		Became *Aosta* in 1774	(1690) Private: black headgear, white cravat, light grey coat with red cuffs, red breeches and stockings, white metal buttons[25]
SC-1	1671	Vittorio Amedeo of Savoy Prince of Piedmont, **Prince de Piémont**		Ceded to France in 1672	(1671) Private: black headgear, blue coat with red cuffs[26]
SC-2	1683	Don Gabriele di Savoia Marquis of Riva (cuirassiers), or **Piemonte Corazze**		Disbanded in 1685	(1680) Private: buff coat, blue coat[27]

22 BRT, *Manoscritto Militare*, Ms. 134.
23 ASTo, *Camerale, Piemonte* (1688), *Saluzzo*.
24 BRT, *Manoscritto Militare*, Ms. 134.
25 ASTo, *Camerale, Piemonte, Contratti* (1690), *Fucilieri*.
26 BRT, *Manoscritto Militare*, Ms. 134.
27 ASTo, *Materie Ecclesiastiche, Cat. I, Negoziati*, 7 March 1685.

APPENDIX II

Cavalry and Dragoons

Id.	Year	Colonel or Denomination	Engagements	History	Uniforms
SD-1	1683	Giuseppe Maria Ignazio Augusto Manfredo Gerolamo Scaglia Count of La Verrua, 1689 Bonifacio Antonio Solaro Count of Macello, or **Sua Altezza Reale** (dragoons)		Merged with *Genevois* dragoons in 1689	(1690) Private: red slouch cap, red coat with blue cuffs, red breeches, white metal buttons, white lanyards[28]
SD-2	1683	Gaspare Roussillon Count of Bernezzo or **Madama Reale** (dragoons)		Disbanded in 1685	(1685) Private: black headgear, blue coat with red cuffs.[29]
SD-3	1689	Louis Deschamps, Marquis of **Chaumont**, or **Genevois** (dragoons)		Became *Dragoni di Sua Altezza Reale* in 1740	(1690) Private: red slouch cap, green coat with red cuffs, green breeches, white metal buttons, withe lanyards.[30]
SD-4	1690	Bonifacio Antonio Solaro, Count of Macello or **Piemonte** (dragoons)		Became *Nizza Cavalleria* in 1848	Private (1690) red slouch cap; yellow coat with black cuffs, red breeches, white metal buttons, withe lanyards, red cloak.[31]

Captain of the Duke of Savoy's company of the Cent Suisses
1648-1665   Ludwig Am Rhyn (from Lucerne)
1665-1671   Jost Am Rhyn (brother of Ludwig, frcm Lucerne)
1671-1700   Johann Anton Schmid (from Uri)
Source: Emmanuel May de Romainmôtier, *Histoire militaire de la Suisse* (Berne, 1772)

1654-1665   Ludwig Dupré (from Freiburg); second in command Jost Am Rhyn (Lucerne)
1665-1676   Jost Am Rhyn
1676-1700   (?)   Johann Anton Schmid (from Uri)
Source: Guillaume de Kalbermatten's manuscript (Valais State Achive, Suisse)

---

28 BRT, *Manoscritto Militare*, Ms. 134.
29 IASTo, *Materie Ecclesiastiche*, Cat. I, *Negoziati*, 7 March 1685.
30 BRT, *Manoscritto Militare*, Ms. 134.
31 ASTo, *Camerale Piemonte, Memoriale a capi con risposte di S.A.R. per la levata di un reggimento di Dragoni, proposto dal Conte di Macello* (1690).

Venetian Infantry Regiments (1686–1690)

Id.	Year	Colonel or Denomination	Nationality	History
VI-1	1686	Maraba	Italian	Disbanded in 1687
VI-2	1686	Geremia	Italian	Disbanded in 1687
VI-3	1686	Graziani	Italian	Disbanded in 1687
VI-4	1686	Corbon, 1687 Magnaini	Italian	Disbanded in 1687
VI-5	1686	Catti	Italian	Disbanded in 1687
VI-6	1686	Corponese	Italian	Disbanded in 1695
VI-7	1686	Scipione Vespasiano Giovine	Italian (Naples)	Disbanded in 1695?
VI-8	1686	Gabrieli	*Oltramontane*	Disbanded in 1687
VI-9	1686	Bartolomeo Manganoni	*Oltramontane*	Reformed as Italian in 1695; mixed in 1698; disbanded in 1702
VI-10	1686	Maron	French	Disbanded in 1687
VI-11	1686	Bonometti	Italian	Disbanded in 1688?
VI-12	1686	Maglian, 1686 Graziani (?), 1687 Tomeo Pompei, 1694 Antonio Sala	Italian	Became Veneto Real in 1698
VI-13	1687	Pistro, 1687 Lancia	Italian	Disbanded in 1689
VI-14	1687	Muazzo, 1688 Furietti, 1697 Marchesini	Italian	Disbanded in 1706
VI-15	1687	Montanasi, 1692 Soardo	Italian	Disbanded in 1706
VI-16	1687	Bianchi, 1696 Michiel,	Italian	Disbanded in 1700
VI-17	1687	Campe, 1693 Magnanini, 1697 Paradisi	Italian	Disbanded in 1705
VI-18	1687	Cittadella,1698 Molin	Italian	Disbanded in 1699
VI-19	1687	Arageti, 1688 Maglian, 1689 Nicolò Rossi	Italian	Disbanded in 1706
VI-20	1687	Lannoye	Swiss	Disbanded in 1688
VI-21	1687	Stader, 1695 Carrara	*Oltramontane*	Disbanded in 1706
VI-22	1689	Maglian, 1695 Bartolomeo Degli Oddi	Italian	Disbanded in 1727
VI-23	1689	Hannibal von Degenfeld, 1691 Maximilian von Degenfeld, 1697 Christoph Ferdinand von Degenfeld	*Oltramontane*	Disbanded in 1699
VI-24	1692	Casile, 1694 Nicolò Grimaldi	Corsican	Disbanded in 1705
VI-25	1692	Trauttmansdorf	*Oltramontane*	Disbanded in 1693?
VI-26	1693	Bacigalupo, 1696 Costanti	Corsican	Disbanded in 1702

APPENDIX II

Id.	Year	Colonel or Denomination	Nationality	History
VI-27	1693	Styrum	Oltramontane	Disbanded in 1693
VI-28	1695	Giuseppe Battaglia	Italian	Disbanded in 1706
VI-29	1695	De Tenach	French	Disbanded in 1703
VI-30	1695	Gianxich	Oltramontane	Disbanded in 1702
VI-31	1696	Corponese, 1698 Bernardini	Italian-mixed	Disbanded in 1726
VI-32	1696	Mauromatti	Oltramontane	Disbanded in 1705

Foreign Infantry Regiments and Battalions in Venetian Service

Year	Denomination (or Colonel's name)	Provenance	Licensed
1684	Prinz Maximilian	Braunschweig-Lüneburg (Hannover)	1687
1684	Podewills	Braunschweig-Lüneburg (Hannover)	1688
1684	Ohr	Braunschweig-Lüneburg (Hannover)	1688
1685	Raugraf	Braunschweig-Lüneburg (Hannover)	1688
1685	Schönfeld	Electorate of Saxe	1686
1685	Troppau	Electorate of Saxe	1687
1685	Kleist	Electorate of Saxe	1686
1686	Oxenstierna	Sweden	1688
1687	Alt-Württemberg	Württemberg	1689
1687	Prinz Friedrich Karl (Jung-Württemberg)	Württemberg	1690
1687	Plissen, 1688 Ramstätt	Württemberg	1690
1687	Prinz Georg (von Hessen Darmstadt)	Württemberg	1690
1687	Prinz Karl	Hessen-Kassel	1689
1687	Sparr	Ansbach-Bayreuth	1690
1687	Venediger	Brandenburg-Bayreuth Culmbach	1690
1687	Zanthier	Braunschweig-Wolfenbüttel	1690
1687	Prinz von Waldeck	Waldeck-Pyrmont	1690
1687	Cleuter	Liege	1688
1688	Riedesel	Württemberg	1690
1688	Würzburg	Würzburg	1689

Year	Denomination (or Colonel's name)	Provenance	Licensed
1691	Hohenlohe	Hohenlohe-Neunstein	1695
1692	Graf von Waldeck	Waldeck-Pyrmont	1710
1693	Bayreuth	Brandenburg Bayreuth-Culmbach	1694
1695	Prinz Karl Alexander	Württemberg	1698
1695	Salzburg	Salzburg	1699

Venetian Dragoon Regiments (1685–1699)

Id.	Year	Colonel or Denomination	Nationality	History
VD-1	1685	Nicolò Grimaldi Marquis de Courbon, 1688 Count Ottavio Fenicio, 1699 Giovanni Municasa	*Oltramontane*	Disbanded in 1715
VD-2	1689	Giovanni Massa	Italian	Disbanded in 1714
VD-3	1690	Giovanni Strel	*Oltramontane*	Disbanded in 1698
VD-4	1691	Domenico Gualtieri, 1699, Brandis	*Oltramontane*	Disbanded in 1704
VD-5	1691	Enrico Onigo	*Oltramontane*	Disbanded in 1699
VD-6	1692	Lasso	*Oltramontane*	Disbanded in 1699
VD-7	1696	Vandreis	Italian (Naples)	Disbanded in 1699

Allied Fleet Strength at the Beginning of the Sea Campaigns Against the Porte

Fleets		1684	1685	1686	1687	1688	1689	1690	1691	1692	1693	1694	1695	1696	1697	1698
Venice	galleys	22	24	22	24	24	22	22	22	22	22	24	24	22	20	20
	galleasses	6	6	5	5	5	6	5	5	5	5	6	6	6	6	6
	sail ships	12	16	16	17	18	20	20	20	20	18	21	23	25	25	24
Malta	galleys	7	7	7	8	8	8	8	8	8	8	7	7	7	7	-
	sail ships	-	2*	2*	2*	3*	3*	1	1	1	1	1	1	1	-	-
Papal State	galleys	5	6	6	5	-	-	5	-	5	5	5	5	5	5	-
	sail ships	-	-	-	-	-	-	4	4	1	1	1	1	1	-	-
Tuscany	galleys	4	4	4	4	4	-	-	-	-	-	-	-	-	-	-
	sail ships	-	2*	2*	2*	2*	-	-	-	-	-	-	-	-	-	-
Genoa	galleys	-	-	1	2	-	2	-	2	-	-	-	-	-	-	-
	sail ships	-	-	-	2*	-	-	3*	-	-	-	-	-	-	-	-

* Included armed merchant vessels or transport ships.

Sources: Nani Mocenigo, *Storia della Marina Veneziana*.

APPENDIX II

Venetian Sieges in Greece (1684–1694)

Year	Fortress	Duration	Casualties	Outcome
1684	Santa Maura (Lefkas)	18 days	127 dead, 128 wounded	Garrison surrender
1684	Prevesa	8 days	Unknown	Garrison surrender
1685	Corone	48 days	653 dead, 762 wounded	Venetian assault
1686	Old Navarrino	1 day	None	Garrison surrender
1686	New Navarrino	11 days	Unknown	Garrison surrender
1686	Modone	12 days	Unknown	Garrison surrender
1686	Nauplia	28 days	About 1,500 dead and wounded	Garrison surrender
1687	Athens	7 days	Unknown	Garrison surrender
1688	Negroponte	80 days	6,135 dead, 2,016 wounded	Venetian retreat
1689-90	Malvasia	17 months	400 dead and wounded	Garrison surrender
1692	Chaniá	34 days	195 dead and wounded	Venetian retreat
1694	Chios	7 days	Unknown	Garrison surrender

Source: Éric Guillaume Luc Pinzelli, *Venise et la Morée: du triomphe à la désillusion (1684–1718)* (Marseille: Université de Provence, Aix-Marseille I, Département d'histoire, 2003), p. 302

Venetian Artillery Classification (1699–1701)

	lb	Weight (kg)	Useful Range (metres)	Calibre (mm)		lb	Weight (kg)	Useful Range (metres)	Calibre (mm)
Falconetto	1	560	208	47	Cannone	40	5,000	486	152
Falconetto	3	1,000	278	60	Cannone	50	6,000	521	170
Falcone	6	1,200	382	73	Colubrina	14	3,200	573	102
Passavolante	9	1,200	451	81	Colubrina	16	3,400	643	115
Sagro	12	2,300	504	91	Colubrina	20	3,900	625	123
Aspide	12	1,600	374	91	Colubrina	30	5,300	660	139
Cannone	12	1,400	330	91	Colubrina	40	6,600	695	152
Cannone	14	2,200	364	91	Colubrina	50	9,600	729	170
Cannone	16	2,400	382	115	Petriere	120	4,000	382	214
Cannone	20	4,000	451	123	Petriere	200	6,500	434	263
Cannone	30	4,400	469	139					

Source: Éric Guillaume Luc Pinzelli, *Venise et la Morée: du triomphe à la désillusion (1684–1718)* (Marseille: Université de Provence, Aix-Marseille I, Département d'histoire, 2003), pp.318–319.

Tuscan Bande (Militia), 1660–1690

Terzi:	Romagna	Lunigiana	Maremma
Infantry:	Pontassieve	Prato	Val d'Elsa
	Mugello	Pistoia	Volterra
	Terra del Sole	Montagna	Casole
	Rocca San Casciano	Pescia	Massa
	Castrocaro	Barga	Castiglione
	San Sepolcro	Fivizzano	Grosseto
	Casentino	Pontremoli	Pitigliano
	Arezzo	Livorno (countryside)	Castel del Piano
	Castiglion Fiorentino	Pisa	Montalcino
	Cortona	Cascina	Radicofani
	Valdarno	Colline di Pisa	Chiusi
		Empoli	Monte Pulciano
			Lucignano
carabinieri:	Firenzuola	Montagna	Volterra
	Romagna	Pescia	Campiglia
	Pieve Santo Stefano	Colline di Pisa	Massa
	Valdichiana	Rosignano	Grosseto
	Casentino		Sovana
	Valdarno		Radicofani
corazze:	Arezzo	Pisa	Montalcino
	Cortona	Pistoia	Sinalunga

APPENDIX II

Genoese Infantry in 1673 (April)

Oltramontani, 1,720 men: 5 German companies, 991 men (including the Palace Guard); 1 Swiss company (Canton of Freiburg), 315 men; 13 Grison companies, 413 men.

Compagnie di fortuna, 4,061 men: 52 companies, 3357 men; 4 terzi, Colonels Peri, Tettamanzi, Bolognetti, Molinari, 704 men.

Paeselli (Ligurians), 9 companies, 720 men

Corsicans, 3,052 men: 9 independent companies, 532 men; 7 *terzi*, *sergente-maggiore* Filippo Gentile's (4 companies), *colonnello* Frediani's (3 companies), *generale* Restori's (6 companies), *sergente-maggiore* Vincentello Gentile's (4 companies), *sergente-maggiore* Francesco Ornano's (4 companies), *sergente-maggiore* Gerolamo Ventimiglia's (4 companies), *sergente-maggiore* Ranuccio Ornano (3 companies); 2,420 men.

Total of 9,552 men.

Grand Master of the Order of Saint John (Malta)

1636–1657: Giovanni Paolo Lascaris di Ventimiglia e Castellar (Savoy-Piedmont)

1657–1660: Martin de Redin (France)

1660: Annet de Clermont-Gessant (France)

1660–1663: Rafael Cotoner (Spain)

1663–1680: Nicolas Cotoner (Spain)

1680–1690: Gregorio Carafa (Spain–Naples)

Appendix III

Currencies in Italy in the Second Half of the Seventeenth Century

Savoy-Piedmont

1 *lira* = 20 *soldi*, 1 *soldo* = 12 *denari*.

The most common coins circulating were the golden *doppia* equal to 24 *lire*. There were also *doppie* of 2.5, 0.50 and 0.25. Silver coins were the *scudo* or *mezzo* equal to 6 *lire*, and the *testone* valued at 1 and 10 *lire*.

Venice

The ordinary trade currency was the *lira* equal to 20 *soldi* or *marchetti*; 1 soldo = 12 *denari piccoli*. An alternative currency was the *ducato*, equal to 24 *grossi* or 12 *grossetti*.

Ordinary golden coins were the *zecchino* or *quadruplo*, valued at 22 *lire*, the *mezzo* and the *quarto*, equal to 11 *lire* and 5 *lire* and 10 *soldi* respectively. Particular and rare golden coins were the *ducato d'oro* and the *pistola*, valued 14 and 38 *lire* respectively. Silver coins were the *scudo*, equal to 12 *lire* and 8 soldi, and the minor *mezzo scudo* (6 *lire* and 5 *soldi*), *quarto di scudo* (3 lire, 2 *soldi* and 5 *denari piccoli*) and *ottavo di scudo* (1 *lira* and 11 *soldi*). Other silver coins were the *ducatore* (11 *lire*) with coinages of ½, ¼ and ⅛; the *ducato veneto* (8 *lire* only in Italy), with coinages of ½ and ¼; the *osella* (3 *lire* and 18 *soldi*) and the *tallero* (10 *lire* and 5 *soldi*, only in the overseas domains).

APPENDIX III

The Papal States

1 *scudo romano* = 100 *baiocchi*.

The ordinary golden coin were the *zecchino* or *doppia* equal to 215 *baiocchi*, with the coinages *decuplo* (12 *scudi romani* and 50 *baiocchi*), *doppio* (4 *scudi romani* and 30 *baiocchi*), and *mezzo* (107 *baiocchi*). Silver coins were the *scudo* (100 *baiocchi*), *mezzo scudo* (50 *baiocchi*), *testone* (30 *baiocchi*) and *paolo* (10 *baiocchi*).

Genoa

1 *lira* = 20 *soldi*, 1 *soldo* = 12 *denari*. There were a further four currencies used for particular trades, including the one used only in Corsica.

The golden coins were the *zecchino* (3 *lire* and 10 *soldi*) *mezzo zecchino* (6 lire and 15 *soldi*); *doppia* (23 *lire* and 12 *soldi*), *quadrupla* (47 *lire* and 4 *soldi*), with further minor coinages equal to half, ¼ and ⅛ of *zecchino*. Silver coins were the *genovina* or *scudo d'argento*, with coinages of double, half, ¼ and ⅛ of the value; the *giorgina* (1 *lira* and 4 *soldi*), *Madonnina* (1 lira), the latter with coinages of double, half and ¼ of the value.

Tuscany

1 *lira* = 20 *soldi*; 1 *soldo* = 12 *denari*. Alongside the Tuscan currency there was the *Livornina*, introduced in 1665 by Grand Duke Ferdinando II, which applied special benefits to trade depending on the goods, and could be advantageously converted by foreign traders.

Golden coins were the *raspone* (40 *lire*), and the *zecchino* (13 *lire* and 10 *soldi*). Silver coins were the *tallero* (6 *lire*), *testone* (2 *lire*), *lira* (1 *lira*), *paolo* (10 *soldi*).

Parma

1 *lira* = 20 *soldi*; 1 *soldo* = 12 *denari*. In Piacenza there was a higher currency since 5 *lire* were equal to 6 *lire* of Parma. Consequently, the value of the coins was adapted according to the currency of one or the other duchy.

Golden coins: *zecchino* (45 *lire* in Parma, 37 *lire* and 10 *soldi* in Piacenza). Silver coins: *scudo* (8 *lire* and 8 *soldi* in Parma; 7 *lire* in Piacenza), with minor coniages of half, 1/4, 1/8 and 1/10 of the value.

Modena

1 *lira* = 20 *soldi*; 1 *soldo* = 12 *denari*. Differences between Modena and Reggio were calculated in the coins according to the currency of the respective city.

Golden coins: *Doppia* (51 *lire* in Modena; 76 *lire* and 10 *soldi* in Reggio); *scudino* (9 *lire* in Modena, 13 *lire* and 10 *soldi* in Reggio). Silver coins: *Ducatone* (17 *lire* and 7 *soldi* in Modena, 16 *lire* and 10 *soldi* in Reggio); *scudo* (15 *lire* in Modena, 22 *lire* and 10 *soldi* in Reggio), *filippo* (9 *lire* in Modena, 13 *lire* and 10 *soldi* in Reggio), *ducato* or *mezzo* (8 lire in Modena, 12 lire in Reggio), with further coniages of half, ¼, ⅛ and ¹⁄₁₀ of the value.

Mantua

1 *lira* = 20 *soldi*; 1 *soldo* = 12 *denari*.

Golden coins: *doppia* (74 *lire* and 17 *soldi*). Silver coins: *ducatone* (25 *lire* and 7 *soldi*), scudo bianco; (19 *lire* and 7 *soldi*), *tallero* (14 *lire* and 8 *soldi*) with further coniages of of half, ¼, ⅛ and ¹⁄₁₀ of the value.

Lucca

1 *lira* = 20 *soldi*; 1 *soldo* = 12 *denari*.

Ordinary coins were the *doppia lucchese* (6 *lire*) and the *scudo* (2 lire and 15 soldi) with further coniages of half, ¼, ⅛ and ¹⁄₁₀ of the value.

Malta

1 *scudo* = 12 *tari*; 1 *taro* = 20 *grana*

Ordinary coins were the *scudo* (12 *tari*)), *doppia* (18 *tari* and 12 *grana*), and *onza* (6 *tari*) with further coniages of half, ¼, ⅛ and ¹⁄₁₀ of the value. Spanish currency and coins were also used for particular trade.

Image Commentaries

Chapter 1

1. Forte Urbano, fresco of the Sala Urbana in Bologna, mid seventeenth century. The construction of the fort was commissioned by Pope Urban VIII in 1626, who entrusted the project to Giulio Buratti of Senigallia. Once completed, the fort presented a star shape with internal walls surrounded by a wide ditch and four bastions with artillery batteries. The maximum external width was 900 metres. Access was through a large gate with three drawbridges.

2. and 3. Plan of Ferrara and its pentagonal citadel, in two prints dating to the first half of the seventeenth century (author's archive). The demographic and economic crises of Italy following the Thirty Years' War did not affect the Pope's territories. The Franco-Spanish conflict that involved Modena, Parma, Savoy-Piedmont and Lombardy until 1659 was prevented thanks to Ferrara and Forte Urbano, apparently confirming the validity of their strategic function of deterrence, a function that seemed to be fulfilled again until the end of the century. Nevertheless, in the following century, the limits of a static apparatus would be seen. The plan of defence was conceptually valid but too reduced in terms of the number and strength of support points and centres of resistance, and therefore ineffective without a mass of manoeuvre represented by a modern field army.

16. Portrait of Doge Agostino di Saluzzo (1631–1700), 122nd Doge of the Republic of Genoa between 1673 and 1675 (author's archive). Genoa's contribution to Spain remained crucial after 1659. The Genoese government sometimes sought to distance itself from Madrid, but there were too many links between the city's richest families and *Los Austrias*. For Genoa, Spain was first of all the guarantor of its independence against Savoy-Piedmont or France. Significantly the *Doge*, Agostino di Saluzzo, elected in 1673 shortly after the war against Savoy-Piedmont, was ordinarily a resident of Naples where he held a fief and business interest.

18. Genoa in a print dating to 1670. The city-port of Genoa was shaped like a crescent, arching round a natural harbour. Bounded by the mountains river valleys of Polcevera and Bisagno, to the north of the city are the steep slopes to the Appennine ridges. After 1634 the city had a double circuit of fortifications 12.25 km long, shaped like a triangle whose two longer sides ran in from the coast to form a sharp apex, on which stood the bastion called *lo Sperone*. To the north were a couple of mountains, *Due Fratelli*, topped by the *Forte Diamante* which commanded the main road from Novi. Forts were built on all the high points, guarded in front by streams, and from where the guns swept the approaches. The city centre of Genoa, namely the area between the right bank of the Bisagno stream and the *Lanterna* tower, was thus enclosed by walls that started from what is now Piazza della Vittoria, where they intersected with the sixteenth-century walls, and continued along the eastern ridge to Forte Sperone, and from there descended southwestwards not far from the *Lanterna*.

21. The *Guardia Alemanna* of Genoa in a painting of an unknown artist, 1670–1680 (thanks to Enea Mattia Solari for this picture). The company was composed of veteran German mercenaries who had served the Republic. The figures wear a red coat with silver laces, red-white striped breeches and red stockings. The only Italian state comparable in complexity to the Venetian one is that of the other ancient maritime republic. Genoa's attitude was more distrustful than Venice itself towards military power and entrenched its foreign policy behind a neutrality that became more passive by the day. The *Superba* not only lacked territorial military commands, entrusting these functions to the civil officers in charge of the four divisions of the domain, but also had no senior officers on active service, with the sole exception of the colonel commanding the German lifeguard.

25. The bombardment of Genoa by the French fleet in May 1684, in an ex-voto preserved in the church of Santa Maria di Castello (author's photograph). The pro-Spanish policy of the Republic was inevitably destined to collide with the Sun King's geostrategy. In 1681, in preparation for an assault by sea, Louis XIV sent spies and recruited informers into the territory of the Republic, with the task of surveying the position of artillery and the city defences. On 17 May 1684, a French fleet of 160 units deployed off the city. After an unsuccessful call to retreat sent by the government, the French ships opened fire, firing more than 16,000 cannonballs and incendiary bombs for days, half of which failed to explode or fell into the sea. Despite the terrible devastation, the city reacted with pride and together with the regular troops, militiamen and volunteers repulsed all the French landing attempts. The fighting ceased on 29 May, when most of the French fleet put to sea again in the direction of Toulon.

27. Cosimo III de'Medici (1642–1723), portrayed as a young prince by Justus Sustermans (Museum of Palazzo Corsini, Rome). During his 53-year reign, he was unable to arrest the decline of the state and slowly the Grand Duchy decayed to the status of a minor power. Foreign policy was marked by neutrality, while maintaining ties with both France and the Empire. As far as domestic politics were concerned, Tuscany experienced one of its least happy periods, due to economic crisis, oppressive religious interference, and rights restrictions on Jewish minorities.

IMAGE COMMENTARIES

32. Portoferraio, on the island of Elba, in a Spanish print dating to the early 1700s (Archivo Histórico Nacional, Madrid). Portoferraio was the only Tuscan domain on the island, home of the actual and only military naval base of the Grand Duchy. The harbour was defended by fortifications designed to withstand modern artillery, and despite the small regular garrison there was a considerable arsenal.

34. The watch tower of Castiglioncello, on the Tyrrhenian coast south of Livorno, in a mid-eighteenth century drawing (author's archive). This tower was one of the many observation posts guarding the Tuscan shores of the Ligurian and Tyrrhenian seas, similar to those existing in other parts of Italy. The main duty of these posts was to survey the coast to prevent contraband and to give alarm in case of raids by the Ottoman or Northern African corsairs. Each tower or fort had its small garrison composed of four to eight professional soldiers or militiamen under one *torriere* as junior officer, and was located at a sufficient distance to maintain contact by means of optical signals at night, or with smoke during the day. The tower of Castiglioncello had been built under Cosimo I in the sixteenth century on a rocky spur overlooking a wide cove, and in the next century was enlarged with a chapel and a small barracks. On the top of the tower a sentry post had been built at which, in the event of danger, the soldier would ring a bell to call the garrison, who would then rush to arms or make fire signals. For this purpose, here as well as in the other posts, there was a sufficient supply of straw and dry corn cobs to light the fire. The arsenal also comprised muskets, *spingarde* (rampart muskets), and a couple of *smerigli* light guns. Reports describe how the tower was in the middle of vast, unhealthy swamps and that 'the troops quartered there always look ill'.

53. The fiery and pompous Prince Cesare Ignazio d'Este of Scandiano (1653–1713), portrayed by Henri Gascard in 1675 (Gallerie Estensi, Modena). After his stay in France until 1673, d'Este de facto governed the Duchy from 1674 to 1685, when under pressure from Louis XIV and the Duke's sister, Mary of Modena, he withdrew from state affairs. The Prince's military policy had caused concern among foreign powers, yet Cesare Ignazio was aware that the duchy's resources would not allow him any appreciable rearmament. Many anecdotes circulated about him, including one regarding an incident that occurred on 23 April 1677. At night, the Prince with his retinue of 'bold' gentlemen wanted to see for themselves the presence of a ghost in a palace of Modena, but the 'paranormal' encounter resulted in the escape 'of the already cheerful brigade, overwhelmed by fright to the point that some had to bleed their blood'.

59. Lucca in the late seventeenth century, copper engraving from *Curioses Staats-Kriegstheatrum in Bayern, Franken, Hispanien, Italien* printed in Hamburg in 1702 author's archive). On 9 May 1646 the General Council of Lucca entrusted Paolo Lipparelli with the task of drawing up a project for the improvement of the defences, including the construction of new works and a new covered road, half-moons and ramparts. In February of the following year, the project was approved, and in spring work began on the bastions of Santa Croce and San Martino. In November the works were considered completed. The results of the modernisation work were judged very positively by authoritative authors such as Gualdo Priorato. Lipparelli had dedicated himself to this project with great dedication to the point of making it his reason for living. In 1666, when he was nearing the end of his laborious existence, he stipulated in his will that the incomes of his estate should be used to provide for the salary of a skilled engineer capable of preserving the good state of the defences. The work was carried out with the help of the *comandate*, namely the militia of the Sei Miglia and the Vicarie. Although theirs was a specifically military task, the ramparts were frequented by civilians, who considered the area an urban space on a par with other places in the city. The government issued proclamations to prevent people 'from walking and riding the ramparts, even banning these areas for pasturing'. Other prohibitions concerned fishing, 'and the maceration of hemp in the ditches around the city'.

70. *Fra'* **Bartolomeo Varisano-Grimaldi di Castrogiovanni (1626–1682), a Sicilian knight who served Venice and the Maltese Order between 1669 and 1681, portrayed as cavaliere di Gran Croce (author's archive).** He took up a military career after his escape from Sicily in 1651, because he was sentenced as an accomplice in a plot against the Spanish Viceroy. Varisano gained considerable experience in artillery matters. Note on the left in the background the town of Corfu, where he participated in the improvement of the fortifications. Varisano was one of the many professional soldiers exchanged between Venice and the Hospitaller Order.

72. Execution of loyalists in Messina in a Spanish print dated 1674 (author's archive). A series of brutal executions happened during the riots of July, and also after the battle of Lombardello, fought on 17 August 1674 between 4,000–5,000 insurgents and 2,400 Spanish regular troops and militiamen, the insurgents accused of killing prisoners. Spanish propaganda was fuelled by the fact that after the battle the rebels brought back to Messina as a trophy the heads of some Spanish officers and soldiers who had died in the fight.

73. The Battle of Augusta (Sicily), fought on 22 April 1676 between the Dutch–Spanish and the French fleets, in the painting of Ambroise-Louis Garneray (Palais de Luxembourg, Paris). The siege of Messina was marked by a series major naval battles fought by these fleets. In 1675 the French fleet had 20 sailing warships, of which nine were men-of-war suited to fight in line. In January the French easily defeated the Spanish in the Battle of the Lipari Islands, and captured the 44-gun frigate *Nuestra Señora del Pueblo*. In 1676 Michiel de Ruyter, in command of a combined Dutch–Spanish fleet, intended to blockade Messina, but in January his attempt failed when a French fleet under Abraham Duquesne engaged him in the indecisive battle of Stromboli. In the following battle of Augusta de Ruyter was fatally wounded; the combined fleet suffered more casualties than the French, but Duquesne was forced to withdraw from Messina. However, despite frustrating the Dutch–Spanish fleet's blockade, the bulk of the French fleet was recalled to France later in the year, and the French evacuated their troops from Messina early in 1678.

Chapter 2

86. Carlo Strassoldo (1647–1685) was a Venetian subject who had served in the Imperial army since the 1670s before entering the Serenissima's service. After Strassoldo's death, the Senate had appointed the Count of Saint-Paul-Longueville as *generale dello sbarco*. Morosini had momentarily replaced him with Baron Hannibal von Degenfeld when the Count became indisposed, but Degenfeld had not been chosen by the Senate, and his conduct in front of Calamata had proved to be quite questionable. The senators were keen to have a prestigious and experienced figure at the head of their army. There had been promotions at the end of the 1685 campaign: Prince Maximilan Wilhelm of Brunswick had been made a 'general' without further specification.

96. Mistra, which surrendered to the Venetians in 1687. The heroic actions related by the Venetian chronicles rarely speak of the terrible consequences for the civilians, especially those belonging to another religion. In Mistra in August 1687, after the surrender of the city, the Muslim population had been forced to accept very harsh conditions. All Laconia was placed under quarantine because suspected cases of disease had been found there, and in winter the food supplies from the Venetian authorities had been inadequate, making the situation even worse. The *Provveditore Straordinario* of Morea, Zorzi Benzon, informed the captain-general about acts of rebellion and violations of the quarantine. Consequently the council of war of 22 January 1688 ordered the arrest of all the Muslims of Mistra – men, women and children – and their deportation to Argos. Here, according to the sources, arrived 2,420 prisoners. All men between the ages of 16 and 50, 778 in total, were assigned to the oars of the galleys at an average of 10 per ship. The 312 children were baptised and distributed to the officers and employed as servants. The women and aged men were released, because Morosini was convinced that the enemy, forced to deal with them, would be greatly hindered. Some mothers and wives, however, preferred to throw themselves into the water and seek death rather than be torn from their families. As stated in the final relation, everything was organised in order to strengthen the army and free the kingdom from the Muslims. Only the Jewish population was authorised to remain in Mistra, but in return for an annual contribution of 1,000 *reali*.

97. A seventeenth-century print depicting Corinth and the Acrocorinth, the latter standing on a rocky outcrop overlooking the city. This was the acropolis of ancient Corinth with some remnants of the Byzantine walls. Due to its water source the Acrocorinth could be improved with new fortifications in order to be used as major stronghold of the Morea, as it was located very close to the Isthmus of Corinth, which connected the peninsula to the rest of Greece and blocked access to an enemy coming from east. This strategic location was carefully considered by the Venetians, who planned a campaign of fortification which lasted until the 1690s.

98. Plan of the Acropolis of Athens, during the Venetian siege of September 1687 (author's archive). The Parthenon explosion was followed by the removal of fragments, which caused even greater damage. Francesco Morosini himself did not abstain from the temptation to bring a trophy to Venice. His attempt, as ambitious as it was, was unfortunately disastrous. He wanted to seize the horses of the goddess Athena's chariot on the west side, which had miraculously remained intact. There was no better war prey to bring home than these two splendid rampant horses to be placed with the four bronze horses captured in Constantinople during the Fourth Crusade. The operation was not carried out with due skill and the sculptures fell ruinously to the ground and shattered. Only four lions could be brought back to Venice. They were placed in front of the gate of the Arsenal, where they are still stand today.

100. The strong natural defences of Negroponte appear in this print after Vincenzo Maria Coronelli (author's archive). Before Negroponte the Venetians and their allies committed a series of inexplicable mistakes. Among these, the decision to leave the fort of Kara Baba in the hands of the enemy and consequently the failure to interrupt the connection with Achaia was one of the greatest, as well as not having foreseen that, given the configuration of the terrain, Negroponte could be rescued by land as the besiegers never considered landing their troops upstream of the city to block access. This type of action was within the reach of the fleet, and also of the landing troops, which had performed even more difficult amphibious actions in previous campaigns. Probably haste to conclude the siege and the excessive confidence that the appearance of the Allied fleet would have on the morale of the defenders played a central role in the whole affair. All these errors, combined with the delay accumulated at the start of the siege which then took place in the hottest months of the Greek summer, as well as the onset of malarial fever, turned the campaigns into an unprecedented disaster.

105. The fortified city port of Malvasia, in a late seventeenth century drawing by Vincenzo Maria Coronelli (author's archive). Malvasia was the last Ottoman stronghold in the Peloponnese, which surrendered to the Venetians in 1690. The conquest of the Morea left an indelible mark on the history of Venice, despite the fact that 30 years later the territory was reconquered by the Ottomans even faster than the Venetians took it. With the conquest of the new 'kingdom', the Republic was faced with more than just military problems. The conquest of such a vast territory brought complex legal and religious questions that the government attempted to address with reforms that were far ahead of their time.

IMAGE COMMENTARIES

108. A print of Giuseppe Maria Mitelli, dating to 1694. The war against the Ottoman Empire was marked by strong propaganda, fuelled by a torrential editorial production including books, gazettes, prints and flying leaflets, which sought to respond to a growing curiosity about arms. Some famous prints by the Bolognese engraver Giuseppe Maria Mitelli illustrate with extraordinary effectiveness the state and use of information tools of the time, in years when a rapid evolution of forms of communication was taking place, driven by a vast demand from the public at all social levels.

110. The battle of Mytilene, fought on 20 September 1698, was the last naval engagement of the war against the Porte. In 1645–71 the Cretan War confirmed the Venetian fleet's superiority over the Ottomans; however, the war ended with the loss of Crete and an even worse economic defeat. In contrast, Venice emerged victorious in the 1684–99 war, but none of the naval campaigns achieved significant successes, especially when compared to the previous conflict. Indeed, on several occasions the Ottomans prevailed, if not from the tactical point of view, then certainly at the strategic level.

111. Portrait of Henri Arnaud (1643–1721). He became the leader of his co-religionists after Vittorio Amedeo II of Savoy expelled them from their valleys in 1686, and most probably visited the Dutch Republic, where William II of Orange certainly gave him help and money. Arnaud occupied himself with organising his 3,000 countrymen who had taken refuge in Switzerland, and who twice attempted to regain their homes. The English revolution of 1688, and the election of William to the throne, encouraged the Waldensians to make yet another attempt. Furnished with detailed instructions from the veteran Giosuć Janavel, Arnaud led the 'glorious return' in Piedmont in 1689. The enterprise of Arnaud and his men was an extraordinary episode, since a handful of volunteers were able not only to defeat regular forces, but also to threaten the 'religious peace' imposed by Louis XIV in France and relations with Savoy-Piedmont.

Colour Plate Commentaries

Plate A – The early 1660s

1. Papal State, *Guardia Corsa*, Musketeer, 1662

This soldier is a reconstruction from the figures depicted by Willem Reuter in the painting illustrating the celebration for the birth of Prince Carlos of Habsburg (later King Carlos II of Spain) in front of the palace of the Spanish Embassy in Rome. Certainly, in the period 1650–1660, and also for the early 1670s, the military clothing of the Italian soldiery appeared obsolete if compared to that of contemporary European armies. This is what happened in the Papal States, where the typically aulic features of the Papal government led the way in matters of style. The broad *rabat* collar is relatively old-fashioned for 1662, while the doublet is decidedly of an obsolete pattern.

2. Grand Duchy of Tuscany, musketeer, 1661

This figure comes from an engraving of a spectacle staged in Florence for the wedding day of Prince Cosimo de' Medici and Marguerite-Louise d'Orléans. The chronicles relating this event report that the Prince had his own escort formed by 200 infantrymen dressed in pink. It is difficult to establish whether these were stage costumes, but it cannot be discounted that part of the garrison in Florence continued to wear these colours until the replacement of the dress, which normally took place every two years.

3. Duchy of Modena, musketeer 1660

Modena's contribution to the Cretan War materialised in 1659, when alongside France, the Duchy gathered a contingent that participated in the unsuccessful attempt to seize Chaniá the following year. Duke Alfonso IV, who had served as *maitre de camp* of a French infantry regiment alongside his brother Almerico until 1658, contributed infantrymen and oarsmen to the expedition. Iconographic sources relating the campaign give some account of the clothing issued to the troops of Modena. This musketeer has a French-style *justaucorps* and equipment, including the musket issued to the French infantry in 1660.

COLOUR PLATE COMMENTARIES

Plate B – 1660–75

1. Republic of Lucca, artilleryman, 1664
It is clear from contemporary iconography that the artillerymen serving in Lucca wore dress closely resembling civilian clothing, except for leather coats or bright-coloured doublets and coats, like that of this gunner. A trend common to all Italian states, with the exception of Savoy-Piedmont and partially Venice, was the outdated style of the clothing of their troops.

2. Republic of Genoa, field officer or galley commander, early 1670s
This figure comes from a painting portraying a nobleman whose Genoese origin is testified by the *Lanterna* depicted in the background. Officers naturally tailored their dress privately, but wore sashes on the shoulder or around the waist. This man chose Spanish-style dress, evidenced by the *carlino* coat and light-coloured headgear.

3. Republic of Genoa, Italian infantry, *compagnia di fortuna*, musketeer 1675
Genoese soldiers were dressed according to a Spanish pattern, and this figure is a reconstruction from different descriptions which confirm this kind of influence. He is armed with a flintlock, possibly one of the 1,000 muskets sold by Lucca in 1672, which performed well during that year's war against Savoy-Piedmont. Until 1670 each captain bought whatever clothes were within his means. However, through contracts called *provvigioni per vestiari*, the *Serenissimo Collegio* authorised the purchase of cloth. Grey and brown (similar to the Spanish *pardo*) was the most usual colour of undyed cloth for uniforms. In 1675 a regular deduction from soldier's pay was established, in order to provide regular clothing. In the same year, uniforms were issued to the foreign infantry. Germans dressed in red with *mostre* (facing) of different colours. *Mostre* means the colour of the coat's cuffs as well as its actual lining, but in other cases it could be applied only to cuffs, the lining being like the coat. Probably, in the same year, the Swiss infantry company of Freiburg wore a blue coat with red facing and lining. In 1677, supplier contracts stipulated that native Ligurian companies should wear grey coats with blue lining and Italian *di fortuna* companies received grey coats with different facings for each company, while German companies wore red coats with distinctive facing: blue for the company of *San Tommaso*, green for Gazappi, yellow for Stanghelin. The 1677 the contracts give no information about the Swiss units, but existing clothing bills tell us that the Swiss Company of Freiburg still wore blue coats with red lining and facing, while Grison companies wore blue coats lined with dark yellow.

Plate C – 1675–80

1. Duchy of Modena, infantry militia NCO, 1675
In the equestrian portrait of Cesare Ignazio d'Este, painted by Henry Gascar in 1681, the Prince is depicted like a French *maréchal* with the attributes

317

of commander-in-chief. With him, a group of well-equipped and dressed footmen appears in the background, wearing blue coats with yellow facings, while a sergeant holds a two-handed sword. He wears a pale yellow coat with blue cuffs, the reversed colours of the infantrymen accompanying Cesare Ignazio.

2. Duchy of Modena, foot militia, pikeman, 1675
In another iconographic source, an Easter procession is escorted by pikemen dressed in blue with yellow facing, like those depicted in the painting of Henry Giscar. In the watercolour is an NCO armed similarly to the previous figure. They are probably members of the company of the *caporioni* (urban militia) of Modena. The tendency of pikemen to lighten their load is noted in most of the military manuals of the latter part of the century.

3. Republic of Lucca: Musketeer 1681–85
In the 1670s, travellers transiting through Lucca noticed that the sumptuary laws introduced at the end of the previous decade prescribed the use of certain colours for clothing. The city therefore appeared 'very dreary' due to the dark clothes worn by citizens of all classes, so much so that some compared Lucca to an open-air monastery of monks. Not even the garrison soldiers escaped this rule. A painting by Filippo Gherardi dateable to after 1681 depicts a group of soldiers on the walls of Lucca wearing dark grey coats and black broad-brimmed caps, whose feathers are the only element of colour in their clothing.

Plate D – Venice's allies, Malta 1680s

1. Knight in livery dress, 1685–88
This figure wears the everyday dress of the Maltese knights and comes from a portrait preserved in a private Italian collection. This dress was typical of the Order's members of all nationalities. Note the Maltese white cross fastened to the coat. Few changes took place in the next years, apart for the application of a white cross of cloth on the coat of the *Gran Croce* knights.

2. Knight in campaign dress, 1686
The red tunic with the large white cross is documented in the Manfroni Manuscript and in other contemporary sources. This item replaced the elaborate livery dress during land and sea campaigns.

3. Marine infantry *battaglione*, musketeer, 1686
Maltese infantrymen wearing green coats with red facings also come from the Manfroni Manuscript. The Maltese marine battalion retained this uniform until the early eighteenth century, when it was replaced by a red coat faced and lined with white.

COLOUR PLATE COMMENTARIES

Plate E – Light infantry and *soldati di fortuna*

1. Republic of Genoa, Corsican infantry, musketeer 1684

Corsica was a valuable recruiting ground, so in time of need the governor turned to loyal local leaders to raise companies expected to serve only for a short time. The Corsicans were accustomed to use firearms and their reputation as brave soldiers when employed in skirmish warfare was considerable, although due to a lack of specific training they were less effective in the open field. Corsican companies typically wore blue coats with red cuffs, but companies were allowed to choose *pavonazzo* (dark blue-violet) coats lined with *cremesile* (crimson-red), paying the difference in cost from their own pockets. According to Paolo Giacomone-Piana, Corsicans who had served in foreign armies introduced these colours, which were largely in use outside Genoa. Quinto Cenni misinterpreted *pavonazzo* (dark blue-violet) as *paonazzo* (dark red) and so mistakenly depicted Corsicans wearing red coats. However, the colour's nuance was far from precise, since 'blue' could be anything from light blue to dark violet. In the 1690s the German palace guards, companies 'of fortune' and Corsican companies wore coats with brass buttons, while Ligurian companies and the Swiss Company of Freiburg had pewter buttons. Musicians' coats usually had a chequered lace on the edges of the coat, cuffs, sleeves and around the pocket flaps. This could be in the Genoese colours – red and white – or in the captain's livery colours. Drums were normally painted with the colour of the Republic's coat of arms, or that of the captain. Sergeants usually wore the company uniform of better-quality cloth, with yellow or white metal buttons and lace.

2. Francesco Morosini's Lifeguard, *schiavone*, 1685–88

The Captain General's Lifeguard of Foot was composed of soldiers selected from Dalmatians and Greek islanders subject to Venice. Morosini held the Greeks in high esteem and considered them excellent fighters, unlike Königsmarck, who held them in lower esteem. This figure is based on descriptions of the uniform distributed to these soldiers, composed of elements of *oltramarine* dress.

3. Duchy of Mantua, *soldato di fortuna*, Musketeer, 1687–88

Italian mercenaries from different regions states were recruited by the Italian states, Mantua included. This figure is a reconstruction from the archival sources preserved in Guastalla, which was annexed by Mantua in 1678. In the 1680s, the uniform distributed to the militiamen of Guastalla was of grey cloth with red facings, in order to distinguish them from the regular troops sent by Duke Ferdinando Carlo Gonzaga, who wore grey coats with yellow facings and stockings of different colours.

Plate F – Heavy cavalry

1. Papal States: German cavalry field officer, 1663

The cavalry recruited in the countries of the House of Austria and sent to Rome in the spring of 1663 was equipped like the coeval regiments of Imperial cuirassiers. This figure comes from a portrait of an Austrian officer dated to the early 1660s. The tight leather *kollet* and the small corselet formed by breast and back are characteristic of this period.

2. Grand Duchy of Tuscany: *Corazza Alemanna*, **1675–80**
The mounted life guard company of the *Serenissimo* Grand Duke consisted mainly of Germans, although it also included other foreigners of various origins. Nevertheless, the appellation 'German Cuirassiers' distinguished the unit until its disbandment in 1738. This figure appears in a painting of PandolfoReschi representing the project for the extension of Piazza Pitti in Florence. Black polished metal corselet and buff coats constituted the main elements of this unit's clothing both on active duty and in the quarter. The broad brimmed headgear replaced the lobster helm in ordinary duties, and only at the end of the century the company received an alternative uniform comprising a carmine-red coat with silver laces, white cravat, and carmine-red breeches and stockings. The silver embroidered Medici coat of arms on the saddle cover is speculative.

Plate G – Palace guards

1. Papal States, *Guardia Svizzera*, **1665**
Since the early seventeenth century the Swiss Guards in Rome were dressed with the traditional uniform comprising yellow, red and blue doublets and breeches. On parade duty, the broad-brimmed hat replaced the bonnet.

2. Grand Duchy of Tuscany *Guardia Ferma de' Lanzi*, **1650–60**
The company of *Lanzi* (the name being an Italian corruption of Landsknechts) was dressed in red, typical of the Swiss, and of *pagonazzo*, which in Tuscany meant grey-violet, and was the dynastic colour of the Medici house. Despite the Swiss style of the uniform, the company was comprised of mostly Germans and other foreigners from northern Europe.

3. Parma and Piacenza, *Guardia Alemanna*, **or** *Arciere Prima Guardia*, **1680–90**
This figure is based on the descriptions of the items manufactured for the *Arcieri*, which included the *colterllazzo* scythe. The weapon distinguished rank, the golden blade indicating the captain-lieutenant. When discharged from the corps the guards were allowed to keep their uniforms, including the large silver buttons which represented a considerable value.

COLOUR PLATE COMMENTARIES

112. Entrance of the Prince Cosimo de' Medici in *Il Mondo Festeggiante* (author's archive). The engraving, by Stefano della Bella, depicts one of the fabulous performances in the Boboli amphitheatre, staged in 1661 for the wedding of the Prince and Marguerite-Louise d'Orléans. Chronicles report that the Prince entered the stage on horseback as Hercules, escorted by 200 soldiers of foot wearing pink uniforms.

Plate H – Savoy-Piedmont ensigns, 1672–73: *Guardie* Regiment

1. Colonel's ensign

2. *Ordinanza* ensign. Reconstruction after Stefano Ales, *Insegne militari preunitarie italiane* (1671–1870). Approximate size 240×240 cm.

Plate I – Savoy-Piedmont ensigns

1. *Ordinanze* for infantry, 1680s–1690s
The white cross of Savoy on red or azure background constituted the usual pattern of the infantry until the 1690s, when some additional designs, such as the coat of arms of the province, were added on the corner close to the pole. The size of the ensign considerably decreased during the reign of Vittorio Amedeo II. Approximate size 190×190 cm.

Plate J – Venetian infantry ensigns, 1680–90

1. Traditional rectangular colour with yellow-golden lion
Venetian colours for infantry were traditionally characterised by a rectangular shape and a yellow-golden lion. As for the Italian infantry, the most common background colour was red, but some ensigns had two colours, while the foreign companies usually carried azure flags. Approximate size 190×190 cm.

2. Ensign, copy from a watercolour of the Bassan collection, Venice
This ensign is a copy from a watercolour of the Bassan collection, preserved in Venice in the Naval History Museum, and it may as well be related to an infantry regiment as to a galley, considering that the colours often had multiple uses. Approximate size 180×190 cm.

3. Colonel's company ensign, *Waldeck* infantry regiment
Three infantry ensigns are preserved in Germany in Friedrichstein castle at Bad Wildungen, which belonged to the *Jung-Waldeck* regiments that fought at Corfu in 1716. It is not unlikely that the same flags were used by the Waldeck contingent already in Venetian service at the end of the previous century. The colonel's ensign employs conventional seventeenth-century rules, therefore is white with the St Mark lion rising from the waves, here coupled with the arms of the German count-princedom. On the other existing ensigns, one on red and another on green background, the same elements appear but oriented in the opposite direction (size 210×210 cm).

4. Company ensign, infantry regiment *Hohenlohe*, 1694
In the painting illustrating the burial service of Franceso Morosini in Napoli di Romania, a large black and yellow striped flag appears in the background, bearing a central medallion depicting what is presumably the St Mark lion.

The colours must have related to some foreign regiment in Venetian service. In 1694 only three German mercenary regiments served in the Venetian army: *Waldeck*, *Bayreuth*, and *Hohenlohe*, and heraldic examination allows us to establish this flag as belonging to the *Hohenlohe* regiment. In 1691 the Count-Prince Johann Friedrich I von Hohenlohe raised one grenadier company and 10 musketeer companies to serve in the Peloponnese until 1695. Ensign approximately 170×200 cm.

Plate K – Papal infantry and cavalry colours

1. Papal States: infantry ensign for the *Guardie di Nostro Signore*, 1667–69
All information and images of seventeenth-century papal flags relate to crimson ensigns with the keys and the pope's coat of arms in the centre, here that of Clement IX Rospigliosi. This ensign comes from a painting depicting a flag with a large gold embroidery around the coat of arms. In the seventeenth-century, crimson and yellow were the colours of the Papal States, before white and gold replaced them in the nineteenth century. Approximate size 190×190 cm.

2. Standard of the *Corazze* company, papacy of Innocent XI Odescalchi (1676–1689)
The infantry cavalry standard had a crimson background and bore the papal arms, with occasionally the heraldry of the unit's commander, here a captain of the Aldobrandini family. These elements suggest that the ensign was modified every time a new pontiff was elected or the command of the unit passed to another officer. Approximate size 65×65 cm.

3. Standard of the second mounted militia company of Bologna, 1689
As above, the coat of arms of pope Alexander VIII Ottoboni, and that of the captain count Bovidei Quaranta, mark the standard. In this case, the background copies the distinctive colour of the company.

Plate L – Genoa and Tuscany infantry colours

1. Genoese infantry ensign
The Republic's coat of arms was the red cross of St John on a white field, and constituted the common pattern for the military ensign for infantry from the beginning of the century. Each infantry company had its ensign, and possibly some of these could carry the heraldry of the officer in charge of the command, in this case the marquises Doria of Dolceacqua. Approximate size 200×200 cm.

2. Tuscan infantry ensign
The Tuscan infantry in the Morea carried the flag of the Order of St Stephen. Approximate size 180×180 cm.

Plate M – Modena and Lucca infantry colours

1. Modena, infantry colour, second half of the seventeenth century.
Information regarding the colours of the Modenese infantry in the 1650s states that these followed the pattern of their French ally, but with the blue cross and the dynastic colours of the Este family variously arranged at the quarters. These characteristics remained unmodified until the following century. Approximate size 180×180 cm.

2. Lucca, infantry colour
In the painting by Gerolamo Scaglia depicting the miracle of St Paolino which occurred on 12 July 1664, an officer is carrying a red and white ensign with the Republic's device in the centre. The large size of the flag more than 240×240 approximately, suggests that it was also used as an insignia on the bastions.

Plate N – Malta and Messina infantry colours

1. Malta, infantry colour, end of the seventeenth century

2. Republic of Messina infantry colour, 1675–77
The first ensign carried by the rebel Sicilian republic was the city's coat of arms: a yellow cross on red background. This pattern became standard when the French troops who arrived in Messina to support the rebels carried their own ensigns with the Armagnac white cross. This ensign is a reconstruction with size and proportion according to the French examples, which in the 1670s could measure up to 250×270 cm.

Plate O – Knight of the Order of St Stephen, 1685

In a painting preserved in the Stibbert Museum collection in Florence, the siege of Corone appears in the background. The figure on the right, with the Knight Cross of the Tuscan Order of St Stephen (Santo Stefano), wearing a dark blue coat with white-vermilion-red livery lace, very similar to that of the Maltese Knights. The knight portrayed here was the tutor of the young man in Ottoman clothing, to whom the painting is dedicated: Abdula Chiapoli. The boy had been captured days before the surrender of August 1685, and was saved from the allied soldiers who, after an accidental cannon shot was fired while the negotiations were taking place, furiously attacked the civilians and killed more than 1,500 including women and children. Abdullah had been converted to Catholicism, and he accompanied the Knights in order to encourage the conversion of the Muslim residents in the Peloponnese. Nothing is known of the young prisoner's eventual fate.

COLOUR PLATE COMMENTARIES

Plate P – Prince Cesare Ignazio d'Este of Scandiano (1653–1713), portrayed by Henri Gascard in 1675 (Gallerie Estensi, Modena)

Fiery and pompous, after his stay in France ended in 1673 the Prince governed the Duchy of Modena de facto from 1674 to 1685, when under pressure of Louis XIV and the Duke's sister, Mary of Modena, he withdrew from state affairs. D'Este's military policy had caused concern among foreign powers, yet Cesare Ignazio was aware that the Duchy's resources would not allow him any appreciable rearmament. Many anecdotes circulated about him, including one concerning an incident that occurred on 23 April 1677. At night, the Prince with his retinue of 'bold' gentlemen, wanted to verify the presence of a ghost into a palace of Modena, but the 'paranormal' encounter resulted in the escape 'of the already cheerful brigade, overwhelmed by fright to the point that some gentlemen had to bleed their blood.'

Bibliography

Archival Sources

Archivio dell'Ufficio Storico dello Stato Maggiore dell'Esercito (AUSSME), Rome

Archivio di Stato di Torino (ASTo), *Sezione I & II, Materie Militari, Ufficio Generale del Soldo e Imprese Militari; Ordini e Regolamenti; Sezione III & IV, Ufficio Generale del Soldo, Ordini Generali Misti; Regolamenti Militari*

Biblioteca Nazionale di Torino (BNT)

Biblioteca Reale di Torino (BRT)

Archivio di Stato di Venezia (ASVe), *Senato Mar, dispacci di Provveditori di Terra e di Mar; Savi alle Scritture; Provveditore sopra le artiglierie*

Biblioteca Museo Correr (BMC), Venice

Biblioteca Nazionale Marciana (BNM), Venice

Biblioteca Querini-Stampalia (BQS), Venice

Archivio di Stato di Genova (ASGe), *Archivio Segreto; Guerra e Marina*

Biblioteca Civica Berio (BCB), Genoa

Archivio di Stato di Roma (ASRo), *Soldatesche e Galere; Congregazioni Particolari Deputate 1600-1760; Congregazioni Particolari*

Archivio Segreto Vaticano (ASV), Rome, *Commissariato Armi; Segreteria di Stato, Soldati*

Biblioteca della Camera Apostolica, Rome (BCA)

Archivio di Stato di Firenze (ASFi), *Mediceo del Principato, Spedizione di sodatesche in Levante; Depositeria Generale, Miscellanea Medicea, Scrittoio delle Fortezze e Fabbriche*

Archivio di Stato di Pisa (ASPi), *Ordine dei Cavalieri di Santo Stefano, Ruoli*

Archivio di Stato di Parma (ASPr), *Governo Farnesiano, Milizie; Memorabilia civitas Parmae, 1688-1708*

Archivio di Stato di Modena (ASMo) *Militaria Estense*

Archivio di Stato di Lucca (ASLu), *Camarlingo Generale*

Archivio di Stato di Mantova (ASMn), *Archivio Gonzaga*

Archivio di Stato della Valletta (ASVa), *Registri delle Camere del Tesoro*

Archives of the Order of Malta (AOM), *Correspondence*

Archivio del Gran Priorato di Venezia e Lombardia del Sovrano Militare Ordine di Malta (ASMOMVe), Venice, *Armamenti, Squadra, Commercio, Corsari, Prede, Schiavi (1430-1699); Marittimi e Commerciali (1684-1700)*

Coeval Works

Biblioteca Naciónal de España, Madrid, *Carta Escrita del Rev. N. al Ill.no continuando la novedades que resultan de las hostilidades, entre la Serenissima Republica di Genova, y el serenissimo*

Ducque de Saboya, y con mas distinta relacion del encuentro de Castel Vecchio (1675); 31. Leg. 2, n. 18.

(Anonymous), *Relazione del Glorioso acquisto della Fortezza di Coron, Capitale del Regno di Morea, fatto sotto il prudente Valoroso Commando dell'Eccellentiss. Signor Cavalier e Procurator Francesco Morosini Capitano Generale da Mar, il giorno 11 Agosto 1685* (Venice, 1685)

(Anonymous), *Esatta Notizia del Peloponneso, volgarmente Penisola della Morea, divisa in otto province.* (Venice, 1687)

(Anonymous), *Diario dell'Assedio di Negroponte assieme a un Giornale delle campagne in Dalmazia* (Venice, 1699)

Alimari, Doroteo, *Instruttioni militari appropriati all'uso moderno di guerreggiare. Opera nuova utile e necessaria a' professori dell'onorata disciplina della milizia* (Nurnberg–Venice, 1692)

Beregani, Nicola, *Historia delle Guerre d'Europa dalla comparsa dell'Armi Ottomane in Ungheria*, Vols I–II (Venice, 1698)

Bizozeri, Simpliciano, *La Sagra Lega contro la Potenza Ottomana* (Milan, 1690)

Bosio, Giacomo, *Dell'Istoria della Sacra Religione et Ill.ma Militia di San Giovanni Gierosolimitano*, Vol. III (Naples, 1684)

Burgo, Giovanni Battista, *Viaggio di cinque anni in Asia, Africa, e Europa*, volls I-IV (Milan, 1688)

Contarini, Camillo, *Istoria della Guerra di Leopoldo I Imperadore e de' Principi Collegati contro il Turco, dall'anno 1683 fino alla Pace*, vols. I–II (Venice, 1710)

Coronelli, Pietro Maria, *Memorie Istorio Grafiche delli Regni di Morea e Negroponte*, vols I–II (Venice, 1687)

Dal Pozzo, Bartolomeo, *Historia della Sacra Religione Militare di San Giovanni Gerosolimitano detta di Malta* (Venice, 1715)

Amelot De La Houssaye, Abraham Nicolas, *Histoire du Gouvernement de Venise*, vol. II (Amsterdam, 1705)

Fontana, Fulvio, *I Pregi della Toscana nell'Imprese più segnalate de' Cavalieri di Santo Stefano* (Florence, 1701)

Foscarini, Michele, *Historia della Republica Veneta* (Venice, 1696)

Garzoni, Pietro, *Istoria della Repubblica di Venezia in tempo della Sacra Lega contra Maometto IV e tre suoi Successori*, Vols I–II (Venice, 1712)

Giustinian, Bernardo, *Historie Cronologiche dell'Origine degli Ordini Militari e di tutte le Legioni Cavalleresche* (Venice, 1692)

Gualdo-Priorato, Galeazzo, *Relatione della Città di Genova e suo Dominio* (Cologne, 1668)

Gualdo-Priorato, Galeazzo, *Relatione della Città di Fiorenza, e del Gran Ducato di Toscana sotto il Regnante Gran Duca Ferdinando II, con tutte le Cose più degne e curiose da sapersi* (Cologne, 1668)

Gualdo-Priorato, Galeazzo, *Relatione della Signoria di Luca e suo Dominio* (Cologne, 1668)

Gude, Heinrich Ludwig, *Staat von Parma und Piacenza, Mirandula und Concordia, Massa und Carrara, Monaco, Doria, St. Piedro, Sesto St. Angelo und dei Fieschi* (1708)

Gude, Heinrich Ludwig, *Staat von Mantua und Monferrat* (1708)

Gude, Heinrich Ludwig, *Der Staat von Florenz, Modena und Reggio* (1708)

Gude, Heinrich Ludwig, *Staat der Republique von Genoua, Lucca und Marino* (1708)

Léonard, Jean, *Histoire des conquêtes des Vénitiens depuis 1684 jusques à présent* (Bruxelles, 1688)

Leti, Gregorio, *Itinerario della Corte di Roma o Vero Teatro Historico, cronologico e politico della Sede Apostolica, Dataria e Cancelleria Romana* (Valenza, 1675), vols I–II.

Locatelli, Alessandro, *Racconto historico della veneta guerra in Levante* (Cologne, 1691)

Marzioli, Francesco, *Precetti Militari* (Bologna, 1678)

Mainenti, Michelangelo (capitano), *Esercizii militari della fanteria secondo l'uso moderno dimostrati* (Venice, 1694)

Moretti, Tommaso, *Trattato dell'Artiglieria* (Venice, 1665)

Muazzo, Antonio, *Guerra coi i Turchi*, Biblioteca Nazionale Marciana, Manoscritti Italiani VII, n. 172 (8187)

Piccinini, Gianfrancesco (ed.), *Il Viaggio di Alessandro II Pico all'Isola di Candia* (Guastalla: Centro Internazionale di Cultura 'Pico della Mirandola', 2009)

Sala, Antonio, *La Prattica in Teorica del Soldato Instruito in Mare* (Venice, 1697)

Siri, Vittorio, *Il Mercurio, overo Historia de' Correnti Tempi*, vols IV–XV (Florence, 1667–82)

Vezzani, Antonio, *L'Esercizio Accademico della Picca* (Parma, 1688)

Viviani della Robbia, Luigi, *Compendio Civile, Economico e Militare della Toscana* (Florence, 1734)

Viceti, Francesco Maria, *Compendioso Racconto De principali Successi della Guerra mossa l'anno 1672 Alla Repubblica di Genova Dal Duca di Savoia Collo stabilimento della Pace nell'Anno 1673 Descritta Dà Francesco M:a Viceti* (Archivio Storico del Comune di Genova, Manoscritti, Ricci, 136, after 1673)

General Documentary Sources

Ales, Stefano, *Insegne militari preunitarie italiane, 1671–1870* (Rome: USSME, 2001)

Botta, Carlo, *Storia d'Italia continuata da quella del Guicciardini*, vols VII–VIII (Paris, 1738)

Cessi, Roberto, *Storia della Repubblica di Venezia* (Florence: Giunti, 1981)

Cont, Alessandro, *Corte Britannica e Stati Italiani, Rapporti politici, diplomatici e culturali (1685–1688)* (Rome: Società Dante Alighieri, 2019), Biblioteca della 'Nuova Rivista Storica' n. 55

Cont, Alessandro, 'L'uomo di corte italiano: identità e comportamenti nobiliari tra XVII e XVIII secolo', in *Rivista Storica Italiana* – a. CXXVI – Fascicolo I, April 2014, pp.94–119

Cremonini, Cinzia and Riccardo Musso (eds), *I feudi imperiali in Italia tra XVI e XVIII secolo* (Rome: Bulzoni, 2010)

Donati, Claudio, 'The Italian Nobilities in the Seventeenth and Eighteenth Centuries', in *The European Nobilities in the Seventeenth and Eighteenth Centuries' Vol. I: Western Europe* (London–New York: Longman, 1995), pp.237–268

Martin, John; Romano, Dennis (editors), *Venice Reconsidered. The History and Civilization of an Italian City-State, 1297–1797* (Baltimore MA: Johns Hopkins University Press, 2000)

Muratori, Ludovico Antonio, *Annali d'Italia e altre Opere Varie*, vols IV–V (Milan, 1837)

Pezzolo, Luciano, 'Stato, Guerra e Finanza nella Repubblica di Venezia fra Medioevo e prima Età Moderna, in acts of the conference *Navies and State Formation* (Volos, 9–12 September 2004), pp.67–112

Pezzolo, Luciano, 'Violenza, costi di protezione e declino commerciale nell'Italia del Seicento' in *Rivista di Storia Economica*, vol. 23 (2007), pp.111–124

Pezzolo, Lucino, 'Le spese degli stati italiani, 1350–1700: modelli a confronto' in *El alimento del estado y la salud de la república: Orígenes, desarrollo y estructura del gasto público en Europa (siglos XIII–XVII)* (Madrid, Instituto de Estudios Fiscales, 2014), pp.381–402

Raviola, Blythe, 'The Imperial System in Early Modern Northern Italy: A Web of Dukedoms, Fiefs and Enclaves along the Po', in P. H. Wilson and R. J. W. Ewans (eds), *The Holy Roman Empire, 1495–1806: A European Perspective* (Leiden–Boston, MS: Brill, 2012), pp. 217–238.

Setton, Kenneth M., *Venice, Austria, and the Turks in the Seventeenth Century* (Philadelphia: The American Philosophical Society, 1991)

Sodini, Carla, *Scrivere e compilare. Galeazzo Gualdo Priorato e le sue relazioni di Stati e città* (Lucca: Pacini Fazzi, 2004)

Spagnoletti, Angelantonio, *Principi italiani e Spagna nell'età barocca* (Milan: Bruno Mondadori, 1996)

Military History

Bercé, Yves-Marie, 'Les guerres dans l'Italie du XVII siécle', in Y. M. Berce, G. Delille, J. M. Sallmann, J. C. Waquet (eds), with a preface of A. Corvisier, *L'Italie au XVIIe siècle* (Paris: C.D.U.-S.E.D.E.S., 1989), pp.313-331

Del Negro, Piero, 'La storia militare dell'Italia moderna nello specchio della Storiografia del Novecento', in *Istituzioni militari in Italia fra Medioevo ed Età Moderna*, Cheiron, 23 (1995), pp.11-33

Donati, Claudio, 'Il 'Militare' nella Storia dell'Italia Moderna dal Rinascimento all'Età Napoleonica', in C. Donati (editor), *Eserciti e carriere militari nell'Italia moderna* (Milan: Unicopli, 1998), pp.7-39

Donati, Claudio, 'Strutture militari degli Stati italiani nella prima età moderna: una rassegna degli studi recenti', in: *Società italiana di Studi Militari. Quaderno 2000*, P. Del Negro (ed.), *La storiografia militare in Italia e in Francia negli ultimi vent'anni. Due esperienze a confronto.* (Venice, 27-28 aprile 2001), Napoli, E.S.I., 2003, pp.45-62

Donati, Claudio, Militärstrukturen der italienischen Staaten in der frühen Neuzeit: ein Forschungsbericht jüngster Studien, in *Militär und Gesellschaft in der Frühen Neuzeit*, 7 (2003), n. 2, pp. 145-167

Hanlon, Gregory, *The Twilight of a Military Tradition. Italian Aristocrats and European Conflicts, 1560-1800* (London: UCL Press, 1998)

Ilari, Virgilio, *Storia del servizio militare in Italia (1506-1870)*, vol. I, *Dall' ordinanza fiorentina di Machiavelli alla costituzione dell'esercito italiano*, Collana del Centro Militare di Studi Strategici (Rome: Rivista Militare, 1990)

Labanca, Nicola (ed.), *Storie di guerre ed eserciti. Gli studi di storia militare italiana negli ultimi venticinque anni* (Milan: Unicopli, 2011)

Lo Basso, Luca, 'Schiavi, forzati e buonevoglie. La gestione dei rematori delle galere dell'Ordine di Santo Stefano e della Repubblica di Venezia. Modelli a confronto' , in *L'Ordine di Santo Stefano e il mare* (Pisa: Edizioni ETS, 2001), pp.171-232

Paoletti, Ciro, *Gli italiani in armi. Cinque secoli di storia militare nazionale 1494-1997* (Rome: USSME, 2001)

Pezzolo, Luciano, 'La 'rivoluzione militare': una prospettiva italiana 1400-1700', in A. Dattero and S. Levati (eds) *Militari in età moderna. La centralità di un tema di confine* (Milan: Cisalpino, 2006), pp.15-62

Pieri, Piero, 'L'evoluzione dell'arte militare nei secoli XV, XVI e XVII e la guerra nel secolo XVIII', in *Nuove questioni di storia moderna,* vol. I (Milan: Marzorati, 1964), pp.1123-1179

Pieri, Piero, 'La storia militare', *in La storiografia italiana negli ultimi venti anni*, vol. II (Milan: Marzorati, 1970)

Stumpo, Enrico, 'La crisi del Seicento in Italia', in M. Firpo and N. Tranfaglia (eds), *La storia. I grandi problemi dal Medioevo all'Età Contemporanea* (Turin: UTET, 1986), vol. V, pp.313-337

Williams, Phillip, 'Mare Nostrum? Reform, Recruitment and the Business of Crusade in the Fleets of the Seventeenth Century Mediterranean', in *Storia Economica*, *XIX* (Edizioni Scientifiche Italiane, 2016), n. 1, pp.77-102

Savoy-Piedmont

Barberis, Walter, *Le armi del Principe. La tradizione militare sabauda* (Turin: Einaudi, 1988)

Bianchi, Paola, 'La riorganizzazione militare del Ducato di Savoia e i rapporti del Piemonte con la Francia e la Spagna. Da Emanuele Filiberto a Carlo Emanuele II' in García Hernán, E. and Maffi, D. (eds), *Guerra y sociedad en la monarquía hispánica: política, estrategia y cultura en la*

Europa moderna (1500-1700) (Madrid: Fundación MAPFRE, Laberinto; Consejo Superior de Investigaciones Científicas, CSIC, 2006), vol. I, pp.189–216

Bianchi, Paola, 'La corte dei Savoia: disciplinamento del servizio e delle fedeltà' in W. Barberis (ed.), *I Savoia. I secoli d'oro di una dinastia europea* (Turin: Einaudi, 2007), pp.135–176

Bianchi, Paola, 'Immagine e realtà dell'eccezione militare del Piemonte' in P. Bianchi (ed.), *Il Piemonte come eccezione? Riflessioni sulla 'Piedmontese exception'* (Turin: Centro Studi Piemontesi, 2008), pp.57–78

Bianchi, Paola, 'Al servizio degli alemanni. Militari piemontesi nell'Impero e negli stati tedeschi fra Sei e Settecento', in P. Bianchi, D. Maffi, E. Stumpo (eds) *Italiani al servizio straniero in età moderna* (Milan, Franco Angeli, 2008)

Bianchi, Paola, *Sotto diverse bandiere: l'internazionale militare nello Stato sabaudo d'antico regime* (Milan: Franco Angeli, 2012)

Bianchi, Paola, *Educare a corte: paggeria ed Accademia Reale fra Sei e Settecento*, in A. Merlotti (ed.), *Paggi e paggerie nelle corti italiane. Educare al comando* (Florence: Olschki, 2021), pp.45–70

Brancaccio, Nicola, *L'esercito del vecchio Piemonte, 1560-1859. Sunti storici dei principali corpi* (Rome, 1922)

Brancaccio, Nicola, *L'esercito del vecchio Piemonte. Gli ordinamenti. Parte I (1560–1814)* (Rome, 1923)

Duboin, Felice Amato, *Raccolta per ordine di materie delle leggi cioè editti, patenti, manifesti, ecc. emanate negli stati di terraferma sino all'8 dicembre 1798 dai sovrani della Real Casa di Savoja*, vols XXVII–XXVIII (Turin, 1848)

Fiora, Paolo, *Bandiere in Piemonte* (Turin: Centro Studi dell'Accademia di San Marciano, 1971)

Gerbaix de Sonnaz, C. A., *Bandiere, Stendardi e Vessilli di Savoia* (Turin, 1896–1911)

Giuliani, Giuseppe, 'Formazione e Struttura dell'Esercito Sabaudo nel XVII secolo e nel XVIII secolo' in *Studi Storico-Militari* (Rome: USSME, 2009), pp.5–56

Guerrini, Domenico, *La Brigata dei Granatieri di Sardegna. Memorie storiche* (Turin, 1902)

Paoletti, Ciro, *Dal Ducato all'Unità. Tre secoli e mezzo di storia militare piemontese* (Rome: USSME, 2011)

Paoletti, Ciro, *William III's Italian Ally. Piedmont and the War of the League of Augsburg 1683–1697* (Warwick: Helion & Company, 2019)

Ricchiardi, Enrico, *Bandiere della Fanteria Nazionale Sabauda (1690–1773)*, Vol. XVII-2 (Turin: Centro Studi Piemontesi, 1988)

Ricchiardi, Enrico, *Bandiere della Fanteria Straniera al soldo dei Savoia (1690–1773)*, Vol. XVIII-2 (Turin: Centro Studi Piemontesi, 1989)

Ricchiardi, Enrico, *Il Costume Militare Sabaudo*, Vol. I (Turin: Centro Studi Piemontesi, 1989)

Saluzzo, Alessandro di, *Histoire Militaire du Piémont*, Vols IV–V (Turin, 1818)

Salvi, Costantino, *Carlo Emanuele II e la guerra contro Genova dell'anno 1672* (Rome, 1933)

Sconfienza, Roberto, 'Sulla prima uniforme e lo stemma del Reggimento Dragoni di Piemonte', in *Armi Antiche. Bollettino dell'Accademia di San Marciano*, 1995 (1998), pp.75–81

Stumpo, Enrico, *Finanza e Stato moderno nel Piemonte del Seicento* (Rome: Istituto storico italiano per l'età moderna e contemporanea, 1979)

Stumpo, Enrico, 'Guerra ed economia: spese e guadagni militari nel Piemonte del Seicento', in *Studi Storici*, XXVII (1986), pp.371–395

Symcox, Geoffrey, *Victor Amadeus II. Absolutism in the Savoyard State, 1675–1730* (Berkeley-Los Angeles, CA: University of California Press, 1983)

Venice

Beltrame, Carlo and Marco Morin, *I Cannoni di Venezia. Artiglierie della Serenissima da fortezze e relitti* (Florence: All'Insegna del Giglio, 2013)

Birtachas, Stathis, 'Stradioti, Cappelletti, Compagnie or Milizie Greche: Greek Mounted and Foot Mercenary Companies in the Venetian State (1400–1700)', in G. Teotokis and A. Yldiz (eds), *A Military History of the Mediterranean Sea. Aspects of War, Diplomacy and Military Elites* (Leiden–Boston: Brill, 2018), pp.325–346

Candiani, Guido, 'L'evoluzione della flotta veneziana durante la prima guerra di Morea', in *Venezia e il Mediterraneo. La Guerra di Morea* (Venice, Fondazione Querini Stampalia – Dipartimento di Studi Storici Università di Venezia, 2001), pp.1–4

Candiani, Guido, *I vascelli della Serenissima. Guerra, politica e costruzioni navali a Venezia in età moderna, 1650-1720* (Venice: Istituto Veneto di Scienze, 2009)

Candiani, Guido, 'Vele, remi e cannoni: l'Impiego congiunto di navi, galee e galeazze nella flotta veneziana, 1572–1718', in G. Candiani and L. Lo Basso (eds), *Mutazioni e Permanenze nella Storia Navale del Mediterraneo, secc. XVI–XIX* (Milan: Franco Angeli, 2010) pp.116–162

Candiani, Guido, *Dalla galea alla nave di linea. Le trasformazioni della marina veneziana (1572-1699)* (Novi Ligure: Città del silenzio, 2012)

Camporota, Bonaventura, *Vita di Francesco Morosini Peloponnesiaco, Doge di Venezia* (Napoli 1865)

Casini, Matteo, 'Immagini dei Capitani Generali da Mar a Venezia in età barocca', *in* M. Fantoni (ed.), *Il 'Perfetto Capitano'. Immagini e realtà (secoli XV–XVII)* (Rome: Bulzoni, 2001), pp.219–270

Casoni, Giovanni, 'Nota sulle Truppe Marittime e Terrestri della Repubblica di Venezia', in *Venezia e le sue Lagune* (Venice, 1847), vol. I, n 2, pp.251–262

Del Negro, Piero, 'Il Leone in Campo: Venezia e gli Oltramarini nelle Guerre di Candia e di Morea', in S. Graciotti (ed.), *Mito e Antimito di Venezia nel Bacino Adriatico (secoli XV–XIX)* (Rome: Il Calamo, 2001, pp.323–344

Levi-Weiss, Dora, 'Le relazioni fra Venezia e la Turchia dal 1670 al 1684 e la formazione della Sacra Lega', in *Archivio Veneto* (1926), pp.97–155

Mayhew, Tea, 'Soldiers, Widows and Families: Social and Political Status of the Professional Warriors of the Venetian Republic (1645-1718)', in B. Waaldijk (ed.), *Professions and social identity: new European historical research on work, gender and society*, Vol. IV (Pisa, 2006), pp.89–101

Morton Paton, James, 'A Florentine officer in the Morea in 1687', in *American Journal of Archaeology*, XXXVIII (1934), pp.59–66

Morton Paton, James, *The Venetians in Athens 1687-1688, from the Istoria of Cristoforo Ivanovich* (Harvard–Cambridge, 1940)

Nani-Mocenigo, Mario, *Storia della marina veneziana* (Rome, 1935)

Ongaro, Giulio, 'Il lavoro militare fra XVI e XVII sec.: contadini-soldato nella Repubblica di Venezia tra subordinazione e agency', in *L'empreinte domestique du travail*, Mélanges de l'École française de Rome – Italie et Méditerranée modernes et contemporaines , n. 131-1 (2019), pp.5–30

Panopoulos, Angeliki G. and Kostas G. Tsiknakis, 'Historical Research on the District of Agyos Georgios in the Second Period of the Venetian Rule', in S. Kourakou-Dragona (ed.), *Nemea Beloved Land of Zeus and Dionysos* (Athens: Foinikas Publications, 2011), pp.115–215

Pezzolo, Luciano, 'L'archibugio e l'aratro. Considerazioni e problemi per una storia delle milizie rurali venete nei secoli XVI e XVII', in *Studi Veneziani vol. 7 (1983)*, pp.59–80

Pezzolo, Luciano, 'Esercito e Stato nella prima età moderna: alcune considerazioni preliminari per una ricerca sulla Repubblica di Venezia', in *Studi Veneziani*, vol. 14 (1987), pp.303–322

Pezzolo, Luciano, 'Fonti e problemi per la storia dell'esercito veneziano nella prima età moderna', in L. Antonelli and C. Donati (eds), *Al di là delle fonti militari* (Catanzaro: Rubbettino, 2004) pp.32–40

Pezzolo, Luciano, 'Stato, Guerra e Finanza nella Repubblica di Venezia fra Medioevo e Prima Età Moderna', in R. Cancila (ed.), *Mediterraneo in armi (sec. XV–XVIII) – Quaderni di Mediterranea* (Palermo, 2007), pp.67–112

Pezzolo, Luciano, 'Una finanza in guerra, 1645–1669', in G. Ortalli, G. Gullino, E. Ivetic (eds), *L'inestinguibile sogno del dominio. Francesco Morosini* (Venice: Istituto Veneto di Scienze, Lettere e Arti, 2021), pp.65–112

Pinzelli, Éric Guillaume Luc, *La défense de l'isthme de Corinthe durant la période vénitienne (1687–1715)* (Marseille: Université de Provence, Aix-Marseille I, Département d'histoire 1996-1997)

Pinzelli, Éric Guillaume Luc, *Venise et la Morée: du triomphe à la désillusion (1684–1718)* (Marseille: Université de Provence, Aix-Marseille I, Département d'histoire, 2003)

Robuschi, Luigi, *La strategia di Francesco Morosini nella guerra di Morea (1684–1699) e il suo contributo alla nascita delle truppe da sbarco* (Centro Alti Studi per la Difesa – 8° Corso Superiore di Stato Maggiore Interforze, 2005–2006)

Schwenke, Alexander, *Geschichte der hannoverschen Truppen in Griechenland 1685-1689, zugleich als Beitrag zur Geschichte der Türkenkriege. Nach archivalischen Quellen* (Hannover, 1854)

Stouraiti, Anastasia, 'Printing Empire: Visual Culture and the Imperial Archive in Seventeenth-Century Venice', in *The Historical Journal* (April 2016), pp.1–34

Tamburrini, Pierluigi, *L'organizzazione militare veneziana nella prima metà del Settecento* (Rome: SISM, 2014)

(Various Authors), *Francesco Morosini, 1619-1694: l'uomo, il doge, il condottiero* (Rome–Venice: Poligrafico e Zecca dello Stato italiano, 2020)

(Various Authors), *Francesco Morosini in guerra a Candia e in Morea* (Exhibition Guide and Catalogue; Venice: Ente Editoriale per il Corpo della Guardia di Finanza, 2020)

Papal States

Bailly, R., 'La garnison pontificale du Palais des Papes aux XVIIe et XVIIIe siècles', in *Mémoires de l'Académie de Vauclouse* (1954), pp.66–77

Brunelli, Giampiero, 'Poteri e Privilegi. L'istituzione degli ordinamenti delle milizie nello Stato Pontificio tra Cinque e Seicento', in *Cheiron*, XII (1995), n. 23, pp.105–129

Brunelli, Giampiero, *Soldati del papa. Politica militare e nobiltà nello Stato della Chiesa (1560-1644)* (Rome: Carocci, 2003)

Brunelli, Giampiero, 'Al vertice dell'istituzione militare pontificia: il Generale di santa Chiesa (sec. XVI-XVII)', in A. Jamme and O. Poncet (eds), *Offices et papauté (XIVe–XVIIe siècle)* (Rome: Publications de l'École Française de Rome, 2013), pp.483–499

Da Mosto, Andrea, 'Milizie dello Stato Romano dal 1600 al 1797', in *Memorie Storico Militari*, n. 22 (Città di Castello, 1914), pp.193–579

Giangolini, Luca, *Le Armi del Papa. L'esercito pontificio tra burocrazia curiale e nobiltà. 1645-1740* (Rome: Università La Sapienza, 2018)

Guglielmotti, Alberto, *La squadra ausiliaria della marina romana a Candia ed alla Morea* (Rome, 1883)

Ilari, Virgilio, 'L'esercito pontificio nel XVIII secolo fino alle Riforme del 1792-93', in *Studi Storico Militari 1985*, USSME (Rome 1986), pp.555–664

Ilari Virgilio, 'Gli antenati della Gendarmeria pontificia: il Battaglione de' Corsi e poi Dei soldati in luogo de' Còrsi (1603–1678)', in *Memorie Storico Militari 1983*; USSME (Rome 1984), pp.751–800

Lutz, Georg, 'L'esercito pontificio nel 1667. Camera apostolica, bilancio militare dello Stato della Chiesa e nepotismo nel primo evo moderno', in *Miscellanea in onore di Monsignor Martino Giusti Prefetto dell'Archivio Segreto Vaticano*, II (Città del Vaticano, Archivio Vaticano, 1978), pp.39–95

Paoletti, Ciro, 'La frontiera padana dello Stato Pontificio nel secolo XVII', in C. Sodini (ed.), *Frontiere e fortificazioni di frontiera* (Florence: EDIFIR, 2001), pp.127–134

Paoletti, Ciro, *Le Armi e le Chiavi – Storia militare degli Stati Pontifici nell'età moderna e contemporanea* (Rome: Commissione Italiana di Storia Militare, 2020)

Savestre, B., 'Les Corses au service du Pape' in *Les Troupes Corse et l'histoire militaire de la Corse*, 'Carnet de la Sabretache' – nouvelle série – n. 20 (Special Issue, 1973), pp.22–29

Genoa

Assereto, Giovanni, *La metamorfosi della Repubblica. Saggi di storia genovese tra il XVI e il XIX secolo* (Savona: Daner, 1999)

Beri Emiliano, *Genova e il suo regno. Ordinamenti militari, poteri locali e controllo del territorio in Corsica fra insurrezioni e guerre civili (1729–1768)* (Genoa: Università degli Studi di Genova, 2009–2010)

Dellepiane, Riccardo, *Mura e fortificazioni di Genova* (Genoa: Nuova Editrice Genovese, 1984)

Ferrante, Riccardo, 'La nazione dei genovesi dall'antico regime alla Restaurazione', in A. De Benedictis, I. Fosi, and L. Mannori (eds), *Nazioni d'Italia. Identità politiche e appartenenze regionali fra Settecento e Ottocento* (Rome: Viella – Società Italiana per la Storia dell'Età Moderna – Società per gli Studi di Storia delle Istituzioni, 2012), pp.346–374

Giacomone Piana, Paolo and Riccardo Dellepiane, *Militarium* (Genoa: Brigati, 2004)

Kirk, Thomas Allison, *Genoa and the Sea: Policy And Power In An Early Modern Maritime Republic, 1559–1684* (Baltimore MD: Johns Hopkins University Press, 2005)

Musso, Riccardo, 'Compagnie scelte e ordinarie nello Stato di Terraferma', in *Liguria*, LIII-1/2 (1986), pp.4–36

Repetti, Giovanni, *L'ochio drito della Repubblica. Amministrazione e vita quotidiana della fortezza genovese del Priamàr di Savona nei secoli XVII e XVIII* (Savona: Elio Ferraris, 1998)

Ornano, Marquis de, *La Corse Militaire* (Paris, 1904)

Ricci, Jean-Baptiste, *Gênes e le maintien de l'ordre aux XVIIe et XVIIIe siècles (1568–1729): les effectifs* (Bastia: Université de Corse, Mémoire de DEA, 1998)

Zanini, Andrea, 'Soldati corsi e famegli. La forza pubblica della Repubblica di Genova nel XVIII secolo', in L. Antonelli and C. Donati (eds), *Corpi armati e ordine pubblico in Italia (XVI–XIX sec.)*, pp.141–180

Tuscany

Angiolini, Franco, *I cavalieri e il principe. L'ordine di Santo Stefano e la società toscana in Età Moderna* (Florence: Edifir, 1996), pp.1–45

Angiolini, Franco, 'Le Bande medicee tra ordine e disordine', in L. Antonelli and C. Donati (eds), *Corpi armati e ordine pubblico in Italia (XVI–XIX sec.)* (Soveria Mannelli CZ: Rubbettino, 2003), pp.9–47

Bonifacio, Gaetano, *Campagne dei cavalieri di S. Stefano in Levante, 1684–1688* (Livorno, 1938)

Capponi, Niccolò, *L'organizzazione militare del Granducato di Toscana sotto Ferdinando II de' Medici* (Padova, Università degli Studi, 1998)

Diaz, Furio, *il Granducato di Toscana. I Medici* (Turin: Utet, 1976)

Ferretti, Jolanda, 'L'organizzazione militare in Toscana durante il governo di Alessandro e Cosimo I de'Medici', in *Rivista storica degli archivi toscani*, I (1929), pp.58–275

Gurrieri, Gino, *I cavalieri di Santo Stefano* (Pisa: Nistri-Lischi, 1960)

Hibbert, Christopher, *The House of Medici. Its Rise and Fall* (New York: HarperCollins, 1980)

Labanca, Nicola, 'Le Panoplie del Granduca', in *Ricerche Storiche*, XXV n. 2 (May–August, 1995), pp.295–364

Mugnai, Bruno, 'Il crepuscolo dell'Ercole Tirreno: l'esercito degli ultimi Medici', in *Rivista Medicea* n. 5 (February 2010), pp.40–53

Pezzolo, Luciano, 'Note sulla finanza dello Stato Fiorentino, 1350-1700', in A. Fornasin and C. Povolo, *Per Furio. Studi in onore di Furio Bianco* (Udine, FORUM, 2014), pp.293–305

Waquet, Jean Claude, *Le Grand Duché de Toscane sous les derniers Medici* (Rome: Ecole Française de Rome, 1990)

Parma and Piacenza

Hanlon, Gregory, 'Parma during the era of Duke Odoardo, 'the Great' (1630-1650)', in G. Bertini (ed.), *Storia di Parma* vol. IV (Parma: Monte Universitaria, 2014), pp.2–33

Zannoni, Mario and Massimo Fiorentino, *L'esercito Farnesiano dal 1694 al 1731* (Parma: Palatina Editrice, 1981)

Modena

Bonacini, Pierpaolo, 'Per il gran bene della pubblica tranquillità e sicurezza … Giustizia e disciplina militare negli Stati estensi di Antico Regime (secoli XVI–XVII)', in *Historia et Ius*, n. 16 (2019), pp.3–70

Menziani, Alberto, 'L'esercito estense ed austro-estense (1598–1859)', in A. Spaggiari and G. Trenti (eds), *Lo Stato di Modena. Una capitale, una dinastia, una civiltà nella storia d'Europa* (Modena, 1998), Saggi 66 – Ministero per i Beni e le Attività Culturali – Direzione Generale per gli Archivi, pp.699–718

Signorotto, Gianvittorio, 'Modena e il mito della sovranità eroica', in E. Fumagalli and G. Signorotto (eds) *La corte estense nel primo Seicento Diplomazia e mecenatismo artistico* (Rome: Viella, 2012), pp.11–50

Mantua and Guastalla

Giuseppe Coniglio, *I Gonzaga* (Milan: Dall'Oglio, 1967)

Raviola, Blythe Alice, *Il Monferrato gonzaghesco: istituzioni ed élites di un micro-stato (1536–1708)* (Florence: Olschki, 2003)

Sulpizi, Giorgio, 'L'organizzazione militare del ducato di Guastalla' in *Archivio Storico degli Antichi Stati Guastallesi* (Guastalla: Associazione Guastallese di Storia Patria, 2000), pp.97–162

Lucca

Nelli, Sergio: 'Indicazioni archivistiche circa la presenza militare in Lucca', in *Le fonti per la storia militare italiana in Età Contemporanea* (Rome: Ministero per i Beni Culturali e Ambientali – Ufficio Centrale per i Beni Archivistici, 1993), pp.267–296

Tommasi, Girolamo and Carlo Minutoli, *Sommario della Storia di Lucca* (Florence, 1847)

Malta

Blouet, Brian W., *The Story of Malta* (London: Faber and Faber, 1967)

Del Negro, Piero, 'L'Ordine di Malta e Venezia nelle storie veneziane del Seicento sulla Guerra di Candia' in *Studi Veneziani*, LX (2010), pp.1179–195

Devrım Atauz, Ayşe, *Trade, Piracy, and Naval Warfare in the Central Mediterranean: The Maritime History and Archaeology of Malta* (Middle East Technical University; M.A., Bilkent University, 2004)

Grech, Ivan, 'Dealing with Manpower Shortages in the Mediterranean: the Order of St John's Labour Force problems during the Long Seventeenth Century', in C. Vassallo and S. Mercieca (eds), *The Port of Malta* (Malta, 2018), pp.75–96

Grech, Ivan, 'The Dread of Violence and the Lure of Conflict. Contrasting Attitudes to Warfare: The Case of the Hospitaller Order of St John', in B. Borstner, S. Gartner, S. Deschler-Erb, C. Dalli, I. M. D'Aprile (eds), *Historicizing Religion. Critical Approaches to Contemporary Concerns* (Pisa: Pisa University Press 2010), pp.145–157

Mori Ubaldini, Ubaldino, *La Marina del sovrano militare Ordine di San Giovanni di Gerusalemme, di Rodi e di Malta* (Rome: Regionale Editrice, 1971)

Restifo, Giuseppe, 'I Cavalieri di Malta', in *Mediterranean Studies* (2014), pp.1–11

Messina

Barbagallo, Salvatore, *La guerra di Messina 1674–1678: 'Chiprotegge li ribelli d'altri principi, invita i propri a ribellarsi'* (Naples: Guida, 2017)

Gazzara, Piero, 'La rivolta antispagnola di Messina e la battaglia di Lombardello (1674)', in F. Imbasi (ed.), *Sicilia Millenaria. Dalla microstoria alla dimensione moderna* (Messina: Università degli Studi, 2019), vol. I, pp.173–196

Laloy, Émile, *L'expédition de Sicile et la politique française en Italie (1674–1678)*, vols I–III (Paris, 1929)

Ribot, Luis, *La Monarquía de España y la guerra de Mesina, 1674–1678* (Madrid: Actas, 2002)